using the Interactive Examples that have this text by the authors!

- The solution for the example in the book is demonstrated using the TI-83 and BA II Plus Professional calculators – reducing the class time needed to teach this. Each step-by-step tutorial will clearly walk you through each problem to help eliminate any confusion.

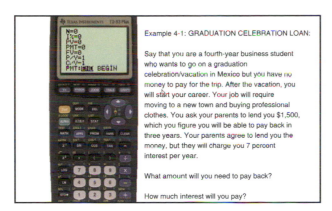

Example 4-1: GRADUATION CELEBRATION LOAN:

Say that you are a fourth-year business student who wants to go on a graduation celebration/vacation in Mexico but you have no money to pay for the trip. After the vacation, you will start your career. Your job will require moving to a new town and buying professional clothes. You ask your parents to lend you $1,500, which you figure you will be able to pay back in three years. Your parents agree to lend you the money, but they will charge you 7 percent interest per year.

What amount will you need to pay back?

How much interest will you pay?

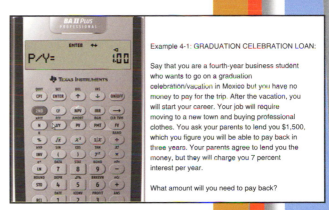

Example 4-1: GRADUATION CELEBRATION LOAN:

Say that you are a fourth-year business student who wants to go on a graduation celebration/vacation in Mexico but you have no money to pay for the trip. After the vacation, you will start your career. Your job will require moving to a new town and buying professional clothes. You ask your parents to lend you $1,500, which you figure you will be able to pay back in three years. Your parents agree to lend you the money, but they will charge you 7 percent interest per year.

What amount will you need to pay back?

- Lastly, the solution for the example in the book is demonstrated using Excel, to help provide a basic understanding on how to set up the spreadsheets.

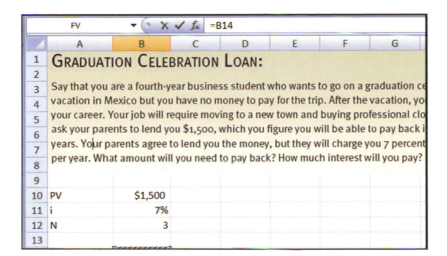

finance

applications & theory

The McGraw-Hill/Irwin Series in Finance, Insurance, and Real Estate

Stephen A. Ross, Franco Modigliani Professor of Finance and Economics,
Sloan School of Management, Massachusetts Institute of Technology, Consulting Editor

FINANCIAL MANAGEMENT

Adair
Excel Applications for Corporate Finance
First Edition

Block, Hirt, and Danielsen
Foundations of Financial Management
Thirteenth Edition

Brealey, Myers, and Allen
Principles of Corporate Finance
Ninth Edition

Brealey, Myers, and Allen
Principles of Corporate Finance, Concise
First Edition

Brealey, Myers and Marcus
Fundamentals of Corporate Finance
Sixth Edition

Brooks
FinGame Online 5.0

Bruner
Case Studies in Finance: Managing for Corporate Value Creation
Fifth Edition

Chew
The New Corporate Finance: Where Theory Meets Practice
Third Edition

Cornett, Adair, and Nofsinger
Finance: Applications and Theory
First Edition

DeMello
Cases in Finance
Second Edition

Grinblatt (editor)
Stephen A. Ross, Mentor: Influence through Generations

Grinblatt and Titman
Financial Markets and Corporate Strategy
Second Edition

Higgins
Analysis for Financial Management
Ninth Edition

Kellison
Theory of Interest
Third Edition

Kester, Ruback, and Tufano
Case Problems in Finance
Twelfth Edition

Ross, Westerfield and Jaffe
Corporate Finance
Eighth Edition

Ross, Westerfield, Jaffe and Jordan
Corporate Finance: Core Principles and Applications
Second Edition

Ross, Westerfield and Jordan
Essentials of Corporate Finance
Sixth Edition

Ross, Westerfield and Jordan
Fundamentals of Corporate Finance
Eighth Edition

Shefrin
Behavioral Corporate Finance: Decisions that Create Value
First Edition

White
Financial Analysis with an Electronic Calculator
Sixth Edition

INVESTMENTS

Bodie, Kane and Marcus
Essentials of Investments
Seventh Edition

Bodie, Kane and Marcus
Investments
Eighth Edition

Hirt and Block
Fundamentals of Investment Management
Ninth Edition

Hirschey and Nofsinger
Investments: Analysis and Behavior
First Edition

Jordan and Miller
Fundamentals of Investments: Valuation and Management
Fifth Edition

FINANCIAL INSTITUTIONS AND MARKETS

Rose and Hudgins
Bank Management and Financial Services
Seventh Edition

Rose and Marquis
Money and Capital Markets: Financial Institutions and Instruments in a Global Marketplace
Tenth Edition

Saunders and Cornett
Financial Institutions Management: A Risk Management Approach
Sixth Edition

Saunders and Cornett
Financial Markets and Institutions
Fourth Edition

INTERNATIONAL FINANCE

Eun and Resnick
International Financial Management
Fifth Edition

Kuemmerle
Case Studies in International Entrepreneurship: Managing and Financing Ventures in the Global Economy
First Edition

REAL ESTATE

Brueggeman and Fisher
Real Estate Finance and Investments
Thirteenth Edition

Ling and Archer
Real Estate Principles: A Value Approach
Second Edition

FINANCIAL PLANNING AND INSURANCE

Allen, Melone, Rosenbloom and Mahoney
Retirement Plans: 401(k)s, IRAs, and Other Deferred Compensation Approaches
Tenth Edition

Altfest
Personal Financial Planning
First Edition

Harrington and Niehaus
Risk Management and Insurance
Second Edition

Kapoor, Dlabay, and Hughes
Focus on Personal Finance: An active approach to help you develop successful financial skills
Second Edition

Kapoor, Dlabay and Hughes
Personal Finance
Ninth Edition

finance
applications & theory

Marcia Millon Cornett
Boston University

Troy A. Adair, Jr.
Wilkes University

John Nofsinger
Washington State University

McGraw-Hill
Irwin

Boston   Burr Ridge, IL   Dubuque, IA   New York   San Francisco   St. Louis
Bangkok   Bogotá   Caracas   Kuala Lumpur   Lisbon   London   Madrid   Mexico City
Milan   Montreal   New Delhi   Santiago   Seoul   Singapore   Sydney   Taipei   Toronto

FINANCE: APPLICATIONS & THEORY

ISBN 978-0-07-338225-8
MHID 0-07-338225-6

Executive editor: *Michele Janicek*
Senior developmental editor: *Christina Kouvelis*
Marketing manager: *Ashley Smith*
Manager of photo, design & publishing tools: *Mary Conzachi*
Full service project manager: *Marilyn Rothenberger*
Lead production supervisor: *Carol A. Bielski*
Lead designer: *Matthew Baldwin*
Senior media project manager: *Kerry Bowler*
Cover and interior design: *Mathew Baldwin*
Typeface: *10.5/12 Minon*
Compositor: *Laserwords Private Limited*
Printer: *R. R. Donnelley*

Library of Congress Cataloging-in-Publication Data

Cornett, Marcia Millon.
    Finance : applications & theory /Marcia Millon Cornett, Troy A. Adair, Jr., John Nofsinger.—1 st ed.
        p. cm.—(The McGraw-Hill/Irwin series in finance, insurance, and real estate)
    Includes index.
    ISBN-13: 978-0-07-338225-8 (alk. paper)
    ISBN-10: 0-07-338225-6 (alk. paper)
    1. Finance. I. Adair, Troy A. (Troy Alton), 1964- II. Nofsinger, John R. III. Title.
HG173.C679 2009
332—dc22
                                                                        2008020876

www.mhhe.com

dedicated

to my parents, Tom and Sue—Marcia Millon Cornett

to my daughter, Genevieve—Troy A. Adair, Jr.

to Anna, my wife and best friend—John Nofsinger

about the authors

Marcia Millon Cornett *Professor of finance in the School of Management at Boston University.* She received her BS degree in economics from Knox College in Galesburg, Illinois, and her MBA and PhD degrees in finance from Indiana University in Bloomington, Indiana. Dr. Cornett has written and published several articles in the areas of bank performance, bank regulation, corporate finance, and investments. Articles authored by Dr. Cornett have appeared in such academic journals as the *Journal of Finance;* the *Journal of Money, Credit, and Banking;* the *Journal of Financial Economics; Financial Management;* and the *Journal of Banking and Finance.* Along with Anthony Saunders (John M. Schiff Professor of Finance and chair of the Department of Finance at the Stern School of Business at New York University), Dr. Cornett has just completed writing the 6th edition of *Financial Institutions Management* (McGraw-Hill/Irwin) and is beginning work on the 4th edition of *Financial Markets and Institutions* (McGraw-Hill/Irwin). She is the guest editor for the *Journal of Financial Services Research* Special Issue on Government Regulation of Banking Firms and *Review of Financial Economics* January 2004 special issue on Commercial Banks: Performance, Regulation, and Market Value. She serves as an associate editor for the *Journal of Financial Services Research, FMA Online,* the *Review of Financial Economics, Financial Review,* and *Multinational Finance Journal.* Dr. Cornett has served as a member of the board of directors, the executive committee, and the finance committee of the SIU Credit Union. Dr. Cornett has also taught at Southern Illinois University at Carbondale, the University of Colorado, Boston College, and Southern Methodist University. She is a member of the Financial Management Association, the American Finance Association, and the Western Finance Association.

Troy Alton Adair, Jr. *Director of educational initiatives at Wilkes University.* He received his BS degree in computers/information science from the University of Alabama at Birmingham, his MBA from the University of North Dakota, and his PhD in finance from Indiana University. Dr. Adair has written articles on bank regulator self-interest, analyst earnings per share forecasting, and capital budgeting in continuous time and is the author of *Corporate Finance Demystified (McGraw-Hill/Irwin), Excel Applications in Corporate Finance,* and *Excel Applications in Investments (McGraw-Hill/Irwin).* He has also served as a consultant on financial data information systems to a number of international banks, and as the faculty representative to the board of trustees investments committee at Alma College. Dr. Adair has also taught at the University of Michigan, Alma College, Hofstra University, Indiana University, and the University of North Carolina at Chapel Hill. He is a member of the Financial Management Association, the American Finance Association, and the Southern Finance Association.

John Nofsinger *A Lang Fellow and associate professor of finance at Washington State University.* He earned his BS degree in electrical engineering from Washington State University, his MBA degree from Chapman University, and his PhD degree in finance from Washington State University. Dr. Nofsinger has written dozens of articles in the areas of investments, corporate finance, and behavioral finance. These papers have appeared in the scholarly journals, the *Journal of Finance, Journal of Business, Journal of Financial and Quantitative Analysis, Financial Management, Journal of Corporate Finance, Journal of Banking and Finance, Journal of Behavioral Decision Making,* among others. Dr. Nofsinger has also authored (or coauthored) six trade books and textbooks that have been translated into six different languages. The most prominent of these books are the industry book, *The Psychology of Investing,* and the textbook, *Investments: Analysis and Behavior* (McGraw-Hill/Irwin, coauthored with Mark Hirschey, the Anderson W. Chandler Professor of Business at the University of Kansas). Dr. Nofsinger is a leading expert in behavioral finance and is a frequent speaker on this topic at industry conferences, universities, and academic conferences. He has often been quoted or appeared in the financial media, including *The Wall Street Journal, Financial Times, Fortune, BusinessWeek, Smart Money, Washington Post, Bloomberg,* and *CNBC,* and other media from *The Dolans* to *TheStreet.com.*

a note from the authors

"There is a lot to cover in this course so I focus on the core concepts, theories, and problems."

"I like to teach the course by using examples from their own individual lives."

"My students come into this course with varying levels of math skills."

How many of the quotes above might you have said while teaching the undergraduate corporate finance course? Our many years of teaching certainly reflect such sentiments, and as we prepared to write this book, we conducted many market research studies that confirm just how much these statements—or ones similar—are common across the country. This critical course covers so many crucial topics that instructors need to focus on core ideas to ensure that students are getting the preparation they need for future classes—and for their lives beyond college.

We did not set out to write this book to change the way finance is taught, but rather to parallel and support the way that instructors from across the country currently teach finance. Nearly 600 instructors teaching this course have shared their class experiences and ideas via a variety of research methods that we used to develop the framework for this text. We are excited to have authored a book that we think you will find to fit your classroom style perfectly.

KEY THEMES

This book's framework emphasizes three themes. See pages xiii–xv for a description of features in our book that support these themes.

- **Finance is about connecting core concepts.** We all struggle with fitting so many topics into this course, so this text strives to make it easier for you by getting back to the core concepts, key research, and current topics. We realize that today's students expect to learn more in class from lectures than in closely studying their textbooks, so we've created brief chapters that clearly lead students to crucial material that they need to review if they are to understand how to approach core financial concepts. Since textbook materials are always more interesting with real-world examples, we've included many current events to illustrate key topics. The text is also organized around learning goals, making it easier for you to prep your course and for students to study the right topics.

- **Finance can be taught using a personal perspective.** Most long-term finance instructors have often heard students ask "How is this course relevant to me?" on the first day of class. We no longer teach classes dedicated solely to finance majors; many of us now must teach the first finance course to a mix of business majors. We need to give finance majors the rigor they need while not overwhelming class members from other majors. For years, instructors have used individual examples to help teach these concepts, but this is the first text to integrate this personal way of teaching into the chapters.

- **Finance focuses on solving problems and decision making.** This isn't to say that concepts and theories aren't important, but students will typically need to solve some kind of mathematical problem—or at least understand the impact of different numerical scenarios—to make the right decision on common finance issues. If you, as an instructor, either assign problems for homework or create exams made up almost entirely of mathematical material, you understand the need for good problems (and plenty of them). You also understand from experience the number of office hours you spend tutoring students and grading homework. Students have different learning styles, and this text aims to address that challenge to allow you more time in class to get through the critical topics.

ORGANIZATION

In our research for this book, we spent a lot of time deciding on the essential topics for an ideal corporate finance course. Our respondents noted many topics and chapters in common, but definite areas of corporate finance arose that not all instructors polled would include in their courses, or topics that instructors would cover only if they had enough time. Therefore, the table of contents will include more topics than you most likely will cover in a typical semester-long class. Our goal, however, is to present the most valued material for this course while still creating one of the briefest books on the market.

Chapter 1 covers what finance entails, how financial management functions within the business world, and why the student will benefit on a personal level from studying financial principles. Along the way, it provides a uniquely intuitive explanation of what finance is and what the various subareas of finance entail, combined with a straightforward explanation of the fundamental difference between individuals' investing decisions and firms' capital budgeting decisions. The chapter also covers the role of finance in the firm, and a brief description of how financial markets and intermediaries interact with the firm.

Chapter 2 provides an overview of the four major financial statements. We briefly examine each statement, identifying its major features. We highlight the differences between the accounting-based (or book) value of a firm reported in these statements and the true market value of a firm, as well as between accounting-based income and actual cash flows. We explain how taxes influence corporate managers' and investors' decisions. We highlight the difference between accounting income and cash flows and then demonstrate how to use a firm's financial statements to calculate its cash flows. Finally, we note that cautions should be taken when examining and making decisions based on financial statements because they might be restated or even shown to be misleading.

Chapter 3 reviews the major financial ratios and identifies the general trend (higher or lower) that managers and investment analysts look for in each ratio. Unique to this text, we discuss how a ratio that seems too good can actually be bad for a company. We also see how ratios interrelate. That is, a change in one ratio may affect the value of several ratios. Finally, we discuss cautions that you should take when using ratio analysis to evaluate firm performance.

PART I: INTRODUCTION

Chapter 1:   Introducing Financial Management

PART II: FINANCIAL STATEMENTS

Chapter 2:   Reviewing Financial Statements
Chapter 3:   Analyzing Financial Statements and Planning

PART III: VALUING OF FUTURE CASH FLOWS

Chapter 4: Time Value of Money 1: Analyzing Single Cash Flows

Chapter 5: Time Value of Money 2: Analyzing Annuity Cash Flows

PART IV: VALUING OF BONDS AND STOCKS

Chapter 6: Valuing Bonds

Chapter 7: Valuing Stocks

Chapter 8: Understanding Financial Markets and Institutions

Chapter 4 is the first of a two-chapter set on the time value of money. This chapter focuses on single cash flows and starts with the creation of the time line. The concepts of future value and present value are presented and quickly followed by examples that are more personal to the student as well as business-related examples to reinforce the theory. We use clear and simple formulas as well as calculator keystrokes. The "quick and dirty" approximation technique using the Rule of 72 is illustrated. We also allow for compounding with different interest rates through time.

Chapter 5 is the second chapter of the two-chapter set on the time value of money and develops the annuity cash flows. Again, there is extensive use of the time line throughout the chapter. The examples of credit card debt, car loans, mortgages, pensions, retirement savings, and growing annuities are particularly relevant to college students. The "retirement" boxed reading is especially surprising to students. Multiple annuities, perpetuities, the APR/EAR issue and amortization schedules are all covered. There is a second set of practice problems that combines some of the topics from both chapters of this two-chapter set.

Chapter 6 examines the valuation and interest rate dynamics of various types of bonds. Bond quotes with detailed descriptions provide a roadmap for discussing the various components of the different types of bonds. We provide a simplified process for the evaluation of various components of a bond followed by excellent examples. We cover current yield along with the yield to maturity. Both interest rate risk and reinvestment rate risk are illustrated. Topics also include the pricing of zero coupon bonds, credit risk dynamics, and tax exempt applications. The chapter also spends some time helping students obtain bond information.

Chapter 7 is often a favorite of students due to the subject matter. We first provide an overview of the stock exchanges and a history of the stock indexes. A section on the mechanics of buying and selling stock gives curious students the information to get started themselves. Stock valuation is developed using the dividend discount model and illustrated with real companies, Coca-Cola and McDonald's. The constant growth rate model, preferred stock valuation, and variable growth rates are all discussed. Relative valuation techniques are also described. Specifically, the dynamics of the price/earnings ratio are illustrated using the 30 DJIA firms. The investor psychology boxed reading gives the chapter a more personal flavor.

Chapter 8 builds upon the information about stocks, bonds, and other securities covered in Chapters 6 and 7 to provide an overview of the U.S. financial system. We look at various financial markets' nature and operations and the financial institutions that participate in those markets. Financial institutions (FIs) allow financial markets to function by providing the least costly and most efficient way to channel funds to and from these markets. FIs play a second crucial role by spreading risk among market participants. Finally, we analyze specific factors that influence interest rates and offer different theories that explain the shape of the term structure of interest rates as well as how forward interest rates derive from the term structure of interest rates. Unique to the chapter is the tie-in to economic concepts of demand and supply, the presentation of WSJ tables, and the citing of increased or decreased risk of the various financial instruments.

Chapter 9 focuses on historical return and risk. We start with the calculation of returns using real companies, Radio Shack and Mattel. Showing their returns over time leads to the idea of return volatility. Computing standard deviation of return is introduced as a measure of risk. Comparisons of the two individual firms' risk and return characteristics with those of the broad asset classes introduce the concept of diversification. Diversification risk reduction is illustrated by adding real companies, one at a time, to a portfolio. This discussion naturally evolves into efficient portfolios and modern portfolio theory. Topics like total risk, diversifiable versus nondiversifiable risk, and the coefficient of variation are covered. The use of real companies throughout this chapter takes this difficult material out of the abstract and really applies it for students.

> **PART V: RISK AND RETURN**
>
> **Chapter 9:** Characterizing Risk and Return
> **Chapter 10:** Estimating Risk and Return
>
> **PART VI: CAPITAL BUDGETING**
>
> **Chapter 11:** Calculating the Cost of Capital
> **Chapter 12:** Estimating Cash Flows on Capital Budgeting Projects
> **Chapter 13:** Weighing Net Present Value and Other Capital Budgeting Criteria

Chapter 10 covers expected returns. The importance of forward-looking returns and risk premiums are discussed. The CAPM is developed through the efficient frontier, capital market line, and security market line. The problems faced in computing beta are discussed and illustrated with real world information about corporate betas. Especially useful is the list of various publicly reported betas for AT&T and the discussion of why these betas differ. We also show the estimation of an expected return using the constant growth rate model as an alternative to the CAPM approach. Capital market efficiency is discussed from the perspective of informational efficiency and is followed by a discussion of behavioral finance. These concepts are tied to the activities of the financial manager.

Chapter 11 explains how to calculate a firm's or a project's cost of capital as a weighted average of the component costs of each type of capital. We cover firmwide, project-specific, and divisional cost of capital calculations and devote a good deal of attention to the costs and benefits associated with using each approach to evaluate a proposed new capital budgeting project. We discuss the trade-off inherent in choosing either a subjective or objective approach to calculating divisional costs of capital. Finally, while other texts tend to focus on one single methodology for incorporating floatation costs, either by adjusting the WACC or by adjusting the initial cash outflow, we cover both approaches.

Chapter 12 uses the concept of free cash flow to illustrate how to calculate expected cash flow for proposed new projects, providing the intuitively appealing explanation of it measuring the operating cash flow minus the necessary reinvestment in assets. In addition to addressing the conventional list of topics associated with cash flow calculation, this chapter does a uniquely thorough job of covering several topics that are usually given very minimal attention: we explain how the half-year convention affects the MACRS depreciation tables, how section 179 deductions can accelerate expensing of fixed assets even further, and why the assumption that changes in NWC must lead sales makes sense.

We also offer tips for making what is admittedly a very complicated process as straightforward as possible. For example, we explicitly state what assumptions should be used when a *project* has a negative EBIT versus when a *firm* has a negative EBIT, and why; and we stress the use of one, common formula for calculating tax consequences when selling an asset for other than depreciated book value, regardless of whether the asset is sold at a loss or a gain against book value.

Chapter 13 covers the major capital budgeting decision techniques: NPV, Payback Discounted Payback, IRR, Modified Payback, and the Profitability Index. We take a very systematic approach to discussing each technique, detailing how to calculate the relevant statistic, what benchmark to compare it with, and the strengths and weaknesses of each technique. We also spend time discussing why so many different types of decision techniques are available, discussing the rationale for the different forms of decision metrics used by the various techniques. Finally, we provide a more thorough explanation of the usual methodology for calculating the crossover point for two NPV profiles than that provided by competing texts.

PART VII: CAPITAL STRUCTURE ISSUES

Chapter 14: Assessing Long-Term Debt, Equity, and Capital Structure

Chapter 15: Sharing Firm Wealth: Dividends, Share Repurchases, and Other Payouts

Chapter 16 Issuing Capital and the Investment Banking Process

PART VIII: WORKING CAPITAL MANAGEMENT

Chapter 17: Addressing Working Capital Policies and Managing Short-Term Assets and Liabilities

Chapter 14 explores the question of the firm's optimal capital structure, detailing how the choice changes when we take a firm in a "perfect world" and add the existence of corporate taxes and the chance of default to the situation. We provide a discussion of active vs. passive capital structures. We provide in-depth examples of how to calculate break-even EBIT, and we use payoff diagrams for debt and equity to explain the overinvestment and underinvestment problems.

Chapter 15 covers how firms go about paying back investors via dividends, share repurchases, and other payouts. We discuss the implications for firms' dividend policies of both the dividend irrelevance theorem and the bird-in-the-hand theory, and we explain how differential taxation of capital gains and dividends leads investors to prefer one form of payout over the other. We do a uniquely thorough job of covering the dividend payment procedures and their implications for expected patterns in stock price. We also cover stock dividends and splits and discuss the advantages and disadvantages of firm share repurchases.

Chapter 16 describes the decisions that firms face when they raise capital. We first look at small firms in their early operating stages. We describe the funding process: with funds coming mainly from banks and venture capital firms. We then look at the process of going public, as well as publicly traded firms' subsequent issues of debt and equity. Then we describe the types of securities that public firms issue and explore the role that investment banks play in the process. As we go through the chapter, note how important financial institutions become in raising capital funds to finance a firm's assets.

Chapter 17 discusses net working capital policy, including the operating and cash cycles of the firm; the trade-off between carrying costs and shortage costs for net working capital; the description and reasons for choosing between flexible and restrictive financing policies; the different sources of short-term capital, including commercial loans, commercial paper, and banker's acceptances; the Baumol and Mill-Orr models for determining optimal cash management policies; descriptions of collection and disbursement float and strategies for managing both; and credit management policies.

Chapter 18 covers the financial aspects of operating in a dynamic international business environment. We first characterize the dynamics of the global economy through international trade, foreign direct investment, and free trade zones. Currency exchange and exchange rate risk are illustrated through the global activities of Starbucks Coffee. Hedging tools and procedures are developed. These tools are backed by the theories of purchasing power parity and interest rate parity. Political risks are also an important barrier for multinational companies. Last, we show how these topics are incorporated into a firm's capital budgeting process.

> **PART IX: OTHER TOPICS IN FINANCE**
>
> **Chapter 18:** Considering International Aspects of Corporate Finance
> **Chapter 19:** Managing Mergers and Acquisitions and Financial Distress

Chapter 19 looks at two ways in which corporations may cease to exist. First, we look at mergers and acquisitions, in which two firms combine assets, liabilities, and equity. We look at the merger and acquisition process and demonstrate how to mathematically value mergers. We then look at a second way that firms cease to exist—financial distress. We discuss methods by which a firm can informally resolve severe financial distress. We differentiate between Chapter 7 and Chapter 11 bankruptcy used to accomplish this. Finally, we discuss statistical models used to predict bankruptcy.

Walk-through of pedagogical features

CONNECTING CORE CONCEPTS

Learning Goals appear at the beginning of each chapter and are indicated throughout the text next to headings, examples, summary, and end-of-chapter problems to which they relate. This helps the student follow how we build larger concepts from smaller steps. It also helps instructors develop their classes and assign readings and homework based on these goals. The accompanying test bank provides instructors with hundreds of questions organized by level and learning goals to make customization even easier!

LG **Learning Goals**

LG1 Define the subareas of finance and their roles in corporate financial management.
LG2 Show why and how finance is at the heart of sound business decisions.
LG3 Apply finance in your personal life.
LG4 Compare and contrast the advantages and disadvantages of the three most common business organizational forms in the United States.
LG5 Differentiate between financial managers' appropriate and inappropriate goals.
LG6 Identify the firm's primary agency relationship and discuss why agency relationships can create conflicts.
LG7 Incorporate ethics into financial management.
LG8 Describe the complex and necessary relationships among firms, financial institutions, and financial markets.

---

finance at work

corporate

THE AMAZING (ONGOING) STORY OF APPLE INC. AND STEVE JOBS

Steven Jobs and Stephen Wozniak started Apple Computer in 1976 as an equal partnership. Together, they built 50 computers in a garage using money borrowed from family, the proceeds from the sale of a VW bus, and credit from the parts distributor.

Jobs and Wozniak then designed the Apple II computer. But a higher production level to make more than 50 computers required more space and employees. They needed much more capital. They could not get a loan until angel investor Mike Markkula (an Intel executive) became a partner in the firm. He invested $92,000 and his personal guarantee induced a bank to loan Apple $250,000. As production ramped up in 1977, Apple Computer incorporated. Most shares were owned by Jobs, Wozniak, and Markkula, but the principles made some shares available to employees. They also hired an experienced manager (Mike Scott) to be the CEO and run the firm. Note that as the firm expanded, Jobs' ownership level and control got diluted. By 1980, Apple Computer had sold a total of 121,000 computers—against a potential demand of millions more. Apple needed even more capital.

At the end of 1980, Apple became a public corporation and sold $65 million worth of stock to public investors. Steve Jobs, cofounder of Apple, still owned more shares than anyone else (7.5 million), but he owned less than half of the firm. He gave up a great deal of ownership to new investors in exchange for the capital to expand the firm. Unhappy with Mike Scott's leadership, Steve Jobs also became CEO of Apple.

After a couple of years, Apple's board of directors felt that Jobs was not experienced enough to steer the firm through its rapid expansion. They hired John Sculley as CEO in 1983. In 1985, a power struggle ensued for control of the firm, and the board backed Sculley over Jobs. Jobs was forced out of Apple and no longer had a say in business operations, even though he was the largest shareholder and an original cofounder of the firm.

So, Steve Jobs bought Pixar in 1986 for $5 million and founded NeXT Computer. Over the next 10 years, Jobs' Pixar produced mega hit movies like *Toy Story*, *A Bug's Life*, and *Monsters, Inc.* This time, he kept 53 percent ownership of Pixar to ensure keeping full control. In the meantime, Apple Computer began to struggle, with losses of $800 million in 1996 and $1 billion in 1997. To get Steve Jobs back into the firm, Apple bought NeXT for $400 million and hired him as Apple's CEO. Over the next few years, Jobs introduced the iMAC, iPod, and iTunes, and Apple became very profitable again! Jobs was given the use of a $90 million Gulfstream jet as a perk. To realign his incentives, he became an Apple owner again via compensation that included options on 10 million shares of stock and 30 million shares of **restricted stock**. Then in 2006, Disney bought Pixar by swapping $7.4 billion worth of Disney stock for Pixar stock. When the deal closed, Steve Jobs became the largest owner of Disney stock (7 percent) and joined Disney's board of directors.

Wow! What a story of accessing capital, business organizational form, company control, and corporate governance.

⚠ want to know more? Key Words to Search For Updates: **Steve Jobs, Apple Computer, Pixar**

Finance at Work boxes highlight current events and hot topics noted in the news. Since these current events and hot topics can quickly date the text material, the *Want to know more?* feature in each box contains suggested words to use for searching the Internet for updates. These features are great to use for class discussion or as homework assignments.

Time Out boxes, featured at the end of each section, test students' understanding of key terms and core concepts just presented. Answers to the Time Out questions appear at the end of each chapter.

TIME OUT 🕐

1-3   Why must an entrepreneur give up some control of the business as it grows into a public corporation?
1-4   What advantages does the corporate form of organization hold over a partnership?

ANSWERS TO TIME OUT 🕐

1-1   The main subareas are investments, financial management, financial institutions and markets, and international finance. Investors interact with the other groups by buying and selling securities through financial markets, being influenced by what to buy and sell by the quality of firms' financial management, and assessing international opportunities for investment and for firm prospects. Financial management acquires and repays capital from investors through financial institutions and markets. Financial managers must also run their businesses in an increasingly internationally integrated

---

key terms

www.mhhe.com/can1e

agency problem, The difficulties that arise when a principle hires an agent and cannot fully monitor the agent's actions. (p. 16)
angel investors, Individuals who provide small amounts of capital and expert business advice to small firms in exchange for an ownership stake in the firm. (p. 11)
auditor, A person who performs an independent assessment of the fairness of a firm's financial statements. (p. 17)

board of directors, The group of directors elected by stockholders to oversee management in a corporation. (p. 17)
chief executive officer (CEO), The highest-ranking corporate manager. (p. 16)
corporate governance, The set of laws, policies, incentives, and monitors designed to handle the issues arising from the separation of ownership and control. (p. 16)

22

Key terms are presented in boldface type when first mentioned. A definition of the term appears in the end-of-chapter material with a page reference for easy recall.

Summary of Learning Goals appears at the end of each chapter to help students connect the learning goals to the concepts introduced in the chapter and to provide a clear recap of those concepts.

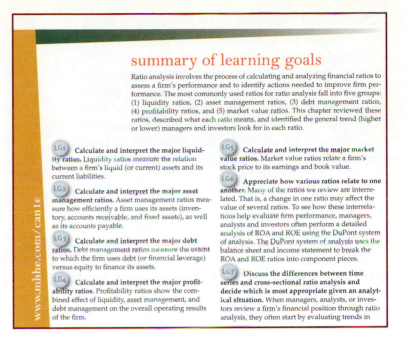

summary of learning goals

Ratio analysis involves the process of calculating and analyzing financial ratios to assess a firm's performance and to identify actions needed to improve firm performance. The most commonly used ratios for ratio analysis fall into five groups: (1) liquidity ratios, (2) asset management ratios, (3) debt management ratios, (4) profitability ratios, and (5) market value ratios. This chapter reviewed these ratios, described what each ratio means, and identified the general trend (higher or lower) managers and investors look for in each ratio.

LG1 Calculate and interpret the major liquidity ratios. Liquidity ratios measure the relation between a firm's liquid (or current) assets and its current liabilities.

LG2 Calculate and interpret the major asset management ratios. Asset management ratios measure how efficiently a firm uses its assets (inventory, accounts receivable, and fixed assets), as well as its accounts payable.

LG3 Calculate and interpret the major debt ratios. Debt management ratios measure the extent to which the firm uses debt (or financial leverage) versus equity to finance its assets.

LG4 Calculate and interpret the major profitability ratios. Profitability ratios show the combined effect of liquidity, asset management, and debt management on the overall operating results of the firm.

LG5 Calculate and interpret the major market value ratios. Market value ratios relate a firm's stock price to its earnings and book value.

LG6 Appreciate how various ratios relate to one another. Many of the ratios we review are interrelated. That is, a change in one ratio may affect the value of several ratios. To see how these interrelations help evaluate firm performance, managers, analysts and investors often perform a detailed analysis of ROA and ROE using the DuPont system of analysis. The DuPont system of analysis uses the balance sheet and income statement to break the ROA and ROE ratios into component pieces.

LG7 Discuss the differences between time series and cross-sectional ratio analysis and decide which is most appropriate given an analytical situation. When managers, analysts, or investors review a firm's financial position through ratio analysis, they often start by evaluating trends in

www.mhhe.com/can1e

research it! Reviewing Financial Statements

Go the Web site of Wal-Mart Stores, Inc. at www.walmartstores.com and get the latest financial statements from the annual report using the following steps.

Go to Wal-Mart Stores, Inc.'s Web site at www.walmartstores.com. Click on Investors, then select Financial Information; next choose Annual Reports; finally, click on the most recent date. This will bring the file onto your computer that contains the relevant data.

Locate the total assets, total equity, net sales, net income, dividends paid, cash flows from operating activities, and cash flows from investing activities for the last two years. How have these items changed over the last two years?

Research It! projects, perfect for individual assignments or as group projects, are included at the end of each chapter and require students to search the Web for data and other information to answer the questions.

Practice tests are available on the book Web site at www.mhhe.com/can1e for students to test their knowledge of concepts prior to starting the material contained within the chapter.

Questions are featured at the end of each chapter that can be used for discussion in class to review chapter concepts or for homework.

PERSONAL PERSPECTIVE

viewpoints

Business Application

Caleb has worked very hard to create and expand his juice stand at the mall. He has finally perfected his products and feels that he is offering the right combination of juice and food. As a result, the stand is making a nice profit. Caleb would like to open more stands at malls all over his state and eventually all over the country.

Caleb knows he needs more money to expand. He needs money to buy more equipment, buy more inventory, and hire and train more people. How can Caleb get the capital he needs to expand? **(See solution on p. 19)**

Personal Application

Dagmar is becoming interested in investing some of her money. However, she has heard about several corporations in which the investors lost all of their money. In the past several years, Dagmar has heard that Enron (2001), WorldCom (2002), and Delta Airlines (2005) have all filed for bankruptcy. These firms' stockholders lost their entire investments in these firms.

Many of the stockholders who lost money were employees of these companies who had invested some of their retirement money in the company stock. She wonders what guarantee she has as an investor against losing her money. **(See solution on p. 19)**

Viewpoints, a unique feature presented at the beginning of each chapter, poses a problem using key chapter topics from a business perspective. This business question is then mirrored by a problem using a personal perspective. These Viewpoints scenarios immediately set a context for the chapter and allow instructors to take class discussion in multiple directions to make key concepts clearer. The Viewpoints Revisited feature, at the end of the chapter, shows how these problems are solved.

Numbered examples in each chapter will feature various perspectives; most examples will highlight corporate perspectives, but some will feature personal/student perspectives to emphasize the relevance of finance problems to people as well as to corporations. Similarly, some **end-of-chapter problems** will also feature personal perspectives, so students gain practice in solving problems in both business and individual contexts.

PROBLEM-SOLVING AND LEARNING STYLES

Interactive examples that accompany the numbered examples are exciting, unique features that detail the solution to a key problem or concept within each chapter. For each example, students can go to the book's Web site at **www.mhhe.com/can1e** to find the following additional support. **(See inside front cover for more information)**

- The exact example in the book is worked out in a visual and narrated format.

- A similar example is presented in a video format, which stops at decision points in the problem and asks the students to identify the next step. The video continues, explaining why the student is correct or incorrect, and continues solving the problem. This feature allows students to apply and check their learning before doing homework.

- The solution for the example in the book is demonstrated using the TI-83 and BA II Plus Professional calculators—reducing the class time needed to teach students how to use their calculators.

- The solution for the example in the book is demonstrated using Excel, to help you and your students get a basic understanding on how to set up the spreadsheets.

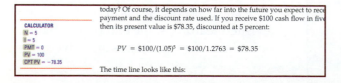

Math Coach boxes are featured in many chapters to help coach students in avoiding the most commonly made mathematical mistakes in a particular problem so students can build confidence in their math skills to solve finance problems.

Calculator keystroke hints are included in the margin next to key examples, if applicable, showing a quick snapshot of how to solve the problem via a business calculator. These can easily be skipped if calculators are not used for your class.

End-of-chapter problems are numerous, are grouped according to level of difficulty, and every odd-numbered problem is mirrored by a similar even-numbered problem. Thus instructors essentially have two different sets of similar problems to assign to different sections. Alternatively, instructors can use one set of problems to work in class and assign the other set.

Self-Test Problems with Solutions appear before the gradable problem sets so students can test themselves before diving into their homework.

Integrated Minicases at the end of each chapter combine the chapter's key concepts into a more complex problem to help students understand how concepts and methods tie together.

Numbered formulas are presented throughout. A concerted effort has been made to reduce the number of different variables used in equations in order to simplify some of the critical financial formulas. A listing of formulas is presented at the end of applicable chapters.

$$\text{Current ratio} = \frac{\text{Current assets}}{\text{Current liabilities}} \qquad (3\text{-}1)$$

$$\text{Quick ratio (acid-test ratio)} = \frac{\text{Current assets} - \text{Inventory}}{\text{Current liabilities}} \qquad (3\text{-}2)$$

$$\text{Cash ratio} = \frac{\text{Cash and marketable securities}}{\text{Current liabilities}} \qquad (3\text{-}3)$$

SUPPLEMENTS FOR THE INSTRUCTOR

INSTRUCTOR'S RESOURCE CD

ISBN-13: 9780073313009
ISBN-10: 0073313009

This comprehensive CD contains all the following instructor supplements. We have compiled them in electronic format for easier access and convenience. Print copies are available through your McGraw-Hill/Irwin representative.

- **Learning Goal Map** Succinctly maps each chapter according to the learning goals chapter narrative, end-of-chapter material, and test bank questions to help instructors organize their course.

- **Test Bank** Peggy Ward, Wichita State University, has developed this test bank with hundreds of questions to complement the material presented in the book. The Test Bank is organized by problem type-questions, problems, and essay. It is also tagged by level of difficulty, learning goal, AACSB's five knowledge categories (ethics, analytics, communication, technology, and diversity) and Bloom's taxonomy—making it easy for instructors to customize exams to reflect the material stressed in class if so desired. The test bank is available in Word files and in McGraw-Hill's flexible electronic testing program *EZ Test Online*. EZ Test Online allows you to create tests or quizzes in this easy to use program.

  Instructors can select questions from multiple McGraw-Hill test banks or author their own, and then either print the test for paper distribution or give it online. This user-friendly program allows instructors to sort questions by format; edit existing questions or add new ones; and scramble questions for multiple versions of the same test. You can export your tests for use in WebCT, Blackboard, PageOut and Apple's iQuiz. Sharing tests with colleagues, adjuncts, TAs is easy! Instant scoring and feedback is provided and EZ Test's grade book is designed to easily export to your grade book.

- **Solutions Manual** Developed by the authors—Marcia Cornett, Troy Adair, and John Nofsinger—this resource contains all the worked-out solutions to the end-of-chapter problems. The solutions have been class-tested and checked by multiple instructors to ensure accuracy.

- **PowerPoint Presentation** Steve Byers, Idaho State University, has developed this unique asset, which is separated into three presentations. The first file contains the lecture notes that closely follows the book content. The second file contains additional problems and questions that can be used for in-class discussion not included within the book, but that serve to further enhance the subject matter in each chapter. Last, the third file contains the electronic files of the figures and tables presented within the book. Instructors can easily customize to suit their classroom needs and various presentation styles.

DVD

ISBN-13: 9780073363653
ISBN-10: 0073363650

McGraw-Hill/Irwin has produced a series of finance videos that present 10-minute case studies of key topics in corporate finance, such as time value of money and capital budgeting.

ASSURANCE OF LEARNING

Many educational institutions today are focused on the notion of assurance of learning, an important element of some accreditation standards. *Finance: Applications and Theory* is designed specifically to support your assurance of learning initiatives with a simple, yet powerful, solution.

Each test bank question for *Finance: Applications and Theory* maps to a specific chapter learning goal listed in the text. You can use the test bank software to easily query for learning goals that directly relate to the learning objectives for your course. You can then use the reporting features of the software to aggregate student results in similar fashion, making the collection and presentation of assurance of learning data simple and easy.

AACSB STATEMENT

The McGraw-Hill Companies is a proud corporate member of AACSB International. Understanding the importance and value of AACSB accreditation, *Finance: applications and theory, 1e* has sought to recognize the curricula guidelines detailed in the AACSB standards for business accreditation by connecting selected questions in the test bank to the general knowledge and skill guidelines found in the AACSB standards.

The statements contained in *Finance: applications and theory, 1e* are provided only as a guide for the users of this text. The AACSB leaves content coverage and assessment within the purview of individual schools, the mission of the school, and the faculty. While *Finance: applications and theory, 1e* and the teaching package make no claim of any specific AACSB qualification or evaluation, we have, within *Finance: applications and theory, 1e* labeled selected questions according to the six general knowledge and skills areas.

FOR THE STUDENT

ONLINE LEARNING CENTER
www.mhhe.com/can1e

A wealth of information is available online at our book Web site. Students will have access to study materials specifically created for this text, such as:

- **Interactive Examples** Examples Each numbered example featured within the book has a series of five different tutorials that accompany it: a narrated example, a related example with interactive solutions and decision points that need to be made by the student, an example using the BA II Plus calculator, another example using the TI-83 calculator, and an example using Excel.

- **Practice Quizzes** These online quizzes offer a quick way to review concepts presented in the chapter. Ten multiple-choice questions are included for each chapter so students can test their knowledge related to specific chapter content.

Instructors will have access to all the material that students can view but will also have password-protected access to the teaching support materials.

PACKAGING OPTIONS

Please contact your McGraw-Hill/Irwin sales representative to find out more about these exciting packaging options now available for your class.

- **McGraw-Hill's Homework Manager®** Are you looking for a way to spend less time grading and to have more flexibility with the problems you assign as homework and tests? McGraw-Hill's Homework Manager® is an exciting new package option developed for this text! McGraw-Hill's Homework Manager® is a Web-based tool for instructors and students for delivering, answering, and grading end-of-chapter problems and tests and for providing a limitless supply of self-graded practice for students.

  Even-numbered problems are represented algorithmically so each student has a unique set of variables for the problems. You create the assignments and control parameters, such as do you want your students to receive hints, is this a graded assignment or practice, and so on. The test bank is also available in McGraw-Hill's Homework Manager®, giving you the ability to use those questions for online tests. Both the problems and the tests are automatically graded and the results are stored in a private grade book, which is created when you set up your class. Detailed results let you see at a glance how each student does on an assignment or an individual problem—you can even see how many tries it took them to solve it. If you order this special package, students will receive a McGraw-Hill's Homework Manager® User's Guide and an access code packaged with their text.

- **McGraw-Hill's Homework Manager Plus™** There is also an enhanced version of McGraw-Hill's Homework Manager® through the McGraw-Hill's Homework Manager Plus™ package option. If you order the text packaged with McGraw-Hill's Homework Manager Plus™, your students will receive McGraw-Hill's Homework Manager® as described above, but with an integrated online text included. When students are in homework manager and need more help to solve a problem, there will be a link that takes them to the section of the text online that explains the concept they are struggling with. If you order this special package, students will receive the McGraw-Hill's Homework Manager Plus™ card packaged with their text, which gives them access to all of these products, as well as an online homework manager User's Guide.

acknowledgments

Development of this book started with a course survey that was completed by 400 instructors across the country. The following is a list of many of the reviewers that became part of the many review stages, focus groups, and class-testing all of which were invaluable to us during the development of this book.

Rebecca Abraham
Nova Southeastern University

Paul Adams
University of Cincinnati at Cincinnati

Pankaj Agrrawal
University of Maine

Aigbe Akhigbe
University of Akron

Anne Anderson
Lehigh University

Murat Aydogdu
Bryant University

Robert Balik
Western Michigan University

Marvin Ball
East Oregon University

Jaclyn Beierlein
East Carolina University

Eli Beracha
East Carolina University

Robert Boldin
Indiana University of Pennsylvania

Denis Boureaux
University of Louisiana

David Bourff
Boise State University

Walter Boyle
Fayetteville Tech Community College

Joe Bracato
Tarleton State University

Cheryl A. Broyler
Preston University

Celso Brunetti
Johns Hopkins University

Sarah K. Bryant
Shippensburg University

James Buck
East Carolina University

Steven Byers
Idaho State University

Stephen Caples
University of Houston, Clear Lake

Bob Castaneda
Robert Morris University

Su-Jane Chen
Metro State College of Denver

Samuel Chinnis
Guilford Tech Community College

Cetin Ciner
University of North Carolina, Wilmington

Julie Dahlquist
University of Texas, San Antonio

Kenneth Daniels
Virginia Commonwealth University

Natalya Delcoure
Sam Houston State University

James DeLoach
Troy University

Michael Devaney
Southeast Missouri State University

Anne Drougas
Dominican University

David Dumpe
Kent State University

Alan Eastman
Indiana University of Pennsylvania

Scott Ehrhorn
Liberty University

Zekeriya Eser
Eastern Kentucky University

Angelo Esposito
University of North Florida

Joe Farinella
University of North Carolina, Wilmington

John Farlin
Ohio Dominican University

John Fay
Santa Clara University

David Fehr
Southern New Hampshire University

Calvin Fink
Bethune-Cookman College

Barbara Fischer
Cardinal Stritch University

Susan Flaherty
Towson University

Frank Flanegin
Robert Morris University

Sharon Garrison
University of Arizona

Victoria Geyfman
Bloomsburg University

Charmaine Glegg
East Carolina University

Cameron Gordon
University of Canberra

Ed Graham
University of North Carolina, Wilmington

Keshav Gupta
Kutztown University

Christine Harrington
State University of New York, Oneonta

James Harriss
Campbell University

Travis Hayes
Chattanooga State University

Heikki Heino
Governors State University

Susan Hendrickson
Robert B. Miller College

Steve Henry
Sam Houston State University

Rodrigo Hernandez
Radford University

James Howard
University of Maryland

Bharat Jain
Towson University

Joel Jankowski
University of Tampa

Steve Johnson
University of Northern Iowa

Jacqueline Griffith Jonnard
Berkley College

Dongmin Ke
Kean University

Francis E. Laatsch
Bowling Green State University

Stephen Lacewell
Murray State University

Baeyong Lee
Fayetteville State University

Adam Lei
Midwestern State University

Fei Leng
University of Washington, Tacoma

Denise Letterman
Robert Morris University

Ralph Lim
Sacred Heart University

Bing-Xuan Lin
University of Rhode Island

Scott W. Lowe
James Madison University

Balasundram Maniam
Sam Houston State University

Kelly Manley
Gainesville State College

Peter Martino
Johnson & Wales University

Mario Mastrandrea
Cleveland State University

Leslie Mathis
University of Memphis

Christine McClatchey
University of Northern Colorado

Bruce L. McManis
Nicholls State University

Kathleen S. McNichol
LaSalle University

James A. Milanese
University of North Carolina, Greensboro

Helen Moser
St. Cloud State University

Tarun Mukherjee
University of New Orleans

Elisa Muresan
Long Island University

James Nelson
East Carolina University

Tom Nelson
University of Colorado, Boulder

Tom C. Nelson
Leeds School of Business

Vivian Okere
Providence College

Elisabeta Pana
Illinois Wesleyan University

Anil Pawar
San Diego State University

Glenn Pettengill
Grand Valley State University

Wendy Pirie
Valparaiso University

Gary E. Porter
John Carroll University

Franklin Potts
Baylor University

Eric Powers
University of South Carolina

Robert Prati
East Carolina University

Lora Reinholz
Marquette University

Nivine Richie
University of North Carolina, Wilmington

Philip Russel
Philadelphia University

Oliver Schnusenberg
University of North Florida

Andrew Spieler
Hofstra University

Jim Sprow
Corban College

Martin S. St. John
Westmoreland County Community College

Gikenn l. Stevens
Franklin & Marshall College

Gordon Stringer
University of Colorado, Colorado Springs

Don Stuhlman
Wilmington University

Jennifer O' Sullivan
Hardin-Simmons University

Janikan Supanvanji
St. Cloud State University

Arun Tandon
University of South Florida, Lakeland

Kudret Topyan
Manhattan College

Michael Toyne
Northeastern State University

Gary Tripp
Southern New Hampshire University

Kuo-Cheng Tseng
California State University, Fresno

James A. Turner
Weber State University

John Upstrom
Loras College

Michael C. Walker
University of Cincinnati

Peggy Ward
Wichita State University

Gwendolyn Webb
Baruch College

Paul Weinstock
Ohio State University

Kyle Wells
University of New Mexico

John B. White
Georgia Southern University

Susan White
University of Maryland

George Young
Liberty University

Emily Norman Zietz
Middle Tennessee State University

We are also indebted to the talented staff at McGraw-Hill/Irwin for their expertise and guidance, specifically Michele Janicek, executive editor; Christina Kouvelis, senior developmental editor; Mary Conzachi, manager of photo, design, and publishing tools; Marilyn Rothenberger, project manager; Trish Taylor, consulting development editor; Ashley Smith, marketing manager; Jennifer Jelinski, marketing specialist; Carol Bielski, production supervisor; Matt Baldwin, lead designer; and Kerry Bowler, media project manager. We would also like to thank Blerina Reca, Weicheng Wang, and Hongyan Fang.

We hope you like the outcome of this text. Research and development is always ongoing, and we are interested in your feedback on how this text has worked for you!

Marcia Millon Cornett
Troy A. Adair, Jr.
John Nofsinger

brief table of contents

PART ONE: INTRODUCTION *2*

1   Introduction to Financial Management *2*

PART TWO: FINANCIAL STATEMENTS *28*

2   Reviewing Financial Statements *28*
3   Analyzing Financial Statements *68*

PART THREE: VALUING OF FUTURE CASH FLOWS *110*

4   Time Value of Money 1: Analyzing Single Cash Flows *110*
5   Time Value of Money 2: Analyzing Annuity Cash Flows *140*

PART FOUR: VALUING OF BONDS AND STOCKS *178*

6   Valuing Bonds *178*
7   Valuing Stocks *218*
8   Understanding Financial Markets and Institutions *254*

PART FIVE: RISK AND RETURN *294*

9   Characterizing Risk and Return *294*
10   Estimating Risk and Return *326*

PART SIX: CAPITAL BUDGETING *358*

11   Calculating the Cost of Capital *358*
12   Estimating Cash Flows on Capital Budgeting Projects *388*
13   Weighing Net Present Value and Other Capital Budgeting Criteria *424*

PART SEVEN: CAPITAL STRUCTURE ISSUES *460*

14   Assessing Long-Term Debt, Equity, and Capital Structure *460*
15   Sharing Firm Wealth: Dividends, Share Repurchases, and Other Payouts *490*
16   Issuing Capital and the Investment Banking Process *512*

PART EIGHT: WORKING CAPITAL MANAGEMENT *538*

17   Addressing Working Capital Policies and Managing Short-Term Assets and Liabilities *538*

PART NINE: OTHER TOPICS IN FINANCE *568*

18   Considering International Aspects of Corporate Finance *568*
19   Managing Mergers and Acquisitions and Financial Distress *598*

table of contents

PART ONE: Introduction 2

1   Introduction to Financial Management 2

1.1 Finance in Business and in Life 4
    What Is Finance? 4
    Subareas of Finance 6
    Application and Theory for Financial Decisions 8
1.2 The Financial Function 9
    The Financial Manager 9
    Finance in Other Business Functions 10
    Finance in Your Personal Life 10
1.3 Business Organization 11
    Sole Proprietorships 11
    Partnerships 12
    Corporations 12
    Hybrid Organizations 13
1.4 Firm Goals 14
1.5 Agency Theory 15
    Agency Problem 15
    Corporate Governance 16
    The Role of Ethics 18
1.6 Financial Markets, Intermediaries, and the Firm 20
Summary of Learning Goals 21

PART TWO: Financial Statements 28

2   Reviewing Financial Statements 28

2.1 Balance Sheet 30
    Assets 30
    Liabilities and Stockholders' Equity 30
    Managing the Balance Sheet 30
2.2 Income Statement 34
    Corporate Income Taxes 35

2.3 Statement of Cash Flows 39
    Sources and Uses of Cash 39
    Free Cash Flow 42
2.4 Statement of Retained Earnings 44
2.5 Cautions in Interpreting Financial Statements 45
Summary of Learning Goals 48

3   Analyzing Financial Statements 68

3.1 Liquidity Ratios 70
3.2 Asset Management Ratios 72
    Inventory Management 72
    Accounts Receivable Management 72
    Accounts Payable Management 73
    Fixed Asset and Working Capital Management 74
    Total Asset Management 74
3.3 Debt Management Ratios 76
    Debt versus Equity Financing 76
    Coverage Ratios 77
3.4 Profitability Ratios 79
3.5 Market Value Ratios 81
3.6 DuPont Analysis 83
3.7 Other Ratios 86
    Spreading the Financial Statements 86
    Internal and Sustainable Growth Rates 87
3.8 Time Series and Cross-Sectional Analysis 88
3.9 Cautions in Using Ratios to Evaluate Firm Performance 89
Summary of Learning Goals 92

PART THREE: Valuing of Future Cash Flows 110

4   Time Value of Money 1: Analyzing Single Cash Flows 110

4.1 Organizing Cash Flows 112

4.2 Future Value *112*

    Single Period Future Value *113*

    Compounding and Future Value *113*

4.3 Present Value *119*

    Discounting *119*

4.4 Using Present Value and Future Value *122*

    Moving Cash Flows *122*

4.5 Computing Interest Rates *124*

    Return Asymmetries *126*

4.6 Solving for Time *126*

Summary of Learning Goals *128*

5   Time Value of Money 2: Analyzing Annuity Cash Flows *140*

5.1 Future Value of Multiple Cash Flows *142*

    Finding the Future Value of Several Cash Flows *142*

    Future Value of Level Cash Flows *143*

    Future Value of Multiple Annuities *144*

5.2 Present Value of Multiple Cash Flows *148*

    Finding the Present Value of Several Cash Flows *148*

    Present Value of Level Cash Flows *148*

    Present Value of Multiple Annuities *151*

    Perpetuity—A Special Annuity *152*

5.3 Ordinary Annuities versus Annuities Due *152*

5.4 Compounding Frequency *154*

    Effect of Compounding Frequency *154*

5.5 Annuity Loans *157*

    What Is the Interest Rate? *157*

    Finding Payments on an Amortized Loan *158*

Summary of Learning Goals *163*

PART FOUR: Valuing of Bonds and Stocks *178*

6   Valuing Bonds *178*

6.1 Bond Market Overview *180*

    Bond Characteristics *180*

    Bond Issuers *182*

    Other Bonds and Bond-Based Securities *183*

    Reading Bond Quotes *185*

6.2 Bond Valuation *187*

    Present Value of Bond Cash Flows *187*

    Bond Prices and Interest Rate Risk *190*

    Bond Prices and the Term Structure of Interest Rates *192*

6.3 Bond Yields *193*

    Current Yield *193*

    Yield to Maturity *194*

    Yield to Call *195*

    Municipal Bonds and Yield *196*

    Summarizing Yields *198*

6.4 Credit Risk *199*

    Bond Ratings *199*

    Credit Risk and Yield *200*

6.5 Bond Markets *202*

    Following the Bond Market *202*

Summary of Learning Goals *205*

7   Valuing Stocks *218*

7.1 Common Stocks *220*

7.2 Stock Markets *220*

    Tracking the Stock Market *223*

    Trading Stocks *225*

7.3 Basic Stock Valuation *227*

    Cash Flows *227*

    Dividend Discount Models *229*

    Preferred Stock *230*

    Expected Return *232*

7.4 Additional Valuation Methods *233*

    Variable-Growth Techniques *233*

    The P/E Model *236*

    Estimating Future Stock Prices *238*

Summary of Learning Goals *241*

8   Understanding Financial Markets and Institutions *254*

8.1 Financial Markets *256*

    Primary Markets versus Secondary Markets *256*

    Money Markets versus Capital Markets *258*

    Other Markets *261*

8.2 Financial Institutions *262*

    Unique Economic Functions Performed by Financial Institutions *264*

8.3 Interest Rates *266*

    Factors that Influence Interest Rates for Individual Securities *266*

Theories Explaining the Shape of the Term Structure of Interest Rates 274

Forecasting Interest Rates 280

Summary of Learning Goals 282

PART FIVE: Risk and Return 294

9 Characterizing Risk and Return 294

9.1 Historical Returns 296

Computing Returns 296

Performance of Asset Classes 298

9.2 Historical Risks 299

Computing Volatility 299

Risk of Asset Classes 302

Risk versus Return 302

9.3 Forming Portfolios 304

Diversifying to Reduce Risk 304

Modern Portfolio Theory 305

Summary of Learning Goals 312

10 Estimating Risk and Return 326

10.1 Expected Returns 328

Expected Return and Risk 328

Risk Premiums 330

10.2 Market Risk 331

The Market Portfolio 331

Beta, a Measure of Market Risk 333

The Security Market Line 334

Finding Beta 337

Concerns about Beta 337

10.3 Capital Market Efficiency 339

Efficient Market Hypothesis 340

Behavioral Finance 341

10.4 Implications for Financial Managers 343

Using the Constant Growth Model for Required Return 343

Summary of Learning Goals 345

PART SIX: Capital Budgeting 358

11 Calculating the Cost of Capital 358

11.1 The WACC Formula 360

Calculating the Component Cost of Equity 360

Calculating the Component Cost of Preferred Stock 362

Calculating the Component Cost of Debt 362

Choosing the Appropriate Tax Rate for the WACC 363

Calculating the Weights 364

11.2 Firm WACC versus Project WACC 365

Project Cost Numbers that We Should Take from the Firm 365

Project Cost Numbers that We Should Not Take from the Firm: The Pure Play Approach 366

11.3 Divisional WACC 369

Advantages and Disadvantages of a Divisional WACC 369

Subjective versus Objective Approaches to Calculating Divisional WACCs 371

11.4 Flotation Costs 374

Adjusting the WACC 375

Summary of Learning Goals 376

12 Estimating Cash Flows on Capital Budgeting Projects 388

12.1 Sample Project Description 390

12.2 Guiding Principles for Cash Flow Estimation 390

Opportunity Costs 391

Sunk Costs 391

Substitutionary and Complementary Effects 391

Stock Dividends and Bond Interest 392

12.3 Total Project Cash Flow 392

Calculating Depreciation 393

Calculating Operating Cash Flow 394

Calculating Changes in Gross Fixed Assets 394

Calculating Changes in Net Working Capital 395

Bringing It All Together 396

12.4 Accelerated Depreciation and the Half-Year Convention 397

MACRS Depreciation Calculation 398

Section 179 Deductions 399

Impact of Accelerated Depreciation 399

12.5 "Special" Cases Aren't Really That Special 400

12.6 Choosing between Alternative Assets with Differing Lives: EAC 402

12.7 Flotation Costs Revisited 404

Summary of Learning Goals 407

13 Weighing Net Present Value and Other Capital Budgeting Criteria 424

13.1 The Set of Capital Budgeting Techniques 426

13.2 The Choice of Decision Statistic Format 426

Decision Statistic Formats 427

13.3 Processing Capital Budgeting Decisions 427

13.4 Net Present Value 427

NPV Statistic 428

NPV Benchmark 428

NPV Strengths and Weaknesses 430

13.5 Payback and Discounted Payback 431

Payback Statistic 431

Payback Benchmark 431

Discounted Payback Statistic 432

Discounted Payback Benchmark 433

Payback and Discounted Payback Strengths and Weaknesses 434

13.6 Internal Rate of Return and Modified Internal Rate of Return 435

Internal Rate of Return Statistic 436

Internal Rate of Return Benchmark 436

Problems with Internal Rate of Return 437

IRR and NPV Profiles with Non-Normal Cash Flows 437

Differing Reinvestment Rate Assumptions of NPV and IRR 438

Modified Internal Rate of Return Statistic 439

IRRs, MIRRs, and NPV Profiles and Mutually Exclusive Projects 440

MIRR Strengths and Weaknesses 444

13.7 Profitability Index 445

Profitability Index Statistic 445

Profitability Index Benchmark 446

Summary of Learning Goals 447

PART SEVEN: Capital Structure Issues 460

14 Assessing Long-Term Debt, Equity, and Capital Structure 460

14.1 Active versus Passive Capital Structure Changes 462

14.2 Capital Structure Theory: The Effect of Financial Leverage 463

Modigliani and Miller's "Perfect World" 463

M&M with Corporate Taxes 468

The Choice to Re-leverage 470

Break-Even EBIT and EBIT Expectations 473

14.3 M&M with Corporate Taxes and Bankruptcy 475

Types of Bankruptcies in the United States 475

Costs of Financial Distress 476

The Value of the Firm with Taxes *and* Bankruptcy 479

14.4 Capital Structure Theory versus Reality 481

Optimal Theoretical Capital Structure 481

Observed Capital Structures 482

Summary of Learning Goals 483

15 Sharing Firm Wealth: Dividends, Share Repurchases, and Other Payouts 490

15.1 Dividends versus Capital Gains 492

Dividend Irrelevance Theory 492

Why Some Investors Favor Dividends 493

Why Some Investors Favor Capital Gains 493

15.2 Other Dividend Policy Issues 494

The Information Effect 494

The Clientele Effect 494

Corporate Control Issues 494

15.3 Real-World Dividend Policy 495

The Residual Dividend Model 495

Extraordinary Dividends 496

15.4 Dividend Payment Logistics 497

Payment Procedures 498

Effect of Dividends on Stock Prices 498

15.5 Stock Dividends and Stock Splits 501

Stock Dividends 501

Stock Splits 502

Effect of Splits and Stock Dividends on Stock Prices 502

15.6 Stock Repurchases 502

Advantages of Repurchases 503

Disadvantages of Repurchases 503

Effect of Repurchases on Stock Prices 504

Summary of Learning Goals 505

16 Issuing Capital and the Investment Banking Process 512

16.1 Sources of Capital for New and Small Firms 514

Debt Financing 514

Equity Financing and Expertise   *517*

The Choice to Go Public   *518*

16.2 Public Firms' Capital Sources   *519*

Debt Financing   *519*

Equity Financing   *523*

Summary of Learning Goals   *529*

PART EIGHT: Working Capital Management   *538*

17 Addressing Working Capital Policies and Managing Short-term Assets and Liabilities   *538*

17.1 Revisiting the Balance-Sheet Model of the Firm   *540*

17.2 Tracing Cash and Net Working Capital   *541*

The Operating Cycle   *541*

The Cash Cycle   *541*

17.3 Some Aspects of Short-Term Financial Policy   *543*

The Size of the Current Assets Investment   *543*

Alternative Financing Policies for Current Assets   *544*

17.4 The Short-Term Financial Plan   *546*

Unsecured Loans   *546*

Secured Loans   *547*

Other Sources   *548*

17.5 Cash Management   *548*

Reasons for Holding Cash   *548*

Determining the Target Cash Balance: The Baumol Model   *549*

Determining the Target Cash Balance: The Miller-Orr Model   *551*

Other Factors Influencing the Target Cash Balance   *552*

17.6 Float Control: Managing the Collection and Disbursement of Cash   *553*

Accelerating Collections   *553*

Delaying Disbursements   *554*

Ethical and Legal Questions   *555*

17.7 Investing Idle Cash   *555*

Why Firms Have Surplus Cash   *556*

What to Do with Surplus Cash   *556*

17.8 Credit Management   *556*

Credit Policy: Terms of the Sale   *556*

Credit Analysis   *557*

Collection Policy   *557*

Summary of Learning Goals   *559*

PART NINE   Other Topics In Finance   *568*

18 Considering International Aspects of Corporate Finance   *568*

18.1 Global Business   *570*

International Opportunities   *570*

Corporate Expansion into Other Countries   *572*

18.2 Foreign Currency Exchange   *574*

Exchange Rates   *574*

Exchange Rate Risk   *576*

The Forward Exchange Rate and Hedging   *577*

Interest Rate Parity   *579*

Purchasing Power Parity (PPP) and Future Exchange Rates   *580*

18.3 Political Risks   *583*

18.4 International Capital Budgeting   *585*

Summary of Learning Goals   *586*

19 Managing Mergers and Acquisitions and Financial Distress   *598*

19.1 Mergers and Acquisitions   *601*

Types of Mergers   *601*

Motives for Mergers and Acquisitions   *602*

Valuing a Merger   *608*

19.2 Financial Distress   *609*

Types and Causes of Financial Distress   *609*

Informal Resolutions of Financial Distress   *610*

Federal Bankruptcy Laws   *611*

Predicting Bankruptcy   *615*

Summary of Learning Goals   *622*

Appendix A *Present Value and Future Value Tables*   *636*

Appendix B *Selected Answers to End of Chapter Problems*   *641*

Index   *647*

finance

applications & theory

chapter 1:
INTRODUCTION TO FINANCIAL MANAGEMENT

Learning Goals

LG1 Define the subareas of finance and their roles in corporate financial management.

LG2 Show why and how finance is at the heart of sound business decisions.

LG3 Apply finance in your personal life.

LG4 Compare and contrast the advantages and disadvantages of the three most common business organizational forms in the United States.

LG5 Differentiate between financial managers' appropriate and inappropriate goals.

LG6 Identify the firm's primary agency relationship and discuss why agency relationships can create conflicts.

LG7 Incorporate ethics into financial management.

LG8 Describe the complex and necessary relationships among firms, financial institutions, and financial markets.

D o you know: What finance entails? How financial management functions within the business world? Why you might benefit from studying financial principles? This chapter is the ideal place to get answers to those questions.

Finance is largely the study of how to value all sorts of things, such as shares of stock, the payments left on a home mortgage, the purchase of an entire company, and the personal decision to retire early. In this text, we're going to focus primarily on one particular area of finance, **financial management,** which tends to concentrate on valuing things from the perspective of a company.

Financial management is critically important to the success of any business organization, and throughout the text, we will concentrate on describing the key financial concepts central to corporate finance. However, many of the tools and techniques we'll learn for handling the financial management of a firm are pretty widely applicable to broader types of financial problems, too, such as personal finance decisions.

In finance, we call the receiving and paying of money *cash flow,* and we'll start our discussion of finance off with a graphical depiction of the cash flows of finance, using this depiction to both help explain what finance is all about and to demonstrate the different aspects of finance.

viewpoints

Business Application

Caleb has worked very hard to create and expand his juice stand at the mall. He has finally perfected his products and feels that he is offering the right combination of juice and food. As a result, the stand is making a nice profit. Caleb would like to open more stands at malls all over his state and eventually all over the country.

Caleb knows he needs more money to expand. He needs money to buy more equipment, buy more inventory, and hire and train more people. How can Caleb get the capital he needs to expand? **(See solution on p. 21)**

Personal Application

Dagmar is becoming interested in investing some of her money. However, she has heard about several corporations in which the investors lost all of their money. In the past several years, Dagmar has heard that Enron (2001), WorldCom (2002), and Delta Airlines (2005) have all filed for bankruptcy. These firms' stockholders lost their entire investments in these firms.

Many of the stockholders who lost money were employees of these companies who had invested some of their retirement money in the company stock. She wonders what guarantee she has as an investor against losing her money. **(See solution on p. 21)**

A practice test can be found on the Online Learning Center at
www.mhhe.com/can1e

The remainder of this chapter will be devoted to a discussion of several important environmental variables that will significantly impact the financial decisions of the firm, including the organizational form of the business, the agency relationship between the managers and owners of a firm, and ethical considerations in the application of finance.

1.1 Finance in Business and in Life

Your perception of what finance is all about may have been negatively skewed by pop-culture entertainment. Most movies portray finance professionals as greedy and unethical people [see, for example, the movies *Trading Places* (1983), *Wall Street* (1987), *Barbarians at the Gate* (1993), *Rogue Trader* (1998), and *Boiler Room* (2000)]. While such characters make for good entertainment, those depictions do not reflect the truth about finance professionals and their contributions to society.

Successfully applying finance theories helps money flow from individuals who want to improve their financial future to businesses that want to expand the scale or scope of their operations. These exchanges lead to an expanding economy and more employment opportunities for people at all levels of society. So, two great things result from this simple exchange: the economy will be more productive now, and individuals' wealth will grow into the future.

In this section, we develop a comprehensive description of finance, its subareas, and the relevant decisions professionals in each subarea must make. As you will see, all of the subareas share a common set of ideas and application tools.

What Is Finance?

To envision what finance is all about, consider segmenting all of the participants in an economy along two dimensions. The first dimension is the availability of "extra" money (i.e., money above and beyond their current spending needs) for investment. The second dimension is the ability to develop economically viable business ideas. Dividing everyone along these two dimensions will result in participants being divided into four groups, as shown in Figure 1.1. Of course, people can move from one group to another over time.

Type 1 people really play no direct role in **financial markets** as either lenders of capital or users of capital, though they will probably play an indirect role by providing their labor to or consuming products from economic enterprises. Our discussion of finance is going to concentrate on only those participants who play a direct role, so we can set the Type 1 participants aside.

Type 4 people will use financial tools to evaluate their own ideas to pick the ones that have the most potential and to create those enterprises that will implement those ideas most efficiently. However, the type 4 individuals have no need for the financial markets because they are self-funded, so the financial tools they use and the types of decisions they make will be fairly narrowly focused. Thus our discussion will not concentrate on type 4 individuals either.

Financial institutions and financial markets enhance the economy by empowering types 2 and 3 people to engage in a mutually advantageous exchange: the type 2 people temporarily lend their money to the type 3 people, who put that money into their good business ideas. In most developed economies, type 2 participants are usually individual **investors**—just as you will likely be for most of your life. Each of us individually may not have a lot of extra money, but by aggregating our available funds, we can provide sizable amounts. Type 3 participants

figure 1.1

	NO EXTRA MONEY	EXTRA MONEY
No Economically Viable Business Ideas	Type 1: No money and no ideas	Type 2: Money, but no ideas
Economically Viable Business Ideas	Type 3: No money, but ideas	Type 4: Both money and ideas

Participants in Our Hypothetical Economy

figure 1.2

$

People with ideas but not enough money (Companies) ← People with money but no ideas/time (Investors)

Capital Flow from Investors to Companies

figure 1.3

Return of Capital to Investors

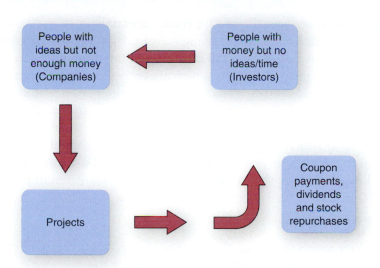

People with ideas but not enough money (Companies) ← People with money but no ideas/time (Investors)

Projects → Coupon payments, dividends and stock repurchases

may be individuals with innovative new ideas, but are more often corporations or other types of companies with Research and Development (R&D) departments dedicated to developing innovative ideas.

Obviously, investors and companies can help one another. If investors lend their "extra" capital to companies, as shown in Figure 1.2, then companies can use this capital to fund expansion projects. Economically successful projects will eventually offer to repay the money (plus profit) to investors, as shown in Figure 1.3. The company has expanded its business, hired more employees, and created a promising future for itself. Meanwhile, the investor has increased wealth for the future.

Of course, not all of the cash will return to the investors. In reality, sources of friction arise in this system, which will reduce the amount of capital returned to investors. Two primary sources of friction will be **retained earnings** (which you can intuitively think of as funds that the firm retains to support ongoing operations) and *taxes*, which the government imposes on the company and individuals

figure 1.4

The Complete Cash
Flows of Finance

to help fund public services. Figure 1.4 shows an analysis of the resulting cash
flows with the associated retained earnings and tax payments. Though simplistic, this figure provides a great overall intuitive explanation of finance in general
and of the major subareas of finance, which are embedded in the figure.

For example, individuals must assess what investment opportunities are right
for their needs and risk tolerance; financial institutions and markets must efficiently distribute the capital; and companies must evaluate their potential projects
and wisely decide which projects to fund, what kind of capital to use, and how
much capital to return to investors. All of these types of decisions deal with the
basic cash flows of finance shown in Figure 1.4, but from different perspectives.

Subareas of Finance

Suppose we look at this set of cash flows from the investor's perspective as shown
in Figure 1.5. The red arrows going into and out of the investor's perspective
(represented by the blue box) represent the concerns of the study of **investments,**
which involves methods and techniques for making appropriate decisions about
what kinds of securities to own (e.g., bonds versus stocks), which firms' securities to buy, and how to pay the investor back in the form that the investor wishes
(e.g., the timing and certainty of the promised cash flows).

The next major subarea of finance, *financial management,* looks at firm decisions in acquiring and utilizing cash received from investors or from retained
earnings, as shown in Figure 1.6. This text will focus primarily on this financial
area, and we'll see that financial management involves decisions about:

- How to organize the firm in a manner that will attract capital.
- How should capital be raised (e.g., via bonds versus stocks).
- Which projects to fund.
- How much capital to retain in the firm for ongoing operations and new
  projects.
- How to minimize taxation.
- How to go about paying back capital providers.

figure 1.5

Investments

figure 1.6

Financial Management

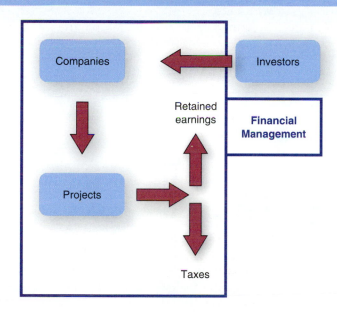

All of these decisions are quite involved, and we will discuss them throughout later chapters.

Another major subarea of finance, shown in Figure 1.7, covers the **financial institutions and markets** that help facilitate the capital flows between investors and companies. This subarea involves the firm initially acquiring capital and then investors' ongoing securities trading. It also involves the function of financial institutions, like banks and pension administrators, and the dynamics of interest rates.

Finally, as the world has transformed into a global economy, finance has had to become much more innovative and sensitive to changes in other countries. As Figure 1.8 shows, investors, companies, business operations, and capital markets may all be located in different countries. Adapting to this environment requires study of **international finance.** Until recently, international financial decisions were considered to be a straightforward application of the other

figure 1.7

Financial Institutions
and Markets

figure 1.8

International Finance

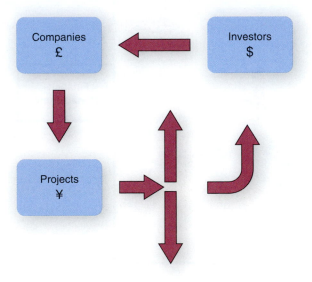

three financial subareas. But experience has shown that the uncertainty about future exchange rates, political risk, and changing country business laws all add enough complexity to these decisions to warrant considering international finance as a subarea in its own right.

Application and Theory for Financial Decisions

Applying finance theory to real decisions requires that we realize that cash flows are neither instantaneous nor guaranteed. Future cash flows are uncertain both in terms of timing and size, and we refer to this uncertainty as **risk.** Investors experience risk about the return of their capital. Companies experience risk in funding and operating their business projects. Most financial decisions involve comparing the rewards of a decision to the risks that decision involves.

Comparing rewards with risks frequently involves assessing the value today of cash flows that we expect to receive in the future. For example, the price of a **financial asset,** like a stock or a bond, should depend on the cash flows you expect to receive from that asset in the future. A stock that's expected to deliver high cash flows in the future will be more valuable today than a stock with low expected future cash flows. Of course, investors would like to buy stocks whose market prices are currently lower then their actual values. They want to get stocks on sale! Similarly, a firm's goal is to fund projects that will give them more value than their costs.

Despite the large number of stories about investors who've struck it rich in the stock market, it's actually more likely that a firm will find "bargain" projects than that investors will find underpriced stocks. Firms can find bargains because business projects involve **real assets** trading in **real markets,** where some level of monopoly power, special knowledge, and expertise can possibly make such projects worth more than they cost. Investors, however, are trading financial assets in *financial markets,* where the assets are more likely to be worth, on average, exactly what they cost.

The method for relating expected cash flows to a present value is called the **time value of money (TVM).** Since the expected cash flows of either a business project or an investment are likely to be uncertain, the TVM analysis must account for both the timing and the risk level of the cash flows.

TIME OUT

1-1   What are the main subareas of finance and how do they interact?

1.2 The Financial Function

In most companies, the financial function is usually closely associated with the accounting function. In a very rough sense, the accountant's job is to keep track of what happened *in the past* to the firm's money, while the finance job uses these historical figures with current information to determine what should happen *now and in the future* with the firm's money. The results of financial decisions will eventually appear in accounting statements, so this close association makes sense. Nevertheless, accounting tends to focus on and characterize the past, while finance focuses on the present and future.

The Financial Manager

The firm's highest-level financial manager is usually the chief financial officer, or CFO. Both the company treasurer and the controller report to the CFO. The treasurer is typically responsible for:

- Managing cash and credit.
- Issuing and repurchasing financial securities such as stocks and bonds.
- Deciding how and when to spend capital for new and existing projects.
- Hedging (reducing the firm's potential risk) against changes in foreign exchange and interest rates.

In larger corporations, the treasurer may also oversee other areas, such as purchasing insurance or managing the firm's pension fund investments. The controller oversees the accounting function, usually managing the tax, cost accounting, financial accounting, and data processing functions.

Finance in Other Business Functions

Though the CFO and treasurer positions tend to be the firm's most visible finance-related positions, finance affects the firm in many ways that are unrelated to such relatively high positions in a company's organizational chart. Finance permeates the entire business organization, providing guidance for both strategic and day-to-day decisions of the firm and collecting information for control and feedback about the firm's financial decisions.

Operational managers use finance daily to determine how much overtime labor to use, or to perform cost/benefit analysis when they consider new production lines or methods. Marketing managers use finance to assess the cost effectiveness of doing follow-up marketing surveys. Human resource managers use finance in evaluating the company's cost for various employee benefit packages. No matter where you work in business, finance can help you do your job better.

 ## Finance in Your Personal Life

Finance can also help you make good financial decisions in your personal life. Consider these common activities you will probably face in your life:

- Borrow money to buy a new car.
- Refinance your home mortgage at a lower rate.
- Make credit card or student loan payments.
- Save for retirement.

You will be able to perform all of these tasks better after learning about finance. Recent changes throughout our economy and the U.S. business environment make knowledge of finance even more valuable to you than before. For example, most companies have switched from providing **defined benefit** retirement plans to employees to offering **defined contribution** plans (such as **401k** plans) and self-funded plans like **individual retirement accounts (IRAs).** Tax changes in the early 1980s made this switch more or less inevitable. It appears that each of us will have to ensure adequate funds for our own retirement—much more so than previous generations.

EXAMPLE 1-1

 For interactive versions of this example visit www.mhhe.com/can1e

 ## FINANCE APPLICATIONS

Chloe realizes how important finance will be for her future business career. However, some of the ways that she will see financial applications seem way off in the future. She is curious about how the theory applies to her personal life, both in the near term and in the long term.

SOLUTION:

Chloe will quickly find that her financial health now and in the future will depend upon many decisions she makes as she goes through life—starting now! For example, she will learn that the same tools that she applies to a business loan analysis can be applied to her own personal debt. After this course, Chloe will be able to evaluate credit card offers and select one that could save her hundreds of dollars per year. When she buys a new car and the dealership offers her a low interest rate loan or a higher rate loan with cash back, she will be able to pick the option that will truly cost her the least. Also, when Chloe gets her first professional job, she will know how to direct her retirement account so that she can earn millions of dollars for her future.

TIME OUT ⏰

1-2   How might the application of finance improve your professional and personal decisions?

1.3 Business Organization

In the United States, people can structure businesses in any of several ways, with the primary driving factor being the number of owners. Traditionally, single owners, partners, and corporations operate businesses. We can express the advantages and disadvantages of each organizational form through several dimensions. In describing these legal forms, we will use the following dimensions:

- Who controls the firm.
- Who owns the firm.
- What the owners' risks are.
- What access to capital exists.
- What the tax ramifications are.

Recently, small businesses have adopted hybrid structures that capture the benefits from multiple organizational forms, and we'll discuss those hybrid structures after we cover the more common, traditional types of business organizations.

Sole Proprietorships

Sole proprietorships represent, by far, the most common type of business in the United States.[1] A sole proprietorship is defined as any unincorporated business owned by a single individual.[2] Perhaps these businesses are so popular because they are relatively easy to start, and they're subject to a much lighter regulatory and paperwork burden than other business forms. The owner, or sole proprietor, of the business has complete control of the firm's activities. The owner also receives all of the firm's profits and is solely responsible for all losses.

The biggest disadvantage that sole proprietorships carry relative to other organizational forms is that they have **unlimited liability** for their companies' debts and actions. The owner's personal assets may be confiscated if the business is sued. The law recognizes no distinction between the owner's business assets and personal assets. The income of the business is also added to the owner's personal income and taxed by the government at the appropriate personal tax rate. Finally, sole proprietors have a difficult time obtaining capital to expand their business operations. Banks and other lenders are not typically interested in lending much money to sole proprietors because small firms have only one person liable for paying back the debt. A sole proprietor could raise capital by issuing **equity** to another investor. **Angel investors** and **venture capitalists** exchange capital for ownership in a business. But this requires re-forming the business as a partnership and the sole proprietor must give up some of the ownership (and thus control) of the firm. Table 1.1 summarizes sole proprietorships' characteristics.

---

[1]According to the IRS' *SOI Tax Stats—Integrated Business Data* for 2002, 71.59% of all businesses in the U.S. were sole proprietorships.

[2]However, if you are the sole member of a domestic limited liability company (LLC, discussed below), you are not a sole proprietor if you elect to treat the LLC as a corporation.

	OWNERSHIP	CONTROL	OWNERSHIP RISK	ACCESS TO CAPITAL	TAXES
Sole Proprietor	Single individual	Proprietor	Unlimited liability	Very limited	Paid by owner
Partnership	Multiple people	Shared by partners	Unlimited liability	Limited	Paid by partners
Corporation	Public investors who own the stock	Company managers	Stockholders can only lose their investment in the firm	Easy access	Corporation pays income tax and stockholders pay taxes on dividends
Hybrids: S-corp, LLP, LLC, LP	Partners or shareholders	Shared	Mostly limited	Limited by firm size restrictions	Paid by partners

Partnerships

A **general partnership,** or as it is more commonly known, a *partnership,* is an organizational form that features multiple individual owners. Each partner can own a different percentage of the firm. Firm control is typically determined by the size of partners' ownership stakes. Businesses' profits are split among the partners according to a prearranged agreement, usually by the percentage of firm ownership. Received profits are added to each partner's personal income and taxed at personal income tax rates.

The partners jointly share unlimited personal liability for the debts of the firm and all are obligated for contracts agreed to by any one of the partners. Banks are more willing to lend to partnerships than to sole proprietorships, because all partners are liable for repaying the debt. Partners would have to give up some ownership and control in the firm to raise more equity capital. In order to raise enough capital for substantial growth, a partnership often changes into a public corporation.

Corporations

Public corporations are legally *independent entities* entirely separate from their owners. This independence dramatically alters the firm's characteristics. Corporations hold many rights and obligations of individual persons, such as the ability to own property, sign binding contracts, and pay taxes. Federal and state governments tax corporate income once at the corporate level. Then shareholders pay taxes again at the personal level when corporate profits are paid out as dividends. This practice is generally known as **double taxation.**

Corporate owners are stockholders, also called *shareholders.* Public corporations typically have thousands of stockholders. The firm must hire managers to direct the firm, since thousands of individual shareholders could not direct day-to-day operations under any sort of consensus. As a result, managers control the company. Strong possibilities of conflicts of interests arise when one group of people owns the business, but another group controls it. We'll discuss conflicts of interest and their resolution later in the chapter.

As individual legal entities, corporations assume liability for their own debts, so the shareholders have only **limited liability.** That is, corporate shareholders cannot lose more money than they originally paid for their shares of stock. This limited liability is one reason that many people feel comfortable owning stock. Corporations are thus able to raise incredible amounts of money by selling stock (equity) and borrowing money. The largest businesses in the world are organized as corporations.

GOOGLE BUYS YOUTUBE

In November 2006, Web search leader Google purchased the online video-sharing phenomenon YouTube for $1.65 billion. Google bought the firm by giving YouTube owners shares of Google stock in exchange for their ownership in YouTube. YouTube was a private corporation owned primarily by cofounders Chad Hurley and Steve Chen, who each received over $300 million of Google stock. Venture capital firm Sequoia Capital had backed YouTube and received $442 million of Google stock. Two dozen YouTube employees also had ownership stakes; some of them became millionaires from the deal.

YouTube was founded in February 2005. Imagine starting a business that was purchased for $1.65 billion less than two years later! Consider how many finance people and applications were needed to organize the buyout. Google's CFO George Reyes and team had to determine the value that YouTube could bring to Google. They also had to convince their own Google stockholders that Google did not overpay

for the purchase. To do so, auditors had to evaluate YouTube's cash flows and the riskiness of those cash flows. The CFO, along with investment banker advisors, had to decide how to pay for YouTube. Google swapped its own stock for the firm but could have paid all cash or used a combination of cash and stock.

YouTube owners also had to assess the value of their stock to ensure that they received a fair price. Google's offer had to be compared to alternatives. For example, YouTube could have waited for a better offer from Google or sought an offer from another firm. Or YouTube owners could have decided to take the company public and sold shares to public investors.

This chapter illustrates the kinds of issues that finance addresses. The rest of the book describes the theories and tools needed to make these judgments. The practice of finance isn't just about numbers—the results of financial analysis are very dynamic and exciting!

 want to know more?   Key Words to Search For Updates: **Google, YouTube**

Hybrid Organizations

To promote the growth of small businesses, the U.S. government allows for several types of business organizations that simultaneously offer both limited personal liability for the owners *and* provide a pass-through of all firm earnings to the owners, so that the earnings are subject only to single taxation.

Hybrid organizations, such as *S corporations, limited liability partnerships (LLPs),* or *limited liability companies (LLCs),* offer single taxation and limited liability to all owners. Others, called *limited partnerships (LPs),* offer single taxation and limited liability to the *limited partners,* but also have *general partners,* who benefit from single taxation but also must bear personal liability for the firm's debts.

The U.S. government typically restricts hybrid organization status to relatively small firms. The government limits the maximum number of shareholders or partners involved,[3] the maximum amount of investment capital allowed, and the lines of business permitted. These restrictions are consistent with the government's stated reason for allowing the formation of these forms of business organization—to encourage the formation and growth of small businesses.

---

[3]For example, current federal regulations limit the number of shareholders in an S corporation to no more than 100.

TIME OUT

1-3   Why must an entrepreneur give up some control of the business as it grows into a public corporation?

1-4   What advantages does the corporate form of organization hold over a partnership?

1.4 Firm Goals

LG5

Tens of thousands of public corporations operate in the United States. Many of them are the largest business organizations in the world. Because U.S. corporations are so large and because there are so many of them, corporations have a tremendous impact on society. Given the power that these huge firms wield, many people question what the corporate goals should be. Two different, well-developed viewpoints have arisen concerning what the goal of the firm should be. The owners' perspective holds that the only appropriate goal is to **maximize shareholder wealth.** The competing viewpoint is from the **stakeholders'** perspective, which emphasizes social responsibility over profitability. This view maintains that managers must maximize the total satisfaction of all stakeholders in a business. These stakeholders include the owners and shareholders, but also include the business's customers, employees, and local communities.

While strong arguments speak in favor of both perspectives, financial practitioners and academics now tend to believe that the manager's primary responsibility should be to maximize shareholder wealth and give only secondary consideration to other stakeholders' welfare. One of the first, and most well-known, proponents of this viewpoint was Adam Smith, an 18th-century economist who argued that, in capitalism, an individual pursuing his own interests tends also to promote the good of his community.[4]

Smith argued that the **invisible hand** of the market, acting through competition and the free price system, would ensure that only those activities most efficient and beneficial to society as a whole would survive in the long run. Thus, those same activities would also profit the individual most. When companies try to implement a goal other than profit maximization, their efforts tend to backfire. Consider the firm that tries to maximize employment. The high number of employees raises costs. Soon the firm will find that its costs are too high to allow it to compete against more efficient firms, especially in a global business environment. When the firm fails, all employees are let go and employment ends up being minimized, not maximized.

Regardless of whether you believe Smith's assertion or not, a more pragmatic reason supports the argument that maximizing owners' wealth is an admirable goal. As we discuss below, the owners of the firm hire managers to work on their behalf, so the manager is morally, ethically, and legally required to act in the owners' best interests. Any relationships between the manager and other firm stakeholders are necessarily secondary to the goal that shareholders give to their hired managers.

Maximizing owners' equity value means carefully considering:

- How best to bring additional funds into the firm.
- Which projects to invest in.
- How best to return the profits from those projects to the owners over time.

[4]See Book IV of his *The Wealth of Nations.*

For corporations, maximizing the value of owners' equity can also be stated as *maximizing the current value per share, or* **stock price,** *of existing shares.* To the extent that the current stock price can be expected to include the present value of any future expected cash flows accruing to the owners, the goal of maximizing stock price provides us with a single, concrete, measurable gauge of value. You may be tempted to choose several other potential goals over maximizing the value of owners' equity. Common alternatives are:

- Maximizing net income or profit.
- Minimizing costs.
- Maximizing market share.

Though each may look appealing, each of these goals has some potentially serious shortcomings. For example, net income is measured on a year-by-year or quarter-by-quarter basis. When we say that we want to maximize profits, to which net income figure are we referring? We can maximize this year's net income in several legitimate ways, but many of these ways impose costs which will reduce future income. Or, current net income can be pushed into future years. Neither of these two extremes will likely encourage the firm's short-term and long-term stability. One more likely goal would be to maximize today's value of *all* future years of net income. Of course, this possible goal is very close to maximizing the current stock price, without the convenient market-oriented measure of the stock price. Another problem with considering maximizing all future profits as the goal is that net income (for reasons we'll go into later) does not really measure how much money the firm is actually earning.

Minimizing costs and *maximizing market share* also have fundamental problems as potential goals. Certainly minimizing costs would not make some stakeholders, like employees, very happy. In addition, without spending the money on R&D and new product development, many companies would not survive long in the ever-evolving economy without improving its products. A firm can always increase market share by lowering price. But if a firm loses money on every product sold, then selling more products will simply drive the firm into fiscal distress.

TIME OUT

1-5 Describe why the primary objective of maximizing shareholder value may actually be the most beneficial for society in the long run.

1.5 Agency Theory

Whenever one party (the *principal*) hires someone else (the *agent*) to work for him or her, their interaction is called an *agency relationship.* The agent is always supposed to act in the principal's best interests. For example, an apartment complex manager should ensure that tenants aren't doing willful damage to the property, that fire codes are enforced, and that the vacancy rate is kept as low as possible, because these are best for the apartment owner.

Agency Problem

In the context of a public corporation, we have already noted that stockholders hire managers to run the firm. Ideally, managers will operate the firm so that the shareholders realize maximum value for their equity. But managers may be tempted to operate the firm to serve their own best interests. Managers could spend company money to improve their own lifestyle instead of earning more profits for shareholders. Sometimes the manager's best interest does not necessarily align with shareholder goals. This creates a situation that we refer to as the **agency problem.**

For example, suppose it is time to buy a new corporate car for the firm's **chief executive officer (CEO).** Assuming that the CEO has no extraordinary driving requirements, shareholders might wish for the CEO to buy a nice, conservative domestic sedan. But suppose that the CEO demands the newest, biggest luxury car available. It's tempting to say that the shareholders could just tell the CEO which car to buy. But remember, the CEO has most of the control in a public corporation. Organizational behavior specialists have identified three basic approaches to minimize this conflict of interest. First, ignore it. If the amount of money involved is small enough relative to the firm's cash flows, or if the suitability of the purchase in question is ambiguous enough, shareholders might be best served to simply overlook the problem. A good deal of research literature suggests that allowing the manager a certain amount of such **perks (perquisites)** might actually enhance owner value, in that such items may boost managers' productivity.[5]

The second approach to mitigating this conflict is to monitor managers' actions. Monitoring at too fine a level of detail is probably counterproductive and prohibitively expensive. However, major firm decisions are usually monitored at least roughly through the accounting auditing process. Also, shareholders can benefit indirectly from the fact that current debt holders with a relatively large stake in the firm will usually engage in at least some additional monitoring of their own to insure their investments.[6]

The final approach for aligning managers' personal interests with those of owners is to make the managers owners—that is, to offer managers an equity stake in the firm so that management participates in any equity value increase. Many corporations take this approach, either through explicitly granting shares to managers, by awarding them **options** on the firm's stock, or by allowing them to purchase shares at a subsidized price through an **employee stock option plan (ESOP).** When firm managers are also firm owners, their incentives are more likely to align with stockholders' best interests.

Corporate Governance

We refer to the process of monitoring managers and aligning their incentives with shareholder goals as **corporate governance.** Theoretically, managers work for shareholders. In reality, because shareholders are usually inactive, the firm actually seems to belong to management. Generally speaking, the investing public does not know what goes on at the firm's operational level. Managers handle day-to-day operations, and they know that their work is mostly

---

[5]See, for example, Raghuram Rajan and Julie Wulf, "Are Perks Really Managerial Excess?" *Journal of Financial Economics* 79(1), 2006, 1–33.

[6]Potential acquirers will also often monitor firms for evidence that assets are being under- or misused by current management. To the extent that these acquirers may submit hostile takeover bids for the company (i.e., bids for enough of the company's shares to take control of the firm because existing management is not using firm assets in their highest use), current shareholders can benefit from this type of indirect monitoring, too.

figure 1.9

Corporate Governance Monitors

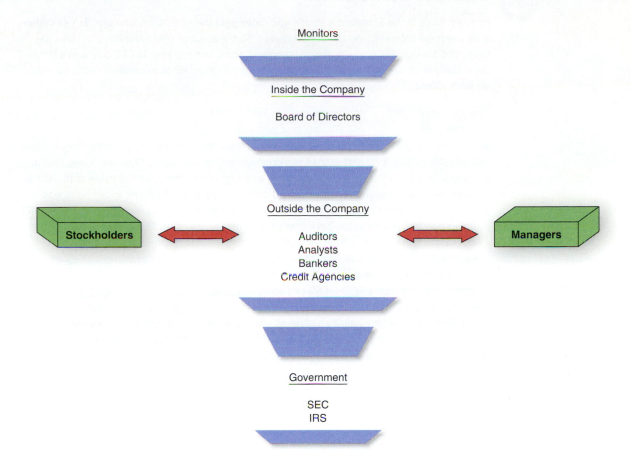

unknown to investors. This lack of supervision demonstrates the need for monitors. Figure 1.9 shows the people and organizations that help monitor corporate activities.

The monitors inside a public firm are the **board of directors,** who are appointed to represent shareholders' interests. The board hires the CEO, evaluates management, and can also design compensation contracts to tie management's salaries to firm performance.

The monitors outside the firm include auditors, analysts, investment banks, and credit rating agencies. **Auditors** examine the firm's accounting systems and comment on whether financial statements fairly represent the firm's financial position. **Investment analysts** follow a firm, conduct their own evaluations of the company's business activities, and report to the investment community. **Investment banks,** which help firms access capital markets and advise managers about how to interact with those capital markets, also monitor firm performance. **Credit analysts** examine a firm's financial strength for its debt holders. The government also monitors business activities through the Securities and Exchange Commission (SEC) and the Internal Revenue Service (IRS).

EXAMPLE 1-2

For interactive versions of this example visit www.mhhe.com/can1e

LG6 EXECUTIVE COMPENSATION

In 2005, firms in the Standard & Poor's 500 Index paid their CEOs, on average, $13.51 million, a 16.1 percent increase over the previous year. So the average CEO compensation was 411 times the average employee's compensation. In 2006, the increase in CEO pay was 8.9 percent. Every year, the controversy over CEO pay arises again. What arguments could be made on both sides?

SOLUTION:

Many people believe that CEOs are paid too much for the services they provide. They receive compensation that is far higher than workers' pay within their firms. Over the years, executive compensation has also increased at a faster and higher rate than has the value of the stockholders' wealth. For example, the return for stockholders of the S&P 500 Index firms was 15.6 percent in 2006 and 4.9 percent in 2005, compared to CEO pay increases of 8.9 percent and 16.1 percent, respectively. Each firm's board of directors sets CEO compensation. However, CEOs may have undue influence over director selection, tenure, and committee assignments—even over selecting the compensation advisors. This practice creates an unhealthy conflict of interest.

Others believe that a skilled CEO can positively affect company performance and that, therefore, the firm needs to offer high compensation and a bundle of perquisites to attract the best talent. To overcome agency problems, managers must be given incentives that pay very well when the company performs very well. If CEOs create a substantial amount of shareholder wealth, then who is to say that they are overpaid?

The Role of Ethics

Ethics must play a strong role in any practice of finance. Finance professionals commonly manage other people's money. For example, corporate managers control the stockholder's firm, bank employees manage deposits, and investment advisors manage people's investment portfolios. These **fiduciary** relationships create tempting opportunities for finance professionals to make decisions that either benefit the client or benefit the advisors themselves. Professional associations (such as for treasurers, bank executives, investment professionals, etc.) place a strong emphasis on ethical behavior and provide ethics training and standards. Nevertheless, as with any profession with millions of practitioners, a few are bound to act unethically.

The agency relationship between corporate managers and stockholders can create ethical dilemmas. Sometimes the corporate governance system has failed to prevent unethical managers from stealing from firms, which ultimately means stealing from shareholders. Governments all over the world have passed laws and regulations meant to ensure compliance with ethical codes of behavior.[7] And if professionals don't act appropriately, governments have set up strong

---

[7]The Sarbanes-Oxley Act of 2002 was passed in response to a number of recent major corporate accounting scandals including those affecting Enron, Tyco International, and WorldCom. The goal of the act was to make the accounting and auditing procedures more transparent and trustworthy.

THE AMAZING (ONGOING) STORY OF APPLE INC. AND STEVE JOBS

Steven Jobs and Stephen Wozniak started Apple Computer in 1976 as an equal partnership. Together, they built 50 computers in a garage using money borrowed from family, the proceeds from the sale of a VW bus, and credit from the parts distributor.

Jobs and Wozniak then designed the Apple II computer. But a higher production level to make more than 50 computers required more space and employees. They needed much more capital. They could not get a loan until angel investor Mike Markkula (an Intel executive) became a partner in the firm. He invested $92,000 and his personal guarantee induced a bank to loan Apple $250,000. As production ramped up in 1977, Apple Computer incorporated. Most shares were owned by Jobs, Wozniak, and Markkula, but the principles made some shares available to employees. They also hired an experienced manager (Mike Scott) to be the CEO and run the firm. Note that as the firm expanded, Jobs' ownership level and control got diluted. By 1980, Apple Computer had sold a total of 121,000 computers—against a potential demand of millions more. Apple needed even more capital.

At the end of 1980, Apple became a public corporation and sold $65 million worth of stock to public investors. Steve Jobs, cofounder of Apple, still owned more shares than anyone else (7.5 million), but he owned less than half of the firm. He gave up a great deal of ownership to new investors in exchange for the capital to expand the firm. Unhappy with Mike Scott's leadership, Steve Jobs also became CEO of Apple.

After a couple of years, Apple's board of directors felt that Jobs was not experienced enough to steer the firm through its rapid expansion. They hired John Sculley as CEO in 1983. In 1985, a power struggle ensued for control of the firm, and the board backed Sculley over Jobs. Jobs was forced out of Apple and no longer had a say in business operations, even though he was the largest shareholder and an original cofounder of the firm.

So, Steve Jobs bought Pixar in 1986 for $5 million and founded NeXT Computer. Over the next 10 years, Jobs' Pixar produced mega hit movies like *Toy Story*, *A Bug's Life*, and *Monsters, Inc.* This time, he kept 53 percent ownership of Pixar to ensure keeping full control. In the meantime, Apple Computer began to struggle, with losses of $800 million in 1996 and $1 billion in 1997. To get Steve Jobs back into the firm, Apple bought NeXT for $400 million and hired him as Apple's CEO. Over the next few years, Jobs introduced the iMAC, iPod, and iTunes, and Apple became very profitable again! Jobs was given the use of a $90 million Gulfstream jet as a perk. To realign his incentives, he became an Apple owner again via compensation that included options on 10 million shares of stock and 30 million shares of **restricted stock.** Then in 2006, Disney bought Pixar by swapping $7.4 billion worth of Disney stock for Pixar stock. When the deal closed, Steve Jobs became the largest owner of Disney stock (7 percent) and joined Disney's board of directors.

Wow! What a story of accessing capital, business organizational form, company control, and corporate governance.

 want to know more?   Key Words to Search For Updates: **Steve Jobs, Apple Computer, Pixar**

punishments for financial malfeasance. In the end, financial managers must realize that they not only owe their shareholders the very best decisions to further shareholder interests, but they also have a broader obligation to society as a whole.

 TIME OUT

1-6   What unethical activities might managers engage in because of the agency problem?

1-7   Explain how the corporate governance system reduces the agency problem.

figure 1.10

Financial Institutions
Cash Flows

 1.6 Financial Markets, Intermediaries, and the Firm

Astute readers will note that we increased our emphasis on the role of financial markets and intermediaries throughout this chapter. This emphasis is intentional, as we feel that you must understand the role and impact of these institutions on the firm if you are to grasp the context in which professionals make financial management decisions.

There is one other important point we want to emphasize about these financial institutions (FI). Very astute readers may wonder how, if financial markets are competitive, investment banks and other financial institutions are able to make such impressive profits. Although FIs assist others with transactions involving financial assets in the financial markets, they do so as paid services. Successful execution of those services takes unique assets and expertise. As shown in Figure 1.10, it's the use of those unique assets and expertise that provides financial institutions with their high profit margins.

 TIME OUT

1-8 What is the role of financial institutions in a capitalist economy?

Business Application Solution

Because Caleb is a sole proprietor of a small business, he will have trouble getting loans for large amounts of money if he wants to expand. Caleb should consider the following options.

First, Caleb can expand slowly. He can get a small loan or self-fund an expansion into one other mall. Once the new juice stand is making a profit, he can expand again. The advantage of this slow expansion is that he retains full ownership and control of his business. One significant risk is that others may copy his idea and open their own stands, thus taking the prime spots in malls before he gets there.

In order to obtain the capital to expand more quickly, Caleb may have to take on a partner. Forming a partnership with an angel investor or a venture capitalist who can provide business expertise and substantial amounts of capital would allow for much faster expansion. The disadvantage of this option is that Caleb will have to give up some ownership of his business.

Personal Application Solution

Dagmar should know that the market gives no guarantees against losing money investing in company stocks. These companies failed for different reasons. Enron and WorldCom went bankrupt because their managers acted unethically to falsely make their company look good. When the truth came out, the firms became so financially troubled that they had to file for bankruptcy. Delta Airlines, however, went bankrupt along with other airline companies because they had trouble competing in their business. They could not profitably deliver their product at market prices. These firms emerged out of bankruptcy court with new stockholders.

Dagmar should also know that the collapse of these firms, and others, has led to a strengthened corporate governance system monitoring managerial actions. We all hope that this new governance system will reduce the number of company failures due to managerial malfeasance. Nevertheless, she can minimize her loss from a corporate bankruptcy by not putting all her "eggs in one basket." Diversification is a finance principle discussed in detail later in this book.

summary of learning goals

Finance is largely about the determination and evaluation of cash flows and value. Financial management is critically important to the success of any business organization. This book will describe the key finance concepts central to corporate finance. The organizational form of a business may impact its cash flow and value. The firm's organizational structure influences managerial goals, incentives, and the agency relationship between management and the firm's owners. Most of these finance principles can be successfully applied to one's personal life.

LG1 **Define the subareas of finance and their roles in corporate financial management.** Subareas or concentrations within finance include investments, financial management, financial institutions and markets, and international finance. Individuals must assess what investment opportunities best meet their needs and their risk tolerances. Financial institutions and markets must efficiently distribute capital between investors and companies. Companies use financial management to evaluate potential projects and decide which to fund, what capital to use, and what kind and amount of capital to return to investors. Finance in a global context is more than just an extension of domestic finance activities. International finance deals with the special risks and opportunities of moving cash flows in a global business.

LG2 **Show why and how finance lies at the heart of sound business decisions.** Finance permeates entire business organizations, providing guidance for the firm's strategic (long-term) and day-to-day decisions. Many nonfinance professionals within a firm can use financial concepts to improve their decisions.

LG3 **Apply finance to your personal life.** Knowing finance theory and applying financial tools will help you make better personal decisions.

LG4 **Compare and contrast the advantages and disadvantages of the three most common business organizational forms in the United States.** Sole proprietors own and control their own businesses. The owner receives all profits and pays taxes at a personal income tax rate. The sole proprietor has unlimited liability for the firm's actions and often may have difficulty obtaining capital for expansion. Similar businesses with multiple owners are known as *partnerships.* The partners share ownership, control, and the profits. Public corporations have thousands of owners—its stockholders. The firm hires managers who control the day-to-day firm operations. Corporations have virtually unlimited access to capital—much more so than other business organizational forms. Corporate profits are taxed twice—first at the corporate level and then again at stockholders' personal tax rate when dividends are paid. Stockholders have limited liability and can only

lose the amount of money they originally invested in the stock.

LG5 **Differentiate between appropriate and inappropriate goals for financial managers.** Most finance professionals agree that maximizing the value of stockholders' equity, as measured by stock price, ensures a financially successful and stable firm for the long run. Financially stable firms are good for stakeholders, such as employees, managers, customers, and local communities. Other goals, like maximizing employment, market share, or profits, do not ensure firm viability over the long run.

LG6 **Identify the firm's primary agency relationship and discuss why agency relationships can create conflicts.** Theoretically, managers work for shareholders. In reality, because shareholders aren't involved in day-to-day firm activities, managers control the firm. Managers might be tempted to operate the firm in such a way as to benefit themselves more than the shareholders. Corporate governance is the system of incentives and monitors that tries to overcome this agency problem. Shareholders can align managers' interests with stockholder interests by making managers part owners of the firm. Then, various monitors follow the firm and report on its activities.

LG7 **Incorporate ethics into financial management.** Because finance professionals commonly manage other people's money in a fiduciary capacity, ethics are of primary importance in finance.

LG8 **Describe the complex and necessary relationships among firms, financial institutions, and financial markets.** Financial institutions assist companies and individuals with transactions involving financial assets in the financial markets. Firms' ability to acquire capital is particularly important.

key terms

agency problem, The difficulties that arise when a principle hires an agent and cannot fully monitor the agent's actions. (p. 16)

angel investors, Individuals who provide small amounts of capital and expert business advice to small firms in exchange for an ownership stake in the firm. (p. 11)

auditor, A person who performs an independent assessment of the fairness of a firm's financial statements. (p. 17)

board of directors, The group of directors elected by stockholders to oversee management in a corporation. (p. 17)

chief executive officer (CEO), The highest-ranking corporate manager. (p. 16)

corporate governance, The set of laws, policies, incentives, and monitors designed to handle the issues arising from the separation of ownership and control. (p. 16)

credit analysts, A person who analyzes a company's ability to repay its debts and reports the findings as a grade. (p. 17)

defined benefit plan, A retirement plan in which the employer sets aside money for the employees' retirement benefits. (p. 10)

defined contribution plan, A retirement plan in which the employee contributes money and directs its investment. The amount of retirement benefits are directly related to the amount of money contributed and the success of its investment. (p. 10)

double taxation, A situation in which two taxes must be paid on the same income. (p. 12)

employee stock option plan (ESOP), An incentive program that grants options to employees (typically managers) as compensation. (p. 16)

equity, An ownership interest in a business enterprise. (p. 11)

ethics, The study of values, morals, and morality. (p. 18)

fiduciary, A legal duty between two parties where one party must act in the interest of the other party. (p. 18)

finance, The ways people and organizations raise and allocate capital, use monetary resources, and account for the risks involved. (p. 2)

financial asset, A general term for securities like stocks, bonds, and other assets that represent ownership in a cash flow. (p. 9)

financial institutions and markets, The organizations that facilitate the flow of capital between investors and companies. (p. 7)

financial management, The process for and the analysis of making financial decisions in the business context. (p. 2)

financial market, The places and processes that facilitate the trading of financial assets between investors. (p. 4)

401k plan, A defined contribution plan that is sponsored by corporate employers. (p. 10)

general partnership, A form of business organization where the partners own the business together and are personally liable for legal actions and debts of the firm. (p. 12)

individual retirement account (IRA), A self-sponsored retirement program. (p. 10)

international finance, The use of finance theory in a global business environment. (p. 7)

investment analysts, A person who analyzes a company's business prospects and gives opinions about its future success. (p. 17)

investment banks, Banks that help companies and governments raise capital. (p. 17)

investment, The analysis and process of choosing securities and other assets to purchase. (p. 6)

investors, Those who buy securities or other assets in hopes of earning a return and getting more money back in the future. (p. 4)

invisible hand, A metaphor used to illustrate how an individual pursuing his own interests also tends to promote the good of the community. (p. 14)

limited liability, Limitation of a person's financial liability to a fixed sum or investment. (p. 12)

maximization of shareholder wealth, A view that management should first and foremost consider the interests of shareholders in its business decisions. (p. 14)

option, The opportunity to buy stock at a fixed price over a specific period of time. (p. 16)

perks/perquisites, Nonwage compensation, often in the form of company car, golf club membership, etc. (p. 16)

public corporation, A company owned by a large number of stockholders from the general public. (p. 12)

real assets, Physical property like gold, machinery, equipment, or real estate. (p. 9)

real markets, The places and processes that facilitate the trading of real assets. (p. 9)

restricted stock, A special type of stock that is not transferable from the current holder to others until specific conditions are satisfied. (p. 19)

retained earnings, The portion of company profits that are kept by the company rather than distributed to the stockholders as cash dividends. (p. 5)

risk, A potential future negative impact to value and/or cash flows. It is often discussed in terms of the probability of loss and the expected magnitude of the loss. (p. 8)

sole proprietorship, A business entity that is not legally separate from its owner. (p. 11)

stakeholder, A person or organization that has a legitimate interest in a corporation. (p. 14)

stock price, The price of a share of stock trading on a stock market. (p. 15)

time value of money (TVM), The theory and application of valuing cash flows at various points in time. (p. 9)

unlimited liability, A situation in which a person's personal assets are at risk from a business liability. (p. 11)

venture capitalists, Similar to angel investors except that they are organized as groups of investors and can provide larger amounts of capital. (p. 11)

self-test problems with solutions

1 **Organizational Form:** Titus founded his own construction wholesale business many years ago. After building a successful firm that supplies materials to real estate developers in his region, he joined with a partner who provided the capital to expand throughout the state. They changed the business to a privately owned corporation of which Titus owns 60 percent of the shares. The partner owns 30 percent of the shares and 10 percent were set aside to give to some employees in a stock ownership plan. The statewide expansion has been a big success. Financial advisors have suggested to Titus that he take the company public. What issues should he consider when thinking about it?

Solution:

Some big advantages accrue to a public corporation. By going public, he could raise much more capital and expand the firm nationally. Being a larger national firm might give him more ability to buy his products at lower costs. Also, the owners (himself, the partner, and some employees) would have greater ability to sell their shares to "cash out" of the firm—or at least to sell some shares and diversify their wealth. This also allows an older entrepreneur to keep both the business wealth he generated and to transition into retirement. Some disadvantages also arise when a firm goes public. Titus will have to give up some fraction of his ownership and thus may eventually lose control of the firm. The profits of the firm will be taxed twice, once at the firm level and then again at the shareholder level. Titus will have to evaluate these advantages and disadvantages to decide whether to go public.

questions

1. Describe the type of people who use the financial markets. *(LG1)*

2. What is the purpose of financial management? Describe the kinds of activities that financial management involves. *(LG1)*

3. What is the difference in perspective between finance and accounting? *(LG2)*

4. What personal decisions can you think of that will benefit from your learning finance? *(LG3)*

5. What are the three basic forms of business ownership? What are the advantages and disadvantages to each? *(LG4)*

6. Between the three basic forms of business ownership, describe the ability of each form to access capital. *(LG4)*

7. Explain how the founder of a business can eventually lose control of the firm. How can the founder ensure this will not happen? *(LG4)*

8. Explain the shareholder wealth maximization goal of the firm and how it can be measured. Make an argument for why it is a better goal than maximizing profit. *(LG5)*

9. Name and describe as many corporate stakeholders as you can. *(LG5)*

10. What conflicts of interest can arise between managers and stockholders? *(LG6)*

11. Figure 1.9 shows firm monitors. In your opinion, which group is in the best position to monitor the firm? Explain. Which group has the potential to be the weakest monitor? Explain. *(LG6)*

12. In recent years, governments all over the world have passed laws that increased the penalties for executives' crimes. Do you think this will deter unethical corporate managers? Explain. *(LG6)*

13. Every year, the media report on the vast amounts of money (sometimes hundreds of millions of dollars) that some CEOs earn from the companies they manage. Are these CEOs worth it? Give examples. *(LG6)*

14. Why is ethical behavior so important in the field of finance? *(LG7)*

15. Does the goal of shareholder wealth maximization conflict with behaving ethically? Explain. *(LG7)*

16. Describe how financial institutions and markets facilitate the expansion of a company's business. *(LG8)*

research it! Corporate Governance

The corporate governance system continues to evolve. After the very visible governance failures in the early 2000s, national focus was placed on this issue. The U.S. government passed new laws regarding auditing, board of directors' composition, and executive behavior. Directors also began to change the form of executive incentive compensation. Some believe the changes went too far and have placed a costly burden on public corporations. Others believe that some new laws did not go far enough to rein in the extreme levels of executive compensation. For information on this ongoing debate, visit the leading independent source for U.S. corporate governance and executive compensation, The Corporate Library, at **www.thecorporatelibrary.com.**

integrated minicase Corporate Citizenship

What is a company's responsibility to society? Proponents of the modern view of stakeholder theory argue that companies have a social obligation to operate in ethically, socially, and environmentally responsible ways. This active approach is referred to as *corporate social responsibility (CSR)* or *corporate citizenship*. The idea of corporate citizenship is that a firm should conduct its business in a manner that meets its economic, legal, ethical, and philanthropic expectations.

The economic responsibilities have the highest priority. A firm must be efficient and survive over the long term in order to be useful to society. It must also execute its business activities in a legal and ethical way. These responsibilities are over and above the ones codified in laws and are in line with societal norms and customs. They are expected by society even though they may be ill-defined. This could include things such as environmental ethics. Philanthropy is the least important priority. The corporate citizenship concept focuses more on engagement with stakeholders to achieve mutual goals.

(continued)

figure 1.11

Top 3 CSR Topics
Getting Attention in
Your Firm

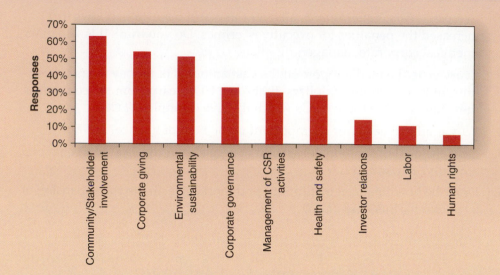

Some corporations have responded to this trend by including CSR-oriented statements in their corporate goals. These statements recognize that CSR has value in a code of conduct or ethics, a commitment to local communities, an interest in employee health and education, an environmental consciousness, and recognition of social issues (diversity, social fairness, etc.). In October 2006, The Conference Board surveyed large U.S. firms on corporate citizenship issues and 198 firms responded. Figure 1.11 shows the results of the survey when firms were asked about the top three CSR topics receiving attention at the company.

What is the motivation for these companies to fund CSR programs? When asked, 92 percent stated that enhancing corporate reputation was very important. Other popular responses were for recruiting and retention (78 percent) and reducing risk (65 percent).

a. Wal-Mart generates over $11 billion in profits per year and is the largest corporate employer in the U.S., with 1.4 million employees. But Wal-Mart also seems to be coming under increasing pressure from different social groups for its business practices. Community groups have worked to keep Wal-Mart from coming to their towns. Wal-Mart claims that its low prices help everyone in the community. Also by giving over $270 million to charity last year, it is the largest corporate cash contributor in the U.S. Go to **www.wakeupwalmart.com** and describe the current stakeholder problems with Wal-Mart. Also go to **www.walmart.com** and describe what Wal-Mart is doing to engage these stakeholders. What is your opinion?

b. What activities might companies engage in to satisfy the four components of corporate citizenship: economic, legal, ethical, and philanthropic?

c. By embracing citizenship goals, assess whether corporations can insulate themselves from many activist actions, thereby avoiding negative media events.

References: Archie B. Carroll, "Corporate Social Responsibility: Evolution of a Definitional Construct," *Business & Society* 38, no. 3 (1999): 268–295, and David Vidal, "Reward Trumps Risk: How Business Perspectives on Corporate Citizenship and Sustainability Are Changing," *Executive Action Series*, The Conference Board, No. 216, November 2006.

ANSWERS TO TIME OUT

1-1   The main subareas are investments, financial management, financial institutions and markets, and international finance. Investors interact with the other groups by buying and selling securities through financial markets, being influenced by what to buy and sell by the quality of firms' financial management, and assessing international opportunities for investment and for firm prospects. Financial management acquires and repays capital from investors through financial institutions and markets. Financial managers must also run their businesses in an increasingly internationally integrated economy. Financial institutions and markets facilitate the allocation of capital between the investment and financial management subareas.

1-2   Finance knowledge and tools help people to understand, evaluate, and deal with financial risks in both their professional and personal lives. In addition, the application of finance helps people manage cash flow and valuation decisions. Making good cash flow and value decisions will help make business operations more successful and personal wealth grow.

1-3   In order for a business to grow very large, it needs a lot of capital. Banks and other lenders do not lend large amounts of money to individual small business owners. This leaves equity, the only other source of capital left to grow. People who provide equity capital become part owners. Owners of a business demand some control of that business. Thus, an entrepreneur must give up some control of the firm in order to access equity capital and become much larger.

1-4   The corporation can have any number of owners (stockholders) and thus can acquire vast amounts of capital. In addition, corporations have an easier time borrowing money from banks and public bond holders. Corporations also hire professional managers.

1-5   Maximizing shareholder value provides many advantages for society. For example, more people will be willing to offer their capital through buying stocks when they believe companies are trying to maximize their value. Since more capital will be offered, then more business, expansion, and employment will result. In addition, this goal gives the best opportunity for long-term existence and stability of the firm, which benefits employees and local communities.

1-6   The most common activity is to use the company's resources to benefit themselves at the expense of the shareholders. Examples include low interest loans and unnecessary or personal use of a corporate jet, homes, or apartments. However, managers may also use their influence to get friends and relatives hired by the company or to steer them business.

1-7   The corporate governance system reduces the agency problem by monitoring management activities through many different groups and people. These people witness and report on different aspects of managers' activities. In addition, incentives may be created to align the manager's own interests with those of the shareholders.

1-8   Financial institutions are critical to the function of a capitalist society. Capitalism requires the flow of capital from those with excess funds to those with good uses for it. There are far more ideas on how to use money than there are sources of money. In other words, money is a scarce resource. The existing money must be able to flow to the best ideas and projects in order to maximize the benefit to the economy and to society. Financial institutions and markets make this happen.

chapter 2:
REVIEWING FINANCIAL STATEMENTS

Corporate managers must issue many reports to the public. Most stockholders, analysts, government entities, and other interested parties pay particular attention to annual reports. An annual report provides four basic **financial statements:** the balance sheet, the income statement, the statement of cash flows, and the statement of retained earnings.

These four statements provide an accounting-based picture of a firm's financial position. While accountants focus on reporting what happened in the past, financial managers use financial statements to draw inferences about the future. The statements often provide key information to firm managers, who make financial decisions, and to investors, who decide whether or not to invest in the firm. In this chapter, we review these four vital financial statements, which you likely saw in accounting classes. We briefly examine each statement to identify its major features and uses. We highlight the differences between the accounting-based (or book) value of a firm as these statements report and the true market value of a firm. We also differentiate between accounting-based income and actual cash flows, which we explore further in Chapter 3 as they are much more relevant to finance.

While firms must follow GAAP (generally accepted accounting principles), managers still have substantial discretion in preparing their firms' financial statements. For example, two firms with exactly the same operations may report financial statements that convey vastly different impressions about their firms' financial strengths, depending on managers' strategic plans for the future. We also discuss cautions that readers should take when they review and analyze financial statements in Chapter 3.

viewpoints

Business Application

The managers of DPH Tree Farm, Inc. believe the firm could double its sales if it had additional factory space and acreage. If DPH purchased the factory space and acreage in 2009, these new assets would cost $27 million to build and would require an additional $1 million in cash, $5 million in accounts receivable, $6 million in inventory, and $4 million in accounts payable. In addition to accounts payable, DPH Tree Farm would finance the new assets with the sale of a combination of long-term debt (40 percent of the total) and common stock (60 percent of the total). Assuming all else stays constant, what will these changes do to DPH Tree Farm's 2009 balance sheet assets, liabilities, and equity? **(See solution on p. 47)**

Personal Application

Chris Ryan is looking to invest in DPH Tree Farm, Inc. Chris has the most recent set of financial statements from DPH Tree Farm's annual report but is not sure how to read them or what they mean. What are the four financial statements that Chris should pay most attention to? What information will these key financial statements contain? **(See solution on p. 47)**

A practice test can be found on the Online Learning Center at
www.mhhe.com/can1e

2.1 Balance Sheet

The **balance sheet** reports a firm's assets, liabilities, and equity at a particular point in time. A firm's assets must equal (balance) the liabilities and equity used to purchase the assets (hence the term *balance sheet*):

$$\text{Assets} = \text{Liabilities} + \text{Equity} \qquad (2\text{-}1)$$

Figure 2.1 illustrates a basic balance sheet and Table 2.1 presents a simple balance sheet for DPH Tree Farm, Inc. as of December 31, 2007 and 2008. The left side of the balance sheet lists assets of the firm and the right side lists liabilities and equity. Both assets and liabilities are listed in descending order of **liquidity,** that is, the time and effort it takes to convert the accounts to cash. The most liquid assets—called *current assets*—appear first on the asset side of the balance sheet. The least liquid, called *fixed assets*, appear last. Similarly, current liabilities—those obligations that the firm must pay within a year, appear first on the right side of the balance sheet. Stockholders' equity, which never matures, appears last on the balance sheet.

Assets

Figure 2.1 shows that assets fall into two major categories: current assets and fixed assets. **Current assets** will normally convert to cash within one year. They include cash and marketable securities, accounts receivable, and inventory. **Fixed assets** have a useful life exceeding one year. This class of assets includes physical (tangible) assets, such as net plant and equipment, and other, less tangible, long-term assets, such as patents and trademarks. We find the value of net plant and equipment by taking the difference between gross plant and equipment (or the fixed assets' original value) and the depreciation accumulated against the fixed assets since their purchase.

Liabilities and Stockholders' Equity

Lenders provide funds, which become **liabilities,** to the firm. Liabilities fall into two categories as well: current or long-term. **Current liabilities** constitute the firm's obligations due within one year, including accrued wages and taxes, accounts payable, and notes payable. **Long-term debt** includes long-term loans and bonds with maturities of more than one year.

The difference between total assets and total liabilities of a firm is the stockholders' (or owners') equity. The firm's preferred and common stock owners provide the funds known as **stockholders' equity. Preferred stock** appears on the balance sheet as the cash proceeds when the firm sells preferred stock in a public offering. Similarly, the proceeds from **common stock and paid-in surplus** appear as the other component of stockholder's equity. If the firm's managers decide to reinvest cumulative earnings rather than pay the dividends to stockholders, the balance sheet will record these funds as **retained earnings.**

Managing the Balance Sheet

Managers must monitor a number of issues underlying items reported on their firms' balance sheets. These include:

- The accounting method for fixed asset depreciation.
- The level of net working capital.
- The liquidity position of the firm.
- The method for financing the firm's assets—equity or debt.
- The difference between the book value reported on the balance sheet and the true market value of the firm.

figure 2.1

The Basic Balance Sheet

Total Assets		Total Liabilities and Equity
Current assets	net working capital	Current liabilities
Cash and marketable securities		Accrued wages and taxes
Accounts receivable		Accounts payable
Inventory		Notes payable
Fixed assets		Long-term debt
Gross plant and equipment		
Less: Depreciation		Stockholders' equity
Net plant and equipment		Preferred stock
Other long-term assets		Common stock and paid-in surplus
		Retained earnings

Balance Sheet for DPH Tree Farm, Inc.

table 2.1

DPH TREE FARM, INC.
Balance Sheet as of December 31, 2007 and 2008
(in millions of dollars)

Assets	2007	2008	Liabilities and Equity	2007	2008
Current assets			**Current liabilities**		
Cash and marketable securities	$ 25	$ 24	Accrued wages and taxes	$ 15	$ 20
Accounts receivable	65	70	Accounts payable	50	55
Inventory	100	111	Notes payable	45	45
Total	190	205	Total	110	120
Fixed assets			Long-term debt	190	195
Gross plant and equipment	300	368	Total debt	300	315
Less: Depreciation	40	53	**Stockholders' equity**		
Net plant and equipment	260	315	Preferred stock (5 million shares)	5	5
Other long-term			Common stock and paid-in surplus (20 million shares)	40	40
assets	50	50	Retained earnings	155	210
Total	310	365	Total	200	255
Total assets	$500	$570	Total liabilities and equity	$500	$570

ACCOUNTING METHOD FOR FIXED ASSET DEPRECIATION Firm managers can choose the accounting method they use to record depreciation against their fixed assets. Two choices include the straight-line method and the modified accelerated cost recovery system (MACRS). Companies often calculate depreciation using MACRS when computing the firm's taxes and the straight-line method when reporting income to the firm's stockholders. The MACRS method accelerates deprecation, which results in higher deprecation expenses and lower taxable income and lower taxes in the early years of a project's life. The straight-line method results in lower depreciation expenses, but also results in higher taxes in the early years of a project's life. Firms seeking to lower their cash outflows from tax payments will favor the MACRS depreciation method.

NET WORKING CAPITAL We arrive at a **net working capital** figure by taking the difference between a firm's current assets and current liabilities. So, clearly, net working capital is positive when the firm has more current assets than current liabilities. Table 2.1 shows the 2007 and 2008 year-end balance sheets for DPH Tree Farm, Inc. At year-end 2007, the firm had $190 million of current assets and $110 million of current liabilities. So the firm's net working capital was $80 million. A firm needs cash and other liquid assets to pay its bills as expenses come due. Liability holders monitor net working capital as a measure of a firm's ability to pay its obligations. Positive net working capital values are usually a sign of a healthy firm.

LIQUIDITY   As we noted above, any firm needs cash and other liquid assets to pay its bills as debts come due. Liquidity actually refers to two dimensions: the ease with which the firm can convert an asset to cash, and the degree to which such a conversion takes place at a fair market value. You can convert any asset to cash quickly if you price the asset low enough. But clearly, you will wish to convert the asset without giving up a great portion of its value. So a highly liquid asset can be sold quickly at its fair market value. An illiquid asset, on the other hand, cannot be sold quickly unless you reduce the price far below fair value.

Current assets, by definition, remain relatively liquid, including cash and assets that will convert to cash within the next year. Inventory is the least liquid of the current assets. Fixed assets, then, remain relatively illiquid. In the normal course of business, the firm would have no plans to liquefy or convert these tangible assets such as buildings and equipment into cash.

Liquidity presents a double-edged sword on a balance sheet. The more liquid assets a firm holds, the less likely the firm will be to experience financial distress. However, liquid assets generate no profits for a firm. For example, cash is the most liquid of all assets, but it earns no return for the firm. In contrast, fixed assets are illiquid, but provide the means to generate revenue. Thus, managers must consider the trade-off between the advantages of liquidity on the balance sheet and the disadvantages of having money sit idle rather than generating profits.

DEBT VERSUS EQUITY FINANCING   Ever since your high school physics class, you have known that levers are very useful and powerful machines—given a long enough lever, you can move almost anything. **Financial leverage** is likewise very powerful. Leverage in the financial sense refers to the extent to which a firm chooses to finance its ventures or assets by issuing debt securities. The more debt a firm issues as a percentage of its total assets, the greater its financial leverage. We discuss in later chapters why financial leverage can greatly magnify the firm's gains *and* losses for the firm's stockholders.

When a firm issues debt securities—usually bonds—to finance its activities and assets, debt holders usually demand first claim to a fixed amount of the firm's cash flows. Their claims are fixed because the firm must only pay the interest owed to bondholders and any principal repayments that come due within any given period. Stockholders—who buy equity securities or stocks—claim any cash flows left after debt holders are paid. When a firm does well, financial leverage increases shareholders' rewards, since the share of the firm's profits promised to debt holders is set and predictable.

However, financial leverage also increases risk. Leverage can create the potential for the firm to experience financial distress and even bankruptcy. If the firm has a bad year and cannot make its scheduled debt payments, debt holders can force the firm into bankruptcy. But managers generally prefer to fund firm activities using debt, precisely because they can calculate the cost of doing business without giving away too much of the firm's value. So managers often walk a fine line as they decide upon the firm's **capital structure**—the amount of debt versus equity financing to hold on the balance sheet—because it can determine whether the firm stays in business or goes bankrupt.

 BOOK VALUE VERSUS MARKET VALUE   Beginning finance students usually have already taken accounting, so they are familiar with the accounting point of view. For example, a firm's balance sheet shows its **book (or historical**

cost) value based on generally accepted accounting principles (GAAP). Under GAAP, assets appear on the balance sheet at what the firm paid for them, regardless of what those assets might be worth today if the firm were to sell them. Inflation and market forces make many assets worth more now than they were when the firm bought them. So in most cases, book values differ widely from the **market values** for the same assets—the amount that the assets would fetch if the firm actually sold them. For the firm's current assets—those that mature within a year—the book value and market value of any particular asset will remain very close. For example, the balance sheet lists cash and marketable securities at their market value. Similarly, firms acquire accounts receivable and inventory and then convert these short-term assets into cash fairly quickly, so the book value of these assets is generally close to their market value.

The "book value versus market value" issue really arises when we try to determine how much a firm's fixed assets are worth. In this case, book value is often very different from market value. For example, if a firm owns land for 100 years, this asset appears on the balance sheet at its historical cost (of 100 years ago). Most likely, the firm would reap a much higher price on the land upon its sale than the historical price would indicate.

Again, accounting tools reflect the past: Balance sheet assets are listed at historical cost. Managers would thus see little relation between the total asset value listed on the balance sheet and the current market value of the firm's assets. Similarly, the stockowners' equity listed on the balance sheet generally differs from the true market value of the equity. In this case, the market value may be higher or lower than the value listed on the firm's accounting books. So financial managers and investors often find that balance sheet values are not always the most relevant numbers. The following example illustrates the difference between the book value and the market value of a firm's assets.

 For interactive versions of this example visit www.mhhe.com/can1e

EXAMPLE 2-1

CALCULATING BOOK VERSUS MARKET VALUE

EZ Toy, Inc. lists fixed assets of $25 million on its balance sheet. The firm's assets have recently been appraised at $32 million. EZ Toy, Inc.'s balance sheet also lists current assets at $10 million. Current assets were appraised at $11 million. Current liabilities' book and market values stand at $6 million and the firm's long-term debt is $15 million. Calculate the book and market values of the firm's stockholders' equity. Construct the book value and market value balance sheets for EZ Toy, Inc.

SOLUTION:

Recall the balance sheet identity in equation 2-1: Assets = Liabilities + Equity. Rearranging this equation: Equity = Assets − Liabilities. Thus, the balance sheets would appear as follows:

Value Assets	BOOK VALUE	MARKET VALUE	Liabilities and Equity	BOOK VALUE	MARKET VALUE
Current assets	$10m.	$ 11m.	Current liabilities	$ 6m.	$ 6m.
Fixed assets	25m.	32m.	Long-term debt	15m.	15m.
			Stockholders' equity	14m.	22m.
Total	$35m.	$43m.	Total	$35m.	$43m.

TIME OUT

2-1   What is a balance sheet?

2-2   Which are the most liquid assets and liabilities on a balance sheet?

2.2 Income Statement

You will recall that **income statements** show the total revenues that a firm earns and the total expenses the firm incurs to generate those revenues over a specific period of time—generally one year. Remember that while the balance sheet reports a firm's position at a point in time, the income statement reports performance over a period of time, for example, over the last year. Figure 2.2 illustrates a basic income statement and Table 2.2 shows a simple income statement for DPH Tree Farm, Inc. for the years ended December 31, 2007 and 2008. DPH's revenues (or net sales) appear at the top of the income statement. The income statement then shows various expenses (cost of goods sold, depreciation, interest, and taxes) subtracted from revenues to arrive at profit or income measures.

The top part of the income statement reports the firm's operating income. First, we subtract the cost of goods sold (the direct costs of producing the firm's product) from net sales to get **gross profit** (so, DPH Tree Farm enjoyed gross profits of $140 million in 2007 and $165 million in 2008). Next, we deduct depreciation from gross profits to get operating profit or earnings before interest and taxes (**EBIT**) (so DPH Tree Farm's EBIT was $128 million in 2007 and $152 million in 2008). The EBIT figure represents the profit earned from the sale of the product without any financing cost or tax considerations.

The bottom part of the income statement summarizes the firm's financial and tax structure. First, we subtract interest expense (the cost to service the firm's debt) from EBIT to get earnings before taxes (**EBT**). So, as we follow our sample income statement, DPH Tree Farm had EBT of $110 million in 2007 and $136 million in 2008. Of course, firms differ in their financial structures and tax situations. These differences can cause two firms with identical operating income to report differing levels of net income. For example, one firm may finance its assets with only debt, while another finances with only common equity. The company with no debt would have no interest expense. Thus, even though EBIT for the two firms is identical, the firm with all-equity financing and no debt would report higher net income. We subtract taxes from EBT to get the last item on the income statement (the "bottom line"), or **net income.** DPH Tree Farm, Inc. reported net income of $70 million in 2007 and $90 million in 2008.

Below the net income, or bottom line, on the income statement, firms often report additional information summarizing income and firm value. For example, with its $90 million of net income in 2008, DPH Tree Farm, Inc. paid its preferred stockholders cash dividends of $10 million and its common stockholders cash dividends of $25 million, and added the remaining $55 million to retained earnings. Table 2.1 shows that retained earnings on the balance sheet increased from $155 million in 2007 to $210 million in 2008. Other items reported below the bottom line include:

$$\text{Earnings per share (EPS)} = \frac{\text{Net income available to common stockholders}}{\text{Total shares of common stock outstanding}} \qquad \textbf{(2-2)}$$

$$\text{Dividends per share (DPS)} = \frac{\text{Common stock dividends paid}}{\text{Number of shares of common stock outstanding}}$$

$$\textbf{(2-3)}$$

figure 2.2

Net sales
Less: Cost of goods sold
Gross profits
Less: Depreciation   } Operating income
Earnings before interest and taxes (EBIT)

Less: Interest
Earnings before taxes (EBT)   } Financing and tax considerations
Less: Taxes

Net income before preferred dividends
Preferred dividends
Net income

Income Statement for DPH Tree Farm, Inc.	table 2.2

DPH TREE FARM, INC.
Income Statement for Years Ending December 31, 2007 and 2008
(in millions of dollars)

	2007	2008
Net sales (all credit)	$275	$315
Less: Cost of goods sold	135	150
Gross profits	140	165
Less: Depreciation	12	13
Earnings before interest and taxes (EBIT)	128	152
Less: Interest	18	16
Earnings before taxes (EBT)	110	136
Less: Taxes	40	46
Net income	$ 70	$ 90
Less: Preferred stock dividends	$ 10	$ 10
Net income available to common stock holders	$ 60	$ 80
Less: Common stock dividends	$ 25	$ 25
Addition to retained earnings	$ 35	$ 55
Per (common) share data:		
Earnings per share (EPS)	$ 3.00	$ 4.00
Dividends per share (DPS)	$ 1.25	$ 1.25
Book value per share (BVPS)	$ 9.75	$ 12.50
Market value (price) per share (MVPS)	$ 15.60	$ 17.25

$$\text{Book value per share (BVPS)} = \frac{\text{Common stockholders equity}}{\text{Number of shares of common stock outstanding}}$$

(2-4)

$$\text{Market value per share (MVPS)} = \text{Market price of the firm's common stock}$$

(2-5)

We discuss these items further in Chapter 3.

Corporate Income Taxes

LG3

Firms pay out a large portion of their earnings in taxes. For example, in 2005, Microsoft had EBT of $16.6 billion. Of this amount, Microsoft paid $4.4 billion (over 26 percent of EBT) in taxes. Congress oversees the U.S. tax code, which determines corporate tax obligations. Corporate taxes can thus change with changes of administration or other changes in the business or public

TAXABLE INCOME	PAY THIS AMOUNT ON BASE INCOME	PLUS THIS PERCENTAGE ON ANYTHING OVER THE BASE
$0 − $50,000	$ 0	15%
$50,001 − $75,000	7,500	25
$75,001 − $100,000	13,500	34
$100,001 − $335,000	22,250	39
$335,001 − $10,000,000	113,900	34
$10,000,001 − $15,000,000	3,400,000	35
$15,000,001 − $18,333,333	5,150,000	38
Over $18,333,333	6,416,667	35

environment. As you might expect, the U.S. tax system is extremely complicated, so we do not attempt to cover it in detail here. However, firms recognize taxes as a major expense item and many financial decisions arise from tax considerations. In this section we provide a general overview of the U.S. corporate tax system.

The 2008 corporate tax schedule appears in Table 2.3. Note from this table that the U.S. tax structure is progressive, meaning that the larger the income, the higher the taxes assessed. However, corporate tax rates do not increase in any kind of linear way based on this progressive nature: They rise from a low of 15 percent to a high of 39 percent, then drop to 34 percent, rise to 38 percent, and finally drop to 35 percent.

In addition to calculating their tax liability, firms also want to know their **average tax rate** and **marginal tax rate.** You can figure the average tax rate as the percentage of each dollar of taxable income that the firm pays in taxes.

$$\text{Average tax rate} = \frac{\text{Tax liability}}{\text{Taxable income}} \qquad \text{(2-6)}$$

From your economics classes, you can probably guess that the firm's marginal tax rate is the amount of additional taxes a firm must pay out for every additional dollar of taxable income it earns.

EXAMPLE 2-2

 For interactive versions of this example visit www.mhhe.com/can1e

CALCULATION OF CORPORATE TAXES

Indian Point Kennels, Inc. earned $16.5 million taxable income (EBT) in 2008. Use the tax schedule in Table 2.3 to determine the firm's 2008 tax liability, its average tax rate, and its marginal tax rate.

SOLUTION:

From Table 2.3, the $16.5 million of taxable income puts Indian Point Kennels in the 38 percent marginal tax bracket. Thus

Tax liability = Tax on base amount + Tax rate (amount over base)

= $5,150,000 + .38 ($16,500,000 − $15,000,000) = $5,720,000

(continued)

Note that the base amount is the maximum dollar value listed in the previous tax bracket. In this example, we take the highest dollar value ($15,000,000) in the preceding tax bracket (35 percent). The additional percentage owed results from multiplying the income above and beyond the $15,000,000 (or $1,500,000) by the marginal tax rate (38%). The *average* tax rate for Indian Point Kennels Inc. comes to:

$$\text{Average tax rate} = \frac{\text{Tax liability}}{\text{Taxable income}}$$

$$= \$5,720,000/\$16,500,000 = 34.67\%$$

If Indian Point Kennels earned $1 more of taxable income, it would pay 38 cents (its tax rate of 38 percent) more in taxes. Thus, the firm's marginal tax rate is 38 percent.

INTEREST AND DIVIDENDS RECEIVED BY CORPORATIONS Any interest that corporations receive is taxable, though a notable exception arises: Interest on state and local government bonds is exempt from federal taxes. The U.S. tax code allows this exception to encourage corporations to be better community citizens by supporting local governments. Another exception of sorts arises when one corporation owns stock in another corporation. Seventy percent of any dividends received from other corporations is tax exempt. Only the remaining 30 percent is taxed at the receiving corporation's tax rate.[1]

 For interactive versions of this example visit www.mhhe.com/can1e

EXAMPLE 2-3

CORPORATE TAXES WITH INTEREST AND DIVIDEND INCOME

In the example above, suppose that in addition to the $16.5 million of taxable income, Indian Point Kennels, Inc. received $250,000 of interest on state-issued bonds and $500,000 of dividends on common stock it owns in DPH Tree Farm, Inc. How do these items affect Indian Point Kennel's tax liability, average tax rate, and marginal tax rate?

SOLUTION:

In this case, interest on the state-issued bonds is not taxable and should not be included in taxable income. Further, the first 70 percent of the dividends received from DPH Tree Farm is not taxable. Thus, only 30 percent of the dividends received are taxed, so:

$$\text{Taxable income} = \$16,500,000 + (.3)\$500,000 = \$16,650,000$$

Now Indian Point Kennel's tax liability will be:

$$\text{Tax liability} = \$5,150,000 + .38\ (\$16,650,000 - \$15,000,000) = \$5,777,000$$

The $500,000 of dividend income increased Indian Point Kennel's tax liability by $57,000. Indian Point Kennels, Inc.'s resulting average tax rate is now:

$$\text{Average tax rate} = \$5,777,000/\$16,650,000 = 34.70\%$$

Finally, if Indian Point Kennels earned $1 more of taxable income, it would still pay 38 cents (based upon its marginal tax rate of 38 percent) more in taxes.

[1]This tax code provision prevents or reduces any triple taxation that could occur: income could be taxed at three levels: (1) on the income from the dividend-paying firm, (2) as income for the dividend-receiving firm, and (3) finally, on the personal income of stockholders who receive dividends.

INTEREST AND DIVIDENDS PAID BY CORPORATIONS Corporate interest payments appear on the balance sheet as an expense item, so we deduct interest payments from operating income when the firm calculates taxable income. But any dividends paid by corporations to their shareholders are not tax deductible. This is one factor that encourages managers to finance projects with debt financing rather than to sell more stock. Suppose one firm uses mainly debt financing and another firm, with identical operations, uses mainly equity financing. The equity-financed firm will have very little interest expense to deduct for tax purposes. Thus, it will have higher taxable income and pay more taxes than the debt-financed firm. The debt-financed firm will pay fewer taxes and be able to pay more of its operating income to asset funders, that is, its bondholders and stockholders. So even stockholders prefer that firms finance assets primarily with debt rather than with stock. The debt-versus-equity financing issue is called *capital structure,* which we address more fully in Part Seven of the book.

EXAMPLE 2-4 For interactive versions of this example visit www.mhhe.com/can1e

EFFECT OF DEBT VERSUS EQUITY FINANCING ON FUNDERS' RETURNS

Suppose that you are considering a stock investment in one of two firms (AllDebt, Inc. and AllEquity, Inc.), both of which operate in the same industry and have identical operating incomes of $5 million. AllDebt, Inc. finances its $12 million in assets with $11 million in debt (on which it pays 10 percent interest) and $1 million in equity. AllEquity, Inc. finances its $12 million in assets with no debt and $12 million in equity. Both firms pay 30 percent tax on their taxable income. Calculate the income that each firm has available to pay its debt and stockholders and the resulting return on assets for the two firms.

SOLUTION:

	ALLDEBT	ALLEQUITY
Operating income	$5.00m.	$5.00m.
Less: Interest	1.10m.	0.00m.
Taxable income	3.90m.	5.00m.
Less: Taxes (30%)	1.17m.	1.50m.
Net income	$2.73m.	$3.50m.
Income available for asset funders (= operating income − taxes)	$3.83m.	$3.50m.
Return on asset-funders' investment	$3.83m/$12m = 31.92%	$3.50m/$12.0m = 29.17%

By financing most of its assets with debt and receiving the associated tax benefits from the interest paid on this debt, AllDebt, Inc. is able to pay more of its operating income to the funders of its assets, i.e., its debt holders and stockholders, than AllEquity, Inc.

TIME OUT

2-3   What is an income statement?

2-4   When a corporation owns stock in another corporation, what percentage of dividends received on the stock is taxed?

2.3 Statement of Cash Flows

LG4

Clearly, income statements and balance sheets are the most common financial documents available to the public. But managers who make financial decisions may find themselves at something of a loss if they only have these two documents—reports on past performance—on which to base their decisions for today and into the future. Consider the following. Company accountants must prepare firm income statements following GAAP principles. GAAP procedures require that the firm recognize revenue at the time of sale, but sometimes the company receives the cash before or after the time of sale. Likewise, GAAP counsels the firm to show production and other expenses on the balance sheet as the sales of those goods take place. So production and other expenses associated with a particular product's sale only appear on the income statement (for example, cost of goods sold and depreciation) when that product sells. Of course, just as with the revenue recognition, actual cash outflows incurred with production may occur at a very different point in time—usually much earlier than GAAP principles allow the firm to formally recognize the expenses.

Further, income statements contain several noncash entries, the largest of which is depreciation. Depreciation attempts to capture the noncash expense incurred as fixed assets deteriorate from the time of purchase to the point when those assets must be replaced. Let's illustrate the effect of depreciation: Suppose a firm purchases a machine for $100,000. The machine has an expected life of five years and at the end of those five years, the machine will have no expected salvage value. The firm lays out a $100,000 cash outflow at the time of purchase. But the entire $100,000 does not appear on the income statement in the year that the firm purchases the machine—in accounting terms, the machine is not *expensed* in the year of purchase. Rather, if the firm's accounting department uses the straight-line depreciation method, it deducts only $100,000/5, or $20,000, each year as an expense. This $20,000 equipment expense is not a cash outflow for the firm. The person in charge of buying the machine knows that the cash flow occurred at the time of purchase—and it totaled $100,000 rather than $20,000.

So, figures shown on an income statement may not represent the actual cash inflows and outflows for a firm during a particular period. Financial managers and investors, however, are far more interested in actual cash flows than they are in the somewhat artificial, backward-looking accounting profit listed on the income statement. This is a very important distinction between the accounting point of view and the finance point of view. Finance professionals know that the firm needs cash, not accounting profit, to pay the firm's obligations as they come due, to fund the firm's operations and growth, and to compensate the firm's ultimate owners: its shareholders. Thus, the **statement of cash flows** is a financial statement that shows the firm's cash flows over a given period of time. This statement reports the amounts of cash that the firm generated and distributed during a particular time period. The bottom line on the statement of cash flows— the difference between cash sources and uses—equals the change in cash on the firm's balance sheet from the previous year's cash account balance. That is, the statement of cash flows reconciles income statement items and noncash balance sheet items to show changes in the cash and marketable securities account on the balance sheet over the particular analysis period.

Sources and Uses of Cash

LG5

In general, some activities increase cash (cash sources) and some decrease cash (cash uses). Figure 2.3 classifies the firm's basic cash sources and uses. Cash sources include increasing liabilities (or equity) or decreasing noncash assets. For example, if a firm sells new common stock, the firm has used primary markets

figure 2.3

Sources and Uses of
Cash

SOURCES OF CASH	USES OF CASH
Decrease a noncash current asset	Increase a noncash current asset
Decrease a fixed asset	Increase a fixed asset
Increase a current liability	Decrease a current liability
Increase long-term debt	Decrease long-term debt
Net income	Net losses
Depreciation	Pay dividends
Sell common or preferred stock	Repurchase common or preferred stock

to raise cash. Likewise, a drop in accounts receivable means that the firm has collected cash from its credit sales—also a cash source. The firm used cash to decrease a liability (paying off a bank loan) or to increase noncash assets (buying inventory). The statement of cash flows separates these cash flows into three categories or sections:

1. Cash flows from operating activities.
2. Cash flows from investing activities.
3. Cash flows from financing activities.

The basic setup of a statement of cash flows is shown in Figure 2.4 and a more detailed statement of cash flows for DPH Tree Farm, Inc. for the year ending December 31, 2008, appears as Table 2.4.

Cash flows from operations are those cash inflows and outflows that result directly from producing and selling the firm's products. These cash flows include:

- Net income.
- Depreciation.
- Working capital accounts other than cash and operations-related short-term debt.

Most finance professionals consider this top section of the statement of cash flows to be the most important. It shows quickly and compactly the firm's cash flows generated by and used for the production process. For example, DPH Tree Farm, Inc. generated $97 million in cash flows from its 2008 production. That is, producing and selling the firm's product resulted in a net cash inflow for the firm. Managers and investors look for positive cash flows from operations as a sign of a successful firm—positive cash flows from the firm's operations is precisely what gives the firm value. Unless the firm has a stable, healthy pattern in its cash flows from operations, it is not financially healthy no matter what its level of cash flow from investing activities or cash flows from financing activities.

Cash flows from investing activities are cash flows associated with buying or selling of fixed or other long-term assets. This section of the statement of cash flows shows cash inflows and outflows from long-term investing activities— most significantly the firm's investment in fixed assets. For example, DPH Tree Farm, Inc. used $68 million in cash to purchase fixed and other long-term assets in 2008. DPH funded this $68 million cash outflow with the $97 million cash surplus DPH Tree Farm produced from its operations.

Cash flows from financing activities are cash flows that result from debt and equity financing transactions. These include raising cash by:

- Issuing short-term debt,
- Issuing long-term debt,
- Issuing stock,
- Using cash to pay dividends,

figure 2.4

A. Cash flows from operating activities

Net income
Additions (sources of cash):
    Depreciation
    Decrease noncash current asset
    Increase accrued wages and taxes
    Increase in accounts payable
Subtractions (uses of cash):
    Increase noncash current asset
    Decrease accrued wages and taxes
    Decrease in accounts payable

B. Cash flows from investing activities

Additions:
    Decrease fixed assets
    Decrease in other long-term assets
Subtractions:
    Increase fixed assets
    Increase in other long-term assets

C. Cash flows from financing activities

Additions:
    Increase in notes payable
    Increase in long-term debt
    Increase in common and preferred stock
Subtraction:
    Decrease in notes payable
    Decrease in long-term debt
    Decrease in common and preferred stock
    Pay dividends

D. Net change in cash and marketable securities

The Statement of Cash Flows

Statement of Cash Flows for DPH Tree Farm, Inc.	table 2.4

DPH TREE FARM, INC.
Statement of Cash Flows for Year Ending December 31, 2008
(in millions of dollars)

	2008
A. Cash flows from operating activities	
Net income	$90
Additions (sources of cash):	
Depreciation	13
Increase accrued wages and taxes	5
Increase in accounts payable	5
Subtractions (uses of cash):	
Increase in accounts receivable	−5
Increase in inventory	−11
Net cash flow from operating activities	$97
B. Cash flows from investing activities	
Subtractions:	
Increase fixed assets	−$68
Increase in other long-term assets	0
Net cash flow from investing activities	−$68
C. Cash flows from financing activities	
Additions:	
Increase in notes payable	$0
Increase in long-term debt	5
Increase in common and preferred stock	0
Subtractions:	
Pay preferred stock dividends	−10
Pay common stock dividends	−25
Net cash flow from financing activities	−$30
D. Net change in cash and marketable securities	−$ 1

- Using cash to pay off debt,
- Using cash to buy back stock.

In 2008, DPH Tree Farm, Inc.'s financing activities produced a net cash outflow of $30 million. As we saw with cash flows from financing activities, this $30 million cash outflow was funded (at least partially) with the $97 million cash surplus DPH Tree Farm produced from its operations. Managers, investors, and analysts normally expect the cash flows from financing activities to include small amounts of net borrowing along with dividend payments. If, however, a firm is going through a major period of expansion, net borrowing could reasonably be much higher.

The bottom line of the statement of cash flows shows the sum of cash flows from operations, investing activities, and financing activities. The bottom line will reconcile to the **net change in cash and marketable securities** account on the balance sheet over the period of analysis. For example, the bottom line of the statement of cash flows for DPH Tree Farm is −$1 million. This is also the change in the cash account on the balance sheet between 2007 and 2008 ($24 million − $25 million = − $1 million). In this case, the firm's operating, investing, and financing activities combined to produce a net drain on the firm's cash during 2008—cash outflows were greater than cash inflows, largely because of the $68 million investment in long-term and fixed assets. Of course, when the bottom line is positive, a firm's cash inflows exceed cash outflows for the period.

Even though a company may report a large amount of net income on its income statement during a year, the firm may actually receive a positive, negative, or zero amount of cash. For example, DPH Tree Farm, Inc. reported net income of $90 million on its income statement (in Table 2.2), yet reported a net change in cash and marketable securities of −$1 million on its statement of cash flows (in Table 2.4). Accounting rules under GAAP create this sense of discord: Net income is the result of accounting rules, or GAAP, that do not necessarily reflect the firm's cash flows. While the income statement shows a firm's accounting-based income, the statement of cash flows more often reflects reality today and is thus more important to managers and investors as they seek to answer such important questions as:

- Does the firm generate sufficient cash to pay its obligations, thus avoiding financial distress?
- Does the firm generate sufficient cash to purchase assets needed for sustained growth?
- Does the firm generate sufficient cash to pay down its outstanding debt obligations?

Free Cash Flow

The statement of cash flows measures net cash flow as net income plus noncash adjustments. However, to maintain cash flows over time, firms must continually replace working capital and depreciating fixed assets and develop new products. Thus, firm managers cannot use the available cash flows any way they please. Of particular interest to investors, **free cash flows** are the cash flows available to pay the firm's stockholders and debt holders after the firm has made the necessary working capital investments, fixed asset investments, and developed the necessary new products to sustain the firm's ongoing operations.

To calculate free cash flow (FCF), we use the mathematical equation that appears below:

$$\text{FCF} = [\text{EBIT} - \text{Taxes} + \text{Depreciation}] - [\Delta\text{Gross fixed assets}$$
$$+ \Delta\text{Net operating working capital}]$$
$$= \text{Operating cash flow} - \text{Investment in operating capital} \qquad (2\text{-}7)$$

To calculate free cash flow, we start with operating cash flow. Firms generate operating cash flow (OCF) after they have paid necessary taxes. Depreciation, a noncash charge, is added back to operating cash flow to determine total OCF. We add other relevant noncash charges, such as amortization and depletion, back as well. Firms either buy physical assets or earmark funds for eventual equipment replacement to sustain firm operations; this is called *investment in operating capital (IOC)*. In accounting terms, IOC includes the firm's net investments (or changes) in fixed assets, current assets, and spontaneous current liabilities (such as accounts payable and accrued wages).

For interactive versions of this example visit www.mhhe.com/can1e

EXAMPLE 2·5

CALCULATING FREE CASH FLOW

From Tables 2.1 and 2.2, in 2008, DPH Tree Farm, Inc. had EBIT of $152 million, paid taxes of $46 million, and expensed deprecation at $13 million. Therefore, DPH Tree Farm's operating cash flow was

$$OCF = EBIT - Taxes + Depreciation$$

$$= (\$152m. - \$46m. + \$13m.) = \$119m.$$

DPH Tree Farm's gross fixed assets increased by $68 million between 2007 and 2008. The firm's current assets increased by $15 million and spontaneous current liabilities increased by $10 million ($5 million in accrued wages and taxes and $5 million in accounts payable). Therefore, DPH's investment in operating capital for 2008 was

$$IOC = \Delta Gross\ fixed\ assets + \Delta Net\ operating\ working\ capital$$

$$= \$68m. + (\$15m. - \$10m.) = \$73m.$$

Accordingly, what was DPH Tree Farm's free cash flow for 2008?

SOLUTION:

$$FCF = Operating\ cash\ flow - Investment\ in\ operating\ capital$$

$$= \$119m. - \$73m. = \$46m.$$

In other words, in 2008, DPH Tree Farm, Inc. had cash flows of $46 million available to pay its stockholders and debt holders.

Like the bottom line shown on the statement of cash flows, the level of free cash flow can be positive, zero, or negative. A positive free cash flow value means that the firm may distribute funds to its investors (debt holders and stockholders.) When the firm's free cash flows come in as zero or negative, however, the firm's operations produce no cash flows available for investors. Of course, if free cash flow is negative because operating cash flow is negative, investors are likely to take up the issue with the firm's management. Negative free cash flows as a result of negative operating cash flows generally indicate that the firm is experiencing operating or managerial problems. A firm with positive operating cash flows, but negative free cash flows, however, is not necessarily a poorly managed firm. Firms that invest heavily in operating capital to support growth often have positive operating cash flows but negative free cash flows, but in this case, the negative free cash flow will likely result in growing future profits.

TIME OUT

2-5   What is a statement of cash flows?

2-6   What do the three main sections on the statement of cash flows measure?

2.4 Statement of Retained Earnings

The **statement of retained earnings** provides additional details about changes in retained earnings during a reporting period. This financial statement reconciles net income earned during a given period and any cash dividends paid within that period on one side with the change in retained earnings between the beginning and ending of the period on the other. Table 2.5 presents DPH Tree Farm, Inc.'s statement of retained earnings as of December 31, 2008. The statement shows that DPH Tree Farms brought in a net income of $90 million during 2008. The firm paid out $10 million in dividends to preferred stockholders and another $25 million to common stockholders. The firm then had $55 million to reinvest back into the firm, which shows as an increase in retained earnings. Thus, the retained earnings account on the balance sheet (Table 2-1) increased from $155 million at year-end 2007 to $210 million at year-end 2008.

Increased retained earnings occur not just because a firm has net income, but rather because the firm's common stockholders agree to let management reinvest net income back into the firm rather than pay it out as dividends. Reinvesting net income into retained earnings allows the firm to use investment to grow through additional funds spent in plant and equipment, inventory, and other assets needed to generate even more profit. So retained earnings represent a claim against all of the firm's assets and not against a particular asset.

EXAMPLE 2-6

 For interactive versions of this example visit www.mhhe.com/can1e

STATEMENT OF RETAINED EARNINGS

Indian Point Kennels, Inc. earned net income in 2008 of $10.78 million. The firm paid out $1 million in cash dividends to its preferred stockholders and $2.5 million in cash dividends to its common stockholders. The firm ended 2007 with $135.75 million in retained earnings. Construct a statement of retained earnings to calculate the year-end 2008 balance of retained earnings.

SOLUTION:

The statement of retained earnings for 2008 is as follows:

INDIAN POINT KENNELS, INC.
Statement of Retained Earnings as of December 31, 2008
(in millions of dollars)

		2008
Balance of retained earnings, December 31, 2007		$135.75
Plus: Net income for 2008		10.78
Less: Cash dividends paid		
Preferred stock	$1.0	
Common stock	2.5	
Total cash dividends paid		3.50
Balance of retained earnings, December 31, 2008		$143.03

DPH TREE FARM, INC.
Statement of Retained Earnings as of December 31, 2008
(in millions of dollars)

		2008
Balance of retained earnings, December 31, 2007		$155
Plus: Net income for 2008		90
Less: Cash dividends paid		
Preferred stock	$10	
Common stock	25	
Total cash dividends paid		35
Balance of retained earnings, December 31, 2008		$210

TIME OUT

2-7   What is a statement of retained earnings?

2-8   If, during a given period, a firm pays out more in dividends than it has net income, what happens to the firm's retained earnings?

2.5 Cautions in Interpreting Financial Statements

As we mentioned earlier in the chapter, firms must prepare their financial statements according to GAAP. GAAP provides a common set of standards intended to produce objective and precise financial statements. But recall also that managers have significant discretion over their reported earnings. Managers and financial analysts have recognized for years that firms use considerable latitude in using accounting rules to manage their reported earnings in a wide variety of contexts. Indeed, within the GAAP framework, firms can "smooth" earnings. That is, firms often take steps to over- or understate earnings at various times. Managers may choose to smooth earnings to show investors that firm assets are growing steadily. Similarly, one firm may be using straight-line depreciation for its fixed assets, while another is using a modified accelerated cost recovery method (MACRS), which causes depreciation to accrue quickly. If the firm uses MACRS accounting methods, they write fixed asset values down quickly; assets will thus have lower book value than if the firm used straight-line depreciation methods.

This process of controlling a firm's earnings is called **earnings management.** At the extreme, earnings management has resulted in some widely reported accounting scandals involving Enron, Merck, WorldCom, and other major U.S. corporations that tried to artificially influence their earnings by manipulating accounting rules. Congress responded to the spate of corporate scandals that emerged after 2001 with the **Sarbanes-Oxley Act,** passed in June 2002. Sarbanes-Oxley requires public companies to ensure that their corporate boards' audit committees have considerable experience applying generally accepted accounting principles (GAAP) for financial statements. The act also requires that any firm's senior management must sign off on the financial statements of the firm, certifying the statements as accurate and representative of the firm's financial condition during the period covered. If a firm's board of directors or senior managers fail to comply with Sarbanes-Oxley (SOX), the firm may be delisted from stock exchanges.

COLDWATER CREEK RECEIVES AUTOMATIC DELISTING NOTICE FROM NASDAQ AS A RESULT OF INCOMPLETE 10-Q FILING

Coldwater Creek Inc. announced today that it received a Nasdaq Staff Determination on June 14, 2006, stating that Coldwater Creek (the "Company") failed to comply with Marketplace Rule 4310(c)(14) because its Quarterly Report on Form 10-Q for the quarter ended April 29, 2006 (the "Form 10-Q") filed on June 8, 2006, was incomplete. NASDAQ Staff Determination notices are generated automatically in these circumstances and indicate that, due to such noncompliance, Coldwater Creek's common stock will be subject to delisting.

As indicated in the Form 10-Q, the Company's independently registered public accounting firm had not completed its review of the financial information included in the Form 10-Q when it made the filing due to the Company's pending restatement of certain historical financial information. As a result, the Company was unable to provide the officer certifications required by . . . the Sarbanes-Oxley Act of 2002 with the Form 10-Q.

In the interim, the Company is working diligently to complete the amendment to its Form 10-K for the fiscal year ended January 28, 2006 to reflect the restated financial information so that the Company's independently registered public accounting firm can complete its review of the financial information in the Form 10-Q. Once this review is completed, the Company intends to file as soon as possible a fully compliant amended Form 10-Q/A, including the certifications required under . . . the Sarbanes-Oxley Act. It is currently expected that the Company's amended Form 10-K filing will be finalized prior to the Nasdaq hearing date, which will enable the Company to file its amended Form 10-Q and return to compliance with Nasdaq's Marketplace Rules.

Source: *The Wall Street Journal,* June 20, 2006, p. A3.

 want to know more? **Key Words to Search for Updates: Sarbanes-Oxley Act of 2002, financial statements, 10Q filing, 10K filing.**

As illustrated in the Finance at Work reading, Coldwater Creek's accounting firm had not completed its review of the firm's financial statements when they were released to the public. As a result, the firm's common stock became subject to delisting. Congress's goal in passing SOX was to prevent deceptive accounting and management practices and to bring stability to jittery stock markets battered in 2002 by accounting and managerial scandals that cost employees their life savings and harmed many innocent shareholders as well.

TIME OUT

2-9   What is earnings management?

Business Application Solution

If the managers of DPH Tree Farm increase the firm's fixed assets by $27 million and net working capital by $8 million in 2009, the balance sheet would look like the one below (Table 2.6). That is, fixed assets increase by $27 million, to $387 million; cash, accounts receivable, and inventory would increase by $1 million, $5 million, and $6 million, respectively. DPH Tree Farm's total assets will thus grow by $39 million to $609 million by year-end 2009. This growth in assets would be financed with $4 million in accounts payable, and the remaining $35 million will be financed with 40 percent long-term debt (.4 × $35m. = $14m.) and 60 percent with common stock (.6 × $35m. = $21m.).

Personal Application Solution

As Chris Ryan examines the 2008 financial statements for DPH Tree Farm, Inc. she needs to remember that the balance sheet reports a firm's assets, liabilities, and equity at a particular point in time, the income statement reports the total revenues and expenses over a specific period of time, the statement of cash flows shows the firm's cash flows over a period of time, and the statement of retained earnings reconciles net income earned during a given period and any cash dividends paid with the change in retained earnings over the period.

GAAP procedures dictate how each financial statement is prepared. GAAP requires that the firm recognizes revenue when the firm sells the product, which is not necessarily when the firm receives the cash. Likewise, under GAAP, expenses appear on the income statement as they match sales. That is, the income statement

(continued)

table 2.6

DPH TREE FARM INC.
Balance Sheet as of December 31, 2009
(in millions of dollars)

Assets	2009		Liabilities and Equity	2009	
Current assets:			Current liabilities:		
Cash	$ 25	($24 + $1)	Accrued wages and taxes	$ 20	
Accounts receivable	75	($70 + $5)	Accounts payable	59	($55 + $4)
Inventory	117	($111 + $6)	Notes payable	45	
Total	217		Total	124	
Fixed assets:					
Gross plant and equipment	395	($368 + $27)	Long-term debt:	209	($195 + .4($39 − $4))
Less: Depreciation	53		Stockholders' equity:		
Net plant and equipment	342		Preferred stock (5 million shares)	5	
Other long-term assets	50		Common stock and paid-in surplus (20 million shares)	61	($40 + .6($39 − $4))
			Retained earnings	210	
Total	392		Total	276	
Total assets	$609	($570 + $39)	Total liabilities and equity	$609	($570 + $39)

Personal Application Solution (concluded)

recognizes production and other expenses associated with sales when the firm sells the product. Again, the actual cash outflow associated with producing the goods may actually occur at a very different time than that reported. In addition, the income statement contains several noncash items, the largest of which is depreciation. As a result, figures shown on an income statement may not be representative of the actual cash inflows and outflows for a firm during any particular period.

For investors like Chris Ryan, the actual cash flows are often more important than the accounting profit listed on the income statement. Cash, not accounting profit, is needed to pay the firm's obligations as they come due: to fund the firm's operations and growth, and to compensate the firm's owners. So Chris is more likely to find the answers she seeks in the statement of cash flows, which shows the firm's cash flows over a given period of time. The statement of cash flows reports the amounts of cash generated and cash distributed by a firm during the time period analyzed.

Finally, Chris must remember that firms are required to prepare their financial statements according to GAAP. GAAP allows managers to have significant discretion over their reported earnings, in other words, to *manage earnings.* Indeed, managers can report their results in such a way that indicates to investors that the firm's assets are growing more steadily than may really be the case. Similarly, the choice of depreciation method—straight line or MACRS—for fixed assets may make two firms with identical fixed assets appear to have very different results. Thus, Chris may need to delve more deeply into research about this firm's—or any firm's—financial condition before she makes any final investment decision.

summary of learning goals

This chapter reviewed the four basic financial statements. We examined each statement's major features. The chapter also discussed cautions that readers of financial statements should take when reviewing the documents.

LG1 **Recall the major financial statements that firms provide to the public.** In any annual report, you will find the four basic financial statements—the balance sheet, the income statement, the statement of cash flows, and the statement of retained earnings. These four statements provide an accounting-based picture of a firm's financial position. These statements often provide a key source of information for firm managers to make financial decisions and for investors to decide whether to invest in the firm.

LG2 **Differentiate between book (or accounting) value and market value.** A firm's balance sheet shows its book (or historical cost) value based on generally accepted accounting principles (GAAP). Under GAAP, assets are listed on the balance sheet at the amount the firm paid for them, regardless of what they might be worth today. Market value is the amount the firm would get if it actually sold an asset. The book value and market value of a firm's current assets are generally very close in value. However, the book value of a firm's fixed assets is often very different from the market value.

LG3 **Explain how taxes influence corporate managers' and investors' decisions.** Firms pay out a large portion of their earnings as taxes. The U.S. Congress sets (and often changes) the U.S. tax code, which in turn determines corporate tax obligations. The U.S. tax system is extremely complicated and we do not attempt to cover it in detail here. However, taxes are a major expense item for a firm and they are a crucial part of many financial decisions.

LG4 **Differentiate between accounting income and cash flows.** The income statement is prepared using GAAP. Following GAAP, revenue is recognized at the time of sale, which is not necessarily when cash is received. Likewise, under GAAP, expenses appear on the income statement as they match sales. That is, production and other expenses associated with the sales reported on the income statement (for example, cost of goods sold and depreciation) are recognized at the time the product is sold. Again, the actual cash outflow associated with these expenses may occur at a very different point in time.

In addition, the income statement contains several noncash items. The largest is depreciation. As a result, figures shown on an income statement may not represent the actual cash inflows and outflows for a firm during a particular period. For the financial manager and investors, however, these cash flows are precisely the most important information available among the financial documents; more

important than the accounting profit listed on the income statement. Cash, not accounting profit, is needed to pay the firm's obligations as they come due, to fund operations and growth, and to compensate firm owners.

LG5 **Demonstrate how to use a firm's financial statements to calculate its cash flows.** The statement of cash flows is the financial statement that shows the firm's cash flows over a given period of time. The statement of cash flows reports how much cash the firm generates and distributes during the time period analyzed. The bottom line of the statement of cash flows—the difference between cash sources and cash uses—equals the change in cash on the firm's balance sheet. That is, the statement of cash flows reconciles income statement items and noncash balance sheet items to get to the change in the cash and marketable securities account on the balance sheet over the period of analysis.

LG6 **Observe cautions that should be taken when examining financial statements.** Firms must prepare their financial statements according to GAAP, which provides a common set of standards intended to produce financial statements that are objective and precise. However, GAAP also allows managers significant discretion over the firm's reported earnings. Managers and financial analysts have recognized for years that firms use considerable latitude in accounting rules to manage their reported earnings in a wide variety of contexts.

chapter equations

2-1 Assets = Liabilities + Equity

2-2 $\text{Earnings per share (EPS)} = \dfrac{\text{Net income available to common stockholders}}{\text{Total shares of common stock outstanding}}$

2-3
$\text{Dividends per share (DPS)} = \dfrac{\text{Common stock dividends paid}}{\text{Number of shares of common stock outstanding}}$

2-4
$\text{Book value per share (BVPS)} = \dfrac{\text{Common stockholders' equity}}{\text{Number of shares of common stock outstanding}}$

$$2\text{-}5 \quad \text{Market value per share (MVPS)} = \text{Market price of the firm's common stock}$$

$$2\text{-}6 \quad \text{Average tax rate} = \frac{\text{Tax liability}}{\text{Taxable income}}$$

$$2\text{-}7 \quad \text{FCF} = [\text{EBIT} - \text{Taxes} + \text{Depreciation}] - [\Delta\text{Gross fixed assets}$$
$$+ \Delta\text{Net operating working capital}]$$
$$= \text{Operating cash flow} - \text{Investment in operating capital}$$

key terms

average tax rate, The average tax rate is the percentage of each dollar of taxable income that the firm pays in taxes. (p. 36)

balance sheet, The financial statement that reports a firm's assets, liabilities, and equity at a particular point in time. (p. 30)

book (or historical cost) value, Assets are listed on the balance sheet at the amount the firm paid for them. (p. 32)

capital structure, The amount of debt versus equity financing to hold on the balance sheet. (p. 32)

cash flows from financing activities, Cash flows that result from debt and equity financing transactions. (p. 40)

cash flows from investing activities, Cash flows associated with the purchase or sale of fixed or other long-term assets. (p. 40)

cash flows from operations, Cash flows that are the direct result of the production and sale of the firm's products. (p. 40)

common stock and paid-in surplus, Cash that common stockholders paid to the firm when it originally issued the stock. (p. 30)

current assets, Assets that will normally convert to cash within one year. (p. 30)

current liabilities, Obligations of the firm that are due within one year. (p. 30)

earnings management, The process of controlling a firm's earnings. (p. 45)

EBIT, Earnings before interest and taxes. (p. 34)

EBT, Earnings before taxes. (p. 34)

financial leverage, The extent to which debt securities are used by a firm. (p. 32)

financial statement, Statement that provides an accounting-based picture of a firm's financial position. (p. 28)

fixed assets, Assets with a useful life exceeding one year. (p. 30)

free cash flow, Cash flows available for payments to stockholders and debt holders of a firm after the firm has made investments in assets necessary to sustain the ongoing operations of the firm. (p. 42)

gross profit, Net sales minus cost of goods sold. (p. 34)

income statement, Financial statement that reports the total revenues and expenses over a specific period of time. (p. 34)

liabilities, Funds provided by lenders to the firm. (p. 30)

liquidity, The ease of conversion of an asset into cash at a fair value. (p. 30)

long-term debt, Obligations of the firm that are due in more than one year. (p. 30)

marginal tax rate, The amount of additional taxes a firm must pay out for every additional dollar of taxable income it earns. (p. 36)

market value, Assets are listed at the amount the firm would get if it sold them. (p. 33)

net change in cash and marketable securities, The sum of the cash flows from operations, investing activities, and financing activities. (p. 42)

net income, The bottom line on the income statement. (p. 34)

net working capital, The difference between a firm's current assets and current liabilities. (p. 31)

preferred stock, Cash that preferred stockholders paid to the firm when it originally issued stock. (p. 30)

retained earnings, The cumulative earnings the firm has reinvested rather than pay out as dividends. (p. 30)

Sarbanes-Oxley Act of 2002, Requires that any firm's senior management must sign off on the financial statements of the firm, certifying the statements as accurate and representative of the firm's financial condition during the period covered. (p. 45)

statement of cash flows, Financial statement that shows the firm's cash flows over a period of time. (p. 39)

statement of retained earnings, Financial statement that reconciles net income earned during a given period and any cash dividends paid with the change in retained earnings over the period. (p. 44)

stockholders' equity, Funds provided by the firm's preferred and common stock owners. (p. 30)

self-test problems with solutions

1 **Financial Statements** Listed below are partial financial statements for Marion & Carter, Inc. Complete each of these statements. Fill in the blanks on the four financial statements.

MARION & CARTER, INC.
Balance Sheet as of December 31, 2007 and 2008
(in millions of dollars)

Assets	2007	2008	Liabilities and Equity	2007	2008
Current assets:			Current liabilities:		
Cash and marketable securities	$ 155	$ 165	Accrued wages and taxes	$ 95	$ 124
Accounts receivable	400	☐	Accounts payable	☐	340
Inventory	620	690	Notes payable	280	342
Total	1,175	1,290	Total	685	806
Fixed assets:			Long-term debt:	☐	1,210
Gross plant and equipment	1,860	☐	Stockholders' equity:		
Less: Depreciation	250	330	Preferred stock (25 million shares)	25	25
Net plant and equipment	1,610	1,950	Common stock and paid-in surplus (200 million shares)	☐	250
Other long-term assets	310	350	Retained earnings	957	1,299
Total	1,920	☐	Total	1,232	1,574
Total assets	$3,095	$3,590	Total liabilities and equity	$ ☐	$3,590

MARION & CARTER, INC.
Income Statement for Years Ending December 31, 2007 and 2008
(in millions of dollars)

	2007	2008
Net sales	$ 1,705	$ ☐
Less: Cost of goods sold	☐	930
Gross profits	868	1,023
Less: Depreciation	75	80
Earnings before interest and taxes (EBIT)	793	943
Less: Interest	112	☐
Earnings before taxes (EBT)	681	844
Less: Taxes	248	☐
Net income	$ 433	$ 559
Less: Preferred stock dividends	$ 62	$ 62

(continued)

Net income available to common stockholders		$ 371	$ 497
Less: Common stock dividends		[____]	155
Addition to retained earnings		$ 216	$ 342
Per (common) share data:			
Earnings per share (EPS)		$ 1.855	$ [____]
Dividends per share (DPS)		$ [____]	$ 0.775
Book value per share (BVPS)		$ 6.035	$ [____]
Market value (price) per share (MVPS)		$21.470	$22.970

MARION & CARTER, INC.
Statement of Cash Flows for Year Ending December 31, 2008
(in millions of dollars)

	2008
A. Cash flows from operating activities	
Net income	$ [____]
Additions (sources of cash):	
Depreciation	80
Increase accrued wages and taxes	[____]
Increase in accounts payable	30
Subtractions (uses of cash):	
Increase in accounts receivable	−35
Increase in inventory	[____]
Net cash flow from operating activities:	[____]
B. Cash flows from investing activities	
Subtractions:	
Increase fixed assets	−420
Increase in other long-term assets	[____]
Net cash flow from investing activities:	[____]
C. Cash flows from financing activities	
Additions:	
Increase in notes payable	[____]
Increase in long-term debt	32
Increase in common and preferred stock	0
Subtractions:	
Pay preferred stock dividends	[____]
Pay common stock dividends	[____]
Net cash flow from financing activities:	[____]
D. Net change in cash and marketable securities	−$10

MARION & CARTER, INC.
Statement of Retained Earnings as of December 31, 2008
(in millions of dollars)

	2008
Balance of retained earnings, December 31, 2007	$ 957
Plus: Net income for 2008	[____]
Less: Cash dividends paid	
Preferred stock	$ [____]
Common stock	[____]
Total cash dividends paid	[____]
Balance of retained earnings, December 31, 2008	$ 1,299

Solution:

MARION & CARTER, INC.
Balance Sheet as of December 31, 2007 and 2008
(in millions of dollars)

Assets	2007	2008	Liabilities and Equity	2007	2008
Current assets:			**Current liabilities:**		
Cash and marketable securities	$ 155	$ 165	Accrued wages and taxes	$ 95	$ 124
Accounts receivable	400	1,290−690−165=435	Accounts payable	685−280−95=310	340
Inventory	620	690	Notes payable	280	342
Total	1,175	1,290	Total	685	806
Fixed assets:			Long-term debt:	$3,095−1,232−685=1,178	1,210
Gross plant and equipment	1,860	1,950−330=2,280	**Stockholders' equity:**		
Less: Depreciation	250	330	Preferred stock (25 million shares)	$ 25	$ 25
Net plant and equipment	1,610	1,950	Common stock and paid-in surplus (200 million shares)	1,232−957−25=250	250
Other long-term assets	310	350	Retained earnings	957	1,299
Total	1,920	1,950+350=2,300	Total	1,232	1,574
Total assets	$3,095	$3,590	Total liabilities and equity	$3,095	$3,590

MARION & CARTER, INC.
Income Statement for Years Ending December 31, 2007 and 2008
(in millions of dollars)

	2007	2008
Net sales	$ 1,705	1,023+930=$1,953
Less: Cost of goods sold	1705−868=837	930
Gross profits	868	1,023
Less: Depreciation	75	80
Earnings before interest and taxes (EBIT)	793	943
Less: Interest	112	943−844=99
Earnings before taxes (EBT)	681	844
Less: Taxes	248	844−559=285
Net income	$ 433	$ 559
Less: Preferred stock dividends	$ 62	$ 62
Net income available to common stock holders	$ 371	$ 497
Less: Common stock dividends	371−216=$155	155
Addition to retained earnings	$ 216	$ 342
Per (common) share data:		
Earnings per share (EPS)	$ 1.855	497/200=$2.485
Dividends per share (DPS)	155/200=$0.775	$ 0.775
Book value per share (BVPS)	$ 6.035	(1,574−25)/200=$7.745
Market value (price) per share (MVPS)	$21.470	$22.970

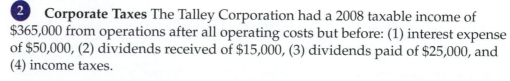

2 **Corporate Taxes** The Talley Corporation had a 2008 taxable income of $365,000 from operations after all operating costs but before: (1) interest expense of $50,000, (2) dividends received of $15,000, (3) dividends paid of $25,000, and (4) income taxes.

a. Calculate Talley 's taxable income.

b. Calculate Talley's income tax liability for 2008.

c. Calculate Talley's after-tax income for 2008.

d. What are the company's average and marginal tax rates on taxable income?

Solution:

a. Taxable income = EBIT − Interest expense + Taxable portion of dividends received

$$= \$365,000 - 50,000 + 15,000(1 - .7) = \$319,500$$

b. Tax liability = Tax on base amount + Tax rate (amount over base)

$$= \$22,250 + .39\ (\$319,500 - \$100,000) = \$107,855$$

c. After-tax income $= \$365,000 - \$50,000 + \$15,000 - \$107,855 = \$222,145$

d. The resulting average tax rate for Talley Corporation Inc. is:

$$\text{Average tax rate} = \frac{\text{Tax liability}}{\text{Taxable income}} = \frac{107,855}{319,500} = 33.76\%$$

Marginal tax rate $= 39\%$

3 **Free Cash Flow** In 2008, Nolen Power, Inc. earned an EBIT of $675 million, paid taxes of $226 million, and computed its depreciation expense as $57 million. Nolen Power's gross fixed assets increased by $58 million from 2007 to 2008. The firm's current assets increased by $30 million and spontaneous current liabilities increased by $15 million ($5 million in accrued wages and taxes and $10 million in accounts payable).

LG5

a. Calculate Nolen Power's operating cash flow for 2008.

b. Calculate Nolen Power's investment in operating capital for 2008.

c. Calculate Nolen Power's free cash flow for 2008.

Solution:

a. Operating cash flow for 2008 is:

OCF = EBIT − Taxes + Depreciation
$$= (\$675m. - \$226m. + \$57m.) = \$506m.$$

b. Investment in operating capital for 2008 is:

IOC = ΔGross fixed assets + ΔNet operating working capital
$$= \$58m. + (\$30m. - \$15m.) = \$73m.$$

c. Free cash flow for 2008 is:

FCF = Operating cash flow − Investment in operating capital
$$= \$506m. - \$73m. = \$433m.$$

In other words, in 2008, Nolen Power, Inc. had cash flows of $433 million available to pay its stockholders and debt holders.

questions

1. List and describe the four major financial statements. *(LG1)*

2. On which of the four major financial statements (balance sheet, income statement, statement of cash flows, or statement of retained earnings) would you find the following items? *(LG1)*

   a. Earnings before taxes.

   b. Net plant and equipment.

   c. Increase in fixed assets.

   d. Gross profits.

   e. Balance of retained earnings, December 31, 20xx.

   f. Common stock and paid-in surplus.

   g. Net cash flow from investing activities.

   h. Accrued wages and taxes.

   i. Increase in inventory.

3. What is the difference between current liabilities and long-term debt? *(LG1)*

4. How does the choice of accounting method used to record fixed asset depreciation affect management of the balance sheet? *(LG1)*

5. What are the costs and benefits of holding liquid securities on a firm's balance sheet? *(LG1)*

6. Why can the book value and market value of a firm differ? *(LG2)*

7. From a firm manager's or investor's point of view, which is more important—the book value of a firm or the market value of the firm? *(LG2)*

8. What do we mean by a progressive tax structure? *(LG3)*

9. What is the difference between an average tax rate and a marginal tax rate? *(LG3)*

10. How does the payment of interest on debt affect the amount of taxes the firm must pay? *(LG3)*

11. The income statement is prepared using GAAP. How does this affect the reported revenue and expense measures listed on the balance sheet? *(LG4)*

12. Why do financial managers and investors find cash flow to be more important than accounting profit? *(LG4)*

13. Which of the following activities result in an increase (decrease) in a firm's cash? *(LG5)*

   a. Decrease fixed assets

   b. Decrease accounts payable

   c. Pay dividends

   d. Sell common stock

   e. Decrease accounts payable.

   f. Increase notes payable

14. What is the difference between net cash flow from operating activities, net cash flow from investing activities, and net cash flow from financing activities? *(LG5)*

15. What are free cash flows for a firm? What does it mean when a firm's free cash flow is negative? *(LG5)*

16. What is earnings management? *(LG6)*

17. What does the Sarbanes-Oxley Act require of firm managers? *(LG6)*

problems

basic problems

2-1 **Balance Sheet** You are evaluating the balance sheet for Goodman's Bees Corporation. From the balance sheet you find the following balances: cash and marketable securities = $400,000, accounts receivable = $1,200,000, inventory = $2,100,000, accrued wages and taxes = $500,000, accounts payable = $800,000, and notes payable = $600,000. Calculate Goodman Bee's net working capital. *(LG1)*

2-2 **Balance Sheet** Zoeckler Mowing & Landscaping's year-end 2009 balance sheet lists current assets of $256,000, fixed assets of $324,000, current liabilities of $245,000, and long-term debt of $185,000. Calculate Zoeckler's total stockholders' equity. *(LG1)*

2-3 **Income Statement** Reed's Birdie Shot, Inc.'s 2008 income statement lists the following income and expenses: EBIT = $538,000, interest expense = $63,000, and net income = $435,000. Calculate the 2008 taxes reported on the income statement. *(LG1)*

2-4 **Income Statement** Reed's Birdie Shot, Inc.'s 2009 income statement lists the following income and expenses: EBIT = $455,000, interest expense = $58,000, and taxes = $138,000. Reed's has no preferred stock outstanding and 100,000 shares of common stock outstanding. Calculate the 2008 earnings per share. *(LG1)*

2-5 **Corporate Taxes** Oakdale Fashions Inc. had $245,000 in 2008 taxable income. Using the tax schedule in Table 2.3, calculate the company's 2008 income taxes. What is the average tax rate? What is the marginal tax rate? *(LG3)*

2-6 **Corporate Taxes** Hunt Taxidermy, Inc. is concerned about the taxes paid by the company in 2008. In addition to $26.5 million of taxable income, the firm received $1,750,000 of interest on state-issued bonds and $600,000 of dividends on common stock it owns in Hunt Taxidermy, Inc. Calculate Hunt Taxidermy's tax liability, average tax rate, and marginal tax rate. *(LG3)*

2-7 **Statement of Cash Flows** Ramakrishnan, Inc. reported 2008 net income of $15 million and depreciation of $2,650,000. The top part of Ramakrishnan, Inc.'s 2007 and 2008 balance sheets is listed below (in millions of dollars).

	2007	2008		2007	2008
Current assets:			Current liabilities:		
Cash and marketable securities	$ 15	$ 20	Accrued wages and taxes	$ 18	$ 19
Accounts receivable	75	84	Accounts payable	45	51
Inventory	110	121	Notes payable	40	45
Total	$200	$225	Total	$103	$115

Calculate the 2008 net cash flow from operating activities for Ramakrishnan, Inc. *(LG4)*

2-8 **Statement of Cash Flows** In 2008, Usher Sports Shop had cash flows from investing activities of −$2,567,000 and cash flows from financing activities of −$3,459,000. The balance in the firm's cash account was $950,000 at the beginning of 2008 and $1,025,000 at the end of the year. Calculate Usher Sports Shop's cash flow from operations for 2008. *(LG4)*

2-9 **Free Cash Flow** You are considering an investment in Fields and Struthers, Inc. and want to evaluate the firm's free cash flow. From the income statement, you see that Fields and Struthers earned an EBIT of $62 million, paid taxes of $17 million, and its depreciation expense was $5 million. Fields and Struthers' gross fixed assets increased by $32 million from 2007 to 2008. The firm's current assets increased by $20 million and spontaneous current liabilities increased by $12 million. Calculate Fields and Struthers' operating cash flow, investment in operating capital, and free cash flow for 2008. *(LG5)*

2-10 **Free Cash Flow** Tater and Pepper Corp. reported free cash flows for 2008 of $23 million and investment in operating capital of $13 million. Tater and Pepper listed $8 million in depreciation expense and $17 million in taxes on its 2008 income statement. Calculate Tater and Pepper's 2008 EBIT. *(LG5)*

2-11 **Statement of Retained Earnings** Mr. Husker's Tuxedos Corp. began the year 2008 with $256 million in retained earnings. The firm earned net income of $33 million in 2008 and paid $5 million to its preferred stockholders and $10 million to its common stock holders. What is the year-end 2008 balance in retained earnings for Mr. Husker's Tuxedos? *(LG1)*

2-12 **Statement of Retained Earnings** Use the following information to find dividends paid to common stock holders during 2008. *(LG1)*

Balance of retained earnings, December 31, 2007		$785m.
Plus: Net income for 2008		25m.
Less: Cash dividends paid		
Preferred stock	$5m.	
Common stock	☐	
Total cash dividends paid		☐
Balance of retained earnings, December 31, 2008		$798m.

intermediate
problems

2-13 **Balance Sheet** Brenda's Bar and Grill has total assets of $15 million of which $5 million are current assets. Cash makes up 10 percent of the current assets and accounts receivable makes up another 40 percent of current assets. Brenda's gross plant and equipment has a book value of $11.5 million and other long-term assets have a book value of $500,000. Using this information, what is the balance of inventory and the balance of depreciation on Brenda Bar and Grill's balance sheet? *(LG1)*

2-14 **Balance Sheet** Ed's Tobacco Shop has total assets of $54 million. Fifty percent of these assets are financed with debt of which $17 million is current liabilities. The firm has no preferred stock but the balance in common stock and paid-in surplus is $12 million. Using this information what is the balance for long-term debt and retained earnings on Ed's Tobacco Shop's balance sheet? *(LG1)*

2-15 **Market Value versus Book Value** Muffin's Masonry, Inc. balance sheet lists net fixed assets as $14 million. The fixed assets could currently be sold for $19 million. Muffin's current balance sheet shows current liabilities of $5.5 million and net working capital of $4.5 million. If all the current accounts were liquidated today, the company would receive $7.25 million cash after paying $5.5 million in liabilities. What is the book value of Muffin's Masonry's assets today? What is the market value of these assets? *(LG2)*

2-16 **Debt versus Equity Financing** You are considering a stock investment in one of two firms (AllDebt, Inc. and AllEquity, Inc.), both of which operate in the same industry and have identical operating income of $12.5 million. AllDebt, Inc. finances its $25 million in assets with $24 million in debt (on which it pays 10 percent interest annually) and $1 million in equity. AllEquity, Inc. finances its $25 million in assets with no debt and $25 million in equity. Both firms pay a tax rate of 30 percent on their taxable income. Calculate the income available to pay the asset funders (the debt holders and stockholders) and resulting return on assets for the two firms. *(LG1)*

2-17 **Income Statement** You have been given the following information for Corky's Bedding Corp.:

a. Net sales = $11,250,000.

b. Cost of goods sold = $7,750,000.

c. Addition to retained earnings = $1,000,000.

d. Dividends paid to preferred and common stock holders = $495,000.

e. Interest expense = $850,000.

The firm's tax rate is 35 percent. Calculate the depreciation expense for Corky's Bedding Corp. *(LG1)*

2-18 **Income Statement** You have been given the following information for Moore's HoneyBee Corp.:

a. Net sales = $54,500,000.

b. Gross profit = $27,500,000.

c. Addition to retained earnings = $8,000,000.

d. Dividends paid to preferred and common stock holders = $5,000,000.

e. Depreciation expense = $5,000,000.

The firm's tax rate is 35 percent. Calculate the cost of goods sold and the interest expense for Moore's HoneyBee Corp. *(LG1)*

2-19 **Corporate Taxes** The Dakota Corporation had a 2008 taxable income of $33,365,000 from operations after all operating costs but before (1) interest charges of $8,500,000; (2) dividends received of $750,000; (3) dividends paid of $5,250,000; and (4) income taxes.

a. Use the tax schedule in Table 2.3 to calculate Dakota's income tax liability. (LG3)

b. What are Dakota's average and marginal tax rates on taxable income? *(LG3)*

2-20 **Corporate Taxes** Suppose that in addition to $10.5 million of taxable income, Texas Taco, Inc. received $650,000 of interest on state-issued bonds and $450,000 of dividends on common stock it owns in Texas Taco, Inc.

a. Use the tax schedule in Table 2.3 to calculate Texas Taco's income tax liability. *(LG3)*

b. What are Texas Taco's average and marginal tax rates on taxable income? *(LG3)*

2-21 **Statement of Cash Flows** Use the balance sheet and income statement below to construct a statement of cash flows for Clancy's Dog Biscuit Corp. *(LG5)*

CLANCY'S DOG BISCUIT CORPORATION
Balance Sheet as of December 31, 2007 and 2008
(in millions of dollars)

Assets	2007	2008	Liabilities and Equity	2007	2008
Current assets:			Current liabilities:		
Cash and marketable securities	$ 5	$ 5	Accrued wages and taxes	$ 6	$ 10
Accounts receivable	19	20	Accounts payable	15	16
Inventory	29	36	Notes payable	13	14
Total	53	61	Total	34	40
Fixed assets:			Long-term debt:	53	57
Gross plant and equipment	88	106	Stockholders' equity:		
Less: Depreciation	11	15	Preferred stock (2 million shares)	2	2
			Common stock and paid-in surplus (5 million shares)	11	11
Net plant and equipment	77	91	Retained earnings	45	57
Other long-term assets	15	15			
Total	92	106	Total	58	70
Total assets	$145	$167	Total liabilities and equity	$145	$167

CLANCY'S DOG BISCUIT CORPORATION
Income Statement for Years Ending December 31, 2007 and 2008
(in millions of dollars)

	2007	2008
Net sales	$80	$76
Less: Cost of goods sold	39	44
Gross profits	41	32
Less: Depreciation	4	4
Earnings before interest and taxes (EBIT)	37	28
Less: Interest	5	5
Earnings before taxes (EBT)	32	23
Less: Taxes	10	7
Net income	$22	$16
Less: Preferred stock dividends	$ 1	$ 1
Net income available to common stock holders	$ 21	$15
Less: Common stock dividends	$ 3	$ 3
Addition to retained earnings	$18	$12
Per (common) share data:		
Earnings per share (EPS)	$ 4.20	$ 3.00
Dividends per share (DPS)	$ 0.60	$ 0.60
Book value per share (BVPS)	$ 11.20	$13.60
Market value (price) per share (MVPS)	$ 14.60	$14.25

2-22 Statement of Cash Flows Use the balance sheet and income statement below to construct a statement of cash flows for Valium's Medical Supply Corp. *(LG5)*

VALIUM'S MEDICAL SUPPLY CORPORATION
Balance Sheet as of December 31, 2007 and 2008
(In thousands of dollars)

Assets	2007	2008	Liabilities and Equity	2007	2008
Current liabilities:			Current assets:		
Cash and marketable securities	$ 123	$ 124	Accrued wages and taxes	$ 76	$ 98
Accounts receivable	321	339	Accounts payable	246	271
Inventory	494	548	Notes payable	222	222
Total	938	1,011	Total	544	591
Fixed assets:			Long-term debt:	937	963
Gross plant and equipment	1,507	1,843	Stockholders' equity:		
Less: Depreciation	197	261	Preferred stock (10 million shares)	10	10
Net plant and equipment	1,310	1,582	Common stock and paid-in surplus (100 million shares)	200	200
Other long-term assets	220	220	Retained earnings	777	1,049
Total	1,530	1,802	Total	987	1,259
Total assets	$2,468	$2,813	Total liabilities and equity	$2,468	$2,813

VALIUM'S MEDICAL SUPPLY CORPORATION
Income Statement for Years Ending December 31, 2007 and 2008
(in thousands of dollars)

	2007	2008
Net sales	$1,357	$1,509
Less: Cost of goods sold	666	740
Gross profits	691	769
Less: Depreciation	59	64
Earnings before interest and taxes (EBIT)	632	705
Less: Interest	68	79
Earnings before taxes (EBT)	564	626
Less: Taxes	190	219
Net income	$ 374	$ 407
Less: Preferred stock dividends	$ 10	$ 10
Net income available to common stock holders	364	397
Less: Common stock dividends	125	125
Addition to retained earnings	$ 239	$ 272
Per (common) share data:		
Earnings per share (EPS)	$ 3.64	$ 3.97
Dividends per share (DPS)	$ 1.25	$ 1.25
Book value per share (BVPS)	$ 9.77	$ 12.49
Market value (price) per share (MVPS)	$ 10.60	$ 14.25

2-23 Statement of Cash Flows Lane's Outdoor Furniture, Inc. has net cash flows from operating activities for the last year of $340 million. The income statement shows that net income is $315 million and depreciation expense is $46 million. During the year, the change in inventory on the balance sheet was $38 million, change in accrued wages and taxes was $15 million, and change in accounts payable was $20 million. At the beginning of the year, the balance of accounts receivable was $50 million. Calculate the end-of-year balance for accounts receivable. (LG5)

2-24 **Statement of Cash Flows** Dogs 4 U Corporation has net cash flow from financing activities for the last year of $20 million. The company paid $105 million in dividends last year. During the year, the change in notes payable on the balance was $23 million and change in common and preferred stock was $0. The end of year balance for long-term debt was $185 million Calculate the beginning of year balance for long-term debt. (LG5)

2-25 **Free Cash Flow** The 2008 income statement for Duffy's Pest Control shows that depreciation expense is $197 million, EBIT is $418 million, EBT is $240 million, and the tax rate is 30 percent. At the beginning of the year, the balance of gross fixed assets was $1,562 million and net operating working capital was $417 million. At the end of the year, gross fixed assets was $1,803 million. Duffy's free cash flow for the year was $424 million. Calculate the end-of-year balance for net operating working capital. (LG5)

2-26 **Free Cash Flow** The 2008 income statement for Egyptian Noise Blasters shows that depreciation expense is $50 million, EBIT is $215 million, and taxes are $70 million. At the end of the year, the balance of gross fixed assets was $385 million. The change in net operating working capital during the year was $43 million. Egyptian's free cash flow for the year was $112 million. Calculate the beginning of year balance for gross fixed assets. (LG5)

2-27 **Statement of Retained Earnings** Thelma and Louie, Inc. started the year with a balance of retained earnings of $543 million and ended the year with retained earnings of $589 million. The company paid dividends of $35 million to the preferred stockholders and $88 million to common stockholders. Calculate Thelma and Louie's net income for the year. (LG1)

2-28 **Statement of Retained Earnings** Jamaica Tours, Inc. started the year with a balance of retained earnings of $1,047 million. The company reported net income for the year of $168 million and paid dividends of $10 million to the preferred stockholders and $35 million to common stockholders. Calculate Jamaica Tour's end of year balance in retained earnings. (LG1)

advanced problems

2-29 **Income Statement** Listed below is the 2008 income statement for Tom and Sue Travels, Inc.

TOM AND SUE TRAVELS, INC.
Income Statement for Year Ending December 31, 2008
(in millions of dollars)

	2008
Net sales	$16.500
Less: Cost of goods sold	10.300
Gross profits	6.200
Less: Depreciation	2.900
Earnings before interest and taxes (EBIT)	3.300
Less: Interest	0.950
Earnings before taxes (EBT)	2.350
Less: Taxes	0.705
Net income	$ 1.645

The CEO of Tom and Sue's wants the company to earn a net income of $2.250 million in 2009. Cost of goods sold is expected to be 60 percent of net sales, depreciation expense is not expected to change, interest expense is expected to increase to $1.050 million, and the firm's tax rate will be 30 percent. Calculate the net sales needed to produce net income of $2.250 million. *(LG1)*

2-30 **Income Statement** You have been given the following information for Kellygirl's Athletic Wear Corp. for the year 2008:

   a. Net sales = $22,500,000.

   b. Cost of goods sold = $16,100,000.

   c. Addition to retained earnings = $1,150,000.

   d. Dividends paid to preferred and common stockholders = $1,125,000.

   e. Interest expense = $1,050,000.

   f. The firm's tax rate is 30 percent.

   g. In 2009, net sales are expected to increase by $2.5 million.

   h. Cost of goods sold is expected to be 70 percent of net sales.

   i. Expensed depreciation is expected to be the same as in 2008.

   j. Interest expense is expected to be $1,200,000.

   k. The tax rate is expected to be 30 percent of EBT.

   l. Dividends paid to preferred and common stock holders will not change.

Calculate the addition to retained earnings expected in 2009. *(LG1)*

2-31 **Free Cash Flow** Michelle's Flowers 4U, Inc. had free cash flow during 2008 of $43 million, EBIT of $110 million, tax expense of $25 million, and depreciation of $14 million. Using this information, fill in the blanks on Michelle's balance sheet below. *(LG5)*

MICHELLE'S FLOWERS 4U, INC.
Balance Sheet as of December 31, 2007 and 2008
(in millions of dollars)

Assets	2007	2008	Liabilities and Equity	2007	2008
Current assets:			Current liabilities:		
Cash and marketable securities	$ 25	$ 28	Accrued wages and taxes	$ 15	$ 17
Accounts receivable	65	75	Accounts payable	50	☐
Inventory	100	118	Notes payable	45	45
Total	190	221	Total	110	118
Fixed assets:			Long-term debt:	190	195
Gross plant and equipment	300	333	Stockholders' equity:		
Less: Depreciation	40	54	Preferred stock (5 million shares)	5	5
Net plant and equipment	260	279	Common stock and paid-in surplus (20 million shares)	40	40
Other long-term assets	50	50	Retained earnings	155	192
Total	310	329	Total	200	237
Total assets	$500	$550	Total liabilities and equity	$500	$550

2-32 **Free Cash Flow** Wondy's Overhead Construction had free cash flow during 2008 of $12 million. The change in gross fixed assets on Wondy's balance sheet during 2008 was $10 million and the change in net operating working capital was $14 million. Using this information, fill in the blanks on Wondy's income statement below. *(LG5)*

WONDY'S OVERHEAD CONSTRUCTION, CORP.
Income Statement for Year Ending December 31, 2008
(in millions of dollars)

	2008
Net sales	$ ___
Less: Cost of goods sold	75.6
Gross profits	31.5
Less: Depreciation	6.0
Earnings before interest and taxes (EBIT)	___
Less: Interest	___
Earnings before taxes (EBT)	___
Less: Taxes (25%)	___
Net income	$ ___

research it: Reviewing Financial Statements

Go the Web site of Wal-Mart Stores, Inc. at **www.walmartstores.com** and get the latest financial statements from the annual report using the following steps.

Go to Wal-Mart Stores, Inc.'s Web site at **www.walmartstores.com.** Click on Investors, then select Financial Information; next choose Annual Reports; finally, click on the most recent date. This will bring the file onto your computer that contains the relevant data.

Locate the total assets, total equity, net sales, net income, dividends paid, cash flows from operating activities, and cash flows from investing activities for the last two years. How have these items changed over the last two years?

integrated minicase: Working with Financial Statements

Shown below are partial financial statements for Garners' Platoon Mental Health Care, Inc. Fill in the blanks on the four financial statements.

(continued)

GARNERS' PLATOON MENTAL HEALTH CARE, INC.
Balance Sheet as of December 31, 2007 and 2008
(in millions of dollars)

Assets	2007	2008	Liabilities and Equity	2007	2008
Current assets:			Current liabilities:		
Cash and marketable securities	$	$ 421	Accrued wages and taxes	$ 242	$ 316
Accounts receivable	1,020		Accounts payable	791	867
Inventory	1,581	1,760	Notes payable	714	
Total		3,290	Total	1,747	2,055
Fixed assets:			Long-term debt:		3,090
Gross plant and equipment	4,743		Stockholders' equity:		
Less: Depreciation	640	840	Preferred stock (25 million shares)	60	60
			Common stock and paid-in surplus (200 million shares)		637
Net plant and equipment		4,972			
Other long-term assets	790		Retained earnings	2,440	3,312
Total	4,893	5,864	Total	3,137	4,009
Total assets	$7,889	$	Total liabilities and equity	$7,889	$9,154

GARNERS' PLATOON MENTAL HEALTH CARE, INC.
Income Statement for Years Ending December 31, 2007 and 2008
(in millions of dollars)

	2007	2008
Net sales	$	$4,980
Less: Cost of goods sold	2,135	
Gross profits	2,213	2,609
Less: Depreciation	191	200
Earnings before interest and taxes (EBIT)		2,409
Less: Interest	285	
Earnings before taxes (EBT)	1,737	2,094
Less: Taxes		
Net income	$ 1,105	$ 1,327
Less: Preferred stock dividends	$	$ 60
Net income available to common stock holders	1,045	1,267
Less: Common stock dividends	395	395
Addition to retained earnings	$	$ 872
Per (common) share data:		
Earnings per share (EPS)	$	$
Dividends per share (DPS)	$	$
Book value per share (BVPS)	$	$
Market value (price) per share (MVPS)	$22.500	$26.850

(continued)

GARNERS' PLATOON MENTAL HEALTH CARE, INC.
Statement of Cash Flows for Year Ending December 31, 2008
(in millions of dollars)

	2008
A. Cash flows from operating activities	
Net income	$☐
Additions (sources of cash):	
Depreciation	☐
Increase accrued wages and taxes	☐
Increase in accounts payable	☐
Subtractions (uses of cash):	
Increase in accounts receivable	☐
Increase in inventory	☐
Net cash flow from operating activities	$☐
B. Cash flows from investing activities	
Subtractions:	
Increase fixed assets	☐
Increase in other long-term assets	☐
Net cash flow from investing activities	$☐
C. Cash flows from financing activities	
Additions:	
Increase in notes payable	$☐
Increase in long-term debt	☐
Increase in common and preferred stock	☐
Subtractions:	
Pay dividends	☐
Net cash flow from financing activities	$☐
D. Net change in cash and marketable securities	−$26

GARNERS' PLATOON MENTAL HEALTH CARE, INC.
Statement of Retained Earnings as of December 31, 2008
(in millions of dollars)

		2008
Balance of retained earnings, December 31, 2007		$2,440
Plus: Net income for 2008		☐
Less: Cash dividends paid		
Preferred stock	$☐	
Common stock	☐	
Total cash dividents paid		☐
Balance of retained earnings, December 31, 2008		$☐

ANSWERS TO TIME OUT

2-1 The most liquid assets—called current assets—appear first on the asset side of the balance sheet.

2-2 The balance sheet reports a firm's assets, liabilities, and equity at a particular point in time. A firm's assets must equal (balance) the liabilities and equity used to purchase the assets (hence the term *balance sheet*).

2-3 Income statements show the total revenues that a firm earns and the total expenses the firm incurs to generate those revenues over a specific period of time—generally one year. Remember that while the balance sheet reports a firm's position at a point in time, the income statement reports performance over a period of time, for example, over the last year.

2-4 When one corporation owns stock in another corporation, 70 percent of any dividends received from other corporations is tax exempt. Only the remaining 30 percent is taxed at the receiving corporation's tax rate.

2-5 The statement of cash flows is a financial statement that shows the firm's cash flows over a given period of time. This statement reports the amounts of cash that the firm generated and distributed during a particular time period. The bottom line on the statement of cash flows—the difference between cash sources and uses—equals the change in cash on the firm's balance sheet from the previous year's cash account balance. That is, the statement of cash flows reconciles income statement items and noncash balance sheet items to show changes in the cash and marketable securities account on the balance sheet over the particular analysis period.

2-6 The statement of cash flows separates these cash flows into three categories or sections: cash flows from operating activities; cash flows from investing activities; and cash flows from financing activities.

2-7 The statement of retained earnings provides additional details about changes in retained earnings during a reporting period. This financial statement reconciles net income earned during a given period and any cash dividends paid within that period on one side with the change in retained earnings between the beginning and ending of the period on the other.

2-8 If a firm pays out more in dividends than it has net income, retained earnings will decrease.

2-9 Managers have significant discretion over their reported earnings. Managers and financial analysts have recognized for years that firms use considerable latitude in using accounting rules to manage their reported earnings in a wide variety of contexts. Indeed, within the GAAP framework, firms can "smooth" earnings. That is, firms often take steps to over or understate earnings at various times. Managers may choose to smooth earnings to show investors that firm assets are growing steadily. Similarly, one firm may be using straight line depreciation for its fixed assets, while another is using a modified accelerated cost recovery method (MACRS), which causes depreciation to accrue quickly. If the firm uses MACRS accounting methods, it writes fixed asset values down quickly; assets will thus have lower book value than if the firm used straight line depreciation methods. This process of controlling a firm's earnings is called *earnings management*.

www.mhhe.com/can1e

chapter 3:

ANALYZING FINANCIAL STATEMENTS

 Learning Goals

LG1   Calculate and interpret major liquidity ratios.

LG2   Calculate and interpret major asset management ratios.

LG3   Calculate and interpret major debt ratios.

LG4   Calculate and interpret major profitability ratios.

LG5   Calculate and interpret major market value ratios.

LG6   Appreciate how various ratios relate to one another.

LG7   Discuss the differences between time series and cross-sectional ratio analysis and decide which is most appropriate given an analytical situation.

LG8   Explain cautions that should be taken when examining financial ratios and financial information in general.

We reviewed the major financial statements in Chapter 2. These financial statements provide information on a firm's financial position at a point in time or its operations over some past period of time. But these financial statements' real value lies in the fact that managers, investors, and analysts can use the information the statements contain to analyze the current financial performance or condition of the firm. More importantly, managers can use this information to plan changes that will improve the firm's future performance and, ultimately, its market value. Most commonly, managers, investors, and analysts use ratios to evaluate financial statements. **Ratio analysis** involves calculating and analyzing financial ratios to assess a firm's performance and to identify actions that could improve firm performance. The most commonly used ratios fall into five groups: (1) liquidity ratios, (2) asset management ratios, (3) debt management ratios, (4) profitability ratios, and (5) market value ratios.

viewpoints

Business Application

The managers of DPH Tree Farm, Inc. have released public statements that the firm's performance surpasses that of other firms in the industry. They cite the firm's liquidity and asset management positions as particularly strong. DPH's superior performance in these areas has resulted in superior overall returns for their stockholders. What are the key financial ratios that DPH Tree Farm, Inc. needs to calculate and evaluate in order to justify these statements? **(See solution on p. 91)**

Personal Application

Chris Ryan is looking to invest in DPH Tree Farm, Inc. Chris has the most recent set of financial statements from DPH Tree Farm's annual report but is not sure how to evaluate them or measure the firm's performance relative to other firms in the industry. What are the financial ratios with which Chris should measure the performance of DPH Tree Farm, Inc.? How can Chris use these ratios to evaluate the firm's performance? **(See solution on p. 91)**

In this chapter, we review these ratios, describe what each ratio means, and identify the general trend (higher or lower) that managers and investment analysts look for in each ratio. Note as we review the ratios that the number calculated for a ratio is not always good or bad and that extreme values (either high or low) can be a bad sign for a firm. We will discuss how a ratio that seems too good can actually be bad for a company. We will also see how ratios interrelate—how a change in one ratio may affect the value of several ratios. It is often hard to make sense of a set of performance ratios. Thus, when managers or investors review a firm's financial position through ratio analysis, they often start by evaluating trends in the firm's financial ratios over time and by comparing their firm's ratios with that of other firms in the same industry. Finally, we discuss cautions that you should take when using ratio analysis to evaluate firm performance. As we go through the chapter, we show sample ratio analysis using the financial statements for DPH Tree Farm, Inc. listed in Tables 2.1 and 2.2.

 ## 3.1 Liquidity Ratios

As we stated in Chapter 2, firms need cash and other liquid assets (or current assets) to pay their bills (or current liabilities) as they come due. **Liquidity ratios** measure the relationship between a firm's liquid (or current) assets and its current liabilities. The three most commonly used liquidity ratios are the current ratio, the quick (or acid-test) ratio, and the cash ratio.

$$\text{Current ratio} = \frac{\text{Current assets}}{\text{Current liabilities}} \tag{3-1}$$

$$\text{Quick ratio (acid-test ratio)} = \frac{\text{Current assets} - \text{Inventory}}{\text{Current liabilities}} \tag{3-2}$$

$$\text{Cash ratio} = \frac{\text{Cash and marketable securities}}{\text{Current liabilities}} \tag{3-3}$$

The broadest liquidity measure, the current ratio, measures the dollars of current assets available to pay each dollar of current liabilities. Inventories are generally the least liquid of a firm's current assets. Further, inventory is the current asset for which book values are the least reliable measures of market value. In practical terms, what this means is that if the firm must sell inventory to pay upcoming bills, the firm is most likely to have to discount inventory items in order to liquidate them, and therefore, they are the current assets on which losses are most likely to occur. Therefore, the quick (or acid-test) ratio measures a firm's ability to pay off short-term obligations without relying on inventory sales. The quick ratio measures the dollars of more liquid assets (cash and marketable securities and accounts receivable) available to pay each dollar of current liabilities.

Likewise, if the firm sells accounts receivable to pay upcoming bills, the firm must often discount the AR items to sell them—the assets once again bring less than their book value. Therefore, the cash ratio measures a firm's ability to pay short-term obligations with its available cash and marketable securities. The cash ratio measures the dollars of cash and marketable securities available to pay each dollar of current liabilities.

CALCULATING LIQUIDITY RATIOS

Use the balance sheet (Table 2.1) and income statement (Table 2.2) for DPH Tree Farm, Inc. to calculate the firm's 2008 values for the liquidity ratios.

SOLUTION:

The liquidity ratios for DPH Tree Farm, Inc. are calculated as follows.

$$\text{Current ratio} = \frac{\$205m.}{\$120m.} = 1.71 \text{ times}$$

Industry average = 1.50 times

$$\text{Quick ratio (acid-test ratio)} = \frac{\$205m. - \$111m.}{\$120m.} = 0.78 \text{ times}$$

Industry average = 0.50 times

$$\text{Cash ratio} = \frac{\$24m.}{\$120m.} = 0.20 \text{ times}$$

Industry average = 0.15 times

All three liquidity ratios show that DPH Tree Farm, Inc. has more liquidity on its balance sheet than the industry average (we discuss the process used to develop an industry average below). Thus, DPH Tree Farm has more cash and other liquid assets (or current assets) available to pay its bills (or current liabilities) as they come due, than does the average firm in the tree farm industry.

Of course, liquidity on the balance sheet is important. The more liquid assets a firm holds, the less likely it is that the firm will experience financial distress. Thus, the higher the liquidity ratios, the less liquidity risk a firm has. But as with everything else in business, high liquidity represents a painful trade-off for the firm. Liquid assets do not generate any profits for the firm. In contrast, fixed assets are illiquid, but generate revenue for the firm. Thus, extremely high levels of liquidity guard against liquidity crises but at the cost of lower returns on assets. High liquidity levels may actually show bad or indecisive firm management. Thus, in deciding the appropriate level of current assets to hold on the balance sheet, managers must consider the trade-off between the advantages of being liquid versus the disadvantages of reduced profits. Note that a company with very predictable cash flows can maintain low levels of liquidity without incurring much liquidity risk.

TIME OUT

3-1 What are the three major liquidity ratios used in evaluating financial statements?

3-2 How do the three major liquidity ratios used in evaluating financial situations differ?

3-3 Does a firm generally want to have high or low liquidity ratios? Why?

3.2 Asset Management Ratios

Asset management ratios measure how efficiently a firm uses its assets (inventory, accounts receivable, and fixed assets), as well as how efficiently the firm manages its accounts payable. The specific ratios allow managers and investors to evaluate whether a firm is holding a reasonable amount of each type of asset and whether management uses each type of asset to effectively generate sales. The most commonly used asset management ratios are listed below, grouped by type of asset.

Inventory Management

The inventory turnover ratio measures the number of dollars of sales produced per dollar of inventory. Cost of goods sold is used in the numerator when managers want to emphasize that inventory is listed on the balance sheet at cost, that is, the cost of production per dollar of inventory purchased (equation 3-4). The days' sales in inventory ratio measures the number of days that inventory is held before the final product is sold (equation 3-5).

$$\text{Inventory turnover ratio} = \frac{\text{Sales or Cost of goods sold}}{\text{Inventory}} \quad \text{(3-4)}$$

$$\text{Days' sales in inventory} = \frac{\text{Inventory} \times 365 \text{ days}}{\text{Sales or Cost of goods sold}} \quad \text{(3-5)}$$

In general, a firm wants to produce a high level of sales per dollar of inventory, that is, it wants to turn inventory over (from raw materials to finished goods to sold goods) as quickly as possible. A high level of sales per dollar of inventory implies reduced warehousing, monitoring, insurance, and any other costs of servicing the inventory. So, a high inventory turnover ratio or a low days' sales in inventory is generally a sign of good management.

However, if the inventory turnover ratio is extremely high and the days' sales in inventory is extremely low, the firm may not be holding sufficient inventory to prevent running out (or stocking out) of the raw materials needed to keep the production process going. Thus, production and sales stop, which wastes the firm's fixed resources. So, extremely high levels for the inventory turnover ratio and low levels for the days' sales in inventory ratio may actually be a sign of bad firm or production management.

As they decide the optimal inventory level to hold on the balance sheet, managers must consider the trade-off between the advantages of holding sufficient levels of inventory to keep the production process going versus the costs of holding large amounts of inventory. Note that companies with very good supply chain relations can maintain lower levels of inventory without incurring as much risk of stockouts.

Accounts Receivable Management

The average collection period (ACP) measures the number of days accounts receivable are held before the firm collects cash from the sale (equation 3-6). The accounts receivable turnover ratio measures the number of dollars of sales produced per dollar of accounts receivable (equation 3-7).

$$\text{Average collection period (ACP)} = \frac{\text{Accounts receivable} \times 365 \text{ days}}{\text{Credit sales}} \quad \text{(3-6)}$$

$$\text{Accounts receivable turnover} = \frac{\text{Credit sales}}{\text{Accounts receivable}} \tag{3-7}$$

In general, a firm wants to produce a high level of sales per dollar of accounts receivable, that is, it wants to collect its accounts receivable as quickly as possible to reduce any cost of financing accounts receivable. These costs include interest expense on liabilities used to finance accounts receivable, and defaults associated with accounts receivable. In general, a high accounts receivable turnover ratio or a low ACP is a sign of good management, which is well aware of financing costs and customer remittance habits.

However, if the accounts receivable turnover ratio is extremely high and the ACP is extremely low, the firm's accounts receivable policy may be so strict that customers prefer to do business with competing firms. Firms offer accounts receivable terms as an incentive to get customers to buy products from their firm rather than a competing firm. By offering customers the accounts receivable privilege, management allows them to buy (more) now and pay later. Without this incentive, customers may choose to buy the goods from the firm's competitors who offer better credit terms. So extremely high accounts receivable turnover ratio levels and low ACP levels may be a sign of bad firm management. As they decide what level of accounts receivable to hold on the firm's balance sheet, managers must consider the trade-off between the advantages of increased sales by offering customers better terms versus the disadvantages of financing large amounts of accounts receivable.

Accounts Payable Management

The average payment period (APP) measures the number of days that the firm holds accounts payable before it has to extend cash to buy raw materials (equation 3-8). The accounts payable turnover ratio measures the dollar cost of goods sold per dollar of accounts payable (equation 3-9).

$$\text{Average payment period (APP)} = \frac{\text{Accounts payable} \times 365 \text{ days}}{\text{Cost of goods sold}} \tag{3-8}$$

$$\text{Accounts payable turnover} = \frac{\text{Cost of goods sold}}{\text{Accounts payable}} \tag{3-9}$$

In general, a firm wants to pay for its purchases as slowly as possible. The slower the firm pays for its supply purchases, the longer it can avoid obtaining other costly sources of financing such as notes payable or long-term debt. Thus, a high APP or a low accounts payable turnover ratio is generally a sign of good management.

However, if the APP is extremely high and the accounts payable turnover ratio is extremely low, the firm may be abusing the credit terms that its raw materials suppliers offer. At some point, the firm's suppliers may revoke its ability to buy raw materials on account and the firm will lose this source of free financing. If this situation is developing, extremely high levels for the APP and low levels for the accounts receivable turnover ratio may point to bad firm management.

As they decide the accounts payable level to hold on the balance sheet, managers must consider the trade-off between maximizing the use of free financing that raw material suppliers offer versus the risk of losing the opportunity to buy on account.

Fixed Asset and Working Capital Management

The fixed asset turnover ratio measures the number of dollars of sales produced per dollar of fixed assets (equation 3-10). Similarly, the sales to working capital ratio measures the number of dollars of sales produced per dollar of net working capital (current assets minus current liabilities) (equation 3-11).

$$\text{Fixed asset turnover ratio} = \frac{\text{Sales}}{\text{Fixed assets}} \qquad (3\text{-}10)$$

$$\text{Sales to working capital} = \frac{\text{Sales}}{\text{Working capital}} \qquad (3\text{-}11)$$

In general, the higher the level of sales per dollar of fixed assets and working capital, the more efficiently the firm is being run. Thus, high fixed asset turnover and sales to working capital ratios are generally signs of good management. However, if either the fixed asset turnover or sales to working capital ratio is extremely high, the firm may be close to its maximum production capacity. If capacity is hit, the firm cannot increase production or sales. Accordingly, extremely high fixed asset turnover and sales to working capital ratio levels may actually indicate bad firm management if managers have allowed the company to approach maximum capacity without making any accommodations for growth.

Note a word of caution here. The age of a firm's fixed assets will affect the fixed asset turnover ratio level. A firm with older fixed assets, listed on its balance sheet at historical cost, will tend to have a higher fixed asset turnover ratio than will a firm that has just replaced its fixed assets and lists them on its balance sheet at a (most likely) higher value. Accordingly, the firm with newer fixed assets would have a lower fixed asset turnover ratio. But this is because it has updated its fixed assets, while the other firm has not. It is *not* correct to conclude that the firm with new assets is underperforming relative to the firm with older fixed assets listed on its balance sheet.

Total Asset Management

The final two asset management ratios put it all together. The total asset turnover ratio measures the number of dollars of sales produced per dollar of total assets (equation 3-12). Similarly, the capital intensity ratio measures the dollars of total assets needed to produce a dollar of sales (equation 3-13).

$$\text{Total assets turnover ratio} = \frac{\text{Sales}}{\text{Total assets}} \qquad (3\text{-}12)$$

$$\text{Capital intensity ratio} = \frac{\text{Total assets}}{\text{Sales}} \qquad (3\text{-}13)$$

In general, a well-managed firm produces many dollars of sales per dollar of total assets, or uses few dollars of assets per dollar of sales. Thus, in general, the higher the total asset turnover and lower the capital intensity ratio, the more efficient the overall asset management of the firm will be. However, if the total asset turnover is extremely high and capital intensity ratio is extremely low, the firm may actually have an asset management problem. As described above, inventory stockouts, capacity problems, or tight account receivables policies can all lead to a high total asset turnover and may actually be signs of poor firm management.

CALCULATING ASSET MANAGEMENT RATIOS

Use the balance sheet (Table 2.1) and income statement (Table 2.2) for DPH Tree Farm, Inc. to calculate the firm's 2008 values for the asset management ratios.

SOLUTION:

We calculate the asset management ratios for DPH Tree Farm, Inc. as follows:

$$\text{Inventory turnover ratio} = \frac{\$315m.}{\$111m.} = 2.84 \text{ times}$$

Industry average = 2.15 times

$$\text{Days' sales in inventory} = \frac{\$111m. \times 365 \text{ days}}{\$315m.} = 129 \text{ days}$$

Industry average = 170 days

$$\text{Average collection period (ACP)} = \frac{\$70m. \times 365 \text{ days}}{\$315m.} = 81 \text{ days}$$

Industry average = 95 days

$$\text{Accounts receivable turnover} = \frac{\$315m.}{\$70m.} = 4.50 \text{ times}$$

Industry average = 3.84 times

$$\text{Average payment period (APP)} = \frac{\$55m. \times 365 \text{ days}}{\$150m.} = 134 \text{ days}$$

Industry average = 102 days

$$\text{Accounts payable turnover} = \frac{\$150m.}{\$55m.} = 2.73 \text{ times}$$

Industry average = 3.55 times

$$\text{Fixed asset turnover ratio} = \frac{\$315m.}{\$315m.} = 1.00 \text{ times}$$

Industry average = 0.85 times

$$\text{Sales to working capital} = \frac{\$315m.}{\$205m. - \$120m.} = 3.71 \text{ times}$$

Industry average = 3.20 times

$$\text{Total assets turnover ratio} = \frac{\$315m.}{\$570m.} = 0.55 \text{ times}$$

Industry average = 0.40 times

$$\text{Capital intensity ratio} = \frac{\$570m.}{\$315m.} = 1.81 \text{ times}$$

Industry average = 2.50 times

In all cases, asset management ratios show that DPH Tree Farm, Inc. is outperforming the industry average. The firm is turning over its inventory faster than the average firm in the tree farm industry, thus producing more dollars of sales per dollar of inventory. It is also collecting its accounts receivable faster and paying its accounts payable slower than the average firm. Further, DPH Tree Farm is producing more sales per dollar of fixed assets, working capital, and total assets than the average firm in the industry.

TIME OUT

3-4 What are the major asset management ratios?

3-5 Does a firm generally want to have high or low values for each of these ratios?

3-6 Explain why many of these ratios are mirror images of one another.

3.3 Debt Management Ratios

As we discussed in Chapter 2, financial leverage refers to the extent to which the firm uses debt securities in its capital structure. The more debt a firm uses as a percentage of its total assets, the greater is its financial leverage. **Debt management ratios** measure the extent to which the firm uses debt (or financial leverage) versus equity to finance its assets. The specific ratios allow managers and investors to evaluate whether a firm is financing its assets with a reasonable amount of debt versus equity financing, as well as whether the firm is generating sufficient earnings or cash to make the promised payments on its debt. The most commonly used debt management ratios are listed below.

Debt versus Equity Financing

The debt ratio measures the percentage of total assets financed with debt (equation 3-14). The debt-to-equity ratio measures the dollars of debt financing used for every dollar of equity financing (equation 3-15). The equity multiplier ratio measures the dollars of assets on the balance sheet for every dollar of equity (or just common stockholders' equity) financing (equation 3-16).

$$\text{Debt ratio} = \frac{\text{Total debt}}{\text{Total assets}} \tag{3-14}$$

$$\text{Debt-to-equity ratio} = \frac{\text{Total debt}}{\text{Total equity}} \tag{3-15}$$

$$\text{Equity multiplier ratio} = \frac{\text{Total assets}}{\text{Total equity}} \text{ or } \frac{\text{Total assets}}{\text{Common stockholders' equity}} \tag{3-16}$$

As you might suspect, all three measures are related.[1] Specifically

$$\text{Debt-to-equity ratio} = \frac{1}{(1/\text{Debt ratio}) - 1} = \text{Equity multiplier ratio} - 1$$

$$\text{Equity multiplier ratio} = \frac{1}{1 - \text{Debt ratio}} = \text{Debt-to-equity ratio} + 1$$

So, the lower the debt, debt-to-equity, or equity multiplier ratios, the less debt and more equity the firm uses to finance its assets (i.e., the bigger the firm's equity cushion).

---

[1]To see this remember the balance sheet identity is Assets (A) = Debt (D) + Equity (E). Dividing each side of this equation by equity, we get A/E = D/E + E/E, or A/E = D/E + 1. Also, rearranging this equation, D/E = A/E − 1.

When a firm issues debt to finance its assets, it gives the debt holders first claim to a fixed amount of its cash flows. Stockholders are entitled to any residual cash flows—those left after debt holders are paid. When a firm does well, financial leverage increases the reward to shareholders since the amount of cash flows promised to debt holders is constant and capped. So when firms do well, financial leverage creates more cash flows to share with stockholders—it magnifies the return to the stockholders of the firm. This magnification is one reason that stockholders encourage the use of debt financing.

However, financial leverage also increases the firm's potential for financial distress and even failure. If the firm has a bad year and cannot make promised debt payments, debt holders can force the firm into bankruptcy. Thus, a firm's current and potential debt holders (and even stockholders) look at equity financing as a safety cushion that can absorb fluctuations in the firm's earnings and asset values and guarantee debt service payments. Clearly, the larger the fluctuations or variability of a firm's cash flows, the greater the need for an equity cushion. Managers' choice of **capital structure**—the amount of debt versus equity to issue—affects the firm's viability as a long-term entity. In deciding the level of debt versus equity financing to hold on the balance sheet, managers must consider the trade-off between maximizing cash flows to the firm's stockholders versus the risk of being unable to make promised debt payments.

Coverage Ratios

The times interest earned ratio measures the number of dollars of operating earnings available to meet each dollar of interest obligations on the firm's debt (equation 3-17). The fixed-charge coverage ratio measures the number of dollars of operating *earnings* available to meet the firm's interest dollars and other fixed charges (equation 3-18). The cash coverage ratio measures the number of dollars of operating *cash* available to meet each dollar of interest and other fixed charges that the firm owes (equation 3-19).

$$\text{Times interest earned} = \frac{\text{EBIT}}{\text{Interest}} \qquad \textbf{(3-17)}$$

$$\text{Fixed-charge coverage ratio} = \frac{\text{Earnings available to meet fixed charges}}{\text{Fixed charges}}$$
$$\textbf{(3-18)}$$

$$\text{Cash coverage ratio} = \frac{\text{EBIT} + \text{Depreciation}}{\text{Fixed charges}} \qquad \textbf{(3-19)}$$

With the help of the times interest earned, fixed-charge coverage, and cash coverage ratios, managers, investors, and analysts can determine whether a firm has taken on a debt burden that is too large. These ratios measure the dollars available to meet debt and other fixed-charge obligations. A value of 1 for these ratios means that $1 of earnings or cash is available to meet each dollar of interest or fixed-charge obligations. A value of less (greater) than 1 means that the firm has less (more) than $1 of earnings or cash available to pay each dollar of interest or fixed-charge obligations.[2] Further, the higher the times interest

---

[2]The fixed-charge and cash coverage ratios can be tailored to a particular firm's situation, depending on what really constitutes fixed charges that must be paid. One version of it follows: (EBIT + Lease payments)/[Interest + Lease payments + Sinking fund/$(1 - t)$], where t is the firm's marginal tax rate. Here, it is assumed that sinking fund payments must be made. They are adjusted by the division of $(1 - t)$ into a before-tax cash outflow so they can be added to other before-tax cash outflows.

earned, fixed-charge coverage, and cash coverage ratios, the more equity and less debt the applicant uses to finance its assets. Thus, low levels of debt will lead to a dilution of the return to stockholders due to a greater increased usage of equity as well as to not taking advantage of the tax deductibility of interest expense.

EXAMPLE 3-3

 For interactive versions of this example visit www.mhhe.com/can1e

CALCULATING DEBT MANAGEMENT RATIOS

Use the balance sheet (Table 2.1) and income statement (Table 2.2) for DPH Tree Farm, Inc. to calculate the firm's 2008 values for the debt management ratios.

SOLUTION:

The debt management ratios for DPH Tree Farm, Inc. are calculated as follows:

$$\text{Debt ratio} = \frac{\$120m. + \$195m.}{\$570m.} = 55.26\%$$

Industry average = 68.50%

$$\text{Debt-to-equity ratio} = \frac{\$120m. + \$195m.}{\$255m.} = 1.24 \text{ times}$$

Industry average = 2.17 times

$$\text{Equity multiplier ratio} = \frac{\$570m.}{\$255m.} = 2.24 \text{ times or } \frac{\$570m.}{\$250m.} = 2.28 \text{ times}$$

Industry average   = 4.10 times   or   4.14 times

$$\text{Times interest earned} = \frac{\$152m.}{\$16m.} = 9.50 \text{ times}$$

Industry average = 5.15 times

$$\text{Fixed-charge coverage ratio} = \frac{\$152m.}{\$16m.} = 9.50 \text{ times}$$

Industry average = 5.70 times

$$\text{Cash coverage ratio} = \frac{\$152m. + 13m.}{\$16m.} = 10.31 \text{ times}$$

Industry average = 7.78 times

In all cases, debt management ratios show that DPH Tree Farm, Inc. holds less debt on its balance sheet than the average firm in the tree farm industry. Further, the firm has more dollars of operating earnings and cash available to meet each dollar of interest obligations (there are no other fixed charges listed on DPH Tree Farm's income statement) on the firm's debt. This lack of financial leverage decreases the firm's potential for financial distress and even failure, but may also decrease equity shareholders' chance for magnified earnings. If the firm has a bad year, it has promised relatively few payments to debt holders. Thus, the risk of bankruptcy is small. However, when DPH Tree Farm, Inc. does well, the low level of financial leverage dilutes the return to the stockholders of the firm. This dilution of profit is likely to upset common stockholders of the firm.

TIME OUT

3-7   What are the major debt management ratios?

3-8   Does a firm generally want to have high or low values for each of these ratios?

3-9   What is the trade-off between using too much financial leverage and not using enough leverage? Who is likely to complain the most in each case?

3.4 Profitability Ratios

The liquidity, asset management, and debt management ratios examined so far allow for an isolated or narrow look at a firm's performance. **Profitability ratios** show the combined effects of liquidity, asset management, and debt management on the overall operating results of the firm. Profitability ratios are among the most watched and best known of the financial ratios. Indeed, firm values (or stock prices) react quickly to unexpected changes in these ratios. The most commonly used profitability ratios are listed below.

The profit margin is the percentage of sales left after all firm expenses are paid (equation 3-20). The basic earnings power ratio measures the operating return on the firm's assets, irrespective of financial leverage and taxes (equation 3-21). This ratio measures the operating profit (EBIT) earned per dollar of assets on the firm's balance sheet. Return on assets (ROA) measures the overall return on the firm's assets, inclusive of financial leverage and taxes (equation 3-22). This ratio is the net income earned per dollar of assets on the firm's balance sheet. Return on equity (ROE) measures the return on the common stockholders' investment in the assets of the firm (equation 3-23). ROE is the net income earned per dollar of common stockholders' equity. The value of a firm's ROE is affected not only by net income, but also by the amount of financial leverage or debt that firm uses. As stated above, financial leverage magnifies the return to the stockholders of the firm. However, financial leverage also increases the firm's potential for financial distress and even failure. Generally, a high ROE is considered to be a positive sign of firm performance. However, if performance comes from a high degree of financial leverage, a high ROE can indicate a firm with an unacceptably high level of bankruptcy risk as well. Finally, the dividend payout ratio is the percentage of net income available to common stockholders that the firm actually pays as cash to these investors (equation 3-24).

$$\text{Profit margin} = \frac{\text{Net income available to common stockholders}}{\text{Sales}} \qquad (3\text{-}20)$$

$$\text{Basic earnings power ratio (BEP)} = \frac{\text{EBIT}}{\text{Total assets}} \qquad (3\text{-}21)$$

$$\text{Return on assets (ROA)} = \frac{\text{Net income available to common stockholders}}{\text{Total assets}} \qquad (3\text{-}22)$$

$$\text{Return on equity (ROE)} = \frac{\text{Net income available to common stockholders}}{\text{Common stockholders' equity}} \qquad (3\text{-}23)$$

$$\text{Dividend payout ratio} = \frac{\text{Common stock dividends}}{\text{Net income available to common stockholders}} \qquad (3\text{-}24)$$

For all but the dividend payout ratio, the higher the value of the ratio, the higher the profitability of the firm. But just as has been the case previously in this chapter, high profitability ratio levels may result from poor management in other areas of the firm as much as superior financial management. A high profit margin means that the firm has low expenses relative to sales. The BEP reflects how much the firm's assets earn from operations, irrespective of financial leverage and taxes. It follows logically that managers, investors, and analysts find BEP a useful ratio when they compare firms that differ in financial leverage and taxes. In contrast, ROA measures the firm's overall performance. It shows how the firm's assets generate a return inclusive of financial leverage and tax decisions made by management.

ROE measures the return on common stockholders' investment. Since managers seek to maximize common stock price, managers, investors, and analysts monitor ROE above all other ratios. The dividend payout ratio measures how much of the profit the firm retains versus how much it pays out to common stockholders as dividends. The lower the dividend payout ratio, the more profits the firm retains for future growth or other projects. A profitable firm that retains its earnings increases its level of equity capital as well as its own value.

EXAMPLE 3-4

For interactive versions of this example visit www.mhhe.com/can1e

CALCULATING PROFITABILITY RATIOS

Use the balance sheet (Table 2.1) and income statement (Table 2.2) for DPH Tree Farm, Inc. to calculate the firm's 2008 values for the profitability ratios.

SOLUTION:

The profitability ratios for DPH Tree Farm, Inc. are calculated as follows:

$$\text{Profit margin} = \frac{\$80\text{m.}}{\$315\text{m.}} = 25.40\%$$

Industry average $= 23.25\%$

$$\text{Basic earnings power ratio (BEP)} = \frac{\$152\text{m.}}{\$570\text{m.}} = 26.67\%$$

Industry average $= 22.85\%$

$$\text{Return on assets (ROA)} = \frac{\$80\text{m.}}{\$570\text{m.}} = 14.04\%$$

Industry average $= 9.30\%$

$$\text{Return on equity (ROE)} = \frac{\$80\text{m.}}{\$40\text{m.} + \$210\text{m.}} = 32.00\%$$

Industry average $= 38.50\%$

$$\text{Dividend payout ratio} = \frac{\$25\text{m.}}{\$80\text{m.}} = 31.25\%$$

Industry average $= 30.90\%$

(continued)

These ratios show that DPH Tree Farm, Inc. is more profitable than the average firm in the tree farm industry. The profit margin, BEP, and ROA are all higher than industry figures. Despite this, the ROE for DPH Tree Farm is much lower than the industry average. DPH's low debt level and high equity level relative to the industry is the main reason for DPH's strong figures relative to the industry. As we mentioned above, DPH's managerial decisions about capital structure dilute its returns, which will likely upset its common stockholders. To counteract common stockholders' discontent, DPH Tree Farm pays out a slightly larger percentage of its income to its common stockholders as cash dividends. Of course, this slightly high dividend payout ratio means that DPH Tree Farm retains less of its profits to reinvest into the business. A profitable firm that retains its earnings increases its equity capital level as well as its own value.

TIME OUT

3-10 What are the major profitability ratios?

3-11 Does a firm generally want to have high or low values for each of these ratios?

3-12 What are the trade-offs to having especially high or low values for these ratios?

3.5 Market Value Ratios

As we note above, ROE is a most important financial statement ratio for managers and investors to monitor. Generally, a high ROE is considered to be a positive sign of firm performance. However, if a high ROE results from a highly leveraged position, it can signal a firm with a high level of bankruptcy risk. While ROE does not directly incorporate this risk, for publicly traded firms, market prices of the firm's stock do. (We look at stock valuation in Chapter 7.) Since the firm's stockholders earn their returns primarily from the firm's stock market value, ratios that incorporate stock market values are equally, and arguably more, important than other financial statement ratios.

The final group of ratios is market value ratios. **Market value ratios** relate a firm's stock price to its earnings and its book value. For publicly traded firms, market value ratios measure what investors think of the company's future performance and risk. The most commonly used market value ratios are

$$\text{Market-to-book ratio} = \frac{\text{Market price per share}}{\text{Book value per share}} \qquad \text{(3-25)}$$

$$\text{Price-earnings (PE) ratio} = \frac{\text{Market price per share}}{\text{Earnings per share}} \qquad \text{(3-26)}$$

The market-to-book ratio measures the amount that investors will pay for the firm's stock per dollar of equity used to finance the firm's assets (equation 3-25). Book value per share is an accounting-based number reflecting the firm's assets' historical costs, and hence historical value (equation 3-26). The market-to-book ratio compares the market (current) value of the firm's equity to its historical cost. In general, the higher the market-to-book ratio, the better the firm. If liquidity, asset management, debt management, and accounting profitability are good for a firm, then the market-to-book ratio will be high. A market-to-book ratio greater than 1 (or 100 percent) means that stockholders will pay a premium over book value for their equity investment in the firm.

Probably the best known and most often quoted figure, the price-earnings (or PE) ratio measures how much investors are willing to pay for each dollar the firm earns per share of its stock. PE ratios are often quoted in multiples—the number of dollars per share—that fund managers, investors, and analysts compare within industry classes. Managers and investors often use PE ratios to evaluate the relative financial performance of the firm's stock. Generally, the higher the PE ratio, the better the firm's performance. Analysts and investors, as well as managers, expect companies with high PE ratios to experience future growth, to have rapid future dividend increases, or both, because retained earnings will support the company's goals. However, for value-seeking investors, high PE firms indicate expensive companies. Further, higher PE ratios carry greater risk because investors are willing to pay higher prices today for a stock in anticipation of higher earnings in the future. These earnings may or may not materialize. Low PE firms are generally companies with little expected growth or low earnings. However, note that earnings depend on many factors (such as financial leverage or taxes) that have nothing to do directly with firm operations.

EXAMPLE 3-5

 For interactive versions of this example visit www.mhhe.com/can1e

CALCULATING MARKET VALUE RATIOS

Use the balance sheet (Table 2.1) and income statement (Table 2.2) for DPH Tree Farm, Inc. to calculate the firm's 2008 values for the market value ratios.

SOLUTION:

The market value ratios for DPH Tree Farm, Inc. are calculated as follows:

$$\text{Market-to-book ratio} = \frac{\$17.25}{\$12.50} = 1.38 \text{ times}$$

Industry average $= 2.15$ times

$$\text{Price-earnings (PE) ratio} = \frac{\$17.25}{\$4.00} = 4.31 \text{ times}$$

Industry average $= 6.25$ times

These ratios show that DPH Tree Farm's investors will not pay as much for a share of DPH's stock per dollar of book value and earnings the average for the industry. DPH's low leverage level and high reliance on equity relative to the industry as likely are main reason for investors' disinterest. As mentioned above, DPH's seemingly intentional return dilution will likely upset the firm's common stockholders. Accordingly, stockholders lower the amount they are willing to invest per dollar of book value and EPS.

TIME OUT

3-13 What are the major market value ratios?

3-14 Does a firm generally want to have high or low values for each of these ratios?

3-15 Discuss the price-earnings ratio and address why it assumes particular importance among all of the other ratios we have presented.

3.6 DuPont Analysis

LG6

Table 3.1 lists the ratios we discuss, their values for DPH Tree Farm, Inc. as of 2008, and the corresponding values for the tree farm industry. The value of each ratio for DPH Tree Farm is highlighted in green if it is generally stronger than the industry and is highlighted in red if it is generally a negative sign for the firm. As we noted in this chapter's introduction, many of the ratios we have discussed thus far are interrelated. So a change in one ratio may well affect the value of several ratios. Often these interrelations can help evaluate firm performance. Managers and investors often perform a detailed analysis of ROA (Return on Assets) and ROE (Return on Equity) using the **DuPont analysis system.** Popularized by the DuPont Corporation, the DuPont analysis system uses the balance sheet and income statement to break the ROA and ROE ratios into component pieces.

The basic DuPont equation looks at ROA as the product of the profit margin and the total asset turnover ratios:

$$\text{ROA} = \text{Profit margin} \times \text{Total asset turnover}$$

$$\frac{\text{Net income available to common stockholders}}{\text{Total assets}} = \frac{\text{Net income available to common stockholders}}{\text{Sales}} \times \frac{\text{Sales}}{\text{Total assets}} \tag{3-27}$$

The basic DuPont equation looks at the firm's overall profitability as a function of the profit the firm earns per dollar of sales (operating efficiency) and the dollar of sales produced per dollar of assets on the balance sheet (efficiency in asset use). With this tool, managers can see the reason for any changes in ROA in more detail. For example, if ROA increases, the DuPont equation may show that the net profit margin was constant, but the total asset turnover (efficiency in using assets) increased, or that total asset turnover remained constant, but profit margins (operating efficiency) increased. Managers can more specifically identify the reasons for an ROA change by using the ratios described above to further break down operating efficiency and efficiency in asset use.

Next, the DuPont system looks at ROE as the product of ROA and the equity multiplier.

$$\text{ROE} = \text{ROA} \times \text{Equity multiplier}$$

$$\frac{\text{Net income available to common stockholders}}{\text{Common stockholders' equity}} = \text{ROA} \times \frac{\text{Total assets}}{\text{Common stockholders' equity}} \tag{3-28}$$

Notice that this version of the equity multiplier uses the return to common stockholders (the firm's owners) only. So the DuPont equity multiplier uses common stockholders' equity only, rather than total equity (which includes preferred stock).

Taking this breakdown one step further, the DuPont system breaks ROE into the product of the profit margin, the total asset turnover, and the equity multiplier.

$$\text{ROE} = \text{Profit margin} \times \text{Total asset turnover} \times \text{Equity multiplier}$$

$$\frac{\text{Net income available to common stockholders}}{\text{Common stockholders' equity}} = \frac{\text{Net income available to common stockholders}}{\text{Sales}} \times \frac{\text{Sales}}{\text{Total assets}} \times \frac{\text{Total assets}}{\text{Common stockholders' equity}} \tag{3-29}$$

RATIO	VALUE FOR DPH TREE FARM, INC.	VALUE FOR THE TREE FARM INDUSTRY
Liquidity ratios:		
Current ratio $= \dfrac{\text{Current assets}}{\text{Current liabilities}}$	1.71 times	1.50 times
Quick ratio (acid-test ratio) $= \dfrac{\text{Current assets} - \text{Inventory}}{\text{Current liabilities}}$	0.78 times	0.50 times
Cash ratio $= \dfrac{\text{Cash and marketable securities}}{\text{Current liabilities}}$	0.20 times	0.15 times
Asset management ratios:		
Inventory turnover ratio $= \dfrac{\text{Sales or Cost of goods sold}}{\text{Inventory}}$	2.84 times	2.15 times
Days' sales in inventory $= \dfrac{\text{Inventory} \times 365 \text{ days}}{\text{Sales}}$	129 days	170 days
Average collection period $= \dfrac{\text{Accounts receivable} \times 365 \text{ days}}{\text{Credit sales}}$	81 days	95 days
Accounts receivable turnover $= \dfrac{\text{Credit sales}}{\text{Accounts receivable}}$	4.50 times	3.84 times
Average payment period (APP) $= \dfrac{\text{Accounts payable} \times 365 \text{ days}}{\text{Cost of goods sold}}$	134 days	102 days
Accounts payable turnover $= \dfrac{\text{Cost of goods sold}}{\text{Accounts payable}}$	2.73 times	3.55 times
Fixed asset turnover ratio $= \dfrac{\text{Sales}}{\text{Fixed assets}}$	1.00 times	0.85 times
Sales to working capital $= \dfrac{\text{Sales}}{\text{Working capital}}$	3.71 times	3.20 times
Total asset turnover ratio $= \dfrac{\text{Sales}}{\text{Total assets}}$	0.55 times	0.40 times
Capital intensity $= \dfrac{\text{Total assets}}{\text{Sales}}$	1.81 times	2.50 times
Debt management ratios:		
Debt ratio $= \dfrac{\text{Total debt}}{\text{Total assets}}$	55.26%	68.50%
Debt-to-equity ratio $= \dfrac{\text{Total debt}}{\text{Total equity}}$	1.24 times	2.17 times
Equity multiplier ratio $= \dfrac{\text{Total assets}}{\text{Total equity}}$	2.24 times	4.10 times
or $\dfrac{\text{Total assets}}{\text{Common stockholders' equity}}$	2.28 times	4.14 times
Times interest earned $= \dfrac{\text{EBIT}}{\text{Interest}}$	9.50 times	5.15 times
Fixed-charge coverage ratio $= \dfrac{\text{Earnings available to meet fixed charges}}{\text{Fixed charges}}$	9.50 times	5.70 times
Cash coverage ratio $= \dfrac{\text{EBIT} + \text{Depreciation}}{\text{Fixed charges}}$	10.31 times	7.78 times
Profitability ratios:		
Profit margin $= \dfrac{\text{Net income available to common stockholders}}{\text{Sales}}$	25.40%	23.25%

(continued)

Basic earnings power ratio $= \dfrac{\text{EBIT}}{\text{Total assets}}$	26.67%	22.85%
Return on assets $= \dfrac{\text{Net income available to common stockholders}}{\text{Total assets}}$	14.04%	9.30%
Return on equity $= \dfrac{\text{Net income available to common stockholders}}{\text{Common stockholders' equity}}$	32.00%	38.50%
Dividend payout ratio $= \dfrac{\text{Common stock dividends}}{\text{Net income available to common stockholders}}$	31.25%	30.90%
Market value ratios:		
Market-to-book ratio $= \dfrac{\text{Market price per share}}{\text{Book value per share}}$	1.38 times	2.15 times
Price-earnings ratio $= \dfrac{\text{Market price per share}}{\text{Earnings per share}}$	4.31 times	6.25 times

figure 3.1

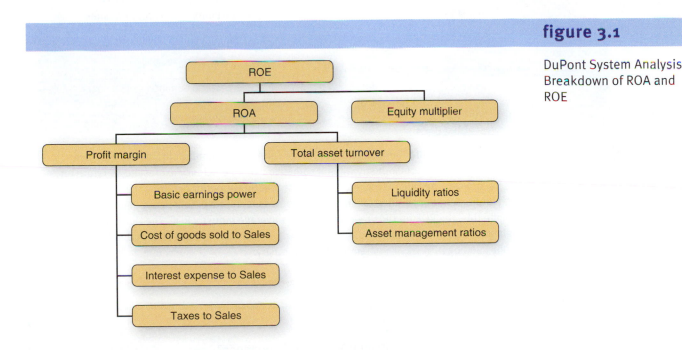

This presentation of ROE allows managers, analysts, and investors to look at the return on equity as a function of the net profit margin (profit per dollar of sales from the income statement), total asset turnover (efficiency in the use of assets from the balance sheet), and the equity multiplier (financial leverage from the balance sheet). Again, we can break these components down to more specifically identify possible causes for a ROE change. Figure 3.1 illustrates the DuPont system analysis breakdown of ROA and ROE.

 For interactive versions of this example visit www.mhhe.com/can1e

EXAMPLE 3-6

APPLICATION OF DuPONT ANALYSIS

Use the balance sheet (Table 2.1) and income statement (Table 2.2) for DPH Tree Farm, Inc. to calculate the firm's 2008 values for the ROA and ROE DuPont equations.

(continued)

The ROA and ROE DuPont equations for DPH Tree Farm, Inc. are calculated as follows:

ROA	=	Profit margin	×	Total asset turnover
14.04%	=	25.39683%	×	0.55263 times
Industry average: 9.30%	=	23.25%	×	0.40 times

$$\frac{\text{Net income available to common stockholders}}{\text{Stockholders' equity}} = \frac{\text{Net income available to common stockholders}}{\text{Sales}} \times \frac{\text{Sales}}{\text{Total assets}}$$

$$\frac{\$80m.}{\$570m.} = \frac{\$80m.}{\$315m.} \times \frac{\$315m.}{\$570m.}$$

ROE	=	Profit margin	×	Total asset turnover	×	Equity multiplier
32.00%	=	25.39683%	×	0.55263 times	×	2.28 times
Industry average: 38.50%	=	23.25%	×	0.40 times	×	4.13978 times

$$\frac{\text{Net income available to common stockholders}}{\text{Common stockholders' equity}} = \frac{\text{Net income available to common stockholders}}{\text{Sales}} \times \frac{\text{Sales}}{\text{Total assets}} \times \frac{\text{Total assets}}{\text{Common stockholders' equity}}$$

$$\frac{\$80m.}{\$40m. + \$210m.} = \frac{\$80m.}{\$315m.} \times \frac{315m.}{\$570m} \times \frac{\$570m.}{\$40m. + \$210m.}$$

As we saw with profitability ratios, DPH Tree Farm, Inc. is more profitable than the average firm in the tree farm industry when it comes to overall efficiency expressed as return on assets, or ROA. The DuPont equation highlights that this superior performance comes from both profit margin (operating efficiency) and total asset turnover (efficiency in asset use). Despite this, the ROE for DPH Tree Farm lags the average industry ROE. The DuPont equation highlights that this inferior performance is due solely to the low level of debt and high level of equity used by DPH Tree Farm relative to the industry.

TIME OUT

3-16 What are the DuPont ROA and ROE equations?

3-17 How do each of these equations help to explain firm performance and pinpoint areas for improvement?

 ## 3.7 Other Ratios

Spreading the Financial Statements

In addition to the many ratios listed above, managers, analysts, and investors can also compute additional ratios by dividing all balance sheet amounts by total assets and all income statement amounts by net sales. These calculations, sometimes called *spreading the financial statements,* yield what we call **common-size financial statements** that correct for sizes. Using common-size financial statements, interested parties can identify changes in corporate performance. Year-to-year growth rates in common-size balance sheets and income statement balances also provide useful ratios for identifying trends. They also allow for an easy comparison of balance sheets and income statements across firms in the industry. Common-size financial statements may provide quantitative clues about the direction that the firm (and perhaps the industry) is moving. They may thus provide roadmaps for managers' next moves.

Internal and Sustainable Growth Rates

Remember again that any firm manager's job is to maximize the firm's market value. The firm's ROA and ROE can be used to evaluate the firm's ability to grow and its market value to be maximized. Specifically, managers, analysts, and investors use these ratios to calculate two growth measures: the internal growth rate and the sustainable growth rate.

The **internal growth rate** is the growth rate a firm can sustain if it uses only internal financing—that is, retained earnings—to finance future growth. Mathematically, the internal growth rate is:

$$\text{Internal growth rate} = \frac{\text{ROA} \times \text{RR}}{1 - (\text{ROA} \times \text{RR})} \qquad (3\text{-}30)$$

where RR is the firm's earnings retention ratio. The retention ratio represents the portion of net income that the firm reinvests as retained earnings:

$$\text{Retention ratio (RR)} = \frac{\text{Addition to retained earnings}}{\text{Net income available to common stockholders}} \qquad (3\text{-}31)$$

Since a firm either pays its net income as dividends to its stockholders or reinvests those funds as retained earnings, the dividend payout and the retention ratios must always add to one:

$$\text{Retention ratio} = 1 - \text{Dividend payout ratio} \qquad (3\text{-}32)$$

A problem arises when a firm relies only on internal financing to support asset growth: Through time, its debt ratio will fall because as asset values grow, total debt stays constant—only retained earnings finance asset growth. If total debt remains constant, as assets grow the debt ratio decreases. As we noted above, shareholders often become disgruntled if, as the firm grows, a decreasing debt ratio (increasing equity financing) dilutes their return. So as firms grow, managers must often try to maintain a debt ratio that they view as optimal. In this case, managers finance asset growth with new debt *and* retained earnings. The maximum growth rate that can be achieved this way is the **sustainable growth rate.** Mathematically, the sustainable growth rate is:

$$\text{Sustainable growth rate} = \frac{\text{ROE} \times \text{RR}}{1 - (\text{ROE} \times \text{RR})} \qquad (3\text{-}33)$$

Maximizing the sustainable growth rate helps firm managers maximize firm value. Applying the DuPont ROE equation here, notice that a firm's sustainable growth depends on four factors:

1. The profit margin (operating efficiency).
2. The total asset turnover (efficiency in asset use).
3. Financial leverage (the use of debt versus equity to finance assets).
4. Profit retention (reinvestment of net income into the firm rather than paying it out as dividends).

Increasing any of these factors increases the firm's sustainable growth rate and hence helps to maximize firm value. Managers, analysts, and investors will want to focus on these areas as they evaluate firm performance and market value.

CALCULATING INTERNAL AND SUSTAINABLE GROWTH RATES

Use the balance sheet (Table 2.1) and income statement (Table 2.2) for DPH Tree Farm, Inc. to calculate the firm's 2008 internal and sustainable growth rates.

SOLUTION:

The internal and sustainable growth rates for DPH Tree Farm, Inc. are calculated as follows.

$$\text{Retention rate (RR)} = \frac{\$55\text{m.}}{\$80\text{m.}} = .6875 \text{ or } 68.75\%$$

$$\text{Industry RR} = 1 - \text{Industry dividend payout ratio}$$

$$= 1 - .3090$$

$$\text{Internal growth rate} = \frac{.1404 \times .6875}{1 - (.1404 \times .6875)} = .1068 \text{ or } 10.68\%$$

$$\text{Industry average internal growth rate} = \frac{.0930 \times (1 - .3090)}{1 - (.0930 \times (1 - .3090))} = .0687 \text{ or } 6.87\%$$

$$\text{Sustainable growth rate} = \frac{.3200 \times .6875}{1 - (.3200 \times .6875)} = .2821 \text{ or } 28.21\%$$

$$\text{Industry average sustainable growth rate} = \frac{.3800 \times (1 - .3090)}{1 - (.3800 \times (1 - .3090))} = .3561 \text{ or } 35.61\%$$

MATH COACH

When putting values into the equation, enter them in decimal format, not percentage format
CORRECT $1 - (.1404 \times .6875)$
NOT CORRECT $1 - (14.04 \times 68.75)$

These ratios show that DPH Tree Farm, Inc. can grow faster than the industry if the firm uses only retained earnings to finance the growth. However, if DPH grows while keeping the debt *ratio* constant (e.g., both debt and retained earnings are used to finance the growth), industry firms can grow much faster than DPH Tree Farm. Once again, DPH's low debt level and high equity level relative to the industry creates this disparity. Therefore, DPH Tree Farm limits its growth as a result of its managerial decisions.

TIME OUT

3-18 What does "spreading the financial statements" mean?

3-19 What are retention rates and internal and sustainable growth rates?

3-20 What factors enter into sustainable growth rates?

 ## 3.8 Time Series and Cross-sectional Analysis

We have explored many ratios that allow managers and investors to examine firm performance. But to really analyze performance in a meaningful way, we must interpret our ratio results against some kind of standard or benchmark. To interpret financial ratios, managers, analysts, and investors use two major types of benchmarks: (1) performance of the firm over time (**time series analysis**) and (2) performance of the firm against one or more companies in the same industry (**cross-sectional analysis**).

Analyzing ratio trends over time, along with absolute ratio levels, gives managers, analysts, and investors information about whether a firm's financial condition is improving or deteriorating. For example, ratio analysis may reveal that the days' sales in inventory is increasing. This suggests that inventories, relative to the sales they support, are not being used as well as they were in the past. If this increase is the result of a deliberate policy to increase inventories to offer customers a wider choice and if it results in higher future sales volumes or increased margins that more than compensate for increased capital tied up in inventory, the increased relative size of the inventories is good for the firm. Managers and investors should be concerned, on the other hand, if increased inventories result from declining sales but steady purchases of supplies and production.

Looking at one firm's financial ratios, even through time, gives managers, analysts, and investors only a limited picture of firm performance. Ratio analysis almost always includes a comparison of one firm's ratios relative to the ratios of other firms in the industry, or cross-sectional analysis. Key to cross-sectional analysis is identifying similar firms that compete in the same markets, have similar assets sizes, and operate in a similar manner to the firm being analyzed. Since no two firms are identical, obtaining such a comparison group is no easy task. Thus, the choice of companies to use in cross-sectional analysis is at best subjective. Note that as we calculated the financial ratios for DPH Tree Farm, Inc. throughout the chapter, we compared them to the industry average. Comparative ratios that can be used in cross-sectional analysis are available from many sources. For example, Value Line Investment Surveys, Robert Morris Associates, Hoover's Online (at **www.hoovers.com**), and MSN Money Web site (at **moneycentral.msn.com**) are examples of four major sources of financial ratios for numerous industries that operate within the U.S. and worldwide.

TIME OUT

3-21 What is time series analysis of a firm's operations?

3-22 What is cross-sectional analysis of a firm's operations?

3-23 How do time-series and cross-sectional analyses differ, and what information would you expect to gain from each?

3.9 Cautions in Using Ratios to Evaluate Firm Performance

Financial statement analysis allows managers, analysts, and investors to better understand a firm's performance. However, data from financial statements should not be received without certain cautions. These include:

1. Financial statement data are historical. Historical data may not reflect future performance. While we can make projections using historical data, we must also remember that projections may be inaccurate if historical performance does not persist.

2. As we discussed in Chapter 2, firms use different accounting procedures. For example, inventory methods can vary. One firm may use FIFO (first-in, first-out), transferring inventory at the first purchase price, while another uses LIFO (last-in, first-out), transferring inventory at the last purchase price. Likewise, the depreciation method used to value a firm's fixed

assets over time may vary across firms. One firm may use straight-line depreciation, while another may use an accelerated depreciation method (e.g., MACRS). Particularly, when reviewing cross-sectional ratios, differences in accounting rules can affect balance sheet values and financial ratios. It is important to know which accounting rules the firms under consideration are using before making any conclusions about its performance from ratio analysis.

3. Similarly, a firm's cross-sectional competitors may often be located around the world. Financial statements for firms based outside the United States do not necessarily conform to GAAP. Even beyond inventory pricing and depreciation methods, different accounting standards and procedures make it hard to compare financial statements and ratios of firms based in different countries.

4. Sales and expenses vary throughout the year. Managers, analysts, and investors need to note the timing of these fund flows when performing cross-sectional analysis, otherwise they may draw conclusions from comparisons that are actually the result of seasonal cash flow differences. Similarly, firms end their fiscal years at different dates. For cross-sectional analysis, this complicates any comparison of balance sheets during the year. Likewise, one-time events, such as a merger, may affect a firm's financial performance. Cross-sectional analysis involving these events can result in misleading conclusions.

5. Large firms often have multiple divisions or business units engaged in different lines of business. In this case, it is difficult to truly compare a set of firms with which managers and investors can perform cross-sectional analysis.

6. Firms often window dress their financial statements to make annual results look better. For example, to improve liquidity ratios calculated with year-end balance sheets, firms often delay payments for raw materials, equipment, loans, and so on to build up their liquid accounts and thus their liquidity ratios. If possible, it is often more accurate to use other than year-end financial statements to conduct ratio analysis.

Financial statement ratio analysis is a major part of evaluating a firm's performance. If managers, analysts, or investors ignore the issues noted here, they may well draw faulty conclusions from their analysis. However, used intelligently and with good judgment, ratio analysis can provide useful information on a firm's current position and hint at future performance.

TIME OUT

3-24 What cautions should managers and investors take when evaluating a firm using ratio analysis?

Business Application Solution

The managers of DPH Tree Farm, Inc. have stated that its performance surpasses that of other firms in the industry. Particularly strong are the firm's liquidity and asset management positions. The superior performance in these areas has resulted in superior overall returns for the stockholders of DPH Tree Farm, Inc., according to DPH management. Having analyzed the financial statements using ratio analysis, we could conclude that these statements are partially true. All three liquidity ratios show that DPH Tree Farm, Inc. holds more liquidity on its balance sheet than the industry average. Thus, DPH Tree Farm has more cash and other liquid assets (or current assets) available to pay its bills (or current liabilities) as they come due than the average firm in the tree farm industry. In all cases, the asset management ratios show that DPH Tree Farm, Inc. is outperforming the industry average in its asset management. The firm is turning over its inventory faster than the average firm in the tree farm industry, thus producing more dollars of sales per dollar of inventory. It is also collecting its accounts receivable faster and paying its accounts payable slower than the average firm. Further, DPH Tree Farm is producing more sales per dollar of fixed assets, working capital, and total assets than the average firm in the industry. The profitability ratios show that DPH Tree Farm, Inc. is more profitable than the average firm in the tree farm industry. The profit margin, BEP, and ROA are all higher than the industry. Despite this, the ROE for DPH Tree Farm is much lower than the average for the industry.

What the managers do not state is that the debt management ratios show that DPH Tree Farm, Inc. holds less debt on its balance sheet than the average firm in the tree farm industry. This is a good sign in that this lack of financial leverage decreases the firm's potential for financial distress and even failure. If the firm has a bad year, it has promised relatively few payments to debt

(continued)

Personal Application Solution

To evaluate DPH Tree Farm, Inc.'s financial statements, Chris Ryan would want to perform ratio analysis in which she uses the financial statements to calculate the most commonly used ratios. These include liquidity ratios, asset management ratios, debt management ratios, profitability ratios, and market value ratios. The value of these ratios for DPH Tree Farms and the tree farming industry are presented in Table 3.1. Chris might also want to spread the financial statements. These calculations yield common-size, easily compared financial statements that can be used to identify changes in corporate performance as well as how DPH Tree Farm compares to other firms in the industry. Having calculated these ratios, Chris can identify any interrelationships in the ratios by performing a detailed analysis of ROA and ROE using the DuPont system of analysis. A critical part of performance analysis lies in the interpretation of these numbers against some benchmark. To interpret the financial ratios, Chris will also want to evaluate the performance of the firm over time (time series analysis) and the performance of the firm against one or more companies in the same industry (cross-sectional analysis). Finally, Chris needs to exercise some cautions when reviewing data from financial statements. For example, the financial statement data are historical and may not be representative of future performance. Further, she needs to know what accounting rules DPH Tree Farm uses before making any comparisons or conclusions about its performance from ratios analysis. Finally, DPH Tree Farm's managers may have window dressed their financial statements to make them look better.

Business Application Solution (concluded)

holders. Thus, the risk of bankruptcy is small. Further, the firm has more dollars of operating earnings and cash available to meet each dollar of interest obligations on the firm's debt. However, when DPH Tree Farm, Inc. does well, the low level of financial leverage dilutes the return to the stockholders of the firm. This profit dilution will likely upset the firm's common stockholders. Indeed, the market value ratios show that DPH Tree Farm's investors will not pay as much for a share of the firm's stock per dollar of book value and earnings as the average for the industry. The low debt level and high equity level used by DPH Tree Farm relative to the industry is likely a main reason for this unenthusiastic response by DPH investors.

summary of learning goals

Ratio analysis involves the process of calculating and analyzing financial ratios to assess a firm's performance and to identify actions needed to improve firm performance. The most commonly used ratios for ratio analysis fall into five groups: (1) liquidity ratios, (2) asset management ratios, (3) debt management ratios, (4) profitability ratios, and (5) market value ratios. This chapter reviewed these ratios, described what each ratio means, and identified the general trend (higher or lower) managers and investors look for in each ratio.

LG1 **Calculate and interpret the major liquidity ratios.** Liquidity ratios measure the relation between a firm's liquid (or current) assets and its current liabilities.

LG2 **Calculate and interpret the major asset management ratios.** Asset management ratios measure how efficiently a firm uses its assets (inventory, accounts receivable, and fixed assets), as well as its accounts payable.

LG3 **Calculate and interpret the major debt ratios.** Debt management ratios measure the extent to which the firm uses debt (or financial leverage) versus equity to finance its assets.

LG4 **Calculate and interpret the major profitability ratios.** Profitability ratios show the combined effect of liquidity, asset management, and debt management on the overall operating results of the firm.

LG5 **Calculate and interpret the major market value ratios.** Market value ratios relate a firm's stock price to its earnings and book value.

LG6 **Appreciate how various ratios relate to one another.** Many of the ratios we review are interrelated. That is, a change in one ratio may affect the value of several ratios. To see how these interrelations help evaluate firm performance, managers, analysts and investors often perform a detailed analysis of ROA and ROE using the DuPont system of analysis. The DuPont system of analysis uses the balance sheet and income statement to break the ROA and ROE ratios into component pieces.

LG7 **Discuss the differences between time series and cross-sectional ratio analysis and decide which is most appropriate given an analytical situation.** When managers, analysts, or investors review a firm's financial position through ratio analysis, they often start by evaluating trends in

www.mhhe.com/can1e

the firm's financial position over time (time series analysis) and by comparing the firm's performance with that of other firms in the same industry (cross-sectional analysis).

Explain cautions that should be taken when examining financial ratios and financial

information in general. The analysis of financial statements allows managers and investors to better understand a firm's performance. However, some cautions should be remembered when reviewing data from financial statements.

chapter equations

3-1 Current ratio $= \dfrac{\text{Current assets}}{\text{Current liabilities}}$

3-2 Quick ratio (acid-test ratio) $= \dfrac{\text{Current assets} - \text{Inventory}}{\text{Current liabilities}}$

3-3 Cash ratio $= \dfrac{\text{Cash and marketable securities}}{\text{Current liabilities}}$

3-4 Inventory turnover ratio $= \dfrac{\text{Sales or Cost of goods sold}}{\text{Inventory}}$

3-5 Days' sales in inventory $= \dfrac{\text{Inventory} \times 365 \text{ days}}{\text{Sales or Cost of goods sold}}$

3-6 Average collection period (ACP) $= \dfrac{\text{Accounts receivable} \times 365 \text{ days}}{\text{Credit sales}}$

3-7 Accounts receivable turnover $= \dfrac{\text{Credit sales}}{\text{Accounts receivable}}$

3-8 Average payment period (APP) $= \dfrac{\text{Accounts payable} \times 365 \text{ days}}{\text{Cost of goods sold}}$

3-9 Accounts payable turnover $= \dfrac{\text{Cost of goods sold}}{\text{Accounts payable}}$

3-10 Fixed asset turnover ratio $= \dfrac{\text{Sales}}{\text{Fixed assets}}$

3-11 Sales to working capital $= \dfrac{\text{Sales}}{\text{Working capital}}$

3-12 Total assets turnover ratio $= \dfrac{\text{Sales}}{\text{Total assets}}$

3-13 Capital intensity ratio $= \dfrac{\text{Total assets}}{\text{Sales}}$

3-14   Debt ratio $= \dfrac{\text{Total debt}}{\text{Total assets}}$

3-15   Debt-to-equity ratio $= \dfrac{\text{Total debt}}{\text{Total equity}}$

3-16   Equity multiplier ratio $= \dfrac{\text{Total assets}}{\text{Total equity}}$ or $\dfrac{\text{Total assets}}{\text{Common stockholders' equity}}$

3-17   Times interest earned $= \dfrac{\text{EBIT}}{\text{Interest}}$

3-18   Fixed-charge coverage ratio $= \dfrac{\text{Earnings available to meet fixed charges}}{\text{Fixed charges}}$

3-19   Cash coverage ratio $= \dfrac{\text{EBIT} + \text{Depreciation}}{\text{Fixed charges}}$

3-20   Profit margin $= \dfrac{\text{Net income available to common stockholders}}{\text{Sales}}$

3-21   Basic earnings power ratio (BEP) $= \dfrac{\text{EBIT}}{\text{Total assets}}$

3-22   Return on assets (ROA) $= \dfrac{\text{Net income available to common stockholders}}{\text{Total assets}}$

3-23   Return on equity (ROE) $= \dfrac{\text{Net income available to common stockholders}}{\text{Common stockholders' equity}}$

3-24   Dividend payout ratio $= \dfrac{\text{Common stock dividends}}{\text{Net income available to common stockholders}}$

3-25   Market-to-book ratio $= \dfrac{\text{Market price per share}}{\text{Book value per share}}$

3-26   Price-earnings (PE) ratio $= \dfrac{\text{Market price per share}}{\text{Earnings per share}}$

3-27   ROA $=$ Profit margin $\times$ Total asset turnover

$$\dfrac{\text{Net income available to common stockholders}}{\text{Total assets}} = \dfrac{\text{Net income available to common stockholders}}{\text{Sales}} \times \dfrac{\text{Sales}}{\text{Total assets}}$$

3-28   ROE $=$ ROA $\times$ equity multiplier

$$\dfrac{\text{Net income available to common stockholders}}{\text{Common stockholders' equity}} = \text{ROA} \times \dfrac{\text{Total assets}}{\text{Common stockholders' equity}}$$

3-29 ROE = Profit margin × Total asset turnover × Equity multiplier

$$\frac{\text{Net income available}}{\text{to common stockholders}} = \frac{\text{Net income available}}{\text{to common stockholders}} \times \frac{\text{Sales}}{\text{Total assets}} \times \frac{\text{Total assets}}{\text{Common stockholders' equity}}$$

3-30 $\text{Internal growth rate} = \dfrac{\text{ROA} \times \text{RR}}{1 - (\text{ROA} \times \text{RR})}$

3-31 $\text{Retention ratio (RR)} = \dfrac{\text{Addition to retained earnings}}{\text{Net income available to common stockholders}}$

3-32 Retention ratio = 1 − Dividend payout ratio

3-33 $\text{Sustainable growth rate} = \dfrac{\text{ROE} \times \text{RR}}{1 - (\text{ROE} \times \text{RR})}$

key terms

asset management ratios, Measure how efficiently a firm uses its assets (inventory, accounts receivable, and fixed assets), as well as its accounts payable. (p. 72)

capital structure, The amount of debt versus equity to hold on the balance sheet. (p. 77)

common-size financial statements, Dividing all balance sheet amounts by total assets and all income statement amounts by net sales. (p. 86)

cross-sectional analysis, Analyzing the performance of a firm against one or more companies in the same industry. (p. 88)

debt management ratios, Measure the extent to which the firm uses debt (or financial leverage) versus equity to finance its assets. (p. 76)

DuPont system of analysis, An analytical method that uses the balance sheet and income statement to break the ROA and ROE ratios into component pieces. (p. 83)

internal growth rate, The growth rate a firm can sustain if it finances growth using only internal financing, that is, retained earnings growth. (p. 87)

liquidity ratios, Measure the relation between a firm's liquid (or current) assets and its current liabilities. (p. 70)

market value ratios, Ratios that relate a firm's stock price to its earnings and book value. (p. 81)

profitability ratios, Ratios that show the combined affect of liquidity, asset management, and debt management on the firm's overall operating results. (p. 79)

ratio analysis, The process of calculating and analyzing financial ratios to assess the firm's performance and to identify actions needed to improve firm performance. (p. 68)

sustainable growth rate, The growth rate a firm can sustain if it finances growth using both debt and internal financing such that the debt ratio remains constant. (p. 87)

time series analysis, Analyzing firm performance by monitoring ratio trends. (p. 88)

self-test problems with solutions

1 **Calculating Ratios** Listed below are the balance sheet and income statement for Marion & Carter, Inc. Use these financial statements to calculate liquidity, asset management, debt management, profitability, and market value ratios for 2008.

MARION & CARTER, INC.
Balance Sheet as of December 31, 2007 and 2008
(in millions of dollars)

Assets	2007	2008	Liabilities and Equity	2007	2008
Current assets:			Current liabilities:		
Cash and marketable securities	$ 155	$ 165	Accrued wages and taxes	$ 95	$ 124
Accounts receivable	400	475	Accounts payable	310	360
Inventory	620	650	Notes payable	280	322
Total	1,175	1,290	Total	685	806
Fixed assets:			Long-term debt:	1,178	1,210
Gross plant and equipment	1,860	2,280	Stockholders' equity:		
Less: Depreciation	250	330	Preferred stock (25 million shares)	25	25
Net plant and equipment	1,610	1,950	Common stock and paid-in surplus (200 million shares)	250	250
Other long-term assets	310	350	Retained earnings	957	1,299
Total	1,920	2,300	Total	1,232	1,574
Total assets	$3,095	$3,590	Total liabilities and equity	$3,095	$3,590

MARION & CARTER, INC.
Income Statement for Years Ending December 31, 2007 and 2008
(in millions of dollars)

	2007	2008
Net sales (all credit)	$ 1,705	$ 2,053
Less: Cost of goods sold	837	1,030
Gross profits	868	1,023
Less: Depreciation	75	80
Earnings before interest and taxes (EBIT)	793	943
Less: Interest	112	99
Earnings before taxes (EBT)	681	844
Less: Taxes	248	285
Net income	$ 433	$ 559
Less: Preferred stock dividends	$ 62	$ 62
Net income available to common stockholders	$ 371	$ 497
Less: Common stock dividends	155	155
Addition to retained earnings	$ 216	$ 342
Per (common) share data:		
Earnings per share (EPS)	$ 1.855	$ 2.485
Dividends per share (DPS)	$ 0.775	$ 0.775
Book value per share (BVPS)	$ 6.035	$ 7.745
Market value (price) per share (MVPS)	$21.470	$22.970

Solution:

Liquidity ratios:

Current ratio $= \dfrac{\$1,290\text{m.}}{\$806\text{m.}} = 1.60$ times

Quick ratio (acid-test ratio) $= \dfrac{\$1,290\text{m.} - \$650\text{m.}}{\$806\text{m.}} = 0.794$ times

Cash ratio $= \dfrac{\$165\text{m.}}{\$806\text{m.}} = 0.20$ times

Asset management ratios:

Inventory turnover ratio $= \dfrac{\$2,053\text{m.}}{\$650\text{m.}} = 3.16$ times

Days' sales in inventory $= \dfrac{\$650\text{m.} \times 365 \text{ days}}{\$2,053\text{m.}} = 115.56$ days

Average collection period $= \dfrac{\$475\text{m.} \times 365 \text{ days}}{\$2,053\text{m.}} = 84.45$ days

Accounts receivable turnover $= \dfrac{\$2,053\text{m.}}{\$475\text{m.}} = 4.32$ times

Average payment period $= \dfrac{\$360\text{m.} \times 365 \text{ days}}{\$930\text{m.}} = 141.29$ days

Accounts payable turnover $= \dfrac{\$930\text{m.}}{\$360\text{m.}} = 2.58$ times

Fixed asset turnover ratio $= \dfrac{\$2,053\text{m.}}{\$1,950\text{m.}} = 1.05$ times

Sales to working capital $= \dfrac{\$2,053\text{m.}}{(\$1,290\text{m.} - \$806\text{m.})} = 4.24$ times

Total asset turnover ratio $= \dfrac{\$2,053\text{m.}}{\$3,590\text{m.}} = 0.57$ times

Capital intensity $= \dfrac{\$3,590\text{m.}}{\$2,053\text{m.}} = 1.75$ times

Debt management ratios:

Debt ratio $= \dfrac{\$806\text{m.} + \$1,210\text{m.}}{\$3,590\text{m.}} = 56.16\%$

Debt-to-equity ratio $= \dfrac{\$806\text{m.} + \$1,210\text{m.}}{\$1,574\text{m.}} = 1.28$ times

Equity multiplier ratio $= \dfrac{\$3,590\text{m.}}{\$1,574\text{m.}} = 2.28$ times

Times interest earned $= \dfrac{\$943\text{m.}}{\$99\text{m.}} = 9.53$ times

Fixed-charge coverage ratio $= \dfrac{\$943\text{m.}}{\$99\text{m.}} = 9.53$ times

Cash coverage ratio $= \dfrac{\$943\text{m.} + \$80\text{m.}}{\$99\text{m.}} = 10.33$ times

Profitability ratios:

Profit margin $= \dfrac{\$497\text{m.}}{\$2,053\text{m.}} = 24.21\%$

Basic earnings power ratio $= \dfrac{\$943\text{m.}}{\$3,590\text{m.}} = 26.27\%$

Return on assets $= \dfrac{\$497\text{m.}}{\$3,590\text{m.}} = 13.84\%$

Return on equity $= \dfrac{\$497\text{m.}}{\$250\text{m.} + \$1,299\text{m.}} = 32.09\%$

Dividend payout ratio $= \dfrac{\$155\text{m.}}{\$497\text{m.}} = 31.19\%$

Market value ratios:

Market-to-book ratio $= \dfrac{\$22.970}{\$7.745} = 2.97$ times

Price-earnings ratio $= \dfrac{\$22.970}{\$2.485} = 9.24$ times

2 **Internal and Sustainable Growth Rates** Calculate the internal growth rate and sustainable growth rate for Marion & Carter, Inc. using the 2008 financial statements.

LG6

Solution:

Retention rate (RR) $= \dfrac{\$342\text{m.}}{\$497\text{m.}} = .6881 \text{ or } 68.81\%$

Internal growth rate $= \dfrac{.1384 \times .6881}{1 - (.1384 \times .6881)} = .1053 \text{ or } 10.53\%$

Sustainable growth rate $= \dfrac{.3209 \times .6881}{1 - (.3209 \times .6881)} = .2834 \text{ or } 28.34\%$

www.mhhe.com/can1e

questions

1. Classify each of the following ratios according to a ratio category (liquidity ratio, asset management ratio, debt management ratio, profitability ratio, or market value ratio). *(LG1–LG5)*

   a. Current ratio

   b. Inventory turnover ratio

   c. Return on assets

   d. Accounts payable period

   e. Times interest earned

   f. Capital intensity ratio

   g. Equity multiplier

   h. Basic earnings power ratio

2. For each of the actions listed below, determine what would happen to the current ratio. Assume nothing else on the balance sheet changes and that net working capital is positive. *(LG1)*

   a. Accounts receivable are paid in cash

   b. Notes payable are paid off with cash

   c. Inventory is sold on account

   d. Inventory is purchased on account

   e. Accrued wages and taxes increase

   f. Long-term debt is paid with cash

   g. Cash from a short-term bank loan is received

3. Explain the meaning and significance of the following ratios *(LG1–LG5)*

   a. Quick ratio

   b. Average collection period

   c. Return on equity

   d. Days' sales in inventory

   e. Debt ratio

   f. Profit margin

   g. Accounts payable turnover

   h. Market-to-book ratio

4. A firm has an average collection period of 10 days. The industry average ACP is 25 days. Is this a good or poor sign about the management of the firm's accounts receivable? *(LG2)*

5. A firm has a debt ratio of 20%. The industry average debt ratio is 65%. Is this a good or poor sign about the management of the firm's financial leverage? *(LG3)*

6. A firm has an ROE of 20%. The industry average ROE is 12%. Is this a good or poor sign about the management of the firm? *(LG4)*

7. Why is the DuPont system of analysis an important tool when evaluating firm performance? *(LG6)*

8. A firm has an ROE of 10%. The industry average ROE is 15%. How can the DuPont system of analysis help the firm's managers identify the reasons for this difference? *(LG6)*

9. What is the difference between the internal growth rate and the sustainable growth rate? *(LG6)*

10. What is the difference between time series analysis and cross-sectional analysis? *(LG7)*

11. What information does time series and cross-sectional analysis provide for firm managers, analysts, and investors? *(LG7)*

12. Why is it important to know a firm's accounting rules before making any conclusions about its performance from ratios analysis? *(LG8)*

13. What does it mean when a firm window dresses its financial statements? *(LG8)*

problems

basic problems

3-1 Liquidity Ratios You are evaluating the balance sheet for Goodman's Bees Corporation. From the balance sheet you find the following balances: cash and marketable securities = $400,000; accounts receivable = $1,200,000; inventory = $2,100,000; accrued wages and taxes = $500,000; accounts payable = $800,000; and notes payable = $600,000. Calculate Goodman Bee's current ratio, quick ratio, and cash ratio. *(LG1)*

3-2 Liquidity Ratios The top part of Ramakrishnan Inc.'s 2008 and 2009 balance sheets is listed below (in millions of dollars).

	2008	2009		2008	2009
Current assets:			Current liabilities:		
Cash and marketable securities	$ 15	$ 20	Accrued wages and taxes	$ 18	$ 19
Accounts receivable	75	84	Accounts payable	45	51
Inventory	110	121	Notes payable	40	45
Total	$200	$225	Total	$103	$115

Calculate Ramakrishnan Inc.'s current ratio, quick ratio, and cash ratio for 2008 and 2009. *(LG1)*

3-3 Asset Management Ratios Tater and Pepper Corp. reported sales for 2008 of $23 million. Tater and Pepper listed $5.6 million of inventory on its balance sheet. Using a 365-day year, how many days did Tater and Pepper's inventory stay on the premises? How many times per year did Tater and Pepper's inventory turn over? *(LG2)*

3-4 Asset Management Ratios Mr. Husker's Tuxedos, Corp. ended the year 2008 with an average collection period of 32 days. The firm's credit sales for 2008 were $33 million. What is the year-end 2008 balance in accounts receivable for Mr. Husker's Tuxedos? *(LG2)*

3-5 Debt Management Ratios Tiggie's Dog Toys, Inc. reported a debt-to-equity ratio of 1.75 times at the end of 2008. If the firm's total debt at year-end was $25 million, how much equity does Tiggie's have on its balance sheet? *(LG3)*

3-6 Debt Management Ratios You are considering a stock investment in one of two firms (LotsofDebt, Inc. and LotsofEquity, Inc.), both of which operate in the same industry. LotsofDebt, Inc. finances its $25 million in assets with $24 million in debt and $1 million in equity. LotsofEquity, Inc. finances its $25 million in assets with $1 million in debt and $24 million in equity. Calculate the debt ratio, equity multiplier, and debt-to-equity ratio for the two firms. *(LG3)*

3-7 Profitability Ratios Maggie's Skunk Removal, Corp.'s 2008 income statement listed net sales of $12.5 million, EBIT of $5.6 million, net income available to common stockholders of $3.2 million, and common stock dividends of $1.2 million. The 2008 year-end balance sheet listed total assets of $52.5 million and common stockholders' equity of $21 million with 2 million shares outstanding. Calculate the profit margin, basic earnings power ratio, ROA, ROE, and dividend payout ratio. *(LG4)*

3-8 Profitability Ratios In 2008, Jake's Jamming Music, Inc. announced an ROA of 8.56%, ROE of 14.5%, and profit margin of 20.5%. The firm had total assets of $16.5 million at year-end 2008. Calculate the 2008 values of net income available to common stockholders, common stockholders' equity, and net sales for Jake's Jamming Music, Inc. *(LG4)*

3-9 Market Value Ratios You are considering an investment in Roxie's Bed & Breakfast, Corp. During the last year the firm's income statement listed an addition to retained earnings of $4.8 million and common stock dividends = $2.2 million. Roxie's year-end balance sheet shows common stockholders' equity of $35 million with 10 million shares of common stock outstanding. The common stock's market price per share was $9.00. What is Roxie's Bed & Breakfast's book value per share and earnings per share? Calculate the market-to-book ratio and PE ratio. *(LG5)*

3-10 Market Value Ratios Gambit Golf's market-to-book ratio is currently 2.5 times and PE ratio is 6.75 times. If Gambit Golf's common stock is currently selling at $12.50 per share, what is the book value per share and earnings per share? *(LG5)*

3-11 DuPont Analysis If Silas 4-Wheeler, Inc. has an ROE of 18%, equity multiplier of 2, a profit margin of 18.75%, what is the total asset turnover ratio and the capital intensity ratio? *(LG6)*

3-12 DuPont Analysis Last year Hassan's Madhatter, Inc. had an ROA of 7.5%, a profit margin of 12%, and sales of $10 million. Calculate Hassan's Madhatter's total assets. *(LG6)*

3-13 Internal Growth Rate Last year Lakesha's Lounge Furniture Corporation had an ROA of 7.5% and a dividend payout ratio of 25%. What is the internal growth rate? *(LG6)*

3-14 Sustainable Growth Rate Last year Lakesha's Lounge Furniture Corporation had an ROE of 12.5% and a dividend payout ratio of 20% What is the sustainable growth rate? *(LG6)*

3-15 **Liquidity Ratios** Brenda's Bar and Grill has current liabilities of $15 million. Cash makes up 10 percent of the current assets and accounts receivable makes up another 40 percent of current assets. Brenda's current ratio is 2.1 times. Calculate the value of inventory listed on the firm's balance sheet. *(LG1)*

3-16 **Liquidity and Asset Management Ratios** Mandesa, Inc. has current liabilities of $5 million, current ratio of 2 times, inventory turnover ratio of 12 times, average collection period of 30 days, and sales of $40 million. Calculate the value of cash and marketable securities. *(LG1, LG2)*

3-17 **Asset Management and Profitability Ratios** You have the following information on Els' Putters, Inc.: sales to working capital is 4.6 times, profit margin is 20%, net income available to common stockholders is $5 million, and current liabilities are $6 million. What is the firm's balance of current assets? *(LG2, LG4)*

3-18 **Asset Management and Debt Management Ratios** Use the following information to complete the balance sheet below. Sales are $5.2 million, capital intensity ratio is 2.10 times, debt ratio is 55%, and fixed asset turnover ratio is 1.2 times. *(LG2, LG3)*

ASSETS		LIABILITIES AND EQUITY	
Current assets	$_____	Total liabilities	$_____
Fixed assets	_____	Total equity	_____
Total assets	$_____	Total liabilities and equity	$_____

3-19 **Debt Management Ratios** Tiggie's Dog Toys, Inc. reported a debt to equity ratio of 1.75 times at the end of 2008. If the firm's total assets at year-end were $25 million, how much of their assets are financed with debt and how much with equity? *(LG3)*

3-20 **Debt Management Ratios** Calculate the times interest earned ratio for LaTonya's Flop Shops, Inc. using the following information. Sales = $1 million, cost of goods sold = $600,000, depreciation expense = $100,000, addition to retained earnings = $97,500, dividends per share = $1, tax rate = 30%, and number of shares of common stock outstanding = 60,000. LaTonya's Flop Shops has no preferred stock outstanding. *(LG3)*

3-21 **Profitability and Asset Management Ratios** You are thinking of investing in Nikki T's, Inc. You have only the following information on the firm at year-end 2008: net income is $250,000, total debt is $2.5 million, and debt ratio is 55%. What is Nikki T's ROE for 2008? *(LG2, LG4)*

3-22 **Profitability Ratios** Rick's Travel Service has asked you to help piece together financial information on the firm for the most current year. Managers give you the following information: sales are $4.8 million, total debt is $1.5 million, debt ratio is 40%, and ROE is 18%. Using this information, calculate Rick's ROA. *(LG4)*

3-23 **Market Value Ratios** Leonatti Labs' year-end price on its common stock is $35. The firm has total assets of $50 million, debt ratio 65%, no preferred stock, and 3 million shares of common stock outstanding. Calculate the market-to-book ratio for Leonatti Labs. *(LG5)*

3-24 **Market Value Ratios** Leonatti Labs' year-end price on its common stock is $15. The firm has a profit margin of 8%, total assets of $25 million, a total asset turnover ratio of 0.75, no preferred stock, and 3 million shares of common stock outstanding. Calculate the PE ratio for Leonatti Labs. *(LG5)*

3-25 **DuPont Analysis** Last year, Stumble-on-Inn, Inc. reported an ROE of 18%. The firm's debt ratio was 55%, sales were $15 million, and the capital intensity ratio was 1.25 times. Calculate the net income for Stumble-on-Inn last year. *(LG6)*

3-26 **DuPont Analysis** You are considering investing in Nuran Security Services. You have been able to locate the following information on the firm: total assets are $16 million, accounts receivable are $2.2 million, ACP is 25 days, net income is $2.5 million, and debt-to-equity ratio is 1.2 times. Calculate the ROE for the firm. *(LG6)*

3-27 **Internal Growth Rate** Dogs R Us reported a profit margin of 10.5%, total asset turnover ratio of 0.75 times, debt-to-equity ratio of 0.80 times, net income of $500,000, and dividends paid to common stockholders of $200,000. The firm has no preferred stock outstanding. What is Dogs R Us's internal growth rate? *(LG6)*

3-28 **Sustainable Growth Rate** You have located the following information on Webb's Heating & Air Conditioning: debt ratio is 54%, capital intensity ratio is 1.10 times, profit margin is 12.5%, and dividend payout ratio is 40%. Calculate the sustainable growth rate for Webb. *(LG6)*

Use the following financial statements for Lake of Egypt Marina to answer Problems 3-29 through 3-32.

LAKE OF EGYPT MARINA, INC.
Balance Sheet as of December 31, 2007 and 2008
(in millions of dollars)

	2007	2008		2007	2008
Assets			**Liabilities and Equity**		
Current assets:			Current liabilities:		
Cash and marketable securities	$ 65	$ 75	Accrued wages and taxes	$ 43	$ 40
Accounts receivable	110	115	Accounts payable	80	90
Inventory	190	200	Notes payable	70	80
Total	365	390	Total	193	210
Fixed assets:			Long-term debt:	280	300
Gross plant and equipment	471	580	Stockholders' equity:		
Less: Depreciation	100	110	Preferred stock (5 million shares)	5	5
Net plant and equipment	371	470	Common stock and paid-in surplus (65 million shares)	65	65
Other long-term assets	49	50	Retained earnings	242	330
Total	420	520	Total	312	400
Total assets	$785	$910	Total liabilities and equity	$785	$910

LAKE OF EGYPT MARINA, INC.
Income Statement for Years Ending December 31, 2007 and 2008
(in millions of dollars)

	2007	2008
Net sales (all credit)	$ 432	$ 515
Less: Cost of goods sold	200	260
Gross profits	232	255
Less: Depreciation	20	22
Earnings before interest and taxes (EBIT)	212	233
Less: Interest	30	33
Earnings before taxes (EBT)	182	200
Less: Taxes	55	57
Net income	$ 127	$ 143
Less: Preferred stock dividends	$ 5	$ 5
Net income available to common stockholders	$ 122	$ 138
Less: Common stock dividends	65	65
Addition to retained earnings	$ 57	$ 73
Per (common) share data:		
Earnings per share (EPS)	$ 1.877	$ 2.123
Dividends per share (DPS)	$ 1.000	$ 1.000
Book value per share (BVPS)	$ 4.723	$ 6.077
Market value (price) per share (MVPS)	$12.550	$14.750

3-29 **Spreading the Financial Statements** Spread the balance sheets and income statements of Lake of Egypt Marina, Inc. for 2007 and 2008. (*LG1–LG7*)

3-30 **Calculating Ratios** Calculate the following ratios for Lake of Egypt Marina, Inc. as of year-end 2008. (*LG1–LG7*)

	LAKE OF EGYPT MARINA, INC.	INDUSTRY
a. Current ratio		2.0 times
b. Quick ratio		1.2 times
c. Cash ratio		0.25 times
d. Inventory turnover ratio		3.60 times
e. Days' sales in inventory		101.39 days
f. Average collection period		32.50 days
g. Average payment period		45 days
h. Fixed asset turnover ratio		1.25 times
i. Sales to working capital		4.25 times
j. Total asset turnover ratio		0.85 times
k. Capital intensity ratio		1.18 times
l. Debt ratio		62.50%
m. Debt-to-equity ratio		1.67 times
n. Equity multiplier		2.67 times
o. Times interest earned		8.50 times
p. Cash coverage ratio		8.75 times
q. Profit margin		28.75%
r. Basic earnings power ratio		32.50%
s. ROA		19.75%
t. ROE		36.88%
u. Dividend payout ratio		35%
v. Market-to-book ratio		2.55 times
w. PE ratio		15.60 times

3-31 DuPont Analysis Construct the DuPont ROA and ROE breakdowns for Lake of Egypt Marina, Inc. (*LG1–LG7*)

3-32 Internal and Sustainable Growth Rates Calculate the internal and sustainable growth rate for Lake of Egypt Marina, Inc. (*LG1–LG7*)

3-33 Cross-Sectional Analysis Using the ratios from Problem 3-30 for Lake of Egypt Marina, Inc. and the industry, what can you conclude about Lake of Egypt Marina's financial performance for 2008? (*LG1–LG7*)

advanced problems

3-34 Ratio Analysis Use the following information to complete the balance sheet below. (*LG1–LG5*)

Current ratio = 2.5 times
Profit margin = 10%
Sales = $2,100m.
ROE = 20%
Long-term debt to Long-term debt and equity = 55%

Current assets	_____	Current liabilities	$370m.
Fixed assets	_____	Long-term debt	_____
		Stockholders' equity	_____
Total assets	$ _____	Total liabilities and equity	$ _____

3-35 Ratio Analysis Use the following information to complete the balance sheet below. (*LG1–LG5*)

Current ratio = 2.2 times
Credit sales = $1,200m.
Average collection period = 60 days
Inventory turnover = 1.50 times
Total asset turnover = 0.75 times
Debt ratio = 60%

Cash	_____		
Accounts receivable	_____	Current liabilities	$500m.
Inventory	_____	Long-term debt	_____
Current assets	_____	Total debt	_____
Fixed assets	_____	Stockholders' equity	_____
Total assets	$ _____	Total liabilities and equity	$ _____

research it! Analyzing Financial Statements

Go the Web site of Wal-Mart Stores, Inc. at **www.walmartstores.com** and get the latest financial statements from the annual report using the following steps.

Click on "Investors." Click on "Financial Information." Click on "Annual Reports." Click on the most recent date. This will bring the file onto your computer that contains the relevant data.

Using the most recent balance sheet and income statement, calculate the financial ratios for the firm, including the internal and sustainable growth rates.

integrated minicase: Working with Financial Statements

Listed below are the 2008 financial statements for Garners' Platoon Mental Health Care, Inc. Spread the balance sheet and income statement. Calculate the financial ratios for the firm, including the internal and sustainable growth rates. Using the DuPont system of analysis and the industry ratios reported below, evaluate the performance of the firm.

GARNERS' PLATOON MENTAL HEALTH CARE, INC.
Balance Sheet as of December 31, 2008
(in millions of dollars)

Assets	2008	Liabilities and Equity	2008
Current assets:		Current liabilities:	
Cash and marketable securities	$ 421	Accrued wages and taxes	$ 316
Accounts receivable	1,109	Accounts payable	867
Inventory	1,760	Notes payable	872
Total	3,290	Total	2,055
Fixed assets:		Long-term debt:	3,090
Gross plant and equipment	5,812	Stockholders' equity:	
Less: Depreciation	840	Preferred stock (25 million shares)	60
Net plant and equipment	4,972	Common stock and paid-in surplus (200 million shares)	637
Other long-term assets	892	Retained earnings	3,312
Total	5,864	Total	4,009
Total assets	$9,154	Total liabilities and equity	$9,154

GARNERS' PLATOON MENTAL HEALTH CARE, INC.
Income Statement for Years Ending December 31, 2008
(in millions of dollars)

	2008
Net sales (all credit)	$ 4,980
Less: Cost of goods sold	2,371
Gross profits	2,609
Less: Depreciation	200
Earnings before interest and taxes (EBIT)	2,409
Less: Interest	315
Earnings before taxes (EBT)	2,094
Less: Taxes	767
Net income	$ 1,327
Less: Preferred stock dividends	60
Net income available to common stockholders	$ 1,267
Less: Common stock dividends	395
Addition to retained earnings	$ 872
Per (common) share data:	
Earnings per share (EPS)	$ 6.335
Dividends per share (DPS)	$ 1.975
Book value per share (BVPS)	$ 19.745
Market value (price) per share (MVPS)	$26.850

(continued)

GARNERS' PLATOON MENTAL HEALTH CARE, INC.	INDUSTRY
Current ratio	2.0 times
Quick ratio	1.2 times
Cash ratio	0.25 times
Inventory turnover ratio	2.50 times
Days' sales in inventory	146.00 days
Average collection period	91.00 days
Average payment period	100.00 days
Fixed asset turnover ratio	1.25 times
Sales to working capital	4.00 times
Total asset turnover ratio	0.50 times
Capital intensity ratio	2.00 times
Debt ratio	50.00%
Debt-to-equity ratio	1.00 times
Equity multiplier	2.00 times
Times interest earned	7.25 times
Cash coverage ratio	8.00 times
Profit margin	18.75%
Basic earnings power ratio	19.90%
ROA	9.375%
ROE	18.75%
Dividend payout ratio	35%
Market-to-book ratio	1.300 times
PE ratio	4.100 times

ANSWERS TO TIME OUT

3-1 The three most commonly used liquidity ratios are the current ratio, the quick (or acid-test) ratio, and the cash ratio.

3-2 The current ratio measures the dollars of current assets available to pay each dollar of current liabilities. The quick ratio measures the dollars of more liquid assets (cash and marketable securities and accounts receivable) available to pay each dollar of current liabilities. The cash ratio measures the dollars of cash and marketable securities available to pay each dollar of current liabilities

3-3 The more liquid assets a firm holds, the less likely it is that the firm will experience financial distress. Thus, the higher the liquidity ratios, the less liquidity risk a firm has. But, liquid assets do not generate any profits for the firm. In contrast, fixed assets are illiquid, but generate revenue for the firm. Thus, extremely high levels of liquidity guard against liquidity crises but at the cost of lower returns on assets.

3-4 The major asset management ratios are the inventory turnover ratio, the days' sales in inventory ratio, the average collection period (ACP), the accounts receivable turnover ratio, the average payment period (APP), the accounts payable turnover ratio, the fixed asset turnover ratio, the sales to working capital ratio, the total asset turnover ratio, and the capital intensity ratio.

3-5 In general, a firm wants to produce a high level of sales per dollar of inventory. That is, it wants to turn inventory over as quickly as possible.

(continued)

However, if the inventory turnover ratio is extremely high and the days' sales in inventory is extremely low, the firm may not be holding sufficient inventory to prevent running out of the raw materials needed to keep the production process going.

In general, a firm wants to collect its accounts receivable as quickly as possible. However, if the accounts receivable turnover ratio is extremely high and the ACP is extremely low, the firm's accounts receivable policy may be so strict that customers prefer to do business with competing firms.

In general, a firm wants to pay for its purchases as slowly as possible. Thus, a high APP or a low accounts payable turnover ratio is generally a sign of good management. However, if the APP is extremely high and the accounts payable turnover ratio is extremely low, the firm may be abusing the credit terms that its raw materials suppliers offer. At some point, the firm's suppliers may revoke its ability to buy raw materials on account and the firm will lose this source of free financing.

In general, high fixed asset turnover and sales to working capital ratios are signs of good management. However, if either the fixed asset turnover or sales to working capital ratio are extremely high, the firm may be close to its maximum production capacity.

In general, the higher the total asset turnover and lower the capital intensity ratio, the more efficient the overall asset management of the firm will be. However, as described above, inventory stockouts, capacity problems, or tight account receivables policies can all lead to a high fixed asset turnover and may actually be signs of poor firm management.

3-6   Many of the ratios are mirror images of one another because the one ratio might be the inverse of another ratio. For example, the inventory turnover ratio measures the number of dollars of sales produced per dollar of inventory, while the days' sales in inventory ratio measures the number of days that inventory is held before the final product is sold.

3-7   The major debt management ratios are the debt ratio, the debt-to-equity ratio, the equity multiplier, the times interest earned ratio, the fixed-charge coverage ratio, and the cash coverage ratio.

3-8   Low levels of debt will lead to a dilution of the return to stockholders due to a greater increased usage of equity as well as not taking advantage of the tax deductibility of interest expense.

3-9   In deciding the level of debt versus equity financing to hold on the balance sheet, managers must consider the trade-off between maximizing cash flows to the firm's stockholders versus the risk of being unable to make promised debt payments. When firms do well, financial leverage creates more cash flows to share with stockholders—it magnifies the return to the stockholders of the firm. This magnification is one reason that firm stockholders encourage the use of debt financing. However, financial leverage also increases the firm's potential for financial distress and even failure. If the firm has a bad year and cannot make promised debt payments, debt holders can force the firm into bankruptcy. Thus, a firm's current and potential debt holders (and even stockholders) look at equity financing as a safety cushion that can absorb fluctuations in the firm's earnings and asset values and guarantee debt service payments.

3-10 The major profitability ratios are the profit margin, the basic earnings power ratio, the return on assets (ROA), the return on equity (ROE), and the dividend payout.

(continued)

www.mhhe.com/can1e

3-11 For all but the dividend payout ratio, the higher the value of the ratio, the higher the profitability of the firm. But just as has been the case previously in this chapter, high profitability ratio levels may result from poor management in other areas of the firm as much as superior financial management.

3-12 Generally, a high ROE is considered to be a positive sign of firm performance. However, if performance comes from a high degree of financial leverage, a high ROE can indicate a firm with an unacceptably high level of bankruptcy risk as well.

3-13 The major market value ratios are the market-to-book ratio and the price-earnings (or PE) ratio.

3-14 Generally, the higher the PE ratio, the better the firm's performance. However, for value-seeking investors, high PE firms indicate expensive companies. Further, higher PE ratios carry greater risk because investors are willing to pay higher prices today for a stock in anticipation of higher earnings in the future. These earnings may or may not materialize. Low PE firms are generally companies with little expected growth or low earnings.

3-15 The price-earnings (or PE) ratio measures how much investors are willing to pay for each dollar the firm earns per share of its stock. PE ratios are often quoted in multiples—the number of dollars per share—which fund managers, investors, and analysts compare within industry classes. Managers and investors often use PE ratios to evaluate the relative financial performance of the firm's stock.

3-16 The basic DuPont equation looks at ROA as the product of the profit margin [the firm's overall profitability as a function of the profit the firm earns per dollar of sales (operating efficiency)] and the total asset turnover ratios [the dollar of sales produced per dollar of assets on the balance sheet (efficiency in asset use)].

3-17 This presentation of ROE allows managers, analysts, and investors to look at the return on equity as a function of the net profit margin (profit per dollar of sales from the income statement), total asset turnover (efficiency in the use of assets from the balance sheet), and the equity multiplier (financial leverage from the balance sheet).

3-18 Managers, analysts, and investors can compute additional ratios by dividing all balance sheet amounts by total assets and all income statement amounts by net sales. These calculations, sometimes called "spreading the financial statements," yield what we call "common-size" financial statements that adjust for sizes.

3-19 The internal growth rate is the growth rate a firm can sustain if it uses only internal financing—that is, retained earnings—to finance future growth. The retention ratio represents the portion of net income that the firm reinvests as retained earnings. Since a firm either pays its net income as dividends to its stockholders or reinvests those funds as retained earnings, the dividend payout and the retention ratios must always add to one. The sustainable growth rate is the maximum growth rate that can be achieved when managers finance asset growth with new debt *and* retained earnings.

3-20 A firm's sustainable growth depends on four factors: (1) the profit margin (operating efficiency), (2) the total asset turnover (efficiency in asset use), (3) financial leverage (the use of debt versus equity to finance assets), and (4) profit retention (reinvestment of net income into the firm rather than paying it out as dividends).

(continued)

ANSWERS TO TIME OUT (concluded)

3-21 Time series analysis involves analyzing ratio trends over time, along with absolute ratio levels. It gives managers, analysts, and investors information about whether a firm's financial condition is improving or deteriorating.

3-22 Cross-sectional analysis involves a comparison of one firm's ratios relative to the ratios of other firms in the industry, or cross-sectional analysis. Key to cross-sectional analysis is identifying similar firms in that they compete in the same markets, have similar asset sizes, and operate in a similar manner to the firm being analyzed.

3-23 Analyzing ratio trends over time, along with absolute ratio levels, gives managers, analysts, and investors information about whether a firm's financial condition is improving or deteriorating. Cross-sectional analysis gives the manager a comparison of one firm's ratios relative to the ratios of other firms in the industry.

3-24 Data from financial statements should not be received without certain cautions. These include: (1) Financial statement data are historical; historical data may not reflect future performance. (2) Firms use different accounting procedures. (3) A firm's cross-sectional competitors may often be located around the world; financial statements for firms based outside the U.S. do not necessarily conform to GAAP. (4) Sales and expenses vary throughout the year. Managers, analysts, and investors need to note the timing of these fund flows when performing cross-sectional analysis. Similarly, firms end their fiscal years at different dates. Likewise, one-time events, such as a merger, may affect a firm's financial performance. (5) Large firms often have multiple divisions or business units engaged in different lines of business. (6) Firms often window dress their financial statements to make annual results look better.

chapter 4:
TIME VALUE OF MONEY 1: ANALYZING SINGLE CASH FLOWS

 Learning Goals

LG1 Create a cash flow time line.

LG2 Compute the future value of money.

LG3 Show how the power of compound interest increases wealth.

LG4 Calculate the present value of a payment made in the future.

LG5 Move cash flows from one year to another.

LG6 Apply the Rule of 72.

LG7 Compute the rate of return realized on selling an investment.

LG8 Calculate the number of years needed to grow an investment to a specific amount of money.

Both this chapter and the next illustrate time value of money (TVM) calculations, which we will use throughout the rest of this book. We hope that you will see what powerfull tools they are for making financial decisions. Whether you're managing the financial or other functional area of a business, or making decisions in your personal life, being able to make TVM calculations will help you make financially sound decisions.

This background will also allow you to understand why CEOs, CFOs, and other professionals make the decisions that they do. Together, this chapter and the next will present all aspects of TVM. Since some students find this topic intimidating, we split the topic into two chapters as a way of providing more examples and practice opportunities. As you see the examples and work the practice problems, we believe that you will find that TVM is not difficult.

Factors to consider when making time value of money decisions include:

- Size of the cash flows.
- Time between the cash flows.
- Rate of return we can earn.

viewpoints

Business Application

As the production manager of Head Phone Gear, Inc., you have received an offer from the supplier who provides the wires used in head sets. Due to poor planning, the supplier has an excess amount of wire and is willing to sell $500,000 worth for only $450,000. You already have one year's supply on hand. It would cost you $2,000 to store the wire until Head Phone Gear needs it next year. What implied interest rate would you be earning if you purchased and stored the wire? Should you make the purchase? **(See solution on p. 127.)**

Personal Application

Payday lending has become a multi-billion-dollar industry across the United States in just a few years. It provides people with short-term loans and gets its name from the fact that the loan is to be paid back at the borrower's next payday. Anthony is short a few hundred dollars and his next paycheck is two weeks away. For a $300 loan, Anthony must pay a $50 "fee" in advance and repay the $300 loan in two weeks. What implied interest rate would Anthony pay for this two-week period? **(See solution on p. 127.)**

A practice test can be found on the Online Learning Center at
www.mhhe.com/can1e

The basic idea behind the time value of money is that $1 today is worth more than $1 promised next year. But how much more? Is $1 today worth $1.05 next year? $1.08? $1.12? The answer varies depending on current interest rates. This chapter describes the time value of money concept and provides the tools needed to analyze single cash flows at different points in time.

4.1 Organizing Cash Flows

Managing cash flow timing is one of the most important tasks in successfully operating a business. A helpful tool for organizing our analysis is the **time line,** which shows the magnitude of cash flows at different points in time, such as monthly, quarterly, semiannually, or yearly. Cash we receive is called an **inflow,** and we denote it with a positive number. Cash that leaves us, like a payment or contribution to a deposit, is an **outflow** designated with a negative number.

The time line below illustrates a $100 deposit you made at a bank that pays 5 percent interest. In one year, the $100 has become $105. *Given that interest rate,* having $100 now (in year 0) has the same value as having $105 in one year.

Here's one way to look at this example: suppose you allowed the bank to rent your $100 for a year at a cost of 5 percent, or $5. This cost is known as the **interest rate.** Interest rates will affect you throughout your life, both in business and in your personal life. Companies borrow money to build factories and expand into new locations and markets. They expect the future revenues generated by these activities to more than cover the interest payments and repay the loan. People borrow money on credit cards and obtain loans for cars and home mortgages. They expect their purchases to give them the satisfaction in the future that compensates them for the interest payments charged on the loan. Understanding the dynamics between interest rates and cash inflows and outflows over time is key to financial success. The best place to start learning these concepts lies in understanding how money grows over time.

TIME OUT

4-1 Why is a dollar worth more today than a dollar received one year from now?

4-2 Drawing on your past classes in accounting, explain why time lines must show one negative cash flow and one positive cash flow.

4-3 Set up a time line, given a 6 percent interest rate, with a cash inflow of $200 and a cash outflow of $212 in one year.

4.2 Future Value

The $105 payment that your bank credits to your account in one year is known as a **future value (FV)** of $100 in one year at a 5 percent annual interest rate. If interest rates were higher than 5 percent, then the future value of your $100 would also be higher. If you left your money in the bank for more than one year, then its future value would continue to grow over time. Let's see why.

| | | Higher Interest Rates Lead to Higher Future Value | | table 4.1 |

TODAY'S CASH FLOW	INTEREST RATE	DOLLAR INTEREST EARNED	NEXT YEAR'S FUTURE VALUE
$ 100.00	5%	$ 5.00	$ 105.00
100.00	6	6.00	106.00
100.00	10	10.00	110.00
500.00	7.50	37.50	537.50
750.00	7.50	56.25	806.25
15,000.00	8	1,200.00	16,200.00
15,000.00	9	1,350.00	16,350.00

Single Period Future Value

Computing the future value of a sum of money one year from today is straight-forward: add the interest cost to today's cash flow. In this case:

$$\text{Value in one year} = \text{Today's Cash flow} + \text{Interest earned}$$
$$\$105 = \$100 + \$5$$

We computed the $5 interest figure by multiplying the interest rate by today's cash flow ($100 × 5%). Note that in equations, interest rates appear in decimal format. So we use 0.05 for 5 percent:

$$\$100 + (\$100 \times 0.05) = \$105$$

Note that this is the same as:

$$\$100 \times (1 + 0.05) = \$105$$

We need the 1 in the parentheses to recapture the original deposit and the 0.05 is for the interest earned. We can generalize this computation to any amount of today's cash flow. In the general form of the future value equation, we call cash today **present value,** or **PV.** We compute the future value one year from now, called FV_1, using the interest rate, i:

$$FV_1 = PV \times (1 + i) \tag{4-1}$$

Notice that this is the same equation we used to figure the future value of your $100. We've simply made it generic so we can use it over and over again. The 1 subscript means that we are calculating for only one period—in this case, one year. If interest rates were 6 percent instead of 5 percent per year, for instance, we could use equation 4-1 to find that the future value of $100 in one year is $106 [=$100 × (1 + 0.06)].

Of course, the higher the interest rate, the larger the future value will be. Table 4.1 shows the interest cost and future value for a sample of different cash flows and interest rates. Notice from the first two lines of the table that, while the difference in interest earned between 5 percent and 6 percent ($1) doesn't seem like much on a $100 deposit, the difference on a $15,000 deposit (the last two lines) is substantial ($150).

Compounding and Future Value

After depositing $100 for one year, you must decide whether to take the $105 or leave the money at the bank for another year to earn another 5 percent (or what-ever interest rate the bank currently pays). In the second year at the bank, the deposit earns 5 percent on the $105 value, which is $5.25 (= $105 × 0.05). Importantly, you get more than the $5 earned the first year, which would be a simple total of $110. The extra 25 cents earned in the second year is interest *on interest that was earned in the first year.* We call this process of earning interest on both the original deposit and on the earlier interest payments **compounding.**

So, let's illustrate a $100 deposit made for two years at 5 percent in the following time line:

Cash flow	−100				?
Period	0	5%	1	5%	2 years

The question mark denotes the amount we want to solve for. As with all TVM problems, we simply have to identify what element we're solving for; in this case, we're looking for the FV. To compute the two-year compounded future value, simply use the one-year equation (4-1) twice.

$$\$100 \times (1 + 0.05) \times (1 + 0.05) = \$110.25$$

So the future value of $100 deposited today at 5 percent interest is $110.25 in period 2. You can see that this represents $10 of interest payments generated from the original $100 ($5 each year) and $0.25 of interest earned in the second year on previously earned interest payments. The $5 of interest earned every year on the original deposit is called **simple interest.** Any amount of interest earned above the $5 in any given year comes from compounding. Over time, the new interest payments earned from compounding can become substantial. The multiyear form of equation 4-1 is the future value in year N, shown as:

$$\text{Future value in N years} = FV_N = PV \times (1 + i)^N \tag{4-2}$$

We can solve the two-year deposit problem more directly using equation 4-2 as $110.25 = $100 × (1.05)². Here, solving for FV in the equation requires solving for only one unknown. In fact, all TVM equations that you will encounter only require figuring out what is unknown in the situation and solving for that one unknown factor.

We can easily adapt equation 4-2 to many different future value problems. What is the future value in 30 years of that $100 earning 5 percent per year? Using equation 4-2, we see that the future value is $100 × (1.05)³⁰ = $432.19. The money has increased substantially! You have made a profit of $332.19 over and above your original $100. Of this profit, only $150 (= $5 × 30 years) came from simple interest earned on the original deposit. The rest, $182.19, is from the compounding effect of earning interest on previously earned interest.

Remember that the difference between earning 5 percent and 6 percent in interest on the $100 was only $1 the first year. So what is the future value difference after 15 years? Is it $15? No, as Figure 4.1 shows, the difference in future value substantially increases over time. The difference is $31.76 in year 15 and $142.15 in year 30.

THE POWER OF COMPOUNDING   Compound interest is indeed a powerful tool for building wealth. Albert Einstein, the German-American physicist who developed the special and general theories of relativity and won the Nobel Prize for Physics in 1921, is supposed to have said, "The most powerful force in the universe is compound interest."[1] Figure 4.2 illustrates this point. It shows

---

[1]No one seems to know exactly what he said, when he said it, or to whom. Similar statements commonly attributed to Einstein are: (1) compound interest is the greatest wonder of the universe, (2) compound interest is the ninth wonder of the world, and (3) it is the greatest mathematical discovery of all time. If he did not say any of these things, he (or someone else) should have!

figure 4.1

figure 4.2

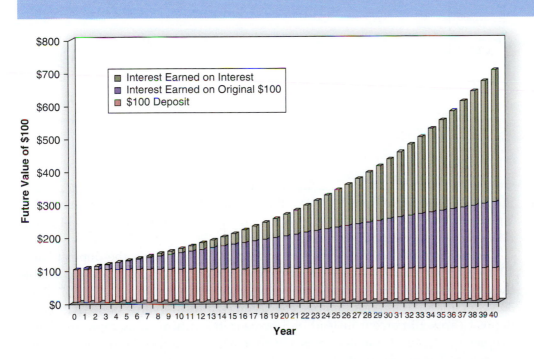

the original $100 deposited, the cumulative interest earned on that deposit, and the cumulative interest-on-interest earned. By the 27th year, the money from the interest-on-interest exceeds the interest earned on the original deposit. By the 40th year, interest-on-interest contributes more than double the interest on the deposit. The longer money can earn interest, the greater the compounding effect.

Earning higher interest rates on the investment for additional time periods magnifies compounding power. Consider the future value of $100 deposited at different interest rates and over different time periods as shown in Table 4.2. The future value of $100 earning 5 percent per year for five years is $127.63, for a profit of $27.63. Would you double your profit by simply investing that same $100 at double the interest rate, 10 percent? No, because compounding changes the nature of the investment so that your money grows exponentially, not in a

Compounding Builds Wealth Over Time				table 4.2

FUTURE VALUE OF $100 DEPOSITED AT 5%, 10%, AND 15% INTEREST RATES

	FUTURE VALUE			
INTEREST RATE EARNED	**5 YEARS**	**10 YEARS**	**20 YEARS**	**30 YEARS**
5%	$127.63	$162.89	$ 265.33	$ 432.19
10	161.05	259.37	672.75	1,744.94
15	201.14	404.56	1,636.65	6,621.18

figure 4.3

The Impact of Time and the Magnitude of the Interest Rate

Future value of $100 deposited at 5%, 10%, and 15% interest rates

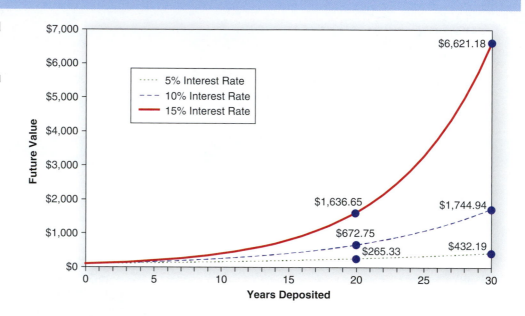

simple linear relationship. The future value of $100 in five years at 10 percent is $161.05. The $61.05 profit is *more* than double the profit of $27.63 earned at 5 percent. Tripling the interest rate to 15 percent shows a profit of $101.14 that is nearly *quadruple* the profit earned at 5 percent.

The same affect occurs when we increase the time. When the deposit earns 10 percent per year for five years, it makes a profit of $61.05. When we double the amount of time to 10 years, the return more than doubles to $159.37. After 30 years, the $100 deposit at 5 percent becomes a future value of $432.19. If the deposit earns 10 percent instead of 5 percent, the future value more than quadruples to $1,744.94. Interest rates and time **are** both important factors in compounding! These relationships are illustrated in Figure 4.3

TIME OUT

4-4 How does compounding help build wealth (or increase debt) over time?

4-5 In the previous example, how much of the $337.56 (= $1,837.56 − $1,500) paid in interest is actually interest-on-interest? (*Hint:* first compute the interest paid on the original $1,500 in each of the three years.)

LG3 **COMPOUNDING AT DIFFERENT INTEREST RATES OVER TIME** Interest rates have varied over time. In the past half-century, banks have offered depositors rates as low as 1 percent and as high as double digit rates. They've

USING A FINANCIAL CALCULATOR

Financial, or business, calculators are programmed to perform the time value of money equations we develop in this chapter and the next. The two most common types of inexpensive financial calculators that can perform such functions are the Hewlett/Packard 10B II Business Calculator and the Texas Instruments BA II (Plus or Professional). Among many useful financial shortcuts these calculators have five specific financial buttons. The relevant financial buttons for time value of money (TVM) calculations are listed below. The HPIOBII calculator buttons look like this.

1. N (for the number of periods),

2. I/YR (for the interest rate),

3. PV (for present value),

4. PMT (for a constant payment every period), and

5. FV (for future value).

Notice that the TI BA II Plus financial calculator buttons appear to be very similar:

A common, more sophisticated and expensive calculator is the TI-83. This calculator has a menu system that includes the financial functions as shown:

To get to the TVM menu, select APPLICATIONS and then choose FINANCE, and finally 1 TVM SOLVER on the previous screens.

Setting Up Your Calculator: Both of these calculators come from the factory with specific settings. You will find it useful to change two of them. The first is to set the number of digits shown after the decimal point on the calculator display. The factory setting is for two digits. However, consider a problem in which we use a 5.6 percent interest rate. The decimal version of this percentage is 0.056, which a two-digit display would round to 0.06. It's less worrisome to set the calculator to display the number of digits necessary to show the right number; this is called a *floating point display*. To set a floating point display for the HP calculator, press the color button, then the DISP button, and finally the decimal (.) button. To set the display for a floating point decimal on the TI calculator, push the 2ND button, followed by the FORMAT button, followed by the 9 button, and finally the ENTER button.

The second change you'll want to make is to set the number of times the calculator compounds each period. The settings may be preset to 12 times per period. Reset this to one time per period. To change the HP calculator to compound once per period, push the 1 button, then the color button, and finally the P/YR button. On the TI calculator, simply push the 2ND button, the P/Y button, the number one, and the ENTER button. These new settings will remain in the calculator until you either change them or remove the calculator's batteries.

Using Your Calculator: The calculators compute time-value problems in similar ways. Enter the cash flows into the time-value buttons (PV, PMT, and FV) consistent with the way they are shown in a time line. In other words, cash inflows should be positive and cash outflows negative. Thus, PV and FV cash flows are nearly always opposite in sign. Enter interest rates (I) in the percentage form, not the decimal form. Also enter the number of periods in the problem (N).

Consider our earlier example of the $100 deposit for two years earning a 5% interest rate.

1. To set the number of years, press 2 and then the N button.

2. To set the interest rate, press 5 and then the I button. (*Note* that interest rates are in percent format for using a financial calculator and in decimal format for using the equations.)

3. To enter the current cash flow: press 100, then make it negative by pressing the +/− button, then press the PV button.

4. We won't use the PMT button, so enter 0 and then the PMT button.

5. To solve for future value, press the compute button (CPT) [for the TI] and then the FV button [press the FV button only for the HP].

6. Solution: the display should show FV = 110.25

Note that the answer is positive, consistent with an inflow and the time line diagram. These values remain in the TVM registers even after the calculator is turned off. So when you start a new problem, you should clear out old values first. For the HP calculator, clear the registers by pressing the shift/orange key before pressing C. You can clear the BAII Plus calculator with the 2nd and CLR Work.

You'll notice that throughout this book we use the equations in the main text to solve time value of money problems. We provide the calculator solutions in the margins.

GRADUATION CELEBRATION LOAN

 Dominic is a fourth-year business student who wants to go on a graduation celebration/vacation in Mexico but he has no money to pay for the trip. After the vacation, Dominic will start his career. His job will require moving to a new town and buying professional clothes. He asked his parents to lend him $1,500, which he figures he will be able to pay back in three years. His parents agree to lend him the money, but they will charge 7 percent interest per year. What amount will Dominic need to pay back? How much interest will he pay?

CALCULATOR
$N = 3$
$I = 7$
$PV = 1500$
$PMT = 0$
$CPT\ FV = -1837.56$

SOLUTION: Dominic will have to pay

$$FV_3 = \$1,500 \times (1.07)^3 = \$1,500 \times 1.225 = \$1,837.56$$

Of the $1,837.56 he owes his parents, $337.56 (= $1,837.56 − $1,500) is interest. We can illustrate this time-value problem in the following time line.

Cash flow	1,500						−1,837.56
Period	0	7%	1	7%	2	7%	3 years

---

also charged interest from about 5.5 percent to 21.6 percent to consumers for various kinds of loans. Let's look at how to compute future value when rates change, so that money earns interest at multiple interest rates over time. In our first example in this chapter, your deposit of $100 earned 5 percent interest. Now consider the future value when the bank announces it will pay 6 percent interest in the second year. How much will you earn now? We can illustrate the question with this time line:

Cash flow	−100				?
Period	0	5%	1	6%	2 years

We already know that the $100 deposit will grow to $105 at the end of the first year. This $105 will then earn 6 percent in the second year and have a value of $111.30 [= $105 × (1.06)] . If we put the two steps together into one equation, the solution appears as $111.30 = $100 × (1.05) × (1.06). From this you should not be surprised that a general equation for future value of multiple interest rates is

$$\text{Future value in N periods} = FV_N = PV \times (1 + i_{\text{period 1}}) \times (1 + i_{\text{period 2}}) \times (1 + i_{\text{period 3}}) \times \cdots \times (1 + i_{\text{period } N}) \qquad \textbf{(4-3)}$$

Note that the future value equation 4-2 is a special case of the more general equation 4-3. If the interest rate every period is the same, we can write equation 4-3 as equation 4-2.

EXAMPLE 4-2

CELEBRATION LOAN WITH PAYBACK INCENTIVE

Reexamine the loan Dominic was seeking from his parents in the previous example. His parents want to give him an incentive to pay off the loan as quickly as possible. They structure the loan so they charge 7 percent interest the first year and increase the rate 1 percent each year until the loan is paid. How much will Dominic owe if he waits three years to pay off the loan? Say that in the third year he considers whether to pay off the loan or wait one more year. How much more will he pay if he waits one more year?

SOLUTION:

For a payment in the third year, Dominic will pay interest of 7 percent the first year, 8 percent the second year, and 9 percent the third year. He will have to pay

$$FV_3 = \$1,500 \times (1.07) \times (1.08) \times (1.09) = \$1,500 \times 1.2596 = \$1,889.41$$

The cash flow time line is

Even worse, if he waits until the fourth year, he will pay one year of interest at 10 percent. The total payment will be

$$FV_4 = \$1,889.41 \times (1.10) = \$2,078.35$$

Because of both the escalating interest rate and the compounding effect, Dominic must make timely and increasing payments the longer he delays in paying off the loan. Deciding in the third year to put off the payment an extra year would cost him an additional $188.94 (= $2,078.35 − $1,889.41).

4.3 Present Value

We asked earlier what happens when you deposit $100 of cash in the bank to earn 5 percent interest for one year—the bank pays you a $105 future value. However, we could have asked the question in reverse. That is, if the bank will pay $105 in one year and interest rates are 5 percent, how much would you be willing to deposit now, to receive that payment in a year? Here, we start with a future value and must find the present value—a different kind of calculation called **discounting.**

Discounting

While the process of a present value growing over time into the future is called *compounding*, the process of figuring out how much an amount that you expect to receive in the future is worth today is discounting. Just as compounding significantly increases the present value into the future, discounting significantly decreases the value of a future amount to the present. Since discounting is the reverse of compounding, we can rearrange equation 4-1 to solve for the present value of a cash flow received one year in the future.

$$\text{Present value of next period's cash flow} = PV = FV_1 \times \frac{1}{(1+i)} = FV_1 \Big/ (1+i)$$

(4-4)

Suppose the bank is going to pay $105 in one year and interest rates are 5 percent. Then the present value of the payment is $105/(1.05) = $100. Present values are always smaller than future values (as long as interest rates are greater than zero!), and the difference between what an investment is worth today and what it's worth when you're supposed to redeem it gets larger as the interest rate increases. Likewise, if the amount of time until the expected payment date increases, the deposit will also increase in value.

DISCOUNTING OVER MULTIPLE PERIODS   Discounting over multiple periods is the reverse process of compounding over multiple periods. If we know that, we can find the general equation for present value by rearranging the terms in equation 4-2 to form:

$$\text{Present value of cash flow made in N years} = PV = FV_N \times \frac{1}{(1+i)^N}$$

$$= \frac{FV_N}{(1+i)^N}$$

(4-5)

The interest rate, i, which we use to calculate present value, is often referred to as the **discount rate**. How much is a $100 payment to be made in the future worth today? Of course, it depends on how far into the future you expect to receive the payment and the discount rate used. If you receive $100 cash flow in five years, then its present value is $78.35, discounted at 5 percent:

$$PV = \$100/(1.05)^5 = \$100/1.2763 = \$78.35$$

The time line looks like this:

Cash flow	−78.35									100
Period	0	5%	1	5%	2	5%	3	5%	4	5%	5 years

If the discount rate rises to 10 percent, the present value of our $100 to be paid to us in five years is only $62.09 today. At a 15 percent interest rate, the present value declines to less than half the future cash flow: $49.72. Higher interest rates discount future cash flows more quickly and dramatically. You can see this principle illustrated in Figure 4.4.

Moving right from point A in the figure, notice that if interest rates are 0 percent, the present value will equal the future value. Also note from the curved lines that when the discount rate is greater than zero, the discounting to present value is not linear through time. The higher the discount rate, the more quickly the cash flow value falls. If the discount rate is 10 percent, a $100 cash flow that you would receive in 25 years is worth less than $10 today, as shown at point B in the figure. With a 15 percent discount rate, the $100 payment to be received in 33 years, at point C, is worth less than $1 today.

figure 4.4

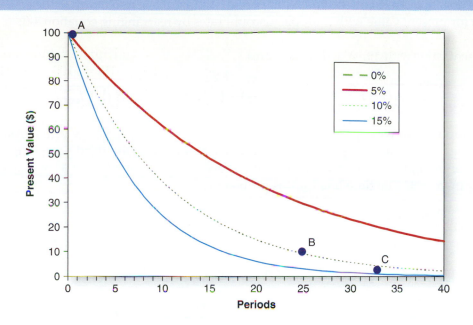

Present Value of a $100 Cash Flow Made in the Future

For interactive versions of this example visit www.mhhe.com/can1e

EXAMPLE 4-3

BUY NOW AND DON'T PAY FOR TWO YEARS

Suppose that a marketing manager for a retail furniture company proposes a sale. Customers can buy now but don't have to pay for their furniture purchases for two years. From a time value of money perspective, selling furniture at full price with payment in two years is equivalent to selling furniture at a sale, or discounted, price with immediate payment. If interest rates are 7.5 percent per year, what is the equivalent sale price of a $1,000 sleeper-sofa when the customer takes the full two years to pay for it?

SOLUTION: The time line for this problem is:

Using equation 4-5, the present value computation is

$$PV = \frac{FV_N}{(1+i)^N} = \frac{\$1,000}{1.075^2} = \frac{\$1,000}{1.1556} = \$865.33$$

CALCULATOR
N = 2
I = 7.5
PMT = 0
FV = 1000
CPT PV = −865.33

In this case, the marketing proposal for delaying payment for two years is equivalent to selling the $1,000 sleeper-sofa for a sale price of $865.33, or a 13.5 percent discount. When stores promote such sales, they often believe that customers will not be able to pay the full amount at the end of the two years and then must pay high interest rate charges and late fees. Customers who do pay on time are getting a good deal.

DISCOUNTING WITH MULTIPLE RATES We can also discount a future cash flow at different interest rates per period. We find the general form of the equation for present value with multiple discount rates by rearranging equation 4-3:

Present value with different discount rates

$$= PV = \frac{FV_N}{(1 + i_{\text{period } 1}) \times (1 + i_{\text{period } 2}) \times (1 + i_{\text{period } 3}) \times \cdots \times (1 + i_{\text{period } N})} \qquad (4\text{-}6)$$

Suppose that we expect interest rates to increase over the next few years, from 6 percent this year, to 8 percent next year, to 8.5 percent in the third year. In this environment, how would we work out the present value of a future $2,500 cash flow in year 3? The time line for this problem is

Cash flow	?							2,500
Period	0	7%	1	8%	2	8.5%	3 years

Using equation 4-6 shows that the present value is $1,993.90:

$$PV = \frac{\$2,500}{(1.07) \times (1.08) \times (1.085)} = \frac{\$2,500}{1.2538} = \$1,993.90$$

TIME OUT

4-6   How are interest rates in the economy related to the way people value future cash payments?

4-7   Explain how discounting is the reverse of compounding.

4.4 Using Present Value and Future Value

Moving Cash Flows

As managers analyze investment projects, debt management, and cash flow, they frequently find it useful to move cash flows to different points in time. While you may be planning to keep money deposited in the bank for three years when you will buy a car, life often has a way of altering plans. What type of car might you purchase if the money earns interest for only two years, or for four years? How is a corporate financial forecast affected if the firm needs to remodel a factory two years sooner than planned? Moving cash flows around in time is important to businesses and individuals alike for sound financial planning and decision making.

Moving cash flows from one point in time to another requires us to use both present value and future value equations. Specifically, use the present value equation for moving cash flows *earlier* in time, and the future value cash flows for moving cash flows *later* in time. For example, what's the value in year 2 of a $200 cash flow to be received in three years, when interest rates are 6 percent? This problem requires moving the $200 payment in the third year to a value in the second year, as shown in the time line:

Cash flow					?		200
Period	0		1		2	6%	3 years

WHEN INTEREST RATES ARE	A CASH FLOW OF	IN YEAR	CAN BE MOVED TO YEAR	WITH EQUATION	EQUIVALENT CASH FLOW
8%	$1,000	5	10	$FV_{10} = PV_5 \times (1 + i)^5 = \$1,000 \times (1.08)^5 =$	$1,469.33
8	1,000	5	2	$PV_2 = FV_5 / (1 + i)^3 = \$1,000 / (1.08)^3 =$	793.83
10	500	9	10	$FV_{10} = PV_9 \times (1 + i)^1 = \$500 \times (1.10)^1 =$	550.00
10	500	9	8	$PV_8 = FV_9 / (1 + i)^1 = \$500 / (1.10)^1 =$	454.55
10	500	9	0	$PV_0 = FV_9 / (1 + i)^9 = \$500 / (1.10)^9 =$	212.05
12	100	4	20	$FV_{20} = PV_4 \times (1 + i)^{16} = \$100 \times (1.12)^{16} =$	613.04
12	100	4	30	$FV_{30} = PV_4 \times (1 + i)^{26} = \$100 \times (1.12)^{26} =$	1,904.01

Since the cash flow is to be moved one year *earlier* in time, we use the present value equation

$$PV_2 = FV_3/(1 + i)^1 = \$200/(1.06)^1 = \$188.68.$$

When interest rates are 6 percent, a $188.68 payment in year 2 equates to a $200 payment in year 3.

What about moving the $200 cash flow to year 5? Since this requires moving the cash flow later in time by two years, we use the future value equation. In this case, the equivalent of $200 in the third year is a fifth-year payment of

$$FV_5 = PV_3 \times (1 + i)^2 = \$200 \times (1.06)^2 = \$200 \times 1.1236 = \$224.72$$

Table 4.3 illustrates how we might move several cash flows. At an 8 percent interest rate, a $1,000 cash flow due in year 5 compounded to year 10 equals $1,469.33. We could also discount that same $1,000 cash flow to a value of $793.83 in year 2. At an 8 percent interest rate, the three cash flows ($793.83 in year 2, $1,000 in year 5, and $1,469.33 in year 10) become equivalent. Table 4.3 illustrates the movement of other cash flows given different interest rates and time periods.

Moving cash flows from one year to another creates an easy way to compare or combine two cash flows. Would you rather receive $150 in year 2 or $160 in year 2? Since both cash flows occur in the same year, the comparison is straightforward. But we can't directly add or compare cash flows in different years until we consider their time value. We can compare cash flows in different years by moving one cash flow to the same time as the other using the present value or future value equations. Once you have the value of each cash flow in the same year, you can directly compare or combine them.

RULE OF 72 Albert Einstein is also credited with popularizing compound interest by introducing a simple mathematical approximation for the number of years required to double an investment. It's called the **Rule of 72.**

$$\text{Approximate number of years to double an investment} = \frac{72}{\text{Interest rate}} \quad \text{(4-7)}$$

The Rule of 72 illustrates the power of compound interest. How many years will it take to double money deposited at 6 percent per year? Using the Rule of 72, we find the answer is 12 years (72/6). A higher interest rate causes faster increases in future value. A 9 percent interest rate allows money to double in just eight years. Remember that this rule provides only a mathematical approximation. It's more

PAY DAMAGES OR APPEAL?

 Timber Inc. lost a lawsuit in a business dispute. The judge ordered the company to pay the plaintiff $175,000 in one year. Timber's attorney advises Timber to appeal the ruling. If so, Timber will likely lose again and will still have to pay the $175,000. But by appealing, Timber moves the $175,000 payment to year 2, along with the attorney's fee of $20,000 for the extra work. The interest rate is 7 percent. What decision should Timber make?

SOLUTION:

CALCULATOR
N = 1
I = 7
PMT = 0
FV = 195000
CPT PV = −182,242.99

Timber executives must decide whether to pay $175,000 in one year or $195,000 in two years. To compare the two choices more directly, move the payment in year 2 to year 1 and then compare it to $175,000. Timber should choose to make the smaller payment. The computation is:

$$PV_1 = FV_2/(1+i)^1 = \$195,000/(1.07)^1 = \$182,242.99$$

The value in year 1 of a year 2 payment of $195,000 is $182,242.99, which is clearly more than the $175,000 year 1 payment. So Timber should *not* appeal and should pay the plaintiff $175,000 in one year (and may want to look for another attorney).

---

accurate with lower interest rates. After all, with a 72 percent interest rate, the rule predicts that it will take one year to double the money. However, we know that it actually takes a 100 percent rate to double money in one year.

We can also use the Rule of 72 to approximate the interest rate needed to double an investment in a specific amount of time. What rate do we need to double an investment in 5 years? Rearranging equation 4-7 shows that the rate needed is 14.4 percent (72/5) per year.

TIME OUT

4-8 In the problem above, could Timber Inc. have performed its analysis by moving the $175,000 to year 2 and comparing? Would the firm then have made the same decision?

4-9 At what interest rate (and number of years) does the Rule of 72 become too inaccurate to use?

4.5 Computing Interest Rates

 Time value of money calculations come in handy when we know two cash flows and need to find the interest rate. The investment industry often uses this analysis. Solving for the interest rate, or rate of return,[2] can answer questions like, "If you bought a gold coin for $350 three years ago and sell it now for $475, what rate of return have you earned?" The time line for this problem looks like this:

| Cash flow | −350 | | | 475 |
| Period | 0 | 1 | ?% 2 | 3 years |

[2]The terms *interest rate* and *rate of return* are referring to the same thing. However, it is a common convention to refer to interest rate when you are the one paying the cash flows and refer to rate of return when you are the one receiving the cash flows.

FAD "INVESTMENTS"

Periodically, seemingly ordinary items become popular "investments." The past several decades have seen the rise and subsequent decline in popularity of collectible baseball cards, Beatles memorabilia, Pokèmon items, POGs, and other items. Without any real rationale, people collected them and treated them like investments.

Remember the Beanie Baby craze of the late 1990s? Beanie Babies are small beanbag animals with cute names like "Bucky" the beaver. Ty, Inc. makes these toys in limited numbers and sells them for about $5 each. As they became popular, people tried to collect them all, insisting that one day their "collections" would become priceless. The demand for Beanie Babies skyrocketed, and so did their price. Many "retired" Beanies sold for $10 one year and $50 the next. Rare Beanies such as Peanut (the Royal

Blue Elephant) sold for over $4,000 in online auctions. If you had bought Peanut for $5 and saw its price rise to $5,000 in three years, your annual return would have been 900 percent per year!

Then, seemingly overnight, the demand for Beanie Babies dried up. People who had bought dozens of the darlings at inflated prices all tried to sell at once. As collectors became sellers, the toys' prices plummeted. If you had bought Peanut for $5,000 at its peak, you would have experienced its price collapse six years later to $5.99, representing a −67.4 annual return. During the same period, Derby the Horse lost 70.8 percent per year; Pinchers the Lobster lost 72.2 percent per year, and Chilly the Polar Bear lost 66.8 percent per year.

Beware the fad "investment."

 want to know more? **Key Words to Search for Updates: collectible, Beanie Baby, bubble, memorabilia**

In general, computing interest rates is easiest with a financial calculator. To compute the answer using the time-value equations, consider how the cash flows fit into the future value equation 4-2:

$$FV_N = PV \times (1 + i)^N$$
$$475 = 350 \times (1 + i)^3$$
Rearranging gives $475/350 = (1 + i)^3$
or, $\quad 1.357 = (1 + i)^3$

CALCULATOR
N = 3
PV = −350
PMT = 0
FV = 475
CPT I = 10.716

To solve for the interest rate, i, take the third root of both sides of the equation. To do this, take 1.357 to the 1/3 power using the y^x button on your calculator.[3] Doing this leads to:

$$1.107 = (1 + i), \text{ or } i = 0.107 = 10.7\%$$

If you buy a gold coin for $350 and sell it three years later for $475, you earn a 10.7 percent return per year.

Time is an important factor in computing the return that you're earning per year. Turning a $100 investment into $200 is a 100 percent return. If your investments earn this much in two years, then they earned a 41.42 percent rate of return per year [computed as: $100 \times (1.4142)^2 = 200$]. Table 4.4 shows the annual interest rate earned for doubling an investment over various time periods. Notice how compounding complicates the solution: It's not as simple as just dividing by the number of years. Getting a 100 percent return in two years means earning 41.42 percent per year, not 50 percent per year. Table 4.4 also shows the Rule of 72 interest rate estimate.

---

[3]The general equation for computing the interest rate is $i = \left(FV_N / PV\right)^{\frac{1}{N}} - 1$.

Interest Rate per Year to Double an Investment		table 4.4
NUMBER OF YEARS TO DOUBLE INVESTMENT	**PRECISE ANNUAL INTEREST RATE**	**RULE OF 72 INTEREST RATE ESTIMATE**
1	100.00%	72.00%
2	41.42	36.00
3	25.99	24.00
4	18.92	18.00
5	14.87	14.40
6	12.25	12.00
7	10.41	10.29
8	9.05	9.00
9	8.01	8.00
10	7.18	7.20
15	4.73	4.80
20	3.53	3.60
25	2.81	2.88
30	2.34	2.40

MATH COACH

When using a financial calculator to compute an interest rate between two cash flows, you must enter one cash flow as a negative number. This is because you must inform the calculator which payments are cash inflows and which are cash outflows. If you input all the cash flows as the same sign, the calculator will show an error when asked to compute the interest rate.

Return Asymmetries

Suppose you bought a gold coin for $700 last year and now the market would only pay you $350. Clearly, the investment earned a negative rate of return. Use a financial calculator or a time-value equation to verify that this is a return of −50 percent. You lost half your money! So, in order to break even and get back to $700, you need to earn a positive 50 percent, right? Wrong. Note that to get from $350 to $700, your money needs to double! You need a 100 percent return to make up for a 50 percent decline. Similarly, you need a gain of 33.33 percent to make up for a 25 percent decline. If your investment declines by 10 percent, you'll need an 11.1 percent gain to offset the loss. In general, only a higher positive return can offset any given negative return.

TIME OUT

4-10   Say you double your money in three years. Explain why the rate of return is NOT 33.3 percent per year.

4-11   Show that you must earn a 25 percent return to offset a 20 percent loss.

4.6 Solving for Time

 LG8

Sometimes you may need to determine the time period needed to accumulate a specific amount of money. If you know the starting cash flow, the interest rate, and the future cash flow (the sum you will need), you can solve the time value equations for the number of years that you will need to accumulate that money. Just as with solving for different interest rates, solving for the number of periods is complicated and requires using natural logarithms.[4] Many people prefer to use a financial calculator to solve for the number of periods.

[4]The equation for solving for the number of periods is $N = \dfrac{\ln\left(FV_N/PV\right)}{\ln(1 + i)}$.

Business Application Solution

You must compare the cash flows of buying the wire now at a discount, or waiting one year. The cost of the wire should include both the supplier's bill and the storage cost, for a total of $452,000. What interest rate is implied by a $452,000 cash flow today versus $500,000 in one year? Using equation 4-2:

$$FV_N = PV \times (1 + i)^N$$
$$500,000 = 452,000 \times (1 + i)^1$$
$$i = 500,000/452,000 - 1 = 0.1062 \text{ or } 10.62\%$$

CALCULATOR
N = 1
PV = −452000
PMT = 0
FV = 500000
CPT I = 10.62

Whether your company should purchase the wire today depends on the cost of the firm's capital (discussed in Chapter 11). If it costs the firm less than 10.6 percent to obtain cash, then you should purchase the wire today. Otherwise, you should not.

Personal Application Solution

Since Anthony's loan of $300 requires an immediate $50 payment, the actual cash flow is $250 (= $300 − $50). He then must repay the full $300. Use equation 4-2 to compute the interest rate you pay for the period:

$$FV_N = PV \times (1 + i)^N$$
$$300 = 250 \times (1 + i)^1$$
$$i = 300/250 - 1 = 0.02 \text{ or } 20\%$$

CALCULATOR
N = 1
PV = −250
PMT = 0
FV = 300
CPTI = = 20.00

Anthony is paying 20 percent for a loan of only two weeks! This is equivalent to paying 11,348 percent per year (this is shown in Chapter 5). He will never be able to build wealth if he continue to pay interest rates like this. Indeed, many people get trapped in a continuing cycle, obtaining one payday loan after another.

When interest rates are 9 percent, how long will it take for a $5,000 investment to double? Finding the solution with a financial calculator entails entering

- I = 9
- PV = −5,000
- PMT = 0
- FV = 10,000

The answer is 8.04 years, or eight years and two weeks. The Rule of 72 closely approximates the answer, which predicts eight years (72 ÷ 9).

 For interactive versions of this example visit www.mhhe.com/can1e

EXAMPLE 4-5

GROWTH IN STAFFING NEEDS

Say that you are the sales manager of a company that produces software for human resource departments. You are planning your staffing needs, which depend on the volume of sales over time. Your company currently sells $350 million of merchandise per year and has grown

(continued)

7 percent per year in the past. If this growth rate continues, how long will it be before the firm reaches $500 million in sales? How long before it reaches $600 million?

SOLUTION:

You could set up the following time line to illustrate the problem:

Cash flow	350			500	
Period	0	1	7%	2	? years

As shown in the margin, $350 million of sales growing at 7 percent per year will reach $500 million in five years and three months. To reach $600 million will take just two weeks short of eight years.

CALCULATOR

I = 7
PV = −350
PMT = 0
FV = 500
CPTN = 5.27

TIME OUT

4-12 In the example above, how long will it take your company to double its sales?

4-13 In what other areas of business can these time-value concepts be used?

summary of learning goals

In this chapter, we introduce the concept of the time value of money. We describe the tools used to determine how money today grows over time. The same tools, once rearranged, also can determine the value of a future cash flow today, as $100 paid in the future is worth less than $100 today. Other useful applications of the time-value equations include determining the rate earned on an investment or figuring out how long it will take an investment to reach a specific amount of money. The next chapter continues with this topic and introduces intra-year compounding and how to handle multiple cash flows.

LG1 Create a cash flow time line. The first step in analyzing a time-value problem is to identify the cash inflows and outflows, the time when they occur, and the pertinent interest rate. Organizing the specific factors that appear in TVM equations makes finding the answers more straightforward.

LG2 Compute the future value of money. Money deposited today at a bank will grow to a larger amount next year. The higher the interest rate, or the longer the money is left to grow, the greater the final amount will be. Future values are larger than present values.

LG3 Show how the power of compound interest increases wealth. The interest payment earned in the first year adds to the deposit for the second

year. In the second year of the deposit with compounding, both the original deposit and the interest earned in the first year will earn interest. Over time, compound interest earned on prior interest payments can become substantial. At times, different interest rates may apply to compound future value over time.

Earning just 1 percent more in interest rate every year results in much higher future values over time. Doubling the interest rate can mean triple or even quadruple earnings over 20 or 30 years. Time has the same effect. Doubling the time that money is invested more than doubles the amount of profits earned.

LG4 Calculate the present value of a payment made in the future. A dollar paid (or received) in the future is not worth as much as a dollar paid today. Computing the present value of a future payment made in the future is called *discounting*. The interest rate used to determine the present value is the discount rate. As long as the discount rate is positive, present values are smaller than future values. Higher discount rates cause the value of the future value to decline more quickly and dramatically.

LG5 **Move cash flows from one year to another.** A cash flow may actually occur in a year other than originally planned. To evaluate the effect, we use the future value equation to move cash flows later in time and the present value equation to move cash flows earlier in time until all cash flows are expressed in the same period. By moving one cash flow to the same year as the other, we can directly compare them.

LG6 **Apply the Rule of 72.** To approximate the length of time needed to double a sum of money, simply divide 72 by the interest rate. The Rule of 72 is useful for estimating interest rates at or below 15

percent but deviates too much from true values at higher interest rates.

LG7 **Compute the rate of return realized on selling an investment.** The number of years between the present and future cash flows is an important factor in determining the annual rate earned. Because we compute rates of return using the beginning-period value of an investment, investments that feature gains and losses may become asymmetric between gains and losses. You double your investment with a 100 percent return but lose all your profits with a 50 percent decline in price.

LG8 **Calculate the number of years needed to grow an investment to a specific amount of money.** You can use the time-value equations and a business calculator to compute the number of years to reach a specific level of desired growth. The higher the interest rate, the shorter the time period needed to achieve the growth.

chapter equations

4-1   Future value $FV_1 = PV \times (1 + i)$

4-2   Future value in N years $= FV_N = PV \times (1 + i)^N$

4-3   Future value in N periods $= FV_N = PV \times (1 + i_{period\ 1}) \times (1 + i_{period\ 2})$
$$\times (1 + i_{period\ 3}) \times \cdots \times (1 + i_{period\ N})$$

4-4   Present value of next period's cash flow $= PV = FV_1/(1 + i)$

4-5   Present value of cash flow made in N years $= PV = \dfrac{FV_N}{(1 + i)^N}$

4-6   Present value with different discount rates
$$= PV = \frac{FV_N}{(1 + i_{period\ 1}) \times (1 + i_{period\ 2}) \times (1 + i_{period\ 3}) \times \cdots \times (1 + i_{period\ N})}$$

4-7   Approximate number of years to double an investment $= \dfrac{72}{\text{Interest rate}}$

key terms

compounding, The process of adding interest earned every period on both the original investment and the reinvested earnings. (p. 114)

discounting, The process of finding present value by reducing future values using the discount, or interest, rate. (p. 119)

discount rate, The interest rate used to discount future cash flow(s) to the present. (p. 120)

future value, The value of an investment after one or more periods. (p. 112)

inflow Cash received, often from income or sale of an investment. (p. 112)

interest rate, The cost of borrowing money denoted as a percent. (p. 112)

outflow, Cash payment, often a cost or the price of an investment or deposit. (p. 112)

present value, The amount a future cash flow is worth today. (p. 113)

Rule of 72, An approximation for the number of years it will take an investment to double in value. (p. 123)

simple interest, Interest earned only on the original deposit. (p. 114)

time line, A graphical representation showing the size and timing of cash flows through time. (p. 112)

self-test problems with solutions

LG2, LG5

1   **Two Future Values** You have entered a consulting deal with a company. You are to complete two projects. The first project will take one year to finish. The second project will take two years and must be started immediately following the first one. The deal includes a provision in which the company will make a $10,000 payment to your retirement plan after the first project and $20,000 after the second project. You have 20 years until retirement and will earn 9 percent per year on your retirement plan money. How much money will you have for retirement from these two payments?

Solution:

The future value of each payment can be computed and then added together in year 20. The $10,000 payment will be paid in one year and compounded for 19 years:

CALCULATOR
N = 19
I = 9
PV = −10000
PMT = 0
CPT FV = 51,416.61

$$FV_N = PV \times (1 + i)^N$$
$$FV_{19} = 10{,}000 \times (1 + 0.09)^{19}$$
$$= 10{,}000 \times 5.1417$$
$$= 51{,}416.61$$

So the first payment will grow to $51,416.61 by your planned retirement.

The $20,000 payment will be paid in three years and compounded for 17 years:

CALCULATOR
N = 17
I = 9
PV = −20000
PMT = 0
CPT FV = 86,552.67

$$FV_N = PV \times (1 + i)^N$$
$$FV_{17} = 20{,}000 \times (1 + 0.09)^{17}$$
$$= 20{,}000 \times 4.328$$
$$= 86{,}552.67$$

So the second payment will grow to $86,552.67. Because both payments are now moved to Year 20, they can be combined. The money available in 20 years will be $137,969.28 (= $51,416.61 + $86,552.67).

LG4

2   **Present Value** You have decided to leave the small advertising firm where you are a partner. The partnership agreement among the partners states that if a partner leaves, that person's ownership in the firm is "cashed out" with an immediate payment consisting of 5 percent of last year's revenue. Last year the firm had revenue of $1 million. But your partners would rather not have to pay out this big cash flow to you this year because they are expecting much more business soon. In fact, they believe that they will be earning revenues of $1.5 million in just two years. So, they offer you a choice between taking 5 percent of last year's revenue now, or taking 4 percent of expected revenue in two years. If you believe an appropriate discount rate is 10 percent, which cash out payment should you accept?

Solution:

You should find the present value of the alternative and compare it to the deal to receive payment now. If things go as expected, waiting two years would result in a payment of $60,000 (= $1.5 million × 0.04). The present value of this future payment can be computed as:

$$PV = FV_N/(1 + i)^N$$
$$PV = 60,000/(1 + 0.10)^2$$
$$= 60,000/1.21$$
$$= \$49,586.78$$

The present value of the "wait two years" alternative is $49,586.78. Getting a cash out payment now would be $50,000 (= $1 million × 0.05). Because the immediate cash out is worth more, on a time-value basis, you should take it now. Also note that the waiting alternative is risky. You might get less if the firm does not grow as expected.

3 **Computing Rates of Return** Say that you invested $1,000 and found two years later that the investment had fallen to $600. Your hopes are that the investment will get back to even during the next two years. What was the annual rate of return earned in the first two years? What rate would need to be earned in the next two years to break even? Show a time line of the problem.

Solution:

The time line for the problem is shown below. The single question mark (?) and double question mark (??) show the two rates to be computed.

Cash flow	−1,000		600		1,000
Period 0	?%	1	?%	2	??% 3 ??% 4 years

To solve for the first two year annual rates, use the future value equation:

$$FV_N = PV \times (1 + i)^N$$
$$600 = 1,000 \times (1 + i)^2$$

rearranging gives:

$$0.6 = (1 + i)^2$$
$$i = -0.2254 \text{ or } -22.54 \text{ percent}$$

The annual return for the first two years was −22.54 percent.

To solve for the next two year annual rate, use the future value equation again:

$$FV_N = PV \times (1 + i)^N$$
$$1,000 = 600 \times (1 + i)^2$$

rearranging gives:

$$1.67 = (1 + i)^2$$
$$i = 0.291 \text{ or } 29.1 \text{ percent}$$

Notice the asymmetry: It will take you two years of 29.10 percent returns to offset two years of −22.54 percent returns.

4 **Computing Time Periods** Consider that you, a college student, have recently been given a trust fund from your grandparents. The grandparents were concerned about giving a large amount of money to a young person with no experience earning, managing, or investing money. Therefore, they set up the trust so that the $1 million inheritance would have to triple in value to $3 million before you can have access to it. They figured this would give you time to learn more about finance. Now you want to estimate how long it will be before you can start spending some of the money. How long will you have to wait if the fund earns an interest rate of 4 percent, 6 percent, or 9 percent per year?

Solution:

Using the financial calculator, you can solve for the number of years. This is done for the 4 percent interest rate; refer to the calculator hint in the margin.
Earning 4 percent per year, it will take 28 years for the trust fund to triple in size. You could easily compute the time it will take earning 6 percent by entering 6 into the interest rate (I) button and recomputing the periods. Earning 6 percent, it will take 18 years, 10 months and two weeks. If the fund earns 9 percent, it will take 12 years and 9 months to triple. It looks like you are going to have plenty of time to learn about money!

CALCULATOR

I	= 4
PV	= −1
PMT	= 0
FV	= 3
CPT N	= 28.01

questions

1. List and describe the purpose of each part of a time line with an initial cash inflow and a future cash outflow. Which cash flows should be negative and which positive? Why? *(LG1)*

2. How are the present value and future value related? *(LG2)*

3. Would you prefer to have in investment earning 5 percent for 40 years or an investment earning 10 percent for 20 years? Explain. *(LG3)*

4. How are present values affected by changes in interest rates? *(LG4)*

5. What do you think about the following statement? "I am going to receive $100 two years from now and $200 three years from now, so I am getting a $300 future value." How could the two cash flows be compared or combined? *(LG5)*

6. Show how the Rule of 72 can be used to approximate the number of years to quadruple an investment. *(LG6)*

7. Without making any computations, indicate which of each pair has a higher interest rate: *(LG7)*

   a. $100 doubles to $200 in five years *or* seven years.

   b. $500 increases in four years to $750 *or* to $800.

   c. $300 increases to $450 in two years *or* increases to $500 in three years.

8. A $1,000 investment has doubled to $2,000 in eight years because of a 9 percent rate of return. How much longer will it take for the investment to reach $4,000 if it continues to earn a 9 percent rate? *(LG8)*

problems

4-1 **Time Line** Show the time line for a $300 cash inflow today, a $363 cash outflow in year 2, and a 10 percent interest rate. *(LG1)*

4-2 **Time Line** Show the time line for a $400 cash outflow today, a $518 cash inflow in year three, and a 9% interest rate. *(LG1)*

4-3 **One Year Future Value** What is the future value of $500 deposited for one year earning a 9 percent interest rate annually? *(LG2)*

4-4 **One Year Future Value** What is the future value of $400 deposited for one year earning an interest rate of 11 percent per year? *(LG2)*

4-5 **Multiyear Future Value** How much would be in your savings account in eight years after depositing $150 today if the bank pays 7 percent per year? *(LG3)*

4-6 **Multiyear Future Value** Compute the value in 25 years of a $1,000 deposit earning 10 percent per year. *(LG3)*

4-7 **Compounding with Different Interest Rates** A deposit of $350 earns the following interest rates:

    a. 8 percent in the first year.

    b. 7 percent in the second year.

    c. 5 percent in the third year.

What would be the third year future value? *(LG3)*

4-8 **Compounding with Different Interest Rates** A deposit of $750 earns interest rates of 10 percent in the first year and 12 percent in the second year. What would be the second year future value? *(LG3)*

4-9 **Discounting One Year** What is the present value of a $250 payment in one year when the discount rate is 10 percent? *(LG4)*

4-10 **Discounting One Year** What is the present value of a $400 payment in one year when the discount rate is 7 percent? *(LG4)*

4-11 **Present Value** What is the present value of a $1,500 payment made in five years when the discount rate is 8 percent? *(LG4)*

4-12 **Present Value** Compute the present value of an $850 payment made in 10 years when the discount rate is 12 percent. *(LG4)*

4-13 **Present Value with Different Discount Rates** Compute the present value of $1,000 paid in three years using the following discount rates: 6 percent in the first year, 7 percent in the second year, and 6 percent in the third year. *(LG4)*

4-14 **Present Value with Different Discount Rates** Compute the present value of $5,000 paid in two years using the following discount rates: 8 percent in the first year and 7 percent in the second year. *(LG4)*

4-15 **Rule of 72** Approximately how many years does it take to double a $100 investment when interest rates are 7 percent per year? *(LG6)*

4-16 **Rule of 72** Approximately how many years does it take to double a $500 investment when interest rates are 10 percent per year? *(LG6)*

4-17 **Rule of 72** Approximately what interest rate is needed to double an investment over five years? *(LG6)*

4-18 Rule of 72 Approximately what interest rate is earned when an investment doubles over 12 years? *(LG6)*

4-19 Rates over One Year Determine the interest rate earned on a $1,500 deposit when $1,700 is paid back in one year. *(LG7)*

4-20 Rates over One Year Determine the interest rate earned on a $2,300 deposit when $2,700 is paid back in one year. *(LG7)*

4-21 Interest-on-Interest Consider a $1,000 deposit earning 8 percent interest per year for five years. What is the future value, and how much total interest is earned on the original deposit vs. how much is interest earned on interest? *(LG3)*

4-22 Interest-on-Interest Consider a $5,000 deposit earning 9 percent interest per year for 10 years. What is the future value, how much total interest is earned on the original deposit, and how much is interest earned on interest? *(LG3)*

4-23 Comparing Cash Flows What would be more valuable, receiving $500 today or receiving $625 in three years if interest rates are 9 percent? Why? *(LG5)*

4-24 Comparing Cash Flows Which cash flow would you rather pay, $400 today or $500 in two years if interest rates are 10 percent? Why? *(LG5)*

4-25 Moving Cash Flows What is the value in year 3 of a $700 cash flow made in year 7 if interest rates are 10 percent? *(LG5)*

4-26 Moving Cash Flows What is the value in year 4 of a $900 cash flow made in year 6 if interest rates are 8 percent? *(LG5)*

4-27 Moving Cash Flows What is the value in year 10 of a $1,000 cash flow made in year 5 if interest rates are 9 percent? *(LG5)*

4-28 Moving Cash Flows What is the value in year 15 of a $250 cash flow made in year 3 if interest rates are 12 percent? *(LG5)*

4-29 Solving for Rates What annual rate of return is earned on a $1,000 investment when it grows to $2,500 in six years? *(LG7)*

4-30 Solving for Rates What annual rate of return is earned on a $5,000 investment when it grows to $9,500 in five years? *(LG7)*

4-31 Solving for Time How many years (and months) will it take $2 million to grow to $5 million with an annual interest rate of 7 percent? *(LG8)*

4-32 Solving for Time How long will it take $2,000 to reach $6,000 when it grows at 10 percent per year? *(LG8)*

4-33 Future Value At age 30 you invest $1,000 that earns 9 percent each year. At age 40 you invest $1,000 that earns 12 percent per year. In which case would you have more money at age 60? *(LG2)*

4-34 Future Value At age 25 you invest a $1,500 that earns 8 percent each year. At age 40 you invest $1,500 that earns 11 percent per year. In which case would you have more money at age 65? *(LG2)*

4-35 Solving for Rates You invested $2,000 in the stock market one year ago. Today, the investment is valued at $1,500. What return did you earn? What return would you need to get next year to break even overall? *(LG7)*

4-36 Solving for Rates You invested $3,000 in the stock market one year ago. Today, the investment is valued at $3,500. What return did you earn?

What return would you suffer next year for your investment to be valued at the original $3,000? *(LG7)*

4-37 **Solving for Rates** What annual rate of return is earned on a $4,000 investment made in year 2 when it grows to $7,000 by the end of year 6? *(LG7)*

4-38 **Solving for Rates** What annual rate of return is implied on a $2,500 loan taken next year when $3,500 must be repaid in year 4? *(LG7)*

4-39 **General TVM** Ten years ago, Hailey invested $2,000 and locked in a 9 percent annual interest rate for 30 years (end 20 years from now). Aidan can make a 20-year investment today and lock in a 10 percent interest rate. How much money should he invest now in order to have the same amount of money in 20 years as Hailey? *(LG2, LG4)*

4-40 **Moving Cash Flows** You are scheduled to *receive* a $500 cash flow in one year, a $1,000 cash flow in two years, and *pay* a $800 payment in three years. If interest rates are 10 percent per year, what is the combined present value of these cash flows? *(LG5)*

4-41 **Excel Problem** Oil prices have increased a great deal in the last decade. The table below shows the average oil price for each year since 1949. Many companies use oil products as a resource in their own business operations (like airline firms and manufacturers of plastic products). Managers of these firms will keep a close watch on how rising oil prices will impact their costs. The interest rate in the PV/FV equations can also be interpreted as a growth rate in sales, costs, profits, and so on (see Example 4-5).

a. Using the 1949 oil price and the 1968 oil price, compute the annual growth rate in oil prices during those 19 years.

b. Compute the annual growth rate between 1969 and 1988 and between 1989 and 2007.

c. Given the price of oil in 2007 and your computed growth rate between 1989 and 2007, compute the future price of oil in 2010, 2015, and 2020.

AVERAGE OIL PRICES

YEAR	PER BARREL	YEAR	PER BARREL	YEAR	PER BARREL
1949	$2.54	1969	$ 3.09	1989	$15.86
1950	$2.51	1970	$ 3.18	1990	$20.03
1951	$2.53	1971	$ 3.39	1991	$16.54
1952	$2.53	1972	$ 3.39	1992	$15.99
1953	$2.68	1973	$ 3.89	1993	$14.25
1954	$2.78	1974	$ 6.87	1994	$13.19
1955	$2.77	1975	$ 7.67	1995	$14.62
1956	$2.79	1976	$ 8.19	1996	$18.46
1957	$3.09	1977	$ 8.57	1997	$17.23
1958	$3.01	1978	$ 9.00	1998	$10.87
1959	$2.90	1979	$12.64	1999	$15.56
1960	$2.88	1980	$21.59	2000	$26.72
1961	$2.89	1981	$31.77	2001	$21.84
1962	$2.90	1982	$28.52	2002	$22.51
1963	$2.89	1983	$26.19	2003	$27.54
1964	$2.88	1984	$25.88	2004	$38.93
1965	$2.86	1985	$24.09	2005	$46.47
1966	$2.88	1986	$12.51	2006	$58.30
1967	$2.92	1987	$15.40	2007	$64.67
1968	$2.94	1988	$12.58		

research it! Stock Market Returns

What kind of returns might you expect in the stock market? One way to measure how the stock market has performed is to examine the rate of return of the S&P 500 Index. To see historical returns of the S&P 500 Index, go to Standard & Poor's Web site at **www.standardandpoors.com.** Click on "Indices" on the side menu and then "view total return" under the S&P 500 title. Lastly, scroll down and click the link "S&P 500 historical returns." This opens an Excel spreadsheet of returns over various periods.

Examine the 1-year, 5-year, and 10-year total returns over time. What do you conclude about the returns during each of these periods?

integrated minicase: Investing in Gold

People have had a fascination with gold for thousands of years. Archaeologists have discovered gold jewelry in Southern Iraq dating to 3000 BC and gold ornaments in Peru dating to 1200 BC. The ancient Egyptians were masters in the use of gold for jewelry, ornaments, and economic exchange. By 1000 BC, squares of gold were a legal form of money in China. The Romans issued a popular gold coin called the Aureus (*aureus* is the Latin word for gold). By 1100 AD, gold coins had been issued by several European countries. Gold has been a highly sought-after asset all over the world and has always retained at least some economic value over thousands of years.

The United States has had a very chaotic history with gold. For example, in the Great Depression, President Franklin D. Roosevelt banned the export of gold and ordered U.S. citizens to hand in all the gold they possessed. It was not until the end of 1974 that the ban on gold ownership by U.S. citizens was lifted. By 1986, the U.S. government's attitude on gold ownership had completely turned around, as evidenced by the resumption of the U.S. Mint's production of gold coins with the American Eagle. However, U.S. investors have little more than 30 years of gold-investing experience. Figure 4.5 shows how the price of gold per Troy ounce has changed since 1974.

These end-of-December prices do not illustrate the true magnitude of the price bubble in gold prices that occurred in 1980. The price of gold increased from $512 at the end of 1979 to a top of $870 on January 21, 1980. The subsequent crash in the price of gold was just as spectacular. The annual returns of gold are shown in Table 4.5. Gold prices have been very volatile, increasing dramatically for one or two years and then experiencing significant declines the next year or two.

a. Compute the rate of return in gold prices that occurred during the three weeks between the last day of 1979 and the January 21, 1980 top.

b. By the end of 1980, gold had dropped to $589.75 per Troy ounce. Compute the rate of return from the top to the end of 1980.

c. Imagine that you invested $1,000 in gold at the end of 1999. Use the returns in Table 4.5 to determine the value of the investment at the end of 2007.

figure 4.5

December Gold Prices Since 1974

Data Source: Kitco (**www.kitco.com**)

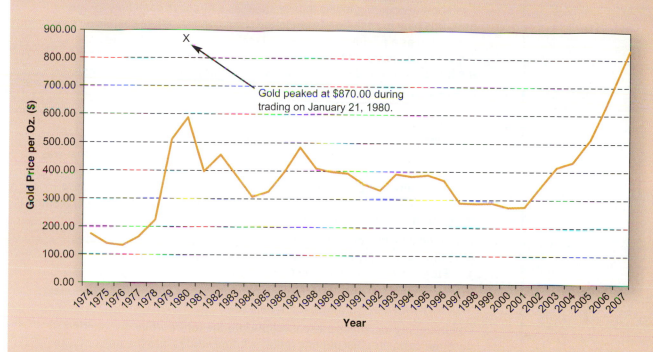

Annual Gold Returns Since 1975			table 4.5

YEAR	ANNUAL GOLD RETURN	YEAR	ANNUAL GOLD RETURN
1975	−19.86%	1992	−5.75%
1976	−4.10%	1993	17.68%
1977	22.64%	1994	−2.17%
1978	37.01%	1995	0.98%
1979	126.55%	1996	−4.59%
1980	15.19%	1997	−21.41%
1981	−32.60%	1998	−0.83%
1982	14.94%	1999	0.85%
1983	−16.31%	2000	−5.44%
1984	−19.19%	2001	0.75%
1985	5.68%	2002	25.57%
1986	21.31%	2003	19.89%
1987	22.21%	2004	4.65%
1988	−15.26%	2005	17.77%
1989	−2.84%	2006	23.20%
1990	−1.47%	2007	31.92%
1991	−10.07%		

ANSWERS TO TIME OUT

4-1 Positive interest rates in the economy mean that $1 deposited today would return more than $1 in the future. To return $1 in the future, deposit less then $1 today. Thus, $1 received one year from now is worth less than $1 today.

4-2 Cash flow accounting labels money spent as a negative cash flow for the firm. This type of cash flow is put in the debit column. When cash is received, it is added as a positive cash flow and registered as a credit. Investments, deposits, and loans all include one cash flow where money leaves your (or the firm's) hands and one cash flow where money goes into your hands.

4-3 Cash flow $200   −$212

Period   0   6%   1 year

4-4 The principle in an investment or debt increases over time by the interest rate. However, compounding causes interest to be earned on money that was previously earned as interest. So, wealth is built from both the principle earning profits and prior profits earning additional profits. If this is a debt whose interest payments are not being paid but added to the principle, then the debt will increase in the same way.

4-5 The original $1,500 owes an interest each year of $1,500 × 0.07 = $105. After three years, the interest from the original $1,500 would be 3 × $105 = $315. So the interest on interest is $337.56 − $315 = $22.56.

4-6 If interest rates are high, then future payments are valued much lower today than they would be if interest rates were low.

4-7 Compounding increases present values into the future while discounting does the opposite. Discounting reduces future values into the present. The TVM equations show the relationship between a present value and a future value. When moving cash flows forward in time, we call it *compounding*. When moving cash flows back in time, we call it *discounting*.

4-8 Yes, the $175,000 could be moved from year 1 to year 2 using the 7 percent interest rate and compared with the $195,000 year 2 payment. The two procedures are equivalent mathematically and will lead to the same decision.

4-9 This depends on what level of accuracy is needed. Interest rates that are too low or too high cause less accurate Rule of 72 estimates. Consider the following interest rates with associated years to double using the Rule of 72 and the TVM equations:

INTEREST RATE	RULE ESTIMATE	TVM ESTIMATE
3%	24.0	23.4
5	14.4	14.2
7	10.3	10.2
9	8.0	8.0
11	6.5	6.6
13	5.5	5.7
15	4.8	5.0
17	4.2	4.4

4-10 The 33.3 percent estimate misses the effect of compounding. Earning interest-on-interest allows money to double in three years at a 26 percent rate.

(continued)

ANSWERS TO TIME OUT (concluded)

4-11 Consider a $100 investment that loses 20 percent to $80. This $80 would have to earn $20 to reach $100 again. A $20 profit on a $80 investment is a $20 ÷ $80 = 0.25, or 25%, return.

4-12 To double the sales at a 7 percent growth rate takes 10.24 years (using TVM calculator).

4-13 TVM concepts can be used in many business areas. Moving cash flows, investment, debt, and growth are important in fields such as accounting, entrepreneurship, marketing, management, and manufacturing.

chapter 5:
TIME VALUE OF MONEY 2: ANALYZING ANNUITY CASH FLOWS

 Learning Goals

LG1 Compound multiple cash flows to the future.

LG2 Compute the future value of frequent, level cash flows.

LG3 Discount multiple cash flows to the present.

LG4 Compute the present value of an annuity.

LG5 Recognize the unique use of TVM methods to figure cash flows and present value of a perpetuity.

LG6 Recognize and adjust values for beginning-of-period annuity payments as opposed to end-of-period annuity payments.

LG7 Explain the impact of compound frequency and the difference between the annual percentage rate and the effective annual rate.

LG8 Compute the interest rate of annuity payments.

LG9 Compute payments and amortization schedules for car and mortgage loans.

LG10 Calculate the number of payments on a loan.

We explained basic time value computations in the previous chapter. Those TVM equations covered moving a single cash flow from one point in time to another. While this circumstance does describe *some* problems that businesses and individuals face, most debt and investment applications of time value of money feature multiple cash flows. In fact, *most* situations require many equal payments over time. Since these situations require a bit more complicated analysis, this chapter continues the TVM topic for applications that require many equal payments over time. For example, car loans and home mortgage loans require the borrower to make the same monthly payment for many months or years. People save for the future through monthly contributions to their pension portfolios. People in retirement must convert their savings into monthly income. Companies also make regular payments. Johnson & Johnson (ticker: JNJ) will pay level semiannual interest payments through 2033 on money they borrowed. General Motors (ticker: GM) paid a 50¢ per

viewpoints

Business Application

Walkabout Music, Inc. issued $20 million in debt 10 years ago to finance their factory construction. The debt allows Walkabout to make interest-only payments at a 7 percent coupon rate, paid semi-annually for 30 years. Debt issued today would carry only 6 percent interest. The company CFO is considering whether or not to issue new debt (for 20 years) to pay off the old debt. To pay off the old debt early, Walkabout would have to pay a special "call premium" totaling $1.4 million to its debt holders. To issue new debt, the firm would have to pay investment bankers a fee of $1.2 million. Should the CFO replace the old debt with new debt? **(See solution on p. 162.)**

Personal Application

Say that you obtained a mortgage for $150,000 three years ago when you purchased your home. You've been paying monthly payments on the 30-year mortgage with a fixed 8 percent interest rate and have $145,920.10 of principal left to pay. Recently, your mortgage broker called to mention that interest rates on new mortgages have declined to 7 percent. He suggested that you could save money every month if you refinanced your mortgage. You could find a 27-year mortgage at the new interest rate for a $1,000 fee. Should you refinance your mortgage? **(See solution p. 162.)**

A practice test can be found on the Online Learning Center at www.mhhe.com/can1e

share quarterly dividend to stockholders for six straight years until 2006, when it switched to a 25¢ dividend. These examples require payments (and compounding) over different time intervals (monthly for car loans and semiannually for company debt). How are we to value these payments into common or comparable terms? In this chapter, we illustrate how to value multiple cash flows over time, including many equal payments, and how to incorporate different compounding frequencies.

5.1 Future Value of Multiple Cash Flows

Chapter 4 illustrated how to take single payments and compound them into the future. To save enough money for a down payment on a house or for retirement, people typically make many contributions over time to their savings account. We can add the future value of each contribution together to see what the total will be worth at some future point in time—such as age 65 for retirement or in two years for a down payment on a house.

Finding the Future Value of Several Cash Flows

Consider the following contributions to a savings account over time. You make a $100 deposit today, followed by a $125 deposit next year, and a $150 deposit at the end of the second year. If interest rates are 7 percent, what's the future value of your deposits at the end of the third year? The time line for this problem is illustrated as:

Cash flow	−100	−125	−150	?
Period	0	1	2	3 years
		7%		

Note that the first deposit will compound for three years. That is, the future value in year 3 of a cash flow in year 0 will compound 3 ($= 3 − 0$) times. The deposit at the end of the first year will compound twice ($= 3 − 1$). In general, a deposit in year m will compound $N − m$ times for a future value in year N. We can find the total amount at the end of three years by computing the future value of each deposit and then adding them together. Using the future value equation from Chapter 4, the future value of today's deposit is $\$100 \times (1 + 0.07)^3 = \$122.50$. Similarly, the future value of the next two deposits are $\$125 \times (1 + 0.07)^2 = \$143.11$ and $\$150 \times (1 + 0.07)^1 = \$160.50$, respectively.

Putting these three individual future value equations together would yield:

$$FV_3 = \$100 \times (1 + 0.07)^3 + \$125 \times (1 + 0.07)^2 + \$150 \times (1 + 0.07)^1 = \$426.11$$

The general equation for computing the future value of multiple and varying cash flows (or payments) is:

$$FV_N = \text{Future value of first cash flow} + \text{Future value of second cash flow}$$
$$+ \cdots + \text{Future value of last cash flow} \tag{5-1}$$
$$= PMT_m \times (1 + i)^{N-m} + PMT_n \times (1 + i)^{N-n} + \cdots$$
$$+ PMT_p \times (1 + i)^{N-p}$$

In this equation, the letters m, n, and p denote when the cash flows occur in time. Each deposit can be different from the others.

SAVING FOR A CAR

Say that as a freshman in college, you will be working as a house painter in each of the next three summers. You intend to set aside some money from each summer's paycheck to buy a car for your senior year. If you can deposit $2,000 from the first summer, $2,500 in the second summer, and $3,000 in the last summer, how much money will you have to buy a car if interest rates are 5 percent?

 LG1

SOLUTION: The time line for the forecast is:

| Cash flow | 0 | | −2,000 | | −2,500 | | −3,000 | ? |
| Period | 0 | | 1 | 5% | 2 | | 3 years | |

The first cash flow, which occurs at the end of the first year, will compound for two years. The second cash flow will be invested for only one year. The last contribution will not have any time to grow before the purchase of the car. Using equation 5-1, the solution is

$$FV_3 = 2,000 \times (1+0.05)^{3-1} + 2,500 \times (1+0.05)^{3-2} + 3,000 \times (1+0.05)^{3-3}$$

$$= 2,000 \times 1.1025 + 2,500 \times 1.05 + 3,000 \times 1 = \$7,830$$

You will have $7,830 in cash to purchase a car for your senior year.

CALCULATOR

FV of 1st cash flow:
N = 2
I = 5
PV = −2000
PMT = 0
CPT FV = 2,205

FV of 2nd cash flow:
N = 1
I = 5
PV = −2500
PMT = 0
CPT FV = 2,625

FV total = 2,205 + 2,625
+ 3,000 = $7,830

Future Value of Level Cash Flows

Now suppose that each cash flow is the same and occurs every year. Level sets of frequent cash flows are common in finance—we call them **annuities**. The first cash flow of an annuity occurs at the end of the first year (or other time period) and continues every year to the last year. We derive the equation for the future value of an annuity from the general equation for future value of multiple cash flows, equation 5-1. Since each cash flow is the same, and the cash flows are every period, the equation appears as:

LG2

$$FVA_N = \text{Future value of first payment} + \text{Future value of second payment}$$
$$+ \cdots + \text{Last payment}$$
$$= PMT \times (1+i)^{N-1} + PMT \times (1+i)^{N-2} + PMT \times (1+i)^{N-3}$$
$$+ \cdots + PMT(1+i)^0$$

The term *FVA* is used to denote that this is the future value of an annuity. Factoring out the common level cash flow, PMT, we can summarize the equation as:

$$FVA_N = PMT \sum_{t=1}^{N} (1+i)^{N-t}$$

And finally, we can reduce to the simpler equation:

$$FVA_N = PMT \times \frac{(1+i)^N - 1}{i} \qquad \text{(5-2)}$$

ANNUITY CASH FLOW	NUMBER OF YEARS	INTEREST RATE	FUTURE VALUE
$ 50	20	6%	$ 1,839.28
100	20	6	3,678.56
100	40	6	15,476.20
100	40	10	44,259.26

Suppose that $100 deposits are made at the end of each year for five years. If interest rates are 8 percent per year, the future value of this annuity stream is computed using equation 5-2 as:

$$FVA_N = \$100 \times \frac{(1 + 0.08)^5 - 1}{0.08} = \$100 \times 5.8666 = \$586.66$$

 We can show these deposits and future value on a time line as:

Five deposits of $100 each were made. So, the $586.66 future value represents $86.66 of interest paid. As with almost any TVM problem, the length of time of the annuity and the interest rate for compounding are very important factors in accumulating wealth within the annuity. Consider the examples in Table 5.1. A $50 deposit made every year for 20 years will grow to $1,839.28 with a 6 percent interest rate. Doubling the annual deposits to $100 also doubles the future value to $3,678.56. However, making $100 deposits for *twice* the amount of time, 40 years, more than *quadruples* the future value to $15,476.20! Longer time periods lead to more total compounding and much more wealth. Interest rates also have this effect. Increasing the interest rate from 6 percent to 10 percent on the 40-year annuity results in nearly tripling the future value to $44,259.26. Think about it: Depositing only $100 per year (about 25 lattes per year) can generate some serious money over time. See Figure 5.1. What would $2,000 annual deposits grow to?

Future Value of Multiple Annuities

At times, multiple annuities can occur in both business and personal life. For example, you may find that you can increase the amount of money you save each year because of a promotion or a new and better job. As an illustration, reconsider the annual $100 deposits made for five years at 8 percent per year. This time, the deposit is able to be increased to $150 for the fourth and fifth year. How can we use the annuity equation to compute the future value when

figure 5.1

Future Value of a $100 Annuity at 6%

 For interactive versions of this example visit www.mhhe.com/can1e

EXAMPLE 5-2

SAVING IN THE COMPANY PENSION PLAN

 LG2

You started your first job after graduating from college. Your company offers a retirement plan for which the company contributes 50 percent of what you contribute each year. So, if you contribute $3,000 per year from your salary, the company adds another $1,500. You get to decide how to invest the total annual contribution from several portfolio choices that the plan administrator provides. Suppose that you pick a mixture of stocks and bonds that is expected to earn 7 percent per year. If you plan to retire in 40 years, how big will you expect that retirement account to be? If you could earn 8 percent per year, how much money would be available?

SOLUTION:

Every year, you and your employer will set aside a total of $4,500 for your retirement. Using equation 5-2 shows that the future value of this annuity is:

$$FVA_{40} = \$4,500 \times \frac{(1+0.07)^{40} - 1}{0.07} = \$4,500 \times 199.635 = \$898,358.00$$

Note that you can build a substantial amount of wealth ($898,358) through your pension plan at work. If you can earn just one percent more each year, 8 percent total, you could be a millionaire!

$$FVA_{40} = \$4,500 \times \frac{(1+0.08)^{40} - 1}{0.08} = \$4,500 \times 259.057 = \$1,165,754.33$$

CALCULATOR

N = 40
I = 7
PV = 0
PMT = −4500
CPT FV = 898,358.00

Now change to
I = 8
CPT FV = 1,165,754.33

WHERE WILL YOUR RETIREMENT INCOME COME FROM?

Though it seems way too early for you to think about planning for your "golden years," financially wise people realize that it's never too early to start. Your retirement income will come from four main sources: Social Security, company or government pensions, income from investment assets, and earnings from jobs you might take after retirement. People between the ages of 65 to 69 years receive an annual income of $17,708 per year, distributed as follows:

- $8,872 from Social Security.
- $5,140 from pensions.
- $3,244 interest or principal from saved assets.
- $452 from other sources.

No wonder, then, that people in this age group continue to work for an additional $10,374 in earned wages each year. People 10 years older (75 to 79) average only $20,278 per year, from these sources:

- $9,772 from Social Security.
- $4,509 from pensions.
- $2,807 from saved assets.
- $2,874 from current jobs.
- $316 from other sources.

We can note several important things about the above. First, Social Security, while the largest contribution to retirees' income, doesn't provide very much money to live on. Second, the average retiree does not enjoy a very high living standard. Third, older people's savings have proved inadequate to provide a comfortable retirement lifestyle. Many of today's retirees aged 65 or above expected Social Security to meet a much greater portion of their income needs in retirement. These retirees also expected that their employers would provide adequate pensions for the retirees to live comfortably in retirement. So, what can you do to avoid the same situation when you retire?

Most company and government employers offer employees defined contribution plans. (The corporate version is called a 401(k) plan; a nonbusiness plan is usually referred to as a 403(b) plan—both named after the legislation that created the plans.) These plans place all of the responsibility on employees to provide for their retirement. Employees contribute from their own paychecks and decide how to invest it. Employees' decisions about how much to contribute and how early to start contributing have a dramatic impact on retirement wealth. Consider employees who earn $50,000 annually for 40 years and then retire. Note that if the employees contribute for 40 years, they must start by age 25 or so—starting early is vitally important! Contributing 5 percent of their salaries ($2,500) to the 401(k) plan every year and having it earn a 4 percent return will generate $237,564 for retirement. A 10 percent contribution ($5,000) would create $475,128 for retirement. Finally, investment decisions that yield an 8 percent return would yield $1.3 million with a 10 percent contribution. This is quite a range of retirement wealth generated from just three important decisions each employee must make—how much to contribute, how to invest the funds, and when to start! Unfortunately, too many people make poor decisions. The average 401(k) account value for people in their 60s is only $136,400—often because people start 401(k) contributions too late to allow the funds to compound much.

Saving and investing money through a defined contribution plan is a good way to build wealth for retirement. But you must Start Early, Save Much, and Don't Touch!

Sources: "Distribution of Older Population's Average Annual Income," *Fast Facts from EBRI*, #18, February 23, 2006, and "401(k) Account Balances, Asset Allocation by the Numbers," *Fast Facts from EBRI*, #08, October 3, 2005.

 want to know more? **Key Words to Search for Updates: See the Employee Benefit Research Institute Web site (www.ebri.org) or Google retirement income.**

 we have two levels of cash flows? In this case, the cash flow can be categorized as two annuities. The first annuity is a $100 cash flow for five years. The second annuity is a $50 cash flow for two years. We demonstrate this as:

						?
					−50	−50
Cash flow	0	−100	−100	−100	−100	−100
Period	0	1	2 8%	3	4	5 years

To determine the future value of these two annuities, compute the future value of each one separately, and then simply add them together. The future value of the

$100 annuity is the same as computed before, $586.66. The future value of the $50 annuity, using the TVM equation for the future value of a cash stream, is:

$$FVA_N = \$50 \times \frac{(1 + 0.08)^2 - 1}{0.08}$$
$$= \$50 \times 2.08 = \$104$$

So, the future value of both of the annuities is $690.66 (= $586.66 + $104). In this same way, we could easily compute the future value if the last two cash flows are $50 *lower* ($50 each), instead of $50 higher ($150 each). To solve this alternative version, we would simply *subtract* the $104 future value instead of adding it.

For interactive versions of this example visit www.mhhe.com/can1e

MATH COACH

SOLVING MULTIPLE ANNUITIES

The trick to solving multiple annuity problems is to disentangle cash flows into groups of level payments ending in the future value year that we've designated.

EXAMPLE 5-3

GROWING RETIREMENT CONTRIBUTIONS

LG2

In the previous example, you are investing a total of $4,500 per year for 40 years in your employer's retirement program. You believe that with raises and promotions, you will eventually be able to contribute more money each year. Consider that halfway through your career, you are able to increase your investment in the retirement program to $6,000 per year (your contribution plus the company match). What would be the future value of your retirement wealth from this program if investments are compounded at 7 percent?

SOLUTION:

You can compute the future value using two annuities. The first annuity is one with payments of $4,500 that lasts 40 years. The second is a $1,500 (= $6,000 − $4,500) annuity that lasts only 20 years. We already computed the future value of the first annuity in the previous example: $898,358. The future value of the second annuity is:

$$FVA_{20} = \$1,500 \times \frac{(1 + 0.07)^{20} - 1}{0.07} = \$1,500 \times 40.9955 = \$61,493.24$$

So, your retirement wealth from this program would be $959,851 (= $898,358 + $61,493).

CALCULATOR
Add to previous answer
N = 20
I = 7
PV = 0
PMT = −1500
CPT FV = 61,493.24

TIME OUT

5-1 Describe how compounding affects the future value computation of an annuity.

5-2 Reconsider your original retirement plan example to invest $4,500 per year for 40 years. Now consider the result if you don't contribute anything for four years (years 19 to 22) while your child goes to college. How many annuity equations will you need to find the future value of your 401(k) in this situation?

5.2 Present Value of Multiple Cash Flows

The future value concept is very useful to understand how to build wealth for the future. The present value concept will help you most particularly for personal applications such as evaluating loans (like car and mortgage loans) and business applications (like determining the value of business opportunities).

Finding the Present Value of Several Cash Flows

LG3

Consider the cash flows that we showed in the very beginning of the chapter: you deposit $100 today, followed by a $125 deposit next year, and a $150 deposit at the end of the second year. In the previous situation, we sought the future value when interest rates are 7 percent. Instead of future value, we compute the present value of these three cash flows. The time line for this problem appears as:

Cash flow	−100	−125	? −150
Period	0	1	7% 2 years

The first cash flow is already in year zero, so its value will not change. We will discount the second cash flow one year and the third cash flow two years. Using the present value equation from the previous chapter, the present value of today's payment is simply $100 ÷ $(1 + 0.07)^0$ = $100. Similarly, the present value of the next two cash flows are $125 ÷ $(1 + 0.07)^1$ = $116.82 and $150 ÷ $(1 + 0.07)^2$ = $131.02, respectively. Therefore, the present value of these cash flows is $347.84 (= $100 + $116.82 + $131.02).

Putting these three individual present value equations together would yield:

$$PV = \$100 \div (1 + 0.07)^0 + \$125 \div (1 + 0.07)^1 + \$150 \div (1 + 0.07)^2$$
$$= \$347.84$$

The general equation for discounting multiple and varying cash flows is:

$$PV = \text{Present value of first cash flow} + \text{Present value of second cash flow}$$
$$+ \cdots + \text{Present value of last cash flow}$$
$$= \frac{PMT_m}{(1+i)^{N-m}} + \frac{PMT_n}{(1+i)^{N-n}} + \cdots + \frac{PMT_p}{(1+i)^{N-p}} \qquad (5\text{-}3)$$

In this equation, the letters m, n, and p denote when the cash flows occur in time. Each deposit can differ from the others in terms of size and timing.

Present Value of Level Cash Flows

LG4

You will find that this present value of an annuity concept will have many business and personal applications throughout your life. Most loans are set up so that the amount borrowed (the present value) is repaid through level payments made every period (the annuity). Lenders will examine borrowers' budgets and determine how much each borrower can afford as a payment. The maximum loan offered will be the present value of that annuity payment. We derived the equation for the present value of an annuity from the general equation for the present value of multiple cash flows, equation 5-3. Since each cash flow is the same, and the borrower pays the cash flows every period, we can write the equation as:

$$PVA_N = \text{Present value of first payment} + \text{Present value of second payment}$$
$$+ \cdots + \text{Present value of last payment}$$
$$= PMT/(1+i)^1 + PMT/(1+i)^2 + PMT/(1+i)^3 + \cdots + PMT/(1+i)^N$$

CALCULATOR
PV of 1st cash flow is $100

PV of 2nd cash flow:
N = 1
I = 7
PMT = 0
FV = −125
CPT PV = 116.82

PV of 3rd cash flow:
N = 2
I = 7
PMT = 0
FV = −150
CPT PV = 131.01

Add the 3 PVs

ANNUITY CASH FLOW	NUMBER OF YEARS	INTEREST RATE	PRESENT VALUE
$ 50	20	6%	$ 573.50
100	20	6	1,146.99
100	40	6	1,504.63
100	40	10	977.91

We denote the present value of an annuity as PVA. If we group the common level cash flow as PMT, the equation becomes

$$PVA_N = PMT \times \sum_{t=1}^{N} \frac{1}{(1 + i)^t}$$

And finally, reduced to a simpler equation:

$$PVA_N = PMT \times \left[\frac{1 - \dfrac{1}{(1 + i)^N}}{i} \right] \qquad \textbf{(5-4)}$$

Suppose that someone makes $100 payments at the end of each year for five years. If interest rates are 8 percent per year, the present value of this annuity stream is computed using equation 5-4 as:

$$PVA_5 = 100 \times \left[\frac{1 - \dfrac{1}{(1 + 0.08)^5}}{0.08} \right] = 100 \times 3.9927 = 399.27$$

The time line for these payments and present value appears as:

Notice that although five payments of $100 each were made, $500 total, the present value is only $399.27. As we've noted previously, the span of time over which the borrower pays the annuity and the interest rate for discounting strongly affect present value computations. When you borrow money from the bank, the bank views the amount they lend as the present value of the annuity they receive over time from the borrower. Consider the examples in Table 5.2. A $50 deposit made every year for 20 years is discounted to $573.50 with a 6 percent discount rate. Doubling the annual cash flow to $100 also doubles the present value to $1,146.99. But extending the time period does not impact the present value as much as you might expect. Making $100 payments for twice the amount of time—40 years—does not double the present value. As you can see in Table 5.2, the present value increases less than 50 percent to only $1,504.63! If the discount rate increases from 6 percent to 10 percent on the 40-year annuity, the present value will shrink to $977.91.

figure 5.2

Present Value of Each
Annuity Cash Flow

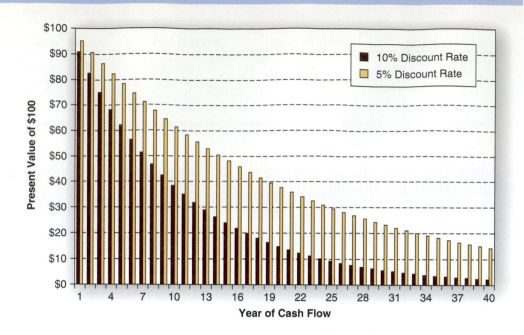

The present value of a cash flow made far into the future is not very valuable today. That's why doubling the number of years in the table from 20 to 40 only increased the present value by approximately 30 percent. Figure 5.2 shows how the present value of $100 annuity payments declines for the cash flows made later in time, especially at higher discount rates. The $100 cash flow in year 20 is worth less than $15 today if we use a 10 percent discount rate; they're worth more than double, at nearly $38 today, if we use a discount rate of 5 percent. The figure also shows how quickly present value declines with a higher discount rate

---

EXAMPLE 5-4

 For interactive versions of this chapter visit www.mhhe.com/can1e

VALUE OF PAYMENTS

 Your firm needs to buy additional physical therapy equipment that costs $20,000. The equipment manufacturer will give you the equipment now if you will pay $6,000 per year for the next four years. If your firm can borrow money at a 9 percent interest rate, should you pay the manufacturer the $20,000 now or accept the four-year annuity offer of $6,000?

SOLUTION:

We can find the cost of the four-year, $6,000 annuity in present value terms using equation 5-4:

CALCULATOR
N = 4
I = 9
PMT = −6000
FV = 0
CPT PV = 19,438.32

$$PVA_4 = \$6,000 \times \left[\frac{1 - \dfrac{1}{(1+0.09)^4}}{0.09} \right] = \$6,000 \times 3.2397 = \$19,438.32$$

The cost of paying for the equipment over time is $19,438.32. This is less, in present value terms, than paying $20,000 cash. The firm should take the annuity payment plan.

relative to a lower rate. As we showed above, the present values of the annuities in the figure are the sums of the present values shown. Since the present values for the 10 percent discount rate are smaller, the present value of an annuity is smaller as interest rates rise.

Present Value of Multiple Annuities

Just as we can combine annuities to solve various future value problems, we can also combine annuities to solve some present value problems with changing level cash flows. Consider Alex Rodriguez's (A-Rod's) baseball contract in 2000 with the Texas Rangers. This contract made A-Rod into the "$252 million man." The contract was structured so that the Rangers paid A-Rod a $10 million signing bonus, $21 million per year in 2001 through 2004, $25 million per year in 2005 and 2006, and $27 million per year in 2007 through 2010.[1] Note that adding the signing bonus to the annual salary equals the $252 million figure. However, Rodriguez will receive the salary in the future. Using an 8 percent discount rate, what is the present value of A-Rod's contract?

We begin by showing the salary cash flows with the time line:

First create a $27 million, 10-year annuity. Here are the associated cash flows:

Now create a $−2 million, six-year annuity:

Notice that creating the $−2 million annuity also resulted in the third annuity of $−4 million for four years. This time line shows three annuities. If you add the cash flows in any year, the sum is A-Rod's salary for that year. Now we can find the present value of each annuity using equation 5-4 three times.

$$PVA_{10} = \$27 \times \left[\frac{1 - \frac{1}{(1 + 0.08)^{10}}}{0.08} \right] = \$27 \times 6.710 = \$181.17 \text{ million}$$

$$PVA_{6} = \$-2 \times \left[\frac{1 - \frac{1}{(1 + 0.08)^{6}}}{0.08} \right] = \$-2 \times 4.623 = \$-9.25 \text{ million}$$

$$PVA_{4} = \$-4 \times \left[\frac{1 - \frac{1}{(1 + 0.08)^{4}}}{0.08} \right] = \$-4 \times 3.312 = \$-13.25 \text{ million}$$

CALCULATOR
N = 10
I = 8
PMT = −27
FV = 0
CPT PV = 181.17

Now change to
N = 6
PMT = 2
CPT PV = −9.25

Now change to
N = 4
PMT = 4
CPT PV = −13.25

[1]The contract actually contains some complications like incentives to play well and salary deferral. We ignore those complicating factors here.

Adding the value of the three annuities reveals that the present value of A-Rod's salary was $158.67 million (= $181.17 − $9.25 − $13.25). Adding in the $10 million signing bonus produces a contract value of $168.67 million. So, the present value of A-Rod's contract turns out to be quite considerable, but you might not call him the $252 million man![2]

Perpetuity—A Special Annuity

A perpetuity is a special type of annuity with a stream of level cash flows that are paid forever. These arrangements are called **perpetuities** because payments are perpetual. Assets that offer investors perpetual payments are preferred stocks and British 2 ½% Consolidated Stock, a debt referred to as **consols**.

The value of an investment like this is the present value of all future annuity payments. As the cash flow continues indefinitely, we can't use equation 5-4. Luckily, mathematicians have figured out that when the number of periods, N, in equation 5-4 goes to infinity, the equation reduces to a very simple one:

$$PV \text{ of a perpetuity} = \frac{PMT}{i} \tag{5-5}$$

For example, the present value of an annual $100 perpetuity discounted at 10 percent is $1,000 (= $100 ÷ 0.10). Compare this to the present value of a $100 annuity of 40 years as shown in Table 5.2. The 40-year annuity's value is $977.91. You'll see that extending the payments from 40 years to an infinite number of years adds only $22.09 (= $1,000 − $977.91) of value. This demonstrates once again how little value today is placed on cash flows paid many years into the future.

TIME OUT

5-3 How important is the magnitude of the discount rate in present value computations? Do significantly higher interest rates lead to significantly higher present values?

5-4 Reconsider the physical therapy equipment example. If interest rates are only 7 percent, should you pay the up-front fee or the annuity?

5.3 Ordinary Annuities versus Annuities Due

So far, we've assumed that every cash flow comes in at the end of every period. But in many instances, cash flows come in at the beginning of each period. An annuity in which the cash flows occur at the beginning of each period is called an **annuity due**.

Consider the five-year $100 annuity due. The cash flow in the beginning of year 1 looks like it's actually a cash flow today.

Note that these five annuity-due cash flows are essentially the same as a payment today and a four-year ordinary annuity.

---

[2]Rodriguez opted out of the contract after the 2007 season and then re-signed with the New York Yankees with a new contract.

TAKE YOUR LOTTERY WINNINGS NOW OR LATER?

On February 18, 2006, a group of ConAgra Foods co-workers won a record Powerball jackpot of $365 million. The group had two choices for payment. They could take a much-discounted lump sum cash payment immediately, or take 30 annuity payments (one immediately and then one every year for 29 years, which is a 30-year annuity due). The annuity payment would be $12.17 million (= $365 million ÷ 30). The lump sum payment offered was $177.3 million. One way to decide between the two alternatives would be to use the time value of money concepts. They might have computed the present value of the annuity and compared it to the lump sum cash payment.

At the time, long-term interest rates were 5 percent. The present value of the annuity offered was $196.38 million. (Compute this yourself.) Notice that winning $365 million does not deliver $365 million of value! If the decision was made from this perspective, the group should take the annuity choice because it has more value than the cash

alternative. However, this group selected the immediate cash option. Most winners do. Financial advisors tend to recommend that lottery winners take the lump sum because they believe that the money can earn a higher return than the 5 percent interest rate.

Good reasons arise for taking the annuity, however. To earn the higher return on the lump sum, the advisor (and the group of owners) would have to take risks. In addition, most of the lump sum would have to be invested. But most people who take a lump sum end up spending much of it in the first couple of years. Stories abound about lottery winners who declare bankruptcy a few years after receiving their money. Taking the money as an annuity helps instill financial discipline, since the winners can't waste money today that they won't receive for years.

Sources: "8 Win Record U.S. Lottery Jackpot, $365 million," *The New York Times*, February 23, 2006, page A24, and **www.powerball.com**.

 want to know more? **Key Words to Search for Updates: See the Powerball Web site (www.powerball.com) or Google Powerball winners.**

FUTURE VALUE OF AN ANNUITY DUE So, how do we calculate the future value of the five-year annuity due shown in the time line? The first cash flow of an ordinary five-year annuity can compound for four years. The last cash flow does not compound at all. From the time line, you can see that the first cash flow of the annuity due essentially occurs in year zero, or today. So the first cash flow compounds for five years. The last cash flow of an annuity due compounds one year. The main difference between an annuity due and an ordinary annuity is that all the cash flows of the annuity due compound one more year than the ordinary annuity. The future value of the annuity due will simply be the future value of the ordinary annuity multiplied by $(1 + i)$:

LG6

$$FVA_N \text{ due} = FVA_N \times (1 + i) \qquad \textbf{(5-6)}$$

Earlier in the chapter, the future value of this ordinary annuity was shown to be $586.66. Therefore, the future value of the annuity due is $633.59 (= $586.66 × 1.08).

PRESENT VALUE OF AN ANNUITY DUE. What is a five-year annuity due, shown above, worth today? Remember that we discount the first cash flow of an ordinary five-year annuity one year. We discount the last cash flow for the full five years. But since the first cash flow of the annuity due is already paid today, we don't

MATH COACH

SETTING FINANCIAL CALCULATORS FOR ANNUITY DUE

Financial calculators can be set for beginning-of-period payments. Once set, you compute future and present values of annuities due just as you would the ordinary annuity. To set the HP calculator, press the color button followed by the BEG/END button. To set the TI calculator for an annuity due, push the 2ND button, followed by the BGN button, followed by the 2ND button again, followed by the SET button, and followed by the 2ND button a third time, finally the QUIT button. To set the HP and TI calculators back to end-of-period cash flows, repeat these procedures.

discount it at all. We discount the last cash flow of an annuity due only four years. Indeed, we discount all the cash flows of the annuity due one year less than we would discount the ordinary annuity. Therefore, the present value of the annuity due is simply the present value of the ordinary annuity multiplied by $(1 + i)$:

$$PVA_N \text{ due} = PVA_N \times (1 + i) \tag{5-7}$$

Earlier in the chapter, we discovered that the present value of this ordinary annuity was $399.27. So the present value of the annuity due is $431.21 (= $399.27 × 1.08).

Interestingly, we make the same adjustment, $(1 + i)$, to both the ordinary annuity present value and future value to compute the annuity due value.

CALCULATOR

Change to BGN

N = 5
I = 8
PMT = −100
FV = 0
CPT PV = 431.21

TIME OUT

5-5 In what situations might you need to use annuity due analysis instead of an ordinary annuity analysis?

5-6 Reconsider your retirement plan earlier in this chapter. What would your retirement wealth grow to be if you started contributing today?

5.4 Compounding Frequency

So far, all of our examples and illustrations have used annual payments and annual compounding or discounting periods. But many situations that use cash flow time-value-of-money analysis require more frequent or less frequent time periods than simple yearly entries. Bonds make semiannual interest payments; stocks pay quarterly dividends. Most consumer loans require monthly payments. Monthly payments require monthly compounding. In this section, we'll discuss the implications of compounding more than once a year.

Effect of Compounding Frequency

Consider a $100 deposit made today with a 12 percent annual interest rate. What's the future value of this deposit in one year? Equation 4-2 from the previous chapter shows that the answer is $112. What would happen if the bank compounded the interest every six months instead of at the end of the year? Halfway through the year, the bank would compute that the deposit has grown 6 percent (half the annual 12 percent rate) to $106. At the end of the year, the bank would compute another 6 percent interest payment. However, this 6 percent is earned on $106, not the original $100 deposit. The end-of-year value is therefore $112.36 (= $106 × 1.06). By compounding twice per year instead of just once, the future value is $0.36 higher. Though this amount may seem negligible, you might be surprised to see how quickly the difference becomes significant.

Instead of compounding annually or semiannually, what might happen if compounding were quarterly? Since each year contains four quarters, the interest rate per quarter would be 3 percent (= 12 percent ÷ 4 quarters). The future value in one year, compounded quarterly, is $112.55 (= $100 × 1.03⁴). Again, the compounding frequency increased and so did the future value. Table 5.3 shows the effect of various compounding frequencies. We'd like to draw your attention to two important points in the table. First, the higher the compound frequency, the higher the future value will be. Second, the relative increase in value from

LG6

LG7

FREQUENCY	PERIOD INTEREST RATE	FUTURE VALUE EQUATION	FUTURE VALUE
		table 5.3 Future Value in One Year and Compounding Frequency of $100 at 12 percent	
Annual	12%	100×1.12^1	$112.00
Semiannual	6	100×1.06^2	112.36
Quarterly	3	100×1.03^4	112.55
Monthly	1	100×1.01^{12}	112.68
Daily	0.032877	$100 \times 1.00032877^{365}$	112.748
Hourly	0.00136986	$100 \times 1.0000136986^{8760}$	112.749

 For interactive versions of this example visit www.mhhe.com/can1e

EXAMPLE 5-5

CAR LOAN DEBT

Now you would like to buy a car. You have reviewed your budget and determined that you can afford to pay $500 per month as a car payment. How much can you borrow if interest rates are 9 percent and you pay the loan over four years? How much could you borrow if you agree to pay for six years instead?

SOLUTION:

The loan amount is the present value of the 48-month, $500 annuity. Note that the loan term will be 48 ($=4 \times 12$) months and the interest rate is 0.75 ($=9 \div 12$) percent. Using equation 5-4, you discover that you can borrow up to $20,092 to buy a car:

$$PVA_{48} = \$500 \times \left[\frac{1 - \dfrac{1}{(1+0.0075)^{48}}}{0.0075} \right] = \$500 \times 40.1848 = \$20,092.39$$

CALCULATOR

N = 48
I = 0.75
PMT = −500
FV = 0
CPT PV = 20,092.39

Then change N to 72
CPT PV = 27,738.42

If you are willing to borrow money for six years instead of four, the small change to the equation results in your ability to borrow $27,738. Although this would allow you to buy a more expensive car, it would also require two more years of $500 payments (an additional $12,000 of payments!).

increasing compounding frequency seems to diminish with increasing frequencies. For example, increasing frequency from annual to semiannual increased the future value by 36 cents. However, increasing frequency from daily to hourly compounding increases the future value by only 0.1 cents.[3]

When we work with annuity cash flows, the compound frequency used is the same as the timing of the cash flows. When annuity cash flows are paid monthly, then interest is also compounded monthly, as seen in the following two examples.

EARS AND APRS If you borrowed $100 at a 12 percent interest rate, you would expect to pay $112 in one year. If the loan compounded monthly, then Table 5.3 shows that you would owe $112.68 at the end of the year. So a 12 percent

[3]It is also possible to continuously compound. The future value of a continuously compounded deposit is $FV_N = PV \times e^{(i \times N)}$, where e has a value of 2.7183.

	The EAR Is Higher than the APR			table 5.4
APR	**COMPOUNDING PERIODS**	**EQUATION**		**= EAR**
5%	1	$(1 + 0.05/1)^1 - 1$		5.00%
5	4	$(1 + 0.05/4)^4 - 1$		5.09
5	12	$(1 + 0.05/12)^{12} - 1$		5.12
9	4	$(1 + 0.09/4)^4 - 1$		9.31
9	12	$(1 + 0.09/12)^{12} - 1$		9.38
12	4	$(1 + 0.12/4)^4 - 1$		12.55
12	12	$(1 + 0.12/12)^{12} - 1$		12.68

EXAMPLE 5-6

For interactive versions of this example visit www.mhhe.com/can1e

MAKING MONTHLY PENSION CONTRIBUTIONS

Reexamine your original plan to contribute to your company retirement plan. Instead of a total contribution of $4,500 per year for 40 years, you are able to contribute monthly. Given your expected 7 percent per year investment return, how much money can you expect in your retirement account?

SOLUTION:

Now your total monthly contribution will be $375 (= $4,500 ÷ 12), which will continue for 480 months and earn a 0.58333 (= 7 ÷ 12) percent monthly return. The results of equation 5-2 show that the future value of this annuity is:

$$FVA_{40} = \$375 \times \frac{(1 + 7 \div 12 \div 100)^{480} - 1}{7 \div 12 \div 100} = \$375 \times 2,624.8135 = \$984,305.02$$

When you made contributions annually, the future value was $898,358. By changing to monthly contributions, your retirement nest egg increased by nearly $90,000 to $984,305!

CALCULATOR
N = 480
I = 7÷12
PV = 0
PMT = −375
CPT FV = 984,305.02

MATH COACH

COMMON MISTAKES

As you figure present and future values of annuity cash flows, check that all terms are consistent: the number of payments, interest rate, and payment size all need to use common terms. If your payments are monthly, then the number of payments must reflect the number of months; the interest rate must be stated as a per-month rate, and the payment must be a monthly payment.

loan compounded monthly means that you really pay more than 12 percent. In fact, you would pay 12.68 percent. In this example, the 12 percent rate is called the **annual percentage rate (APR).** The higher rate, 12.68 percent, is called the **effective annual rate (EAR)**—a more accurate measurement of what you will actually pay.

Lenders are legally required to show potential borrowers the APR on any loan offered. While the difference in APR and EAR is not that large in this example, it's interesting that the law requires only the less accurate (and lower) one to be shown. Since the EAR is a more accurate measure of what you will pay, it's useful to know how to convert a stated APR to an EAR. Equation 5-8 shows this conversion with a compounding frequency of *m* times per year:

$$EAR = \left(1 + \frac{APR}{m}\right)^m - 1 \tag{5-8}$$

Table 5.4 shows various EAR conversions. If compounding occurs annually, you will see that the EAR and the APR will be the same. If compounding happens more than once a year, then the EAR will be higher than the APR. The table also demonstrates that the compound frequency effect grows substantially for higher interest rates or longer term loans. Compounded quarterly, the EAR is hardly different at all from a 5 percent APR: 5.09 percent versus 5 percent. The difference is larger when the APR is 12 percent. Compounded quarterly, the EAR is higher at 12.55 percent.

 For interactive versions of this example visit www.mhhe.com/can1e

EXAMPLE 5-7

EVALUATING CREDIT CARD OFFERS

As a college student, you probably receive many credit card offers in the mail. Consider these two offers. The first card charges a 16 percent APR. An examination of the footnotes reveals that this card compounds monthly. The second credit card charges 15.5 percent APR and compounds weekly. Which card has a lower effective annual rate?

SOLUTION:

Compute the EAR of each card to compare them in common (and realistic) terms. The first card has an EAR of:

$$EAR = \left(1 + \frac{0.16}{12}\right)^{12} - 1 = 0.17227 = 17.23\%$$

The EAR of the second card is:

$$EAR = \left(1 + \frac{0.155}{52}\right)^{52} - 1 = 0.16739 = 16.74\%$$

You should pick the second credit card because it has a lower effective annual rate. But note also that you will always be better off if you pay off your credit card balance whenever the bill comes due.

 TIME OUT

5-7 Why is EAR a more accurate measure of the rate actually paid than APR?

5-8 What would have a smaller present value, a future sum discounted annually or one discounted monthly?

5.5 Annuity Loans

In this chapter, we've focused on computing the future and present value of annuities. But in many situations, these values are already known and what we really need to compare are the payments or implied interest rate—usually, the highest interest rate offered.

What Is the Interest Rate?

Many business and personal applications already state the cost of an investment, as well as the annuity cash flows and time period. We need, then, to solve for the implied interest rate of this investment. Unfortunately, we have no general, easy equation to solve for the interest rate. Even financial calculators use an iterating process, which causes it to "think" a little longer before displaying the estimated interest rate result.

Consider the plight of a manager of a small doctor's office who has the opportunity to buy a piece of imaging equipment for $100,000. The equipment will allow the office to generate $25,000 in profits for six years, at which time the equipment will be worn out and without value in the U.S.[4] What rate of return does this purchase offer the doctor's office? The time line for this problem appears as

Cash flow	−100,000	25,000	25,000	25,000	25,000	25,000	25,000
Period	0	1	2	3	4	5	6 years

For the financial calculator solution, input N = 6, PV = −100000, PMT = 25000, and FV = 0. The interest rate result is then 12.98 percent. So, if this is a high enough return relative to other uses of the $100,000, the doctor's office should seriously consider purchasing the imaging machine.

EXAMPLE 5-8

 For interactive versions of this example visit www.mhhe.com/can1e

COMPUTING INTEREST RATE NEEDED

 LG8

After saving diligently your entire career, you and your spouse are finally ready to retire with a nest egg of $800,000. You need to invest this money in a mix of stocks and bonds that will allow you to earn $6,000 per month for 30 years. What interest rate do you need to earn?

SOLUTION:

Use a financial calculator and input N = 360, PV = −800000, PMT = 6000, and FV = 0. The interest rate result is 0.6860 percent. But remember, since the periods and payments are in months, the interest rate is too. It is customary to report this as an APR: 8.23 percent (= 0.6860 percent × 12). However, the EAR more accurately reflects the true interest rate, 8.55 percent (= $1.00686^{12} - 1$). In order for your money to last for 30 years while funding a $6,000 per month income, you must earn at least an 8.23 APR per year return.

Finding Payments on an Amortized Loan

Many consumers and small business owners already know how much money they want to borrow and the level of current interest rates. Usually, they really need to translate this information into the actual payments to determine if they can really afford the purchase. A loan structured for annuity payments that completely pay off the debt is called an **amortized loan**. To compute the annuity cash flow of an amortized loan, rearrange the present value of an annuity formula, equation 5-4, to solve for the payment:

 LG9

$$PMT_N = PV \times \left[\frac{i}{1 - \dfrac{1}{(1 + i)^N}} \right]$$ **(5-9)**

---

[4]Some charities are now gathering "obsolete" U.S. medical equipment and sending the materials to less developed countries—a situation in which everybody wins.

Monthly Payments on a $225,000 Loan		table 5.5
APR INTEREST RATE (%)	YEARS TO REPAY LOAN	MONTHLY PAYMENT ($)
10	30	1,974.54
8	30	1,650.97
7	30	1,496.93
6	30	1,348.99
8	15	2,150.22
7	15	2,022.36
6	15	1,898.68

Most car loans require monthly payments for three to five years. Assume that you need a $10,000 loan to buy a car. The loan is for four years and interest rates are 9 percent per year APR. To implement equation 5-9, use an interest rate of 0.75 percent (= 9 percent / 12) and 48 periods (= 4 × 12) as:

$$PMT_{48} = \$10,000 \times \left[\frac{0.0075}{1 - \dfrac{1}{(1 + 0.0075)^{48}}} \right] = \$10,000 \times 0.024885 = \$248.85$$

CALCULATOR
N = 48
I = 0.75
PV = 10000
FV = 0
CPT PMT = −248.85

So, when interest rates are 9 percent, it takes monthly payments of $248.85 to pay off a $10,000 loan in four years.

Interest rate levels and loan length strongly affect how large your payments will be. Table 5.5 shows the monthly payments needed to pay off a mortgage debt at various interest rates and lengths of time. (Try computing the payments yourself!) Note that as the interest rate declines, the monthly payment also declines. This is why people rush to refinance their mortgage after interest rates fall. A decline of 1 or 2 percent can save a homeowner hundreds of dollars every month. You will also see from the table that paying off a mortgage in only 15 years requires larger payments, but generally saves thousands in interest.

AMORTIZED LOAN SCHEDULES When you pay a car loan or home mortgage, you will often find it useful to know how much of the debt, or **loan principal,** you still owe. For example, consider a case wherein you bought a car two years ago using a four-year loan. In order to sell the car now, the loan balance will have to be paid off. Being able to compute this principal balance may influence your chances of selling the car.

An interest-only loan allows the borrower to make payments that consist totally of interest payments, so none of the debt is reduced. A $10,000 interest-only loan with a 9 percent APR paid monthly will cost $75 per month (= $10,000 × 0.09 ÷ 12). Amortizing this loan over four years requires monthly payments of $248.85 (see earlier car loan problem). The difference in the first month's payment on the two loans is $173.85 (= $248.85 − $75) and represents the amount of the regular amortized loan's payment that goes to reducing the principal balance. So after the first month's payment, the amortized loan's balance has fallen to $9,826.15, while the interest-only loan still has a balance of $10,000.

In the second month, the interest incurred on the regular amortized loan is $73.70 (= $9,826.15 × 0.09 ÷ 12), so the $248.85 second month payment represents principal payment of $175.15. These numbers are shown in the **amortization schedule** of Table 5.6. The table will show you that the early payments on a car loan go mostly to paying the interest rather than reducing the principal. That interest component declines over time, and then the principal balance declines.

MONTH	BEGINNING BALANCE	TOTAL PAYMENT	INTEREST PAID	PRINCIPAL PAID	ENDING BALANCE	MONTH	BEGINNING BALANCE	TOTAL PAYMENT	INTEREST PAID	PRINCIPAL PAID	ENDING BALANCE
1	$10,000.00	$248.85	$75.00	$173.85	$9,826.15	25	$5,447.13	$248.85	$40.85	$208.00	$5,239.14
2	9,826.15	248.85	73.70	175.15	9,651.00	26	5,239.14	248.85	39.29	209.56	5,029.58
3	9,651.00	248.85	72.38	176.47	9,474.53	27	5,029.58	248.85	37.72	211.13	4,818.45
4	9,474.53	248.85	71.06	177.79	9,296.74	28	4,818.45	248.85	36.14	212.71	4,605.74
5	9,296.74	248.85	69.73	179.12	9,117.61	29	4,605.74	248.85	34.54	214.31	4,391.43
6	9,117.61	248.85	68.38	180.47	8,937.15	30	4,391.43	248.85	32.94	215.91	4,175.52
7	8,937.15	248.85	67.03	181.82	8,755.32	31	4,175.52	248.85	31.32	217.53	3,957.99
8	8,755.32	248.85	65.66	183.19	8,572.14	32	3,957.99	248.85	29.68	219.17	3,738.82
9	8,572.14	248.85	64.29	184.56	8,387.58	33	3,738.82	248.85	28.04	220.81	3,518.01
10	8,387.58	248.85	62.91	185.94	8,201.64	34	3,518.01	248.85	26.39	222.46	3,295.55
11	8,201.64	248.85	61.51	187.34	8,014.30	35	3,295.55	248.85	24.72	224.13	3,071.41
12	8,014.30	248.85	60.11	188.74	7,825.56	36	3,071.41	248.85	23.04	225.81	2,845.60
13	7,825.56	248.85	58.69	190.16	7,635.40	37	2,845.60	248.85	21.34	227.51	2,618.09
14	7,635.40	248.85	57.27	191.58	7,443.81	38	2,618.09	248.85	19.64	229.21	2,388.88
15	7,443.81	248.85	55.83	193.02	7,250.79	39	2,388.88	248.85	17.92	230.93	2,157.94
16	7,250.79	248.85	54.38	194.47	7,056.32	40	2,157.94	248.85	16.18	232.67	1,925.28
17	7,056.32	248.85	52.92	195.93	6,860.40	41	1,925.28	248.85	14.44	234.41	1,690.87
18	6,860.40	248.85	51.45	197.40	6,663.00	42	1,690.87	248.85	12.68	236.17	1,454.70
19	6,663.00	248.85	49.97	198.88	6,464.12	43	1,454.70	248.85	10.91	237.94	1,216.76
20	6,464.12	248.85	48.48	200.37	6,263.75	44	1,216.76	248.85	9.13	239.72	977.04
21	6,263.75	248.85	46.98	201.87	6,061.88	45	977.04	248.85	7.33	241.52	735.51
22	6,061.88	248.85	45.46	203.39	5,858.49	46	735.51	248.85	5.52	243.33	492.18
23	5,858.49	248.85	43.94	204.91	5,653.58	47	492.18	248.85	3.69	245.16	247.02
24	5,653.58	248.85	42.40	206.45	5,447.13	48	247.02	248.87	1.85	247.02	0.00

EXAMPLE 5-9

For interactive versions of this example visit www.mhhe.com/can1e

MONTHLY MORTGAGE PAYMENTS

LG9

Say that you have your heart set on purchasing a beautiful, old Tudor-style house for $250,000. A mortgage broker says that you can qualify for a mortgage for 80 percent (or $200,000) of the price. If you get a 15-year mortgage, the interest rate will be 6.1 percent APR. A 30-year mortgage costs 6.4 percent. One of the factors that will help you decide which mortgage to take is the magnitude of the monthly payments. What will they be?[5]

SOLUTION:

To pay off the mortgage in only 15 years, the payments would have to be larger than for the 30-year mortgage. The higher payment will be eased somewhat because the interest rate is lower on the 15-year mortgage. The payment for the 15-year mortgage is

$$PMT_{180} = \$200,000 \times \left[\frac{0.0050833}{1 - \dfrac{1}{(1+0.0050833)^{180}}} \right] = \$200,000 \times 0.0849269 = \$1,698.54$$

(continued)

[5]Most homeowners are actually most interested in their total payment, which will include hazard insurance for the home and property taxes. Such payments are referred to as PITI—principal, interest, taxes, and insurance. For simplicity, we use only PI payments here—principal and interest only.

The payment for the 30-year mortgage would be:

$$PMT_{360} = \$200,000 \times \left[\dfrac{0.0053333}{1 - \dfrac{1}{(1 + 0.0053333)^{360}}} \right] = \$200,000 \times 0.00622551 = \$1,251.01$$

So, the payments on the 15-year mortgage are nearly $450 more each month than the 30-year mortgage payments. You must decide whether the cost of paying the extra $450 each month is worth it to own the house with no debt 15 years sooner. The decision would depend on your financial budget and the strength of your desire to be debt free.

CALCULATOR
N = 180
I = 6.1 ÷ 12
PV = 200000
FV = 0
CPT PMT = −1,698.54

For 30-year mortgage:
N = 360
I = 6.4 ÷ 12
CPT PMT = −1,251.01

The schedule shows that if you wish to sell the car after two years, you will have to pay the loan company a car loan (principal) debt of $5,447.13. Of course, if you had an interest-only loan, you would still owe the full principal of $10,000 after two years. Amortization schedules are also useful for determining other things, like the total amount of interest that you will pay over the life of the loan. In this case, if you take a regular loan in which you pay both principal and interest, you pay $10,000 in principal and nearly $1,945 in interest during the four years of the loan. The interest component is an even larger component of longer-term loans, like 30-year mortgages. Depending on the interest rate charged, the first payment in a mortgage consists of 75 percent to 95 percent interest. The home mortgage principal balance falls very slowly in the first years of the loan.

We construct amortization schedules by showing the loan's principal balance at the beginning of the month. This is the same as the balance at the end of the previous month (except for the very first payment). Then we compute the interest owed on that balance for the month. After paying that interest, what's left of the monthly payment reduces the loan balance for the next month. Because of these repetitive computations, spreadsheets make amortization schedules easy to construct.

COMPUTE THE TIME PERIOD You might well also find it useful to know how long it will take to pay off a loan with specific annuity payments. To find the number of periods, you can solve equation 5-9 for N—the number of payments—but the equation becomes quite complicated.[6] Many people just use a financial calculator or spreadsheet. We can check to see if the $248.85 monthly payment would indeed pay off the $10,000, 9 percent, car loan in four years. Finding the solution with a financial calculator entails entering I = 0.75, PV = 10000, PMT = −248.85, and FV = 0. The answer is 48 months.

[6]The equation for solving for the number of periods in an annuity is

$$N = \dfrac{\ln\left(PMT / (PMT - PVA_N \times i) \right)}{\ln(1 + i)}.$$

viewpoints REVISITED

Business Application Solution

Walkabout Music, Inc. pays $700,000 (= $20 million $\times$ 0.07 $\div$ 2) in interest every six months on its existing debt. The new debt would require payments of $600,000 (= $20 million $\times$ 0.06 $\div$ 2) every six months, which represents a $100,000 savings semiannually.

The present value of these savings over the next 20 years is computed using 40 semiannual periods and a 3 percent interest rate per period:

$$PVA_N = \$100,000 \times \left[\frac{1 - \frac{1}{(1 + 0.03)^{40}}}{0.03} \right]$$

$$= \$2,311,477$$

CALCULATOR
N = 20 $\times$ 2 = 40
I/Y = 6 $\div$ 2 = 3
PMT = 100,000
FV = 0
CPT PV = $-2,311,477.20$

Since this savings is less than the $2.6 million cost of refinancing, the CFO should not refinance the old debt at this time. The company should wait until it can find more favorable terms.

Personal Application Solution

Should you switch to a new home mortgage with a lower interest rate? To answer this question, first find the monthly savings with the new mortgage. Then compare the present value of the savings to the cost of getting the new mortgage.

The current monthly mortgage payments are

$$PMT_N = \$150,000 \times \left[\frac{0.00667}{1 - \frac{1}{(1 + 0.00667)^{360}}} \right] = \$1,100.65$$

CALCULATOR
N = 30 $\times$ 12 = 360
I/Y = 8 $\div$ 12 = 0.667
PV = 150,000
FV = 0
CPT PMT = $-1,100.65$

CALCULATOR
N = 27 $\times$ 12 = 324
I/Y = 7 $\div$ 12 = 0.5833
PV = 145,920.10
FV = 0
CPT PMT = $-1,003.66$

The new mortgage would payments would be

$$PMT_N = \$145,920.10 \times \left[\frac{0.00583}{1 - \frac{1}{(1 + 0.00583)^{324}}} \right] = \$1,003.66$$

The new mortgage would save you $96.99 per month for the next 27 years.

The present value of these savings at the current 7 percent interest rate is

$$PVA_N = \$96.99 \times \left[\frac{1 - \frac{1}{(1 + 0.00583)^{324}}}{0.00583} \right] = \$14,101.14$$

CALCULATOR
N = 27 $\times$ 12 = 324
I/Y = 7 $\div$ 12 = 0.5833
PMT = 96.99
FV = 0
CPT PV = $-14,101.14$

Since the present value of the monthly savings is greater than the $1,000 broker fee, you should refinance the mortgage.

TIME TO PAY OFF A CREDIT CARD BALANCE

Through poor financial management, your friend has racked up $5,000 in debt on his credit card. The card charges a 19 percent APR and compounds monthly. His latest bill shows that he must pay a minimum of $150 this month. At this rate, how long will it take the friend to pay off his credit card debt?

SOLUTION:

Using the financial calculator, input I = 1.58333, PV = 5000, PMT = −150, FV = 0. The answer is 48 months, or 4 years. If the friend pays the minimum payment, then it will be a long time before he will be out of debt. The credit card company is very content to continue to earn the high return for many years—essentially, the interest on the loan and a very small portion of the principal. Your friend should pay more than the minimum charge to reduce his debt quicker.

TIME OUT

5-9 How might credit card companies keep their cardholders in debt for a long time? What payment do the credit card companies expect your friend to make so that he never pays down the debt?

5-10 Can you find the interest rate if you know the annuity payments and a future value? Under what circumstances might you want to solve this kind of problem? Which equation would you use?

---

summary of learning goals

In this chapter, we extend the concept of the time value of money to multiple cash flows and traditional types of loans and investment plans. Common loans and investment programs are in the form of frequent, consistent, and level cash flows, called *annuities*. We've introduced and illustrated the tools used to describe the dynamics of present and future value of annuity payments. You might well find other useful applications of annuity equations to determine loan payments, the interest rate associated with an annuity stream, or how long it will take to repay a debt.

LG1 **Compound multiple cash flows to the future.** In Chapter 4, we illustrated how a deposit today increases in value over time. But many situations include multiple deposits over time. Each of these deposits compound and can be added together at some future point in time.

LG2 **Compute the future value of frequent, level cash flows.** We call any frequent, consistent, series of level cash flows an annuity. Many retirement savings plans include contributing the same amount of money every month to a portfolio. We can compute the future value of your retirement nest egg if the portfolio is invested to earn a specific interest rate. We describe and work through many future value of an annuity tools that you can use in many applications.

Compounding makes the magnitude of the interest rate earned have a distinct impact on future value. Higher interest rates lead to more interest earnings, which in turn lead to more interest-on-interest growth. The number of annuity cash flows also strongly affects the size of the future value of a stream of cash flows.

LG3   **Discount multiple cash flows to the present.** You will find that you will often need to figure the present value of many cash flows. First, compute the present value of each individual cash flow using the appropriate discount rate. Once each cash flow is discounted to the present, they will be in common terms and thus can be added together.

LG4   **Compute the present value of an annuity.** You'll find that the present value of an annuity concept has many applications. Most car and home mortgage loans are set up so that the amount borrowed (the present value) is repaid through level payments made every period (the annuity). Given the amount of money a borrower can afford to pay (the annuity), lenders will compute its present value to determine the amount of a loan they are willing to offer. Your credit rating and current economic conditions will determine the interest rate that the lender will offer.

Borrowers can borrow more money when interest rates are lower. The present value of an annuity declines quickly for higher (interest) discount rates. Indeed, the present value of annuity payments made far into the future are worth very little today.

LG5   **Recognize the unique uses of TVM methods to figure the cash flows and present value of perpetuities.** The perpetuity, a special form of annuity, pays cash flows continuously forever. The present value of perpetuities has some applications in the investment industry.

LG6   **Recognize and adjust values for beginning-of-period annuity payments.** Most ordinary annuities assume that cash flows are paid at the end of each period. Many people who want to start investing for their future want to start today, not at the end of the month or year. Starting today implies an annuity stream that is paid at the beginning of the period. Beginning-of-period cash flows are referred to as *annuities due.* You can compute the present or future value of an annuity due by computing the value of an ordinary annuity and then multiplying by $(1 + i)$.

LG7   **Explain the impact of compound frequency and the difference between the annual percentage rate and the effective annual rate.** Many cash flows are made monthly, quarterly, or semi-annually. In these cases, the interest rate is compounded multiple times within the year. When computing the future value of an annuity, the higher the compound frequency, the higher will be the future value. While the future value will increase as compounding frequency increases, the size of each increase in future value diminishes as compounding frequencies increase.

So, the future value of a 12 percent interest rate compounded annually is lower than if it were compounded monthly. This simple form of an annualized interest rate is called the *annual percentage rate (APR).* Compounding monthly causes the interest rate to be effectively higher, and thus the future value grows. This *effective annual rate (EAR)* is a more accurate measure of the interest rate paid. The law requires lenders to show potential borrowers the APR. While the difference in APR and EAR is not that large, note that the law requires the less accurate (and lower) one to be shown except for large and extended loans such as mortgages.

LG8   **Compute the interest rate of annuity payments.** If you can compute the implied rate of return in a series of cash flows, you can more easily evaluate investment opportunities for both business and individual applications. This computation typically requires the use of a financial calculator or spreadsheet.

LG9   **Compute payments and amortization schedules for car and mortgage loans.** When you take out a loan for a car or home mortgage, you usually already know the amount (or present value) you want to borrow. You will usually find monthly payment at today's interest rates more relevant for your budget. Obviously, lower interest rates require lower payments. This is why people refinance their home mortgage when rates fall. People also frequently try to lower the periodic payments by extending the time period (or term) of the loan. Loan amortization schedules show the principal balance and interest paid per period.

LG10   **Calculate the number of payments on a loan.** When you get your credit card bill, it will offer a minimum payment, which usually only pays the accrued interest and a small amount of principal. If you want to pay down credit card debt, you can using the TVM tools we illustrate in the chapter and this minimum payment to figure the time period it will take to pay off the credit card. Making larger payments will reduce this payoff time. Better yet, paying the balance in full every period will keep you from accumulating large credit card balances. Pay the most you can every month.

chapter equations

5-1 FV_N = Future value of first cash flow + Future value of second cash flow
$$+ \cdots + \text{Future value of last cash flow}$$
$$= PMT_m \times (1+i)^{N-m} + PMT_n \times (1+i)^{N-n} + \cdots + PMT_p \times (1+i)^{N-p}$$

5-2 $$FVA_N = PMT \times \frac{(1+i)^N - 1}{i}$$

5-3 PV = Present value of first cash flow + present value of second cash flow
$$+ \cdots + \text{Present value of last cash flow}$$
$$= \frac{PMT_m}{(1+i)^{N-m}} + \frac{PMT_n}{(1+i)^{N-n}} + \cdots + \frac{PMT_p}{(1+i)^{N-p}}$$

5-4 $$PVA_N = PMT \times \left[\frac{1 - \dfrac{1}{(1+i)^N}}{i} \right]$$

5-5 $$PV \text{ of a perpetuity} = \frac{PMT}{i}$$

5-6 $$FVA_N \text{ due} = FVA_N \times (1+i)$$

5-7 $$PVA_N \text{ due} = PVA_N \times (1+i)$$

5-8 $$EAR = \left(1 + \frac{APR}{m}\right)^m - 1$$

5-9 $$PMT_N = PV \times \left[\frac{i}{1 - \dfrac{1}{(1+i)^N}} \right]$$

key terms

amortized loan, A loan in which the borrower pays interest and principal over time. (p. 158)
amortization schedule, A table detailing the periodic loan payment, interest payment, and debt balance over the life of the loan. (p. 159)

annual percentage rate (APR), The interest rate per period times the number of periods in a year. (p. 156)
annuity, A stream of level and frequent cash flows paid at the end of each time period—often referred to as an *ordinary annuity*. (p. 143)

annuity due, An annuity in which cash flows are paid at the beginning of each time period. (p. 152)
consols, Investment assets structured as perpetuities. (p. 152)
effective annual rate (EAR), An interest rate that reflects annualizing with compounding figured in. (p. 156)

loan principal, The balance yet to be paid on a loan. (p. 159)
perpetuity, An annuity with cash flows that continue forever. (p. 152)

self-test problems with solutions

1 **Future Value and Annuity Payments** Chandler and Monica are trying to decide if they will have enough money to retire early in 12 years, at age 60. Their current assets are $300,000 in retirement plans and they have $100,000 in other investments. Together, they contribute $28,000 per year to their retirement plans and another $6,000 to other investments. If their assets grow at 8 percent per year, how much money will they have when they turn 60? After they retire, they will invest their wealth more conservatively and it will earn 5 percent per year. Is this enough to fund a $100,000 per year retirement for 40 years?

Solution:

Chandler and Monica's current assets of $400,000 will grow to $1,007,268 (= $400,000 \times 1.08^{12}$) in 12 years. Their annuity contributions of $34,000 will add another

$$FVA_{12} = \$34,000 \times \frac{(1 + 0.08)^{12} - 1}{0.08} = \$34,000 \times 18.977 = \$645,222$$

So their total retirement wealth is $1,652,490. To determine the income this wealth generates over 40 years, compute the annual annuity payments as

$$PMT_{40} = \$1,652,490 \times \left[\frac{0.05}{1 - \frac{1}{(1 + 0.05)^{40}}} \right] = \$1,652,490 \times 0.058278$$

$$= \$96,304$$

It appears that Chandler and Monica would not quite make their $100,000 income requirement. However, a few years after they retire, they would be eligible for Social Security. Though relatively meager, the Social Security payments will be enough to comfortably put their income over the $100,000 level.

2 **Present Value of an Annuity** Kevin and Kody are identical twins, have identical jobs, and earn the same salary. However, Kody has been far more financially responsible. He pays his bills on time and pays off his credit card debt quickly. Kevin has been less financially responsible. He often forgets to pay bills and has allowed his credit card balance to balloon. If he is short on cash for the month, he simply decides not to pay even the minimum balance. Now Kevin and Kody are each looking to buy houses. They both decide that they can afford a $1,000 monthly mortgage payment. On Kody's trip to the mortgage broker, he learns that he can obtain a mortgage for a 7 percent APR. Because of Kevin's bad credit rating, he will be charged 10 percent. How is Kevin's bad credit going to impact his house search?

LG2, LG9

LG4

www.mhhe.com/can1e

Solution:

With $1,000 monthly payments and 7 percent interest rate, Kody uses the present value of an annuity equation and computes the amount he can borrow as:

$$PVA_{360} = \$1,000 \times \left[\frac{1 - \dfrac{1}{(1 + 0.0058333)^{360}}}{0.0058333} \right] = \$1,000 \times 150.3076$$

$$= \$150,308$$

With a 20 percent down payment on the house, Kody can look for houses that cost about $187,900 (= $150,308 ÷ 0.8). Kevin must pay a higher interest rate and computes that he can borrow a total of:

$$PVA_{360} = \$1,000 \times \left[\frac{1 - \dfrac{1}{(1 + 0.008333)^{360}}}{0.008333} \right] = \$1,000 \times 113.9509$$

$$= \$113,951$$

If Kevin can find a 20 percent down payment, he can look for houses in the price range of $142,400. Because of Kevin's poor credit management, he must buy a house that is over $45,000 less expensive than Kody can buy, even though Kevin is paying exactly the same monthly mortgage payment as Kody.

CALCULATOR

For Kody
N = 360
I = 0.58333
PMT = −1000
FV = 0
CPT PV = 150,307.57

For Kevin
I = 0.83333
CPT PV = 113,950.82

3 Compound Frequency Say that you own a small business, which you plan to expand. Your expansion plans include borrowing $50,000 from the bank with a three-year, amortized loan. The bank has given you these loan choices:

Annual payments, 10 percent APR
Quarterly payments, 9.8 percent APR
Monthly payments, 9.5 percent APR

Which loan would have a lower effective annual rate?

Solution:

The effective annual rate for the annual payment loan is:

$$EAR = \left(1 + \frac{0.10}{1} \right)^1 - 1 = 0.10 = 10\%$$

The effective annual rate for the quarterly payment loan is:

$$EAR = \left(1 + \frac{0.098}{4} \right)^4 - 1 = 0.1017 = 10.17\%$$

The effective annual rate for the monthly payment loan is:

$$EAR = \left(1 + \frac{0.095}{12} \right)^{12} - 1 = 0.0992 = 9.92\%$$

So, the lowest cost loan is the monthly one.

4 Annuity Payments and Amortization Schedule Consider Rachel and Ross, a young couple who wish to buy their first home. To do this, they will need to borrow $20,000 from her parents to fund some of the down payment. Rachel's parents will charge them a 7 percent rate. They will make monthly payments over three years to repay the loan. Ross wants to deduct the loan's interest from his taxes, so they need to know how much in interest they will pay

LG7

LG9, LG10

www.mhhe.com/can1e

each year. Compute monthly payments and create an amortization schedule table to determine the interest paid each year.

Solution:

The loan will be repaid over 36 months and use a 0.5833 percent (= 7 percent ÷ 12) monthly interest rate. Therefore, the monthly payments will be:

$$PMT_{36} = \$20{,}000 \times \left[\frac{0.005833}{1 - \dfrac{1}{(1 + 0.005833)^{36}}} \right] = \$20{,}000 \times 0.030877$$

$$= \$617.54$$

The following table shows the amortization schedule.

MONTH	BEGINNING BALANCE	TOTAL PAYMENT	INTEREST PAID	PRINCIPAL PAID	ENDING BALANCE
1	$20,000.00	$617.54	$116.67	$500.87	$19,499.13
2	19,499.13	617.54	113.74	503.80	18,995.33
3	18,995.33	617.54	110.81	506.73	18,488.60
4	18,488.60	617.54	107.85	509.69	17,978.91
5	17,978.91	617.54	104.88	512.66	17,466.24
6	17,466.24	617.54	101.89	515.65	16,950.59
7	16,950.59	617.54	98.88	518.66	16,431.93
8	16,431.93	617.54	95.85	521.69	15,910.24
9	15,910.24	617.54	92.81	524.73	15,385.51
10	15,385.51	617.54	89.75	527.79	14,857.72
11	14,857.72	617.54	86.67	530.87	14,326.85
12	14,326.85	617.54	83.57	533.97	13,792.88
13	13,792.88	617.54	80.46	537.08	13,255.80
14	13,255.80	617.54	77.33	540.21	12,715.59
15	12,715.59	617.54	74.17	543.37	12,172.22
16	12,172.22	617.54	71.00	546.54	11,625.69
17	11,625.69	617.54	67.82	549.72	11,075.96
18	11,075.96	617.54	64.61	552.93	10,523.03
19	10,523.03	617.54	61.38	556.16	9,966.88
20	9,966.88	617.54	58.14	559.40	9,407.48
21	9,407.48	617.54	54.88	562.66	8,844.82
22	8,844.82	617.54	51.59	565.95	8,278.87
23	8,278.87	617.54	48.29	569.25	7,709.62
24	7,709.62	617.54	44.97	572.57	7,137.06
25	7,137.06	617.54	41.63	575.91	6,561.15
26	6,561.15	617.54	38.27	579.27	5,981.88
27	5,981.88	617.54	34.89	582.65	5,399.24
28	5,399.24	617.54	31.50	586.04	4,813.19
29	4,813.19	617.54	28.08	589.46	4,223.73
30	4,223.73	617.54	24.64	592.90	3,630.83
31	3,630.83	617.54	21.18	596.36	3,034.47
32	3,034.47	617.54	17.70	599.84	2,434.63
33	2,434.63	617.54	14.20	603.34	1,831.29
34	1,831.29	617.54	10.68	606.86	1,224.43
35	1,224.43	617.54	7.14	610.40	614.04
36	614.04	617.62	3.58	614.04	0.00

Year 1 interest = $1,203.36
Year 2 interest = $754.65
Year 3 interest = $273.50

Ross and Rachel will pay $1,203.36 in interest the first year, $754.65 in the second year, and $273.50 in the third year.

questions

1. How can you add a cash flow in year 2 and a cash flow in year 4 in year 7? *(LG1)*

2. People can become millionaires in their retirement years quite easily if they start saving early in employer 401(k) or 403(b) programs (or even if their employers don't offer such programs). Demonstrate the growth of a $250 monthly contribution for 40 years earning 9 percent APR. *(LG2)*

3. When you discount multiple cash flows, how does the future period that a cash flow is paid affect its present value and its contribution to the value of all the cash flows? *(LG3)*

4. How can you use the present value of an annuity concept to determine the price of a house you can afford? *(LG4)*

5. Since perpetuity payments continue forever, how can a present value be computed? Why isn't the present value infinite? *(LG5)*

6. Explain why you use the same adjustment factor, $(1 + i)$, when you adjust annuity due payments for both future value and present value. *(LG6)*

7. Use the idea of compound interest to explain why EAR is larger than APR. *(LG7)*

8. Would you rather pay $10,000 for a 5-year, $2,500 annuity or a 10-year $1,250 annuity? Why? *(LG8)*

9. The interest on your home mortgage is tax deductible. Why are the early years of the mortgage more helpful in reducing taxes than in the later years? *(LG9)*

10. How can you use the concepts illustrated in computing the number of payments in an annuity to figure how to pay off a credit card balance? How does the magnitude of the payment impact the number of months? *(LG10)*

problems

basic
problems

5-1 **Future Value** Compute the future value in year 8 of a $1,000 deposit in year 1 and another $1,500 deposit at the end of year 3 using a 10 percent interest rate. *(LG1)*

5-2 **Future Value** Compute the future value in year 7 of a $2,000 deposit in year 1 and another $2,500 deposit at the end of year 4 using a 8 percent interest rate. *(LG1)*

5-3 **Future Value of an Annuity** What is the future value of a $500 annuity payment over five years if interest rates are 9 percent? *(LG2)*

5-4 **Future Value of an Annuity** What is the future value of a $700 annuity payment over four years if interest rates are 10 percent? *(LG2)*

5-5 **Present Value** Compute the present value of a $1,000 deposit in year 1 and another $1,500 deposit at the end of year 3 if interest rates are 10 percent. *(LG3)*

5-6 **Present Value** Compute the present value of a $2,000 deposit in year 1 and another $2,500 deposit at the end of year 4 using an 8 percent interest rate. *(LG3)*

5-7 **Present Value of an Annuity** What's the present value of a $500 annuity payment over five years if interest rates are 9 percent? *(LG4)*

5-8 **Present Value of an Annuity** What's the present value of a $700 annuity payment over four years if interest rates are 10 percent? *(LG4)*

5-9 **Present Value of a Perpetuity** What's the present value, when interest rates are 7.5 percent, of a $50 payment made every year forever? *(LG5)*

5-10 **Present Value of a Perpetuity** What's the present value, when interest rates are 8.5 percent, of a $75 payment made every year forever? *(LG5)*

5-11 **Present Value of an Annuity Due** If the present value of an ordinary, seven-year annuity is $6,500 and interest rates are 8.5 percent, what's the present value of the same annuity due? *(LG6)*

5-12 **Present Value of an Annuity Due** If the present value of an ordinary, six-year annuity is $8,500 and interest rates are 9.5 percent, what's the present value of the same annuity due? *(LG6)*

5-13 **Future Value of an Annuity Due** If the future value of an ordinary, seven-year annuity is $6,500 and interest rates are 8.5 percent, what is the future value of the same annuity due? *(LG6)*

5-14 **Future Value of an Annuity Due** If the future value of an ordinary, six-year annuity is $8,500 and interest rates are 9.5 percent, what's the future value of the same annuity due? *(LG6)*

5-15 **Effective Annual Rate** A loan is offered with monthly payments and an 11 percent APR. What's the loan's effective annual rate (EAR)? *(LG7)*

5-16 **Effective Annual Rate** A loan is offered with monthly payments and a 12 percent APR. What's the loan's effective annual rate (EAR)? *(LG7)*

intermediate problems

5-17 **Future Value** Given a 6 percent interest rate, compute the year 6 future value of deposits made in years 1, 2, 3, and 4 of $1,000, $1,200, $1,200, and $1,500. *(LG1)*

5-18 **Future Value** Given a 7 percent interest rate, compute the year 6 future value of deposits made in years 1, 2, 3, and 4 of $1,000, $1,300, $1,300, and $1,400. *(LG1)*

5-19 **Future Value of Multiple Annuities** Assume that you contribute $200 per month to a retirement plan for 20 years. Then you are able to increase the contribution to $400 per month for another 20 years. Given a 7 percent interest rate, what is the value of your retirement plan after the 40 years? *(LG2)*

5-20 **Future Value of Multiple Annuities** Assume that you contribute $150 per month to a retirement plan for 15 years. Then you are able to increase the contribution to $350 per month for the next 25 years. Given an 8 percent interest rate, what is the value of your retirement plan after the 40 years? *(LG2)*

5-21 **Present Value** Given a 6 percent interest rate, compute the present value of payments made in years 1, 2, 3, and 4 of $1,000, $1,200, $1,200, and $1,500. *(LG3)*

5-22 Present Value Given a 7 percent interest rate, compute the present value of payments made in years 1, 2, 3, and 4 of $1,000, $1,300, $1,300, and $1,400. *(LG3)*

5-23 Present Value of Multiple Annuities A small business owner visits his bank to ask for a loan. The owner states that she can repay a loan at $1,000 per month for the next three years and then $2,000 per month for two years after that. If the bank is charging customers 7.5 percent APR, how much would it be willing to lend the business owner? *(LG2)*

5-24 Present Value of Multiple Annuities A small business owner visits his bank to ask for a loan. The owner states that she can repay a loan at $1,500 per month for the next three years and then $500 per month for two years after that. If the bank is charging customers 8.5 percent APR, how much would it be willing to lend the business owner? *(LG2)*

5-25 Present Value of a Perpetuity A perpetuity pays $100 per year and interest rates are 7.5 percent. How much would its value change if interest rates increased to 8.5 percent? Did the value increase or decrease? *(LG5)*

5-26 Present Value of a Perpetuity A perpetuity pays $50 per year and interest rates are 9 percent. How much would its value change if interest rates decreased to 8 percent? Did the value increase or decrease? *(LG5)*

5-27 Future and Present Value of an Annuity Due If you start making $50 monthly contributions today and continue them for five years, what's their future value if the compounding rate is 10 percent APR? What is the present value of this annuity? *(LG6)*

5-28 Future and Present Value of an Annuity Due If you start making $75 monthly contributions today and continue them for four years, what is their future value if the compounding rate is 12 percent APR? What is the present value of this annuity? *(LG6)*

5-29 Compound Frequency Payday loans are very short-term loans that charge very high interest rates. You can borrow $250 today and repay $300 in two weeks. What is the compounded *annual* rate implied by this 20 percent rate charged for only two weeks? *(LG7)*

5-30 Compound Frequency Payday loans are very short-term loans that charge very high interest rates. You can borrow $500 today and repay $575 in two weeks. What is the compounded *annual* rate implied by this 15 percent rate charged for only two weeks? *(LG7)*

5-31 Annuity Interest Rate What's the interest rate of a five-year, annual $5,000 annuity with present value of $20,000? *(LG8)*

5-32 Annuity Interest Rate What's the interest rate of a seven-year, annual $4,000 annuity with present value of $20,000? *(LG8)*

5-33 Annuity Interest Rate What annual interest rate would you need to earn if you wanted a $1,000 per month contribution to grow to $75,000 in five years?

5-34 Annuity Interest Rate What annual interest rate would you need to earn if you wanted a $500 per month contribution to grow to $45,000 in six years? *(LG8)*

5-35 Loan Payments You wish to buy a $25,000 car. The dealer offers you a four-year loan with a 10 percent APR. What are the monthly payments? How would the payment differ if you paid interest only? What would the consequences of such a decision be? *(LG9)*

5-36 Loan Payments You wish to buy a $10,000 dining room set. The furniture store offers you a three-year loan with an 11 percent APR. What are the monthly payments? How would the payment differ if you paid interest only? What would the consequences of such a decision be?

5-37 Number of Annuity Payments Joey realizes that he has charged too much on his credit card and has racked up $5,000 in debt. If he can pay $150 each month and the card charges 17 percent APR (compounded monthly), how long will it take him to pay off the debt? *(LG9)*

5-38 Number of Annuity Payments Phoebe realizes that she has charged too much on her credit card and has racked up $6,000 in debt. If she can pay $200 each month and the card charges 18 percent APR (compounded monthly), how long will it take her to pay off the debt? *(LG10)*

advanced
problems

5-39 Future Value Given an 8 percent interest rate, compute the year 7 future value if deposits of $1,000 and $2,000 are made in years 1 and 3, respectively, and a withdrawal of $500 is made in year 4. *(LG1)*

5-40 Future Value Given a 9 percent interest rate, compute the year 6 future value if deposits of $1,500 and $2,500 are made in years 2 and 3, respectively, and a withdrawal of $700 is made in year 5. *(LG1)*

5-41 Low Financing or Cash Back? A car company is offering a choice of deals. You can receive $500 cash back on the purchase, or a 3 percent APR, four-year loan. The price of the car is $15,000 and you could obtain a four-year loan from your credit union, at 7 percent APR. Which deal is cheaper? *(LG4, LG9)*

5-42 Low Financing or Cash Back? A car company is offering a choice of deals. You can receive $1,000 cash back on the purchase, or a 2 percent APR, five-year loan. The price of the car is $20,000 and you could obtain a five-year loan from your credit union, at 7 percent APR. Which deal is cheaper? *(LG4, LG9)*

5-43 Amortization Schedule Create the amortization schedule for a loan of $15,000, paid monthly over three years using a 9 percent APR. *(LG9)*

5-44 Amortization Schedule Create the amortization schedule for a loan of $5,000, paid monthly over two years using an 8 percent APR. *(LG9)*

5-45 Investing for Retirement Monica has decided that she wants to build enough retirement wealth that, if invested at 8 percent per year, will provide her with $3,500 of monthly income for 30 years. To date, she has saved nothing, but she still has 25 years until she retires. How much money does she need to contribute per month to reach her goal? *(LG4, LG9)*

5-46 Investing for Retirement Ross has decided that he wants to build enough retirement wealth that, if invested at 7 percent per year, will provide him with $4,000 of monthly income for 30 years. To date, he has saved nothing, but he still has 20 years until he retires. How much money does he need to contribute per month to reach his goal? *(LG4, LG9)*

5-47 Loan Balance Rachel purchased a $15,000 car two years ago using an 8 percent, four-year loan. She has decided that she would sell the car now, if she could get a price that would pay off the balance of her loan. What is the minimum price Rachel would need to receive for her car? *(LG9)*

5-48 Loan Balance Hank purchased a $20,000 car two years ago using a 9 percent, five-year loan. He has decided that he would sell the car now, if he could get a price that would pay off the balance of his loan. What's the minimum price Hank would need to receive for his car? *(LG9)*

5-49 **Teaser Rate Mortgage** A mortgage broker is offering a $183,900 30-year mortgage with a teaser rate. In the first two years of the mortgage, the borrower makes monthly payments on only a 4 percent APR interest rate. After the second year, the mortgage interest rate charged increases to 7 percent APR. What are the monthly payments in the first two years? What are the monthly payments after the second year? *(LG9)*

5-50 **Teaser Rate Mortgage** A mortgage broker is offering a $279,000 30-year mortgage with a teaser rate. In the first two years of the mortgage, the borrower makes monthly payments on only a 4.5 percent APR interest rate. After the second year, the mortgage interest rate charged increases to 7.5 percent APR. What are the monthly payments in the first two years? What are the monthly payments after the second year? *(LG9)*

5-51 **Excel Problem** Consider a person who begins contributing to a retirement plan at age 25 and contributes for 40 years until retirement at age 65. For the first 10 years, she contributes $3,000 per year. She increases the contribution rate to $5,000 per year in years 11 through 20. This is followed by increases to $10,000 per year in years 21 through 31 and to $15,000 per year for the last 10 years. This money earns a 9 percent return. First compute the value of the retirement plan when she turns age 65. Then compute the annual payment she would receive over the next 40 years if the wealth was converted to an annuity payment at 8 percent. *(LG2, LG9)*

combined chapter 4 and chapter 5 problems

4&5-1 **Future Value** Consider that you are 35 years old and have just changed to a new job. You have $80,000 in the retirement plan from your former employer. You can roll that money into the retirement plan of the new employer. You will also contribute $5,000 each year into your new employer's plan. If the rolled-over money and the new contributions both earn a 7 percent return, how much should you expect to have when you retire in 30 years?

4&5-2 **Future Value** Consider that you are 45 years old and have just changed to a new job. You have $150,000 in the retirement plan from your former employer. You can roll that money into the retirement plan of the new employer. You will also contribute $8,000 each year into your new employer's plan. If the rolled-over money and the new contributions both earn an 8 percent return, how much should you expect to have when you retire in 20 years?

4&5-3 **Future Value and Number of Annuity Payments** Your client has been given a trust fund valued at $1 million. He cannot access the money until he turns 65 years old, which is in 25 years. At that time, he can withdraw $25,000 per month. If the trust fund is invested at a 5.5 percent rate, how many months will it last your client once he starts to withdraw the money?

4&5-4 **Future Value and Number of Annuity Payments** Your client has been given a trust fund valued at $1.5 million. She cannot access the money until she turns 65 years old, which is in 15 years. At that time, she can withdraw $20,000 per month. If the trust fund is invested at a 5 percent rate, how many months will it last your client once she starts to withdraw the money?

4&5-5 **Present Value and Annuity Payments** A local furniture store is advertising a deal in which you buy a $3,000 dining room set and do not need to pay for two years (no interest cost is incurred). How much money would you have to deposit now in a savings account earning 5 percent APR, compounded monthly, to pay the $3,000 bill in two years? Alternatively, how much would you have to deposit in the savings account each month to be able to pay the bill?

4&5-6 **Present Value and Annuity Payments** A local furniture store is advertising a deal in which you buy a $5,000 living room set with three years before you need to make any payments (no interest cost is incurred). How much money would you have to deposit now in a savings account earning 4 percent APR, compounded monthly, to pay the $5,000 bill in three years? Alternatively, how much would you have to deposit in the savings account each month to be able to pay the bill?

4&5-7 **House Appreciation and Mortgage Payments** Say that you purchase a house for $200,000 by getting a mortgage for $180,000 and paying a $20,000 down payment. If you get a 30-year mortgage with a 7 percent interest rate, what are the monthly payments? What would the loan balance be in 10 years? If the house appreciates at 3 percent per year, what will be the value of the house in 10 years? How much of this value is your equity?

4&5-8 **House Appreciation and Mortgage Payments** Say that you purchase a house for $150,000 by getting a mortgage for $135,000 and paying a $15,000 down payment. If you get a 15-year mortgage with a 7 percent interest rate, what are the monthly payments? What would the loan balance be in five years? If the house appreciates at 4 percent per year, what will be the value of the house in five years? How much of this value is your equity?

4&5-9 **Construction Loan** You have secured a loan from your bank for two years to build your home. The terms of the loan are that you will borrow $100,000 now and an additional $100,000 in one year. Interest of 10 percent APR will be charged on the balance monthly. Since no payments will be made during the two-year loan, the balance will grow at the 10 percent compounded rate. At the end of the two years, the balance will be converted to a traditional 30-year mortgage at a 6 percent interest rate. What will you be paying as monthly mortgage payments (principal and interest only)?

4&5-10 **Construction Loan** You have secured a loan from your bank for two years to build your home. The terms of the loan are that you will borrow $100,000 now and an additional $50,000 in one year. Interest of 9 percent APR will be charged on the balance monthly. Since no payments will be made during the two-year loan, the balance will grow. At the end of the two years, the balance will be converted to a traditional 30-year mortgage at a 7 percent interest rate. What will you pay as monthly mortgage payments (principal and interest only)?

research it! Retirement Income Calculators

The Internet provides some excellent retirement income calculators. You can find one by Googling "retirement income calculator." Many of the calculators allow you to determine your predicted annual income from a retirement nest egg under different assumptions. For example, you can spend only the investment income generated from the nest egg. Most retirees try not to touch the principal. Or, you can spend both the income and the nest egg itself. These calculators let you input the size of the retirement wealth and the investment return to be earned. They then make time value computations to determine the annual income the nest egg will provide.

Go to a retirement income calculator like the one at MSN Money. Use the calculator to create a retirement scenario. Use the TVM equations or a financial calculator to check the Internet results.
(http://moneycentral.msn.com/investor/calcs/n_retire/main.asp)

integrated minicase: Paying on your Stafford Loan

Consider Gavin, a new freshman who has just received a Stafford student loan and started college. He plans to obtain the maximum loan from Stafford at the beginning of each year. Although Gavin does not have to make any payments while he is in school, the 6.8 percent interest owed (compounded monthly) accrues and is added to the balance of the loan.

STAFFORD LOAN LIMITS	
Freshman	$2,625
Sophomore	3,500
Junior	5,500
Senior	5,500

After graduation, Gavin gets a six-month grace period. This means that monthly payments are still not required, but interest is still accruing. After the grace period, the standard repayment plan is to amortize the debt using monthly payments for 10 years.

a. Show a time line of when the loans will be taken.

b. What will be the loan balance when Gavin graduates after his fourth year of school?

c. What is the loan balance six months after graduation?

d. Using the standard repayment plan and a 6.8 percent APR interest rate, compute the monthly payments Gavin owes after the grace period.

ANSWERS TO TIME OUT

5-1 Compounding allows for the earning of interest on the interest that was earned earlier in time. When this occurs more often, more money will be built. So, the greater the compounding frequency, the higher the future value of the annuity.

5-2 You can solve this several ways. First, you can use one annuity of $4,500 for the entire period. Then use a second annuity of $4,500 starting in year 19 and continuing to the end. The future value of this second annuity would be subtracted from the first annuity. Last, add a third annuity of $4,500 starting in year 23. Another way to solve this problem is to start with the $4,500 annuity for the entire period. Then subtract the future values of each of the four individual nonpayments of $4,500.

5-3 The magnitude of the discount rate is very important in the present value computation. The longer the discount period, the more important the interest rate magnitude becomes. No, higher interest rates lead to lower present values.

5-4 The present value of the annuity at 7 percent is $20,323. In this case, the fee of $20,000 appears cheaper.

5-5 Annuity due is good to use in cases where one of the annuity payments is made immediately instead of waiting to the end of the period (year, month, etc.).

5-6 It is easy to switch from the regular annuity future value to the future value of this annuity due. You simply multiply the future value previously found by $(1 + i)$.

5-7 The APR is an easy number to compute and understand, but it does not account for the extra money paid because of compounding. EAR is more difficult to compute, but does incorporate the compounding effect.

5-8 If both discounting examples have the same APR, then the one discounted monthly will result in a smaller present value. This is because it will have a higher EAR.

5-9 Credit card companies allow a small minimum payment each month. This small payment is often mostly interest and entails little principal. Therefore, the cardholder does not pay down very much of the debt and remains in debt for a long time. If the minimum payment is only interest, then the debt will never be paid off.

5-10 If you know the annuity payments, the future value, and the number of payments, then you can determine the implied interest rate. You should solve for the interest rate using a financial calculator as it is quite difficult using the TVM equations.

chapter 6:

VALUING BONDS

 Learning Goals

LG1 Describe bond characteristics.

LG2 Identify various bond issuers and their motivation for issuing debt.

LG3 Read and interpret bond quotes.

LG4 Compute bond prices using present value concepts.

LG5 Explain the relationship between bond prices and interest rates.

LG6 Compute bond yields.

LG7 Find bond ratings and assess credit risk's effects on bond yields.

LG8 Assess bond market performance.

How important are bonds and the bond market to a capitalist economy? Those unfamiliar with the financial markets may have the impression that the stock market dominates capital markets in the United States and in other countries. Stock market performance appears constantly on 24-hour TV news channels and on the evening news. By contrast, we seldom hear any mention of the bond market. While bonds may not generate the same excitement that stocks do, they are an even more important capital source for companies, governments, and other organizations. The bond market is actually larger than the stock market. In late 2007, the U.S. bond market represented roughly $29.2 trillion in outstanding debt obligations. At the same time, the market value of all common stock issues was worth about half the value of the bond market, at roughly $14.2 trillion.

Bonds also trade in great volume and frequency. In 2007, the total average daily trading in all types of U.S. bonds reached over $970 billion. Investors are often attracted to the stock market because it offers the potential for high investor returns—but great risks come with that high potential return. While some bonds offer more safe and stable returns than stocks, other bonds also offer high potential rewards and, consequently, higher risk.

viewpoints

Business Application

You are the chief financial officer (CFO) for Beach Sand Resorts. The firm needs $150 million of new capital to renovate a hotel property. As you discuss the firm's plans with a credit rating agency, you learn that if 15-year bonds are used to raise this capital, the bonds will be rated BB and will have to offer a 7 percent return. How many bonds will you have to issue to raise the necessary capital? What semi annual interest payments will Beach Sand have to make? **(See solution on p. 205)**

Personal Application

You would like to invest in bonds. Your broker suggests two different bonds. The first bond, issued by Liberty Media, will mature in 2013. Its price is quoted at 96.21 and it pays a 5.7 percent coupon. The second bond suggested, issued by Alcoa, Inc., also matures in 2013. This bond's price is 101.94 and pays a 5.375 percent coupon. To help you decide between the bonds, you want to know how much money it will cost to buy 10 bonds, what interest payments you will receive, and what return the bonds offer. Also, you want to understand the differences between what the two bonds imply about their risk. **(See solution on p. 205)**

A practice test can be found on the Online Learning Center at
www.mhhe.com/can1e

In this chapter, we will explore bond characteristics and their price dynamics. You will see that bond pricing uses many time value of money principles that we've used in the preceding chapters.

6.1 Bond Market Overview

Bond Characteristics

Bonds are debt obligation securities that corporations, the federal government or its agencies, or states and local governments issue to fund various projects or operations. All of these organizations periodically need to raise capital for various reasons, which we formally discuss in Chapter 8. Bonds are also known as **fixed-income securities** because bondholders (investors) know both how much they will receive in interest payments and when their principal will be returned. From the bond issuer's point of view, the bond is a loan that requires regular interest payments and an eventual repayment of the borrowed **principal.** Investors—often pension funds, banks, and mutual funds—buy bonds to earn investment returns. Most bonds follow a relatively standard structure. A legal contract called the **indenture agreement** outlines the precise terms between the issuer and the bondholders. Any bond's main characteristics include:

- The date the principal will be repaid (the **maturity date**).
- The **par value** or face value of each bond, which is the principal loan amount that the borrower must repay.
- The interest rate.
- A description of any property to be pledged as collateral.
- Steps that the bondholder can take in the event that the issuer fails to pay the interest or principal.

Table 6.1 describes par value and other bond characteristics. Most bonds have a par value of $1,000. This is the amount of principal the issuer has promised to repay. Bonds have fixed lives. The bond's life ends when the issuer repays the par value to the buyer on the bond's maturity date. Although a bond will mature on a specific calendar date, the bond is usually referenced by its **time to maturity,** that is, 2 years, 5 years, 20 years, and so on. In fact, the market groups bonds together by their time to maturity and classifies them as either short-term bonds, medium-term bonds, or long-term bonds, regardless of issuer. Long-term bonds carry 20 or 30 years to maturity. Of course, over time, the 30-year bond becomes a 20-year bond, 10-year bond, and eventually matures. But other time-periods-to-maturity do exist. For example, Ford Motor issued bonds with 100 years to maturity on May 15, 1997. The bonds have a coupon (interest) rate of 7.70 percent and mature in 2097.

When interest rates economywide fall several percentage points (which often takes several years), homeowners everywhere seek to refinance their home mortgages. They want to make lower interest payments (and sometimes want to pay down their mortgage principal) every month. Corporations that have outstanding bond debt will also want to refinance those bonds. Sometimes the indenture contract allows companies to do so; sometimes the indenture prohibits refinancing. Bonds that can be refinanced have a **call** feature, which means that the issuer can "call" the bonds back and repay the principal before the maturity date. To compensate the bondholders for getting the bond called, the issuer pays the principal and a **call premium.** The most common call premium is one year's worth of interest payments. In some indentures, the call premium declines over time.

	Typical Bond Features		table 6.1
CHARACTERISTIC	**DESCRIPTION**		**COMMON VALUES**
Par value	The amount of the loan to be repaid. This is often referred to as the *principal* of the bond.		$1,000
Time to maturity	The number of years left until the maturity date.		1 year to 30 years
Call	The opportunity for the issuer to repay the principal before the maturity date, usually because interest rates have fallen or issuer's circumstances have changed. When calling a bond, the issuer commonly pays the principal and one year of interest payments.		Many bonds are not callable. For those that are, a common feature is that the bond can be called any time after 10 years of issuance.
Coupon rate	The interest rate used to compute the bond's interest payment each year. Listed as a percentage of par value, the actual payments usually arrive twice per year.		2 to 10 percent
Bond price	The bond's market price reported as a percentage of par value.		80 to 120 percent of par value

The bond's **coupon rate** determines the dollar amount of interest paid to bondholders. The coupon rate appears on the bond and is listed as a percentage of the par value. So a 5 percent coupon rate means that the issuer will pay 5 percent of $1,000, or $50, in interest every year, usually divided into two equal semi annual payments. So a 5 percent coupon bond will pay $25 every six months. The name *coupon* is a holdover from the past, when bonds were actually issued with a coupon book. Every six months a bondholder would tear out a coupon and mail it to the issuer, who would then make the interest payment. These are sometimes referred to as *bearer bonds* (often a feature of spy or mystery movies,) because whoever held the coupon book could receive the payments. Nowadays, issuers register bond owners and automatically wire interest payments to the owner's bank or brokerage account. Nevertheless, the term *coupon* persists today.

At original issue, bonds typically sell at par value, unless interest rates are very volatile. Bondholders recoup the par value on the bond's maturity date. However, at all times in between these two dates, bonds might trade among investors in the secondary bond market. The **bond's price** as it trades in the secondary market will not likely be the par value. Bonds trade for higher and lower prices than their par values. We'll thoroughly demonstrate the reasons for bond pricing in a later section of this chapter. Bond prices are quoted in terms of percent of par value rather than in dollar terms. Sources of trading information list a bond that traded at $1,150 as 115, and a bond that traded for $870 as 87.

 For interactive versions of this example visit www.mhhe.com/can1e

EXAMPLE 6-1

BOND CHARACTERISTICS

 LG1

Consider a bond issued ten years ago with an at-issue time to maturity of 30 years. The bond's coupon rate is 8 percent and it currently trades in the bond market for 109. Assuming a par value of $1,000, what is the bond's current time to maturity, semi annual interest payment, and bond price in dollars?

SOLUTION:

Time to maturity = 30 years − 10 years = 20 years

Annual payment = 8 percent × $1,000 = $80, so semi-annual payment is $40

Bond price = 109 percent × $1,000 = $1,090

figure 6.1

Amount of Capital
Raised Yearly from
Bonds Issued by Local
and Federal Govern-
ment and Corporations

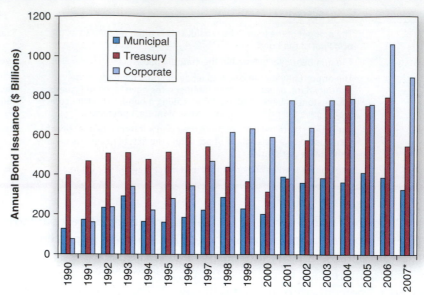

*Through September, *Data Source*: Securities Industry and Financial Markets Association

Bond Issuers

LG2 For many years, bonds were considered stodgy, overly conservative investments. Not anymore! The fixed-income industry has seen tremendous innovation in the past couple of decades. The financial industry has created and issued many new types of bonds and fixed-income securities, some with odd-sounding acronyms, like TIGRs, CATS, COUGRs, and PINEs, all of which are securities based on U.S. Treasuries. Even with all the innovation, the traditional three main bond issuers remain: U.S. treasury bonds, corporate bonds, and municipal bonds. Figure 6.1 shows the amount of money that these bond issuers have raised each year.

LG2 **TREASURY BONDS** Treasury bonds carry the "full-faith-and-credit" backing of the U.S. government and investors have long considered them among the safest fixed-income investments in the world. The federal government sells Treasury securities through public auctions to finance the federal deficit. When the deficit is large, more bonds come to auction. In addition, the Federal Reserve System (the Fed) uses Treasury securities to implement monetary policy. Technically, Treasury securities issued with 1 to 10 years until maturity are Treasury notes. Securities issued with 10 to 30 years until maturities are Treasury bonds. The figure shows that the number of new Treasuries being offered actually declined in the late 1990s as the federal budget deficit declined. However, this dramatically reversed in 2002 when the trend toward issuing more federal debt reversed.

CORPORATE BONDS Corporations raise capital to finance investments in inventory, plant and equipment, research and development, and general business expansion. As managers decide how to raise capital, corporations can issue debt, equity (stocks), or a mixture of both. The driving force behind a corporation's financing strategy is the desire to minimize its total capital costs. Through much of the 1990s, corporations tended to issue equity (stocks) to raise capital. Beginning in 1998 and into 2007, corporations switched to raising capital by issuing bonds to take advantage of low interest rates and issued $6.3 trillion in new bonds.

MUNICIPAL BONDS State and local governments borrow money to build, repair, or improve streets, highways, hospitals, schools, sewer systems, and so on. The interest and principal on these municipal bonds are repaid in two ways. Projects that benefit the entire community, such as courthouses, schools, and municipal office buildings, are typically funded by general obligation bonds and repaid using tax revenues. Projects that benefit only certain groups of people, such as toll roads and airports, are typically funded by revenue bonds and repaid from user fees. Interest payments paid to municipal bondholders are not taxed at the federal level, or by the state for which the bond is issued.

Other Bonds and Bond-Based Securities

Treasury inflation-protected securities (TIPS) have proved one of the most successful recent innovations in the bond market. The U.S. Treasury began issuing this new type of Treasury bond, which is indexed to inflation, in 1997. TIPS have fixed coupon rates like traditional Treasuries. The new aspect is that the federal government adjusts the par value of the TIPS bond for inflation. Specifically, it increases at the rate of inflation (measured by Consumer Price Index, CPI). As the bond's par value changes over time, interest payments also change. At maturity, investors receive an inflation-adjusted principal amount. If inflation has been high, investors will expect that the adjusted principal amount will be substantially higher than the original $1,000. Consider a new 10-year TIPS issued on January 15, 2005, that pays a 1 5/8 percent coupon. The reference CPI for these bonds is 190.94516. Three years later (on January 15, 2008) the reference CPI was 209.49645. So the par value of the TIPS in early 2008 was $1,097.16 (= $1,000 × 209.49645 ÷ 190.94516). Therefore, the 1 5/8 percent coupon (paid semi annually) would be $8.91 (= 1 5/8% × $1,097.16 ÷ 2). A TIPS' total return comes from both the interest payments and the inflation adjustment to the par value.

 For interactive versions of this example visit www.mhhe.com/can1e

EXAMPLE 6-2

TIPS PAYMENTS

A TIPS bond was issued on July 15, 2006 that pays a 2 ½ percent coupon. The reference CPI at issue was 201.95. The reference CPI for the following interest payments were:

January 2007	201.66
July 2007	207.26
January 2008	209.50

Given these numbers, what is the par value and interest payment of the TIPS at the three interest payments?

SOLUTION:

Compute the TIPS index ratio for each period as current CPI divided by the at-issue CPI: The par value for January 2007 is $1,000 × 201.66 ÷ 201.95 = $998.56, so the interest payment is 2 ½% × $998.56 ÷ 2 = $12.48. The answers for the next two dates are:

July 2007	par value = $1,026.29	interest payment = $12.83
January 2008	par value = $1,037.39	interest payment = $12.97

personal finance

BUY TREASURIES DIRECT!

Treasury bonds are U.S. government-issued debt securities that investors trade on secondary markets. The government also issues nonmarketable debt, called "savings bonds," directly to investors. The common EE savings bonds, introduced in 1980, do not pay regular interest payments. Instead, interest accrues and adds to the bond's value. After a one-year holding period, they can be redeemed at almost any bank or credit union. You can now purchase savings bonds and other Treasury securities (bills, notes, bonds, and TIPS) electronically through the U.S. Treasury's web site, TreasuryDirect. You can set up an account in minutes and buy savings bonds with cash from your bank account. You can also redeem your bonds and transfer the proceeds back to your bank account. Bonds can be purchased 24 hours a day, 7 days a week at no cost.

When bondholders redeem savings bonds, they receive the original value paid plus the accrued interest. Paper bonds sell at half of the face value; if investors hold them for the full 30 years, they receive the par value. Investors buy electronic bonds at face value and earn interest in addition to the par value. Unlike with other bonds, savers need not report income from these interest payments to the IRS until they actually redeem the bonds. So savings bonds count as tax-deferred investments.

About one in six Americans own savings bonds. Savings bonds are used for a variety of purposes, such as personal savings instruments or gifts from grandparents to grandchildren. After the September 11, 2001, terrorist attacks, many Americans wanted to show support for the government. In December 2001, banks selling government EE savings bonds began printing "Patriot bond" on them. So EE savings bonds are now often called Patriot Bonds.

 want to know more?   **Key Words to Search for Updates: See the TreasuryDirect Web site (www.treasurydirect.gov).**

U.S. government agency securities are debt securities issued to provide low-cost financing for desirable private-sector activities such as home ownership, education, and farming. Fannie Mae, Freddie Mac, Student Loan Marketing Association (Sallie Mae), Federal Farm Credit System, Federal Home Loan Banks, and the Small Business Administration, among others, issue these **agency bonds** to support particular sectors of the economy. Agency securities do not carry the federal government's full-faith-and-credit guarantee, but the government has never let one of its agencies fail. Because investors believe that the federal government will continue in this watchdog role, agency bonds are thought to be very safe and may provide a slightly higher return than Treasury securities do.

U.S. government agencies invented one popular type of debt security: **mortgage-backed securities** (MBS). Fannie Mae and Freddie Mac offer subsidies or mortgage guarantees for people who wouldn't otherwise qualify for mortgages, especially first-time homeowners. Fannie Mae started out as a government-owned enterprise in 1938 and became a publicly held corporation in 1968. Freddie Mac was chartered as a publicly held corporation at its inception in 1970. To increase the amount of money available (liquidity) for the home mortgage market, Fannie Mae and Freddie Mac purchase home mortgages from banks, credit unions, and other lenders. They combine the mortgages into diversified portfolios of such loans and then issue mortgage-backed securities (MBS), which represent a share in the mortgage debt, to investors. As homeowners pay off or refinance the underlying portfolio of mortgage loans, MBS investors receive interest and principal payments. After selling mortgages to Fannie Mae or Freddie Mac, mortgage lenders have "new" cash to provide more mortgage loans.

We could apply the same concept to any type of loans; indeed, the financial markets have already invented many such pooled-debt securities. Typical examples include credit card debt, auto loans, home equity loans, and equipment leases. Like mortgage-backed securities, investors receive interest and principal

Bond Quote Examples
table 6.2

Treasury Securities

MATURITY RATE	MO/YR	BID	ASKED	CHG	ASK YLD
6.500	Feb 10n	105:19	105:20	−9	4.57

Corporate Bond

COMPANY	COUPON	LAST MATURITY	LAST PRICE	YIELD
Southwest Airlines Co.	5.570	Dec 15, 2016	97.876	6.036

Municipal Bond

ISSUE	COUPON	MATURITY	PRICE	CHG	BID YLD
NYC Muni Wtr Fin Auth	4.500	06-15-37	100.046	−.538	4.49

from **asset-backed securities** as borrowers pay off their consumer loans. The asset-backed securities market is one of the fastest-growing areas in the financial services sector.

Reading Bond Quotes

To those familiar with bond terminology, bond quotes provide all of the information needed to make informed investment decisions. The volume of Treasury securities traded each day is substantial. Treasury bonds and notes average more than a half billion dollars in trading daily. Investors exhibit much less enthusiasm for corporate or municipal bonds, perhaps because the markets for each particular bond or bonds with the same maturity, coupon rate, and credit ratings are much thinner and, therefore, less liquid. Most bond quote tables report only a small fraction of the outstanding bonds on any given day. Bond quotes can be found in *The Wall Street Journal* and online at places like Yahoo! Finance **(yahoo. finance.com)** and BondsOnline **(www.bonds-online.com).** Table 6.2 shows three bond quote examples.

A typical listing for Treasury bonds appears first. Here, this Treasury bond pays bondholders a coupon of 6.500 percent. On a $1,000 par value bond, this interest income would be $65 annual, paid as $32.50 every six months per bond. The bond will mature in February of 2010—since this is fairly soon, the bond is considered a short-term bond. The "n" in the quote indicates that this bond was originally issued as a note (1–10 years maturity). Both the bid and the ask quotes for the bond appear, expressed as percentages of the bond's par value of $1,000. The bid price is the price at which investors can sell the bond. Numbers after the colon represent 32nds of 1 percent. A bid of 105:19 means that a buyer paid $1,055.94 (= $1,000 × 105 19/32%). Investors can buy this bond at the ask price of 105:20, or $1,056.25. Since the price is higher than the par value of the bond, the bond is selling at a premium to par because its coupon rate is higher than current rates. Thus, investors call this kind of security a **premium bond.**

Notice that the ask price is higher than the bid price. The difference is known as the bid-ask spread. Investors buy at the higher price and sell at the lower price. The bid-ask spread is thus the cost of actively trading bonds. Investors buy and sell with a bond dealer. Since the bond dealer takes the opposite side of the transaction, the dealer buys at the low price and sells at the higher price. The bid-ask spread is part of the dealer's compensation for taking on risk. An investor who bought this bond and held it to maturity would experience a $56.25 capital loss (slightly more than −5.3 percent [= −$56.25/$1,056.25]). The bond lost −9/32 percent of its value during the day's trading—a change of −$2.81 for a $1,000 par value bond. Last, the bond is offering investors who purchase it at the ask price and hold it to maturity a 4.57 percent annual return.

Corporate bond quotes provide similar information. The table shows the quote for a Southwest Airlines, Co., bond, which offers bondholders a coupon of 5.570 percent, or $27.85 semi annually (= $1,000 × 5.57% ÷ 2). The bond would be considered a mid-term bond (usually 10–20 years to maturity), since it matures in the year 2016. Corporate bonds are also quoted in percentage of par value, but (thankfully) the 32nds convention is not used. The price quote of 97.876 indicates that the last trade occurred at a price of $978.76 per bond. Since the bond is selling for a price lower than its $1,000 par value, it's called a **discount bond.** An investor who bought this bond would reap a $21.24 capital gain if the bond were held to maturity. The Southwest bond represents an annual return of 6.036 percent for the investor who purchases the bond at $978.76. Notice that this corporate bond offers a higher return than does the Treasury bond's 4.57 percent return. This price relationship is no coincidence; it is consistent with financial theory. Southwest Airlines doesn't enjoy the luxury of virtually unlimited resources as the U.S. government does. The company therefore is more likely to have difficulty paying back its debt than the U.S. government would have in repaying its bond. Since the Southwest bond represents a riskier investment, it should offer investors a higher rate of return.

Companies set a bond's coupon rate when they originally issue the bond. A number of factors determine that coupon rate:

- The amount of uncertainty about whether the company will be able to make all the payments.
- The term of the loan.
- The level of interest rates in the overall economy at the time.

Bonds from different companies carry different coupon rates because some, or all, of these determining factors differ. Even a single company that has raised capital through bond issues many times may carry very different coupon rates on its various issues, because the bond issues would be offered in different years when the overall economic condition and interest rates differ.

Table 6.2 also shows a quote for a municipal bond issued by the New York City Municipal Water Finance Authority. This city government agency has raised capital by issuing municipal bonds to build reservoir facilities to provide water to New York City. The bond pays a 4.500 percent coupon, and since it matures in 2037, it's considered a long-term bond. According to Table 6.2, the bond is trading at a price close to par value—100.046 percent. Most municipal bonds, unlike other bonds, feature a $5,000 face value rather than the typical par value of $1,000. So, the 100.046 percent price quote represents a dollar amount of $5,002.30 (= 100.046% × $5,000). The low rate of return relative to Treasury bonds with similar maturities also has an explanation. Municipal bondholders do not have to pay federal income taxes on the interest payments that they receive from those securities. We explore this (sometimes) substantial advantage further in a later section of this chapter.

The Kohls' corporate bond pays a semi annual interest payment of $36.88 (= 7.375% × $1,000 ÷ 2) and its price is $1,100.10 (= 110.01% × $1,000). This premium bond's 7.375% rate is likely well above market rates, which is why an investor would be willing to pay a premium for it.

The state of Florida issued the muni bond to fund bridge construction. With a $5,000 par value, the interest payments are $125 (= 5.0% × $5,000 ÷ 2) every six months. The bonds are priced at $5,339.00 (= 106.78% × $5,000).

EXAMPLE 6-3

BOND QUOTES

You note the following bond quotes and wish to determine each bond's price, term, and interest payments.

 LG3

Treasury Securities

MATURITY RATE	MO/YR	BID	ASKED	CHG	ASK YLD
9.00	Nov 18	137:19	137:20	−5	4.80

Corporate Bond

COMPANY	COUPON	MATURITY	LAST PRICE	LAST YIELD	
Kohls Corp	7.375	Oct 15, 2011	110.01	4.991	

Municipal Bond

ISSUE	COUPON	MATURITY	PRICE	YLD TO MAT	
Florida St Aquis & Bridge Constr	5.00	July 1, 2025	106.78	4.458	

SOLUTION:

The Treasury bond matures in November of 2018 and pays 9 percent interest. Investors receive cash interest payment of $45 (= 9% × $1,000 ÷ 2) semi annually. Since the bond matures in less than 10 years but more than 1 year, we would consider it a mid-term bond. Since no "n" appears next to the maturity date, we can also tell that the security was issued as a bond that would mature in 30 years. Investors could sell this bond for $1,375.94 (= 137 19/32% × $1,000) and buy it for $1,376.25 (= 137 20/32% × $1,000). The price fell on this particular day by $1.56 (= −5/32% × $1,000). The dealer earned 31 cents on each trade of these premium bonds.

TIME OUT

6-1 Describe the different reasons that the U.S. government, local governments, and corporations would issue bonds.

6-2 What is the following bond's price and what dollar amount will the bond pay for its semi annual interest payment?

COMPANY	COUPON	MATURITY	PRICE	YIELD
Home Depot Inc.	5.40	Mar 1, 2016	100.06	5.391

6.2 Bond Valuation

Present Value of Bond Cash Flows

 LG4

Any bond's value computation directly applies time value of money concepts. Bondholders know the interest payments that they are scheduled to receive and the repayment of the par value at maturity. The current price of a bond is, therefore, the *present value of these future cash flows discounted at the prevailing market interest rate.* The prevailing market interest rate will depend on the bond's term to maturity, credit quality, and tax status.

The simplest type of bond for time value of money calculations is a **zero coupon bond.** As you might guess from its name, a zero coupon bond makes no interest payments. Instead, the bond pays only the par value payment at its maturity date. So a zero-coupon bond sells at a substantial discount from is par value. For example, a bond with a par value of $1,000, maturing in 20 years, and priced to yield 6% might be purchased for about $306.56. At the end of 20 years, the bond investor will receive $1,000. The difference between $1,000 and $306.56 (which is $693.44) represents the interest income received over the 20 years based upon the discount rate of 6 percent. The time line for this zero coupon bond valuation appears as

We compute the zero's price by finding the present value of the $1,000 cash flow received in 20 years. However, to be consistent with regular coupon-paying bonds, zero-coupon bonds are priced using semi annual compounding. So the formula and calculator valuation would use 40 semi annual periods at a 3 percent interest rate rather than 20 periods at 6%. Using the present value equation of Chapter 4 results in

$$PV = \frac{FV_N}{(1 + i)^N} = \frac{\$1,000}{1.03^{40}} = \frac{\$1,000}{3.262} = \$306.56$$

So the zero coupon bond's price is indeed a steep discount to its par value. This makes sense because investors would only buy a security that pays $1,000 in many years for a price that is much lower to make enough profit to make up for the forgone semi annual interest payments. For comparison sake, instead of the 20-year zero, consider a 20-year bond with a 7 percent coupon. So this 20-year maturity bond pays $35 in interest payments every six months. We can think of these interest payments as an annuity stream. If the market discount rate is 6 percent annually, the time line appears as

The time line shows the 40 semi annual payments (with the accompanying semi annual interest rate at 3%) of $35 and the par value payment at the bond's maturity. Think through this: When bonds pay semi annual payments, the discount rate must be a semi annual rate. Thus, the 6 percent annual rate becomes a 3 percent semi annual rate. So we then compute the price of this bond by adding the present value of the interest payment annuity cash flow to the present value of the future par value. A combination of the present value equations for the annuity cash flows and the value of the par redemption appear in the bond valuation equation 6-1:

Present value of bond = Present value of interest payments + Present value of par value

$$= PMT \times \left[\frac{1 - \frac{1}{(1 + i)^N}}{i} \right] + \frac{1,000}{(1 + i)^N} \qquad \textbf{(6-1)}$$

where PMT is the interest payment, *N* is the number of periods until maturity, and *i* is the market interest rate per period on securities with the same bond characteristics. If this bond paid interest annually, then these variables would take yearly period values. Since this bond pays semi annually, *PMT, N,* and *i* are all denoted in semi annual periods. The price of this coupon bond should be

$$\text{Bond price} = \$35 \times \left[\frac{1 - \dfrac{1}{(1+0.03)^{40}}}{0.03} \right] + \frac{1,000}{(1+0.03)^{40}}$$

$$= \$809.017 + \$306.557 = \$1,115.57$$

Of the \$1,115.57 bond price, most of the value comes from the semi annual \$35 coupon payments (\$809.017) and not the value from the future par value payment (\$306.557).

Because equation 6-1 is quite complex, we usually compute bond prices using a financial calculator or computer program. An investor would compute the bond value using a financial calculator by entering $N = 40, I = 3, \text{PMT} = 35,$

 For interactive versions of this example visit www.mhhe.com/can1e

EXAMPLE 6-4

FIND THE VALUE OF A BOND

Consider a 15-year bond that has a 5.5 percent coupon, paid semi annually. If the current market interest rates is 6.5 percent, and the bond is priced at \$940, should you buy this bond?

 LG4

SOLUTION:

Compute the value of the bond using equation 6.1. Use semi annual compounding ($N = 2 \times 15 = 30$ and $I = 6.5 \div 2 = 3.25$, and $PMT = 5.5\% \times \$1,000 \div 2 = \$27.50$) as:

$$\text{Bond value} = \$27.50 \times \left[\frac{1 - \dfrac{1}{(1+0.0325)^{30}}}{0.0325} \right] + \frac{1,000}{(1+0.0325)^{30}} = \$522.00 + \$383.09 = \$905.09$$

CALCULATOR
$N = 30$
$I = 3.25$
$\text{PMT} = 27.50$
$\text{FV} = 1000$
$\text{CPT PV} = -905.09$

So this bond's value is \$905.09, which is less than the \$940 price. The bond is overvalued in the market and you should not buy it.

MATH COACH

BOND PRICING AND PERIODS

Since most bonds have semi annual interest payments, we must use semi annual periods to discount the cash flows. Most errors in computing a bond price occur in the adjustment for semi annual periods. The errors happen whether you are using either the bond pricing equation or a financial calculator. To convert to semi annual periods, be sure to adjust the three variables: number of periods, interest rate, and payments.

The number of years needs to be multiplied by 2 for the number of semi annual periods. The interest rate should be divided by 2 for a six-month rate. Divide the annual coupon payment. Remember to adjust all three inputs for the semi annual periods.

A coupon paying bond's price should hover reasonably around the par value of the bond. For a \$1,000 par value bond, we could expect a price in the range of \$700 to \$1,300. If you compute a price outside this range, check to see whether you made the semi annual period adjustments correctly.

figure 6.2

A Demonstration of the Price and Market Interest Rate over Time of a 30-Year Treasury Bond Issued in 1977 with a Coupon of 7.8 Percent

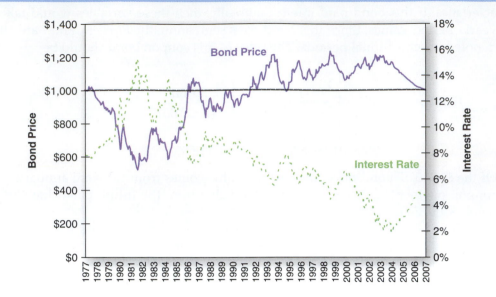

FV = 1000, and computing the present value (PV). The calculator solution is $1,115.57.[1]

 ### Bond Prices and Interest Rate Risk

At the time of purchase, the bond's interest payments and par value expected at maturity are fixed and known. Over time, economy-wide interest rates change, but the bond's coupon rate remains fixed. A rise in prevailing interest rates (also called *increasing the discount rate*) reduces all bonds' values. If interest rates fall, all bonds will enjoy rising values. Consider that when interest rates rise, newly issued bonds offer to pay higher interest rates than the rates offered on existing bonds. So to sell an existing bond with its lower coupon rate, its market price must fall so that the buyer can expect a profit similar to that offered by newly issued bonds. Similarly, when prevailing interest rates fall, market prices for outstanding bonds rise to bring the offered return on older bonds with higher coupon rates into line with new issues.

Figure 6.2 demonstrates how the price of a 30-year Treasury bond may change over time. The 7.8 percent coupon exactly matches prevailing interest rate when the bond is issued in 1977. Consequently, the bond sells for its par value of $1,000. Shortly thereafter, interest rates quickly rose to very high levels (over 15 percent) in the economy. As interest rates rose, bond prices had to decline. Then in 1984, interest rates started a prolonged descent to a low of 5 percent in 1993. Of course, bond prices rose during this nine-year period. Since the early 1990s, interest rates have generally declined, but have done so with many fluctuations. Note that while a bond is issued at $1,000 and returns $1,000 at maturity, its price can vary a great deal in between. Bond investors must be aware that bond prices fluctuate on a day-to-day basis as interest rates fluctuate. Bondholders can incur large capital gains or capital losses.

The fact that, as prevailing interest rates change, the prices of existing bonds will change has a specific name in the financial industry—interest rate risk. **Interest rate risk** means that during periods when interest rates change substantially

---

[1] In order to focus on the valuation concepts, we present these examples with the full 6-months until the bond's next interest payment. However, bonds can be sold anytime between interest payments. When this occurs, we simply add the interest accrued since the last payment to the price.

table 6.3

TIME TO MATURITY	COUPON	PRICE AT 6%	PRICE AT 7%	CHANGE
30 years	0%	$ 174.11	$ 131.37	−24.5%
30 years	5	861.62	750.55	−12.9
30 years	7	1,138.38	1,000.00	−12.2
30 years	10	1,553.51	1,374.17	−11.5
20 years	5	884.43	786.45	−11.1
10 years	5	925.61	857.88	−7.3
5 years	5	957.35	916.83	−4.2
2 years	5	981.41	963.27	−1.8

(and quickly), bondholders experience distinct gains and losses in their bond inventories. But interest rate risk does not affect all bonds exactly the same. Very short-term bonds experience little or no fluctuation in their prices, and thus expose the bondholder to little interest rate risk. Long-term bondholders experience substantial interest rate risk. Table 6.3 illustrates the impact of interest rate risk on bonds with different coupons and times to maturity.[2]

The first four rows show the prices and price changes for 30-year bonds with different coupon rates. Notice that the bonds with higher coupon rates also have higher prices. Bondholders as a rule find it more valuable to receive the large annuity payments. Also notice that a 1 percent increase in interest rates from 6 percent to 7 percent causes bond prices to fall. Bondholders with higher coupon bonds are not affected as much by interest rate increases because they can take the large coupon payments and reinvest those cash flows in new bonds that offer higher returns.

The price decline is greater for bonds with lower coupons because of **reinvestment rate risk.** When interest rates increase, these bondholders' lower future cash flows—both periodic payments and final payoff at maturity—are discounted at a higher rate, decreasing a bond's value. Because the cash flows from low-coupon bonds are smaller, the holder of such bonds will have less money available from interest payments to buy the new, higher coupon bonds. Thus bondholders of lower coupon bonds have their capital tied up in assets that are not making them as much money. They face a bad dilemma: they can sell their lower coupon bonds and take a greater capital loss, using the (smaller) proceeds to buy new bonds with higher coupon rates. Or they can continue to receive the small income payments and hold their lower coupon bonds to maturity to avoid locking in the capital loss. Either way, they lose money relative to those bondholders with higher coupon rates. You can see this illustrated in the 30-year bonds shown in Table 6.3. Reinvestment rates tend to help partially offset changing discount rates for higher coupon paying bonds.

Another factor that influences the amount of reinvestment risk bondholders face is their bonds' time to maturity. The last four bonds in the table all have a 5 percent coupon but have different times to maturity. Note that when interest rates increase, the bond prices of longer-term bonds decline more than shorter-term bonds. This shows that bonds with longer maturities and lower coupons have the higher interest rate risk. Short-term bonds with high coupons have the lowest interest rate risk. High interest rate risk bonds experience considerable price declines when interest rates are rising. However, these bonds also experience dramatic capital gains when interest rates are falling. While a 1 percent change in market interest rates is not commonly seen on a daily or monthly basis, such a change is not unusual over the course of several months or a year.

LG5

[2]The prices are computed using semi annual periods, except for zero coupon bonds, which use annual periods.

CAPITAL GAINS IN THE BOND MARKET

LG5 Say that you anticipate falling long-term interest rates from 6 percent to 5.5 percent during the next year. If this occurs, what will be the total return for a 20-year, 6.5 percent coupon bond through the interest rate decline?

SOLUTION:

To determine the total return, compute the capital gain or loss and the interest paid over the year. The capital gain or loss is determined from the change in price. The current bond price is:

CALCULATOR

N = 40
I = 3
PMT = 32.50
FV = 1000

CPT PV = −1057.79

$$\text{Bond price} = \$32.50 \times \left[\frac{1 - \frac{1}{(1+0.03)^{40}}}{0.03} \right] + \frac{1,000}{(1+0.03)^{40}} = \$751.230 + \$306.557 = \$1,057.79$$

The price in one year would be:

Then change

N = 38
I = 2.75

CPT PV = −1116.97

$$\text{Bond price} = \$32.50 \times \left[\frac{1 - \frac{1}{(1+0.0275)^{38}}}{0.0275} \right] + \frac{1,000}{(1+0.0275)^{38}} = \$760.276 + \$356.690 = \$1,116.97$$

So, the capital gain is $59.18 (= $1,116.97 − $1057.79). The interest payment during the year is $65 (= 6.5% × $1,000). If interest rates fall to 5.5 percent, then this bond should provide a total return of $124.18, which would be an 11.74 percent return (= $124.18 ÷ $1057.79). Of course, this is only an anticipated interest rate change and it may not occur.

LG5

Bond Prices and the Term Structure of Interest Rates

It may surprise you to discover that different interest rates apply to bonds with different terms to maturity. This concept is known as the **term structure of interest rates.** Consider the four Treasury bond quotes shown in Table 6.4. The price quote for each of the four bonds is associated with the yield shown. Note how the bonds with shorter time to maturity have smaller yields.

The maturity and yields of these bonds are depicted as dots in Figure 6.3. Connecting the dots shows the yield curve. This is an upward-sloping yield curve that demonstrates the interest rate for each Treasury bond, defined by its time to maturity. In an upward-sloping curve, longer-term bonds use higher interest rates. Notice that in this environment, even if interest rates do not change in the overall economy (which they always do!), a 20-year bond's interest rate will change over time because one year later, it becomes a 19-year bond, and two years later it becomes an 18-year bond, and so on. As the bond's time to maturity gets shorter, it uses the appropriate interest rate for that maturity to determine its price.

While the upward-sloping example characterizes the relationship between interest rates and bond term to maturity during many periods in history, the yield curve can be flat, humped, and even downward sloping. The dynamics between time to maturity and interest rates is a very important topic. The relationship hints as to how interest rates might change in the future. Predicting future changes in interest rates can influence what bonds a company might issue or an investor may want to own. We'll explore these topics on a more macro level

Treasury Bond Information, December 19, 2007		table 6.4
TIME TO MATURITY	**PRICE QUOTE**	**YIELD**
2 years	100:00	3.11%
5 years	99:21	3.49
10 years	101:20	4.04
30 years	108:27	4.45

figure 6.3

Interest Rates and Term to Maturity

in Chapter 8. For this chapter, it's important to know that different maturities are associated with different interest rates. You can easily determine the current term structure of interest rates through financial Web sites. For example, you can choose the "Bonds" menu of Yahoo! Finance (**finance.yahoo.com**) or the "Bonds and Rates" menu of CNN Money.com (**money.cnn.com**).

TIME OUT

6-3   Show the time line and compute the present value for an 8.5 percent coupon bond (paid semi annually) with 12 years left to maturity and a market interest rate of 7.5 percent.

6-4   Describe the relationship between interest rate changes and bond prices.

6.3 Bond Yields

Current Yield

LG6

Although we speak about "the prevailing interest rate," bond relationships reflect many interest rates (also called *yields*). Some rates are difficult to calculate but accurately reflect the return the bond is offering. Others, like the **current yield,** are easy to compute but only approximate the bond's true return. A bond's current yield is defined as the bond's annual coupon rate divided by the bond's current market price. Current yield measures the rate of return a bondholder would earn annually from the coupon interest payments alone if the bond were purchased at a stated price. Current yield does not measure the total expected return because it does not account for any capital gains or losses that will occur from purchasing the bond at a discount or premium to par.

Yield to Maturity

Yield to maturity is a more meaningful equation for investors than the simple current yield calculation. The yield to maturity calculation tells bond investors the total rate of return that they might expect if the bond were bought at a particular price and held to maturity. While the yield to maturity calculation provides more information than the current yield calculation, it's also more difficult to compute, because we must compute the bond's cash flows' internal rate of return. This calculation seeks to equate the bond's current market price with the value of all anticipated future interest and par value payments. In other words, it is the discount rate that equates the present value of all future cash flows with the current price of the bond. To calculate yield to maturity, investors must solve for the interest rate, i, in equation 6-2, or solve for i in

$$\text{Bond price} = \text{PV of annuity }(pmt,\ i,\ N) + \text{PV }(FV,\ i,\ N) \qquad \textbf{(6-2)}$$

Investors commonly compute the yield to maturity using financial calculators. For example, consider a 7 percent coupon bond (paid semi annually) with eight years to maturity and a current price of $1,150. The return that the bond offers investors, the yield to maturity, is computed as $N = 16$, $PV = -1150$, $PMT = 35$, and $FV = 1000$. Computing the interest rate (I) gives us 2.36 percent. We must remember, however, that 2.36 percent is only the return for six months because the bond pays semi annually. Yield to maturity always means an annual return. So, this bond's yield to maturity is 4.72 percent (2 × 2.36 percent).

Notice the link between a bond's yield to maturity and the prevailing market interest rates used to determine a bond's price as we discussed in the previous section. We use the market interest rate to compute the bond's value. We use the actual bond price to compute its yield to maturity. If the bond is correctly priced at its economic value, then the market interest rate will equal the yield to maturity. Thus, the relationship that we previously identified between bond prices and market interest rates applies to yields as well. Bond prices and bond yields are

---

EXAMPLE 6-6

 For interactive versions of this example visit www.mhhe.com/can1e

COMPUTING CURRENT YIELD AND YIELD TO MATURITY

 You have identified a 3.5 percent Treasury bond with four years left to maturity and a quoted price of 96:09. Calculate the bond's current yield and yield to maturity.

SOLUTION:

(1) First, identify that the bond's price is $962.81 (= 96 09/32% × $1,000).

(2) The annual $35 in interest payments is paid in two $17.50 semi annual payments. Therefore, the current yield of the bond is 3.64 percent (= $35 ÷ $962.81).

(3) The yield to maturity is computed using equation 6-2 and the financial calculator as $N = 8$, $PV = -962.81$, $PMT = 17.50$, and $FV = 1,000$. Computing the interest rate (I) results in 2.26 percent and multiplying by 2 gives the yield to maturity of 4.53 percent.

(4) Note that the current yield is less than the yield to maturity because it does not account for the capital gain to be earned if held to maturity.

inversely related. As a bond's price falls, its yield to maturity increases and a rising bond price accompanies a falling yield. Look back at Figure 6.2 and you will see this relationship clearly.

Yield to Call

The yield to maturity computation assumes that the bondholder will hold the bond to its maturity. But remember that many bonds have call provisions that allow the issuers to repay the bondholder's par value prior to its scheduled maturity. Issuers often call bonds after large drops in market interest rates. In such cases, issuers commonly pay bondholders the bond's par value plus one year of interest payments. The reasons behind early bond redemptions are obvious. When interest rates fall, issuers can sell new bonds at lower interest rates. Companies want to refinance their debt—just as homeowners do—to reduce their interest payments.

Issuers gain important advantages with call provisions because they allow refinancing opportunities. Of course, the same provisions are disadvantages for bond investors. When bonds are called, investors receive the par value and call premium, but then investors must seek equally profitable bonds to buy with the proceeds. You will recall that investors can face reinvestment risk—the available bonds aren't as profitable because interest rates have declined. Bonds are called away at the worst time for investors. In addition, bond prices will rise as market interest rates fall, which could provide issuers opportunities to sell the bonds at a profit. But the price increases will be limited by the fact that the bond will likely be called early. The possibility that bonds can be called early dampens their upside price potential. We can even compute the price of a bond that's likely to be called from the equation

Price of a callable bond = Present value of interest payments to call date + Present value of call price

$$= PMT \times \left[\frac{1 - \dfrac{1}{(1 + i)^N}}{i} \right] + \frac{\text{Call price}}{(1 + i)^N} \qquad \text{(6-3)}$$

In this case, N is the number of periods until the bond can be called and i is the prevailing market rate. The prevailing market interest rate will probably differ from the rate for a noncallable bond. The previous section demonstrated via the yield curve that bonds with different maturities have different yields. A bond that matures in 20 years, but is likely to be called in 5 years, will carry a yield appropriate for a 5-year bond.

Now, reconsider the 20-year bond with a 7 percent coupon that we discussed previously. If the bond can be called in five years with a call price of $1,070, the appropriate discount rate happens to be 5.75 percent annually at that time (instead of the 6 percent in the original problem). This time line would be

Cash flow	?	35	35	35	35	...	35	35	35	1,070 35
Period	0	1	2	3	4	...	7	8	9	10

2.875% semi annual periods

CALLING BONDS

Many bond issues carry call provisions that allow the issuer to retire the bonds prior to the stated maturity. An issuer will typically call bonds when prevailing interest rates drop, making reinvestment less desirable for the buyer. Many corporate bonds have a call feature, but so do some Treasury bonds and municipal bonds.

The U.S. Treasury does not currently issue callable bonds. However, they did issue callable bonds in the early 1980s and some of these bonds still exist. In July of 2007, the Treasury announced that they were "calling" the 10 3/8% Treasury bonds originally issued on November 15, 1982, which were to mature November 15, 2012. These bonds were redemption at par on November 15, 2007. There were $10.1 billion of these bonds outstanding. These bonds were called

for a very simple reason—the 10 3/8% interest rate was significantly above the interest rate that could be financed for the five years remaining of their maturity. The Treasury estimated interest savings from the call and refinancing to be about $2.0 billion.

When the Treasury announced it would call a bond in 1991, it was quite distressful to the bond market. Previously, the Treasury had not called a bond since 1962. Investors had not believed that the Treasury would call any of their bonds and prices on all callable Treasuries subsequently dropped. Throughout the 1990s and 2000s, the Treasury has periodically called one of its issues. Bond investors now expect such moves by the Treasury.

 want to know more? **Key Words to Search for Updates: See the TreasuryDirect Web site (www.savingsbonds.gov) or Google Treasury calls**

The changes in this time line are only 10 semi annual payments of $35 (rather than 40 such semi annual payments), a 2.875 percent semi annual discount rate, and the call price payment of $1,070. The price of this callable bond would be

$$\text{Bond price} = \$35 \times \left[\frac{1 - \dfrac{1}{(1 + 0.02875)^{10}}}{0.02875} \right] + \frac{1{,}070}{(1 + 0.02875)^{10}}$$

$$= \$300.47 + \$805.91 = \$1{,}106.38$$

In this example, the callable bond would be priced at $1,106.38, which is slightly lower than an identical bond that was not callable, priced at $1,115.57.

If a bond is likely to be called, then the yield to maturity calculation does not give investors a good estimate of their return. Bondholders can use instead a **yield to call** calculation, which differs from the yield to maturity only in that its calculation assumes that the investor will receive the par value and call premium at the call date. For example, reconsider the 7 percent coupon bond (paid semi annually) with 8 years to maturity, which we examined previously. The current bond price is $1,130 (which is slightly lower than the yield to maturity bond price of $1,150). If the bond can be called in three years at a specific call price of the par value plus one annual coupon, then what is the yield to call? The yield to call is computed as $N = 6, PV = -1130, PMT = 35,$ and $FV = 1070$. The resulting interest rate (I) is 2.26 percent. The yield to call for this bond is thus 4.52 percent (= 2 × 2.26 percent).

 ## Municipal Bonds and Yield

Municipal bonds (munis) seem to offer low yields to maturity compared to the return that corporate bonds and Treasury securities offer. Munis offer lower rates because the interest income they generate for investors is tax-exempt—at least at the federal level.[3] Specifically, income from municipal bonds is not subject to taxation by the federal government or the state government where the bonds are issued. As a result, municipal bond investors willingly accept lower yields than those they can obtain from taxable bonds. Generally speaking, investors compare the after-tax interest income earned on taxable bonds against the return earned on municipal bonds. For example, suppose an investor in the 35 percent *marginal* income tax bracket has $100,000 to invest in either corporate or municipal bonds. The $100,000 investment would earn a taxable $7,000 annually from 7 percent corporate bonds or $5,000 from tax exempt 5 percent municipal bonds. After taxes, the corporate bond leaves the investor with $4,550 [= (1 − 0.35) × $7,000]. Obviously, this is less than the tax-free income of $5,000 generated by the muni bond.

A common way to compare yields from muni bonds versus that from taxable bonds is to convert the yield to maturity of the muni to a **taxable equivalent yield,** as shown in equation 6-4.

$$\text{Equivalent taxable yield} = \frac{\text{Muni yield}}{1 - \text{Tax rate}} \qquad \textbf{(6-4)}$$

For high-income investors (in the 35 percent marginal tax bracket) a 5 percent muni bond has an equivalent taxable yield of 7.69 percent [= 5% ÷ (1 − 0.35)]. The 5 percent muni is more attractive for this investor than a 7 percent corporate bond. However, for an investor with lower income (in the 28 percent marginal tax bracket) the equivalent taxable yield is only 6.9 percent. The corporate bond provides more after-tax profit than the muni for this investor. It's easy to see why muni bonds are popular among high-income investors (those with substantial marginal tax rates).

 For interactive versions of this example visit www.mhhe.com/can1e

EXAMPLE 6-7

WHICH BOND HAS A BETTER AFTER-TAX YIELD?

Imagine a time when you have a high income, placing you in the 31 percent marginal tax bracket. You are interested in investing some money in a bond issue and have three alternatives. The first is a corporate bond with a 6.4 percent yield to maturity. The second bond is a Treasury that offers a 5.7 percent yield. The third choice is a municipal bond priced at a yield to maturity of 4.0 percent. Which bond gives you the highest after-tax yield?

 LG6

SOLUTION:

The Treasury and corporate bonds are both taxable, so we can compare them directly with each other. The yield of 6.4 percent on the corporate is clearly higher than the 5.7 percent yield offered by the Treasury bond. To include a comparison with the non-taxable municipal bond, compute its equivalent taxable yield as in equation 6-4:

$$\text{Equivalent taxable yield} = \frac{4.0\%}{1 - 0.31} = 5.80\%$$

The municipal bond's equivalent taxable yield of 5.80 percent is higher than the Treasury but lower than the corporate bond.

---

[3]States have differing rules about whether they tax the income from a particular municipal bond—they will generally tax income from munis issued out of state. Further, capital gains arising from municipal bond sales may be taxed, and the income from municipal bonds must be added to overall income when determining the Alternative Minimum Tax consequences.

	PRICE	COUPON RATE	CURRENT YIELD	YIELD TO MATURITY	YIELD TO CALL (IN 5 YEARS)	TAXABLE EQUIVALENT YIELD (35% TAX RATE)
(1) Treasury	$1,000.00	5%	5%	5%		5%
(2) Treasury	1,100.00	5	4.55	3.79		3.79
(3) Treasury	900.00	5	5.56	6.37		6.37
(4) Corporate	1,000.00	6	6	6	6%	6
(5) Corporate	1,110.00	6	5.41	4.61	4.59	4.61
(6) Corporate	900.00	6	6.67	7.44	9.52	7.44
(7) Muni	1,000.00	4	4	4		6.15
(8) Muni	1,100.00	4	3.34	2.84		4.37
(9) Muni	900.00	4	4.44	5.30		8.16

Summarizing Yields

In this section, we have presented several different types of interest rates, or yields, associated with bonds. Many of these yields relate to one another. Consider the bonds and associated yields reported in Table 6.5. Treasury bonds (1) to (3) show how coupon rates, current yield, and yield to maturity relate. When a bond trades at its par value (usually $1,000), then the coupon rate, current yield, and yield to maturity are all the same. When that bond is priced at a premium (bond 2), then both the current yield and the yield to maturity will be lower than the coupon rate. They are both higher than the coupon rate when the bond trades at a discount. Notice that yield to maturity is higher than current yield for discount bonds, and that yield to maturity is lower than current yield for premium bonds. In other words, the current yield always lies between the coupon rate and the yield to maturity. Both the current yield and the yield to maturity move in the opposite direction to the bond's price.

Bonds (4) to (6) are callable corporate bonds. Recall that all the yields (current yield, yield to maturity, and yield to call) are identical when the bond trades at par value. When interest rates fall and bond prices increase, as with bond (5), the issuing corporation has a strong incentive to call the bond after five years, as allowed in the indenture agreement. So investors should base their purchase decisions on the yield to call. When interest rates increase, bond prices decline (as bond 6 shows). In this case, investors could compute the yield to call (as shown), but the information isn't useful because the company will not likely call the bond while interest rates are high.

The last three bonds shown in the table are municipal bonds. Recall that these bonds typically offer lower yields because the income from munis is tax exempt. It is easier to compare municipal bonds with Treasuries and corporate bonds if you compute the municipal bond's taxable equivalent yield first. Here, we use a marginal tax rate of 35 percent in the calculation. The last column of the table shows that the taxable equivalent yield of the municipal bonds is really quite competitive with corporate bond yields. Any investor with income taxed at the 35 percent marginal tax bracket would prefer the municipal bond over the corporate bond if the muni's taxable equivalent yield is higher than the yield to maturity (or yield to call) of the corporate bond.

The table also shows that Treasury securities offer lower yields than corporate bonds with similar terms to maturity. The difference (or spread) between Treasury and corporate yields gives rise to a discussion of bond credit risk, which follows.

TIME OUT

6-5   Calculate the yield to maturity for a zero coupon bond with a price of $525 and 10 years left to maturity.

6-6   Which is higher for a discount bond, the yield to maturity or the coupon rate? Why?

6.4 Credit Risk

Bond Ratings

Will a bond issuer make the promised interest and par value payments over the next 10, 20, or even 30 years? **Credit quality risk** is the chance that the bond issuer will not be able to make timely payments. To assess this risk, independent **bond rating** agencies, such as Moody's and Standard & Poor's, monitor corporate, U.S. agency, or municipal developments during the bond's lifetime and report their findings as a grade or rating. The U.S. government issues the highest credit quality debt; in fact, it's such high quality that it carries no rating. Rating agencies rate all other bonds and issuers who want to sell debt securities in the United States.

Bond credit rating agencies in the United States include Moody's Investors Service, Standard & Poor's Corporation, Fitch IBCA Inc., Dominion Bond Rating Service, and A.M. Best Co. Each of these credit analysis firms assigns similar ratings based on detailed analyses of issuers' financial condition, general economic and credit market conditions, and the economic value of any underlying collateral. The Standard & Poor's ratings are shown in Table 6.6. Their highest credit-quality rating is AAA. Bonds rated AAA, AA, A, or BBB are considered **investment grade** bonds. The issuers of these securities have the highest chance of making all interest and par value payments promised in the indenture agreement.

The investment community considers bonds rated BB and below to be below-investment grade bonds, and some investors, such as pension funds or other fiduciaries, cannot purchase these securities for their portfolios. These bonds are considered to be speculative because they carry a significant risk that the issuer will not make current or future payments. Speculative bonds are sometimes called **junk bonds** because of this risk. In order to attract buyers, issuers sell these bonds at a considerable discount from par and a high associated yield to maturity. Agencies often enhance ratings from "AA" to "CCC" with the addition of a plus (+) or minus (−) sign to show relative standing within the major rating categories. For example, PPG Industries, a manufacturer of coatings, glass, and chemicals, and member of the S&P 500 Index, saw its bonds downgraded from A to A− by Standards & Poor's on January 2, 2008.

Standard & Poor's signals that it's considering a rating change by placing an individual bond, or all of a given issuer's bonds, on CreditWatch (S&P). Rating agencies make their ratings information available to the public through their ratings information desks. In addition to published reports, ratings are made available in many public libraries and over the Internet.

Credit rating agencies conduct general economic analyses of companies' business and analyze firms' specific financial situations. A single company may carry several outstanding bond issues. If these issues feature fundamental differences,

CREDIT RISK	CREDIT RATING	DESCRIPTION
Investment Grade		
Highest quality	AAA	The obligor's (issuer's) capacity to meet its financial commitment on the obligation is extremely strong.
High quality	AA	The obligor's capacity to meet its financial commitment on the obligation is very strong.
Upper medium grade	A	The obligor's capacity to meet its financial commitment on the obligation is still strong, though somewhat susceptible to the adverse effects of changes in circumstances and economic conditions.
Medium grade	BBB	The obligor exhibits adequate protection. However, adverse economic conditions or changing circumstances are more likely to lead to a weakened capacity to meet its financial commitment.
Below Investment Grade		
Somewhat speculative	BB	Faces major ongoing uncertainties or exposure to adverse business, financial, or economic conditions which could lead to the obligor's inadequate capacity to meet its financial commitment.
Speculative	B	Adverse business, financial, or economic conditions will likely impair the obligor's capacity or willingness to meet its financial commitment.
Highly speculative	CCC	Currently vulnerable to nonpayment, and is dependent upon favorable business, financial, and economic conditions for the obligor to meet its financial commitment.
Most speculative	CC	Currently highly vulnerable to nonpayment.
Imminent default	C	Used to cover a situation where a bankruptcy petition has been filed or similar action taken, but payments on this obligation are being continued.
Default	D	Obligations are in default or the filing of a bankruptcy petition has occurred and payments are jeopardized.

Source: Standard & Poor's Web page.

then they may have different credit level risks. For example, **unsecured corporate bonds,** or **debentures,** are backed only by the reputation and financial stability of the corporation. A **senior bond** has a priority claim over junior (more recently issued) securities in the event of default or bankruptcy. So, senior bonds carry less credit risk than junior bonds. Some bonds are secured with collateral. When you buy a car using a loan, the car is collateral for that loan. If you don't make the loan payments, the bank will repossess the car. Companies can also offer collateral when issuing bonds. When a firm uses collateral such as real estate or factory equipment, the bonds are called **mortgage bonds** or **equipment trust certificates,** respectively. Bonds issued with no collateral generally carry higher credit risk.

 ## Credit Risk and Yield

Investors will only purchase higher risk bonds if those securities offer higher returns. Therefore, issuers price bonds with high credit risk to offer high yields to maturity. So another common name for junk bonds is **high-yield bonds.** Differences in credit risk are a prime source of differences in yields between government and various corporate bonds. Figure 6.4 shows the historical average annual yields for long-term Treasury bonds and corporate bonds with credit ratings of AAA and BBB since 1980. Riskier low-quality bonds always offer a higher yield than the higher quality bonds. However, the yield spread between high- and low-quality bonds varies substantially over time. The yield difference between BBB bonds and Treasuries was as high as 3.7 percent and 3.3 percent in 1982 and 2003, respectively. The spread has been as narrow as 1.3 percent and 1.4 percent in 1994 and 2006, respectively.

MICHAEL MILKEN, CONTROVERSIAL FINANCIER

Michael Milken may be the most controversial financial figure of modern times. Some people consider him a financial genius. Others believe that he is a criminal who provided the capital to corporate raiders to break up companies and lay off masses of employees. Controversial indeed! Milken pioneered an active high-yield bond market in the late 1970s and 1980s that provided much needed capital to entrepreneurs and financial innovators, helping to drive the record-breaking stock market of the 1980s and early 90s.

Before the 1970s, the only junk bonds were those issued by once financially stable companies that had fallen on hard times, known as "fallen angels." When a bond was downgraded to junk status, its trading market dried up. Investors were simply unwilling to buy bonds with high credit risk. Using scholarly research, Milken showed investors that, historically, junk bonds rarely defaulted and offered a very high return to those willing to assume the risk of owning them. As investors became interested in buying these bonds, Milken and Drexel Burnham Lambert, the firm for which he worked, developed the market. When banks reduced the amount of risky capital they offered to the market in the 1970s, Milken used the strong demand for high-yield bonds to issue new junk bonds for growing companies and pioneers like Bill McGowan (telecommunications), Ted Turner (cable television), Craig McCaw (cellular telephones), and Steve Wynn (resorts). During the 1980s, Milken also used junk bonds to finance a new class of corporate raiders, such as Kohlberg Kravis Roberts, who carried out numerous mergers, acquisitions, hostile takeovers, and leveraged buyouts.

Nicknamed "The Junk Bond King" in the 1980s, Milken earned $296 million in 1986 and $550 million in 1987 from trading more than $1 billion per day in bonds. He took much criticism for his obscene pay and for the lives ruined at companies targeted by corporate raiders, who tended to break companies up into smaller operating units and lay off many employees in the process. But in 1989, the government charged him with securities fraud. He originally faced a 98-count indictment, but pleaded guilty to only five of the more trivial offenses. He was sentenced to 10 years in prison and a $200 million fine. He paid an additional $750 million in civil settlements. He was released from prison after 22 months but is banned from the securities industry.

Milken has remained very active since being released from prison. He launched a venture called FastCures that is addressing cancer cures (he had prostate cancer). He also created an education empire formally known as Knowledge Universe (it has since changed its name to Monte LLC). The *Forbes* 2006 estimate of Milken's wealth was $2.1 billion. The junk bond market that he pioneered decades ago still thrives today.

Sources: Norman Barry, *Business Ethics,* Ichor Business Books, 1999, and "The Forbes 400," *Forbes,* October 19, 2006, Vol. 178, Issue 7.

 want to know more? **Key Words to Search for Updates: See the Milken Institute (www.MilkenInstitute.org) or Google Michael Milken.**

figure 6.4

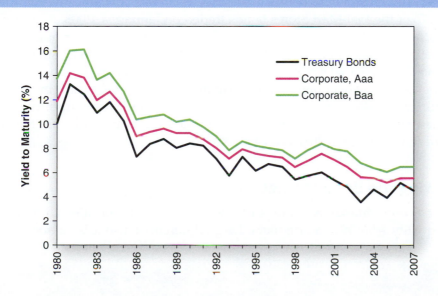

Yield to Maturity on Long-Term Bonds of Different Credit Risk, 1980 to 2007

How do some corporations' debt obligations become junk bonds? Some companies that aren't economically sound or those that use a high degree of financial leverage issue junk bonds. In other cases, financially strong companies issue investment grade bonds and then, over time, begin to have trouble. Eventually a company's bonds can be downgraded to junk status. For example, General Motors (GM) bonds were considered of the highest quality from the 1950s through the 1980s and much of the 1990s. On May 9, 2005, Standard & Poor's downgraded GM bonds to junk status. Junk bonds that were originally issued at investment grade status are still called *fallen angels*.

Bonds that experience credit-rating downgrades must offer a higher yield. As all the future cash flows are fixed, the bond price must fall to create a higher yield to maturity. Alternatively, bonds that are upgraded experience price increases and yield decreases. Bond upgrades often occur during strong economic periods because corporate issuers tend to perform better financially at these times. In a weak economy, high-yield bonds lose their luster because the default risk rises. More credit downgrades occur during economic recessions.

TIME OUT

6-7 Explain why a change in a bond's credit rating will cause its price to change.

6-8 One company has issued two bond classes. One issue is a mortgage bond and the other is a debenture. Which issue will have a higher bond rating and which will offer a higher yield?

 ## 6.5 Bond Markets

The majority of trading volume in the bond market occurs in a decentralized, over-the-counter market. Most trades occur between bond dealers and large institutions (like mutual funds, pension funds, and insurance companies). Dealers bid for bonds that investors seek to sell and offer bonds from their own inventory when investors want to buy. This is especially true for the very active Treasury securities market. However, a small number of corporate bonds are listed on centralized exchanges.

The NYSE operates the largest centralized U.S. bond market. The majority of bond volume at the NYSE is in corporate debt, shown in Figure 6.5. Notice that even the most active bonds experience relatively low trading volume. A total of 73 of the Wal-Mart Stores bonds traded on January 4, 2008. At a price of 100.744 percent of par value, the 73 bonds represent $73,543 of trading value. This is a paltry amount compared to the $930 million of Wal-Mart stock traded the same day. Note that some of the bonds traded are short-term—the Goldman Sachs bond has just over one year left to maturity. Other bonds have many years to maturity, like 48 years for the Gulf Mobile & Ohio RR debenture. While the Goldman bond pays a 7.35 percent coupon, the mid-term bond from Hewlett-Packard that matures in 2017 is a zero coupon bond.

Following the Bond Market

The entire bond market encompasses a wide variety of securities with varying credit quality from different issuers. Large differences also arise among bonds

figure 6.5

Daily Bond Trading Summary on the New York Stock Exchange

Powered by NYSE Euronext Data	as of 16:40 ET 4 Jan 2008	Market data delayed 10 min.				
Most Active Bonds by Volume					See Daily Bond Activity
Name		**Symbol**	**Volume**	**Last Sale**	**Change**
MISSOURI PACIFIC RR CO 4 3/4% 1/1/30		UNP/30	79	87.000	+2.000
GMAC LLO 6% DEEP DISC 4/1/11		GMA11	75	83.000	−0.510
Wal Mart Stores Inc 4.550% NTS 05/01/13		WMT13	73	100.744	+6.744
GOLDMAN SACHS GROUP 7.350% NTS 10/01/2009		GS09	60	104.875	+0.225
Countrywide Home Loans 5.625% SER K 07/15/09		CFC/09A	50	75.000	−6.000
Countrywide Home Loans 6.250% NTS 04/15/09		CFC/09	50	77.000	
HEWLETT-PACKARD CO ZR CPN LYON 10/14/2017		HPQ17Z	50	83.000	+3.000
Verizon Global Funding Co 4.375% NTS 06/01/13		VZ/13	12	97.586	
GULF MOBILE & OHIO RR 5% 12/1/56		GFO56	10	73.000	−4.625
Goldman Sachs Group 6.650% NTS 05/15/09		GS09A	7	101.000	−0.500

Source: NYSE Bond Web page.

in terms of their characteristics such as term to maturity and size of the coupon. The biggest factor associated with changes in bond prices is changes in interest rates. So, one common way to describe the direction of bond prices is simply to report the change in interest rates, since we know that interest rate changes will affect all bonds the same way. The interest rate referenced is the yield to maturity and daily yield change for the 10-year Treasury. Knowing how this interest rate changed today gives bond investors a good idea of the general price movement of all types of bonds.

Bond indexes track specific segments of the bond market. Various brokerage firms, such as Lehman Brothers or Merrill Lynch, maintain these indexes that capture bond price and yield changes in particular segments. You can find information about major bond indices on the Internet and in publications like *The Wall Street Journal* (both in print and online). Figure 6.6 shows indices that track bonds by type of issuer (federal government, corporation, local government, etc.) and time to maturity (short, intermediate, and long).

The Lehman Brothers Aggregate Bond Index tracks more than 5,000 government, investment-grade corporate, and mortgage-backed bonds. The Merrill Lynch Taxable Bond Indexes provide value-weighted total returns (coupon plus capital change) for a range of bond types. The Bond Buyer Municipal Bond Index tracks price and yield trends for long-term tax-free municipal bonds.

TIME OUT

6-9 Why can we use various interest rates to describe the performance of the entire bond market?

6-10 What bond segments are measured by which bond indexes?

figure 6.6

Major Bond Indexes as Reported in *The Wall Street Journal* and on the Internet, January 3, 2008

Index	Close	% Chg	YTD total return	52-wk % Chg	YIELD (%), 52-WEEK RANGE		
					Latest	Low	High
Broad Market Lehman Brothers							
U.S. Government/Credit	1486.21	−0.06	0.72	7.71	4.370	4.340	5.730
Aggregate Lehman	1290.52	−0.01	0.64	7.34	4.760	4.760	5.850
Hourly Treasury Indexes Lehman Brothers							
Composite (Price Return)	1355.59	0.02	0.74	4.46	3.420	−1.850	5.170
Composite (Total Return)	10213.61	0.03	0.78	9.52	3.420	0.210	5.170
Intermediate (Price Return)	1221.74	0.07	0.65	4.52	3.180	−1.160	5.120
Intermediate (Total Return)	8803.54	0.08	0.69	9.34	3.180	0.820	5.120
Long-Term (Price Return)	1803.61	−0.17	1.08	4.27	4.310	−4.420	5.390
Long-Term (Total Return)	15397.93	−0.16	1.13	10.22	4.310	−2.030	5.390
Mortgage-Backed Merrill Lynch							
Ginnie Mae (GNMA)	513.43	0.12	0.66	6.60	5.218	5.218	6.240
Fannie Mae (FNMA)	505.90	0.06	0.41	6.28	5.067	5.067	6.324
Freddie Mae (FHLMC)	312..01	0.08	0.43	6.21	5.207	5.207	6.354
U.S. Corporate Debt Merrill Lynch							
1-10 Year Maturities	1208.73	−0.03	0.67	5.28	5.418	3.373	6.007
10+ Year Maturities	1418.27	−0.31	0.92	3.21	6.351	5.950	6.694
Corporate Master	1701.60	−0.10	0.74	4.75	5.668	5.460	6.180
High Yield	845.80	−0.29	−0.30	1.61	9.676	7.353	9.676
Yankee Bonds	1274.70	−0.08	0.69	6.44	5.176	5.066	6.765
Tax-Exempt Merrill Lynch							
Muni Master	348.36	0.22	0.49	4.39	3.720	3.720	4.294
7-12 years	231.40	0.35	0.56	5.13	3.631	3.631	4.256
12-22 years	249.22	0.38	0.74	3.65	4.205	3.970	4.733
22-plus years	238.50	0.04	0.53	1.01	4.847	4.197	5.154
Bond Buyer 6% Muni	112.69	unch	0.61	−3.53	4.820	4.510	5.070

Source: The Wall Street Journal Online, Major Bond Indexes Web page.

Business Application Solution

To raise $150 million, Beach Sand Resorts would need to issue 150,000 bonds at the customary $1,000 par value (= $150 million ÷ $1,000). The bonds will have to offer a 7 percent coupon. This means that Beach Sand Resorts will pay $35 in interest every six months for each bond issued (= 7.0% × $1,000 ÷ 2). So for all 150,000 bonds, they will pay $5.25 million semi annually (= $35 × 150,000).

Personal Application Solution

You can calculate that buying 10 of the Liberty Media bonds at the quoted price of 96.21 will cost $9,621 (= 96.21% × $1,000 × 10) and would generate $285 (= 5.7% × $1,000 × 10

CALCULATOR	
N = 12	
PV = −1019.40	
PMT = 26.875	
FV = 1000	
CPT I = 2.50	
2.50 × 2 = 5.0	

÷ 2) in interest payments every six months. Buying the bond in 2007, it is priced to offer a 6.48 percent yield to maturity. Ten of the Alcoa bonds would cost $10,194 (= 101.94% × $1,000 × 10) and pay $268.75 (= 5.375% × $1,000 × 10 ÷ 2) in interest payments every six months. This bond is priced to offer a 5.0 percent yield to maturity. The Liberty bonds cost less to purchase, pay more in interest, and offer a higher return than the Alcoa bonds. This is because the Liberty bonds have higher credit risk. You must decide if the higher return of the Liberty bonds is worth taking the extra risk.

summary of learning goals

This chapter describes the bond market. Debt is an important source of capital for companies and governments. A well-functioning bond market contributes to a successful economy. Investors can benefit from bond ownership. Before buying bonds, people should understand how they work.

LG1 **Describe bond characteristics.** Bonds are debt securities that pay a rate of interest called the *coupon rate*. The dollar amount of interest is based on the par value (typically $1,000) of the bond. Interest is usually paid semi annually throughout the time to maturity. At the bond's maturity date, the par value is repaid in full. The bond's legal contract, the indenture agreement, states whether the bond has a call provision that allows the issuer

to redeem the bond prior to scheduled maturity. If the bond is called, the issuer pays the bondholder the par value and a call premium.

LG2 **Identify various bond issuers and their motivations for issuing debt.** Treasury securities are obligations of the U.S. government. The U.S. government uses this debt to fund spending that exceeds its revenue. Treasury bills are extremely short term, usually 30–90 days until maturity. Treasury notes are issued with 1 to 10 years to maturity, while Treasury bonds are issued with 10 to 30 years. Corporations borrow money by issuing bonds as a source of capital to invest in expansion and new business opportunities. State and local governments borrow money by issuing municipal bonds. The interest income from municipal bonds is, for the most part, tax exempt and therefore appeals to investors in the highest tax brackets.

LG3 **Read and interpret bond quotes.** A bond's price and coupon rate is expressed as percentages of the bond's par value. The bid price is the price at which investors can sell the bond and the ask price is the price at which investors buy a bond. For Treasury securities, the numbers after the colons represent 32nds of 1 percent. When a quoted price is higher than the par value of the bond, the bond can be referred to as a *premium bond*. A bond that carries a price lower than 100 percent of par value is called a *discount bond*.

LG4 **Compute bond prices using present value concepts.** The current price of a bond is computed by discounting the future cash flows received: interest payments and par value repayment. The prevailing market interest rate for a bond with similar term to maturity, credit quality, and tax status is used as the discount rate.

LG5 **Explain the relationship between bond prices and interest rates.** As prevailing interest rates change in the economy, bond prices also change. Interest rates and bond prices move in opposite directions. A rise in interest rates increases the discount rate and thus reduces a bond's value. The value of a bond will rise when interest rates fall. Changes in interest rates create risk factors for bonds called *reinvestment risk* and *interest rate risk*.

There is also a term structure of interest rates, which describes the relationship between the time to maturity of a bond and the appropriate interest rate.

LG6 **Compute bond yields.** The simplest bond yield computation is the current yield—simply one year of interest payments divided by the current bond price. Current yield measures the return earned from the interest payments of the bond. However, many bondholders will experience a capital gain or loss in addition to the return from interest payments. The total rate that would be earned if a bond is purchased and held to maturity is the bond's yield to maturity. If a bond is callable, investors may compute the yield to call to assess the return earned if the bond ends up being called. Since municipal bonds pay tax-exempt interest payments, investors commonly compute a taxable equivalent yield to properly compare municipal returns to taxable bond returns.

LG7 **Find bond ratings and assess credit risk's effects on bond yields.** Credit quality risk measures the possibility that the bond issuer will fail to make timely interest and principal payments or that the issuer may even default on the debt. Credit rating agencies grade bond risks and report bond ratings. High quality corporate bonds are considered investment grade, while higher credit risk bonds are speculative, also called *junk bonds* and *high-yield bonds*.

LG8 **Assess bond market performance.** Investors can follow the bond market through prevailing market interest rates because interest rates and bond prices move in the opposite direction. Bond indexes track specific segments of the bond market. Popular bond segments are short-term bonds, long-term bonds, Treasuries, high grade corporate bonds, high yield bonds, and municipal bonds.

chapter equations

6-1 Present value of bond = Present value of interest payments

+ present value of par value

$$= PMT \times \left[\frac{1 - \frac{1}{(1+i)^N}}{i} \right] + \frac{1{,}000}{(1+i)^N}$$

6-2   Solve for i in Bond price $= PV$ of annuity $(pmt, i, N) + PV (FV, i, N)$

6-3   Price of a callable bond $=$ Present value of interest payments to call date

$+$ present value of call price

$$= PMT \times \left[\frac{1 - \dfrac{1}{(1+i)^N}}{i} \right] + \frac{\text{Call price}}{(1+i)^N}$$

6-4   Equivalent taxable yield $= \dfrac{\text{Muni yield}}{1 - \text{Tax rate}}$

key terms

agency bonds, Bonds issued by U.S. government agencies. (p. 184)

asset-backed securities, Debt securities whose payments originate from other loans, such as credit car debt, auto loans, and home equity loans. (p. 185)

bond, Publicly traded form of debt. (p. 180)

bond price, Current price that the bond sells for in the bond market. (p. 181)

bond rating, A grade of credit quality as reported by credit rating agencies. (p. 199)

call, An issuer redeeming the bond before the scheduled maturity date. (p. 180)

call premium, The amount in addition to the par value paid by the issuer when calling a bond. (p. 180)

coupon rate, The annual amount of interest paid expressed as a percentage of the bond's par value. (p. 181)

credit quality risk, The chance that the issuer will not make timely interest payments or even default. (p. 199)

current yield, Return from interest payments; computed as the annual interest payment divided by the current bond price. (p. 193)

debentures, Unsecured bonds. (p. 200)

discount bond, A bond selling for lower than its par value. (p. 186)

equipment trust certificates, Bonds secured with factory and equipment as collateral. (p. 200)

fixed income securities, Any securities that make fixed payments. (p. 180)

high-yield bonds, Bonds with low credit quality that offer a high yield to maturity, also called junk bonds. (p. 200)

indenture agreement, Legal contract describing the bond characteristics and the bondholder and issuer rights. (p. 180)

interest rate risk, The chance of a capital loss due to interest rate fluctuations. (p. 190)

investment grade, High credit quality corporate bonds. (p. 199)

junk bonds, Low credit quality corporate bonds, also called speculative bonds or high-yield bonds. (p. 199)

maturity date, The calendar date on which the bond principal comes due. (p. 180)

mortgage bonds, Bonds secured with real estate as collateral. (p. 200)

mortgage-backed securities, Debt securities whose interest and par value payments originate from real estate mortgage payments. (p. 184)

par value, Amount of debt borrowed to be repaid; face value. (p. 180)

premium bond, A bond selling for greater than its par value. (p. 185)

principal, Face amount, or par value, of debt. (p. 180)

reinvestment rate risk, The chance that future interest payments will have to be reinvested at a lower interest rate. (p. 191)

senior bonds, Older bonds that carry a higher claim to the issuer's assets. (p. 200)

taxable equivalent yield, Modification of a municipal bond's yield to maturity used to compare muni bond yields to taxable bond yields. (p. 197)

term structure of interest rates, A comparison of market yields on securities, assuming all characteristics except maturity are the same. (p. 192)

time to maturity, The length of time (in years) until the bond matures and the issuer repays the par value. (p. 180)

treasury inflation-protected securities, TIPS are U.S. government bonds the par value of which changes with inflation. (p. 183)

unsecured corporate bonds, Corporate debt not secured by collateral such as land, buildings, or equipment. (p. 200)

yield to call, The total return that the bond offers if purchased at the current price and held until the bond is called. (p. 196)

yield to maturity, The total return the bond offers if purchased at the current price and held to maturity. (p. 194)

zero coupon bond, A bond that does not make interest payments but generally sells at a deep discount and then pays the par value at the maturity date. (p. 188)

self-test problems with solutions

LG3, LG4

1 **Bond Quotes and Value** Sheila's broker has given her the following bond quote for a bond issued by Home Depot. What is the price she would pay to buy this bond? Before buying the bond, Sheila notices that other bonds with the same time to maturity and credit rating are offering a 5.08 yield to maturity. What is the bond price at the 5.08 yield? Should Sheila buy this bond? The date is March 2, 2007.

PRICE	COUPON (%)	MATURITY	YTM (%)	CURRENT YIELD (%)	FITCH RATINGS	CALLABLE
101.57	5.200	1-Mar-2011	4.777	5.119	AA	No

Solution:

Sheila knows that the bond quote means that it would cost her $1,015.70 (= 101.57% × $1,000) to purchase now. However, this bond is priced to offer a lower yield to maturity (4.777%) than that offered by similar bonds (5.08%), so it appears mispriced. The value of this bond using the 5.08 percent market interest rate can be computed using equation 6-1. The semi annual interest payment is $26 (= 5.2% × $1,000 ÷ 2) and will be paid eight more times. The bond's value is

$$\text{Bond value} = \$26.00 \times \left[\frac{1 - \dfrac{1}{(1 + 0.0254)^8}}{0.0254} \right] + \frac{1,000}{(1 + 0.0254)^8}$$

$$= \$186.10 + \$818.19 = \$1,004.29$$

Since the bond's value is $1,004.29 and the price is $1,015.70, it appears to be overpriced by $11.41. Sheila may want to consider other bonds that offer an appropriate yield for their level of risk.

LG6

2 **Yield to Maturity and Yield to Call** Kaito is considering a bond issued from Sirius Satellite Radio. The bond has a 9.625 percent coupon and will mature on August 1, 2013. The current market price for the bond is 101.50

and the date is February 2, 2007. Kaito wants to know the current yield and yield to maturity that the bond is offering. In addition, the bond can be called on August 1, 2009, at a price of 104.813. So he wants to know the yield to call as well.

Solution:

The Sirius bond pays $48.125 (= 9.625% × $1,000 ÷ 2) in interest every six months and has six and a half years until it matures. At a price of 101.50, the bond's current yield is 9.48 percent ($96.25 ÷ $1,015.00). The yield to maturity can be found with equation 6-2 and the financial calculator as N = 13, PV = −1015, PMT = 48.125, and FV = 1000. Computing the interest rate (I) results in 4.656 percent and multiplying by 2 gives the yield to maturity of 9.31 percent. Kaito knows that Sirius could call the bond early. To compute the yield to call, the number of periods and the future price need to be changed. In that case, the yield to call would be computed as N = 5, PV = −1015, PMT = 48.125, and FV = 1048.13 Computing the interest rate (I) results in 5.33 percent and multiplying by 2 gives the yield call of 10.66 percent.

③ Municipal Bonds and Income Tax Brackets Shane is a securities broker with many clients. His company has acquired a large number of municipal bonds issued for the Atlanta, Georgia, airport. These bonds pay a coupon of 5 percent, mature on January 1, 2034, have an AAA credit rating, and carry a price of 107.091. Assume that it is January 2, 2008, and that the par value of the bond is $5,000. As an alternative, corporate bonds with similar risk and time to maturity offer a 6.35 percent yield to maturity. Shane is trying to determine which of his clients these bonds would benefit the most.

LG6

Solution:

Since these municipal bonds are issued in the state of Georgia, the bondholders in Georgia will not have to pay either federal or state income tax on the interest payments. Therefore, Shane should focus on his clients who live in Georgia. This bond offers investors a yield to maturity that can be computed using equation 6-2. Using the financial calculator, enter N = 52, PV = −5354.55, PMT = 125, and FV = 5000. Computing the interest rate (I) results in 2.266 percent and multiplying by 2 gives the yield to maturity of 4.53 percent. The tax savings provide a larger benefit for people in a higher marginal tax bracket. Investors in the 35 percent tax bracket can compare the muni bond yield to a taxable corporate yield by converting the muni to an equivalent taxable yield as in equation 6-4:

$$\text{Equivalent taxable yield} = \frac{4.53\%}{1 - 0.35} = 6.97\%$$

So people in the highest tax bracket will prefer this municipal bond to the similar corporate bonds offering only 6.35 percent. The table below shows the equivalent taxable yield for the marginal tax brackets of 2006. Shane notes that in this case, his clients in the upper two marginal tax brackets would benefit from these municipal bonds. Investors in the lower brackets would do better purchasing the corporate bonds.

Marginal Tax Bracket (%)	10	15	25	28	33	35
Equivalent Taxable Yield (%)	5.03	5.33	6.04	6.29	6.77	6.97

www.mhhe.com/can1e

4 **Credit Risk and Bond Costs** Monica is CFO of a manufacturing company that wants to raise capital for several new business projects. The firm's current bonds are rated "A." Monica is working closely with the credit rating agencies to determine what the credit rating would be on new bonds issued under two different circumstances. In the first case, the firm would issue $50 million in new bonds to fund a project. In the second case, the firm would issue $150 million to fund two new projects. The credit rating agency says that the first alternative would result in a "BBB" rating and the second case would result in a "BB" rating. Monica uses the current market yield table below to assess the interest cost of the two alternatives. What would the interest rate cost (in dollars) be in each case?

Credit Rating	AAA	AA	A	BBB	BB	B
20-Year Average Yield	5.7	5.9	6.1	6.5	7.1	8.4

Solution:

If Monica goes with the first case and raises $50 million with a bond issue, the bonds will be rated BBB, the lowest investment grade rating. She would issue the bonds with the market rate 6.5 percent as the coupon rate. This means that she will have to pay $3.25 million (= 6.5% × $50 million) every year in interest payments. If she decides to issue $150 million in bonds instead, they will be rated BB, and be known as junk bonds. She will need to offer the higher interest rate of 7.1 percent as the coupon rate. Therefore, she will have to pay $10.65 million (= 7.1% × $150 million) every year in interest payments. The difference in the two options is due to both the difference in coupon rate and the amount of money borrowed. One other issue Monica may want to consider is the reputation impact of having bonds rated in the junk bond range. Other people in the industry often use bond ratings as a signal about the financial stability of the firm. Her suppliers may begin to worry about the firm if it has a BB rating and may not be willing to extend credit. In other words, the second case may create some financial problems in other parts of the company.

questions

1. What does a call provision allow the issuer to do, and why would they do it? *(LG1)*

2. List the differences between the new TIPS and traditional Treasury bonds. *(LG2)*

3. Explain how mortgage-backed securities work. *(LG2)*

4. Provide the definitions of a discount bond and a premium bond. Give examples. *(LG3)*

5. Describe the differences in interest payments and bond price between a 5 percent coupon bond and a zero coupon bond. *(LG4)*

6. All else equal, which bond's price is more effected by a change in interest rates, a short-term bond or a longer-term bond? Why? *(LG5)*

7. All else equal, which bond's price is more affected by a change in interest rates, a bond with a large coupon or a small coupon? Why? *(LG5)*

8. Explain how a bond's interest rate can change over time even if interest rates in the economy do not change. *(LG5)*

9. Compare and contrast the advantages and disadvantages of the current yield computation versus yield to maturity calculations. *(LG6)*

10. What is the yield to call and why is it important to a bond investor? *(LG6)*

11. What is the purpose of computing the equivalent taxable yield of a municipal bond? *(LG6)*

12. Explain why high income and wealthy people are more likely to buy a municipal bond than a corporate bond. *(LG6)*

13. Why does a Treasury bond offer a lower yield than a corporate bond with the same time to maturity? Could a corporate bond with a different time to maturity offer a lower yield? Explain. *(LG7)*

14. Describe the difference between a bond issued as a high-yield bond and one that has become a "fallen angel." *(LG7)*

15. What is the difference in the trading volume between Treasury bonds and corporate bonds? Give examples and/or evidence. *(LG8)*

16. Explain how the Lehman Brothers Intermediate Bond Index might increase one day while the Merrill Lynch High Yield Index decreases the same day. *(LG8)*

problems

basic
problems

6-1 **Interest Payments** Determine the interest payment for the following three bonds: 3 ½ percent coupon corporate bond (paid semi annually), 4.25 percent coupon Treasury note, and a corporate zero coupon bond maturing in 10 years. (Assume a $1,000 par value.) *(LG1)*

6-2 **Interest Payments** Determine the interest payment for the following three bonds: 4 ½ percent coupon corporate bond (paid semi annually), 5.15 percent coupon Treasury note, and a corporate zero coupon bond maturing in 15 years. (Assume a $1,000 par value.) *(LG1)*

6-3 **Time to Maturity** A bond issued by Ford on May 15, 1997 is scheduled to mature on May 15, 2097. If today is November 16, 2008, what is this bond's time to maturity? *(LG1)*

6-4 **Time to Maturity** A bond issued by IBM on December 1, 1996 is scheduled to mature on December 1, 2096. If today is December 2, 2007, what is this bond's time to maturity? *(LG1)*

6-5 **Call Premium** A 7 percent corporate coupon bond is callable in five years for a call premium of one year of coupon payments. Assuming a par value of $1,000, what is the price paid to the bondholder if the issuer calls the bond? *(LG1)*

6-6 **Call Premium** A 6.5 percent corporate coupon bond is callable in 10 years for a call premium of 1 year of coupon payments. Assuming a par value of $1,000, what is the price paid to the bondholder if the issuer calls the bond? *(LG1)*

6-7   **TIPS Interest and Par Value** A 2 ¾ percent TIPS has an original reference CPI of 185.4. If the current CPI is 210.7, what is the current interest payment and par value of the TIPS? *(LG2)*

6-8   **TIPS Interest and Par Value** A 3 1/8 percent TIPS has an original reference CPI of 180.5. If the current CPI is 206.8, what is the current interest payment and par value of the TIPS? *(LG2)*

6-9   **Bond Quotes** Consider the following three bond quotes; a Treasury note quoted at 97:27, a corporate bond quoted at 103.25, and a municipal bond quoted at 101.90. If the Treasury and corporate bonds have a par value of $1,000 and the municipal bond has a par value of $5,000, what is the price of these three bonds in dollars? *(LG3)*

6-10   **Bond Quotes** Consider the following three bond quotes: a Treasury bond quoted at 106:14, a corporate bond quoted at 96.55, and a municipal bond quoted at 100.95. If the Treasury and corporate bonds have a par value of $1,000 and the municipal bond has a par value of $5,000, what is the price of these three bonds in dollars? *(LG3)*

6-11   **Zero Coupon Bond Price** Calculate the price of a zero coupon bond that matures in 20 years if the market interest rate is 6.5 percent. *(LG4)*

6-12   **Zero Coupon Bond Price** Calculate the price of a zero coupon bond that matures in 15 years if the market interest rate is 7.25 percent. *(LG4)*

6-13   **Current Yield** What's the current yield of a 5.5 percent coupon corporate bond quoted at a price of 102.08? *(LG6)*

6-14   **Current Yield** What's the current yield of a 7.2 percent coupon corporate bond quoted at a price of 96.78? *(LG6)*

6-15   **Taxable Equivalent Yield** What's the taxable equivalent yield on a municipal bond with a yield to maturity of 3.5 percent for an investor in the 28 percent marginal tax bracket? *(LG6)*

6-16   **Taxable Equivalent Yield** What's the taxable equivalent yield on a municipal bond with a yield to maturity of 2.9 percent for an investor in the 33 percent marginal tax bracket? *(LG6)*

6-17   **Credit Risk and Yield** Rank from highest credit risk to lowest risk the following bonds, with the same time to maturity, by their yield to maturity: Treasury bond with yield of 5.55 percent, IBM bond with yield of 7.49 percent, Trump Casino bond with yield of 8.76 percent, and Banc One bond with a yield of 5.99 percent. *(LG7)*

6-18   **Credit Risk and Yield** Rank the following bonds in order from lowest credit risk to highest risk all with the same time to maturity, by their yield to maturity: Treasury bond with yield of 4.65 percent, United Airline bond with yield of 9.07 percent, Bank of America bond with a yield of 6.25 percent, and Hewlett/Packard bond with yield of 6.78 percent. *(LG7)*

intermediate
problems

6-19   **TIPS Capital Return** Consider a 3.5% TIPS with an issue CPI reference of 185.6. At the beginning of this year, the CPI was 196.2 and was at 201.3 at the end of the year. What was the capital gain of the TIPS in dollars and in percentage terms? *(LG2)*

6-20   **TIPS Capital Return** Consider a 2.25% TIPS with an issue CPI reference of 183.5. At the beginning of this year, the CPI was 197.1 and was at 203.8 at the end of the year. What was the capital gain of the TIPS in dollars and in percentage terms? *(LG2)*

6-21 **Compute Bond Price** Compute the price of a 4.5 percent coupon bond with 15 years left to maturity and a market interest rate of 6.8 percent. (Assume interest payments are semi annual.) Is this a discount or premium bond? *(LG4)*

6-22 **Compute Bond Price** Compute the price of a 5.6 percent coupon bond with 10 years left to maturity and a market interest rate of 7.0 percent. (Assume interest payments are semi annual.) Is this a discount or premium bond? *(LG4)*

6-23 **Compute Bond Price** Calculate the price of a 6.2 percent coupon bond with 18 years left to maturity and a market interest rate of 5.9 percent. (Assume interest payments are semi annual.) Is this a discount or premium bond? *(LG4)*

6-24 **Compute Bond Price** Calculate the price of a 5.7 percent coupon bond with 25 years left to maturity and a market interest rate of 4.8 percent. (Assume interest payments are semi annual.) Is this a discount or premium bond? *(LG4)*

6-25 **Bond Prices and Interest Rate Changes** A 5.75 percent coupon bond with 10 years left to maturity is priced to offer a 6.5 percent yield to maturity. You believe that in one year, the yield to maturity will be 6.0 percent. What is the change in price the bond will experience in dollars? *(LG5)*

6-26 **Bond Prices and Interest Rate Changes** A 6.5 percent coupon bond with 14 years left to maturity is priced to offer a 7.2 percent yield to maturity. You believe that in one year, the yield to maturity will be 6.8 percent. What is the change in price the bond will experience in dollars? *(LG5)*

6-27 **Yield to Maturity** A 6.85 percent coupon bond with 26 years left to maturity is offered for sale at $1,035.25. What yield to maturity is the bond offering? (Assume interest payments are paid semi annually.) *(LG6)*

6-28 **Yield to Maturity** A 5.25 percent coupon bond with 14 years left to maturity is offered for sale at $955.75. What yield to maturity is the bond offering? (Assume interest payments are paid semi annually.) *(LG6)*

6-29 **Yield to Call** A 6.75 percent coupon bond with 26 years left to maturity can be called in 6 years. The call premium is one year of coupon payments. It is offered for sale at $1,135.25. What is the yield to call of the bond? (Assume that interest payments are paid semi annually.) *(LG6)*

6-30 **Yield to Call** A 5.25 percent coupon bond with 14 years left to maturity can be called in 4 years. The call premium is one year of coupon payments. It is offered for sale at $1,075.50. What is the yield to call of the bond? (Assume that interest payments are paid semi annually.) *(LG6)*

6-31 **Comparing Bond Yields** A client in the 33 percent marginal tax bracket is comparing a municipal bond that offers a 4.5 percent yield to maturity and a similar-risk corporate bond that offers a 6.45 percent yield. Which bond will give the client more profit after taxes? *(LG6)*

6-32 **Comparing Bond Yields** A client in the 28 percent marginal tax bracket is comparing a municipal bond that offers a 4.5 percent yield to maturity and a similar-risk corporate bond that offers a 6.45 percent yield. Which bond will give the client more profit after taxes? *(LG6)*

advanced problems

6-33 **TIPS Total Return** Reconsider the 3.5% TIPS discussed in problem 6-19. It was issued with CPI reference of 185.6. The bond is purchased at the beginning of the year (after the interest payment), when the CPI was

196.2. For the interest payment in the middle of the year, the CPI was 199.6. Now, at the end of the year, the CPI is 201.3 and the interest payment has been made. What is the total return of the TIPS in dollars and in percentage terms for the year? *(LG2)*

6-34 **TIPS Total Return** Reconsider the 2.25% TIPS discussed in problem 6-20. It was issued with CPI reference of 183.5. The bond is purchased at the beginning of the year (after the interest payment), when the CPI was 197.1. For the interest payment in the middle of the year, the CPI was 200.1. Now, at the end of the year, the CPI is 203.8 and the interest payment has been made. What is the total return of the TIPS in dollars and in percentage terms for the year? *(LG2)*

6-35 **Bond Prices and Interest Rate Changes** A 6.25 percent coupon bond with 22 years left to maturity is priced to offer a 5.5 percent yield to maturity. You believe that in one year, the yield to maturity will be 6.0 percent. If this occurs, what would be the total return of the bond in dollars and percent? *(LG5)*

6-36 **Bond Prices and Interest Rate Changes** A 7.5 percent coupon bond with 13 years left to maturity is priced to offer a 6.25 percent yield to maturity. You believe that in one year, the yield to maturity will be 7.0 percent. If this occurs, what would be the total return of the bond in dollars and percentage terms? *(LG5)*

6-37 **Yields of a Bond** A 3.75 percent coupon municipal bond has 14 years left to maturity and has a price quote of 98.45. The bond can be called in four years. The call premium is one year of coupon payments. Compute and discuss the bond's current yield, yield to maturity, taxable equivalent yield (for an investor in the 35 percent marginal tax bracket), and yield to call. (Assume interest payments are paid semi annually and a par value of $5,000.) *(LG6)*

6-38 **Yields of a Bond** A 4.25 percent coupon municipal bond has 18 years left to maturity and has a price quote of 97.65. The bond can be called in eight years. The call premium is one year of coupon payments. Compute and discuss the bond's current yield, yield to maturity, taxable equivalent yield (for an investor in the 35 percent marginal tax bracket), and yield to call. (Assume interest payments are paid semi annually and a par value of $5,000.) *(LG6)*

6-39 **Bond Ratings and Prices** A corporate bond with a 6.5 percent coupon has 15 years left to maturity. It has had a credit rating of BBB and a yield to maturity of 7.2 percent. The firm has recently gotten into some trouble and the rating agency is downgrading the bonds to BB. The new appropriate discount rate will be 8.5 percent. What will be the change in the bond's price in dollars and percentage terms? (Assume interest payments are paid semi annually.) *(LG7)*

6-40 **Bond Ratings and Prices** A corporate bond with a 6.75 percent coupon has 10 years left to maturity. It has had a credit rating of BB and a yield to maturity of 8.2 percent. The firm has recently become more financially stable and the rating agency is upgrading the bonds to BBB. The new appropriate discount rate will be 7.1 percent. What will be the change in the bond's price in dollars and percentage terms? (Assume interest payments are paid semi annually.) *(LG7)*

 6-41 **Excel Problem** Say that in June of 2008, a company issued bonds that are scheduled to mature in June of 2011. The coupon rate is 5.75% and is paid semi annually. The bond issue was rated AAA.

a. Build a spreadsheet that shows how much money the firm pays for each interest rate payment and when those payments will occur if the bond issue sells 50,000 bonds.

b. If the bond issue rating would have been BBB, then the coupon rate would have been 6.30%. Show the interest payments with this rating. Explain why bond ratings are important to firms issuing capital debt.

c. Consider that interest rates in the economy increased in the first half of 2008. If the firm would have issued the bonds in January of 2008, then the interest rates would have only been 5.40%. How much extra money per year is the firm paying because it issued the bonds in June instead of January?

research it! Bond Information Online

Information on the bond market is widely available in papers like *The Wall Street Journal* and *Barron's*. Bond information can also be found online at financial web sites like finance.yahoo.com, the Bond Market Association (**www.bondmarkets.com**), nasdbondinflo.com. The bond credit rating agencies also maintain web sites with their own bond market news.

You can follow the bond market easily at places like the Yahoo! Finance website. Click on the Bond link in the menu to go to their Bond Center. Bond yields for various maturity Treasury securities are shown for today and for previous days. The Bond Composite Rates link shows similar comparisons for municipal and corporate bonds too.

Bond calculators are also available for free on the Web. Compare a bond price result from your calculator or the price equation with the online bond calculator result at Investopedia. (**www.investopedia.com/calculator/BondPrice.aspx**)

integrated minicase: Corporate Bond Credit Risk Changes and Bond Prices

Land'o'Toys is a profitable, medium-sized, retail company. Several years ago it issued a 6½ percent coupon bond, which pays interest semi annually. The bond will mature in 10 years and is currently priced in the market as $1,037.19. The average yields to maturity for 10-year corporate bonds are reported in the following table by bond rating.

BOND RATING	YIELD (%)	BOND RATING	YIELD (%)
AAA	5.4	BB	7.3
AA	5.7	B	8.2
A	6.0	CCC	9.2
BBB	6.5	CC	10.5
		C	12.0
		D	14.5

(continued)

Periodically, one company will purchase another by buying all of the target firm's stock. The bonds of the target firm continue to exist. The debt obligation is assumed by the new firm. The credit risk of the bonds often changes because of this type of an event.

Suppose that the firm Treasure Toys makes an announcement that they are purchasing Land'o'Toys. Due to Treasury Toys' projected financial structure after the purchase, Standard & Poor's states that the bond rating for Land'o'Toys bonds will change to BB.

a. Compute the yield to maturity of Land'o'Toys bonds before the purchase announcement and use it to determine the likely bond rating.

b. Assume the bond's price changes to reflect the new credit rating. What is the new price? Did the price increase or decrease?

c. What is the dollar change and percentage change in the bond price?

d. How do the bond investors feel about the announcement?

ANSWERS TO TIME OUT

6-1 The federal government issues bonds to fund its annual spending deficit and to refund old bonds that are maturing. Local government and corporations issue bonds to raise the capital needed to fund projects. For local governments, those projects might be the building of roads, bridges, sewer systems, schools, airports, etc. For companies, the projects tend to be expansions of their businesses, which might entail a large factory, new facilities in different geographical locations, and even the purchase of existing business lines from other companies.

6-2 The current price is 100.06% of $1,000, which is $1,000.60. It will pay a semi annual payment of 5.40% × $1,000 ÷ 2 = $27.

6-3

Cash flow	?	42.5	42.5	42.5	42.5	. . .	42.5	42.5	42.5	1,000 42.5
Period	0	1	2	3	4	. . .	21	22	23	24

3.75%   semi annual periods

$$\text{Bond price} = \$42.50 \times \left[\frac{1 - \dfrac{1}{(1+0.0375)^{24}}}{0.0375} \right] + \frac{1,000}{(1+0.0375)^{24}} = \$664.90 + \$413.32 = \$1,078.22$$

6-4 The relationship is one of opposite directions. Increases in market interest rates are associated with decreases in the price of existing bonds. Decreases in interest rates accompany increases in bond prices.

6-5 Using the calculator with settings of N = 20, PV = −525, PMT = 0, FV = 1000, solving for I gives 3.27%. Multiplying this semi annual yield by 2 gives a 6.55% yield to maturity.

6-6 The yield to maturity is higher than the coupon rate for a discount bond. By definition, bonds become discount bonds when the market interest rate (known as the yield to maturity for a bond) rises above the fixed coupon rate.

(continued)

ANSWERS TO TIME OUT (concluded)

6-7 A credit rating change will change the appropriate discount for the bond. An increase in the rating calls for a lower discount rate to be used while a decrease in the rating calls for a higher discount rate. This change in the discount rate directly impacts the bond price.

6-8 The mortgage bond has real estate collateral whereas the debenture has no collateral. Therefore, the mortgage bond is considered a safer security for investors and will be given a higher rating. With the lower bond rating, the debenture will have to offer a lower yield.

6-9 Since bond prices move in the opposite direction as interest rates, the change in interest rates provides much of the information for knowing the change in bond prices.

6-10 Figure 6.6 illustrates many of the popular bond indexes. For example, the Lehman Brothers report indexes on short-term, intermediate-term, and long-term Treasury bonds. For corporate bonds, Merrill Lynch reports indexes for medium-term investment grade, long-term investment grade, and speculative grade. Merrill Lynch also has municipal bond indexes.

chapter 7:

VALUING STOCKS

 Learning Goals

LG1   Understand the rights and returns that come with common stock ownership.

LG2   Know how stock exchanges function.

LG3   Track the wider stock market with stock indices and differentiate among the kinds of information each index provides.

LG4   Know the terminology of stock trading.

LG5   Compute stock values using dividend discount and constant-growth models.

LG6   Calculate the stock value of a variable-growth-rate company.

LG7   Assess relative stock values using the P/E ratio model.

Businesses need capital to start up operations, expand product lines and services, and serve new markets. In the last chapter, we discussed debt, which is one source of financial capital upon which businesses can draw. Their other source of capital is called *equity,* or *business ownership*. Public corporations share business ownership and raise money by issuing stocks to investors. When the company sells this form of equity ownership to raise money, it gives up some ownership—and thus some control—over the business. Investors buy stock to receive the benefits of business ownership. Most citizens do not have the time or expertise to operate their own businesses. Buying stock allows them to participate in the profits of economic activities. Access to equity capital has allowed entrepreneurs like Steve Jobs of Apple (ticker: AAPL) and Larry Page of Google (ticker: GOOG) to take their companies public so that their businesses can become large corporations. Both the company founders and the new owners (stock investors) have amassed much wealth over the years under this arrangement. One very important reason that investors are willing to buy company stock as an investment is that they know that they can sell the stock during any trading day. Investors buy and sell stocks among themselves at stock markets. Well-functioning stock markets are critical to any capitalistic economy. In this chapter, we'll discuss stock market operations and stock valuation.

viewpoints

Business Application

As CEO of your firm, Dawa Tech, which makes computer components, you have been able to grow its dividends by 8 percent per year to a recent $2 per share. You expect this growth to continue. As a result, the stock price has risen to $65 and has a P/E ratio of 16.25.

Tomorrow, you are scheduled to meet with some stockholders and financial analysts. To prepare for the meeting, you should know what return the shareholders seem to expect and estimate where the Dawa stock price may be in three years. How will you go about preparing for this meeting? **(See solution on p. 240)**

Personal Application

You are impressed with the news and entertainment firm, CBC Newscorp. The per-share dividends have increased from $1.25 per year three years ago to the recent $1.68 annual dividend. Then you discover that 15 analysts are following the firm and that their mean growth estimate for the future is 10.1 percent. Now you want to know if the current selling price of $54 seems like a good deal if the appropriate required return for the stock is 13.5 percent. **(See solution on p. 240)**

A practice test can be found on the Online Learning Center at
www.mhhe.com/can1e

7.1 Common Stock

Equity securities (stocks) represent ownership shares in a corporation. **Common stock** offers buyers the potential for current income from dividends and capital appreciation from any stock price increases. Over time, some corporate profits are reinvested in the firm, which increases the value of each shareholder's stake in the business. At any point in time, the market value of a firm's common stock depends on many factors, including:

- The company's profitability.
- Growth prospects for the future.
- Current market interest rates.
- Conditions in the overall stock market.

Over periods of 30 to 40 years, stocks have offered investors the best opportunities to increase wealth. Since stocks are also susceptible to price declines and stock price fluctuations can be very volatile over short periods of time, stock investing requires a longer-term outlook.

Virtually any business firm that is organized as a corporation (see Chapter 1) may choose to issue publicly traded stock. Common stockholders vote to elect the board of directors; they also vote on various other proposals requested by other shareholders or the management team. As owners of the firm, common stockholders are considered to be **residual claimants.** This means that common stockholders have the right to claim any cash flows or value after all other claimants have received what they are owed. As a company earns cash flows, it must pay suppliers, employees, expenses, taxes, and debt interest payments. Stockholders claim the leftover (or residual) cash flow. These profits can be used to reinvest in the firm to foster growth, pay out as dividends to shareholders, or a combination of the two.

Stocks of growing firms are valuable. Stocks in firms that pay dividends to shareholders are also valuable. Stocks issued by firms that have greater amounts of residual cash flow are more valuable. The value is reflected in the stock price. Therefore, stock price values arise from the company's underlying business success. Many different investors and analysts may estimate a stock's fundamental value based upon some outlook or theory. But the actual stock price is determined on stock exchanges when investors seek to trade with one another. Let's discuss this trading process and then explore how stocks are valued.

7.2 Stock Markets

In general, people will only invest significant amounts of their wealth in stocks if they know that they can convert their shares into cash at any time. Stock exchanges provide this liquidity, allowing buyers and sellers the means to transact stock trades with each other. This liquidity gives many people the confidence to invest in the first place and makes stocks (as well as bonds) attractive investments relative to less-liquid assets like real estate or fine collectibles—which can be difficult to sell quickly at full value. The most well-known stock exchange in the world is the **New York Stock Exchange (NYSE).**

The New York Stock Exchange, located in New York City on the corner of Wall Street and Broad Street, is the largest U.S. stock exchange as measured by the value of companies listed and the dollar value of trading activity. The NYSE is the largest equities marketplace in the world and is home to nearly 2,700 companies (many with multiple securities listed). While other exchanges may boast more companies listed, the largest companies in the world tend to list in New York.

Much of the stock buying and selling at the NYSE occurs at 17 stations, called **trading posts,** on the trading floor. Each post is staffed by a **specialist,** who oversees the orderly trading of the specific stocks assigned to that post. **Brokers,** located around the perimeter of the floor, act as agents for those buying and selling stocks. Brokers execute orders by matching buy and sell orders. Once the buy and sell orders match, the transaction is completed and the trade appears on trading screens viewed by people all over the world.

Consider this trade illustration. You decide to buy shares of McDonald's stock because of their new menu items and other initiatives. You place a buy order for 100 shares with your broker—either with a simple phone call or through an online brokerage service. The broker then sends the order to the NYSE electronically via the SuperDOT® System to the trading post assigned for McDonald's stock. At the trading post, the specialist makes sure the transaction is executed in a fair and orderly manner. Your buy order competes with other orders at the point of sale for the best price and an on-floor broker executes your purchase. You will receive a trade confirmation from your broker describing the trade and noting the exact amount you owe for the 100 shares of McDonald's plus any applicable commissions. The NYSE reports the transaction and it appears within seconds on displays across the country and around the world. Note that buy and sell orders are electronically routed from all over the world to the NYSE, which then routes trade results back. Since most of the trade orders are already in electronic form, why not electronically match buy and sell orders and bypass any human intervention in floor trading? Indeed, the NYSE has joined many other exchanges in becoming increasingly electronic. Some floor specialist firms can see a time when no human intervention will be a part of floor trading at the NYSE. Their claim that human intervention can detect and prevent problems with electronic trades has been widely questioned.

The NYSE will trade hundreds of thousands, even millions, of McDonald's stock shares in a given day. An intraday (during trading hours) stock quote for McDonald's stock, **ticker symbol** MCD, is shown in Figure 7.1. On January 8, 2008, over 5 million McDonald's shares traded by early afternoon. The stock traded at $58.12 per share, which was 4 cents higher than the closing price of the previous day. At this price, McDonald's stock is currently much closer to its 52-week high of $63.69 than to its 52-week low of $42.31.

To list its stock on the NYSE, a company must meet minimum requirements for its:

- Total number of stockholders.
- Level of trading volume.
- Corporate earnings.
- Firm size.

The Exchange also charges an initial list fee and an annual fee. Listing standards and fees are higher for the NYSE than for other stock exchanges, so many firms cannot (or choose not to) list their stocks there. They can find one alternative right down the street at the **American Stock Exchange (AMEX),** which uses a specialist trading system like the NYSE. As the nation's second largest floor-based stock auction exchange, the AMEX processes trades in both listed equities and equity derivative securities (options).

Another popular stock trading system is the **Nasdaq Stock Market,** an electronic stock market without a physical trading floor. Today, Nasdaq features many of the big-name high-tech companies investors have come to know, like Apple Computer (ticker: AAPL), Intel (ticker: INTC), Microsoft (ticker: MSFT), and Qualcomm (ticker: QCOM). Many newer high-tech companies like Google (ticker: GOOG), Netflix (ticker: NFLX), and Sirius Satellite Radio (ticker: SIRI),

figure 7.1

Read a Stock Quote, January 8, 2008, Yahoo! Finance

Stock Name and Ticker Symbol: The corporate name and unique symbol used for trading and quotes.

52-Week Range: The highest and lowest price the stock has traded for in the past 12 months. ($)

MCDONALDS CP (NYSE:MCD)				Edit
Last Trade:	**58.12**	Day's Range:	57.29 - 58.64	New! Try our new Charts in Beta
Trade Time:	1:49PM ET	52wk Range:	42.31 - 63.69	MCD 8–Jan 1:45pm (C)Yahoo!
Change:	↑ 0.09 (0.16%)	Volume:	5,557,141	
Prev Close:	58.03	Avg Vol (3m):	8,367,260	
Open:	58.44	Market Cap:	68.74B	
Bid:	N/A	P/E (ttm):	30.06	
Ask:	N/A	EPS (ttm):	1.93	1d 5d 3m 6m 1y 2y 5y max
1y Target Est:	65.04	Div & Yield:	1.50 (2.60%)	Annual Report for MCD

Last Price and Change: Last traded price and the change from the prior day. ($)

Dividend: Per share amount of dividends paid in last 12 months. ($)

Dividend Yield: Defined as annual dividends divided by current stock price. (%)

PE Ratio: Defined as current price dividend by last four quarters of earnings.

Volume of Trading: Total number of shares traded during the previous day.

are also listed on Nasdaq. Nasdaq ranks second, behind the NYSE, among the world's equity markets in terms of total dollar volume. Nasdaq lists nearly 3,100 domestic and foreign companies.

Instead of having a trading floor, Nasdaq uses a vast electronic trading system that executes trades via computer rather than in person. Instead of one specialist overseeing the process for an individual stock on a trading floor, Nasdaq's system uses multiple **market makers,** called **dealers.** Market makers use their own stock inventory and capital to compete with other dealers to buy and sell the stocks they represent. When an investor places an order through a stockbroker for a Nasdaq-listed stock, the electronic system routes the order and the investor buys shares from the dealer offering the best (lowest) price. Typical Nasdaq stocks support 10 market makers actively competing with one another for investor trades.

Table 7.1 shows trading activity on the three main stock exchanges for one day in January 2008. The NYSE and Nasdaq each show over 3,000 securities trading, with a total volume of well over 1 billion shares each. Trading on the AMEX is much smaller at less than 50 million shares traded.

The business of providing platforms or forums for investors and speculators to trade stocks and other financial assets has been changing rapidly. Many exchanges that previously used physical floor trading systems with specialists and public outcry to establish stock prices are shifting to electronic systems with no trading floors. Long-standing, traditional exchanges are also merging with other domestic and international exchanges to create fewer, but larger, forums that focus not just on U.S. securities but on many more internationally focused financial assets. The wider range of represented securities allows traders new opportunities to explore trading relationships among securities traded across

	NYSE	NASDAQ	AMEX
Number of securities traded	3,369	3,066	1,331
Advances	1,800	1,400	690
Declines	1,491	1,554	531
Unchanged	78	112	110
New high	53	60	33
New low	291	271	69
Total volume of shares	2,692,343,087	1,504,089,921	686,316,450

Source: Yahoo! Finance (http://finance.yahoo.com/advances)

the world. This worldwide trading will establish economically sound prices and additional financial stability around the world. Many exchanges have become public companies themselves. For example, in April of 2007, the NYSE became a publicly traded company for the first time in its history when it merged with Euronext and became NYSE Euronext. So now, the common stock for the NYSE Euronext company is traded on the NYSE exchange under the ticker symbol: NYX. The Nasdaq stock exchange became a public company in 2002 and trades on its own exchange under the ticker symbol: NDAQ.

TIME OUT

7-1 What are three primary stock exchanges in the United States and where are they located? For which of the exchanges does physical location matter? Why?

7-2 Describe differences in trading procedures on the NYSE versus the Nasdaq. Which do you think is most fair to investors? Why?

Tracking the Stock Market

With thousands of stocks trading every minute, many stock prices rise while others fall. Table 7.1 also shows that, throughout the trading day, 1,800 stocks increased in price on the NYSE while 1,491 stocks decreased in price. On the AMEX, too, more stocks increased in price than decreased but not on Nasdaq. In addition to the number of stocks advancing and declining, the table also shows the number of stocks that hit new 52-week price highs (53 listed on the NYSE) and new lows (291 on the NYSE) on that day. So, was this a good day or a bad day in the stock market?

To say anything about the *general* direction of the stock market, **stock indices** are useful. Dozens of stock indices are designed to track the overall market; many more track different market segments. The three most recognized indices are the **Dow Jones Industrial Average** (DJIA), the **Standard & Poor's 500 Index (S&P 500),** and the **Nasdaq Composite Index.**

Charles H. Dow invented the first stock average in 1884. At the turn of the 20th century, railroads were the first major corporations. So he began with 11 stocks, mostly railroads. Dow created a price average by simply added up 11 stock prices and divided by the number 11. Two years later, Dow began tracking a 12-stock industrial average. This industrial average would eventually evolve into the modern DJIA, which is a price average of 30 large, industry-leading stocks that together represent roughly 30 percent of the total stock value of all U.S. equities. DJIA level changes describe how the largest companies that participate in the stock market performed over a given period. The DJIA was at 12,866.59, a change of +39.10 (or 0.30 percent), on the day illustrated in Table 7.1.

The Standard & Poor's Corp. introduced its 500-stock index in 1957. Standard & Poor's chooses companies to include in the S&P 500 Index to represent the 10 sectors of the economy:

- Financial
- Information technology
- Health care
- Industrials
- Consumer discretionary
- Consumer staples
- Energy
- Telecom services
- Utilities
- Materials

S&P uses **market capitalization** (a measure of company size using stock price times shares outstanding), not just stock prices, of the largest 500 U.S. firms to compute the index. These 500 firms represent roughly 80 percent of the overall stock market capitalization (number of shares times share price). Although the DJIA is a long-time favorite with the media and individual investors, the S&P 500 is much preferred in the investment industry because of its broader representation of the market as a whole. S&P 500 performance provides a standard against which most U.S. money managers and pension plan sponsors can compare their investment performance. During trading on January 8, 2008, the S&P 500 gained 8.124 (0.57 percent) to close at 1,424.30.

The Nasdaq Composite Index measures the market capitalization of all common stocks listed on the Nasdaq stock exchange. Since the Nasdaq lists so many large, technology-oriented companies, many investors and analysts consider this index to reflect the tech sector performance more than that of the overall stock market. The Nasdaq Composite gained 17.54 to 2,517.00 on January 8, 2008, a gain of 0.70 percent. Because all three popular indexes were up on this day, most reports would reflect a good day for the stock market.

Figure 7.2 shows the levels of all these stock indexes since 1980. The DJIA (black line) level appears on the left-hand axis. Both the S&P 500 (green line) and the Nasdaq Composite (orange line) run from the right-hand axis. The rapid price appreciation for Nasdaq stocks during the late 1990s—the tech boom years—is unprecedented for such a large and widely followed market index. The Nasdaq Composite soared from 817 in March 1995 to peak on March 10, 2000, at 5,048.62, for a 518 percent total return in only five years—a 43.9 percent annual rate of share-price appreciation for Nasdaq stocks. The Nasdaq index performed much better than did the DJIA (19.0 percent per year) or the S&P 500 (22.7 percent per year). The Nasdaq "price bubble" set the stage for one of the most dramatic stock price declines in history: The Nasdaq Composite Index plunged to 1,114.11 on October 9, 2002, losing 78 percent of its value. The other index values also fell during this period, albeit not as sharply. Note that the DJIA didn't climb back to its 2000 high until March 2006. The S&P 500 Index finally recovered in May 2007. The Nasdaq Composite still has a long way to go to recover from its fall from pre-2000 levels.

figure 7.2

TIME OUT

7-3 Discuss why the day's market return may be different when measured by the DJIA, S&P 500 Index, and Nasdaq Composite taken separately.

7-4 Why might the "market bubble" phenomenon appear more dramatic because it occurred in the Nasdaq Composite rather than by the DJIA or S&P 500 Index?

7-5 If you followed the market regularly, to which index would you give the most credence? Why?

Trading Stocks

People who wish to buy and sell stocks need to open stock brokerage accounts. Traditional, full-service stockbrokers (e.g., Smith Barney, Merrill Lynch, Dean Witter) provide clients with research and advice in addition to executing trades. Their clients pay for this research and advice: Commission fees for these services may run well over $100 per trade. Discount brokerage firms (e.g., e-trade, Scot-trade, TD Ameritrade) charge a much lower commission, $5 to $30 per trade, but do not provide the additional services. Investors at discount brokerages usually place trades through the brokerage's Internet sites.

Buy and sell orders go through the brokerage firm to a market maker (a dealer or a specialist) at a stock exchange. The quoted **bid** is the highest price at which the *market maker* offers to pay for the stock. Investors have little choice but to accept this selling price, because regardless of the broker used, the market maker offers the only place to sell the stock. The quoted **ask price** is the lowest price at which a market maker will sell a stock—so investors buy at the ask price. The difference between the bid and the ask price may be only 1 cent for high volume stocks and can be as high as 20 cents for less-often traded companies. The spread

behavioral

INVESTOR PSYCHOLOGY

To us today, it seems ludicrous that in the years 1634 to 1636, near the height of the "Tulip Mania" in Holland, the price for a single rare tulip bulb approached the equivalent of $35,000. Then, the bubble burst and tulip prices quickly plunged to less than the equivalent of $1. We may call those people who invested in a $35,000 tulip bulb irrational or even "crazy."

But this type of story seems to repeat itself throughout history. Investors paid extremely high prices for the new computer stocks in the 1960s, the "nifty fifty" companies in the 1970s, and Japanese stocks during the 1980s. And of course, the recent technology and Internet stock bubble of the late 1990s reflected equally irrational buying. The mania for stocks like Iomega drove its price from an equivalent of $1 per share in January of 1995 to over $75 in just 16 months. When the bubble burst, the price fell hard. Many years later, in 2007, the stock still trades for only about $3.50. But that's just one company. A portfolio full of Internet stocks experienced a similar price mania followed by a severe fall. Investors created a stock index (TheStreet.com Internet Index) designed to track Internet stocks in late 1998, but by that time, part-time investors and veterans alike were already well into the craze. The Internet index started at 250, quickly rose to 1,270 by March of 2000, and subsequently fell

to a low of 63 in October of 2002. In retrospect, irrational bubble-like prices are not confined to tulips and the 17th century in Holland.

Seemingly irrational behavior may not occur only during highly emotional periods of a price bubble. Recently, a growing recognition has arisen that "normal" investors often behave in a way that might not be described as fully rational. Investors, being human, are subject to cognitive biases and emotions. Studies of investor behavior have discovered that investors commonly succumb to psychological biases and:

- Trade too much.
- Sell winners too soon.
- Refuse to realize losses.
- Become overconfident—especially when trading online.
- Seek stocks that have already increased in price—perhaps up to their full potential price.
- Consider and react to what's happening with each stock in isolation, rather than remembering the purpose for forming an overall portfolio.

Investors who succeed in the long run are those who learn to avoid these psychological biases.

 want to know more? Key Words to Search for Updates: **irrational exuberance, price bubble, mania**

between the bid and the ask price is a cost to the investor and a profit for the market maker. This profit compensates the market maker for providing a market and liquidity for that stock.

Investors can place a buy or sell **market order.** A market order to buy stock will be filled immediately at the current ask price when routed to the stock exchange. A sell market order will be filled at the current bid price. The advantage of a market order is that it executes immediately at the best available price. The disadvantage of a market order is that the investor does not know in advance what that fill price will be. Investors can name their own prices by using **limit orders,** in which investors specify the price at which they are willing to execute the buy or sell order. With a buy limit order, a trade is executed if the ask quote is at or below the price target. For a sell limit order, a trade is executed if the bid quote moves through the specified price. If the current quote does not meet the price cited in the limit order, the trade is not executed. The advantage of a limit order is that the investor makes the trade at the desired price; the disadvantage is that the trade might not be executed at all.

Consider a quote of McDonald's stock with a bid price of $58.10 and an ask price of $58.10. An investor placing a market buy order would purchase the stock at $58.10. A market sell order would execute as the price rises through $58.10.

Note that an investor who simultaneously bought and sold 100 shares would pay $5,815 and receive $5,810—losing $5. An investor who places a buy limit order at $58.13 will only purchase the shares if the ask price falls to $58.13 or lower. If the ask does not fall, the order will not execute. Bid and ask prices tell investors at what prices the stock can currently be traded in general. But being able to buy at the ask price does not guarantee that the stock should be *valued* at that price. We'll discuss various ways to arrive at reasonable per-share stock values in the next section.

TIME OUT

7-6   Explain how the difference in the bid and ask prices might be considered a hidden cost to the investor.

7-7   The bid and ask prices for Amazon.com are $37.79 and $37.85. If these quotes occur when a trade order is made, at what price would a market buy order execute? Would a limit sell order execute with a target price of $37.75?

7.3 Basic Stock Valuation

Cash Flows

In the previous chapter, we showed how we value bonds by finding the present value of the future interest payments and the future par value. Stock valuation uses the same concept of finding the present value of future dividends and the future selling price. But of course uncertainty about both price appreciation and future dividend payment streams complicate stock valuation. Consider the simple case of valuing a stock to be held for one year shown in the time line.

Cash flow	?		$D_1 + P_1$
Period	0	i	1 year

The value of such a stock today, P_0, is the present value of the dividend to be received in the first year, D_1, plus the present value of the expected sales price in one year, P_1. The interest rate used to discount the cash flows is shown as i. Using the present value equation from Chapter 4 results in:

$$P_0 = \frac{D_1 + P_1}{1 + i} \tag{7-1}$$

Whenever investors deal with future stock prices and future dividend payments, they must use expected values, not certain ones. Companies rarely decrease their dividends; most companies' dividends either remain constant or slowly grow. Examining a firm's dividend history over the past few years will give clues to that company's future dividend policy. For example, The Coca-Cola Company (ticker: KO) paid a $0.22 per share dividend for each quarter in 2003. The firm then raised the quarterly dividend to $0.25 for each quarterly dividend in 2004. The company paid quarterly dividends in 2005, 2006, and 2007 of $0.28, $0.31, and $0.34 respectively. This increase of 3¢ in the dividend every year seems fairly stable.

Stock prices, though, show much more volatility than dividend histories do. We face much uncertainty in trying to predict stock prices in the short term.

Using a longer holding period to estimate stock value reduces *some*, but by no means all, of the uncertainty. A two-year holding period appears like this:

Cash flow	?		D_1		$D_2 + P_2$
Period	0	i	1		2 years

The present value of the cash flows in years 1 and 2 is today's stock value:

$$P_0 = \frac{D_1}{1+i} + \frac{D_2 + P_2}{(1+i)^2} \tag{7-2}$$

Notice that the divisor for the second term on the right-hand side of equation 7.2 is raised to the second power. This reflects the two years over which those cash flows must be discounted. You can do this analysis over any holding period. For a holding period of n years, the value of a stock is measured by the present value of dividends over the n years, and the eventual sale price, P_n.

$$P_0 = \text{sum of the present value of each payment received}$$

$$P_0 = \frac{D_1}{1+i} + \frac{D_2}{(1+i)^2} + \cdots + \frac{D_n + P_n}{(1+i)^n} \tag{7-3}$$

This formula incorporates both dividend income and capital appreciation or capital loss. It fully includes both major components of the investor's total return from investment.

EXAMPLE 7-1

 For interactive versions of this example visit www.mhhe.com/can1e

VALUING COCA-COLA STOCK

 In January, 2008, you are valuing Coca-Cola stock at the beginning of 2008 to compare its value to its market price. The current market price is $63.50. Given the history of Coca-Cola's dividends, you believe that the company will pay total dividends in 2008 of $1.48 (= 4 × $0.37). Your analysis indicates that the total dividends in 2009 and 2010 will be $1.60 and $1.72, respectively. In addition, you believe that the price of Coca-Cola stock at the end of 2010 will be $84 per share. If the appropriate discount rate is 11.5 percent, what is the value of Coca-Cola stock?

CALCULATOR

1st cash flow:
N = 1. I = 11.5
PMT = 0, FV = 1.48
CPT PV = −1.33
2nd cash flow:
N = 2. I = 11.5
PMT = 0, FV = 1.60
CPT PV = −1.29
3rd cash flow:
N = 3. I = 11.5
PMT = 0, FV = 85.72
CPT PV = −61.84
Value = 1.33 + 1.29 + 61.84
       = 64.46

SOLUTION: To organize your data, you first create the following timeline:

Cash flow	?		$1.48	$1.60	$1.72+$84
Period	0	11.5%	1	2	3 years

Using equation 7-3, you compute the stock value as:

$$P_0 = \frac{\$1.48}{1+0.115} + \frac{\$1.60}{(1+0.115)^2} + \frac{\$1.72 + \$84}{(1+0.115)^3} = \$1.33 + \$1.29 + \$61.84 = \$64.46$$

Since your analysis shows that Coca-Cola's stock should be valued at nearly $64.50 while it's selling for only $63.50, the stock appears to be slightly undervalued. You believe that this might be a good time to buy some Coca-Cola stock.

figure 7.3

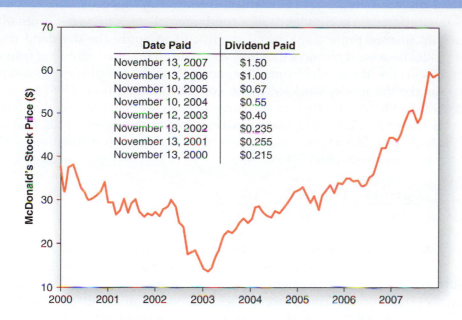

Date Paid	Dividend Paid
November 13, 2007	$1.50
November 13, 2006	$1.00
November 10, 2005	$0.67
November 10, 2004	$0.55
November 12, 2003	$0.40
November 13, 2002	$0.235
November 13, 2001	$0.255
November 13, 2000	$0.215

As is often the case in finance, implementing equation 7.3 presents problems for some firms in practical terms. What will the future dividends of the firm be? What will the stock price be in 3, 5, or 10 years? While it seems that the dividend growth of Coca-Cola will be constant, consider the actual dividends and stock price of McDonald's Corp. since 2000 shown in Figure 7.3.

Unlike most firms, which pay quarterly dividends, McDonald's pays an annual dividend during the second week of November. On November 13, 2000, it paid a $0.215 per share dividend. McDonald's was able to increase that by 4¢ per share the following year (an 18.6 percent increase), but had to cut the dividend by 2¢ per share in 2002 (an 8.9 percent decline). However, since 2002, McDonald's has been able to increase its dividend every year—sometimes substantial increases. The dividend increases in 2003 and 2007 were 70.2 percent and 50.0 percent, respectively. The figure also shows that McDonald's stock price has been very volatile. The price fell from $37 in 2000 to nearly $12 in 2003 and then rapidly increased to over $58 by the end of 2007. An investor in 2000 would have had a very difficult time accurately forecasting these future dividends and stock prices. Indeed, short-term stock price changes seem almost random. Stock valuation can really only be viewed from a long-term perspective. Because predicting future dividends is uncertain at best, it's better to project valuation as a likely range of prices under reasonable assumptions rather than as a single price.

Dividend Discount Models

We can extend the discounted cash flow approach in equation 7-3 for an infinite stream of dividends, $n \to \infty$, and no final future selling price. If stockholders receive all future cash flows as future dividends, the stock's value to the investor is the present value of all these future dividends. In other words, embedded in any stock price is the value of all future dividends. We can demonstrate this value as:

$$P_0 = \frac{D_1}{1+i} + \frac{D_2}{(1+i)^2} + \frac{D_3}{(1+i)^3} + \cdots \qquad \textbf{(7-4)}$$

This equation shows the general case of the **dividend discount model.** The dividend discount model provides a useful theoretical basis because it illustrates the importance of dividends as a fundamental stock price determinant. But, again, finance professionals find it difficult to apply the dividend discount model because it requires that they estimate an infinite number of future dividends. To use the model in practice, analysts make simplifying assumptions to make the model workable. One common assumption: The firm has a constant dividend growth rate, g. If this is the case, next year's dividend is simply this year's dividend that grew one year at the growth rate, that is, $D_1 = D_0 \times (1 + g)$. In fact, we can express each dividend as a function of D_0 and we can rewrite equation 7-4 as:

$$P_0 = \frac{D_0(1 + g)}{1 + i} + \frac{D_0(1 + g)^2}{(1 + i)^2} + \frac{D_0(1 + g)^3}{(1 + i)^3} + \cdots \qquad (7\text{-}5)$$

So, with this version of the model, we need not forecast an infinite string of dividends, D_0 and g take care of that. However, we must still compute an infinite sum of numbers. Luckily, mathematicians know equations like these; they're known as power series. This power series can be simplified to the **constant-growth model,** and it assumes that the growth rate is smaller than the discount rate (i.e., for $g < i$):

$$\text{Constant growth model} = P_0 = \frac{D_0(1 + g)}{i - g} = \frac{D_1}{i - g} \qquad (7\text{-}6)$$

If $g \geq i$, then the denominator would be zero or negative. Economically and mathematically, this is a nonsensical result. In the short run, a firm can grow very quickly. In the long run, no company can grow faster than the overall economic growth rate forever. You may hear the constant-growth model referred to as the *Gordon growth model,* after financial economist Myron J. Gordon.

Investors use several methods to estimate a firm's growth rate for this model. They can project the dividend trend into the future and determine the implied growth rate, compute the past growth rate, or even consider a financial analyst's growth rate predictions. Consider Coca-Cola's dividend behavior. If the 2007 dividend was $1.36 and the projected dividends will grow to $1.90 in 2011, the implied projected dividend growth rate is therefore 8.72 percent (N = 4, PV = − 1.36, PMT = 0, FV = 1.72, CPT I = 8.14) annually. The growth rate in dividend changes from 2003 to 2007 was 11.50 percent (N = 4, PV = −0.88, PMT = 0, FV = 1.36, CPT I = 11.50) per year. You can find analyst forecasts many places online. The Yahoo! Finance Web page for Coca-Cola has an Analyst Estimates link, which shows the average analysts' forecast for the firm's growth in the next five years at 9.37 percent.

Preferred Stock

A special case of the constant-growth model occurs when the dividend does not grow but is the same every year. This zero-growth rate case describes a **preferred stock.** The phrase *preferred* comes from the fact that this type of stock takes preference over common stock in bankruptcy proceedings. Preferred stockholders have a higher priority for receiving proceeds from bankruptcy proceedings than do common stockholders. Preferred stock is largely owned by other companies, rather than by individual investors, because its dividends are mostly nontaxable income (70 percent of the income is exempt from taxes) to other corporations. Preferred stockholders do not have voting rights like common

For interactive versions of this example visit www.mhhe.com/can1e

EXAMPLE 7-2

CONSTANT GROWTH AND COCA-COLA STOCK

Assume that you are valuing Coca-Cola stock again. This time you are using the constant-growth model, assuming a discount rate of 11.5 percent.

SOLUTION:

You have a choice of three growth rates to use. The implied projected dividend growth rate is 8.72 percent. Past dividend growth has been 11.50 percent and analysts forecast a 9.37 percent growth. The 11.50 percent growth rate is the same as the 11.5 percent discount rate and is therefore not appropriate for the constant growth rate model. Compute the stock value using both the 8.72 percent and 9.37 percent growth rates.

Using a dividend growth rate of 8.72 percent and equation 7-6, the stock value is $53.24:

$$P_0 = \frac{\$1.36 \times (1 + 0.0872)}{0.115 - 0.0872} = \frac{\$1.48}{0.0278} = \$53.24$$

Using a dividend growth rate of 9.37 percent, the stock value is $69.83:

$$P_0 = \frac{\$1.36 \times (1 + 0.0937)}{0.115 - 0.0937} = \$69.83$$

Notice how a small change in the growth rate has a large impact on the stock value in this model. At a current price of $63.50 per share, Coca-Cola would be considered undervalued if future dividend growth is 9.37 percent and overvalued if dividends grow at 8.72 percent.

---

stockholders, though, which prevents one company from controlling another through preferred stock ownership.

An interesting characteristic of preferred stock is that it pays a constant dividend. Because the dividend does not change, the preferred stock can be valued using the constant-growth-rate model with a zero growth rate expressed as $P = D/i$. What would Coca-Cola's stock be worth if its dividend stayed at $1.36 and never grew? Using the same 11.5 percent discount rate, the stock would be valued at $11.83 (= $1.36 ÷ 0.115). Given Coca-Cola's current stock price of $63.50, over 81 percent [= ($63.50 − $11.83) ÷ $63.50] of its stock value comes from the expectation that Coca-Cola's dividend will grow. In other words, investors value highly a growing firm.

Most companies issue only common stock, but nearly 1,000 preferred stock issues still exist. Table 7.2 compares the common stock and preferred stock for 10 firms. Many of the preferred stocks come from the finance, energy, and real estate sectors. Notice that the **dividend yield** for preferred stock is higher than for the common stock, because preferred stock investors should only expect a return from dividend payments. Common stockholders will also expect a return from capital appreciation over time. Common stocks also trade much more frequently than preferred stocks do.

> **MATH COACH**
>
> ### USING THE CONSTANT-GROWTH-RATE MODEL
>
> The distinction between the recent year's dividends, D_0, and next year's dividends, D_1, can be confusing in the constant-growth-rate model. The model's equation presents two different numerators. If you are given information about dividends last year or just paid, use the $D_0(1 + g)$ version of the equation. If you have information about expected dividends or next year's dividend, use the D_1 version of the equation.

COMPANY	COMMON STOCK				PREFERRED STOCK			
	TICKER	PRICE	ANNUAL DIVIDEND (YIELD%)	VOLUME	TICKER	PRICE	ANNUAL DIVIDEND (YIELD%)	VOLUME
Alcoa Inc.	AA	$42.43	$0.68(1.5)	11,751,400	AA.PR	$71.75	$3.75(5.2)	1,300
Bear Stearns Cos.	BSC	138.03	1.28(0.9)	6,085,000	BSCPRG	48.40	2.74(5.7)	500
CIT Group Inc.	CIT	55.41	1.00(1.8)	1,110,100	CITPRA	24.85	1.59(6.4)	5,200
El Du Pont de Nemours & Co.	DD	51.18	1.48(2.9)	4,553,200	DDPRA	67.70	3.50(5.2)	300
Ford Motor Co.	F	8.90	0.20(2.5)	69,500,800	FPRS	39.24	3.25(8.3)	4,451,000
Host Hotels & Resorts Inc.	HST	24.53	0.80(3.3)	3,323,200	HSTPRE	26.80	2.22(8.3)	900
LaSalle Hotel Properties	LHO	47.53	2.04(4.3)	316,000	LHOD	24.10	1.88(7.7)	700
Northrop Grumman Corp.	NOC	76.79	1.48(1.9)	966,500	NOCPRB	140.96	7.00(4.9)	4,200
PG&E Corp.	PCG	44.80	1.44(3.2)	1,911,700	PCG.PRA	24.55	1.50(6.1)	300
Public Storage Inc.	PSA	76.55	2.00(2.6)	831,400	PSAPRL	24.27	1.68(6.9)	11,900

Source: New York Stock Exchange (**www.nyse.com**)

The zero-growth-rate version of the constant-growth valuation model shows that, since dividends are fixed, a preferred stock's price changes because of changes in the discount rate, *i*. When interest rates throughout the economy change, the discount rate also changes. Preferred stock prices thus tend to act like bond prices. When interest rates rise, preferred stock prices fall. When interest rates decline, preferred stock prices rise. Preferred stock is usually categorized with bonds in the fixed-income security group because it acts so much like debt securities, even though a preferred stock represents equity ownership, like common stock.

Expected Return

Stock valuation models require a discount rate, *i*, in order to compute the present value of the future cash flows. The discount rate used should reflect the investment risk level. Higher risk investments should be evaluated using higher interest rates. For example, the previous chapter on bonds demonstrated that higher risk bonds, such as junk bonds, offer higher rates of return. Similarly, investors demand higher returns from higher risk stocks than they do from lower risk stocks. We discuss stock risk measurement and appropriate expected returns in the next section of this book.

However, one method for determining what return stock investors require from a stock is to use the constant-growth-rate model. If the current stock price fairly reflects its value, then the discount rate, *i*, in equation 7-6 should be the expected return for the stock. Solving for this expected return results in equation 7-7:

$$\text{Expected return} = i = \frac{D_1}{P_0} + g = \text{Dividend yield} + \text{Capital gain} \qquad \text{(7-7)}$$

Note that the expected return comes again from two sources: dividend yield and expected appreciation of the stock price, or capital gain. For example, consider that Coca-Cola's dividend next year (2008), D_1, is expected to be $1.48 per share. At a current price of $63.50, Coca-Cola offers a dividend yield of 2.33 percent (= $1.48 ÷ $63.50). Since analysts believe that the firm's stock price will grow at 9.37 percent in the future, investors expect a total return of 11.7 percent (= $2.33% + 9.37%). Dividend yield can represent a substantial portion of the

FINANCIAL ANALYSTS' PREDICTIONS AND OPINIONS

Financial analysts examine a firm's business and financial success and assess long-term prospects and management effectiveness. They combine this microeconomic analysis with a macroeconomic view of the conditions of the economy, financial markets, and industry outlooks. Their evaluation results in earnings predictions, stock price targets, and opinions about whether investors should buy the stock. Such recommendations can help investors decide whether to buy, hold, or sell the stock.

Analysts hired by brokerage firms and investment banks are called *sell-side analysts* because their firms make money by selling stocks and bonds. These analysts publicize their predictions and opinions publicly and in company "tip sheets" that are passed along to clients. Keep in mind that sell-side analysts often have incentives to be optimistic. Pension funds and mutual funds often hire analysts to give fund managers private opinions about securities. These analysts are referred to as *buy-side analysts* because they are hired by investment firms looking for advice on what stocks to buy for their portfolios. Because this is private, little buy-side research is made public.

Consider the 14 sell-side analyst predictions reported for Coca-Cola on the Yahoo! Finance Web site. The average five-year share price growth prediction from these analysts is 9.37 percent. This is lower than the growth prediction for the industry (9.51 percent) and sector (9.80 percent). While the current stock price for Coca-Cola this day was $63.50, the average target price that the analysts cited was $65.08, with the target prices ranging from $60 to $69. Last, analysts give opinions on whether investors should buy, sell, or hold Coca-Cola stock. Recommendations come in five levels: Strong Buy, Buy, Hold, Sell, and Strong Sell. Of the 17 analysts, five recommend a Strong Buy, eight recommend a Buy, and four recommend a Hold. Note that even though the analysts predict lower than average growth for the industry and sector, and that the analysts provide meager price targets, none of the analysts recommend a Sell or Strong Sell of the stock. This optimism in analysts' opinions is common. Knowledgeable investors know that a "hold" recommendation is as negative as most public or sell-side analysts get, and therefore a "hold" may actually represent a signal to sell.

 want to know more? **Key Words to Search for Updates: analyst opinion, financial analyst bias**

profits for an investor. Many people get too enamored of high **growth stocks** that do not pay dividends and therefore miss out on an important source of stable returns.

Corporate managers conduct an important application of the expected return concept to determine the return that their shareholders expect of them. We will discuss this application in detail in Part Six: Capital Budgeting.

TIME OUT

7-8   Explain how valuable a firm's (and therefore its stock) growth is. Demonstrate this with growth and no-growth examples.

7-9   What proportion of the 11.7 percent of Coca-Cola's expected return above comes from dividend yield?

7.4 Additional Valuation Methods

Variable-Growth Techniques

Some companies grow at such a high rate that we can't use the constant-growth-rate model to forecast their value. High growth rates might be sustainable for several years, but cannot continue forever. Consider what happens to a high-growth

figure 7.4

Variable Dividend
Growth

figure 7.5

Stage 1 Dividends

firm. Other companies will surely notice the market potential for high growth rates and will enter those product markets to compete with the high-growth firm. The competition will soon drive down the growth rates for all companies in that product market. Companies that experience unusually high growth tend to see that growth become only average in the future unless they possess some kind of entry barrier such as a patent or government regulation due to economies of scale.

Remember that the constant-growth-rate model doesn't work for companies where $g > i$. And of course, we don't really expect the growth rate for these fast-growing firms to remain constant. To value these firms, we must use a **variable-growth-rate** technique. The variable-growth-rate method combines the present-value cash flow from equation 7-3 and the constant-growth-rate model from equation 7-6.

First, the investor chooses two different growth rates for two stages of the analysis. The first and higher growth rate, g_1, is the current growth rate, which we expect to last only a few years. A few years from now, we expect the firm to grow at a slower but more sustainable rate of growth, g_2. Figure 7.4 shows the cash flow time line when the first growth rate applies for the first n years, followed by the second growth rate, which applies forever.

When we analyze a variable growth rate stock like the one in the figure, we know the recent dividend, D_0, and the two expected growth rates. Therefore, we can calculate each of the dividends shown in general terms (i.e., D_1). For example, the dividend in the first year (D_1) is the year zero dividend that grows at g_1, specifically $D_1 = D_0 \times (1 + g_1)$. The dividend then grows at g_1 again for the second year dividend, $D_2 = D_0 \times (1 + g_1)^2$. The dividend continues to grow through the first stage to year n at $D_n = D_0 \times (1 + g_1)^n$. Figure 7.5 shows the first-stage dividends.

At this point, the company starts to move into stage 2 at the more modest growth rate, g_2, and the dividends reflect that slower growth rate. So D_{n+1} is the dividend D_n that grew at the rate g_2, or $D_{n+1} = D_0 \times (1 + g_1)^n \times (1 + g_2)$. Similarly, the dividend in year $n + 2$ is $D_{n+2} = D_0 \times (1 + g_1)^n \times (1 + g_2)^2$. We can now substitute the known dividends as presented in Figure 7.5 into Figure 7.6.

figure 7.6

Details of the Variable
Growth Dividends

Dividends	D_0	$D_0(1+g_1)$	$D_0(1+g_1)^2$	$D_0(1+g_1)^3$		$D_0(1+g_1)^n$	$D_0(1+g_1)^n\times(1+g_2)$	$D_0(1+g_1)^n\times(1+g_2)^2$

Stage 1, high growth rate, g_1 — Stage 2, stable growth rate, g_2

| Period | 0 | i | 1 | 2 | 3 | ... | n | $n+1$ | $n+2$ year |

figure 7.7

New Stage 1 of the
Variable Growth
Dividend Technique

| Dividends | D_0 | $D_0(1+g_1)$ | $D_0(1+g_1)^2$ | $D_0(1+g_1)^3$ | ... | $D_0(1+g_1)^n+D_0(1+g_1)^n(1+g_2)/(1-g_2)$ |

| Period | 0 | i | 1 | 2 | 3 | | n year |

Once we've calculated all of the dividends, we can begin finding the value of the variable growth stock by focusing on Stage 2 of the problem. Assume that the dividends in Stage 2 are growing at a modest rate, g_2, forever. As long as $g_2 < i$, Stage 2 can use the constant-growth-rate model, equation 7-6. Remember that the constant-growth-rate model, $P_0 = D_1/(i - g)$, replaces all future dividends with one value in the previous period. In previous applications, the growth began in year 1, so the value used for all future dividends came from the year 0 dividend. In this case, the change in the dividend rate occurs in year $n + 1$, so we will use the value from year n. So, using the constant-growth-rate model, we can replace all the cash flows in stage 2 with one value from year n, as:

$$P_n = \frac{D_{n+1}}{i - g_2} = \frac{D_0(1 + g_1)^n(1 + g_2)}{i - g_2}$$

The cash flows from Figure 7.6 now appear as shown in Figure 7.7.

By replacing all the Stage 2 cash flows that continued indefinitely with one terminal price in year n, we reduce the problem to a fixed number of cash flows. The value of this variable growth rate stock is finally computed as the present value of these cash flows, as solved with equation 7-3. Substituting the cash flows shown in Figure 7.7 into equation 7-3 gives us the general formula for finding the value of a variable growth rate stock:

General two-stage growth valuation model

$$P_0 = \frac{D_0(1 + g_1)}{1 + i} + \frac{D_0(1 + g_1)^2}{(1 + i)^2} + \frac{D_0(1 + g_1)^3}{(1 + i)^3} + \cdots$$

$$+ \frac{D_0(1 + g_1)^n + \dfrac{D_0(1 + g_1)^n(1 + g^2)}{i - g_2}}{(1 + i)^n}$$

(7-8)

The practical application of the variable growth rate valuation technique requires the investor to decide how long the current high-growth rate will last before declining to a more stable rate.

EXAMPLE 7-3

 For interactive versions of this example visit www.mhhe.com/can1e

VARIABLE GROWTH AND MCDONALD'S STOCK

 The dividend has grown from $0.40 per share on November 12, 2003, to $1.50 on November 13, 2007. This represents an annual growth rate of 39.2 percent (N = 4, PV = −0.40, PMT = 0, FV = 1.50, CPT I = 39.16). You think this growth rate will continue for three years and then fall to the long-term growth rate of 9.4 percent predicted by analysts. You assume a 14 percent discount rate.

SOLUTION:

Figure 7.3 shows a $1.50 per share recent annual dividend. Modify equation 7-8 for a Stage 1 length of three years and then substitute $i = 0.14$, $g_1 = 0.392$, $g_2 = 0.094$, and $D_0 = \$1.50$. The valuation equation and solution becomes:

$$P_0 = \frac{\$1.50(1+0.392)}{1+0.14} + \frac{\$1.50(1+0.392)^2}{(1+0.14)^2} + \frac{\$1.50(1+0.392)^3 + \dfrac{\$1.50(1+0.392)^3(1+0.094)}{0.14-0.094}}{(1+0.14)^3}$$

$$= \$1.83 + \$2.24 + \frac{\$4.05 + \$96.22}{1.482}$$

$$= \$71.73$$

Given these parameters, McDonald's stock is worth nearly $72 per share. Figure 7.3 shows that the stock price at the end of 2007 was around $58. Comparing the stock's value to its market price, the stock is undervalued.

TIME OUT

7-10 Explain how the variable-growth-rate technique could be used for a firm whose dividend is not expected to grow for three years and then will grow at 5 percent indefinitely.

7-11 Set up and solve the McDonald's valuation problem assuming that the first stage growth will last only two years.

The P/E Model

 The valuation models that we've presented thus far help investors attempt to compute a stock's fundamental value based upon its cash flows to the investor. Another common approach is to assess a stock's **relative value.** This approach compares one company's stock valuation to other firms' stock values to evaluate whether your target company's stock is appropriately priced. The price of a stock taken in isolation doesn't give us a good measure of how expensive it is. Let's use an analogy: At the grocery store, we're less concerned with the total price of

figure 7.8

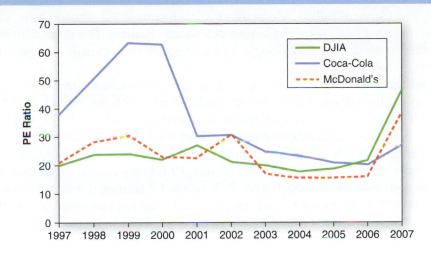

a bag of sugar than we are with the price per pound. Similarly, the price of the stock matters less than its price per one dollar of earnings.

Consider one company that earned $5 per share in profits for the year. Its stock sells for $100. Another company earned $2 per share and its stock price is $50 per share. At first glance, the first stock appears to be more expensive because its price is a high $100 compared to the lower $50 price of the second stock. However, the first company generated higher per-share profits than did the second company. Buying the first stock means that you purchase $5 in earnings. The $100 stock price implies a cost of $20 for every $1 in earnings (= $100 ÷ $5) generated. The $50 price of the second stock implies a cost of $25 for every $1 in earnings (=$50 ÷ $2). So in this regard, the second company becomes more expensive. The **price-earnings (P/E) ratio** represents the most common valuation yardstick in the investment industry; it allows investors to quickly compare the cost of earnings. The P/E ratio is simply the current price of the stock divided by the last four quarters of earnings per share:

$$P/E = \frac{\text{Current stock price}}{\text{Per share earnings for last 12 months}} \qquad (7\text{-}9)$$

More accurately, this figure is the **trailing P/E ratio** and it's often denoted as P/E_0, where the 0 subscript denotes the past (or trailing) earnings.

Figure 7.8 shows two companies' trailing P/E ratios: Coca-Cola and McDonald's, as well as the Dow Jones Industrial Average's trailing P/E ratio over a 10-year period. The P/E ratio for the DJIA changes slowly and mostly stays in the 18-27 range. Historically, the DJIA's P/E ratio has fallen as low as single digits and climbed to over 30. Over the last decade, the P/E ratio for McDonald's has varied more than has the index's P/E ratio. The P/E ratio for Coca-Cola has experienced wild changes—as high as 63 and as low as 21. Figure 7.8 shows that investors valued Coca-Cola more than McDonald's in the late 1990s, but valued them nearly the same by the beginning of 2008.

Variations in P/E ratios between popular companies can be quite large. For example, in January of 2008, the P/E ratio for Google was 51, while the ratio for ConocoPhillips was only 13.1. Google stock is much more expensive than ConocoPhillips. But this does not mean the ConocoPhillips stock is a better deal than Google stock. Investors are willing to pay much more in relative terms for Google because they expect Google will grow much faster than ConocoPhillips.

Indeed, analysts predict an annual growth rate of 34.4 percent per year for Google over the next five years, while they expect a growth rate of only 10.7 percent for ConocoPhillips. Remember that Example 7.2 shows how small changes in growth can result in large stock value changes. The large difference in expected growth between Google and ConocoPhillips causes a large difference in their relative value.

We can more directly see the impact that growth can have on the P/E ratio by modifying the constant-growth-rate model. Begin with the model, $P_0 = D_1 \div (i - g)$. Then divide both sides by the firm's earnings results in $P_0/E_0 = (D_1/E_0) \div (i - g)$. Note that the dividend payout ratio of the firm (D/E), the discount rate (i), and the growth rate (g), taken together, determine the P/E ratio. All else held equal, larger growth rates will lead to larger P/E ratios. Also, firms that have higher payout ratios will have higher P/E ratios. Of course, if a firm pays out a high portion of its earnings as dividends, then it may not have the cash to fund high growth. Thus, high dividend payout firms tend not to be the same as high growth firms.

The value of a stock, and thus its price, relates directly to its future success. Note that valuation models use estimates of future dividends and growth rates. Because of this focus on the future, many people prefer to use a P/E ratio that also looks forward rather than trailing. A **forward P/E ratio** uses analyst estimates of the earnings in the next 12 months instead of the past 12 months and can be denoted as P/E_1. The forward P/E ratio has the advantage over the trailing P/E ratio in that it incorporates investors' expectations of the firm's upcoming profits. A disadvantage is that expected earnings are harder to estimate and thus less accurate than past earnings. The media uses the trailing P/E ratio, while financial managers and investors use the forward P/E ratio more.

Knowledgeable investors who use the P/E ratio as a relative measure of value compare it to the firm's expected growth rate. Table 7.3 shows the forward P/E ratio and analysts' expected growth rates for the 27 of the 30 Dow Jones Industrial Average firms with positive earnings. The firms are sorted by their forward P/E ratios. Investors consider companies with high P/E ratios and high growth rates to be appropriately priced. Companies with low P/E ratios and low growth also seem to be appropriately priced. Investors should be concerned about firms with high P/E ratios and only single digit growth rates. As such, Coca-Cola, McDonald's, Merck, and Verizon may be too expensive for their expected growth rates. Many investors like to buy growth stocks. They seek companies with high growth rates. But growth stock investors are also concerned about paying too much for a stock. While examining growth stocks, they can use the P/E ratio to assess how expensive the stock is. On the other hand, investors consider companies with low P/E ratios and high expected growth to be undervalued, and they are often referred to as **value stocks.** Caterpillar, Wal Mart, and Home Depot would qualify as value stocks. Many investors like to buy value stocks because they feel they are getting a bargain price for a stable company.

Estimating Future Stock Prices

We can often find it useful to estimate a stock's future price. Consider equation 7-3's cash flow discount valuation model. The model requires estimates of future dividends and a future price. How can investors estimate this future price? They can use the P/E ratio model for this purpose. Upon reflection, you will see that multiplying the P/E ratio by earnings results in a stock price. So, in order to

TICKER	COMPANY NAME	STOCK PRICE	FORWARD P/E RATIO	NEXT 5 YEARS GROWTH (%)
INTC	INTEL CP	$ 25.88	18.34	17.07
KO	COCA COLA CO THE	$ 52.27	18.15	9.12
PG	PROCTER GAMBLE	$ 62.74	17.69	11.69
MSFT	MICROSOFT CP	$ 29.90	17.25	12.24
MCD	MCDONALDS CP	$ 51.58	17.14	8.92
HON	HONEYWELL INTL IN	$ 60.33	16.69	11.83
MMM	3M COMPANY	$ 89.46	16.27	11.12
DIS	WALT DISNEY-DISNE	$ 34.15	16.26	13.24
MRK	MERCK CO INC	$ 50.52	15.88	9.28
AXP	AMER EXPRESS INC	$ 62.99	15.62	12.32
VZ	VERIZON COMMUN	$ 41.23	15.45	7.28
MO	ALTRIA GROUP INC	$ 71.95	15.44	7.25
UTX	UNITED TECH	$ 73.66	15.37	11.48
GE	GEN ELECTRIC CO	$ 38.28	15.34	10.56
DD	DU PONT E I DE NE	$ 51.34	14.92	7.27
JNJ	JOHNSON AND JOHNS	$ 63.20	14.65	8.31
HPQ	HEWLETT PACKARD C	$ 47.14	14.63	13.95
IBM	INTL BUSINESS MAC	$109.00	14.11	10.71
HD	HOME DEPOT INC	$ 40.80	13.96	12.18
WMT	WAL MART STORES	$ 48.85	13.51	12.31
XOM	EXXON MOBIL CP	$ 89.10	13.19	5.07
CAT	CATERPILLAR INC	$ 84.07	12.98	12.83
T	AT&T INC.	$ 40.24	12.97	7.37
PFE	PFIZER INC	$ 25.89	10.88	5.47
C	CITIGROUP INC	$ 52.82	10.18	10.03
GM	GEN MOTORS	$ 37.42	10.09	7.90
JPM	JP MORGAN CHASE C	$ 49.25	10.03	9.98

Source: Yahoo! Finance Screener

estimate a future price, simply multiply the expected P/E ratio by the expected earnings. This concept is captured in the following equation:

$$P_n = \left(\frac{P}{E}\right)_n \times E_n \qquad (7\text{-}10)$$
$$= \left(\frac{P}{E}\right)_n \times E_0 \times (1 + g)^n$$

As the formula shows, we can use assumptions about the earnings growth rate to estimate earnings in year n. Many investors believe the firm's P/E ratio in year n is best estimated using today's P/E ratio. However, if today's P/E ratio seems unusual compared with similar firms or even compared with a stock index, then adjustments might be wise.

TIME OUT

7-12 Consider two firms with the same P/E ratio. Explain how one could be described as expensive compared to the other.

7-13 Compute the stock price for Caterpillar in five years if you expect the P/E ratio to decline to 11.

viewpoints REVISITED

Business Application Solution

You can compute the expected return using equation 7-7 as,

$$i = \frac{\$2 \times (1 + 0.08)}{\$65} + 0.08 = 0.033 + 0.08 = 0.113$$

Investors expect an 11.3 percent return.

The P/E ratio of 16.25 and the stock price of $65 indicates that earnings were $4.00 per share (= $65 ÷ 16.25). If the P/E ratio of 16.25 continues, then the price of the stock in three years may be $81.88 [= $16.25 \times \$4 \times (1.08)^3]$. However, a P/E ratio of 16.25 may seem a little high for a firm with an 8 percent growth rate. So the P/E ratio might decline a bit to 15. If so, the stock price in three years would be $75.60. On the other hand, P/E ratios in the stock market may increase in general, thereby inflating this firm's ratio to 17. In this case, the price would be $85.68.

You should report an expected stock price range of $75.60 to $85.68 with a target of $81.88.

Personal Application Solution

The information provided allows for two growth rate estimates for stock valuation. The dividend growth from $1.25 to $1.68 in three years implies a 10.36 percent historical growth rate (N = 3, PV = −1.25, PMT = 0, FV = 1.68, CPT I = 10.36). Since analysts' mean growth estimate is 10.1 percent, you can use either, or both, rates in the constant-growth-rate model using a 13.5 percent discount rate:

$$P_0 = \frac{\$1.68 \times (1 + 0.1036)}{0.135 - 0.1036} = \$59.05$$

$$P_0 = \frac{\$1.68 \times (1 + 0.101)}{0.135 - 0.101} = \$54.40$$

Both valuation estimates exceed the current price of $54. The current stock price does not appear overvalued, so you can consider the purchase.

EXAMPLE 7-4

 For interactive versions of this example visit www.mhhe.com/can1e

THE P/E RATIO MODEL FOR CATERPILLAR

Look at Table 7.3 and notice that the P/E ratio for Caterpillar seems low at 12.98 relative to the growth (12.8 percent) that analysts expect. Caterpillar earned $5.05 per share and paid a $1.10 dividend last year. You decide to explore this seeming anomaly and figure out what Caterpillar's stock price might reach in five years.

SOLUTION:

Compute the expected future price in five years under two different scenarios. The first assumption is that Caterpillar's P/E ratio will be the same in five years as it is today. But since this P/E ratio seems a bit low, the second scenario allows for a rise in the P/E ratio to 15. Under these two scenarios, the future price estimates are:

$$P_5 = \left(\frac{P}{E}\right)_n \times E_0 \times (1+g)^n = 12.98 \times \$5.05 \times (1+0.128)^5 = \$119.70$$

$$P_5 = \left(\frac{P}{E}\right)_n \times E_0 \times (1+g)^n = 15 \times \$5.05 \times (1+0.128)^5 = \$138.33$$

Note that if the P/E ratio increases from 12.98 to 15 in five years, the future price could be more than 15 percent higher than analysts expect without the change.

summary of learning goals

This chapter describes stock ownership and discusses why efficient and fair stock markets are vital in capitalist economies. Investors can benefit from owning common stock. The existence of the stock exchanges allows for easy transfer of stock from one investor to another, providing much more liquidity than would investments with similar returns on investment. The media commonly reports stock market performance using stock indexes. Before buying or selling a stock, investors should determine the stock's value. Many stock valuation methods apply time value of money principles.

LG1 **Understand common stock ownership.** Common stockholders own the corporations in which they hold stock. Stockholders earn investment returns from receiving dividends and from stock price appreciation. As residual claimants, common stockholders claim any cash flows to the firm that remain after the firm pays all other claims—creditors, bondholders, and preferred stockholders. When residual cash flows are high (low), stock values will be high (low).

LG2 **Know how stock exchanges function.** Stock exchanges allow investors to quickly and inexpensively buy and sell thousands of stock shares. Trading at physical exchanges like the New York Stock Exchange and the American Stock Exchange takes place at brokers' trading posts on the floor by open outcry. Specialists and/or market makers oversee brokers and trades to ensure smooth trading in the stocks for which the specialists or dealers are responsible. Dealers create market liquidity in the Nasdaq's electronic stock market; the AMEX and the NYSE process increasing percentages of their trades electronically as open outcry trading becomes increasingly rare. Billions of shares of stock trade every day on each of the exchanges.

LG3 **Track the stock market with stock indices, and differentiate among the kinds of information each index provides.** General stock market performance is measured with popular stock indices like the Dow Jones Industrial Average, the Standard & Poor's 500 Index, and the Nasdaq Composite. The DJIA includes 30 of the largest (market capitalization) and most active companies in the U.S. economy. The S&P 500 Index combines the 500 firms that are the largest in their respective economic sectors. Lastly, the Nasdaq Composite includes all the stock listed on the Nasdaq Stock Exchange. Because so many very large technology firms trade on the

Nasdaq, investors consider this index's performance a bellwether of the tech sector.

LG4 **Know the terminology of stock trading.** Investors buy stock at the quoted ask price and sell at the bid price. The difference between the bid and ask price is the spread—usually a small amount that reimburses the specialist or dealer for expenses. A market order will be immediately executed at quoted prices when the order arrives at the exchange. A limit order will only be executed if the order's price conditions are met; if the price conditions don't materialize a limit order will not be executed and the trade will not take place.

LG5 **Compute stock values using dividend discount and constant-growth models.** We can estimate a stock's value by discounting the future dividends and future stock price appreciation using an appropriate required rate of return as the discount rate. Because future dividends and future stock prices are highly uncertain, we simplify the models if we can reasonably assume conditions such as a constant dividend growth rate. We value preferred stock as a special zero-growth case of the constant-growth-rate model. Valuation model dynamics make clear that lower discount rates lead to higher valuations. Higher growth rates also lead to higher valuations.

LG6 **Calculate the value of a variable-growth-rate company.** Many companies grow very fast at first; we can expect slower future growth. We call such companies "variable-growth-rate" firms. We value these firms using a two-stage process with both the constant-growth model and the discounted cash flow model.

LG7 **Assess relative stock value using the P/E ratio model.** Many investors use the P/E ratio as the most popular relative stock valuation measure. Both individual firm and overall market P/E ratios fluctuate over time. High P/E ratios are associated with high growth stocks. Firms with high P/E ratios but low growth rates are considered relatively expensive. However, firms with low P/E ratios and high growth are considered cheap and we thus refer to them as value stocks. We often use the P/E ratio model with the firm's growth rate to estimate a stock's future price.

chapter equations

$$\text{7-1} \quad P_0 = \frac{D_1 + P_1}{1 + i}$$

$$\text{7-2} \quad P_0 = \frac{D_1}{1 + i} + \frac{D_2 + P_2}{(1 + i)^2}$$

$$\text{7-3} \quad P_0 = \frac{D_1}{1 + i} + \frac{D_2}{(1 + i)^2} + \cdots + \frac{D_n + P_n}{(1 + i)^n}$$

$$\text{7-4} \quad P_0 = \frac{D_1}{1 + i} + \frac{D_2}{(1 + i)^2} + \frac{D_3}{(1 + i)^3} + \cdots$$

$$\text{7-5} \quad P_0 = \frac{D_0(1 + g)}{1 + i} + \frac{D_0(1 + g)^2}{(1 + i)^2} + \frac{D_0(1 + g)^3}{(1 + i)^3} + \cdots$$

$$\text{7-6} \quad \text{Constant growth model} = P_0 = \frac{D_0(1 + g)}{i - g} = \frac{D_1}{i - g}$$

$$\text{7-7} \quad \text{Expected return} = i = \frac{D_1}{P_0} + g = \text{Dividend yield} + \text{Capital gain}$$

$$\text{7-8} \quad P_0 = \frac{D_0(1 + g_1)}{1 + i} + \frac{D_0(1 + g_1)^2}{(1 + i)^2} + \frac{D_0(1 + g_1)^3}{(1 + i)^3}$$
$$+ \cdots + \frac{D_0(1 + g_1)^n + \dfrac{D_0(1 + g_1)^n(1 + g_2)}{i - g_2}}{(1 + i)^n}$$

$$\text{7-9} \quad \text{P/E} = \frac{\text{Current stock price}}{\text{Per share earnings for last 12 months}}$$

$$\text{7-10} \quad P_n = \left(\frac{P}{E}\right)_n \times E_n$$
$$= \left(\frac{P}{E}\right)_n \times E_0 \times (1 + g)^n$$

key terms

American Stock Exchange, Stock exchange with a trading floor. (p. 221)
ask, The quoted price investors are likely to pay when they buy stock. (p. 225)

bid, The quoted price investors are likely to receive when they sell stock. (p. 225)
brokers, Floor traders who execute orders for others and themselves. (p. 221)

common stock, An ownership stake in a public corporation. (p. 220)

constant-growth model, A valuation method based on constantly growing dividends. (p. 230)

dealers, Nasdaq market makers who uses their own capital to trade with investors. (p. 222)

dividend discount model, A valuation approach based on future dividend income. (p. 230)

dividend yield, Last four quarters of dividend income expressed as a percentage of the current stock price. (p. 231)

Dow Jones Industrial Average, A popular index of 30 large, industry-leading firms. (p. 233)

financial analyst, Industry professional who makes predictions about a firm's future earnings and growth, and who may provide buy/sell/hold opinions to investors. (p. 233)

forward P/E ratio, The P/E ratio computed using the *estimated* next four quarters of earning per share. (p. 241)

growth stocks, Companies expected to have above-average rates of growth in revenue, earnings and/or dividends. (p. 233)

limit order, A stock buy or sell order at a specific price. It will only be executed if the market price meets the specified price. (p. 226)

market capitalization, The size of the firm measured as the current stock price multiplied by the number of shares outstanding. (p. 224)

market makers, Dealers and specialists who oversee an orderly trading process. (p. 222)

market order, A stock buy or sell order to be immediately executed at the current market price. (p. 226)

Nasdaq Composite Index, A technology-firm weighted index of stocks listed on the Nasdaq Stock Exchange. (p. 223)

Nasdaq Stock Market, Large electronic stock exchange. (p. 221)

New York Stock Exchange, Large and prestigious stock exchange with a trading floor. (p. 220)

preferred stock, A class of stock with fixed dividends. (p. 230)

price-earnings (P/E) ratio, Current stock price divided four quarters of earnings per share. (p. 237)

relative value, A stock's pricy-ness measured relative to other stocks. (p. 236)

residual claimants, Ownership of cash flows and value after other claimants are paid. (p. 220)

specialist, Person charged with managing the trading process for several individual stocks on the trading floor. (p. 221)

Standard & Poor's 500 Index, A stock index of 500 large companies. (p. 223)

stock index, Index of market prices of a particular group of stocks. The index is used to measure those stocks' performance. (p. 223)

ticker symbol, Unique code for a company consisting of one to five letters. (p. 221)

trading posts, Trading location on the floor of a stock exchange. (p. 221)

trailing P/E ratio, The P/E ratio computed using the *past* four quarters of earning per share. (p. 237)

value stocks, Companies considered to be temporarily undervalued. (p. 238)

variable growth rate, A valuation technique used when a firm's current growth rate is expected to change some time in the future. (p. 234)

self-test problems with solutions

1 **Discounting Dividends and Future Price** You are checking a financial analyst's recommendation. The analyst projects a company's stock price to be $72 per share in three years. The most recent annual dividend was $1.68 per share. The analyst expects that dividend to grow at 9.8 percent annually. Given a 13.5 percent required return, the analyst claims the stock is undervalued at the current price of $54; thus he strongly urges investors to buy it. Using these assumptions, is the stock really undervalued?

Solution:

Using the $72 target price and expected dividends, you can use equation 7-3 to value the cash flows. Since the dividends grow at 9.8 percent, the next three annual dividends will be $D_1 = \$1.84$ (=$\$1.68 \times 1.098$), $D_2 = \$2.03$ (=$\$1.84 \times 1.098$), and $D_3 = \$2.22$ (=$\$2.03 \times 1.098$). Discounting these cash flows results in a value of $53.96:

$$P_0 = \frac{\$1.84}{1 + 0.135} + \frac{\$2.03}{(1 + 0.135)^2} + \frac{\$2.22 + \$72}{(1 + 0.135)^3} = \$1.63 + \$1.58 + \$50.76$$
$$= \$53.96$$

At the current $54 per share price, the stock does not appear undervalued. It appears fairly valued.

LG5

2 **Growth Rates, Required Return, and Value** Consider that a company is about to embark on a large high-risk project. You believe that when this news is publicly announced, shareholders will react by requiring a higher return from the company and by expecting faster growth. The company is expected to pay a $1.75 per share dividend next year. You think that the current price of $70 is fair, given the expected 9 percent growth rate. However, after the announcement investors will expect a 10 percent growth rate and increase the required return by 1.2 percent. If this occurs as you predict, how will the stock price change because of the announcement?

Solution:

It's not initially clear whether this will be good or bad news for the stock price. A rise in the growth rate increases the stock's value. But a higher required return lowers the value. The two changes somewhat offset one another. Since the current $70 stock price is fair, investors require a return of 11.5 percent (= $1.75 \div 70 + 0.09$) before the announcement. After the announcement, investors will require a 12.7 percent return (= $0.115 + 0.012$) and expect a 10 percent growth rate. Therefore, the new stock price should be $64.81 per share, a decline of $5.19 ($-7.4$ percent).

$$P_0 = \frac{\$1.75}{0.127 - 0.10} = \$64.81$$

This was bad news for the stock price.

LG6

3 **Variable Growth Rates** Years Young Match is an online dating firm that finds matches for active people over 55. It has seen substantial growth in revenue and profits as the baby-boom generation ages. The firm will pay its first-ever dividend of 20¢ per share (5¢ per quarter) next year. The dividend is expected to grow at 20 percent per year for the next three years. In the fifth year and afterwards, the Years Young dividend will grow at a steady 9.5 percent per year. If the appropriate discount rate for Years Young is 11 percent, what is the value of the stock?

Solution:

The variable growth rate technique should be used to value this stock. First, calculate the dividends for the first five years. The first dividend is given as $D_1 = \$0.20$. Using the 20 percent growth rate, the rest of the first stage dividends are $D_2 = \$0.24$ (= $\$0.20 \times 1.20$), $D_3 = \$0.288$ (= $\$0.24 \times 1.20$), and $D_4 = \$0.346$ (= $\$0.288 \times 1.20$). The first dividend in the second growth stage is $D_5 = \$0.378$ (= $\$0.346 \times 1.095$). Next, use the constant-growth-rate model and the 11 percent discount rate to convert the rest of the dividends to a terminal price in year four:

$$P_4 = \frac{\$0.378}{0.11 - 0.095} = \$25.20$$

Finally, equation 7-3 can be used to discount all the cash flows as:

$$P_0 = \frac{\$0.20}{1 + 0.11} + \frac{\$0.24}{(1 + 0.11)^2} + \frac{\$0.288}{(1 + 0.11)^3} + \frac{\$0.346 + \$25.20}{(1 + 0.11)^4}$$

$$= \$0.18 + \$0.195 + \$0.211 + \$16.828 = \$17.41$$

The stock for the Years Young Match company is valued at $17.41.

4 **The P/E Ratio and Relative Value** Table 7.3 shows that Home Depot is expected to grow at 12.2 percent per year. HD's P/E ratio is only 14.0. Four other firms in the table are also expected to grow at a similar rate: Microsoft, American Express, Wal-Mart, and Honeywell International. The P/E ratios of these firms range from 13.5 to 17.3, with an average of 15.8. If investors decided that HD should be equally expensive as these other firms, what price would the stock rise to in order for it to have a P/E ratio of 15.8? What return would result from this change in price?

LG7

Solution:
Since the price of HD is $40.80 and the P/E ratio is 14.0, then the expected earnings of HD are $2.91 per share (= $40.80 ÷ 14.0). For the P/E ratio to be 15.8, the price would have to climb to $46.05 (= 15.8 × $2.91). The $5.25 increase would represent a 12.9 percent (= $5.25 ÷ $40.80) capital gain in the price.[1]

questions

1. As owners, what rights and advantages do shareholders obtain? *(LG1)*

2. Describe how being a residual claimant can be very valuable. *(LG1)*

3. Obtain a current quote of McDonald's (MCD) from the Internet. Describe what has changed since the quote in Figure 7.1. *(LG2)*

4. Get the trading statistics for the three main U.S. stock exchanges. Compare the trading activity to that of Table 7.1. *(LG2)*

5. Why might the Standard & Poor's 500 Index be a better measure of stock market performance than the Dow Jones Industrial Average? Why is the DJIA more popular than the S&P 500?*(LG3)*

6. Explain how it is possible for the DJIA to increase one day while the Nasdaq Composite decreases during the same day. *(LG3)*

7. Which is higher, the ask quote or the bid quote? Why? *(LG4)*

8. Illustrate through examples how trading commission costs impact an investor's return. *(LG4)*

9. Describe the difference in the timing of trade execution and the certainty of trade price between market orders and limit orders. *(LG4)*

10. What are the differences between common stock and preferred stock? *(LG5)*

[1]An alternative solution is to recognize that a change in the P/E ratio from 14.0 to 15.8 represents a 12.9 percent change. Thus the price would have to change by the same proportion.

www.mhhe.com/can1e

11. How important is growth to a stock's value? Illustrate with examples. *(LG5)*

12. Under what conditions would the constant-growth-rate model *not* be appropriate? *(LG5)*

13. The expected return derived from the constant-growth-rate model relies on dividend yield and capital gain. Where do these two parts of the return come from? *(LG5)*

14. Describe, in words, how to use the variable-growth-rate technique to value a stock. *(LG6)*

15. Can the variable-growth-rate model be used to value a firm that has a negative growth rate in Stage 1 and a stable and positive growth in Stage 2? Explain. *(LG6)*

16. Explain why using the P/E relative value approach may be useful for companies that do not pay dividends. *(LG7)*

17. How is a firm's changing P/E ratio reflected in the stock price? Give examples. *(LG7)*

18. Differentiate the characteristics of growth stocks and value stocks. *(LG7)*

19. What's the relationship between the P/E ratio and a firm's growth rate? *(LG7)*

20. Describe the process for using the P/E ratio to estimate a future stock price. *(LG7)*

problems

basic problems

7-1 **Stock Index Performance** On January 16, 2007, the Dow Jones Industrial Average set a new high. The index closed at 12,582.59, which was up 26.51 that day. What was the return (in percent) of the stock market that day? *(LG3)*

7-2 **Stock Index Performance** On January 16, 2007, the Standard & Poor's 500 Index reached the highest it had been since 2000. The index closed at 1,431.90, which was up 1.17 that day. What was the return (in percent) of the stock market that day? *(LG3)*

7-3 **Buying Stock with Commissions** At your discount brokerage firm, it costs $8.95 per stock trade. How much money do you need to buy 200 shares of Pfizer, Inc. (PFE), which trades at $27.22? *(LG4)*

7-4 **Buying Stock with Commissions** At your discount brokerage firm, it costs $9.50 per stock trade. How much money do you need to buy 300 shares of Time Warner, Inc. (TWX), which trades at $22.62? *(LG4)*

7-5 **Selling Stock with Commissions** At your full-service brokerage firm, it costs $120 per stock trade. How much money do you receive after selling 150 shares of Nokia Corporation (NOK), which trades at $20.13? *(LG4)*

7-6 **Selling Stock with Commissions** At your full-service brokerage firm, it costs $135 per stock trade. How much money do you receive after selling 250 shares of International Business Machines (IBM), which trades at $96.17? *(LG4)*

7-7 **Buying Stock with a Market Order** You would like to buy shares of Sirius Satellite Radio (SIRI). The current ask and bid quotes are $3.96 and $3.93, respectively. You place a market buy-order for 500 shares that executes at these quoted prices. How much money did it cost to buy these shares? *(LG4)*

7-8 **Buying Stock with a Market Order** You would like to buy shares of Coldwater Creek, Inc. (CWTR). The current ask and bid quotes are $20.70 and $20.66, respectively. You place a market buy-order for 200 shares that executes at these quoted prices. How much money did it cost to buy these shares? *(LG4)*

7-9 **Selling Stock with a Limit Order** You would like to sell 200 shares of WorldSpace, Inc. (WRSP). The current ask and bid quotes are $4.66 and $4.62, respectively. You place a limit sell-order at $4.65. If the trade executes, how much money do you receive from the buyer? *(LG4)*

7-10 **Selling Stock with a Limit Order** You would like to sell 100 shares of eCollege.com (ECLG). The current ask and bid quotes are $15.33 and $15.28, respectively. You place a limit sell-order at $15.31. If the trade executes, how much money do you receive from the buyer? *(LG4)*

7-11 **Value of a Preferred Stock** A preferred stock from Duquesne Light Company (DQUPRA) pays $2.10 in annual dividends. If the required return on the preferred stock is 5.4 percent, what's the value of the stock? *(LG5)*

7-12 **Value of a Preferred Stock** A preferred stock from Hecla Mining Co. (HLPRB) pays $3.50 in annual dividends. If the required return on the preferred stock is 6.8 percent, what is the value of the stock? *(LG5)*

7-13 **P/E Ratio and Stock Price** Ultra Petroleum (UPL) has earnings per share of $1.56 and a P/E ratio of 32.48. What's the stock price? *(LG7)*

7-14 **P/E Ratio and Stock Price** JP Morgan Chase Co. (JPM) has earnings per share of $3.53 and a P/E ratio of 13.81. What is the price of the stock? *(LG7)*

intermediate problems

7-15 **Value of Dividends and Future Price** A firm is expected to pay a dividend of $1.35 next year and $1.50 the following year. Financial Analysts believe the stock will be at their price target of $75 in two years. Compute the value of this stock with a required return of 11.5 percent. *(LG5)*

7-16 **Value of Dividends and Future Price** A firm is expected to pay a dividend of $2.05 next year and $2.35 the following year. Financial Analysts believe the stock will be at their price target of $110 in two years. Compute the value of this stock with a required return of 12 percent. *(LG5)*

7-17 **Dividend Growth** Annual dividends of AT&T Corp (T) grew from $0.96 in 2000 to $1.33 in 2006. What was the annual growth rate? *(LG5)*

7-18 **Dividend Growth** Annual dividends of General Electric (GE) grew from $0.66 in 2001 to $1.03 in 2006. What was the annual growth rate? *(LG5)*

7-19 **Value a Constant Growth Stock** Financial analysts forecast Safeco Corp. (SAF) growth for the future to be 10 percent. Safeco's recent dividend was $1.20. What is the value of Safeco stock when the required return is 12 percent? *(LG5)*

7-20 **Value a Constant Growth Stock** Financial analysts forecast Limited Brands (LTD) growth for the future to be 12.5 percent. LTD's recent dividend was $0.60. What is the value of Limited Brands stock when the required return is 14.5 percent? *(LG5)*

7-21 **Expected Return** Ecolap Inc. (ECL) recently paid a $0.46 dividend. The dividend is expected to grow at a 14.5 percent rate. At a current stock price of $44.12, what is the return shareholders are expecting? *(LG5)*

7-22 **Expected Return** Paychex Inc. (PAYX) recently paid an $0.84 dividend. The dividend is expected to grow at a 15 percent rate. At a current stock price of $40.11, what is the return shareholders are expecting? *(LG5)*

7-23 **Dividend Initiation and Stock Value** A firm does not pay a dividend. It is expected to pay its first dividend of $0.20 per share in three years. This dividend will grow at 11 percent indefinitely. Using a 12 percent discount rate, compute the value of this stock. *(LG6)*

7-24 **Dividend Initiation and Stock Value** A firm does not pay a dividend. It is expected to pay its first dividend of $0.25 per share in two years. This dividend will grow at 10 percent indefinitely. Using an 11.5 percent discount rate, compute the value of this stock. *(LG6)*

7-25 **P/E Ratio Model and Future Price** Kellogg Co. (K) recently earned a profit of $2.52 earnings per share and has a P/E ratio of 19.86. The dividend has been growing at a 5 percent rate over the past few years. If this growth rate continues, what would be the stock price in five years if the P/E ratio remained unchanged? What would the price be if the P/E ratio declined to 15 in five years? *(LG7)*

7-26 **P/E Ratio Model and Future Price** New York Times Co. (NYT) recently earned a profit of $1.21 earnings per share and has a P/E ratio of 19.59. The dividend has been growing at a 7.25 percent rate over the past six years. If this growth rate continues, what would be the stock price in five years if the P/E ratio remained unchanged? What would the price be if the P/E ratio increased to 22 in five years? *(LG7)*

advanced problems

7-27 **Value of Future Cash Flows** A firm recently paid a $0.45 annual dividend. The dividend is expected to increase by 10 percent in each of the next four years. In the fourth year, the stock price is expected to be $80. If the required return for this stock is 13.5 percent, what is its value? *(LG5)*

7-28 **Value of Future Cash Flows** A firm recently paid a $0.60 annual dividend. The dividend is expected to increase by 12 percent in each of the next four years. In the fourth year, the stock price is expected to be $110. If the required return for this stock is 14.5 percent, what is its value? *(LG5)*

7-29 **Constant Growth Stock Valuation** Walgreen Co. (WAG) paid a $0.137 dividend per share in 2000, which grew to $0.286 in 2006. This growth is expected to continue. What is the value of this stock at the beginning of 2007 when the required return is 13.7 percent? *(LG5)*

7-30 **Constant Growth Stock Valuation** Campbell Soup Co. (CPB) paid a $0.632 dividend per share in 2003, which grew to $0.76 in 2006. This growth is expected to continue. What is the value of this stock at the beginning of 2007 when the required return is 8.7 percent? *(LG5)*

7-31 **Changes in Growth and Stock Valuation** Consider a firm that had been priced using a 10 percent growth rate and a 12 percent required return. The firm recently paid a $1.20 dividend. The firm has just announced that because of a new joint venture, it will likely grow at a 10.5 percent rate. How much should the stock price change (in dollars and percentage)? *(LG5)*

7-32 **Changes in Growth and Stock Valuation** Consider a firm that had been priced using an 11.5 percent growth rate and a 13.5 percent required return. The firm recently paid a $1.50 dividend. The firm has just announced that because of a new joint venture, it will likely grow at a 12 percent rate. How much should the stock price change (in dollars and percentage)? *(LG5)*

7-33 **Variable Growth** A fast-growing firm recently paid a dividend of $0.35 per share. The dividend is expected to increase at a 20 percent rate for the next 3 years. Afterwards, a more stable 12 percent growth rate can be assumed. If a 13 percent discount rate is appropriate for this stock, what is its value? *(LG6)*

7-34 **Variable Growth** A fast-growing firm recently paid a dividend of $0.40 per share. The dividend is expected to increase at a 25 percent rate for the next four years. Afterwards, a more stable 11 percent growth rate can be assumed. If a 12.5 percent discount rate is appropriate for this stock, what is its value? *(LG6)*

7-35 **P/E Model and Cash Flow Valuation** Suppose that a firm's recent earnings per share and dividend per share are $2.50 and $1.30, respectively. Both are expected to grow at 8 percent. However, the firm's current P/E ratio of 22 seems high for this growth rate. The P/E ratio is expected to fall to 18 within five years. Compute a value for this stock by first estimating the dividends over the next five years and the stock price in five years. Then discount these cash flows using a 10 percent required rate. *(LG5, LG7)*

7-36 **P/E Model and Cash Flow Valuation** Suppose that a firm's recent earnings per share and dividend per share are $2.75 and $1.60, respectively. Both are expected to grow at 9 percent. However, the firm's current P/E ratio of 23 seems high for this growth rate. The P/E ratio is expected to fall to 19 within five years. Compute a value for this stock by first estimating the dividends over the next five years and the stock price in five years. Then discount these cash flows using an 11 percent required rate. *(LG5, LG7)*

7-37 **Excel Problem** Spreadsheets are especially useful for computing stock value under different assumptions. Consider a firm that is expected to pay the following dividends:

Year 1	2	3	4	5	6	
$1.20	$1.20	$1.50	$1.50	$1.75	$1.90	and grow at 5% thereafter

    a. Using an 11 percent discount rate, what would be the value of this stock?

    b. What is the value of the stock using a 10 percent discount rate? A 12 percent discount rate?

    c. What would the value be using a 6 percent growth rate after Year 6 instead of the 5 percent rate using each of these three discount rates?

    d. What do you conclude about stock valuation and its assumptions?

research it! Stock Screener

Investors can choose from many thousands of stocks. The large number to choose from can be quite daunting to new investors. Fortunately, some good stock screeners are available for free on the Internet that will find only the kinds of companies the investor is looking for. Looking for small value companies? A stock screen at Yahoo! Finance will show all the stocks that meet the three criteria of (1) market capitalization between $250 million and $1 billion, (2) P/E ratio less than or equal to 10, and (3) a quick ratio greater or equal to 1.0. In January of 2007, 86 firms met all three of these criteria. Yahoo! Finance provides 19 screens like this one to choose from. Pick one of these preset screens. Discuss the kinds of stocks the screen will find and report on those companies. (**http://screener.finance.yahoo.com/presetscreens.html**)

integrated minicase: Valuing Carnival Corporation

Carnival Corp. provides cruises to major vacation destinations. Carnival operates 79 cruise ships with a total capacity of 136,960 passengers in North America, Europe, the United Kingdom, Germany, Australia, and New Zealand. The company also operates hotels, sightseeing motor coaches and rail cars, and luxury day boats. These activities generated earnings per share of $2.73 for 2006. The stock price in January of 2007 was $51.95. The previous stock prices and dividends are shown in the following table.

	2000	2001	2002	2003	2004	2005	2006
Annual dividend	$ 0.42	$ 0.42	$ 0.42	$ 0.44	$ 0.525	$ 0.80	$ 1.025
Stock price in January	$40.30	$29.35	$24.96	$22.59	$42.26	$55.44	$50.58

Carnival is a firm in the General Entertainment industry, which is in the Services sector. The following table shows some key statistics for Carnival, the industry, and the sector.

KEY STATISTIC	CARNIVAL	GENERAL ENTERTAINMENT	SERVICES SECTOR
P/E ratio	30.37	26.20	25.66
Dividend yield	0.50%	2.09%	1.33%
Next 5-year growth	15.0%	13.28%	13.44%

Use the various valuation models and relative value measures to assess whether Carnival stock is correctly valued. Compute value estimates from multiple models. The appropriate required rate of return is 15 percent.

www.mhhe.com/can1e

ANSWERS TO TIME OUT

7-1 The New York Stock Exchange (NYSE) has a physical location in New York City near the American Exchange. The Nasdaq Exchange is an electronic network and therefore does not have a specific location per se.

7-2 The NYSE uses a specialist at each trading post on the floor to manage the trading in the stocks assigned to that post. Orders come to the floor through stock brokers worldwide. The trades are executed through an auction system with the floor brokers. The Nasdaq uses an electronic network that ties together many dealers that are interested in trading the stock. These dealers compete with each other to offer the best price. Orders come in from stock brokers and are executed with the dealer that has the best price. Both of these systems are good and each exchange works diligently to make their system effective and efficient for investors.

7-3 First, these indexes are composed of different stocks. Second, the type of stocks in each index may be weighted toward different industries. Last, the indexes are computed using different methodologies.

7-4 The bubble mostly occurred in the Internet and other technology oriented firms. These firms, especially the smaller ones, made up a much larger portion of the Nasdaq Composite than the DJIA or the S&P 500. Therefore, the dramatic price rise and fall for these companies had a bigger impact on the Nasdaq. This is visually seen in the figure.

7-5 Of the popular indexes, the S&P 500 Index includes the largest portion of the market capitalization and therefore gives the best indication of what is happening in the stock market.

7-6 An investor buys at the higher ask price and sells at the lower bid price. Thus, the difference between the bid and ask price is a cost to the trader. If the bid-ask spread is 5 cents, this cost seems small for a $80 stock and high for a $5 stock.

7-7 A market buy order would execute at the ask price of $37.85. Yes, the limit sell order at $37.75 executes if the bid is at or higher. So, the order would execute at the bid of $37.79.

7-8 Firm growth is very valuable to the value of a stock. Consider three firms with the same $1 dividend and 12 percent discount rate but with growth of 10 percent, 5 percent, and 0 percent, respectively. Using the Gordon growth model, the stock price estimates are:

$$P_0 = \frac{\$1 \times (1 + 0.1)}{0.12 - 0.10} = \$55 \qquad P_0 = \frac{\$1 \times (1 + 0.05)}{0.12 - 0.05} = \$15 \qquad P_0 = \frac{\$1 \times (1 + 0)}{0.12 - 0} = \$8.33$$

Note how dramatically different the price estimates are.

7-9 The dividend yield for Coca-Cola was 2.3 percent. This is a 19.7 percent (= 2.3 ÷ 11.7) proportion of the total expected return. The rest comes from growth expectations.

7-10 The variable growth rate model was demonstrated using an initially high growth rate that reduced to a long-term growth rate. However, it is valid with any initial growth rate (high, low, zero, and even negative). The key is that it must settle into a long-term constant growth rate that is lower than the discount rate.

(continued)

7-11 $P_0 = \dfrac{\$1.50(1+0.392)}{1+0.14} + \dfrac{\$1.50(1+0.392)^2 + \dfrac{\$1.50(1+0.392)^2(1+0.094)}{0.14-0.094}}{(1+0.14)^2}$

$= \$1.83 + \dfrac{\$2.91 + \$69.12}{1.30}$

$= \$57.24$

7-12 Rearranging the Gordon growth model, $P_0/E_0 = (D_1/E_0) \div (i - g)$, we see that the P/E ratio is related to the firm's growth rate. Higher P/E ratios are expected for firms with higher growth rates. If two firms have the same P/E ratio, the one with the higher growth rate might be described as cheap compared to the firm with the lower growth rate.

7-13 $P_5 = \left(\dfrac{P}{E}\right) \times E_0 \times (1+g)^5 = 11 \times \$5.05 \times (1+0.128)^5 = \$101.44$

chapter 8:
UNDERSTANDING FINANCIAL MARKETS AND INSTITUTIONS

Learning Goals

LG1 Differentiate between primary and secondary markets and between money and capital markets.

LG2 List the types of securities traded in money and capital markets.

LG3 Identify different types of financial institutions and the services that each financial institution provides.

LG4 Analyze specific factors that influence interest rates.

LG5 Offer different theories that explain the shape of the term structure of interest rates.

LG6 Demonstrate how forward interest rates derive from the term structure of interest rates.

Individual investors and financial managers who wish to make sound decisions must understand how funds flow throughout the economy and how financial markets operate and relate to one another. Investors' funds flow through financial markets such as the New York Stock Exchange and mortgage markets. Financial institutions such as commercial banks (e.g., Bank of America), investment banks (e.g., Merrill Lynch), and mutual funds (e.g., Fidelity) act as intermediaries to channel funds from individual savers or investors to financial markets. In this chapter, we build on the information about stocks, bonds, and other securities covered in Chapters 6 and 7 to provide an overview of the U.S. financial system. That is, we look at various financial markets' nature and operations and the financial institutions (FIs) that participate in those markets.

We generally differentiate financial markets by their primary financial instruments' characteristics (such as bond maturities) or the market's location. FIs allow financial markets to function by providing the least costly and most efficient way to channel funds to and from these markets. FIs play a second crucial role by spreading risk among market participants. This risk-spreading function is vital to entrepreneurial efforts, for few firms or individuals could afford the risk of launching an expensive new product or process by themselves. Individual investors take on pieces of the risk by buying shares in risky enterprises. Investors then mitigate their own risks by diversifying their holdings into appropriate portfolios, which we cover in Chapters 9 and 10.

viewpoints

Business Application

DPH Corporation needs to issue new bonds either this year or in two years. DPH Corp. is a profitable firm, but if the U.S. economy were to experience a downturn, the company would see a big drop in sales over the next two years as its products are very sensitive to changes in the overall economy. DPH Corp. currently has $10 million in public debt outstanding, but its bonds are not actively traded. What questions must DPH Corp. consider as its managers decide whether to issue bonds today or in two years? How can DPH Corp. get these bonds to potential buyers and thus raise the needed capital? **(See solution on p. 281)**

Personal Application

John Adams wants to invest in one of two corporate bonds issued by separate firms. One bond yields 8.00% with a 10-year maturity; the other offers a 10.00% yield and a 9-year maturity. The second bond *seems* to be the better deal. Is it necessarily the bond in which John should invest? Once he decides which bond represents the better investment, how can John go about buying the bond? **(See solution on p. 281)**

A practice test can be found on the Online Learning Center at
www.mhhe.com/can1e

8.1 Financial Markets

Financial markets exist to manage the flow of funds from investors to borrowers. We can distinguish markets along two major dimensions:

- Primary versus secondary markets.
- Money versus capital markets.

 ### Primary Markets versus Secondary Markets

Primary markets provide a forum in which demanders of funds (e.g., corporations or government entities such as IBM or the U.S. Treasury) raise funds by issuing new financial instruments, such as stocks and bonds. Corporations or government entities continually have new projects or expanded production needs, but do not have sufficient internally generated funds (such as retained earnings) to support their capital needs. Thus, corporations and governments issue securities in external primary markets to raise additional funds. Businesses sell new financial instrument issues to initial fund suppliers (e.g., households) in exchange for the funds (money) that the issuer requires.

In the U.S., financial institutions called **investment banks** arrange most primary market transactions for businesses. Some of the best-known examples of U.S. investment banks include Morgan Stanley, Goldman Sachs, or Lehman Brothers. These firms intermediate between issuing parties (fund demanders) and investors (fund suppliers). Investment banks provide fund demanders with a number of services, including advising the company or government agency about the securities issue (such as an appropriate offer price and number of securities to issue) and attracting initial public purchasers of the customer's securities offerings. Firms that need funds are seldom expert at raising capital themselves, so they avert risk and lower their costs by turning to expert investment banks to issue their primary market securities.

Figure 8.1 illustrates a time line for the primary market exchange of funds for a new issue of corporate bonds or equity. We will further discuss how companies, the U.S. Treasury, and government agencies market primary government securities, such as Ginnie Mae and Freddie Mac, go about selling primary market securities in Chapter 16. Throughout this text, we focus on government securities from the *buyer's,* rather than the seller's, point of view. You can find in-depth discussions of government securities from the sellers' point of view in a public finance text.

Primary market financial instruments include stock issues from firms initially going public (e.g., allowing their equity shares to be publicly traded on stock markets for the first time). We usually refer to these first-time issues as **initial public offerings (IPOs).** For example, on April 29, 2004, Google announced a $2.7 billion IPO of its common stock. Google used several investment banks, including Morgan Stanley, to underwrite the company's stock. Publicly traded firms may issue additional bonds or stocks as primary market securities. For example, in May 23, 2006, AngioDynamics Inc. announced that it would sell an additional 2,760,000 shares of common stock (at $24.07 per share) underwritten by investment banks such as RBC Capital Markets, KeyBank Capital Markets, and First Albany Capital. These funds augmented AngioDynamics, Inc.'s existing capital (equity) of $400 million.

SECONDARY MARKETS   Once firms issue financial instruments in primary markets, these same stocks and bonds are then traded—that is, bought and resold—in **secondary markets.** The New York Stock Exchange (NYSE), the

figure 8.1

Primary Market Transfer of Funds

Primary Markets
(Where new issues of financial instruments are offered for sale)

→→→→→ Financial instrument flow
←←←← Funds flow

figure 8.2

Secondary Market Transfer of Funds

Secondary Markets
(Where financial instruments, once issued, are traded)

→→→→→→ Financial instruments flow
←←←←← Funds flow

American Stock Exchange (AMEX), and the National Association of Securities Dealers Automated Quotation (NASDAQ) system are three well-known examples of secondary markets for trading stocks, as you learned in Chapters 6 and 7. In addition to stocks and bonds, secondary markets also exist for financial instruments backed by mortgages and other assets, foreign exchange, and futures and options (i.e., derivative securities).

Buyers find sellers of secondary market securities in economic agents that need funds (fund demanders). Secondary markets provide a centralized marketplace where economic agents know that they can buy or sell most securities quickly and efficiently. Secondary markets, therefore, save economic agents the search costs of finding buyers or sellers on their own. Figure 8.2 illustrates a secondary market transfer of funds. Secondary market buyers often use securities brokers such as Charles Schwab or other brokerage firms to act as intermediaries as they exchange funds for securities (see Chapter 7). An important note: the firm that originally issued the stock or bond is not involved in secondary market transactions in any way—no money accrues to the company itself when its stock trades in a secondary market.

Secondary markets offer benefits to both investors (fund suppliers) and issuers (fund demanders). Investors gain liquidity and diversification benefits (see Chapter 10). And although corporate security issuers are not directly involved in secondary market transactions, issuers do gain information about their securities' current market value. Publicly traded firms can thus observe how investors perceive their corporate value and their corporate decisions by tracking

figure 8.3

Money versus Capital
Market Maturities

	Capital Market Securities		
Money market securities	Notes and bonds	Stocks (equities)	Maturity
0	1 year to maturity	30 years to maturity	No specified maturity

their firms' securities' secondary market prices. Such price information allows issuers to evaluate how well they are using internal funds as well as the funds generated from previously issued stocks and bonds and provides indications about how well any subsequent bond or stock offerings might be received—and at what price.

Secondary market **trading volume** can be quite large. Trading volume is defined as the number of shares of a security that are simultaneously bought and sold during a given period. Each seller and each buyer actually contract with the exchange's clearinghouse, which then matches sell and buy orders for each transaction. The clearinghouse is a company whose stock trades on the exchange, and the clearinghouse runs on a for-profit basis.

The exchange and the clearinghouse can process many transactions in a single day. For example, on October 28, 1997, NYSE trading volume exceeded 1 billion shares for the first time ever. On August 16, 2007, NYSE trading volume topped 5.8 billion shares, the highest level to date. In contrast, during the mid-1980s, an NYSE trading day during which 250 million shares traded was considered a high-volume day.

 ## Money Markets versus Capital Markets

We noted above that financial markets are differentiated in part by the maturity dates of the instruments traded. This distinction becomes important when we differentiate money markets from capital markets. Both of these markets deal in debt securities; the question becomes one of when the securities come due.

MONEY MARKETS **Money markets** feature debt securities or instruments with maturities of one year or less (see Figure 8.3). Economic agents with short-term excess funds can lend these excess funds (that is, they can buy money market instruments) to economic agents who need short-term funds (so, they sell money market instruments to raise funds). Because money market instruments trade for only short periods of time, fluctuations in secondary-market prices are usually quite small. With less volatility, money market securities are thus less risky than longer-term instruments. In the United States, many money market securities do not trade in a specific location; rather, transactions occur via telephones, wire transfers, and computer trading. Thus, most U.S. money markets are said to be **over-the-counter** (OTC) **markets.**

 MONEY MARKET INSTRUMENTS Corporations and government entities issue a variety of money market securities to obtain short-term funds. These securities include:

- Treasury bills.
- Federal funds and repurchase agreements.
- Commercial paper.
- Negotiable certificates of deposit.
- Banker's acceptances.

Treasury bills: short-term U.S. government obligations.

Federal funds: short-term funds transferred between financial institutions, usually for no more than one day.

Repurchase agreements (repos): agreements involving security sales by one party to another, with the promise to reverse the transaction at a specified date and price, usually at a discounted price.

Commercial paper (sometimes called Paper): short-term unsecured promissory notes that companies issue to raise short-term cash.

Negotiable certificates of deposit: bank-issued time deposits that specify an interest rate and maturity date and are negotiable—that is, traded on an exchange. Their face value is usually at least $100,000.

Banker acceptances (BAs): bank-guaranteed time drafts payable to a vendor of goods.

figure 8.4

Money Market Instruments Outstanding

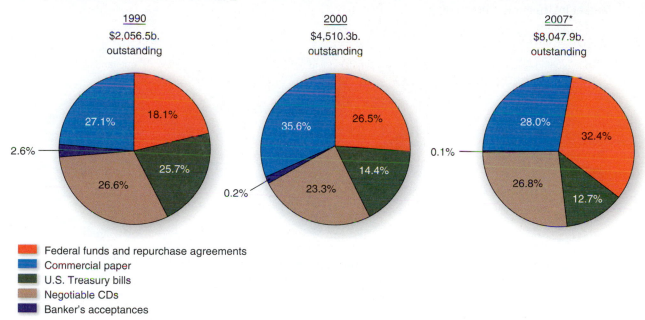

1990
$2,056.5b.
outstanding

2000
$4,510.3b.
outstanding

2007*
$8,047.9b.
outstanding

- Federal funds and repurchase agreements
- Commercial paper
- U.S. Treasury bills
- Negotiable CDs
- Banker's acceptances

* As of the second quarter of the year.

Source: Federal Reserve Board, "Flow of Fund Accounts," *Statistical Releases*, Washington, DC, various issues. **www.federalreserve.gov**

Table 8.1 lists and defines each money market security. Figure 8.4 lists the total dollar value of all money market instruments outstanding and the percentages of the dollar value of each type of money market instruments in the United States in 1990, 2000, and 2007—that is, the breakdown by percentage of each money market instrument traded. Notice that, in 2007, federal funds and repurchase agreements commanded the highest dollar value of all money market instruments, followed by commercial paper, negotiable CDs, and Treasury bills.

CAPITAL MARKETS **Capital markets** are markets in which parties trade equity (stocks) and debt (bonds) instruments that mature in more than one year (see Figure 8.3). Given their longer maturities, capital market instruments are subject to wider price fluctuations than are money market instruments (see the term structure discussion in Chapter 6).

CAPITAL MARKET INSTRUMENTS Capital market securities include:

- U.S. Treasury notes and bonds.
- State and local government bonds.

Treasury notes and bonds: U.S. Treasury long-term obligations to finance the national debt and pay for other federal government expenditures.
State and local government bonds: debt securities issued by state and local (e.g., county, city, school) governments, usually to cover capital (long-term) improvements.
Mortgages: long-term loans to individuals or businesses to purchase homes, pieces of land, or other real property.
Mortgage-backed securities: long-term debt securities that offer expected principal and interest payments as collateral. These securities, made up of many mortgages, are gathered into a pool and are thus "backed" by promised principle and interest cash flows.
Corporate bonds: long-term bonds issued by corporations.
Corporate stocks: long-term equity securities issued by public corporations; stock shares represent fundamental corporate ownership claims.

figure 8.5

Capital Market Instruments Outstanding

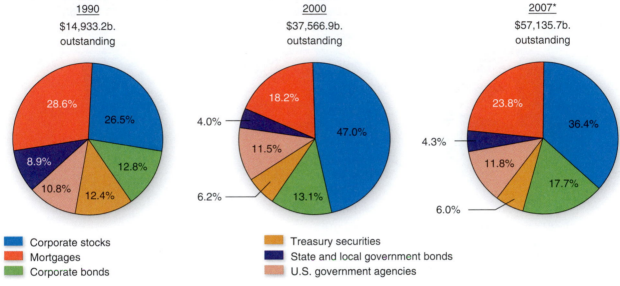

1990	2000	2007*
$14,933.2b. outstanding	$37,566.9b. outstanding	$57,135.7b. outstanding

■ Corporate stocks
■ Mortgages
■ Corporate bonds
■ Treasury securities
■ State and local government bonds
■ U.S. government agencies

*As of the second quarter of the year.

Source: Federal Reserve Board, "Flow of Fund Accounts," *Statistical Releases,* Washington, DC, various issues. **www.federalreserve.gov**

- U.S government agency bonds.
- Mortgages and mortgage backed securities.
- Corporate bonds.
- Corporate stocks.

Table 8.2 lists and defines each capital market security. Figure 8.5 lists the total dollar value of all capital market instruments outstanding and the percentages of these instruments by type traded in the United States in 1990, 2000, and 2007. Note that corporate stocks (equities) represent the largest capital market instrument, followed by mortgage and mortgage-backed securities and then corporate bonds. The relative size of capital markets depends on two factors: the number of securities issued and their market prices. The 1990s saw consistently rising bull markets; hence the sharp increase in equities' dollar value outstanding. Stock values fell in the early 2000s as the U.S. economy experienced a downturn—partly because of 9/11 and partly because interest rates began to rise—and stock prices fell. Stock prices in most sectors subsequently recovered and even surpassed their 1999 levels.

Other Markets

FOREIGN EXCHANGE MARKETS Today, most U.S.-based companies operate globally. Competent financial managers understand how events and movements in financial markets in other countries can potentially affect their own companies' profitability and performance. For example, in late 2001, Argentina's currency and economic crisis hurt U.S. stock markets. The Coca-Cola Co., which derived about 2 percent of its sales from Argentina, attributed a 5 percent decline in its 2002 operating profits to unfavorable currency movements between the Argentinian peso and the U.S. dollar.

Foreign exchange markets trade currencies for immediate (also called "spot") or for some future stated delivery. When a U.S. corporation sells securities or goods overseas, the resulting cash flows denominated in a foreign currency expose the firm to **foreign exchange risk.** This is the risk arising from the unknown value at which foreign currency cash flows can be converted into U.S. dollars. Investors who deal in foreign-denominated securities face the same risk. For example, the actual number of U.S. dollars that a firm receives on a foreign investment depends on the exchange rate between the U.S. dollar and the foreign currency just as much as it does on the investment's performance. They will have to convert the foreign currency into U.S. dollars at the prevailing exchange rate. If the foreign currency depreciates (falls in value) relative to the U.S. dollar (say from $.1679 dollars per unit of foreign currency to $.1550 dollars per unit of foreign currency) over the investment period (i.e., the period between when a foreign investment is made and the time it comes to fruition), the dollar value of cash flows received will fall. If the foreign currency appreciates, or rises in value, relative to the U.S. dollar, the dollar value of cash flows received from the foreign investment will increase.

Foreign currency exchange rates are variable. They vary day to day with demand and supply of foreign currency and with demand and supply of dollars worldwide. Central governments sometimes intervene in foreign exchange markets directly—such as China's recent valuing of the yuan at artificially high rates relative to the dollar. Governments also affect foreign exchange rates indirectly by altering prevailing interest rates within their own countries. You will learn more about foreign exchange markets in Chapter 18.

DERIVATIVE SECURITIES MARKETS A **derivative security** is a financial security (such as a futures contract, option contract, or swap contract) linked to another, underlying security, such as a stock traded in capital markets or British pounds sterling traded in foreign exchange (forex) markets. Derivative securities generally involve an agreement between two parties to exchange a standard quantity of an asset or cash flow at a predetermined price and at a specified date in the future. As the value of the underlying security changes, the value of the derivative security changes.

While derivative security contracts, especially for physical commodities like corn or gold, have existed for centuries, derivative securities markets grew increasingly popular in the 1970s, 1980s, and 1990s as traders, firms, and academics figured out how to spread risk for more and more underlying commodities and securities by using derivative contracts. Derivative contracts generally feature a high degree of leverage; that is, the investor only has to put up a very small portion of the underlying commodity or security's value to affect or control the underlying commodity or security.

Derivative securities markets are the newest—and potentially the riskiest—financial security market. Derivative securities traders can be either users of derivative contracts (for hedging and other purposes) or dealers (such as banks) that act as counterparties in customer trades for fees. An example of hedging involves commodities such as corn, wheat, or soybeans. For example, suppose you run a flour mill and will need to buy either soft wheat (Chicago) or hard red winter wheat (Kansas City) in the future. If you are concerned that the price of wheat will rise, you might lock in a price today to meet your needs six months from now by buying wheat futures on a commodities exchange. If you are correct and wheat prices rise over the six months, you may purchase the wheat by closing out your futures positions, buying the wheat at the futures price rather than the higher market price. Likewise, if you know that you will be delivering a large shipment to, say, Europe, in three months, you might take an offsetting position in euro futures contracts to lock in the exchange rate between the dollar and the euro as it stands today—and (you hope) eliminate foreign exchange risk from the transaction.

TIME OUT

8-1 How do primary and secondary markets differ?

8-2 What are foreign exchange markets?

8-3 What are derivatives securities?

8.2 Financial Institutions

Financial institutions (e.g., banks, thrifts, insurance companies, mutual funds) perform vital functions to securities markets of all sorts. Institutions channel funds from those with surplus funds (suppliers of funds) to those with shortages of funds (demanders of funds). In other words, FIs operate financial markets. Table 8.3 lists and summarizes the various types of FIs. The Finance at Work box highlights Wal-Mart's ultimately unsuccessful attempts to operate as a financial institution.

To understand just how important FIs are to the efficient operation of financial markets, imagine a simple world in which FIs did not exist. In such a world, suppliers of funds (e.g., households), generating excess savings by consuming less than they earn, would have a basic choice. They could either hold cash as an asset or directly transfer that cash in the securities issued by users of funds (e.g., corporations, governments, or retail borrowers). In general, demanders (users) of funds issue financial claims (e.g., equity and debt securities) to finance the gap between their investment expenditures and their internally generated savings, such as retained earnings or tax funds. As shown in Figure 8.6, in a world without financial institutions, we would have **direct transfers** of funds from fund suppliers to fund users. In return, financial claims would flow directly from fund users to fund suppliers.

In this economy without FIs, the amount of funds flowing between fund suppliers and fund users through financial markets would likely be quite low for several reasons:

- Once they have lent money in exchange for financial claims, fund suppliers would need to monitor continually the use of their funds. Fund suppliers must ensure that fund users neither steal the funds outright nor waste the funds on projects that have low or negative returns, since either theft or waste would lower fund suppliers' chances of being repaid and/or earning a positive return on their investments (such as through the receipt of dividends or interest). Monitoring against theft, misuse, or underuse of their funds would cost any given fund supplier a lot of time and effort,

Commercial banks: depository institutions whose major assets are loans and whose major liabilities are deposits. Commercial bank loans cover a broader range, including consumer, commercial, and real estate loans, than do loans from other depository institutions. Because they are larger and more likely to have access to public securities markets, commercial bank liabilities generally include more nondeposit sources of funds, such as subordinate notes and debentures, than do those of other depository institutions.

Thrifts: depository institutions including savings associations, savings banks, and credit unions. Thrifts generally perform services similar to commercial banks, but they tend to concentrate their loans in one segment, such as real estate loans or consumer loans. Credit unions operate on a not-for-profit basis for particular groups of individuals, such as a labor union or a particular company's employees.

Insurance companies: protect individuals and corporations (policyholders) from financially adverse events. Life insurance companies provide protection in the event of untimely death or illness, and help in planning retirement. Property casualty insurance protects against personal injury and liability due to accidents, theft, fire, and so on.

Securities firms and investment banks: underwrite securities and engage in related activities such as securities brokerage, securities trading, and making markets in which securities trade.

Finance companies: make loans to both individuals and businesses. Unlike depository institutions, finance companies do not accept deposits, but instead rely on short- and long-term debt for funding, and many of their loans are collateralized with some kind of durable good, such as washer/dryers, furniture, carpets, and the like.

Mutual funds: pool many individuals' and companies' financial resources and invest those resources in diversified asset portfolios.

Pension funds: offer savings plans through which fund participants accumulate savings during their working years. Participants then withdraw their pension resources (which have presumably earned additional returns in the interim) during their retirement years. Funds originally invested in and accumulated in a pension fund are exempt from current taxation. Participants pay taxes on distributions taken after age 55, when their tax brackets are (presumably) lower.

figure 8.6

Financial claims
(equity and debt instruments)

Users of funds
(corporations)

Suppliers of funds
(household)

Cash

Flow of Funds in a World without FIs

and of course each fund supplier, regardless of the dollar value of the investment, would have to carry out the same costly and time-consuming process. Further, many investors do not have the financial training to understand the necessary business information to assess whether a securities issuer is making the best use of their funds. In fact, so many investment opportunities are available to fund suppliers, that even those trained in financial analysis rarely have the time to monitor how their funds are used in all of their investments. The resulting lack of monitoring increases the risk of directly investing in financial claims. Given these challenges, fund suppliers would likely prefer to delegate the task of monitoring fund borrowers to ensure good performance to others.

• Many financial claims feature a long-term commitment (e.g., mortgages, corporate stock, and bonds) for fund suppliers, thus creating another disincentive for fund suppliers to hold direct financial claims that fund users may issue. Specifically, given the choice between holding cash or holding long-term securities, fund suppliers may well choose to hold cash for its **liquidity,** especially if they plan to use their savings to finance consumption expenditures before their creditors expect to repay them. Fund suppliers may also fear that they will not find anyone to purchase their financial claim and free up their funds. When financial markets are not very developed, or deep, in terms of the number of active buyers and sellers in the market, such liquidity concerns arise.

• Even though real-world financial markets provide some liquidity services by allowing fund suppliers to trade financial securities among themselves, fund suppliers face **price risk** when they buy securities—fund suppliers

RETAIL GIANT TO BATTLE OVER BANK PLANS

Wal-Mart Stores Inc., ever looking for ways to expand its already huge empire, has asked the government for permission to move into an entirely different industry: running its own in-house bank. The world's largest retailer asked the Federal Deposit Insurance Corp. for permission to open a bank that can process millions of checks and credit card payments each month, operating out of its many stores. The company says it's not interested in running a consumer bank as well, but some of its opponents still fear that allowing Wal-Mart into the banking industry in any way could hurt local banks in much the same way that Wal-Mart decimated mom-and-pop stores during Wal-Mart's rapid—some would even say ruthless—expansion.

This is Wal-Mart's fourth bid at establishing its own bank—and its previous requests unleashed an unprecedented flood of comments to the FDIC. . . . "It's a landmark battle in both U.S. business and financial services history," said Jerry Comizio, a financial services lawyer for Thacher, Proffitt & Wood LLP in Washington D.C., and former senior attorney with the Securities and Exchange Commission and deputy general counsel of the U.S. Department of the Treasury's Office of Thrift Supervision.

Wal-Mart says consumers and retail banks have nothing to fear. The retail giant pledges to stay out of branch banking and says it will not provide consumer lending, but for opponents, those assurances ring hollow. "There is reason to believe that these (Wal-Mart's) plans could be expansive. Wal-Mart has attempted on several occasions to enter the full-service banking business," said American Bankers Association's head of government relations Art Johnson, in testimony prepared for the FDIC hearing. "The ABA believes that banking is too important to the nation to try such a risky experiment."

Wal-Mart says that it can save money if allowed to operate an in-house bank to handle the 140 million credit, debit card, and electronic check payments it handles each year. Concerns are twofold. One is the mixing of banking and commerce—parts of the economy that have traditionally been kept separate until the repeal of the Glass-Steagall Act in 1999. The other worry stems from the fact that a Wal-Mart bank could swallow local banks with its national presence and deep pockets, outcompeting even large institutions such as Bank of America, Chase, and Wachovia that have also grown at the expense of local ownership.

Source: *The Wall Street Journal*, April 8, 2006, p. A3.

 want to know more? **Key Words to Search for Updates: Wal-Mart, banking; FDIC; ABA; Glass-Steagall repeal; electronic check payments**

may not get their principal back, let alone any return on their investment. Trading securities on secondary markets involves various transaction costs. The price at which investors can sell a security on secondary markets such as the New York Stock Exchange (NYSE) or NASDAQ may well differ from the price they initially paid for the security. The investment community as a whole may change the security's valuation between the time the fund supplier bought it and the time the fund supplier sold it. Further, dealers, acting as intermediaries between buyers and sellers, charge transaction costs for completing a trade. So even if an investor bought a security and then sold it the next day, the investor would likely lose money from transaction and other costs.

 ## Unique Economic Functions Performed by Financial Institutions

Because of (1) monitoring costs, (2) liquidity costs, and (3) price risk, most average investors may well view direct investment in financial claims and markets as an unattractive proposition and, as fund suppliers, they will likely prefer to hold cash. As a result, financial market activity (and therefore savings and investment)

figure 8.7

would likely remain quite low. However, the financial system has developed an alternative, indirect way for investors (or fund suppliers) to channel funds to users of funds: financial intermediaries **indirectly transfer** funds to ultimate fund users. Because of monitoring, liquidity risk, and price risk costs, fund suppliers often prefer to hold financial intermediaries' financial claims rather than those directly issued by the ultimate fund users. Consider Figure 8.7, which more closely represents the way that funds flow in the U.S. financial system than does Figure 8.6. Notice how financial institutions stand—or intermediate—between fund suppliers and fund users. That is, FIs channel funds from ultimate suppliers to ultimate fund users. Fund suppliers and users use these FIs to channel funds because of financial intermediaries' unique ability to reduce monitoring costs, liquidity costs, and price risk.

MONITORING COSTS As we noted above, a fund supplier who directly invests in a fund user's financial claims faces a high cost of comprehensively monitoring the fund user's actions in a timely way. One solution to this problem is that a large number of small investors can group their funds together by holding claims issued by an FI. In turn, the FI will invest in direct financial claims that fund users issue. Financial institutions' aggregation of funds from fund suppliers resolves a number of problems:

- First, large FIs now have much greater incentive to collect information and monitor the ultimate fund user's actions, because the FI has far more at stake than any small individual fund supplier would have.

- Second, the FI performs the necessary monitoring function via its own internal experts, alleviating the "free-rider" problem that arises when small fund suppliers leave it to each other to collect information and monitor a fund user. In an economic sense, fund suppliers appoint the FI as a **delegated monitor** to act on their behalf. For example, full-service securities firms such as Merrill Lynch carry out investment research on new issues and make investment recommendations for their retail clients (investors), while commercial banks collect deposits from fund suppliers and lend these funds to ultimate users, such as corporations. An important part of these FIs' functions is their ability and incentive to monitor ultimate fund users.

LIQUIDITY AND PRICE RISK In addition to providing more and better information about fund users' activities, financial intermediaries provide additional liquidity to fund suppliers, acting as **asset transformers** as follows: FIs purchase the financial claims that fund users issue—primary securities such as mortgages, bonds, and stocks—and finance these purchases by selling financial claims to household investors and other fund suppliers as deposits, insurance policies, or other **secondary securities.** The secondary securities—packages or pools of primary claims—that FIs collect and then issue are often more liquid than are the primary securities themselves. For example, banks and thrift institutions (e.g., savings associations) offer draft deposit accounts with fixed principal values and (often) guaranteed interest rates. Fund suppliers can generally access the funds in those accounts on demand. Money market mutual funds issue shares to household savers that allow the savers to maintain almost fixed principal amounts while earning somewhat higher interest rates than on bank deposits. Further, savers can also withdraw these funds on demand whenever the saver writes a check on the account. Even life insurance companies allow policyholders to borrow against their company-held policy balances at very short notice.

TIME OUT

8-4 List the major types of financial institutions.

8-5 What three main issues would deter fund suppliers from directly purchasing securities?

8.3 Interest Rates

We often speak of "the interest rate" as if only one rate applies to all financial situations or transactions. In fact, we can list tens or hundreds of interest rates that are appropriate in various conditions or situations within the U.S. economy on any particular day. Let's explore a bit how the financial sector sets these rates and how the rates relate to one another. We actually observe **nominal interest rates** in financial markets—these are the rates most often quoted by financial news services. As we saw in Chapters 6 and 7, nominal interest rates (or, simply, interest rates) directly affect most tradable securities' value or price. Since any change in nominal interest rates has such profound effects on security prices, financial managers and individual investors spend a lot of time and effort trying to identify factors that may influence future interest rate levels.

Of course, interest rate changes influence investment performance and trigger buy or sell decisions for individual investors, businesses, and governmental units alike. Figure 8.8 illustrates the movement of several key U.S. interest rates over the past 35 years:

- The prime commercial loan rate.
- The three-month T-bill rate.
- The high-grade corporate bond rate.
- The home mortgage rate.

Figure 8.8 shows how interest rates vary over time. For example, the prime rate hit highs of over 20 percent in the early 1980s, yet fell as low as 4.75 percent in the early 1970s. The prime rate stayed below 10 percent throughout much of the 1990s, and fell back further to 4.00 percent in the early 2000s.

 Factors that Influence Interest Rates for Individual Securities

Specific factors that affect nominal interest rates for any particular security include:

- Inflation.
- The real interest rate.

figure 8.8

Key U.S. Interest Rates, 1972–2007

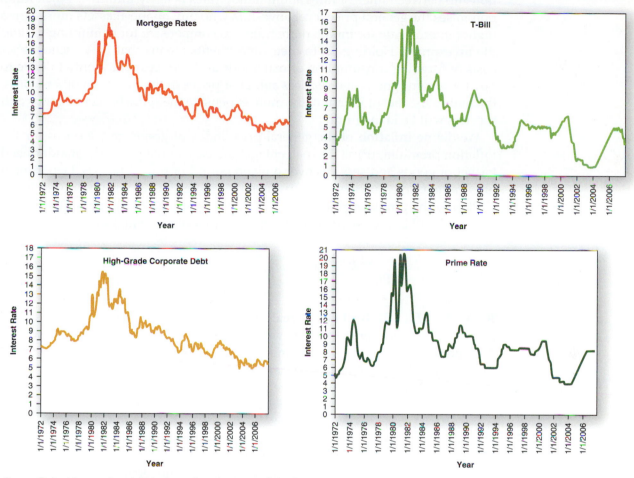

Source: Federal Reserve Board, Web site, various dates. **www.federalreserve.gov**

Factors Affecting Nominal Interest Rates

table 8.4

Inflation: A continual increase in the price level of a basket of goods and services throughout the economy as a whole.

Real interest rate: interest rate adjusted for inflation; generally lower than nominal interest rates at any particular time; interest rate adjusted so that a chosen date represents the base year. Thus, we can validly compare interest rates over various periods based upon a common denominator.

Default risk: risk that a security issuer will miss an interest or principal payment or continue to miss such payments.

Liquidity risk: risk that a security cannot be sold at a price relatively close to its value with low transaction costs on short notice.

Special provisions: provisions (e.g., taxability, convertibility, and callability) that impact a security holder beneficially or adversely and as such are reflected in the interest rates on securities that contain such provisions.

Time to maturity: length of time until a security is repaid, used in debt securities as the date upon which the security holders get their principal back.

- Default risk.
- Liquidity risk.
- Special provisions regarding the use of funds raised by a particular security issuer.
- The security's term to maturity.

We will discuss each of these factors after summarizing them in Table 8.4.

INFLATION The first factor that influences interest rates is the economy-wide *actual or expected inflation rate*. Specifically, the higher the level of actual or expected inflation, the higher will be the level of interest rates. The positive relationship between interest rates and inflation rates is fairly intuitive: When inflation raises the general price level, investors who buy financial assets must earn a higher interest rate (or inflation premium) to compensate for continuing to hold the investment. Holding on to their investments means that they incur higher costs of forgoing consumption of real goods and services today, only to have to buy these same goods and services at higher prices in the future. In other words, the higher the rate of inflation, the more expensive the same basket of goods and services will be in the future.

We define **inflation** of the general price index of goods and services (or the inflation premium, IP) as the (percentage) increase in the price of a standardized basket of goods and services over a given period of time. The U.S. Department of Commerce measures inflation using indexes such as the consumer price index (CPI) and the producer price index (PPI). For example, the annual inflation rate using the CPI index between years t and $t + 1$ would be equal to:

$$IP = \frac{CPI_{t+1} - CPI_t}{CPI_t} \times 100 \qquad \text{(8-1)}$$

REAL INTEREST RATES A **real interest rate** is the rate that a security would pay if no inflation were expected over its holding period (e.g., a year). As such, it measures only society's relative time preference for consuming today rather than tomorrow. The higher society's preference to consume today (i.e., the higher its time value of money or rate of time preference), the higher the real interest rate (RIR) will be.

Fisher Effect Economists often refer to the relationship among real interest rates (RIR), expected inflation (expected IP), and nominal interest rates (i), described above, as the Fisher effect, named for Irving Fisher, who identified these economic relationships early last century. The Fisher effect theorizes that nominal interest rates that we observe in financial markets must compensate investors for

- Any inflation-related reduction in purchasing power lost on funds lent or principal due.
- An additional premium above the expected rate of inflation for forgoing present consumption (which reflects the real interest rate issue discussed above).

$$i = \text{Expected } IP + RIR \qquad \text{(8-2)}$$

Thus, the nominal interest rate will equal the real interest rate only when market participants expect inflation to be zero: Expected $IP = 0$. Similarly, the nominal interest rate will equal the expected inflation rate only when the real interest rate is zero. We can rearrange the nominal interest rate equation to show what determines the real interest rate:[1]

$$RIR = i - \text{Expected } IP \qquad \text{(8-3)}$$

---

[1]Often the Fisher effect formula is written as: $(1 + i) = (1 + IP) \times (1 + RIR)$ which, when solved for i, becomes: $i = \text{Expected } IP + RIR + (\text{Expected } IP \times RIR)$ where $RIR \times \text{Expected } IP$ is the inflation premium for the loss of purchasing power on the promised nominal interest rate payments due to inflation. For small values of RIR and Expected IP this term is negligible. The approximation formula used here assumes these values are small.

figure 8.9

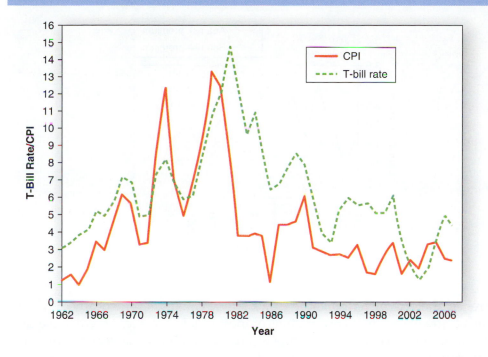

Nominal Interest Rates versus Inflation

Source: Federal Reserve Board and U.S. Department of Labor, Web sites, various dates. **www.federalreserve.gov** and **www.states.bls.gov/cpi/home.htm**

For interactive versions of this example visit www.mhhe.com/can1e

EXAMPLE 8-1

CALCULATING REAL INTEREST RATES

One-year Treasury bill rates in 2007 averaged 4.93 percent and inflation (measured by the consumer price index) for the year was 1.80 percent. If investors had expected the same inflation rate as that actually realized, calculate the real interest rate for 2007 according to the Fisher effect.

SOLUTION:

$$4.93\% - 1.80\% = 3.13\%$$

The one-year T-bill rate in 2004 was 1.89 percent, while the CPI for the year was 3.30 percent, which implies a real interest rate of −1.41 percent—that is, the real interest rate was actually negative. Thus, the real value of investments actually decreased in that year.

Figure 8.9 shows the nominal interest rate (one-year T-bill rate) versus the change in the CPI from 1962 through 2007. The expected inflation rate is difficult to estimate accurately, so the real interest rate can be difficult to measure accurately. Investors' expectations are not always realized either.

DEFAULT OR CREDIT RISK **Default risk** is the risk that a security issuer may fail to make its promised interest and principal payments to its bondholders (or its dividend in the case of preferred stockholders). The higher the default risk, the higher the interest rate that security buyers will demand to compensate them for this default (or credit) risk relative to default-risk-free U.S. Treasury securities. Since the U.S. government has taxation powers and can print

figure 8.10

Default Risk Premiums
on Corporate Bonds

Source: Federal Reserve Board,
web site, various dates. **www.
federalreserve.gov**

currency, the risk of its defaulting on debt payments is practically zero. But some borrowers, such as corporations or individuals, have less predictable cash flows (and no powers to tax anyone to raise funds immediately). So investors must charge issuers other than the U.S. government a premium for any perceived probability of default and the cost of potentially recovering the amount loaned built into their regular interest rate premium. The difference between a quoted interest rate on a security (security j) and a Treasury security with similar maturity, liquidity, tax, and other features is called a *default* or *credit risk premium* (DRP_j). That is:

$$DRP_j = i_{jt} - i_{Tt} \qquad\qquad (8\text{-}4)$$

where i_{jt} = Interest rate on a security issued by a non-Treasury issuer (issuer j) of maturity m at time t.

           i_{Tt} = Interest rate on a security issued by the U.S. Treasury of maturity m at time t.

Various rating agencies, including Moody's and Standard & Poor's, evaluate and categorize the potential default risk on many corporate bonds, some state and municipal bonds, and some stocks. We cover these ratings in more detail in Chapter 7. For example, in 2007, the 10-year Treasury rate was 4.18 percent. Moody's Aaa-rated and Baa-rated corporate debt carried interest rates of 5.53 percent and 6.68 percent, respectively. Thus, the average default risk premiums on the Aaa-rated and Baa-rated corporate debt were:

$$DRP_{Aaa} = 5.53\% - 4.18\% = 1.35\%$$
$$DRP_{Baa} = 6.68\% - 4.18\% = 2.50\%$$

Figure 8.10 presents these risk premiums for the stated creditworthiness categories of bonds from 1977 through 2007. Notice from this figure and Figure 8.9 that default risk premiums tend to increase when the economy is contracting and decrease when the economy is expanding. For example, from 1981 to 1982, real interest rates (T-bills – CPI in Figure 8.9) increased from 5.90 percent to 8.47 percent. Over the same period, default risk premiums on Aaa-rated bonds increased from 0.25 percent to 0.78 percent. Baa-rated bonds showed a default risk premium increase from 2.12 percent to 3.10 percent.

LIQUIDITY RISK A highly liquid asset can be sold at a predictable price with low transaction costs. That is, the holder can convert the asset at its fair market value at short notice. The interest rate on a security reflects its relative liquidity, with highly liquid assets carrying the lowest interest rates (all other characteristics remaining the same). Likewise, if a security is illiquid, investors add a **liquidity risk** premium (LRP) to the interest rate on the security. In the United States, most government securities sell in liquid markets, as do large corporations' stocks and bonds. Securities issued by smaller companies trade in relatively less liquid markets.

A different type of liquidity risk premium may also exist if investors dislike long-term securities because their prices (present values, as discussed in Chapters 4 and 6) react more to interest rate changes than short-term securities do. In this case, a higher liquidity risk premium may be added to a security with a longer maturity because of its greater exposure to price risk (loss of capital value) on the longer-term security as interest rates change.

SPECIAL PROVISIONS OR COVENANTS Sometimes a security's issuing party attaches special provisions or covenants to the security issued. Such provisions affect the interest rates on these securities relative to securities without such provisions attached to them. Some of these special provisions include the security's taxability, convertibility, and callability. For example, investors pay no federal taxes on interest payments received from municipal securities. So a municipal bond holder may demand a lower interest rate than that demanded on a comparable taxable bond—such as a Treasury bond (which is taxable at the federal level but not at the state or local levels) or a corporate bond (the interest on which is taxable at the state, local, and federal levels.)

Another special covenant is convertibility: A convertible bond offers the holder the opportunity to exchange the bond for another type of the issuer's security—usually preferred or common stock—at a preset price (see Chapter 6). This conversion option can be valuable to purchasers, so convertible security buyers require lower interest rates than a comparable nonconvertible security holder would require (all else equal). In general, special provisions that benefit security holders (e.g., tax-free status and convertibility) bring with them lower interest rates, and special provisions that benefit security issuers (e.g., callability, by which an issuer has the option to retire, or call, the security prior to maturity at a preset price) require higher interest rates to encourage purchase.

TERM TO MATURITY Interest rates also change—sometimes daily—because of a bond's term to maturity. As we noted in Chapter 6, financial professionals refer to this daily or even hourly changeability in interest rates as the **term structure of interest rates,** or the yield curve. As we explained in Chapter 6, the shape of the yield curve derives directly from time value of money principles. The term structure of interest rates compares interest rates on debt securities based on their time to maturity, assuming that all characteristics (i.e., default risk, liquidity risk) are equal. Interest rates change as the maturity of a debt security changes; in general, the longer the term to maturity, the higher the required interest rate buyers will demand. This addition to the required interest rate is the maturity premium (MP). The MP, which is the difference between the required yield on long-versus short-term securities of the same characteristics except maturity, can be positive, negative, or zero.

The financial industry most often reports and analyzes the yield curve for U.S. Treasury securities. The yield curve for U.S. Treasury securities has taken many shapes over the years, but the three most common shapes appear in Figure 8.11. In graph (a), the yield curve on August 12, 2004, yields rise steadily

figure 8.11

Common Shapes for
Yield Curves on
Treasury Securities

Source: U.S. Treasury, Office of
Debt Management, Daily Treasury Yield Curves, various dates.
www.ustreas.gov

Panel A

Panel B

Yield Curve, February 28, 2006

Panel C

with maturity when the yield curve slopes upward. This is the most common yield curve. On average, the MP is positive, as you might expect. Graph (b) shows an inverted, or downward-sloping, yield curve, reported on November 27, 2000, in which yields decline as maturity increases. Inverted yield curves do not generally last very long. In this case, the yield curve inverted as the U.S. Treasury began retiring long-term (30 year) bonds as the country began to pay off the national debt. Finally, graph (c) shows a flat yield curve, reported on February 28, 2006, when the yield-to-maturity is virtually unaffected by the term-to-maturity.

Note that yield curves may reflect factors other than investor's preferences for the maturity of a security. In reality, liquidity differences may arise among the securities traded at different points along the yield curve. For example, newly issued 20-year Treasury bonds offer a lower rate of return than previously issued Treasury bonds, all else being equal (so-called seasoned issues). Ten-year Treasury bonds may be more liquid if investors prefer new ("on the run") securities to previously issued ("off the run") securities. Specifically, since the U.S. Treasury has historically only issued new 10-year notes and 20-year bonds at the long end of the maturity spectrum, a seasoned 10-year Treasury bond would have to have been issued 10 years previously (i.e., it was originally a 20-year bond when it was issued 10 years previously). Increased demand for previously issued (and thus more liquid) 20-year Treasury bonds relative to the newly issued but less liquid 10-year Treasury bonds can be large enough to push the equilibrium interest rate on the 20-year Treasury bonds below that for the 10-year Treasury bonds and even below short-term rates. In the next section, we will review three major theories that financial analysts often use to explain the shape of the yield to maturity curve (or the shape of the term structure of interest rates).

Putting together the factors that affect interest rates in different markets, we can use the following general equation to note the influence of the factors that functionally impact the fair interest rate—the rate necessary to compensate investors for all security risks—(i_j^*) on an individual (jth) financial security.

$$i_j^* = f(IP, RIR, DRP_j, LRP_j, SCP_j, MP_j) \qquad \text{(8-5)}$$

where
- IP = Inflation premium.
- RIR = Real interest rate.
- DRP_j = Default risk premium on the jth security.
- LRP_j = Liquidity risk premium on the jth security.
- SCP_j = Special covenant premium on the jth security.
- MP_j = Maturity premium on the jth security.

The first two factors, IP and RIR, are common to all financial securities, while the other factors can uniquely influence the price of a single security.

TIME OUT

8-6 What is the difference between nominal and real interest rates?

8-7 What does "the term structure of interest rates" mean?

8-8 What shape does the term structure usually take? Why?

Theories Explaining the Shape of the Term Structure of Interest Rates

We just explained the necessity of a maturity premium, the relationship between a security's interest rate and its remaining term to maturity. We can illustrate these issues by showing that the term structure of interest rates can take a number of different shapes. As you might expect, economists and financial theorists with various viewpoints differ among themselves in theorizing why the yield curve takes different shapes. Explanations for the yield curve's shape fall predominantly into three categories:

- The unbiased expectations theory.
- The liquidity premium theory.
- The market segmentation theory.

Look again at Figure 8.11 (a), which presents the Treasury yield curve as of August 12, 2004. We see that the yield curve on this date reflected the normal upward-sloping relationship between yield and maturity. Now let's turn to explanations for this shape based on the three predominant theories noted above.

UNBIASED EXPECTATIONS THEORY According to the unbiased expectations theory of the term structure of interest rates, at any given point in time, the yield curve reflects the *market's current expectations of future short-term rates*. As illustrated in Figure 8.12, the intuition behind the unbiased expectations theory is this: If investors have a four-year investment horizon, they could either buy current four-year bonds and earn the current (or spot) yield on a four-year bond ($_1R_4$, if held to maturity) each year, or they could invest in four successive

figure 8.12

one-year bonds (of which they know only the current one-year spot rate ($_1R_1$). But investors also expect what the unknown future one-year rates [$E(_2r_1)$, $E(_3r_1)$, and $E(_4r_1)$] will be. Note that each interest rate term has two subscripts, e.g., $_1R_4$. The first subscript indicates the period in which the security is bought, so that 1 represents the purchase of a security in period 1. The second subscript indicates the maturity on the security. Thus, 4 represents the purchase of a security with a four-year life. Similarly, $E(_3r_1)$ is the expected return on a security with a one-year life purchased in period 3.

According to the unbiased expectations theory, the return for holding a four-year bond to maturity should equal the expected return for investing in four successive one-year bonds, (as long as the market is in equilibrium). If this equality does not hold, an arbitrage opportunity exists. That is, if investors could earn more on the one-year bond investments, they could short (or sell) the four-year bond, use the proceeds to buy the four successive one-year bonds, and earn a guaranteed profit over the four-year investment horizon. So, according to the unbiased expectations hypothesis, if the market expects future one-year rates to rise each successive year into the future, then the yield curve will slope upwards. Specifically, the current four-year T-bond rate or return will exceed the three-year bond rate, which will exceed the two-year bond rate, and so on. Similarly, if the market expects future one-year rates to remain constant each successive year into the future, then the four-year bond rate will equal the three-year bond rate. That is, the term structure of interest rates will remain constant (flat) over the relevant time period. Specifically, the unbiased expectation theory states that current long-term interest rates are geometric averages of current and expected *future* short-term interest rates. The mathematical equation representing this relationship is

$$(1 + {}_1R_N)^N = (1 + {}_1R_1)[1 + E(_2r_1)] \ldots [1 + E(_Nr_1)] \tag{8-6}$$

therefore:

$$_1R_N = \{[1 + {}_1R_1][1 + E(_2r_1)] \ldots [1 + E(_Nr_1)]\}^{1/N} - 1 \tag{8-7}$$

where $_1R_N$ = Actual N-period rate today (i.e., the first day of year 1).

  N = Term to maturity.

  $_1R_1$ = Actual one-year rate today.

  $E(_tr_1)$ = Expected one-year rates for years 2, 3, 4, . . . N in the future.

Notice, as above, that uppercase interest rate terms, $_1R_t$, are the actual current interest rates on securities purchased today with a maturity of t years. Lowercase interest rate terms, $_tr_1$, represent estimates of future one-year interest rates starting t years into the future.

EXAMPLE 8-2

CALCULATING YIELD CURVES

Suppose that the current one-year rate (one-year spot rate) and expected one-year T-bond rates over the following three years (i.e., years 2, 3, and 4, respectively) are as follows:

$$_1R_1 = 2.94\% \qquad E(_2r_1) = 4\% \qquad E(_3r_1) = 4.74\% \qquad E(_4r_1) = 5.10\%$$

Construct a yield curve using the unbiased expectations theory.

SOLUTION:

Using the unbiased expectations theory, current (or today's) rates for one-, two-, three-, and four-year maturity Treasury securities should be:

$$_1R_1 = 2.94\% \quad \text{(Expected return of security with one-year life purchased in period 1)}$$

$$_1R_2 = [(1 + .0294)(1 + .04)]^{1/2} - 1 = 3.469\%$$

$$_1R_3 = [(1 + .0294)(1 + .04)(1 + .0474)]^{1/3} - 1 = 3.891\%$$

$$_1R_4 = [(1 + .0294)(1 + .04)(1 + .0474)(1 + .051)]^{1/4} - 1 = 4.192\%$$

and the current yield to maturity curve will be upward sloping as shown:

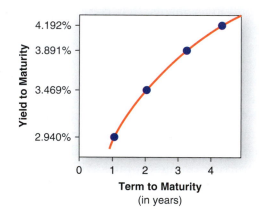

This upward-sloping yield curve reflects the market's expectation of persistently rising one-year (short-term) interest rates over the future horizon.[2]

MATH COACH:

When putting interest rates into the equation, enter them in decimal format, not percentage format:
Correct: $(1 + .0294)$
Not correct: $(1 + 2.94)$

LIQUIDITY PREMIUM THEORY The second popular explanation—the liquidity premium theory of the term structure of interest rates—builds on the unbiased expectations theory. The liquidity premium idea is as follows: Investors will hold long-term maturities only if these securities with longer term maturities are offered at a premium to compensate for future uncertainty in the security's value. Of course, uncertainty or risk increases with an asset's maturity. This theory is thus consistent with our discussions of market risk and liquidity risk, above. Specifically, in a world of uncertainty, short-term securities provide greater marketability (due to their more active secondary markets) and have less

---

[2] That is, $E(_4r_1) > E(_3r_1) > E(_2r_1) > _1R_1$.

figure 8.13

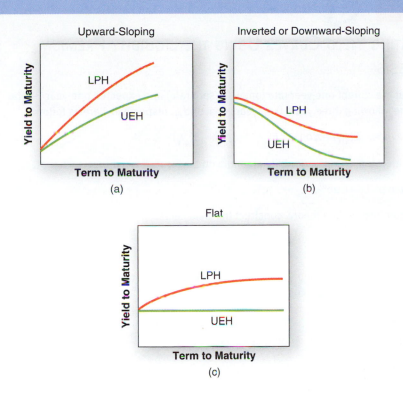

Upward-Sloping

Inverted or Downward-Sloping

Flat

price risk than long-term securities do. As a result, (due to smaller price fluctuations for a given change in interest rates) investors will prefer to hold shorter-term securities because this kind of paper can be converted into cash with little market risk. Said another way, investors face little risk of a capital loss, i.e., a fall in the price of the security below its original purchase price. So, investors must be offered a liquidity premium to buy longer-term securities that carry higher capital loss risk. This difference in market and liquidity risk can be directly related to the fact that longer-term securities are more sensitive to interest rate changes in the market than are shorter-term securities—Chapter 6 discussed bond interest rate sensitivity and the link to a bond's maturity. Because longer maturities on securities mean greater market and liquidity risk, the liquidity premium increases as maturity increases.

The liquidity premium theory states that long-term rates are equal to geometric averages of current and expected short-term rates (like the unbiased expectations theory), plus liquidity risk premiums that increase with the security's maturity (this is the extension of the liquidity premium added to the unbiased expectations theory). Figure 8.13 illustrates the differences in the shape of the yield curve under the unbiased expectations hypothesis versus the liquidity premium hypothesis. For example, according to the liquidity premium theory, an upward-sloping yield curve may reflect investors' expectations that future short-term rates will be flat, but because liquidity premiums increase with maturity, the yield curve will nevertheless slope upward. Indeed, an upward-sloping yield curve may reflect expectations that future interest rates will rise, be flat, or even fall as long as the liquidity premium increases with maturity fast enough to produce an upward-sloping yield curve. The liquidity premium theory can be mathematically represented as

$$_1R_N = \{[1 + {}_1R_1][1 + E(_2r_1) + L_2] \ldots [1 + E(_Nr_1) + L_N]\}^{1/N} - 1 \qquad (8\text{-}8)$$

where L_t = Liquidity premium for a period t and $L_2 < L_3 < L_N$.

CALCULATING YIELD CURVES USING THE LIQUIDITY PREMIUM HYPOTHESIS

Suppose that the current one-year rate (one-year spot rate) and expected one-year T-bond rates over the following three years (i.e., years 2, 3, and 4, respectively) are as follows:

$$_1R_1 = 2.94\%, \quad E(_2r_1) = 4.00\%, \quad E(_3r_1) = 4.74\% \quad E(_4r_1) = 5.10\%$$

In addition, investors charge a liquidity premium on longer-term securities such that,

$$L_2 = 0.10\% \quad L_3 = 0.20\%, \quad L_4 = 0.30\%$$

Using the liquidity premium theory, construct the yield curve.

SOLUTION:

Using the liquidity premium theory, current rates for one-, two-, three-, and four- year maturity Treasury securities should be:

$$_1R_1 = 2.94\%$$

$$_1R_2 = [(1 + .0294)(1 + .04 + .001)]^{1/2} - 1 = 3.52\%$$

$$_1R_3 = [(1 + .0294)(1 + .04 + .001)(1 + .0474 + .002)]^{1/3} - 1 = 3.99\%$$

$$_1R_4 = [(1 + .0294)(1 + .04 + .001)(1 + .0474 + .002)(1 + .051 + .003)]^{1/4} - 1 = 4.34\%$$

and the current yield to maturity curve will be upward sloping as shown:

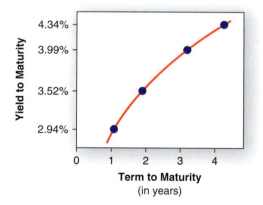

Comparing the yield curves in Examples 8.2 (using the unbiased expectations hypothesis) and 8.3, notice that the liquidity premium in year 2 (L_2 = 0.10%) produces a 0.05 percent premium on the yield to maturity on a two-year T-note, the liquidity premium for year 3 (L_3 = 0.20%) produces a 0.10 percent premium on the yield to maturity on the three-year T-note, and the liquidity premium for year 4 (L_4 = 0.30%) produces a 0.15 percent premium on the yield to maturity on the four-year T-note.

MARKET SEGMENTATION THEORY   The market segmentation theory does not build on the unbiased expectations theory or the liquidity premium hypothesis, but rather argues that individual investors and FIs have specific maturity preferences, and convincing them to hold securities with maturities

figure 8.14

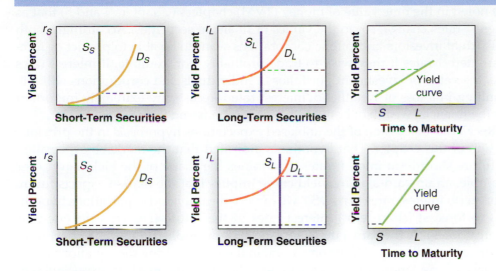

Market Segmentation
and Determination of
the Slope of Yield Curve

other than their most preferred requires a higher interest rate (maturity premium). The main thrust of the market segmentation theory is that investors do not consider securities with different maturities as perfect substitutes. Rather, individual investors and FIs have distinctly preferred investment horizons dictated by the dates when their liabilities will come due. For example, banks might prefer to hold relatively short-term U.S. Treasury bonds because their deposit liabilities also tend to be short-term—recall that bank customers can access their funds on demand. Insurance companies, on the other hand, may prefer to hold long-term U.S. Treasury bonds because life insurance contracts usually expose insurance firms to long-term liabilities. Accordingly, distinct supply and demand conditions within a particular maturity segment—such as the short end and long end of the bond market—determine interest rates under the market segmentation theory.

The market segmentation theory assumes that investors and borrowers generally do not want to shift from one maturity sector to another without adequate compensation—that is, an interest rate premium. Figure 8.14 demonstrates how changes in supply for short- versus long-term bond market segments result in changing shapes of the yield to maturity curve. Specifically, as shown in Figure 8.14, the higher the yield on securities is (which means the lower the price), the higher the demand for those securities is.[3] Thus, as the supply of securities decreases in the short-term market and increases in the long-term market, the slope of the yield curve becomes steeper. If the supply of short-term securities had increased while the supply of long-term securities had decreased, the yield curve would have a flatter slope and might even have sloped downward. Indeed, the U.S. Treasury's large-scale repurchases of long-term Treasury bonds (i.e., reductions in supply) in early 2000 has been viewed as the major cause of the inverted yield curve that appeared in February 2000.

TIME OUT

8-9   What three theories explain the shape of the yield curve?

8-10   Explain how arbitrage plays a role in the unbiased expectations explanation of the shape of the yield curve.

[3]In general, the price and yield on a bond are inversely related. Thus, as the price of a bond falls (becomes cheaper), the demand for the bond will rise. This is the same as saying that as the yield on a bond rises, it becomes cheaper and the demand for it increases. See Chapter 6.

Forecasting Interest Rates

LG6

We noted in the time value of money (TVM) chapters (Chapters 4 and 5) that as interest rates change, so do the values of financial securities. Accordingly, both individual investors and public corporations want to be able to predict or forecast interest rates if they wish to trade profitably. For example, if interest rates rise, the value of investment portfolios of individuals and corporations will fall, resulting in a loss of wealth. So, interest rate forecasts are extremely important for the financial wealth of both public corporations and individuals.

Recall our discussion of the unbiased expectations hypothesis in the previous section of this chapter. That hypothesis indicated that the market's expectation of future short-term interest rates determines the shape of the yield curve. For example, an upward-sloping yield curve implies that the market expects future short-term interest rates to rise. So, we can use the unbiased expectations hypothesis to forecast (short-term) interest rates in the future (i.e., forward one-year interest rates). A **forward rate** is an expected, or implied, rate on a short-term security that will originate at some point in the future. Using the equations in the unbiased expectations theory, we can directly derive the market's expectation of forward rates from existing or actual rates on spot market securities.

To find an implied forward rate on a one-year security to be issued one year from today, we can rewrite the unbiased expectations hypothesis equation as follows:

$$_1R_2 = \{[1 + {_1R_1}][1 + ({_2f_1})]\}^{1/2} - 1 \tag{8-9}$$

where $_2f_1$ = expected one-year rate for year 2, or the implied forward one-year rate for next year.

Saying that $_2f_1$ is the expected one-year rate for year 2 is the same as saying that, once we isolate the $_2f_1$ term, the equation will give us the market's estimate of the expected one-year rate for year 2. Solving for $_2f_1$ we get:

$$_2f_1 = [(1 + {_1R_2})^2 / (1 + {_1R_1})] - 1 \tag{8-10}$$

In general, we can find the forward rate for any year, N, into the future using the following generalized equation derived from the unbiased expectations hypothesis:

$$_Nf_1 = [(1 + {_1R_N})^N / (1 + {_1R_{N-1}})^{N-1}] - 1 \tag{8-11}$$

EXAMPLE 8-4

 For interactive versions of this example visit www.mhhe.com/can1e

ESTIMATING FORWARD RATES

In the mid-2000s, the existing or current (spot) one-year, two-year, three-year, and four-year zero-coupon Treasury security rates were as follows:

$$_1R_1 = 5.00\%, \quad _1R_2 = 4.95\%, \quad _1R_3 = 4.93\%, \quad _1R_4 = 4.94\%$$

Using the unbiased expectations theory, calculate one-year forward rates on zero-coupon Treasury bonds for years two, three, and four.

SOLUTION:

$$2f1 = [(1.0495)^2 / (1.0500)] - 1 = 4.900\%$$

$$3f1 = [(1.0493)^3 / (1.0495)^2] - 1 = 4.890\%$$

$$4f1 = [(1.0494)^4 / (1.0493)^3] - 1 = 4.970\%$$

viewpoints REVISITED

Business Application Solution

In deciding when to issue new debt, DPH Corporation needs to consider two main factors. First, what might happen to specific factors that affect interest rates on any debt the firm may issue? Such specific factors include changes in the firm's default risk, liquidity risk, any special provisions regarding the use of funds raised by the firm's security issuance, and the debt's term to maturity. An increase (decrease) in any of these risks over the next two years would increase (decrease) the rate of interest DPH Corp. would be required to pay to holders of the new debt and make the debt issue in two years less (more) attractive. Second, what might happen to the general level of interest rates in the U.S. economy over the next two years? This involves an analysis of any changes in inflation or the "real" interest rate. DPH can estimate how interest rates may change by examining the term structure of interest rates or the current yield curve. In addition to any internal analysis of these factors, DPH Corp. can get expert advice about the timing of its debt issue and get the new debt to the capital market with help from an investment bank. These financial institutions underwrite securities and engage in related activities, such as making a market in which securities can trade.

Personal Application Solution

In deciding which corporate bond to buy, John Adams needs to consider specific factors that affect differences in interest rates on debt. These specific factors include the general level of inflation and the "real" interest rate in the U.S. economy, as well as the default risk, liquidity risk, any special provisions regarding the use of funds raised by a security issuance, and the term to maturity of the two debt issues. While one bond earns more (10.00%) than the other (8.00%), it may be that the higher yielding bond has more default, liquidity, or other risk than the lower-yielding bond. Thus, the higher yield brings with it more risk. John Adams must consider whether he is willing to incur higher risk to get higher returns. In addition to his own analysis of these factors, John Adams can get expert advice about which bond to buy and then buy the bond with a securities firm's help. These financial institutions engage in activities such as securities brokerage, securities trading, and making markets in which securities can trade.

TIME OUT

8-11 What is a forward rate?

8-12 How can we obtain an implied forward rate from current short- and long-term interest rates?

8-13 Why is it useful to calculate forward rates?

summary of learning goals

In this chapter, we reviewed the basic operations of financial markets and institutions. We described the ways in which funds flow through an economic system from lenders to borrowers and outlined the markets and instruments that lenders and borrowers employ to complete this process. We also reviewed factors that determine nominal interest rates and interest rates' effects on security prices and values in financial markets. We described how the level of interest rates and its movements over time are determined. Finally, the chapter introduced theories regarding the determination of the shape of the term structure of interest rates. The learning goals for the chapter included:

LG1 **Differentiate between primary and secondary markets and between money and capital markets.** Primary markets are markets in which demanders of funds (e.g., corporations) raise funds through new issues of financial instruments, such as stocks and bonds. Once financial instruments such as stocks are issued in primary markets, they are then traded—that is, rebought and resold in secondary markets. Money markets are markets that trade debt securities or instruments with maturities of one year or less. Capital markets are markets that trade equity (stocks) and debt (bonds) instruments with maturities of more than one year.

LG2 **List the types of securities traded in money and capital markets.** A variety of money market securities are issued by corporations and government units to obtain short-term funds. These securities include Treasury bills, federal funds and repurchase agreements, commercial paper, negotiable certificates of deposit, and banker's acceptances. Capital market securities include Treasury notes and bonds, state and local government bonds, U.S government agency bonds, mortgages and mortgage-backed securities, corporate bonds, and corporate stocks.

LG3 **Identify different types of financial institutions and the services that each financial institution provides.** Financial institutions (banks, thrifts, insurance companies, securities firms and investment banks, finance companies, mutual funds, and pension funds) perform the essential function of channeling funds from those with surplus funds (suppliers of funds) to those with shortages of funds (demanders of funds).

LG4 **Analyze specific factors that influence interest rates.** Specific factors that affect differences in interest rates include inflation, the real interest rate, default risk, liquidity risk, special provisions regarding the use of funds raised by a security issuance, and the term to maturity of the security.

LG5 **Offer different theories that explain the shape of the term structure of interest rates.** Explanations for the shape of the yield curve fall predominantly into three theories: the unbiased expectations theory, the liquidity premium theory, and the market segmentation theory.

LG6 **Demonstrate how forward interest rates derive from the term structure of interest rates.** A forward rate is an expected, or implied, rate on a short-term security that is to be originated at some point in the future. Using the equations representing unbiased expectations theory, the market's expectation of forward rates can be derived directly from existing or actual rates on securities currently traded in the spot market.

chapter equations

8-1 $\text{Inflation}\,(IP) = \dfrac{CPI_{t+1} - CPI_t}{CPI_t} \times 100$

8-2 $i = \text{Expected}\,(IP) + RIR$

8-3 $\quad RIR = i - \text{Expected } (IP)$

8-4 $\quad DRP_j = i_{jt} - i_{Tt}$

8-5 $\quad i_j{}^* = f(IP, RIR, DRP_j, LRP_j, SCP_j, MP_j)$

8-6 $\quad (1 + {}_1R_N)^N = [1 + {}_1R_1][1 + E({}_2r_1)] \ldots [1 + E({}_Nr_1)]$

8-7 $\quad {}_1R_N = \{[1 + {}_1R_1][1 + E({}_2r_1)] \ldots [1 + E({}_Nr_1)]\}^{1/N} - 1$

8-8 $\quad {}_1R_N = \{[1 + {}_1R_1][1 + E({}_2r_1) + L_2] \ldots [1 + E({}_Nr_1) + L_N]\}^{1/N} - 1$

8-9 $\quad {}_1R_2 = \{[1 + {}_1R_1][1 + ({}_2f_1)]\}^{1/2} - 1$

8-10 $\quad {}_2f_1 = [(1 + {}_1R_2)^2/(1 + {}_1R_1)] - 1$

8-11 $\quad {}_Nf_1 = [(1 + {}_1R_N)^N/(1 + {}_1R_{N-1})^N - 1] - 1$

key terms

asset transformer, Service provided by financial institutions in which financial claims issued by an FI are more attractive to investors than are the claims directly issued by corporations. (p. 265)

capital markets, Markets that trade debt (bonds) and equity (stock) instruments with maturities of more than one year. (p. 259)

default risk, The risk that a security issuer will default on that security by being late on or missing an interest or principal payment. (p. 269)

delegated monitor, An economic agent appointed to act on behalf of smaller investors in collecting information and/or investing funds on their behalf. (p. 265)

derivative security, A security formalizing an agreement between two parties to exchange a standard quantity of an asset at a predetermined price on a specified date in the future. (p. 261)

direct transfer, The process used when a corporation sells its stock or debt directly to investors without going through a financial institution. (p. 262)

financial institutions, Institutions that perform the essential function of channeling funds from those with surplus funds to those with shortages of funds. (p. 262)

financial markets, The arenas through which funds flow. (p. 256)

foreign exchange markets, Markets in which foreign currency is traded for immediate or future delivery. (p. 261)

foreign exchange risk, Risk arising from the unknown value at which foreign currency cash flows can be converted into U.S. dollars. (p. 261)

forward rate, An expected rate (quoted today) on a security that originates at some point in the future. (p. 280)

indirect transfer, A transfer of funds between suppliers and users of funds through a financial institution. (p. 265)

inflation, The continual increase in the price level of a basket of goods and services. (p. 268)

initial public offerings (IPOs), The first public issue of financial instruments by a firm. (p. 256)

investment banks, Financial institutions that arrange primary market transactions for businesses. (p. 256)

liquidity, The ease with which an asset can be converted into cash. (p. 263)

liquidity risk, The risk that a security can be sold at a predictable price with low transaction costs on short notice. (p. 271)

money markets, Markets that trade debt securities or instruments with maturities of less than one year. (p. 258)

nominal interest rates, The interest rates actually observed in financial markets. (p. 266)

over-the-counter market, Markets that do not operate in a specific fixed location—rather, transactions occur via telephones, wire transfers, and computer trading. (p. 258)

price risk, The risk that an asset's sale price will be lower than its purchase price. (p. 263)

primary markets, Markets in which corporations raise funds through new issues of securities. (p. 256)

real interest rate, The interest rate that would exist on a default free security if no inflation were expected. (p. 268)

secondary markets, Markets that trade financial instruments once they are issued. (p. 256)

secondary securities, Packages or pools of primary claims. (p. 266)

term structure of interest rates, A comparison of market yields on securities, assuming all character-istics except maturity are the same. (p. 271)

trading volume, The number of shares of a security that are simultaneously bought and sold during a period. (p. 258)

self-test problems with solutions

1 **Determinants of Interest Rates for Individual Securities** *The Wall Street Journal* reports that the rate on 2-year Treasury securities is 5.08 percent, and the 6-year Treasury rate is 5.64 percent. From discussions with your broker, you have determined that expected inflation premium is 1.25 percent next year, 1.50 percent in Year 2, and 2.10 percent in Year 3 and beyond. Further, you expect that real interest rates will be 3.6 percent annually for the foreseeable future.

a. Calculate the maturity risk premium on the two-year Treasury security.

b. Calculate the maturity risk premium on the six-year Treasury security.

Solution:

a.

YEAR	INFLATION PREMIUM		REAL INTEREST RATE		1-YEAR TREASURY RATE
1	1.25%	+	3.60%	=	4.85%
2	1.50	+	3.60	=	5.10

Two-year Treasury rate with no market risk premium = $_1R_2$ = $[(1 + .0485)(1 + .051)]^{1/2} - 1 = 4.97\%$.

Thus, the maturity risk premium on the two-year Treasury security = $5.08\% - 4.97\% = 0.11\%$.

b.

YEAR	INFLATION PREMIUM		REAL INTEREST RATE		1-YEAR TREASURY RATE
3	2.10%	+	3.60%	=	5.70%
4	2.10	+	3.60	=	5.70
5	2.10	+	3.60	=	5.70
6	2.10	+	3.60	=	5.70

Six-year Treasury rate with no market risk premium =

$$_1R_6 = [(1 + .0485)(1 + .051)(1 + .057)(1 + .057)(1 + .057)(1 + .057)]^{1/6} - 1$$
$$= 5.46\%.$$

Thus, the maturity risk premium on the 6-year Treasury security = $5.64\% - 5.46\% = 0.28\%$.

2 **Unbiased Expectations Theory** *The Wall Street Journal* reports that the rate on three-year Treasury securities is 5.60 percent and the rate on four-year Treasury securities is 5.65 percent. According to the unbiased expectations hypothesis, what does the market expect the one-year Treasury rate to be three years from today, $E(_4r_1)$?

Solution:

$$_1R_4 = [(1 + _1R_1)(1 + E(_2r_1))(1 + E(_3r_1))(1 + E(_4r_1))]^{1/4} - 1$$

Thus, $0.0565 = [(1 + .056)^3(1 + E(_4r_1))]^{1/4} - 1$

and $E(_4r_1) = [(1 + .0565)^4/(1 + .056)^3] - 1 = 5.80\%$

questions

1. Classify the following transactions as taking place in the primary or secondary markets *(LG1)*:

   a. IBM issues $200 million of new common stock.

   b. The New Company issues $50 million of common stock in an IPO.

   c. IBM sells $5 million of GM preferred stock out of its marketable securities portfolio.

   d. The Magellan Fund buys $100 million of previously issued IBM bonds.

   e. Prudential Insurance Co. sells $10 million of GM common stock.

2. Classify the following financial instruments as money market securities or capital market securities *(LG2)*:

   a. Federal Funds

   b. Common Stock

   c. Corporate Bonds

   d. Mortgages

   e. Negotiable Certificates of Deposit

   f. U.S. Treasury Bills

   g. U.S. Treasury Notes

   h. U.S. Treasury Bonds

   i. State and Government Bonds

3. What are the different types of financial institutions? Include a description of the main services offered by each. *(LG3)*

4. How would economic transactions between suppliers of funds (e.g., households) and users of funds (e.g., corporations) occur in a world without FIs? *(LG3)*

5. Why would a world limited to the direct transfer of funds from suppliers of funds to users of funds likely result in quite low levels of fund flows? *(LG3)*

6. How do FIs reduce monitoring costs associated with the flow of funds from fund suppliers to fund investors? *(LG3)*

www.mhhe.com/can1e

7. How do FIs alleviate the problem of liquidity risk faced by investors wishing to invest in securities of corporations? *(LG3)*

8. What are six factors that determine the nominal interest rate on a security? *(LG4)*

9. What should happen to a security's equilibrium interest rate as the security's liquidity risk increases? *(LG4)*

10. Discuss and compare the three explanations for the shape of the yield curve. *(LG5)*

11. Are the unbiased expectations and liquidity hypothesis explanations for the shape of the yield curve completely independent theories? Explain why or why not. *(LG5)*

12. What is a forward interest rate? *(LG6)*

13. If we observe a one-year Treasury security rate higher than the two-year Treasury security rate, what can we infer about the one-year rate expected one year from now? *(LG6)*

problems

basic problems

8-1 **Determinants of Interest Rates for Individual Securities** A particular security's default risk premium is 2 percent. For all securities, the inflation risk premium is 1.75 percent and the real interest rate is 3.5 percent. The security's liquidity risk premium is 0.25 percent and maturity risk premium is 0.85 percent. The security has no special covenants. Calculate the security's equilibrium rate of return. *(LG4)*

8-2 **Determinants of Interest Rates for Individual Securities** You are considering an investment in 30-year bonds issued by Moore Corporation. The bonds have no special covenants. *The Wall Street Journal* reports that one-year T-bills are currently earning 3.25 percent. Your broker has determined the following information about economic activity and Moore Corporation bonds:

Real interest rate = 2.25%

Default risk premium = 1.15%

Liquidity risk premium = 0.50%

Maturity risk premium = 1.75%

   a. What is the inflation premium? *(LG4)*

   b. What is the fair interest rate on Moore Corporation 30-year bonds? *(LG4)*

8-3 **Determinants of Interest Rates for Individual Securities** Dakota Corporation 15-year bonds have an equilibrium rate of return is 8 percent. For all securities, the inflation risk premium is 1.75 percent and the real interest rate is 3.5 percent. The security's liquidity risk premium is 0.25 percent and maturity risk premium is 0.85 percent. The security has no special covenants. Calculate the bond's default risk premium. *(LG4)*

8-4 **Determinants of Interest Rates for Individual Securities** A 2-year Treasury security currently earns 4.14 percent. Over the next two years, the real interest rate is expected to be 2.25 percent per year and the inflation premium is expected to be 1.75 percent per year. Calculate the maturity risk premium on the 2-year Treasury security. *(LG4)*

8-5 **Unbiased Expectations Theory** Suppose that the current one-year rate (one-year spot rate) and expected one-year T-bill rates over the following three years (i.e., years 2, 3, and 4, respectively) are as follows:

$$_1R_1 = 6\%, \quad E(_2r_1) = 7\%, \quad E(_3r_1) = 7.5\%, \quad E(_4r_1) = 7.85\%$$

Using the unbiased expectations theory, calculate the current (long-term) rates for one-, two-, three-, and four-year-maturity Treasury securities. Plot the resulting yield curve. *(LG5)*

8-6 **Unbiased Expectations Theory** One-year Treasury bills currently earn 3.45 percent. You expected that one year from now, one-year Treasury bill rates will increase to 3.65 percent. If the unbiased expectations theory is correct, what should the current rate be on two-year Treasury securities? *(LG5)*

8-7 **Liquidity Premium Hypothesis** One-year Treasury bills currently earn 3.45 percent. You expect that one year from now, one-year Treasury bill rates will increase to 3.65 percent. The liquidity premium on two-year securities is 0.05 percent. If the liquidity theory is correct, what should the current rate be on two-year Treasury securities? *(LG5)*

8-8 **Liquidity Premium Hypothesis** Based on economists' forecasts and analysis, one-year Treasury bill rates and liquidity premiums for the next four years are expected to be as follows:

$$R_1 = 5.65\%$$
$$E(_2r_1) = 6.75\% \qquad L_2 = 0.05\%$$
$$E(_3r_1) = 6.85\% \qquad L_3 = 0.10\%$$
$$E(_4r_1) = 7.15\% \qquad L_4 = 0.12\%$$

Using the liquidity premium hypothesis, plot the current yield curve. Make sure you label the axes on the graph and identify the four annual rates on the curve both on the axes and on the yield curve itself. *(LG5)*

8-9 **Determinants of Interest Rates for Individual Securities** *The Wall Street Journal* reports that the rate on three-year Treasury securities is 6.00 percent, and the six-year Treasury rate is 6.20 percent. From discussions with your broker, you have determined that expected inflation premium is 2.25 percent next year, 2.50 percent in Year 2, and 2.60 percent in Year 3 and beyond. Further, you expect that real interest rates will be 3.4 percent annually for the foreseeable future.

    a. Calculate the maturity risk premium on the three-year Treasury security. *(LG4)*

    b. Calculate the maturity risk premium on the six-year Treasury security. *(LG4)*

8-10 **Determinants of Interest Rates for Individual Securities** Nikki G's Corporation's 10-year bonds are currently yielding a return of 8.15 percent. The expected inflation premium is 2.5 percent annually and the real interest rate is expected to be 3.10 percent annually over the next 10 years. The liquidity risk premium on Nikki G's bonds is 0.25 percent. The maturity risk premium is 0.10 percent on two-year securities and increases by

0.05 percent for each additional year to maturity. Calculate the default risk premium on Nikki G's 10-year bonds. *(LG4)*

8-11 **Unbiased Expectations Theory** Suppose we observe the following rates: $_1R_1 = 8\%$, $_1R_2 = 10\%$. If the unbiased expectations theory of the term structure of interest rates holds, what is the one-year interest rate expected one year from now, $E(_2r_1)$? *(LG4)*

8-12 **Unbiased Expectations Theory** *The Wall Street Journal* reports that the rate on four-year Treasury securities is 5.60 percent and the rate on five-year Treasury securities is 6.15 percent. According to the unbiased expectations hypotheses, what does the market expect the one-year Treasury rate to be four years from today, $E(_5r_1)$? *(LG5)*

8-13 **Liquidity Premium Hypothesis** *The Wall Street Journal* reports that the rate on three-year Treasury securities is 5.25 percent and the rate on four-year Treasury securities is 5.50 percent. The one-year interest rate expected in three years is, $E(_4r_1)$, is 6.10 percent. According to the liquidity premium hypotheses, what is the liquidity premium on the four-year Treasury security, L_4? *(LG5)*

8-14 **Liquidity Premium Hypothesis** Suppose we observe the following rates: $_1R_1 = 10\%$, $_1R_2 = 14\%$, and $E(_2r_1) = 10\%$. If the liquidity premium theory of the term structure of interest rates holds, what is the liquidity premium for year 2, L_2? *(LG5)*

8-15 **Forecasting Interest Rates** You note the following yield curve in *The Wall Street Journal*. According to the unbiased expectations hypothesis, what is the one-year forward rate for the period beginning one year from today, $_2f_1$? *(LG6)*

MATURITY	YIELD
One day	2.00%
One year	5.50
Two years	6.50
Three years	9.00

8-16 **Forecasting Interest Rates** On May 23, 20XX, the existing or current (spot) one-year, two-year, three-year, and four-year zero-coupon Treasury security rates were as follows:

$$_1R_1 = 4.75\%, \qquad _1R_2 = 4.95\%, \qquad _1R_3 = 5.25\%, \qquad _1R_4 = 5.65\%$$

Using the unbiased expectations theory, calculate the one-year forward rates on zero-coupon Treasury bonds for years 2, 3, and 4 as of May 23, 20XX. *(LG6)*

advanced problems

8-17 **Determinants of Interest Rates for Individual Securities** *The Wall Street Journal* reports that the current rate on 10-year Treasury bonds is 7.25 percent, on 20-year Treasury bonds is 7.85 percent, and on a 20-year corporate bond is 8.75 percent. Assume that the maturity risk premium is zero. If the default risk premium and liquidity risk premium on a 10-year corporate bond is the same as that on the 20-year corporate bond, calculate the current rate on a 10-year corporate bond. *(LG4)*

8-18 **Determinants of Interest Rates for Individual Securities** *The Wall Street Journal* reports that the current rate on five-year Treasury bonds is 6.85 percent and on 10-year Treasury bonds is 7.35 percent. Assume that the maturity risk premium is zero. Calculate the expected rate on a five-year Treasury bond purchased four years from today, $E(_5r_5)$. *(LG4)*

8-19 **Unbiased Expectations Theory** Suppose we observe the three-year Treasury security rate ($_1R_3$) to be 8 percent, the expected one-year rate next year—$E(_2r_1)$—to be 4 percent, and the expected one-year rate the following year—$E(_3r_1)$—to be 6 percent. If the unbiased expectations theory of the term structure of interest rates holds, what is the one-year Treasury security rate, $_1R_1$? *(LG5)*

8-20 **Unbiased Expectations Theory** *The Wall Street Journal* reports that the rate on three-year Treasury securities is 5.60 percent and the rate on five-year Treasury securities is 6.15 percent. According to the unbiased expectations hypothesis, what does the market expect the two-year Treasury rate to be two years from today, $E(_3r_2)$? *(LG5)*

8-21 **Forecasting Interest Rates** Assume the current interest rate on a one-year Treasury bond ($_1R_1$) is 4.50 percent, the current rate on a two-year Treasury bond ($_1R_2$) is 5.25 percent, and the current rate on a three-year Treasury bond ($_1R_3$) is 6.50 percent. If the unbiased expectations theory of the term structure of interest rates is correct, what is the one-year interest rate expected on Treasury bills during year 3, $_3f_1$? *(LG6)*

8-22 **Forecasting Interest Rates** A recent edition of *The Wall Street Journal* reported interest rates of 2.25 percent, 2.60 percent, 2.98 percent, and 3.25 percent for three-year, four-year, five-year, and six-year Treasury security yields, respectively. According to the unbiased expectation theory of the term structure of interest rates, what are the expected one-year rates for years 4, 5, and 6? *(LG6)*

research it! Spreads

Go to the Federal Reserve Board's Web site at **www.federalreserve.gov** and get the latest rates on 10-year T-bills and Aaa- and Baa-rated corporate bonds using the following steps.

Go to the Federal Reserve's Web site at **www.federalreserve.gov.** Click on "Economic Research and Data," then click on "Statistics: Releases and Historical Data." Go to "Weekly Releases: Selected Interest Rates: Releases." Click on the most recent date. This will bring the file onto your computer that contains the relevant data. Calculate the current spread of Aaa- and Baa-rated bonds over the 10-year Treasury-bond rate. How have these spreads changed over the last two years?

integrated minicase: Calculating Interest Rates

From discussions with your broker, you have determined that the expected inflation premium is 1.35 percent next year, 1.50 percent in year 2, 1.75 percent in year 3, and 2.00 percent in year 4 and beyond. Further, you expect that real interest rates will be 3.20 percent next year, 3.30 percent in year 2, 3.75 percent in year 3, and 3.80 percent in year 4 and beyond. You are considering an investment in either five-year Treasury securities or five-year bonds issued by PeeWee Corporation. The bonds have no special covenants. Your broker has determined the following information about economic activity and PeeWee Corporation five-year bonds:

Default risk premium = 2.10%

Liquidity risk premium = 1.75%

Maturity risk premium = 0.75%

Further, the maturity risk premium on Treasury securities is 0.15 percent per year, starting in year 2 and on PeeWee bonds is 0.1875 percent per year starting in year 2. PeeWee's default risk premium and liquidity risk premium do not change with bond maturity.

a. What is the fair interest rate on PeeWee Corporation five-year bonds?

b. What is the fair interest rate on five-year Treasury securities?

c. Plot the five-year yield curve for the Treasury securities.

d. Plot the five-year yield curve for the PeeWee Corporation bonds.

ANSWERS TO TIME OUT

8-1 Primary markets provide a forum in which demanders of funds (e.g., corporations or government entities such as IBM or the U.S. Treasury) raise funds by issuing new financial instruments, such as stocks and bonds. Corporations or government entities continually have new projects or expanded production needs, but do not have sufficient internally generated funds (such as retained earnings) to support their capital needs. Thus, corporations and governments issue securities in external primary markets to raise additional funds. Once firms issue financial instruments in primary markets, these same stocks and bonds are then traded—that is, bought and resold—in secondary markets.

8-2 Foreign exchange markets trade currencies for immediate (also called *spot*) or for some future stated delivery.

8-3 A derivative security is a financial security (such as a futures contract, option contract, or swap contract) linked to another, underlying security, such as a stock traded in capital markets or British pounds sterling traded in foreign exchange (forex) markets. Derivative securities generally involve an agreement between two parties to exchange a standard quantity of an asset or cash flow at a predetermined price and at a specified date in the future. As the value of the underlying security changes, the value of the derivative security changes.

(continued)

ANSWERS TO TIME OUT (continued)

8-4 The major types of financial institutions are:

Commercial Banks: depository institutions whose major assets are loans and whose major liabilities are deposits.

Thrifts: depository institutions, including savings associations, savings banks, and credit unions, that generally perform services similar to commercial banks but tend to concentrate their loans in one segment, such as real estate loans or consumer loans.

Insurance Companies: protect individuals and corporations (policyholders) from financially adverse events, such as untimely death, illness, retirement, and personal injury and liability due to accidents, theft, fire, and so on.

Securities Firms and Investment Banks: underwrite securities and engage in related activities such as securities brokerage, securities trading, and making markets in which securities trade.

Finance Companies: make loans to both individuals and businesses. The loans are funded by short- and long-term debt, and many are collateralized with some kind of durable good, such as washer/dryers, furniture, carpets, and the like.

Mutual Funds: pool many individuals' and companies' financial resources and invest those resources in diversified asset portfolios.

Pension Funds: offer savings plans through which fund participants accumulate savings during their working years.

8-5 First, once they have lent money in exchange for financial claims, fund suppliers would need to continually monitor the use of their funds to guard against theft and waste. Second, many financial claims feature a long-term commitment (e.g., mortgages, corporate stock, and bonds) for fund suppliers, thus creating another disincentive for fund suppliers to hold direct financial claims that fund users may issue. Third, even though real world financial markets provide some liquidity services by allowing fund suppliers to trade financial securities among themselves, fund suppliers face price risk when they buy securities—fund suppliers may not get their principal back, let alone any return on their investment.

8-6 We actually observe nominal interest rates in financial markets—these are the rates most often quoted by financial news services. Real interest rates are interest rate adjusted for inflation; generally lower than nominal interest rates at any particular time; interest rate adjusted so that a chosen date represents the base year.

8-7 The term structure of interest rates compares interest rates on debt securities based on their time to maturity, assuming that all characteristics (i.e., default risk, liquidity risk) are equal.

8-8 The yield curve for U.S. Treasury securities has taken many shapes over the years, but the three most common shapes are: (1) the upward-sloping yield curve (most common) where yields rise steadily with maturity; (2) an inverted or downward-sloping yield curve in which yields decline as maturity increases; and (3) a flat yield curve, when the yield-to-maturity is virtually unaffected by the term-to-maturity.

8-9 Explanations for the yield curve's shape fall predominantly into three categories: the unbiased expectations theory, the liquidity premium theory, and the market segmentation theory.

(continued)

8-10   According to the unbiased expectations theory, the return for holding a four-year bond to maturity should equal the expected return for investing in four successive one-year bonds (as long as the market is in equilibrium). If this equality does not hold, an arbitrage opportunity exists. That is, if investors could earn more on the one-year bond investments, they could short (or sell) the four-year bond, use the proceeds to buy the four successive one-year bonds, and earn a guaranteed profit over the four-year investment horizon.

8-11   A forward rate is an expected, or implied, rate on a short-term security that will originate at some point in the future.

8-12   To find an implied forward rate on a one-year security to be issued one year from today, we can rewrite the unbiased expectations hypothesis equation as follows:

$$_1R_2 = [(1 + {}_1R_1)(1 + ({}_2f_1))]^{1/2} - 1 \qquad\qquad \textbf{(8-9)}$$

where $_2f_1$ = Expected one-year rate for year 2, or the implied forward one-year rate for next year. Saying that $_2f_1$ is the expected one-year rate for year 2 is the same as saying that, once we isolate the $_2f_1$ term, the equation will give us the market's estimate of the expected one-year rate for year 2.

8-13   As interest rates change, so do the values of financial securities. Accordingly, both individual investors and public corporations want to be able to predict or forecast interest rates if they wish to trade profitability. For example, if interest rates rise, the value of investment portfolios of individuals and corporations will fall, resulting in a loss of wealth. So, interest rate forecasts are extremely important for the financial wealth of both public corporations and individuals.

chapter 9:
CHARACTERIZING RISK AND RETURN

 Learning Goals

LG1 Compute an investment's dollar and percentage return.

LG2 Find information about the historical returns and volatility for the stock, bond, and cash markets.

LG3 Measure and evaluate the total risk of an investment using several methods.

LG4 Recognize the risk / return relationship and its implications.

LG5 Plan investments that take advantage of diversification and its impact on total risk.

LG6 Find efficient and optimal portfolios.

LG7 Compute a portfolio's return.

The risk-return relationship fundamentally affects finance theory. You can invest your money very safely by opening a savings account at a bank or by buying Treasury bills. If you can take advantage of these low-risk opportunities, why would you invest your money on risky stocks and bonds? The answer: Very low risk investments also provide a very low return. Investors take on higher risk investments in expectation of earning higher returns. Likewise, businesses also take on risky capital investments only if they expect to earn higher returns that at least cover their costs, including investors' required return. Both investor and business sentiments create a positive relationship between risk and expected return. Of course, taking risk means that you get no guarantee that you will recoup your investment. In the short run, higher risk investments often significantly underperform lower risk investments. Companies and investors should expect higher risk investments to earn higher returns only over the long term (many years). In addition, not all forms of risk are rewarded. In this chapter, we focus on using historical information to characterize past returns and risks. We show how you can diversify to eliminate some risk and expect the highest return possible for your desired risk level. In Chapter 10, we'll turn to estimating the risks and returns you should expect in the future.

viewpoints

Business Application

Managers from the production and marketing departments have proposed some risky new business projects for your firm. These new ideas appear to be riskier than the firm's current business operations.

You are concerned that taking on these new projects will make the firm's stock too risky. However, you also know that diversifying the firm's product offerings could reduce the firm's overall risk. How can you determine whether these project ideas would make the firm's stock riskier or less risky? **(See solution on p. 312)**

Personal Application

Suppose an investor owns a portfolio of 100 percent long-term Treasury bonds because the owner prefers low risk. The investor has avoided owning stocks because of their high volatility.

The investor's stockbroker claims that putting 10 percent of the portfolio in stocks would actually reduce total risk and increase the portfolio's expected return. The investor knows that stocks are riskier than bonds. How can adding the risky stocks to the bond portfolio reduce the risk level? **(See solution on p. 312)**

A practice test can be found on the Online Learning Center at
www.mhhe.com/can1e

9.1 Historical Returns

Let's begin our discussion of risk and return by characterizing the concept of return. First, we need a method for calculating returns. After computing a return, investors need to assess whether it was a good, average, or bad investment return. Examining returns from the past gives us a general idea of what we might expect to see in the future. We should think in terms of return for the long run because a return for any one year can be quite different from the average returns from the past couple of decades.

Computing Returns

How much have you earned on each of your investments? Two ways to determine this are to compute the actual dollar return or compute the dollar return as a percentage of the money invested.

DOLLAR RETURN The **dollar return** earned includes any capital gain (or loss) that occurred as well as any income that you received over the period. Equation 9-1 illustrates the dollar return calculation:

$$\text{Dollar return} = (\text{Capital gain or loss}) + \text{Income} \qquad \textbf{(9-1)}$$
$$= (\text{Ending value} - \text{Beginning value}) + \text{Income}$$

For example, say you held 200 shares of RadioShack Corp's (RSH) stock. The consumer electronic goods retailer had a market price of $16.78 per share at the end of 2006. RadioShack also paid 25¢ in dividends per share during 2006. At the end of 2007, RadioShack's stock price was $16.86. For the whole of 2007, you earned a capital gain of ($16.86 − $16.78) × 200 shares, or $16, and received a dividend payment of 200 shares × $0.25, or $50. So the total dollar return on your investment was $66 (= $16 + $50) for 2007.

In RadioShack's case, the stock price increased slightly, so you experienced a capital gain. On the other hand, the stock price of toy and game producer Mattel Inc. (MAT) started the year at $22.66 per share, paid a 75¢ dividend, and ended 2007 at $19.04. If you owned 200 shares of Mattel, you would have experienced a capital loss of $724. This loss would have been partially offset by the $150 of dividends received. However, the total dollar return would still have been −$574. Stock prices can fluctuate substantially and cause large positive or negative dollar returns.

Does your dollar return depend on whether you continue to hold the Mattel and RadioShack stock or sell it? No. In general, finance deals with *market* values. RadioShack stock was worth $16.86 at the end of 2007 regardless of whether you held the stock or sold it. If you sell it, then we refer to your gains as "realized" gains. If you continue to hold the stock, the gains are "unrealized" gains.

PERCENTAGE RETURN We usually find it more useful to characterize investment earnings as **percentage returns** so that we can easily compare one investment's return to other alternatives' returns. We calculate percentage return by dividing the dollar return by the investment's value at the beginning of the time period.

$$\text{Percentage return} = \frac{\text{Ending value} - \text{Beginning value} + \text{Income}}{\text{Beginning value}} \times 100\% \quad \textbf{(9-2)}$$

Because it's standardized, we can use percentage returns for almost any type of investment. We can use beginning and ending values for stock positions, bond prices, real estate values, and so on. Investment income may be stock dividends, bond interest payments, or other receipts. The percentage return for holding the RadioShack stock during calendar year 2007 was 1.97 percent, computed as:

$$\text{RadioShack percentage return} = \frac{\$16.86 \times 200 - \$16.78 \times 200 + \$0.25 \times 200}{\$16.78 \times 200}$$

$$= 0.0197, \text{ or } 1.97\%$$

The return for the Mattel position during the same period was -12.7 percent:

$$\text{Mattel percentage return} = \frac{\$19.04 \times 200 - \$22.66 \times 200 + \$0.75 \times 200}{\$22.66 \times 200}$$

$$= -0.1266, \text{ or } -12.7\%$$

The 2007 return of -12.7 percent is quite poor for Mattel. Both firms belong to the S&P 500 Index, which earned 3.5 percent in 2007.

 For interactive versions of this example visit www.mhhe.com/can1e

EXAMPLE 9-1

COMPUTING RETURNS

You are evaluating a stock's short-term performance. On January 29, 2007, pharmaceutical giant Bristol-Myers Squibb (BMY) saw its stock price surge on merger news regarding another firm, Schering-Plough. Bristol-Myers stock had closed the previous trading day at $26.21 and was up to $27.69 within hours of trading. BMY had ended 2006 at $26.32 and paid a 28¢ dividend in January. What is the dollar return and percentage return of 300 shares of BMY for the day and year to date?

 LG1

SOLUTION:

For the day, realize that no income is paid. Therefore, the dollar return is $444 = 300 × ($27.69 − $26.21) + 0 and the percent return is 5.65% = $444 ÷ (300 × $26.21). The year to date (YTD) return does include dividend income. So the dollar YTD return is $495 = 300 × ($27.69 − $26.32) + (300 × $0.28). The Bristol-Myer YTD percentage return is

$$\text{BMY YTD return} = \frac{(\$27.69 \times 300) - (\$26.32 \times 300) + (\$0.28 \times 300)}{\$26.32 \times 300} = 0.063, \text{ or } 6.3\%$$

Note that most of the YTD return of 6.3% occurred during the 5.65% return from one day of trading.

Are the 2007 returns for Mattel and RadioShack typical? We look to **average returns** to examine performance over time. The arithmetic average return provides an estimate for how the investment has performed over longer periods of time. The formula for the average return is:

$$\text{Average return} = \frac{\displaystyle\sum_{t=1}^{N} \text{Return}_t}{N} \qquad \textbf{(9-3)}$$

	MATTEL	RADIOSHACK			MATTEL	RADIOSHACK
1985	20.0%	68.0%	1997		36.6%	77.5%
1986	−32.9	4.3	1998		−35.8	7.7
1987	−16.8	−21.2	1999		−42.2	140.1
1988	38.8	26.0	2000		13.9	−12.6
1989	107.5	3.2	2001		20.0	−29.3
1990	2.9	−23.7	2002		11.6	−37.1
1991	108.8	0.8	2003		2.8	65.1
1992	16.9	5.3	2004		3.6	8.0
1993	11.0	69.3	2005		−16.3	−35.3
1994	15.8	2.6	2006		47.3	−19.0
1995	55.8	−15.7	2007		−12.7	2.0
1996	14.8	7.9	**Average =**		**16.1**	**12.5**

Data Source: Yahoo! Finance

where the return for each subperiod is summed up and divided by the number of subperiods. You can state the returns in either percentage or decimal format. Table 9.1 shows the annual returns for Mattel and RadioShack during 1985 to 2007. First, notice that over time, the returns are quite varied for both firms. The stock return for Mattel has ranged from a low of −42.2 percent in 1999 to a high of 108.8 percent in 1991. RadioShack's stock return varied between −37.1 percent (2002) to 140.1 percent (1999). Also note that the returns appear unpredictable or random. Sometimes a large negative return is followed by another bad year, like Mattel's returns in 1986 and 1987. Other times, a poor year is followed by a very good year, like 1987 and 1988 for RadioShack. The table also reports average annual returns for Mattel and RadioShack of 16.1 percent and 12.5 percent, respectively. Over the years, these stocks have earned investors a good average rate of return.

Performance of Asset Classes

During any given year, the stock market may perform better than the bond market, or it may perform worse. Over longer time periods, how do stocks, bonds, or cash securities perform? Historically, stocks have performed better than either bonds or cash. Table 9.2 shows the average returns for these three asset classes over the period 1950 to 2007, as well as over various subperiods. Over the entire period, stocks (as measured by the S&P 500 Index) earned an average 13.2 percent return per year. This is double the 6.4 percent return earned by long-term Treasury bonds. Cash securities, measured by U.S. Treasury bills, earned an average 4.9 percent return.

The table also shows each asset class's average return for each decade since 1950. The best decade for the stock market was the 1950s, when stocks earned an average 20.9 percent per year. The 1990s ran a close second with a 19 percent per year return. The best decade for the bond market was the 1980s, when it earned an average 13.5 percent per year return due to capital gains as interest rates fell. Stocks have outperformed bonds in every decade since 1950. Notice that the average return in the stock and bond markets has not been negative during any decade since 1950. But average stock returns do not really paint a very accurate picture of annual returns. Individual annual returns from 2000 to 2007 show that returns can vary strongly and be quite negative in any particular year. Indeed, this annual variability defines risk. Note that even the bond market outperformed the stock market between 2000 and 2007.

table 9.2

		STOCKS (S&P 500)	LONG-TERM TREASURY BONDS	T-BILLS
1950 to 2007	Average	13.2%	6.4%	4.9%
1950 to 1959	Average	20.9	0.0	2.0
1960 to 1969	Average	8.7	1.6	4.0
1970 to 1979	Average	7.5	5.7	6.3
1980 to 1989	Average	18.2	13.5	8.9
1990 to 1999	Average	19.0	9.5	4.9
2000	Annual return	−9.1	20.1	5.9
2001	Annual return	−11.9	4.6	3.5
2002	Annual return	−22.1	17.2	1.6
2003	Annual return	28.7	2.1	1.0
2004	Annual return	10.9	7.7	1.4
2005	Annual return	4.9	6.5	3.1
2006	Annual return	15.8	1.9	4.7
2007	Annual return	3.5	9.8	3.4
2000 to 2007	Average	2.6	8.7	3.1

TIME OUT

9-1 How important were dividend payments to the total returns that Mattel and RadioShack offered investors?

9-2 Using the average returns shown in Table 9.2, compute how much a $10,000 investment made in each asset class at the beginning of each decade would become at the end of each decade.

9.2 Historical Risks

When you purchase a U.S. Treasury bill, you know exactly what your dollar and percentage return are going to be. Many people find comfort in the certainty from this safe investment. On the other hand, when you purchase a stock, you do not know what your return is going to be—either in the short term or in the long run. This uncertainty is precisely what makes stock investing risky. It's useful to evaluate this uncertainty quantitatively so that we can compare risk among different stocks and asset classes.

Computing Volatility

Financial theory suggests that investors should look at an investment's historical returns to assess how much uncertainty to expect in the future. If you see high variability in historical returns, you should expect a high degree of future uncertainty. Table 9.2 shows that between 2000 and 2007, the stock market experienced a range of −22.2 percent return in 2002 to a 28.7 percent return in 2003. Bonds experienced a smaller variability—1.9 percent return in 2006 to 20.1 percent return in 2000. Examining the range of historical returns provides just one way to express the return volatility that we can expect. In practical terms, the finance industry uses a statistical return volatility measure known as the **standard deviation** of percentage returns. We calculate standard deviation as the square root of the variance, and this figure represents the security's or portfolio's **total risk.** We'll discuss other risk measurements in the next chapter.

	MATTEL RETURN	DEVIATION	SQUARED DEVIATION
	Computation of Mattel Stock Return Standard Deviation		**table 9.3**
1985	20.0%	3.9%	0.1%
1986	−32.9	−49.0	24.1
1987	−16.8	−32.9	10.9
1988	38.8	22.7	5.1
1989	107.5	91.4	83.4
1990	2.9	−13.2	1.8
1991	108.8	92.7	85.8
1992	16.9	0.8	0.0
1993	11.0	−5.1	0.3
1994	15.8	−0.3	0.0
1995	55.8	39.7	15.7
1996	14.8	−1.3	0.0
1997	36.6	20.5	4.2
1998	−35.8	−51.9	27.0
1999	−42.2	−58.3	34.0
2000	13.9	−2.2	0.1
2001	20.0	3.9	0.1
2002	11.6	−4.5	0.2
2003	2.8	−13.3	1.8
2004	3.6	−12.5	1.6
2005	−16.3	−32.4	10.5
2006	47.3	31.2	9.7
2007	−12.7	−28.8	8.3
Average =	**16.1**		
		Sum =	324.9
		Variance =	14.8
		Std Dev =	38.4

Data Source: Yahoo! Finance

Our process of computing standard deviation starts with the average return over the period. The average annual return for the stock market since 1950 is 13.2 percent. How much can the return in any given year deviate from this average? We compute the actual annual deviation by subtracting the return each year from this average return like: Return$_{(1950)}$ − Average return; Return$_{(1951)}$ − Average return; Return$_{(1952)}$ − Average return, and so on. Note that many of these deviations will be negative (from a lower-than-average return that year) and others will be positive (from a higher-than-average return). If we computed the *average* of these return deviations, our result would be zero. Large positive deviations cancel out large negative deviations and hide the variability. To really see the size of the variations without the distractions that come with including a positive or negative sign, we square each deviation before adding them up. Dividing by the number of returns in the sample minus one provides the return *variance.*[1] The square root of the return variance is the standard deviation:

$$\text{Standard deviation} = \sqrt{\frac{\sum_{t=1}^{N}(\text{Return}_t - \text{Average return})^2}{N-1}}$$

(9-4)

A large standard deviation indicates greater return volatility—or high risk. Table 9.3 shows the standard deviations of Mattel stock returns over 23 years. The Deviation column shows the annual return minus Mattel's average return

[1]We use the denominator of $N-1$ to compute a sample's standard deviation, which is the most common for finance applications. We would divide the standard deviation of a population simply by N.

of 16.1 percent. The last column squares each deviation. Then we sum up these squared deviations, divide the result by the number of observations less one (22), to compute the return variance. If we want to use a measure that makes sense in the real world (how would you interpret a squared percentage, anyway?), we take the square root of the variance to get the standard deviation. Mattel's standard deviation of returns during this sample period comes to 38.4 percent. In comparison, the standard deviation of RadioShack stock returns for this same period is 43.6 percent. Since RadioShack's standard deviation is higher, its stock features more total risk than Mattel's stock does.

Although analysts and investors use a stock return's standard deviation as an important and common measure of risk, it's laborious to compute by hand. Most people use a spreadsheet or statistical software to calculate stock return standard deviations.

 For interactive versions of this example visit www.mhhe.com/can1e

EXAMPLE 9-2

RISK AND RETURN

Find the average return and risk (as measured by standard deviation) for Mattel since 2000. Table 9.3 shows the annual returns for years 2000 to 2007.

LG1, LG3

SOLUTION:

First, compute the average annual return for the period. Using equation 9-3:

$$\frac{13.9\% + 20.0\% + 11.6\% + 2.8\% + 3.6\% - 16.3\% + 47.3\% - 12.7\%}{8} = \frac{70.2\%}{8} = 8.8\%$$

Mattel has averaged an 8.8 percent return per year since 2000. To compute the risk, use the standard deviation equation 9-4. First, find the deviations of return for each year:

YEAR 2000	2001	2002	2003	2004	2005	2006	2007
13.9%−8.8%	20.0%−8.8%	11.6%−8.8%	2.8%−8.8%	3.6%−8.8%	−16.3%−8.8%	47.3%−8.8%	−12.7%−8.8%

Square those deviations:

YEAR 2000	2001	2002	2003	2004	2005	2006	2007
$(13.9\%-8.8\%)^2$	$(20.0\%-8.8\%)^2$	$(11.6\%-8.8\%)^2$	$(2.8\%-8.8\%)^2$	$(3.6\%-8.8\%)^2$	$(-16.3\%-8.8\%)^2$	$(47.3\%-8.8\%)^2$	$(-12.7\%-8.8\%)^2$

Then add them up, divide by $N-1$, and take the square root:

$$\sqrt{\frac{\begin{array}{c}(13.9\%-8.8\%)^2 + (20.0\%-8.8\%)^2 + (11.6\%-8.8\%)^2 + (2.8\%-8.8\%)^2 + (3.6\%-8.8\%)^2 \\ +(-16.3\%-8.8\%)^2 + (47.3\%-8.8\%)^2 + (-12.7\%-8.8\%)^2\end{array}}{8-1}}$$

$$= \sqrt{\frac{26.01 + 125.44 + 7.84 + 36.00 + 27.04 + 630.01 + 1482.25 + 462.25}{7}} = \sqrt{399.549} = 19.99\%$$

Mattel stock has averaged an 8.8 percent return with a standard deviation of 19.99 percent since 2000.

		table 9.4
Annual Standard Deviation of Returns for Stocks, Bonds, and T-Bills, 1950 to 2007		

	STOCKS	LONG-TERM TREASURY BONDS	T-BILLS
1950 to 2007	17.0%	10.3%	2.8%
1950 to 1959	19.8	4.9	0.8
1960 to 1969	14.4	6.2	1.3
1970 to 1979	19.2	6.8	1.8
1980 to 1989	12.7	15.1	2.6
1990 to 1999	14.2	12.8	1.2
2000 to 2007	16.4	6.7	1.7

Risk of Asset Classes

We report the standard deviations of return for stocks, bonds, and T-bills in Table 9.4 for 1950 to 2007 and for each decade since 1950. Over the entire sample, the stock market returns' standard deviation is 17.0 percent. As we would expect, stock market volatility is higher than bond market volatility (10.3 percent) or for T-bills (2.8 percent). These volatility estimates are consistent with our previously stated position that the stock market carries more risk than the bond or cash markets do. Every decade since 1950 has seen a lot of stock market volatility. The bond market experienced the most volatility in the 1980s and 1990s as interest rates varied.

You will recall from Chapter 6 that since any bond's par value and coupon rate are fixed, bond prices must fluctuate to adjust for changes in interest rates. Bond prices respond inversely to interest rate changes: As interest rates rise, bond prices fall, and if interest rates fall, bond prices rise. T-bills returns have experienced very low volatility over each decade. Indeed, T-bills are commonly considered to be one of the only risk-free assets. Higher-risk investments offer higher returns over time. But short-term fluctuations in the value of higher risk investments can be substantial. The stock market is risky—while it has offered a good annual return of 13.2 percent, that return comes with volatility of 17.0 percent standard deviation. Many investors may intellectually understand that this high risk means that they may receive very poor returns in the short term. Investors really felt the full force of this risk when the stock market declined three years in a row (2000 to 2002). Some investors even decided that this was too much risk for them and they sold out of the stock market before the 2003 rally.

The stock market return standard deviations that appear in Table 9.4 are all considerably lower than the standard deviations of Mattel and of RadioShack stocks (38.4 percent and 43.6 percent, respectively). In this case, we measure stock market return and standard deviation using the S&P 500 Index. Mattel and RadioShack are both included in the S&P 500 Index. Why do these two large firms have measures of total risk—standard deviations—that are at least twice as large as the standard deviations on the stock market returns? Are Mattel and RadioShack just two of the most risky firms in the Index? Actually, no. The differences in standard deviations between these individual companies and the entire market have much more to do with *diversification*. Owning 500 companies, such as all of those included in the S&P 500 Index, generates much less risk than owning just one company. This phenomenon appears in the standard deviation measure. We'll discuss the effects of diversification in detail later in this chapter.

Risk versus Return

Investors can buy very safe T-bills. Or they can take some risk to seek higher returns. How much extra return can you expect for taking more risk? This is known as the *trade-off between risk and return*. The **coefficient of variation** (CoV) is a common *relative* measure of this risk-vs-reward relationship. The equation for the coefficient of variation is simply the standard deviation divided by average return. It is interpreted as the amount of risk (measured by volatility) per unit of return:

$$\text{Coefficient of variation} = \frac{\text{Standard deviation}}{\text{Average return}} \tag{9-5}$$

As an investor, you would want to receive a very high return (the denominator in the equation) with a very low risk (the numerator). So, a smaller CoV indicates a better risk-reward relationship. Since the average return and standard deviation for Mattel stock are 16.1 percent and 38.4 percent, its CoV is 2.39 (= 38.4 ÷ 16.1). This is better than RadioShack's CoV of 3.49 (= 43.6 ÷ 12.5). For all asset classes since 1950, the stock market earned a higher return than bonds and was also riskier. But which one had a better risk-return relationship? The CoV for common stock is 1.29 (= 17.0 ÷ 13.2). For Treasury bonds, the coefficient of a variation is 1.61 (= 10.3 ÷ 6.4). Even though stocks are riskier than bonds, they involve a somewhat better risk-reward trade-off.

 For interactive versions of this example visit www.mhhe.com/can1e

EXAMPLE 9-3

RISK VERSUS RETURN

You are interested in the risk-return relationship of stocks in each decade since 1950. Obtain the average returns and risks in Tables 9.2 and 9.4.

 LG4

SOLUTION:

Using the coefficient of variation, the average returns, and standard deviation of return, compute the following risk-return relationships:

$$CoV_{1950s} = \frac{19.8\%}{20.9\%} = 0.95 \qquad CoV_{1960s} = \frac{14.4\%}{8.7\%} = 1.66$$

$$CoV_{1970s} = \frac{19.2\%}{7.5\%} = 2.56 \qquad CoV_{1980s} = \frac{12.7\%}{18.2\%} = 0.70$$

$$CoV_{1990s} = \frac{14.2\%}{19.0\%} = 0.75 \qquad CoV_{2000s} = \frac{16.4\%}{2.6\%} = 6.31$$

Note that over short time periods, the stock risk-return relationship varies significantly.

 TIME OUT

9-3 What volatility measure can we use to evaluate and compare risk among different investment alternatives?

9-4 Explain why the coefficients of variation for Mattel and RadioShack are so much higher than the CoV for the stock market as a whole.

9.3 Forming Portfolios

As we noted previously, Mattel and RadioShack stocks' risk as measured by their standard deviations appear quite high compared to the standard deviation of the S&P 500 Index. This is by no means a coincidence. Combining stocks into **portfolios** can reduce many sources of stock risk. **Diversification** reduces risk. The S&P 500 Index, for example, tracks 500 companies, which allows for a great deal of diversification.

 ## Diversifying to Reduce Risk

Think about a stock's total risk as having two components. The first component includes risks that are both specific to that company and common to other companies in the same industry. We call this risk **firm-specific risk.** The stock's other risk component is general risk that all firms—and all individuals, for that matter—face based upon economic strength both domestically and globally. We call this type of risk **market risk.** These risks appear in the equation:

$$\text{Total risk} = \text{Firm-specific risk} + \text{Market risk} \tag{9-6}$$

Standard deviations measure total risk. Individual stocks are subject to many firm-specific risks. We can reduce firm-specific risk by combining stocks into a portfolio. Since we can reduce firm-specific risk by diversifying, this risk is sometimes referred to as **diversifiable risk.** If RadioShack announces lower-than-expected profits, its stock price will decline. However, since this news is *specific* to RadioShack, the news should not affect Mattel stock's price. On the other hand, if the government announces a change in unemployment, both stocks' prices will change to some degree. Macroeconomic events represent market risks because such events—unemployment claims, interest rate changes, national budget deficits or surpluses—affect all companies.

Suppose that you own only RadioShack stock and have earned the annual returns shown in Table 9.5. Then someone suggests that you add Mattel to your RadioShack stock to form a two-stock portfolio. Both Mattel and RadioShack stocks carry a lot of total risk. But look at the risk and return characteristics of a portfolio consisting of 50 percent RadioShack stock and 50 percent Mattel stock. You start with RadioShack stock, which provided an average return of 12.5 percent with a risk of 43.6 percent. The two-stock portfolio earns an average 14.3 percent return with a standard deviation of only 26.2 percent. You added a high-risk stock to a high-risk stock and you ended up with a portfolio with much lower risk! This is a hallmark of most portfolios, which pool market risk but often provide offsetting, reduced firm-specific risks overall.

Next, add IBM stock to your Mattel and RadioShack stock portfolio. Figure 9.1 shows that the total risk of this three-stock portfolio declines to 20.8 percent. Note that adding Newmont Mining, Disney, and General Electric also reduces the total risk of the stock portfolio. As you add more stocks, the firm-specific risk portion of the total portfolio risk declines. The total risk falls rapidly as we add the first few stocks. Diversification's power to reduce firm-specific risk weakens for the later stocks added to the portfolio, because we have already eliminated much of the firm-specific risk. We could continue to add stocks until the portfolio comprises all S&P 500 Index firms, in which case the standard deviation of the portfolio would be 17.0 percent. At this point, virtually all of the firm-specific risk has been purged and the portfolio carries only market risk, which is sometimes called **nondiversifiable risk.**

	RADIOSHACK	MATTEL	PORTFOLIO OF RADIOSHACK AND MATTEL
1985	68.0%	20.0%	44.0%
1986	4.3	−32.9	−14.3
1987	−212	−16.8	−19.0
1988	26.0	38.8	32.4
1989	−3.2	107.5	52.2
1990	−23.	2.9	−10.4
1991	0.8	108.8	54.8
1992	5.3	16.9	11.1
1993	69.3	11.0	40.2
1994	2.6	15.8	9.2
1995	−15.7	55.8	20.1
1996	7.9	14.8	11.4
1997	77.5	36.6	57.1
1998	7.7	−35.8	−14.1
1999	140.1	−42.2	49.0
2000	−12.6	13.9	0.7
2001	−29.3	20.0	−4.7
2002	−37.1	11.6	−12.8
2003	65.1	2.8	34.0
2004	8.0	3.6	5.8
2005	−35.3	−16.3	−25.8
2006	−19.0	47.3	14.2
2007	2.0	−12.7	−5.3
Average =	**12.5**	**16.1**	**14.3**
Std Dev =	**43.6**	**38.4**	**26.2**

Data Source: Yahoo! Finance

figure 9.1

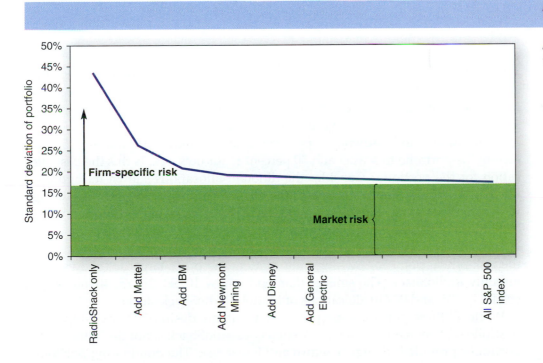

Adding Stocks to a Portfolio Reduces Risk

Modern Portfolio Theory

The concept that diversification reduces risk was formalized in the early 1950s by Harry Markowitz, who eventually won the Nobel Prize in Economics for his work. Markowitz's **modern portfolio theory** shows how risk reduction occurs when securities are combined. The theory also describes how to combine stocks to

INVESTOR DIVERSIFICATION PROBLEMS

Experts have examined investor behavior using detailed datasets of stock brokerage accounts, employee pension plans, and the Survey of Consumer Finances. Studies have identified many investor behaviors that are inconsistent with the principle of full diversification:

- Many households own relatively few individual stocks—they held a median number of two stocks until 2001, when it rose to three. Of course, many households own equity indirectly, through mutual funds or retirement accounts, and these indirect holdings tend to be much better diversified.

- Ten to fifteen percent of households with between $100,000 and $1 million in financial asset wealth own no stocks (neither directly nor indirectly through funds).

- Investors seem to prefer securities of local firms. Many geographic regions feature companies that are heavily concentrated in few industries. Thus, a local preference could reduce diversification opportunities.

- Many employees hold mostly their employers' stocks (more than 50 percent of employee holdings), particularly within their 401(k) retirement savings accounts. Holding a lot of a single stock creates a "portfolio" with high total risk.

Finance professionals and the investment industry have established diversification concepts for many decades and can help investors maximize their returns with appropriate risk levels. But many investors do not consult professionals; they fail to diversify and thus take unnecessary diversifiable risk.

Sources: John Y. Campbell, "Household Finance," *Journal of Finance* 61 (2006): 1553–1604, Valery Polkovichenko, "Household Portfolio Diversification: A Case for Rank-Dependent Preferences," *Review of Financial Studies* 18 (2005): 1467–1500, and Shlomo Benartzi, Richard Thaler, Stephen Utkus, and Cass Sunstein, "The Law and Economics of Company Stock in 401(k) Plans," *Journal of Law and Economics* 50 (2007):45–79.

 want to know more? Key Words to Search for Updates: diversification, pension plan choices, asset allocation

achieve the lowest total risk possible for a given expected return. Or, said differently, it describes how to achieve the highest expected return for the desired risk level. The combination of securities that achieves the highest expected return for a given risk level is called the investor's **optimal portfolio.**

In our Mattel and RadioShack portfolio example above, we allocated 50 percent of the portfolio to Mattel and 50 percent to RadioShack. Is this the best allocation for the portfolio? Consider the different allocations shown in Figure 9.2 for the two stocks. The graph shows the expected return (computed as average return) and risk (computed as standard deviation) of various portfolios. It would be terrific if you could find a portfolio located in the upper left-hand corner. That is, investors would like a high expected return with low risk. One large dot shows the risk-return point for owning only Mattel. The other large dot shows owning only RadioShack. The smaller diamonds show 10/90, 25/75, 40/60, 50/50, 60/40, 75/25, and 90/10 allocations of Mattel/RadioShack stocks.

While all these portfolios are possible, not all are desirable. For example, the portfolio of 25 percent Mattel and 75 percent RadioShack is not desirable. Other portfolios provide *both* higher return and lower risk. The dominating portfolios appear higher and to the left in the figure. One such portfolio consists of 75 percent Mattel stock and 25 percent RadioShack stock. The 50/50 portfolio (circled in the figure) is also better than the 25/75 portfolio. However, the 50/50 portfolio isn't desirable because a portfolio with slightly higher return and slightly lower risk appears above and to the left of the 50/50 portfolio: the 60/40 portfolio. Portfolios with the highest return possible for each risk level are called **efficient portfolios.** Notice that if you drew a line connecting the dots, the figure would

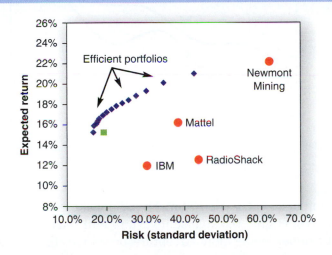

figure 9.3

Efficient Portfolios from
Four Stocks

appear like the end of a bullet. The portfolios on the top of the bullet dominate the portfolios on the bottom; the top portfolio dots show the efficient portfolios for these two stocks.

Figure 9.3 shows efficient portfolios for combining the four stocks: RadioShack, Mattel, IBM, and Newmont Mining. These portfolios appear as diamonds in the figure with each diamond representing a different allocation of the four stocks. The single square represents the portfolio that consists of 25 percent in each of the four stocks. We used this portfolio to demonstrate how diversification reduces risk in Figure 9.1. Notice that other, efficient portfolios dominate this portfolio.

If we showed all efficient portfolios, they would appear as a line that connects the upper side of the bullet shape. If we added all available securities to the graph, then all of the efficient portfolios of those securities form the **efficient frontier.** Efficient frontier portfolios dominate all other possible stock portfolios. The shape of the efficient frontier implies that diminishing returns apply to risk-taking in the investment world. To gain ever-higher expected rates of return, investors must be willing to take on ever-increasing amounts of risk. The optimal portfolio for you is one on the efficient frontier that reflects the amount of risk

figure 9.4

Efficient Portfolios from
Four Stocks

Panel A: Two stocks that move together over time

Panel B: Two stocks that move differently over time

that you're willing to take. Clearly, optimal portfolio choice depends on individual risk preferences. Highly risk-averse investors will select low-risk portfolios on the efficient frontier, while more adventuresome investors will select higher-risk portfolios. Any choice may be appropriate, given differences in individual risk preferences.

 HOW DOES DIVERSIFICATION WORK?   Will combining any two stocks greatly reduce total risk as much as combining RadioShack and Mattel did? The answer is no. If two stocks are subject to exactly the same kinds of events such that their returns always behave the same way over time, then we have no need to own both stocks—simply pick the one that performs better. Diversification comes when two stocks are subject to different kinds of events such that their returns differ over time.

Consider the illustration in Figure 9.4. You own Stock A in Panel A of the figure. The stock features risk, as demonstrated by its price volatility over time. You would like to reduce the risk by combining your position in Stock A with an equal position in Stock B. In this case, the alternative stock, Stock B, moves the same way over time as Stock A does. When Stock A goes up, so does Stock B. They also decline together. A portfolio of both stocks is illustrated. Notice how the portfolio has the same volatility of Stocks A and B separately. Combining these two stocks didn't reduce volatility, or total risk.

Panel A: Company Annual Returns, 1985 to 2007

	RADIOSHACK	MATTEL	IBM	NEWMONT MINING	DISNEY	GENERAL ELECTRIC	CITIGROUP
RadioShack	1						
Mattel	−0.188	1					
IBM	0.253	−0.197	1				
Newmont Mining	−0.053	−0.152	−0.241	1			
Disney	0.256	0.317	−0.128	0.206	1		
General Electric	0.625	0.203	0.339	−0.079	0.508	1	
Citigroup	0.493	0.368	0.056	−0.220	0.298	0.725	1
Bank of New York	0.265	0.466	0.043	−0.372	0.405	0.583	0.598

Panel B: Asset Class Annual Returns, 1950 to 2007

	STOCKS	LONG-TERM TREASURY BONDS	T-BILLS
Stocks	1		
Long-term Treasury bonds	0.106	1	
T-bills	−0.109	0.203	1

Now consider Stock C, shown in Panel B. Stock C has the same volatility as Stock A, but its price moves in different directions than does the price of Stock A. When Stock A's price increases, Stock C's price increases sometimes and decreases sometimes. As shown, a portfolio of Stock A and Stock C features much lower volatility than either Stock A or Stock C alone. Combining Stocks A and C reduces risk because their price movements often counteract one another. In short, combining stocks with similar characteristics does not provide much diversification and thus risk reduction. Combining stocks with many differences does provide diversification and thus lowers risk.

The ways that stocks co-move over time determines how much diversification and thus risk reduction we can achieve by combining them. So what we need is some measure of co-movement to help investors form diversified portfolios. That measure, called **correlation,** is denoted with Greek symbol ρ (rho). Correlation is a statistical measure with some very useful characteristics that makes it easy to interpret. Its value is bounded between −1 and +1. A correlation value of +1 means that returns from two different securities move perfectly in sync. They change lock-step up and down together. A value of −1 means that returns from two securities are perfectly inversely correlated—they move exactly opposite. A value of 0 means that the movements of the two returns over time are unrelated to one another. Investors seeking diversification look for stocks where the returns have low or negative correlations with each other.

What return correlations are common between stocks? Panel A of Table 9.6 shows the correlations between many companies. One high correlation shown is the 0.598 correlation between Citigroup and the Bank of New York. This shouldn't be surprising, because these are two similar firms in the same industry. Combining these two stocks wouldn't reduce risk very much in a portfolio. The largest negative correlation is the correlation of −0.372 between Newmont Mining and the Bank of New York. These firms practice in very different industries and provide large risk reduction possibilities. Note that the correlation between RadioShack and Mattel is −0.188. This negative correlation gives us an answer to the question of why total risk (in the form of standard deviations) fell so much when we combined the two stocks relative to their individual standard deviations as shown in Figure 9.2. Most of the correlations in Table 9.6 are positive. Because most stocks are positively correlated, we typically add many stocks together to fully eliminate all the firm-specific risk in the portfolio, as we showed in Figure 9.1.

INTERNATIONAL OPPORTUNITIES FOR DIVERSIFICATION

The U.S. stock market represents nearly 47 percent of all stock value worldwide. Japanese and U.K. stock markets represent 11 percent and 8 percent of the worldwide stock market value, respectively. Many investment and diversification opportunities present themselves internationally! However, most people allocate very little or none of their portfolios to international securities. If worldwide opportunities can create greater diversification, then those who don't invest in international stocks miss out on an important opportunity to reduce risk in their portfolios.

MSCI Barra is the leading provider of global stock market indexes. Some MSCI Barra indices follow individual countries. In addition, MSCI Barra compiles composite indexes for groups of companies in developed markets, emerging markets, frontier markets, and by geographic regions. Investment managers use the MSCI World Index, the MSCI EAFE (Europe, Australasia, Far East) Index, and the MSCI Emerging Markets Index as premier benchmarks to measure global stock market performance.

The table below shows the average annual returns and standard deviations for the U.S. stock market, Treasury bonds, and the MSCI EAFE and MSCI Emerging Markets indexes for the period 1988 to 2007. Note that both the EAFE and the Emerging Markets indexes feature higher risk than the S&P 500 Index. The Emerging Markets return has been high, but the EAFE return has been low compared to the U.S. stock and bond markets.

	S&P 500	BONDS	EAFE	EMERGING MARKETS
Average	13.4%	9.6%	8.3%	16.8%
Std. Deviation	17.0	10.2	18.6	32.6

The correlations among these markets appear below:

CORRELATION	S&P 500	BONDS	EAFE
S&P 500	1		
Bonds	0.17	1	
EAFE	0.63	−0.13	1
Emerging Markets	0.33	−0.14	0.66

The correlation between the S&P 500 Index and the MSCI EAFE is 0.63 and between the Emerging Markets is 0.33. These correlations indicate that diversification might work. Even better diversification appears to be possible between the U.S. Treasury Bond Market and the EAFE and Emerging Markets indexes—look at the negative correlations!

Source: **www.mscibarra.com**

 want to know more?   **Key Words to Search for Updates: international diversification, global asset allocation**

 Panel B of Table 9.6 shows correlations between stocks, bonds, and T-bills. At 0.11, the correlation between stocks and bonds is fairly small. The small correlation allows for the possibility of good risk reduction by adding bonds to a stock portfolio. Therefore, a well-diversified portfolio will contain both stocks and bonds.

 PORTFOLIO RETURN   A portfolio's return calculation is straightforward. A portfolio's return comes directly from the returns of the portfolio securities and the proportion of the portfolio invested in each security. For example, Disney stock earned −4.8 percent in 2007. The Bank of New York earned 19.4 percent over the same period. If you had invested a quarter of your money in Disney stock and three quarters of it in Bank of New York stock, then your portfolio return would be:

$$\text{Return contribution from Disney} + \text{Contribution from BNY}$$
$$= (0.25 \times -4.8\%) + (0.75 \times 19.4\%) = 13.35\%$$

To calculate the return on a three-stock portfolio, you will need the proportion of each stock in the portfolio and each stock's return. We typically call these proportions *weights*, signified by *w*. So, a portfolio with *n* securities will have a return of

$$R_p = (\text{Proportion of portfolio in first stock} \times \text{That stock's return}) \quad \textbf{(9-7)}$$
$$+ (\text{Second stock portion} \times \text{Second stock return}) + \cdots$$
$$= (w_1 \times R_1) + (w_2 \times R_2) + (w_3 \times R_3) + \cdots + (w_n \times R_n) = \sum_{i=1}^{n} w_i R_i$$

where the sum of the weights, *w*, must equal one. The portfolio's rate of return is a simple weighted sum of the returns of each stock in the portfolio. Investors choose portfolio weights by determining how much of each stock they want in their portfolios. Ideally, investors will choose weights for their portfolios located on the efficient frontier (shown in Figure 9.3).

MATH COACH

When computing portfolio returns, use the decimal format for the portfolio weights and the percentage format for the security returns. The result of equation 9-7 will then be in percentage format.

 For interactive versions of this example visit www.mhhe.com/can1e

EXAMPLE 9-4

COMPUTING PORTFOLIO RETURNS

At the beginning of 2007, you owned $5,000 of Disney stock, $10,000 of Bank of New York stock, and $15,000 of IBM stock. In 2007, Disney, Bank of New York, and IBM returned −4.8 percent, 19.4 percent, and 12.8 percent, respectively. What is your portfolio's return?

LG7

SOLUTION:

First determine your portfolio weights. The three stocks make up a $30,000 portfolio. Disney makes up a 16.67 percent (= $5,000 ÷ $30,000) portion of the portfolio. Bank of New York stock makes up a 33.33 percent (=$10,000 ÷ $30,000) portion and IBM a 50.0 percent (=$15,000 ÷ $30,000) portion. The portfolio return can now be computed as:

$$R_p = (0.1667 \times -4.8\%) + (0.3333 \times 19.4\%) + (0.50 \times 12.8\%) = -0.80\% + 6.47\% + 6.40\% = 12.07\%$$

TIME OUT

9-5   Describe characteristics of companies that would be good to combine into a portfolio.

9-6   Explain why one portfolio made up of the same companies (but not in the same proportions) as another portfolio can be undesirable in comparison.

9-7   Combining which two companies in Table 9.6 would reduce risk the most? Combining which two would create the least diversification?

Business Application Solution

We can apply diversification concepts and modern portfolio theory to many more applications than just investment portfolios. For example, a manufacturing facility can be more efficient by producing different products during the year as demand dictates the need for one product over another. Salespeople can reduce the volatility of their commission incomes by having many different products to sell.

Although new project ideas have more risk, they could actually reduce the firm's overall risk if the projects diversify the firm's current business operations. You could evaluate this possibility by determining the correlation between the expected cash flows from each project idea with the expected cash flows of the firm's current business operations. A low or negative correlation would mean that the new projects could actually reduce risk for the firm. Note that some firms may find that their position is too conservative and that they wish to increase their risk to increase the possibility of earning a higher return.

Personal Application Solution

Since 1950, Tables 9.2 and 9.4 show that the bond market experienced an average return and standard deviation of 6.4 percent and 10.3 percent, respectively. Stocks earned a 13.2 percent return with a 17.0 percent standard deviation. The investor is correct in the belief that the stock market is riskier than the bond market.

However, Table 9.6 shows that the correlation between the stock and bond market is very low, at 0.11. This result allows some diversification opportunity. Indeed, a portfolio of 10 percent stocks and 90 percent bonds would have experienced an average annual return of 7.1 percent with a standard deviation of 9.7 percent since 1950. The broker is correct; adding a small portion of stocks to a bond portfolio actually reduces total risk!

summary of learning goals

In this chapter, we described how to measure investment risk and return. In the long run, higher risk should be associated with higher returns. In the short term, though, high-risk investments experience a great deal of volatility and produce extreme returns. Recall that the market does not reward all risks. We can, for example, reduce firm-specific risk by diversifying our holdings. We get the best diversification opportunities when we combine securities that have very different return characteristics.

LG1 **Compute an investment's dollar and percentage return.** Dollar returns on an investment include both the capital gain (or loss) from any price change in the investment and any income received. Stocks pay dividend income and fixed income securities, such as bonds, pay regularly scheduled interest payments as income. We can find the percentage return by dividing the dollar return by the investment's value at the beginning of the period. Percentage return is a more useful measure to compare performance among different securities. To make meaningful comparisons, we typically average annual percentage returns to assess the investment's historical performance.

LG2 **Find information about the historical returns and volatility for the stock, bond, and cash markets.** Stocks have earned an average 13.2 percent return per year since 1950. However, stock market performance can be very volatile. Investors have frequently seen double digit percentage stock price declines as well as spectacular increases. This high volatility is illustrated by the stock market's standard deviation of 17.0% on average returns of 13.2%.

Bonds have earned lower average returns of 6.4 percent annually, but have also experienced less risk (standard deviation of 10.3 percent). The cash market, as measured by T-bill performance, shows an average return and standard deviation of 4.9 percent and 2.8 percent, respectively.

LG3 **Measure and evaluate the total risk of an investment using standard deviations.** An investment's total risk encompasses the total range of expected outcomes. We measure the likelihood of any particular expected outcome by the past return volatility of the security. We calculate volatility using the statistical concept of the standard deviation of returns. A larger standard deviation indicates higher total risk.

LG4 **Recognize the risk/return relationship and its implications.** When low-return, safe investments are available, why would an investor take risk? The motivation for taking on riskier investments is that they offer a higher return. The performance and risk of the stock and bond markets over a long period of time illustrate the direct risk return relationship that lies at the heart of investment philosophy. Recognize that this relationship can be interpreted in the reverse. When an investment achieves a high return, know that it must be risky.

We commonly measure the risk-return relationship using the coefficient of variation (CoV). The CoV is the standard deviation of an investment's returns divided by its average return. The CoV reports the amount of risk taken for every one percent of return earned. So lower CoV values indicate more favorable risk-return relationships.

LG5 **Plan investments that take advantage of diversification and its impact on total risk.** Recall that an investment's total risk comprises firm-specific risk and market risk. Combining stocks can potentially reduce firm-specific risk in the portfolio. Firms whose returns differ from each other offer the best diversification possibilities. A correlation measures how two different stocks have performed over time relative to one another. Correlations range between −1 and +1. Combining stocks with low or negative correlations can significantly reduce firm-specific risk and thus reduce total risk in an investor's portfolio.

LG6 **Find efficient and optimal portfolios.** Investors want the highest return possible for their preferred risk level. If two portfolios have the same risk level, the one that gives the higher expected return dominates the other. A portfolio that has the highest expected return for its risk level dominates all other portfolios with same risk level; we call this dominating mix an efficient portfolio. The set of all efficient portfolios forms the efficient frontier. Investors pick the efficient portfolio with their own desired risk level to find their optimal portfolios.

LG7 **Compute a portfolio's return.** A portfolio's return comes directly from the returns of the securities in the portfolio and the proportions, or weights, of each investment in the portfolio. In other words, the portfolio return is the weighted average of the portfolio's securities' returns.

chapter equations

9-1   Dollar return = (Capital gain or loss) + Income
           = (Ending value − Beginning value) + Income

9-2   Percentage return = $\dfrac{\text{Ending value} - \text{Beginning value} + \text{Income}}{\text{Beginning value}} \times 100\%$

$$9\text{-}3 \quad \text{Average return} = \frac{\sum\limits_{t=1}^{N} \text{Return}_t}{N}$$

$$9\text{-}4 \quad \text{Standard deviation} = \sqrt{\frac{\sum\limits_{t=1}^{N} (\text{Return}_t - \text{Average return})^2}{N-1}}$$

$$9\text{-}5 \quad \text{Coefficient of variation} = \frac{\text{Standard deviation}}{\text{Average return}}$$

$$9\text{-}6 \quad \text{Total risk} = \text{Firm-specific risk} + \text{Market risk}$$

$$9\text{-}7 \quad R_p = (w_1 \times R_1) + (w_2 \times R_2) + (w_3 \times R_3) + \cdots + (w_n \times R_n) = \sum\limits_{i=1}^{n} w_i R_i$$

key terms

average returns, A measure summarizing the past performance of an investment. (p. 297)

coefficient of variation, A measure of risk to reward (standard deviation divided by average return) earned by an investment over a specific period of time. (p. 303)

correlation, A measurement of the co-movement between two variables that ranges between −1 and +1. (p. 309)

diversification, The process of putting money in different types of investments for the purpose of reducing the overall risk of the portfolio. (p. 304)

diversifiable risk, Another term for firm-specific risk. (p. 304)

dollar return, The amount of profit or loss from an investment denoted in dollars. (p. 296)

efficient portfolios, The set of portfolios that have the maximum expected return for each level of risk. (p. 306)

firm-specific risk, The portion of total risk that is attributable to firm or industry factors.

Firm-specific risk can be reduced through diversification. (p. 304)

market risk, The portion of total risk that is attributable to overall economic factors. (p. 304)

modern portfolio theory, A concept and procedure for combining securities into a portfolio to minimize risk. (p. 305)

nondiversifiable risk, Another term for market risk. (p. 304)

optimal portfolio, The best portfolio of securities for the investor's level of risk aversion. (p. 306)

percentage return, The dollar return characterized as a percentage of money invested. (p. 296)

portfolio, A combination of investment assets held by an investor. (p. 304)

standard deviation, A measure of past return volatility, or risk, of an investment. (p. 299)

total risk, The volatility of an investment, which includes current portions of firm-specific risk and market risk. (p. 299)

self-test problems with solutions

LG1, LG7

① Computing Returns Consider that you own the following position at the beginning of the year: 200 shares of US Bancorp at $29.89 per share, 300 shares of Micron Technology at $13.31 per share, and 250 shares of Hilton Hotels at $24.11 per share. During the year, US Bancorp and Hilton Hotels both paid a dividend of $1.39 and $0.16, respectively. At the end of the year, the stock prices of US Bancorp, Micron, and Hilton Hotels were $36.19, $13.12, and $34.90, respectively. What are the dollar and percentage return of the stocks and the return of the portfolio?

Solution:

You can compute the dollar and percentage returns as:

$$\text{US Bancorp dollar return} = 200 \times (\$36.19 - \$29.89 + \$1.39) = \$1,535.00$$
$$\text{Percent return} = \$1,535.00 \div (200 \times \$29.89) = 25.73\%$$
$$\text{Micron dollar return} = 300 \times (\$13.12 - \$13.31) = \$-57.00$$
$$\text{Percent return} = \$-57.00 \div (300 \times \$13.31) = -1.43\%$$
$$\text{Hilton Hotels dollar return} = 250 \times (\$34.90 - \$24.11 + \$0.16) = \$2,737.50$$
$$\text{Percent return} = \$2,737.50 \div (250 \times \$24.11) = 45.42\%$$

Now you need the portfolio weights of each stock. The total value of the portfolio at the beginning of the year was:

$$\text{Beginning of year value} = 200 \times \$29.89 + 300 \times \$13.31 + 250 \times \$24.11$$
$$= \$15,998.50$$

So the stock weights are:

$$\text{US Bancorp weight} = 200 \times \$29.89 \div \$15,998.50 = 0.3737$$
$$\text{Micron weight} = 300 \times \$13.31 \div \$15,998.50 = 0.2496$$
$$\text{Hilton Hotels weight} = 250 \times \$24.11 \div \$15,998.50 = 0.3768$$

Now compute the portfolio return as:

$$\text{Portfolio return} = 0.3737 \times 25.73\% + 0.2496 \times -1.43\% + 0.3768 \times 45.42\%$$
$$= 26.37\%$$

2 **Risk and Returns** The annual returns for GlaxoSmithKline and for Aetna are show in the table.

	GLAXOSMITHKLINE	AETNA
2006	7.94%	−8.34%
2005	9.87	51.28
2004	5.63	84.70
2003	28.73	64.49
2002	−21.59	24.70

What is the average return and standard deviation of returns for these two firms? What is the average return and risk of a portfolio consisting of 75 percent of GlaxoSmithKline and 25 percent Aetna?

Solution:

Using the average and standard deviation equations for the GlaxoSmithKline returns results in

$$\text{Average} = \frac{7.94\% + 9.87\% + 5.36\% + 28.73\% - 21.59\%}{5}$$
$$= \frac{30.57\%}{5} = 6.11\%$$

315

and Standard deviation of

$$\sqrt{\frac{\begin{array}{c}(7.94\% - 6.11\%)^2 + (9.87\% - 6.11\%)^2 + (5.36\% - 6.11\%)^2 \\ +(28.73\% - 6.11\%)^2 + (-21.59\% - 6.11\%)^2\end{array}}{5-1}}$$
$$= \sqrt{324.00} = 18.00\%$$

For the portfolio, to compute the return for the portfolio each year, use the 75 percent and 25 percent weights:

$$0.75 \times 7.94\% + 0.25 \times -8.34\% = 3.87\%.$$

The risk and return of these two stocks and the portfolio are:

	GLAXOSMITHKLINE	AETNA	75/25 PORTFOLIO
2006	7.94%	−8.34%	3.87%
2005	9.87	51.28	20.22
2004	5.63	84.70	25.39
2003	28.73	64.49	37.67
2002	−21.59	24.70	−10.02
Average	6.11	43.36	15.43
Std. Dev	18.00	36.19	18.70

This combination of the two stocks forms a portfolio that is only slightly riskier than GlaxoSmithKline alone, but earns more than twice the return of GlaxoSmithKline.

 LG4

3 **Risk versus Return** You have gathered average return and standard deviation data for five stocks (A–E). How have these stocks performed on a risk-versus-return basis? Compute the coefficient of variation for each one.

ANNUAL RETURN	COMPANY A	B	C	D	E
Average	13%	14%	9%	11%	9%
Standard deviation	35	44	18	25	30

Solution:
Compute the CoVs as:

$$CoV_A = \frac{35\%}{13\%} = 2.69 \qquad CoV_B = \frac{44\%}{14\%} = 3.14$$

$$CoV_C = \frac{18\%}{9\%} = 2.00 \qquad CoV_D = \frac{25\%}{11\%} = 2.27$$

$$CoV_E = \frac{30\%}{9\%} = 3.33$$

Since lower values represent a better risk-reward trade-off, the stocks can be ordered from best to worst as C, D, A, B, and E.

4 **Diversification Opportunities** You have also computed the correlation between each of the five stocks in ST-3. These correlations are reported in the table below. Assess which stocks should be combined into a portfolio.

CORRELATIONS	A	B	C	D
B	0.45			
C	0.32	0.25		
D	0.11	−0.18	0.33	
E	0.20	−0.07	0.35	0.95

Solution:

First, note that stocks D and E do not seem to provide much diversification potential with each other because they have a correlation of nearly 1, at 0.95. They also have similar correlations with the other stocks. For example, stock D has a correlation with stock C of 0.33 while stock E has a correlation with stock C of 0.35. Realize that you gain very little in owning both stock D and stock E. Therefore, select stock D for the portfolio because it has exhibited a better risk-reward relationship (see ST-3). Also note that all of the other stocks appear to have reasonably low correlations with one another and therefore would benefit a portfolio. You should look into forming a portfolio of stocks A, B, C, and D.

questions

1. Why is the percentage return a more useful measure than the dollar return? *(LG1)*

2. Characterize the historical return, risk, and risk-return relationship of the stock, bond, and cash markets. *(LG2)*

3. How do we define risk in this chapter and how do we measure it? *(LG3)*

4. What are the two components of total risk? Which component is part of the risk-return relationship? Why? *(LG3)*

5. What's the source of firm-specific risk? What's the source of market risk? *(LG3)*

6. Which company is likely to have lower total risk, General Electric or Coca-Cola? Why? *(LG3)*

7. Can a company change its total risk level over time? How? *(LG3)*

8. What does the coefficient of variation measure? Why is a lower value better for the investor? *(LG4)*

9. You receive an investment newsletter advertisement in the mail. The letter claims that you should invest in a stock that has doubled the return of the S&P 500 Index over the last three months. It also claims that this stock is a surefire safe bet for the future. Explain how these two claims are inconsistent with finance theory. *(LG4)*

10. What does diversification do to the risk and return characteristics of a portfolio? *(LG5)*

11. Describe the diversification potential of two assets with a −0.8 correlation. What's the potential if the correlation is +0.8? *(LG5)*

12. You are a risk averse investor with a low-risk portfolio of bonds. How is it possible that adding some stocks (which are riskier than bonds) to the portfolio can lower the total risk of the portfolio? *(LG5)*

13. You own only two stocks in your portfolio but want to add more. When you add a third stock, the total risk of your portfolio declines. When you add a tenth stock to the portfolio, the total risk declines. Adding which stock, the third or the tenth, likely reduced the total risk more? Why? *(LG5)*

14. Many employees believe that their employer's stock is less likely to lose half of its value than a well diversified portfolio of stocks. Explain why this belief is erroneous. *(LG5)*

15. Explain what we mean when we say that one portfolio dominates another portfolio. *(LG6)*

16. Explain what the efficient frontier is and why it is important to investors. *(LG6)*

17. If an investor's desired risk level changes over time, should the investor change the composition of his or her portfolio? How? *(LG6)*

18. Say you own 200 shares of Mattel and 100 shares of RadioShack. Would your portfolio return be different if you instead owned 100 shares of Mattel and 200 shares of RadioShack? Why? *(LG7)*

problems

basic problems

9-1 **Investment Return** FedEx Corp stock ended the previous year at $103.39 per share. It paid a $0.35 per share dividend last year. It ended last year at $106.69. If you owned 300 shares of FedEx, what was your dollar return and percent return? *(LG1)*

9-2 **Investment Return** Sprint Nextel Corp stock ended the previous year at $23.36 per share. It paid a $2.37 per share dividend last year. It ended last year at $18.89. If you owned 500 shares of Sprint, what was your dollar return and percent return? *(LG1)*

9-3 **Total Risk** Rank the following three stocks by their level of total risk, highest to lowest. Rail Haul has an average return of 12 percent and standard deviation of 25 percent. The average return and standard deviation of Idol Staff are 15 percent and 35 percent; and of Poker-R-Us are 9 percent and 20 percent. *(LG3)*

9-4 **Total Risk** Rank the following three stocks by their total risk level, highest to lowest. Night Ryder has an average return of 13 percent and standard deviation of 29 percent. The average return and standard deviation of WholeMart are 11 percent and 25 percent; and of Fruit Fly are 16 percent and 40 percent. *(LG3)*

9-5 **Risk versus Return** Rank the following three stocks by their risk-return relationship, best to worst. Rail Haul has an average return of 12 percent and standard deviation of 25 percent. The average return and standard deviation of Idol Staff are 15 percent and 35 percent; and of Poker-R-Us are 9 percent and 20 percent. *(LG4)*

9-6 **Risk versus Return** Rank the following three stocks by their risk-return relationship, best to worst. Night Ryder has an average return of 13 percent and standard deviation of 29 percent. The average return and standard deviation of WholeMart are 11 percent and 25 percent; and of Fruit Fly are 16 percent and 40 percent. *(LG4)*

9-7 **Dominant Portfolios** Determine which one of these three portfolios dominates another. Name the dominated portfolio and the portfolio that dominates it. Portfolio Blue has an expected return of 12 percent and risk of 18 percent. The expected return and risk of portfolio Yellow are 13 percent and 17 percent, and for the Purple portfolio are 14 percent and 20 percent. *(LG6)*

9-8 **Dominant Portfolios** Determine which one of the three portfolios dominates another. Name the dominated portfolio and the portfolio that dominates it. Portfolio Green has an expected return of 15 percent and risk of 21 percent. The expected return and risk of portfolio Red are 13 percent and 17 percent, and for the Orange portfolio are 13 percent and 16 percent. *(LG6)*

9-9 **Portfolio Weights** An investor owns $4,000 of Adobe Systems stock, $5,000 of Dow Chemical, and $6,000 of Office Depot. What are the portfolio weights of each stock? *(LG7)*

9-10 **Portfolio Weights** An investor owns $3,000 of Adobe Systems stock, $6,000 of Dow Chemical, and $7,000 of Office Depot. What are the portfolio weights of each stock? *(LG7)*

9-11 **Portfolio Return** Year-to-date, Oracle had earned a −1.34 percent return. During the same time period, Valero Energy earned 7.96 percent and McDonald's earned 0.88 percent. If you have a portfolio made up of 30 percent Oracle, 20 percent Valero Energy, and 50 percent McDonald's, what is your portfolio return? *(LG7)*

9-12 **Portfolio Return** Year-to-date, Yum Brands had earned a 3.80 percent return. During the same time period, Raytheon earned 4.26 percent and Coca-Cola earned −0.46 percent. If you have a portfolio made up of 30 percent Yum Brands, 30 percent Raytheon, and 40 percent Coca-Cola, what is your portfolio return? *(LG7)*

intermediate problems

9-13 **Average Return** The past five monthly returns for Kohls are 3.54 percent, 3.62 percent, −1.68 percent, −1.42 percent, and 8.75 percent. What is the average monthly return? *(LG1)*

9-14 **Average Return** The past five monthly returns for PG&E are 2.14 percent, −1.37 percent, 3.77 percent, 6.47 percent, and 3.58 percent. What is the average monthly return? *(LG1)*

9-15 **Standard Deviation** Compute the standard deviation of Kohls' monthly returns shown in problem 9-13. *(LG3)*

9-16 **Standard Deviation** Compute the standard deviation of PG&E's monthly returns shown in problem 9-14. *(LG3)*

9-17 **Risk versus Return in Bonds** Assess the risk-return relationship of the bond market (see Tables 9.2 and 9.4) during each decade since 1950. *(LG2, LG4)*

9-18 **Risk versus Return in T-bills** Assess the risk-return relationship in T-bills (see Tables 9.2 and 9.4) during each decade since 1950. *(LG2, LG4)*

9-19 **Diversifying** Consider the characteristics of the following three stocks:

	EXPECTED RETURN	STANDARD DEVIATION
Thumb Devices	13%	23%
Air Comfort	10%	19%
Sport Garb	10%	17%

The correlation between Thumb Devices and Air Comfort is −0.12. The correlation between Thumb Devices and Sport Garb is −0.13. The correlation between Air Comfort and Sport Garb is 0.85. If you can pick only two stocks for your portfolio, which would you pick? Why? *(LG4, LG5)*

9-20 **Diversifying** Consider the characteristics of the following three stocks:

	EXPECTED RETURN	STANDARD DEVIATION
Pic Image	11%	19%
Tax Help	10%	19%
Warm Wear	14%	24%

The correlation between Pic Image and Tax Help is 0.88. The correlation between Pic Image and Warm Wear is −0.21. The correlation between Tax Help and Warm Wear is −0.19. If you can pick only two stocks for your portfolio, which would you pick? Why? *(LG4, LG5)*

9-21 **Portfolio Weights** If you own 300 shares of Alaska Air at $42.88, 350 shares of Best Buy at $51.32, and 250 shares of Ford Motor at $8.51, what are the portfolio weights of each stock? *(LG7)*

9-22 **Portfolio Weights** If you own 400 shares of Xerox at $17.34, 500 shares of Qwest at $8.15, and 350 shares of Liz Claiborne at $44.73, what are the portfolio weights of each stock? *(LG7)*

9-23 **Portfolio Return** At the beginning of the month, you owned $5,500 of General Motors, $7,500 of Starbucks, and $9,000 of Nike. The monthly returns for General Motors, Starbucks, and Nike were 6.80 percent, −1.36 percent, and −0.22 percent. What is your portfolio return? *(LG7)*

9-24 **Portfolio Return** At the beginning of the month, you owned $6,000 of News Corp, $5,000 of First Data, and $8,500 of Whirlpool. The monthly returns for News Corp, First Data, and Whirlpool were 8.24 percent, −2.59 percent, and 10.13 percent. What's your portfolio return? *(LG7)*

advanced problems

9-25 **Asset Allocation** You have a portfolio with an asset allocation of 50 percent stocks, 40 percent long-term Treasury bonds, and 10 percent T-bills. Use these weights and the returns in Table 9.2 to compute the return of the portfolio in the year 2000 and each year since. Then compute the average annual return and standard deviation of the portfolio and compare them with the risk and return profile of each individual asset class. *(LG2, LG5)*

9-26 **Asset Allocation** You have a portfolio with an asset allocation of 60 percent stocks, 30 percent long-term Treasury bonds, and 10 percent T-bills. Use these weights and the returns in Table 9.2 to compute the return of the portfolio in the year 2000 and each year since. Then compute the average annual return and standard deviation of the portfolio and compare them with the risk and return profile of each individual asset class. *(LG2, LG5)*

9-27 **Portfolio Weights** You have $15,000 to invest. You want to purchase shares of Alaska Air at $42.88, Best Buy at $51.32, and Ford Motor at $8.51. How many shares of each company should you purchase so that your portfolio consists of 30 percent Alaska Air, 40 percent Best Buy, and 30 percent Ford Motor? Report only whole stock shares. *(LG7)*

9-28 **Portfolio Weights** You have $20,000 to invest. You want to purchase shares of Xerox at $17.34, Qwest at $8.15, and Liz Claiborne at $44.73.

How many shares of each company should you purchase so that your portfolio consists of 25 percent Xerox, 40 percent Qwest, and 35 percent Liz Claiborne? Report only whole stock shares. *(LG7)*

9-29 Portfolio Return The table below shows your stock positions at the beginning of the year, the dividends that each stock paid during the year, and the stock prices at the end of the year. What is your portfolio dollar return and percentage return? *(LG7)*

COMPANY	SHARES	BEGINNING OF YEAR PRICE	DIVIDEND PER SHARE	END OF YEAR PRICE
Washington Mutual	300	$43.50	$2.06	$43.43
Pepsico	200	59.08	1.16	62.55
JDS Uniphase	500	18.88		16.66
Duke Energy	250	27.45	1.26	33.21

9-30 Portfolio Return The table below shows your stock positions at the beginning of the year, the dividends that each stock paid during the year, and the stock prices at the end of the year. What is your portfolio dollar return and percentage return? *(LG7)*

COMPANY	SHARES	BEGINNING OF YEAR PRICE	DIVIDEND PER SHARE	END OF YEAR PRICE
Johnson Controls	300	$72.91	$1.17	$85.92
Medtronic	200	57.57	0.41	53.51
Direct TV	500	24.94		24.39
Qualcomm	250	43.08	0.45	37.79

9-31 Risk, Return, and Their Relationship Consider the following annual returns of Estee Lauder and Lowe's Companies:

	ESTEE LAUDER	LOWE'S COMPANIES
2006	23.4%	−6.0%
2005	−26.0	16.1
2004	17.6	4.2
2003	49.9	48.0
2002	−16.8	−19.0

Compute each stock's average return, standard deviation, and coefficient of variation. Which stock appears better? Why? *(LG3, LG4)*

9-32 Risk, Return, and Their Relationship Consider the following annual returns of Molson Coors and International Paper:

	MOLSON COORS	INTERNATIONAL PAPER
2006	16.3%	4.5%
2005	−9.7	−17.5
2004	36.5	−0.2
2003	−6.9	26.6
2002	16.2	−11.1

Compute each stock's average return, standard deviation, and coefficient of variation. Which stock appears better? Why? *(LG3, LG4)*

9-33 **Excel Problem** Below are the monthly returns for May 2002 to June 2007 of three international stock indices: All Ordinaries of Australia, Nikkei 225 of Japan, and FTSE 100 of England.

DATE	ALL ORDINARIES (AUSTRALIA)	NIKKEI 225 (JAPAN)	FTSE 100 (ENGLAND)	DATE	ALL ORDINARIES (AUSTRALIA)	NIKKEI 225 (JAPAN)	FTSE 100 (ENGLAND)
Jun 2007	1.82%	0.55%	1.65%	Nov 2004	2.80%	5.41%	2.36%
May 2007	−0.49	1.47	−0.20	Oct 2004	4.13	1.19	1.71
Apr 2007	2.98	2.73	2.67	Sep 2004	3.04	−0.48	1.17
Mar 2007	3.00	0.65	2.24	Aug 2004	3.17	−2.33	2.50
Feb 2007	2.79	−1.80	2.21	Jul 2004	0.45	−2.15	1.05
Jan 2007	1.02	1.27	−0.51	Jun 2004	0.45	−4.50	−1.14
Dec 2006	2.01	0.91	−0.28	May 2004	2.12	5.54	0.75
Nov 2006	3.35	5.85	2.84	Apr 2004	1.44	−4.47	−1.31
Oct 2006	2.03	−0.76	−1.31	Mar 2004	−0.25	0.40	2.37
Sep 2006	4.69	1.69	2.83	Feb 2004	1.30	6.10	−2.37
Aug 2006	0.65	−0.08	0.93	Jan 2004	2.71	2.40	2.31
Jul 2006	2.48	4.42	−0.37	Dec 2003	−0.68	1.00	−1.93
Jun 2006	−1.53	−0.31	1.63	Nov 2003	3.45	5.70	3.09
May 2006	1.24	0.24	1.91	Oct 2003	−2.64	−4.35	1.28
Apr 2006	−4.51	−8.51	−4.97	Sep 2003	3.34	3.33	4.80
Mar 2006	2.35	−0.90	0.98	Aug 2003	−0.83	−1.20	−1.68
Feb 2006	4.28	5.27	2.99	Jul 2003	3.10	8.16	0.10
Jan 2006	−0.04	−2.67	0.54	Jun 2003	3.59	5.29	3.12
Dec 2005	3.64	3.34	2.52	May 2003	0.64	7.82	−0.42
Nov 2005	2.73	8.33	3.61	Apr 2003	0.30	7.57	3.11
Oct 2005	3.87	9.30	1.99	Mar 2003	4.29	−1.77	8.65
Sep 2005	−3.92	0.24	−2.93	Feb 2003	2.53	−4.67	−1.16
Aug 2005	4.06	9.35	3.41	Jan 2003	−5.35	0.28	2.47
Jul 2005	1.54	4.32	0.28	Dec 2002	−1.35	−2.79	−9.47
Jun 2005	2.76	2.72	3.31	Nov 2002	−1.64	−6.91	−5.49
May 2005	3.92	2.73	3.01	Oct 2002	1.01	6.66	3.21
Apr 2005	3.23	2.43	3.38	Sep 2002	2.28	−7.92	8.54
Mar 2005	−3.84	−5.66	−1.89	Aug 2002	−4.73	−2.45	−11.96
Feb 2005	−1.34	−0.61	−1.49	Jul 2002	1.36	−2.62	−0.45
Jan 2005	1.21	3.10	2.39	Jun 2002	−4.13	−7.00	−8.81
Dec 2004	1.32	−0.88	0.79	May 2002	−4.87	−9.71	−8.43

a. Compute and compare each indices' monthly average return and standard deviation.

b. Compute the correlation between (1) All Ordinaries and Nikkei 225, (2) All Ordinaries and FTSE 100, and (3) Nikkei 225 and FTSE 100, and compare them.

c. Form a portfolio consisting of one-third of each of the indices and show the portfolio return each year, and the portfolio's return and standard deviation.

 research it! Following a Portfolio

Following stocks in a portfolio is easier than ever. Many financial Web sites have the capability to follow the stocks in your portfolio over time. Just enter your stocks, the number of shares, your purchase price, and your commission cost and you can see how your portfolio is doing. These portfolio managers will update your portfolio as stock prices change, minute to minute. Yahoo! Finance has a portfolio management tool. Go to the site and start a portfolio to watch (which requires free registration). Try entering symbols EBAY, T, LMT, DUK, and GSK. As a start, assume you own 200 shares of each. You watch the value of the portfolio change and see how each stock is doing every day. (http://finance.yahoo.com)

www.mhhe.com/can1e

integrated minicase: Diversifying with Other Asset Classes

Many more types of investments are available besides stocks, bonds, and cash securities. Many people invest in real estate and in precious metals, primarily gold. What are the risk and return characteristics of these investments and do they provide diversification opportunities to the typical stock investor?

You can invest in real estate in many ways. You can build properties, own rental units, and trade raw land. These activities take enormous time and expertise. One of the easiest ways to invest in real estate is through *real estate investment trusts* (REITs) that trade like stocks on the stock exchanges. A REIT represents ownership in a portfolio consisting of a pool of real estate assets. An index of all REITs is a good measure of the performance of the real estate market. The table below shows the annual returns for the All REITs Index alongside the returns of the S&P 500 Index.

	S&P 500 INDEX	ALL REITs INDEX	GOLD PRICE CHANGES
1975	37.2%	36.3%	−19.9%
1976	23.8	49.0	−4.1
1977	−7.2	19.1	22.6
1978	6.6	−1.6	37.0
1979	18.4	30.5	126.5
1980	32.4	28.0	15.2
1981	−4.9	8.6	−32.6
1982	21.4	31.6	14.9
1983	22.5	25.5	−16.3
1984	6.3	14.8	−19.2
1985	32.2	5.9	5.7
1986	18.5	19.2	21.3
1987	5.2	−10.7	22.2
1988	16.8	11.4	−15.3
1989	31.5	−1.8	−2.8
1990	−3.2	−17.3	−1.5
1991	30.6	35.7	−10.1
1992	7.7	12.2	−5.7
1993	10.0	18.5	17.7
1994	1.3	0.8	−2.2
1995	37.4	18.3	1.0
1996	23.1	35.8	−4.6
1997	33.4	18.9	−21.4
1998	28.6	−18.8	−0.8
1999	21.0	−6.5	0.9
2000	−9.1	25.9	−5.4
2001	−11.9	15.5	0.7
2002	−22.1	5.2	25.6
2003	28.7	38.5	19.9
2004	10.9	30.4	4.6
2005	4.9	8.3	17.8
2006	15.8	34.4	24.0
2007	3.5	−17.8	31.1

Gold has been a highly sought-after asset all over the world, and has retained at least some economic value over thousands of years. The United States has had a very chaotic history with gold. Americans have sought to "strike it rich" through gold rushes in North Carolina (early 1800s), California and Nevada

(continued)

(mid-1800s), and Alaska (late 1800s). Struggling in the Great Depression, President Franklin D. Roosevelt ordered U.S. citizens to hand in all the gold they possessed. The ban on U.S. citizens owning gold was not lifted until the end of 1974. The table also shows the return from gold prices.

The returns for stocks, real estate, and gold are all volatile. However, during many years, the return of one asset is up while the others are down. This looks promising for diversification opportunities.

a. Using a spreadsheet, compute the average return and standard deviation of each of the three asset classes.

b. Compute the annual returns of a portfolio consisting of 50% stocks/40% real estate/10% gold. What is the average return and standard deviation of this portfolio? Also compute the average return and standard deviation of the following portfolios: 75%/20%/5% and 80%/5%/15%. How do these portfolios perform compared to owning just stocks?

c. Plot the average return and standard deviation of the three assets and the three portfolios on a risk-return graph like Figure 9.3.

ANSWERS TO TIME OUT

9-1   Dividends are a large portion of the return realized by stockholders in the long run. In any given year, the capital gain or loss may dominate the dividend. In many years, the capital gain is low and thus the dividend is a larger portion of the return. Since the capital gain is frequently negative and the dividend is always positive, the dividend plays an important role over time.

9-2   Use the future value equation. For example, for stocks $FV_{\text{end of 1950s}} = \$10,000 \times (1 + 0.209)^{10} = \$66,721$.

Answers are:

	IN STOCKS	IN BONDS	IN CASH
1950s	$66,721	$10,000	$12,190
1960s	23,030	11,720	14,802
1970s	20,610	17,408	18,422
1980s	53,232	35,478	23,457
1990s	56,947	24,782	16,134
2000s	12,279	19,491	12,766

9-3   Standard deviation of returns measures the variability of returns over time. This variability gives investors an idea of the likely range of potential returns.

9-4   The standard deviation (the numerator in the CoV equation) for individual companies is much higher than for the stock market as a whole. This is because it is a measure of total risk, which includes much firm-specific risk for firms. But firm-specific risk is diversified away in the overall market.

9-5   It is useful to find companies whose returns behave differently from each other over time. This comes about from companies that have different

(continued)

businesses. This is measured by the statistical tool, correlation. It is also good if these companies have high expected returns.

9-6   The return on a portfolio depends on the proportions of each asset owned in the portfolio and the returns that each of those assets generates. If the first portfolio is weighted toward poor-performing stocks and the second owns more of the high-performing stocks, the first portfolio will be undesirable in comparison.

9-7   The lowest correlation in Table 9.6 is between the Bank of New York and Newmont Mining. So this combination has the best chance of reducing risk. The least opportunity for diversification is between General Electric and Citigroup because they have the highest correlation.

chapter 10:
ESTIMATING RISK AND RETURN

 Learning Goals

LG1 Compute forward-looking expected return and risk.

LG2 Understand risk premiums.

LG3 Know and apply the Capital Asset Pricing Model (CAPM).

LG4 Calculate and apply beta, a measure of market risk.

LG5 Differentiate among the different levels of market efficiency and their implications.

LG6 Calculate and explain investors' required return and risk.

LG7 Use the constant growth rate model to compute required return.

I n Chapters 9 and 10, we explore methods to find the return that individual or institutional investors require to make a particular investment attractive. In Chapter 9, we established a positive relationship between risk and return using historical data. Risk and return play an undeniable role as investors seek the best return for the least risk. But financial managers and investors must make investment decisions armed only with their *expectations* about future risk and return. We need an exact specification that shows directly the amount of reward required for investors to take the level of risk in a given firm's stock or portfolio of securities.

Investors need to know how much risk they have to take to confidently expect a 10 percent return. Managers also want to know what return shareholders require, so that they can decide how to meet those expectations. In Chapter 11, we'll explore how managers conduct financial analysis to find the shareholders' required return. If we want to specify the exact risk-return relationship, we need to develop a better measure of *risk* for individuals and institutional investors. As we saw in Chapter 9, any firm's total risk is specific to that particular firm. But the market doesn't reward firm-specific risk, because investors can easily diversify away any single firm's specific risks by owning other offsetting firms' stocks to create a portfolio subject only to market or undiversifiable risk. So, we need to find just the market risk portion of total risk for

viewpoints

Business Application

Consider that you work in the finance department of a large corporation. Your team is analyzing several new projects the firm can pursue. To complete the analysis, the team needs to know what return stockholders require from the firm.

You are to estimate this required return. Shareholders' expected return will depend on your company's risk level. What information do you need to gather and how might you compute this return? **(See solution on p. 345)**

Personal Application

You have just started your first job in the corporate world and need to make some retirement plan decisions. The company's 401(k) retirement plan offers three investment choices: a stock portfolio, a bond portfolio, and a money market deposit. For your allocation, you decide to contribute $200 per month to the stock portfolio, $100 to the bond portfolio, and $50 to the money market deposit.

What risk level are you taking in your retirement portfolio and what return should you expect over the long-run? **(See solution on p. 345)**

A practice test can be found on the Online Learning Center at
www.mhhe.com/can1e

investors. The theory to find the market risk portion of stock ownership extends modern portfolio theory. Our search to find market risk will lead us to the capital asset pricing model (CAPM), which utilizes a measure of market risk called beta. CAPM's risk-return specification provides us a powerful tool to make better investment decisions.

Corporate finance managers and investment professionals use the beta measure commonly. But like any theory, CAPM has its limitations. We'll discuss the CAPM's limitations and concerns about beta and propose an alternate required return measure. Whether beta or any other risk-return specification is useful relies in part on whether a stock's price represents a fair estimate of the true company value. Stock price validity and reliability—their general correctness—is vitally important both to investors and corporate managers.

 ## 10.1 Expected Returns

In the previous chapter, we characterized risk and return in historical terms. We defined a stock's return as the actual profit realized while holding the stock or the average return over a longer period. We described risk simply as the standard deviation of those returns—a term already familiar to you from your statistics classes. So, we did a good job describing the risk and return that the stock experienced *in the past.* But do those risk-and-return figures hold into the future? Firms can quite possibly change their stocks' risk level by substantially changing their business. If a firm takes on riskier new projects over time, or changes the nature of its business, the firm itself will become riskier. Similarly, firms can reduce their risk level—and hence, their stock's riskiness—by choosing low-risk new projects. Both investors and firms find expected return, a forward-looking return calculation that includes risk measures, very useful to estimate future stock performance.

 ### Expected Return and Risk

We can attribute a company's business success over a year partly to its management talent, strategies, and other firm-specific activities. Overall economic conditions will also affect a firm's level of success or failure. Consider a steel manufacturer—Nucor Corp. The steel business closely follows economic trends. In a good economy, demand for steel is strong as builders and manufacturers step up building and production. During economic recessions, demand for steel falls off quickly. So, if we want to assess Nucor's probabilities for success next year, we know that we must look partly at Nucor's managerial ability and partly at the economic outlook.

Unfortunately, we cannot accurately predict what the economy will be like next year. Predicting economic activity is like predicting the weather—forecasts give the **probability** of rain or sunshine. Economists cannot say for sure whether the economy will be good or bad next year. Instead, they may forecast a 70 percent chance that the economy will be good and a 30 percent chance of a recession. Similarly, analysts might say that given Nucor's managerial talent, if the economy is good, Nucor will perform well and the stock will increase 20 percent. If the economy goes into a recession, then Nucor's stock will fall 10 percent. So what return do you expect from Nucor? The return still depends on the state of the economy.

This leads us directly to a key concept: **expected return.** We compute expected return by multiplying each possible return by the probability, *p,* of that return occurring. We then sum them (recall that all probabilities must add to one). In Nucor's case, the expected return would be 11 percent [= (0.7 × 20%) + (0.3 × −10%)]. Of course, nothing is quite that simple. Economists seldom predict simple two-state views of the economy as in the above example. Rather, economists give much more detailed forecasts (like three states: red-hot economy, average expansion, and recession). So our general equation for a stock's expected return with *S* different conditions of the economy is:

$$\text{Expected return} = (p_1 \times \text{Return}_1) + (p_2 \times \text{Return}_2) + (p_3 \times \text{Return}_3) \quad \textbf{(10-1)}$$

$$+ \cdots + p_s \times \text{Return}_s = \sum_{j=1}^{s} p_j \times \text{Return}_j$$

The result of this expected return calculation has some interesting properties. First, the expected return figure expresses what the average return would be over time if the probabilistic states of the economy occur as predicted. For example, the 70/30 **probability distribution** for good/recession economic states suggests that the economy will be good in 7 of the next 10 years, earning Nucor shareholders a 20 percent return in each of those years. Shareholders would lose 10 percent in each of the three recession years. So the *average return* over those 10 years would be 11 percent, the same as the expected return. The second interesting property: The expected return itself will not likely occur during any one year. Remember that Nucor will earn either a return of 20 percent or −10 percent. Yet its expected return is 11 percent, a value that it cannot earn because we have no economic condition for which the return is 11 percent. This illustration seems extreme because we used only two economic states. Any real economic forecast would instead include a probability distribution of many potential economic conditions.

We can also characterize risk via this expected return figure. The expected return procedure shows potential return possibilities, but we don't know which one will actually occur, so we face uncertainty. In the last chapter, we measured risk using the standard deviation of returns over time. We can use the same principle to measure risk for expected return. What range of different expected returns will Nucor exhibit from the expected return of 11 percent? In our two-state description of the economy, the deviation could be either 9 percent (= 20% − 11%) or −21 percent (= −10% − 11%). We compute the standard deviation of expected returns the same way we did for historical returns. We square the deviations, then multiply by the probability of that deviation occurring, and then sum them all up. So Nucor's return variance is 189.0 [= (0.7 × 9²) + (0.3 × −21²)]. As a final step, we take the square root of our result to put the figure back into sensible terms.

The standard deviation for Nucor is 13.75 percent (= √189). The general equation for the standard deviation of *S* different economic states is:

$$\text{Standard deviation} = \sqrt{\begin{array}{l} p_1 \times (\text{Return}_1 - \text{Expected return})^2 + p_2 \\ \times (\text{Return}_2 - \text{Expected return})^2 + \cdots \end{array}} \quad \textbf{(10-2)}$$

$$= \sqrt{\sum_{j=1}^{s} p_j \times (\text{Return}_j - \text{Expected return})^2}$$

EXAMPLE 10-1

For interactive versions of this example visit www.mhhe.com/can1e

EXPECTED RETURN AND RISK

 Bailey has a probability distribution for four possible states of the economy, as shown below. She has also calculated the return that Motor Music stock would earn in each state. Given this information, what's Motor Music's expected return and risk?

ECONOMIC STATE	PROBABILITY	RETURN
Fast growth	0.15	25%
Slow growth	0.60	15%
Recession	0.20	−5%
Depression	0.05	−20%

SOLUTION:

Bailey can compute the expected return using equation 10-1:

$$\text{Expected return} = (0.15 \times 25\%) + (0.60 \times 15\%) + (0.20 \times -5\%) + (0.05 \times -20\%) = 10.75\%$$

Then Bailey can compute the expected return by computing the standard deviation using equation 10-2:

$$\text{Standard deviation} = \sqrt{\begin{array}{l} 0.15 \times (25\% - 10.75\%)^2 + 0.60 \times (15\% - 10.75\%)^2 + 0.20 \\ \times (-5\% - 10.75\%)^2 + 0.05 \times (-20\% - 10.75\%)^2 \end{array}}$$

$$= \sqrt{30.46 + 10.84 + 49.61 + 47.28} = 11.76\%$$

The expected return and standard deviation are 10.75 percent and 11.76 percent, respectively. We could also show these equations in a table, such as:

ECONOMIC STATE	PROBABILITY	RETURN	$p \times$ RETURN	DEVIATION	SQUARED DEV.	$\times\, p$
Fast growth	0.15	25%	3.75%	14.25%	203.06	30.46
Slow growth	0.60	15	9.00	4.25	18.06	10.84
Recession	0.20	−5	−1.00	−15.75	248.06	49.61
Depression	0.05	−20	−1.00	−30.75	945.56	47.28
Sum =	1.0		10.75%	Square root =	138.19	11.76%

 ## Risk Premiums

Throughout the book, we have mentioned the positive relationship between expected return and risk. Consider this key question: You have a riskless investment available to you. The short-term government debt security, the T-bill, offers you a low return with no risk. Why would you invest in anything risky, when you could simply buy T-bills? The answer, of course, is that some investors want a higher return and are willing to take some risk to raise their returns. Investors who take on a little risk should expect a slightly higher return than the T-bill rate. People who take on higher risk levels should expect higher returns. Indeed, it's only logical that investors require this extra return to willingly take the added risk.

The expected return of an investment is often expressed in two parts, a risk-free return and a risky contribution. The return investors require for the risk level they take is called the **required return**:

$$\textbf{Required return} = \textbf{Risk-free rate} + \textbf{Risk premium} \qquad \textbf{(10-3)}$$

The Realized Average Annual Risk Premium for Stocks							table 10.1
	1950 to 2007	1950 to 1959	1960 to 1969	1970 to 1979	1980 to 1989	1990 to 1999	2000 to 2007
Risk premium	8.2%	18.8%	4.7%	1.2%	9.3%	14.1%	−0.5%

S&P 500 Index and T-bill rate data.

The *risk-free rate* is typically considered the return on U.S. government bonds and bills and equals the real interest rate and the expected inflation premium that we discussed in Chapter 8. The **risk premium** is the reward investors require for taking risk. How large are the rewards for taking risk? As we discussed in the previous chapter, the market doesn't reward all risks. The firm-specific portion of total risk for any stock can be diversified away, and since the investor takes on such risk out of ignorance or by mistake, an efficient market will not reward anyone for taking on this "superfluous" risk. So as we examine historical risk premiums, we do so with a diversified portfolio that contains no firm-specific risk.

Table 10.1 shows the average annual return on the S&P 500 Index minus the T-bill rate for different time periods. The remainder after we subtract the T-bill rate is the risk premium; in this case, it's the **market risk premium**—the reward for taking general (unsystematic) stock market risk. Since 1950, the average market risk premium has been 8.2 percent per year. Over the long run, this is the reward for taking stock market risk. The actual, realized risk premium during particular decades has varied. The average risk premium has been as high as 18.8 percent for the 1950s and as low as 1.2 percent during the 1970s. So far in the 2000s, the stock market return has been so poor that it has not beaten the risk-free rate. Investors require a risk premium for taking on market risk. But taking that risk also means that they will periodically experience poor returns.

TIME OUT

10-1 Describe the similarities between computing average return and expected return. Also, describe the similarities between expected return risk and historical risk.

10-2 Why would people take risks by investing their hard-earned money?

10.2 Market Risk

How much risk should you take to achieve the return you want over time? In the previous chapter we demonstrated that individual stocks and different portfolios exhibit different levels of total risk. Recall that the rewards for carrying risk apply only to the market risk (or undiversifiable) portion of total risk. But how do investors know how much of the 38.8 percent standard deviation of returns for Mattel Inc. is firm-specific risk and how much of that deviation is market risk? The answer to this important question will determine how much of a risk premium investors should require for Mattel. The attempt to specify an equation that relates a stock's required return to an appropriate risk premium is known as **asset pricing.**

The Market Portfolio

The best-known asset pricing equation is the **capital asset pricing model,** typically referred to as CAPM. Though many theorists formulated theories that, in the end, supported the CAPM's effectiveness, credit for the model goes to

figure 10.1

Maximizing Expected
Return

Panel A The Efficient Frontier

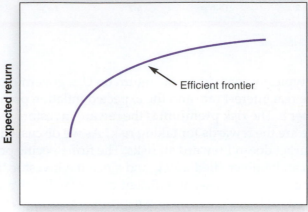

Panel B Add a Risk-free Asset and Do Even Better

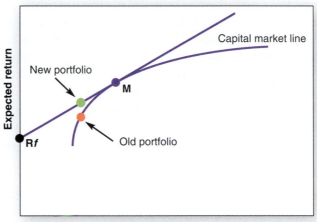

William Sharpe and John Lintner. Sharpe eventually won a Nobel Prize for his work in 1990. (Lintner passed away in 1983, and Nobel Prizes are not awarded posthumously.) Today, both investors and corporate finance professionals use CAPM widely. In developing the CAPM, Lintner and Sharpe sought to emphasize the individual investor's best strategy to maximize returns for a given amount of market risk.

CAPM starts with modern portfolio theory. Remember from the previous chapter that when you combine securities into a portfolio, you can find a set of portfolios that dominate all others. The best combinations possible use all the risky securities available (but not the risk-free asset) to create efficient frontier portfolios, as shown by the curved line in Figure 10.1, panel A. These portfolios represent combinations of various risky securities that give the highest expected return for each potential level of risk.

The idea of a risk premium in equation 10-3 implies a risk-free investment, like T-bills. Panel B shows where the risk-free asset would appear on the **capital market line** (CML). The risk-free asset must lie on the *y*-axis precisely because it carries no risk. Now we draw a line from the risk-free security to a point tangent to the efficient frontier. The CML relationship appears as a line because investments show a direct risk-reward relationship. You may recall from your economics classes that only one tangency point will be possible between this kind of curve and a straight line. The spot where the tangency occurs is called the **market**

portfolio, which has a special significance. The market portfolio represents ownership in all traded assets in the economy, so this portfolio provides maximum diversification. You can locate your optimal portfolio on this line by owning various combinations of the risk-free security and the market portfolio. If most of your money is invested in the market portfolio, then you will have a portfolio on the line that lies just to the left of the market portfolio dot in the graph. If you own just a little of the market portfolio and hold mostly risk-free securities, then your portfolio will lie on the line near the risk-free security dot. For your investments to lie on the line to the right of the market portfolio, you would have to invest all your money in the market portfolio, then borrow more money and invest these additional funds in the market portfolio. Borrowing money to invest is known as using **financial leverage.** Using financial leverage increases the overall risk of the portfolio.

Notice that if you had a portfolio on the efficient frontier (labeled "old portfolio"), you could do better. Instead of owning the old portfolio, you can put some of your money in the market portfolio and some in the risk-free security to obtain the "new portfolio." See how the new portfolio dominates that old one? It carries the same risk level, but offers a higher return. In fact, notice that the line drawn between the risk-free investment and the market portfolio dominates all of the efficient frontier portfolios (except the market portfolio itself). All portfolio allocations between the risk-free security and the market portfolio constitute the capital market line. All investors should want to locate their portfolios on the CML, rather than the efficient frontier. Portfolios on the CML offer the highest expected return for any level of desired risk, which the investor controls by deciding how much of the market portfolio and how much of the risk-free asset to hold. Risk-averse investors can put more of their money in T-bills and less into the market portfolio. Investors willing to take on higher risk for larger returns can put more of their money in the market portfolio.

Beta, a Measure of Market Risk

The CML demonstrates that the market portfolio is crucial. Indeed, its return less the risk-free rate represents the expected average market risk premium. The market portfolio features no firm-specific risk; all such risk is diversified away. So the market portfolio carries only market risk. So the market portfolio's risk factor allows us to compute a measure of firm-specific risk for any individual stock or portfolio. We can now examine the question posed at the beginning of this section: "How much of Mattel's total risk is attributable to market risk?" The standard deviation of returns includes all of Mattel stock's risk—it quantifies how much the stock price rises and falls. The market risk portion will rise and fall along with the market portfolio. If we subtract the market risk portion from the total risk measure, we're left with firm-specific risk. This part of risk rises and falls in ways unrelated to market changes.

Remember that portfolio theory describes a measure—correlation—that measures how two stocks move together through time. Instead of measuring how any two stocks or portfolios move together, we now want to know how a stock or portfolio moves relative to market portfolio movements. This measure is known as **beta (β).** Beta measures the comovement between a stock and the market portfolio.

If Mattel's total risk level is measured by its standard deviation, σ_{Mattel}, then we can find the risk contribution attributable to the market in general by multiplying Mattel's total risk by its correlation with the market portfolio, $\sigma_{Mattel} \times \rho_{Mattel, Market}$. The beta computation is scaled so that the market portfolio itself has a beta of one and is done by dividing by standard deviation of the market portfolio;

Dow Jones Industrial Average Stock Betas | table 10.2

COMPANY	BETA	COMPANY	BETA
3M Company	0.75	Home Depot	1.08
Alcoa	1.69	Honeywell International	1.38
Altria	0.24	Intel	1.44
American International	1.38	International Business Mach.	1.59
American Express	1.12	Johnson & Johnson	0.14
AT&T	1.01	JP Morgan	0.99
Boeing	0.81	McDonald's	1.67
Citigroup	1.20	Merck	1.11
Caterpillar	1.43	Microsoft	1.36
Coca-Cola	0.62	Pfizer	1.16
Du Pont de Nemours	1.10	Procter & Gamble	0.61
ExxonMobil	1.26	United Technologies	0.64
General Electric	0.59	Verizon Communications	1.11
General Motors	1.94	Wal-Mart	0.05
Hewlett-Packard	1.24	Walt Disney	0.56

Data Source: Yahoo! Finance, January 18, 2008

$\sigma_{\text{Mattel}} \times \rho_{\text{Mattel,Market}} \div \sigma_{\text{Market}}$.[1] Stocks with betas larger than one are considered riskier than the market portfolio, while betas of less then one indicate lower risk. Mattel has a beta of 1.5, meaning that Mattel stock is very sensitive to market risk. When the market portfolio moves, you can expect Mattel stock to move in the same direction. Technically, you should expect Mattel's realized risk premium to be 50 percent more than the realized market risk premium.

Table 10.2 shows the beta for each of the 30 companies in the Dow Jones Industrial Average. Investors consider many of these companies high risk, like General Motors ($\beta = 1.94$) and Alcoa (1.69). These firms' stocks carry high market risk because the demand for their products is very sensitive to the overall economy's strength. People buy new cars and firms buy more construction materials when the economy is good. They buy less when they think that the economy is likely to go sour. Investors consider other companies safe bets with low risk, like Wal-Mart (0.05), Johnson & Johnson (0.14), and Altria (0.24). Many lower-beta firms sell consumer goods that we consider the necessities of life, which we will buy whether the economy is in recession or expansion. The demand for these products is price inelastic and not sensitive to economic conditions. Some companies have nearly the same risk as the market portfolio, like JP Morgan (0.99) and AT&T (1.01).

The Security Market Line

Beta indicates the market risk that each stock represents to investors. So the higher the beta, the higher the risk premium investors will demand to undertake that security's market risk. Since beta sums up precisely what investors want to know about risk, we often replace the standard deviation risk measure shown in Figure 10.1 with beta. Figure 10.2 shows required return versus beta risk. We call the line in this figure the **security market line** (SML), which illustrates how required return relates to risk at any particular time, all else held equal. The SML also shows the market portfolio's risk premium or any stock's risk premium. When a stock like Home Depot carries a beta greater than one, then its risk premium must be larger than the market risk premium. A stock like Boeing carries a lower beta than does the overall market; therefore Boeing would offer a lower risk premium to investors.

[1] A mathematically equivalent equation for beta is $\beta = \text{cov}(R_s, R_M)/\text{var}(R_M)$, where cov() is the covariance between the stock and market portfolio returns, and var() is the variance of the market portfolio.

figure 10.2

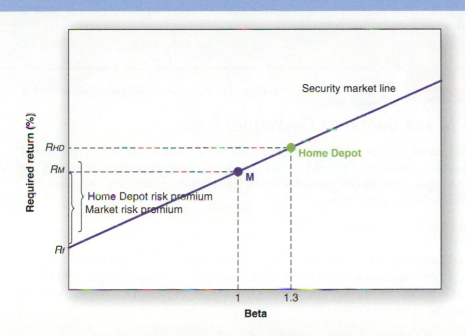

Required Returns for DJIA Stocks		table 10.3	
COMPANY	**REQUIRED RETURN**	**COMPANY**	**REQUIRED RETURN**
3M Company	10.2%	Home Depot	12.6%
Alcoa	16.8	Honeywell International	14.7
Altria	6.7	Intel	15.1
American International	14.7	International Business Mach.	16.1
American Express	12.8	Johnson & Johnson	6.0
AT&T	12.1	JP Morgan	11.9
Boeing	10.7	McDonald's	16.7
Citigroup	13.4	Merck	12.8
Caterpillar	15.0	Microsoft	14.5
Coca-Cola	9.3	Pfizer	13.1
Du Pont de Nemours	12.7	Procter & Gamble	9.3
ExxonMobil	13.8	United Technologies	9.5
General Electric	9.1	Verizon Communications	12.8
General Motors	18.6	Wal-Mart	5.4
Hewlett-Packard	13.7	Walt Disney	8.9

Assumptions: market return = 12% and risk-free rate = 5%.

We can use the SML to shows the relationship between risk and return for any stock or portfolio. To precisely quantify this relationship, we need the equation for the SML. The equation of any line can be defined as $y = b + m\,x$, were b is the intercept and m is the slope. In this case, the y axis is Required Return and the x axis is Beta. The intercept is R_f. You may remember that the slope is the "rise over run" between two points on the line. The rise between the risk-free security and the market portfolio is $R_M - R_f$ and the run is $1 - 0$. Substituting into the line equation results in the CAPM:

$$\text{Required return} = R_f + \beta(R_M - R_f) \tag{10-4}$$

So, we have determined a way to estimate any stock's required return once we have determined its beta. Consider this: We expect the market portfolio to earn 12 percent and T-bill yields are 5 percent. Then Home Depot's required return, with a $\beta = 1.08$, is $5\% + 1.08 \times (12\% - 5\%) = 12.56$ percent. Table 10.3 shows the 30 Dow Jones Industrial Average stocks' required return, using these same market and risk-free rate assumptions. Higher-risk companies have higher betas, and thus require higher returns.

EXAMPLE 10-2

 For interactive versions of this example visit www.mhhe.com/can1e

CAPM AND UNDER- OR OVERVALUED STOCK

Say that you are a corporate CFO. You know that the risk-free rate is currently 4.5 percent and you expect the market to earn 11 percent this year. Through your own analysis of the firm, you think it will earn a 13.5 percent return this year. If the beta of the company is 1.2, should you consider the firm undervalued or overvalued?

SOLUTION:

You can compute shareholders' required return with CAPM as 4.5% + 1.2 × (11% − 4.5%) = 12.3%. Since you think the firm will actually earn more than this required return, the firm appears to be currently undervalued. That is, its price must rise more then predicted by CAPM to obtain the return you estimated.

PORTFOLIO BETA As you might expect, a stock **portfolio's beta** is the weighted average of the portfolio stocks' betas. The portfolio beta equation resembles equation 9-7, which gives the return of a portfolio:

$$\beta_p = (w_1 \times \beta_1) + (w_2 \times \beta_2) + (w_3 \times \beta_3) + \cdots + (w_n \times \beta_n) = \sum_{j=1}^{n} w_j \beta_j \qquad \textbf{(10-5)}$$

With this equation, you can easily determine whether adding a particular stock to the portfolio will increase or decrease the portfolio's total market risk. If you add a stock with a higher beta than the existing portfolio, then the new portfolio will carry higher market risk than the old one did. Although we can find the effects on total portfolio risk of adding particular stocks using beta, the same is not necessarily true if we use standard deviations as our risk measure. The new stock, however risky, might have low correlations with the other stocks in the portfolio—offsetting (negative) correlations would reduce total risk.

EXAMPLE 10-3

 For interactive versions of this example visit www.mhhe.com/can1e

PORTFOLIO BETA

You have a portfolio consisting of 20 percent Boeing stock ($\beta = 0.81$), 40 percent Hewlett-Packard stock ($\beta = 1.24$), and 40 percent McDonald's stock ($\beta = 1.67$). How much market risk does the portfolio have?

SOLUTION:

Compute a beta for the portfolio. Using equation 10-5, the portfolio beta is 0.2 × 0.81 + 0.4 × 1.24 + 0.4 × 1.67 = 1.33. Note that this portfolio carries 33 percent more market risk than the general market does.

Finding Beta

The CAPM is an elegant explanation that relates the return you should require for taking on various levels of market risk. Although CAPM provides many practical applications, you need a company's beta to use those applications. Where or how can you obtain a beta? You have two ways to get beta. First, given the returns of the company and the market portfolio, you can compute the beta yourself. Second, you can find the beta that others have computed through financial information data providers.

Many financial outlets publish company betas. One publication that your library may have been subscribing to for decades is the *Value Line Investment Survey*. Value Line prints a terrific one-page summary of each company that includes beta. Value Line is now also online **(www.valueline.com),** but you need to subscribe to access this information. Nevertheless, many Web sites provide company betas for free: Hoovers, MSN Money, Yahoo! Finance, and Zacks, to name just a few. For example, in January 2008, the beta these Web sites listed for AT&T were: Hoovers (1.2), MSN Money (1.14), Yahoo! Finance (1.01), and Zacks (1.23). Note that these reported betas have some differences. To know why differences might arise, consider how you would go about gathering information and computing beta yourself.

To compute your own beta, first obtain historical returns for the company of interest and of the market portfolio. Then run a regression of the company return as the dependent variable and the market portfolio return as the independent variable. The resulting market portfolio return coefficient is beta. Many important questions may come to mind. First, what do you use as the market portfolio? People typically use a major stock index like the S&P 500 Index to proxy for the market portfolio. Second, what time frame should you use? You can use daily, weekly, monthly, or even annual returns. Using monthly returns is the most common. How long of a time series is needed? As you will recall, statistical estimates become more reliable and valid as more data are used. But you'll have to weigh those statistical advantages against the fact that companies change their business enterprises and thus their risk levels over time. Using data from too far back will distort your beta estimate, reflecting both risk today and risk from previous company activities. Generally speaking, using a time series data of three to five years is common. Whatever decisions you make to address these questions, be consistent by making the same decisions for all the company betas you compute. You'll find an example of computing beta in the Excel problem to this chapter. (It's not a calculation that you would want to make by hand!)

Concerns about Beta

Consider the estimation choices just mentioned. Say you estimate a firm's beta using monthly data for five years and the Dow Jones Industrial Average return as the market portfolio. Suppose that the result is a beta of 1.3. Then you try again using weekly returns for three years and the return from the S&P 500 Index as the market portfolio's yield, resulting in a beta of 0.9. These estimates are quite different and would create a large variation in required return if you plugged them into the CAPM. So, which is the more accurate estimate? Unfortunately, we may not be able to determine which is most representative, or "true." In general, you may estimate a little different beta using different market portfolio proxies, different return intervals (like monthly returns versus annual returns), and different time periods. A problem at the end of this chapter explores these differences.

In addition to these estimation problems, a company can change its risk level, and thus its beta, by changing the way it operates within its business, by

ASSET PRICING AND HEDGE FUNDS

Hedge funds are professionally managed portfolios, much like mutual funds. But differences between the two fund types carry very important ramifications for investors. While mutual funds typically just buy stocks and bonds, hedge funds often take short positions—that is, they sell stock they don't even own by borrowing it because they anticipate price declines. Once the price falls, the short seller covers the short by buying back the securities and returning them to the original owner to close out the transaction. Hedge funds short stocks and take sophisticated positions in commodities, futures, options, and other complicated derivative securities. They also maintain secrecy about their holdings, trading, and strategies. In return for the ability to use these kinds of strategies and maintain privacy, they can't advertise for new clients, so they are limited to sophisticated investors (a net worth in excess of $1 million or an annual income of greater than $200,000). Over $1.2 trillion is currently invested in hedge funds worldwide and the hedge fund industry is growing fast as more and more money managers think that they understand complex positions and can "make a killing" with unorthodox positions and financial instruments.

Some hedge funds use sophisticated asset pricing models to assess risks and rewards of unusual investment strategies. But just as with beta, sometimes asset prices do not behave as indicated in the models. This can lead to spectacular "blow ups." The most famous hedge funds implosion was the Long Term Capital Management debacle in 1998. Partners in LTCM included the likes of David Mullins (former Harvard Business School professor and vice chairman of the Federal Reserve Board) and Nobel Laureates Myron Scholes (from Stanford University) and Robert Merton (from MIT)— very smart and sophisticated investors indeed. The LTCM's traders, economists, and mathematicians used computers to detect suspected mispricings in bond and financial derivative values.

In August 1998, LTCM took a huge position based on their assumption that the "spread" or difference in interest rates between U.S. Treasury bonds and Danish mortgage securities would narrow. They were very wrong. Like many hedge funds, they had taken on enormous financial leverage. Say that you have $100 to invest and you buy a very safe investment. Say further that this investment will very likely pay you profit of $1. You also face a slight risk that you may lose $1. This is a low risk endeavor! Now say that you *borrow* an additional $9,900 to buy more of this safe investment. Now you are financially leveraged to a high degree. The investment will *likely* pay you a total of $100, in which case you will have doubled your $100 investment. But remember that slight chance that you will lose $100, which is all of your money. Either way, you must repay the borrowed $9,900 plus whatever interest you owe on that sum. The leverage you have taken on magnifies your return—and your risk. A low risk investment with no leverage can become a high risk investment when levered. LTCM made a low risk investment, but it was so highly levered that the loss wiped out more than 90 percent of the hedge fund value—a loss of two billion dollars!

The LTCM loss pales in comparison to the Amaranth hedge fund implosion in the fall of 2006. Amaranth lost $6.6 billion by taking a highly leveraged position based on their belief that short-term natural gas prices would rise. Instead, short-term gas prices fell.

Incidents like these can create ripple effects throughout the economy. So the U.S. Securities and Exchange Commission (SEC) has decided to monitor the hedge fund industry more closely, though the Commission has stopped short of actually regulating the industry at this time.

 want to know more? **Key Words to Search for Updates: hedge funds, U.S. SEC, LTCM, Amaranth**

expanding into new businesses and/or by changing its debt load. So even if beta is an accurate measure of what the firm's risk level was in the past, does it apply to the future? Beta's applicability will depend on the firm's future plans.

Both financial managers and investors share these concerns about beta. In the end, beta's usefulness depends on its reliability. Unfortunately, beta's empirical record is not as good as we would like. We should expect that companies with high betas yield higher returns than companies with low betas. On average, though, this does not turn out to be the case. A company's beta does not appear to predict its future return very well. Since characterizing the risk-return relationship is so important, finance researchers have introduced other asset pricing models. One promising model adds more risk factors to the predictive relationship other than just market risk. Firm size and book-to-market ratio have had some success predicting returns, so new models often include factors derived from these characteristics along with beta as a measure of market risk.

TIME OUT

10-3 Explain why portfolios that lie on the capital market line offer better risk-return trade-offs than those that lie on the efficient frontier.

10-4 Examine the betas in Table 10.2. Which seem about right to you and which seem to indicate too much or too little risk for that firm?

10.3 Capital Market Efficiency

The risk and return relationship rests on an underlying assumption that stock prices are generally "correct"—they are not predictably too high or too low. Imagine having a system that identified undervalued stocks with low risks (i.e., relatively high returns with a low beta). Because those stocks are undervalued, they will earn you a high return, on average, as their stock prices rise to their correct value. Note that the CAPM's risk-return relationship would be incorrect. You would be consistently getting high returns with low risk. On the other hand, if you consistently picked overvalued stocks, you wouldn't be earning enough return to compensate you for the risks you are taking. Investors move their money to the best alternatives by selling overvalued stocks and buying undervalued stocks. This causes the prices of the overvalued stocks to drop and the prices of the undervalued stocks to rise until both stocks' returns stand more in line with their riskiness. Thus, the risk-return relationship relies on the idea that prices are generally accurate.

What conditions are necessary for an **efficient market**? Efficient, or perfectly competitive, markets feature:

- Many buyers and sellers.
- No prohibitively high barriers to entry.
- Free and readily available information available to all participants.
- Low trading or transaction costs.

Are these conditions met for the U.S. stock market? Certainly millions of stock investors trade every day, buying and selling securities. With discount brokers and online traders, the costs to trade are fairly minimal and don't represent any real barriers to enter the market. Information is increasingly accessible from many sources and trading philosophies, and commission costs and bid-ask spreads have steadily declined. With millions of the larger companies' shares (say the S&P 500) of stock trading every day, the U.S. stock exchanges appear to meet efficiency conditions. But other segments of the market, like those exchanges that trade in **penny stocks,** feature very thin trading. The prices of these very small companies' stock may not be fair and these equities may be manipulated in fraudulent scams. In the 1970s and 1980s, penny stock king Meyer Blinder and his firm Blinder-Robinson was known as "blind 'em and rob 'em" as they practiced penny stock price manipulation to rob many small investors of their entire investments in these small markets. These days, penny stock price manipulation is typically conducted through e-mail and Web posting scams.

Efficient Market Hypothesis

Our concept of market efficiency provides a good framework for understanding how stock prices change over time. This theory is described in the **efficient market hypothesis (EMH),** which states that *security prices fully reflect all available information.* At any point in time, the price for any stock or bond reflects the collective wisdom of market participants about the company's future prospects. Security prices change as new information becomes available. Since we cannot predict whether new information about a company will be good news or bad news, we cannot predict whether its stock price will go up or go down. This makes short-term stock-price movements unpredictable. But in the longer run, stock prices will adjust to their proper level as market participants gather and digest all available information.

The EMH brings us to the question of what type of information is embedded within current stock prices. Segmenting information into three categories leads to the three basic levels of market efficiency, described as:

1. Weak-form efficiency—current prices reflect all information derived from trading. This stock market information generally includes current and past stock prices and trading volume.

2. Semistrong-form efficiency—current prices reflect all **public information**. This includes all information that has already been revealed to the public, like financial statements, news, analyst opinions, and so on.

3. Strong-form efficiency—current prices reflect *all* information. In addition to public information, prices reflect the **privately held information** that has not yet been released to the public, but may be known to some people, like managers, accountants, auditors, and so on.

Each of the EMH's three forms rests on different assumptions regarding the extent of information that is incorporated into stock prices at any point in time. A fourth possibility—that markets may not be efficient and prices may not reflect all the information known about a company—also arises.

The *weak-form* efficiency level involves the lowest information hurdle, stating that stock prices reflect all past price and trading volume activity. If true, this level of efficiency would have important ramifications. A segment of the investment industry uses price and volume charts to make investment timing decisions. Technical analysis has a large following and its own vocabulary of patterns and trends (resistance, support, breakout, momentum, etc.). If the market is at least weak-form efficient, then prices already reflect this information and these activities would not result in useful predictions about future price changes, and thus would be a waste of time. Indeed, the people who make the most money from price charting services are the people who sell the services, not the investors who buy and use those services.

The *semistrong-form* efficiency level assumes that stock prices include all public information. Notice that past stock prices and volumes are publicly available information, so this level includes the weak form as a subset. Important investment implications arise if markets are efficient to public information. Many investors conduct security analysis in which they obtain financial data and other public information to assess whether a company's stock is undervalued or overvalued. But in a semistrong-form efficient market, stock prices already reflect this information and are thus "correct." Using only public information, you would not be able to determine whether a stock is misvalued because that information is already reflected in the price.

If prices reflect all public information, then those prices will react as traders hear new (or private) information. Consider a company that announces surprisingly good quarterly profits. Traders and investors will have factored the old

figure 10.3

profit expectations into the stock price. As they incorporate the new information, the stock price will quickly rise to a new and accurate price as shown in the solid black line in Figure 10.3. Note that the stock price was $35 before the announcement and $40 immediately following. If you tried to buy the stock after hearing the news, then you would have bought at $40 and not received any benefit of the good quarterly profit news. On the other hand, if the market is not semistrong-form efficient, then the price might react quickly, but not accurately. The dashed green line shows a reaction in a non-semistrong efficient market where the price continues to drift up well after the announcement. This gradual drift to the "correct" price indicates that the market initially underreacted to the news. In this case, you could have bought the stock after the announcement and still earned a profit. The dotted blue line shows an overreaction to the firm's better-than-expected profits announcement. If markets consistently either underreact or consistently overreact to announcements that would change stock prices (earnings, stock split, dividend, etc.), then we would believe that the market is not semistrong efficient.

The *strong-form* market efficiency level presents the highest hurdle to test market reaction to information. The strong-form level includes information considered by the weak-form, the semistrong-form, as well as privately known information. People within firms, like CEOs and CFOs, know information that has not yet been released to the public. They may trade on this privately held, or insider, information and their trading may cause stock prices to change as it reflects that private information. In this way, stock prices could reflect even privately known information. Note that the firm managers, accountants, and auditors know several days in advance that a firm has earned unexpectedly high quarterly profits. If the stock price already incorporated this closely held private knowledge, then the big price reaction shown in Figure 10.3 would not occur.

So, is the stock market efficient? If it is, at what level? This has been a hotly debated topic for decades and continues to be. It is not likely that the market is strong-form efficient. Since insider trading is punished, insider information must be valuable. However, much evidence suggests that the market could be weak-form or semistrong-form efficient. Of course, we also have evidence that the market is not efficient at any of the three levels.

Behavioral Finance

The argument for the market being efficient works as follows: Many individual and professional investors constantly look for mispriced stocks. If they find a stock that is undervalued, they will buy it and drive up its price until it's correctly priced. Likewise, investors would sell an overpriced stock, driving down its price

BUBBLE TROUBLE

Many professionals criticize the EMH because the overall market sometimes seems too high or too low. A very dramatic example of the market level being artificially high is the market bubble. During a market bubble, the market quickly inflates on rampant speculation and subsequently crashes. Investors who buy near the peak of the bubble risk losing nearly all their investment.

One of the United States' earliest stock market bubbles was the bubble and crash of 1929. Note from the figure that the DJIA started in 1927 at around 160. By October 1929, the DJIA had reached nearly 400 and then crashed. By mid-1932, the DJIA had fallen to the 40s. The sustained fall coincided with an economic depression. Panel A of the figure also shows a price bubble in gold. The price of gold was $230 per ounce in January 1979. The late 1970s and early 1980s saw double-digit inflation throughout the economy, and many investors felt that gold represented a safe and inflation-

proof investment. Just one year later, the price had skyrocketed to $870. It then fell below $300 in less than two and a half years.

See the spectacular tech bubble during the 1990s? The Nasdaq 100, which started in 1985 at 250, soared to a peak of 4,816.35 on March 24, 2000. It then fell to less than 1,000 in two and a half years. The rise and fall of the Nasdaq 100 seems much more pronounced than the Japanese stock bubble of the 1980s. From a January 2, 1985, start at 11,543, the Nikkei 225 soared to a closing high of 38,916 on December 29, 1989. The bubble then burst and the Japanese stock market plummeted. The Nikkei has yet to fully recover, trading today at around the 16,500 level.

EMH critics do not believe that the entire stock market, or a substantial segment of it, can be correctly valued before, during, or after a bubble. It certainly appears to be overvalued during the time the bubble is inflating.

want to know more?   Key Words to Search for Updates: stock bubble, irrational exuberance

until it's correctly valued. With so many investors looking for market "mistakes," it's unlikely that any mispriced stock opportunities will be left in the market.

The argument against the market being efficient is equally convincing. The market comprises many people transacting with one another. When someone makes trading decisions influenced by emotion or psychological bias, those decisions may not seem rational. When many people fall under such influences, their trading decisions may actually drive stock prices away from the correct price as emotion carries the traders away from rationality. For example, many people believe that investors were "irrationally exuberant" about technology stocks in the late 1990s—and that their buying excitement drove prices to an artificially high level. In 2000, the excitement wore off and tech stock prices plummeted. Whenever a set of stock prices go unnaturally high and subsequently crash down, the market experiences what we call a **stock market bubble**.

In the past couple of decades, finance researchers have studied **behavioral finance** and found that people often behave in ways that are very likely "irrational." At times, investors appear to be too optimistic, as though they are looking through rose-colored glasses. At other times they appear to be too pessimistic. Common investment decisions aren't necessarily optimal ones, which flies in the face of the economist's expectation of rational economic actors. Perhaps, then, capital markets don't represent perfectly competitive or efficient markets if buyers and sellers do not always make rational choices.

TIME OUT

10-5 Can the market be semistrong-form efficient but not weak-form efficient? Explain.

10-6 If the market usually overreacts to bad news announcements, what would your return be like if you bought after you heard the bad news?

10.4 Implications for Financial Managers

Financial managers must understand the crucial relationship between risk and return for several reasons. First, while the relationship between risk and return is demonstrated here using the capital markets, it equally applies to many business decisions. A firm's product mix, marketing campaign combination, and research and development programs all entail risk and potential rewards. Being able to understand and characterize these decisions within a risk and return framework can help managers make better decisions. In addition, managers must understand what return their stockholders require at various times of firm operations. After all, a firm must receive enough revenue from its variously risky activities to pay its business costs, debt costs, and reward the owners (the stockholders). Managers must thus include the return to shareholders when they analyze new business opportunities.

Firms and capital markets also interact directly. For example, a good understanding of market efficiency helps managers understand how their stock prices will react to different types of decisions (like dividend changes) and news announcements (like unexpectedly high or low profitability). In fact, many managers own company stock and are thus compensated through programs that rely on the stock price, like **restricted stock** and **executive stock options.** Companies also periodically issue (sell) additional shares of stock to raise more capital, and these sales depend upon market efficiency assumptions. The firm would not want to sell additional shares if the stock price is too low (i.e., undervalued). They *would* want to sell more shares at any time that they thought their shares are overvalued. Other times, firms repurchase (buy back) shares of stock. The firm might want to do this if its shares were undervalued, but not if its shares were overvalued. Of course, valuation is not an issue if security markets are efficient.

Using the Constant-Growth Model for Required Return

For decades, financial managers have used the CAPM to compute shareholders' required return. Given recent concerns about beta's limitations, many see the CAPM as a less useful model for calculating appropriate returns. Some have turned instead to another model useful for computing required return—the constant growth rate model discussed in Chapter 7. We can arrange the terms of that model as:

$$i = \frac{D_1}{P_0} + g = \text{Dividend yield} + \text{Constant growth} \qquad \text{(10-6)}$$

Of course, this model assumes that the stock is efficiently priced. This model holds an advantage in that it uses current firm data (dividend, D, and price, P_0) and a simple forward estimate (growth, g) to assess what investors currently expect the stock to return, i. For example, Table 10.2 shows Wal-Mart's beta as 0.05. Using this beta, Table 10.3 shows that shareholders require only 5.4 percent return to hold Wal-Mart stock, given its low risk profile. You may find it hard to believe that Wal-Mart's owners (the shareholders) expect such a low return from one of the world's most profitable firms. So perhaps this is a case in which the CAPM result isn't very useful. Applying the constant-growth model looks something like this: Wal-Mart is expected to pay a $1 dividend this year and say the stock price currently stands at $48 per share. Financial analysts believe Wal-Mart will grow at 12 percent per year for the next five years. The constant growth rate model suggests that Wal-Mart shareholders expect a 14.1 percent [= ($1 ÷ $48) + 0.12] return. So, which required return seems more likely, the 5.4 percent computed from CAPM or the 14.1 percent suggested by the constant growth rate model? Since Wal-Mart shareholders have enjoyed an average annual return of 15.8 percent per year for the past 10 years, the constant growth rate estimate looks better and more accurate.

Financial managers need an estimate of their shareholders' required return in order to make appropriate decisions about their companies' future growth. Good financial managers will compute shareholders' required return using as many methods as they can to determine the most realistic value possible.

EXAMPLE 10-4

 For interactive versions of this example visit www.mhhe.com/can1e

REQUIRED RETURN

Note from Table 10.3 that the required return for 3M, Home Depot, and Intel are 10.2 percent, 12.6 percent, and 15.1 percent, respectively. These expectations may seem quite far apart, considering that all three firms are in the DJIA and are leaders in their market sectors. Use the following information to compute the constant growth rate model estimate of the required return:

	EXPECTED DIVIDEND	CURRENT PRICE	ANALYST GROWTH ESTIMATE
3M Company	$2.00	$75.40	10.9%
Home Depot	0.90	26.30	12.3
Intel	0.50	19.00	17.0

SOLUTION:

You can now use equation 10-6 to find each company's required return as:

$$3M \text{ required return} = (\$2.00 \div \$75.40) + 0.109 = 13.6\%$$

$$\text{Home Depot required return} = (\$0.90 \div \$26.30) + 0.123 = 15.7\%$$

$$\text{Intel required return} = (\$0.50 \div \$19.00) + 0.170 = 19.6\%$$

Note that the constant growth rate model estimates are 2 to 5 percent higher than the CAPM estimates. When the CAPM estimate seems too high or too low, it's a good idea to check the constant growth rate model estimate.

TIME OUT

10-7 Why is the shareholders' required return important to corporate managers?

Business Application Solution

You need to determine the firm's level of market risk. If you can obtain a beta, then you can make a required return estimate using CAPM. To assess the result, you can use the constant growth rate model to check the CAPM estimated required return for comparison's sake.

If you find the beta of the firm to be 1.8, assume a market return of 11 percent, and note a 5 percent T-bill rate, the CAPM computations would be:

$$5\% + 1.8 \times (11\% - 5\%) = 15.8 \text{ percent}$$

The firm will pay a \$0.50 dividend next year and the current stock price is \$32. Managers believe the company will grow at 13 percent per year for the foreseeable future. The constant growth rate model computation gives:

$$\$0.50 \div \$32 + 0.13 = 0.146, \text{ or } 14.6 \text{ percent}$$

You can now take these estimates to the team.

Personal Application Solution

You are investing 57.1 percent (= \$200 ÷ \$350) of your monthly contribution in stocks. You are also contributing 28.6 percent in bonds and 14.3 percent into a money market deposit. The diversified stock portfolio has a beta of 1. The long-term bond portfolio has a beta of 0.18. By definition, the money market deposit is risk-free and thus has a beta of zero.

The beta of this portfolio is therefore:

$$0.571 \times (1) + 0.286 \times (0.18) + 0.143 \times (0) = 0.62$$

With a portfolio beta of 0.62, a market return of 11 percent, and a risk-free rate of 5 percent, you can expect a return of:

$$5\% + 0.62 \times (11\% - 5\%) = 8.7 \text{ percent}$$

If you want a higher expected return, you will have to take more risk. You can do that by contributing a higher proportion of your funds to the stock portfolio.

summary of learning goals

In this chapter, we explored the theory and application of expected return. As an incentive to take market risk, investors require a commensurate return. We developed more precise specifications of the risk and required return relationship here via the CAPM and then discussed whether the underlying assumptions of the CAPM hold well enough in reality for CAPM required return estimates to give realistic insight into what investors really expect.

LG1 **Compute forward-looking expected return and risk.** A firm's stock return performance relates closely to the strength of the economy. We can compute expected return and risk using the probabilities of various good and bad economic states occurring in the future as predicted by macroeconomists.

LG2 **Understand risk premiums.** Investors will take on risk if they are given positive risk premiums. The risk premium of the stock market itself is defined as the market return minus the risk-free rate. The market risk premium provides a basis for us to understand the rewards for taking risk. Any particular stock's risk premium will be jointly

www.mhhe.com/can1e

345

determined by the market risk premium and the stock's sensitivity to market risk.

LG3 **Know and apply the capital asset pricing model (CAPM).** Adding a risk-free security to any portfolio along the efficient frontier gives the investor a higher required return. Investors should own combinations of the market portfolio and the risk-free security. As we change the amounts of the market portfolio and risk-free securities that investors may choose according to their risk preferences, we derive the security market line. The security market line's equation is known as CAPM, which specifies a direct relationship between required return and market risk. Any stock's required return comprises the risk-free rate plus the stock's risk premium. That risk premium is determined by the amount of market risk to which the stock is subject, as measured by beta.

LG4 **Calculate and apply beta, a measure of market risk.** We can use a stock's standard deviation to measure a stock's volatility. The market only rewards investors for taking on the portion of risk or volatility that arises due to general, economy-wide volatility, as shown in the market portfolio. The market risk portion of total risk is scaled so that a beta of one represents the risk of the overall stock market. A beta means that the stock exhibits only half of the overall stock market risk, while a beta of 2 means that the stock exhibits twice the risk that the overall market shows. A riskless security—such as a U.S. Treasury bill—has a zero beta. We can compute betas using past stock returns and the returns from a market portfolio proxy, like the S&P 500 Index. Many financial publications and financial Web sites also provide their own beta estimates for particular stocks.

LG5 **Differentiate among the different levels of market efficiency and their implications.** Financial risk-reward relationships rely upon the assumption that stock market prices are generally "right," given known company information. Various levels of the efficient market hypothesis (EMH) are characterized by the information types that stock prices reflect. The weak-form level of market efficiency states that stock prices incorporate all trading information, like past prices and trading volume. The semistrong form efficiency level states that current stock prices reflect all public information. Note that publicly known information includes the weak-form efficiency information and financial statements, analyst opinions, news, etc. Information that is not publicly known, but that is known by some corporate officers and other insiders, is called privately held information. The strong-form market efficiency level of the EMH claims that stock prices incorporate all information, public and private. Note that all U.S. stock exchanges forbid corporate officers and other people privy to closely held information from profiting from such information—an activity known as insider trading. The fourth possibility of the EMH is that stock prices are not efficient and thus are not always correct. If this is the case, investors can profit from mispricings.

LG6 **Calculate and explain investors' required return and risk.** Financial managers—and all managers, for that matter—must have a firm grasp upon the trade-off between risk and return. This trade-off arises in many business decisions involving product mix, marketing campaigns, and research and development. Financial managers in particular must understanding the return that shareholders require from the firm when they analyze new business opportunities.

LG7 **Use the constant growth rate model to compute required return.** The constant growth rate model provides a useful alternative to the CAPM for computing shareholders' required return. This model requires only the current stock price, an estimate of next year's dividends, and an estimate of the firm's growth rate. To make the best assessment of the required return, compute estimates from both the CAPM and the constant growth rate model and compare them, judging which seems more in line with investors' actual expectations.

chapter equations

10-1 $\text{Expected return} = p_1 \times \text{Return}_1 + p_2 \times \text{Return}_2 + p_3 \times \text{Return}_3$

$$+ \ldots + p_s \times \text{Return}_s = \sum_{j=1}^{s} p_j \times \text{Return}_j$$

10-2 $\text{Standard deviation} = \sqrt{\begin{array}{l} p_1 \times (\text{Return}_1 - \text{Expected return})^2 + p_2 \\ \times (\text{Return}_2 - \text{Expected return})^2 + \cdots \end{array}}$

$$= \sqrt{\sum_{j=1}^{s} p_j \times (\text{Return}_j - \text{Expected return})^2}$$

10-3 $\text{Required return} = \text{Risk-free rate} + \text{Premium for taking risk}$

10-4 $\text{Expected return} = R_f + \beta(R_M - R_f)$

10-5 $\beta_p = w_1 \times \beta_1 + w_2 \times \beta_2 + w_3 \times \beta_3 + \ldots + w_n \times \beta_n = \sum_{j=1}^{n} w_j \beta_j$

10-6 $i = \dfrac{D_1}{P_0} + g = \text{Dividend yield} + \text{Constant growth}$

key terms

asset pricing, The process of directly specifying the relationship between required return and risk. (p. 331)

behavioral finance, The study of the cognitive processes and biases associated with making financial and economic decisions. (p. 343)

beta, A measure of the sensitivity of a stock or portfolio to market risk. (p. 333)

capital asset pricing model (CAPM), An asset pricing theory based on a beta, a measure of market risk. (p. 331)

capital market line, The line on a graph of return and risk (standard deviation) from the risk-free rate through the market portfolio. (p. 332)

efficient market, A securities market in which prices fully reflect available information on each security. (p. 339)

efficient market hypothesis, A theory that describes what types of information are reflected in current stock prices. (p. 340)

executive stock options, Special rights given to corporate executives to buy a specific number of shares of the company stock at a fixed price during a specific period of time. (p. 343)

expected return, The average of the possible returns weighted by the likelihood of those returns occurring. (p. 328)

financial leverage, The use of debt to increase an investment position. (p. 332)

hedge fund, An investment fund structured to avoid regulation. (p. 338)

market portfolio, In theory, the market portfolio is the combination of securities that places the portfolio on the efficient frontier and on a line tangent

from the risk-free rate. In practice, the S&P 500 Index is used to proxy for the market portfolio. (p. 332)

market risk premium, The return on the market portfolio minus the risk-free rate. Risk premiums for specific firms are based on the market risk premium. (p. 331)

penny stocks, The stocks of small companies that are priced below $1 per share. (p. 339)

portfolio beta, The combination of the individual company beta's in an investor's portfolio. (p. 336)

privately held information, The set of information that has not been released to the public, but is known by few individuals, likely company insiders. (p. 340)

probability, The likelihood of occurrence. (p. 328)

probability distribution, The set of probabilities for all possible occurrences. (p. 329)

public information, The set of information that has been publicly released. Public information includes data on past stock prices and volume, financial statements, corporate news, analyst opinion, etc. (p. 340)

required return, The level of total return needed to be compensated for the risk taken. It is made up of a risk-free rate and a risk premium. (p. 330)

restricted stock, Shares of stock issued to executives that have limitations on when they can be sold. (p. 343)

risk premium, The portion of the required return that represents the reward for taking risk. (p. 331)

security market line, Similar to the capital market line except risk is characterized by beta instead of standard deviation. (p. 334)

stock market bubble, Investor enthusiasm causes an inflated bull market that drives prices too high, ending in a dramatic collapse in prices. (p. 342)

www.mhhe.com/can1e

self-test problems with solutions

1 **Expected Return and Risk** An economist has determined that the probability of the economy being in various states is shown in the following table.

ECONOMIC STATE	PROBABILITY	RETURN
Fast growth	0.13	40%
Slow growth	0.42	15
No growth	0.25	5
Recession	0.17	−15
Depression	0.03	−30

You have added the return that your firm will achieve in each economic state. Given this information, you can compute the expected return and risk of the firm.

Solution:

Use equations 10-1 and 10-2 to complete the following table:

ECONOMY	PROBABILITY	RETURN	$p \times$ RETURN	DEVIATION	DEVIATION^2	$\times p$
Fast growth	0.13	40%	5.20%	30.70%	942.49	122.52
Slow growth	0.42	15	6.30	5.70	32.49	13.65
No growth	0.25	5	1.25	−4.30	18.49	4.62
Recession	0.17	−15	−2.55	−24.30	590.49	100.38
Depression	0.03	−30	−0.90	−39.30	1544.49	46.33
sum =	1		9.30%			287.51
					Square root =	16.96%

The expected return for the firm is 9.3 percent and the standard deviation risk is 16.96 percent.

2 **Portfolio Beta and Required Return** You have a stock portfolio that consists of the following positions:

	SHARES	PRICE	BETA
Apple Inc.	50	$89.00	2.40
Fiserv	100	55.00	1.34
Monster Worldwide	150	52.00	2.37
Ross Stores	200	34.00	1.27
Whole Foods	100	51.00	1.66

The beta of each stock is also shown. What is the portfolio beta? If the market return is expected to be 12 percent and the risk-free rate is 4 percent, what is the required return of the portfolio?

Solution:

To compute the portfolio beta, you must first calculate the portfolio weights for each stock. The position of each stock is denoted by the number of shares multiplied by the price of the stock. Adding all of the positions results in a total

www.mhhe.com/can1e

portfolio value of $29,650. The portion that each stock represents in the portfolio is shown as its weight and is computed by dividing each position by the total portfolio value. Once the weights are known, then equation 10-5 can be used. The last column shows the computations for the portfolio beta.

	SHARE	PRICE	POSITION	WEIGHT	BETA	w × BETA
Apple Inc.	50	$89.00	$4,450	0.15	2.40	0.36
Fiserv	100	$55.00	$5,500	0.19	1.34	0.25
Monster Worldwide	150	$52.00	$7,800	0.26	2.37	0.62
Ross Stores	200	$34.00	$6,800	0.23	1.27	0.29
Whole Foods	100	$ 51.00	$5,100	0.17	1.66	0.29
	sum =		$29,650	1.00		1.81

The beta of this portfolio is 1.81. This is a high-risk portfolio. You can now use the CAPM to compute the required return of the portfolio as

$$4\% + 1.81 \times (12\% - 4\%) = 18.48 \text{ percent}$$

③ Required Return Compute the required return for three stocks: Anheuser Busch, Hilton Hotels, and Tribune Co. To be thorough, compute required return using both the CAPM and the constant growth rate model.

LG4, LG7

For the CAPM analysis, see the following market risk information: Anheuser Busch ($\beta = 0.37$), Hilton Hotels ($\beta = 1.51$), and Tribune ($\beta = 0.46$). Assume that the risk-free rate is 4.5 percent and the market risk premium is 6 percent.

For the constant growth rate model, the stock price, dividend, and growth information is:

	PRICE	DIVIDEND	GROWTH RATE
Anheuser Busch	$50.05	$1.20	9.0%
Hilton Hotels	36.70	0.16	15.0
Tribune	30.65	0.76	11.0

Solution:

Start by calculating the required return using CAPM. Note that it was the market risk premium that was given instead of the market return. Since the market risk premium is what goes in the parenthesis of the equation, the results are:

$$\text{Anheuser Busch}: \quad 4.5\% + 0.37 \times (6\%) = 6.72 \text{ percent}$$
$$\text{Hilton Hotels}: \quad 4.5\% + 1.51 \times (6\%) = 13.56 \text{ percent}$$
$$\text{Tribune}: \quad 4.5\% + 0.46 \times (6\%) = 7.26 \text{ percent}$$

The required returns for Anheuser Busch and for Tribune seem a little low. So you should also compute the required return using the constant growth rate model:

$$\text{Anheuser Busch}: \quad (\$1.20 \div \$50.05) + 0.09 = 11.4\%$$
$$\text{Hilton Hotels}: \quad (\$0.16 \div \$36.70) + 0.15 = 15.4\%$$
$$\text{Tribune}: \quad (\$0.76 \div \$30.65) + 0.11 = 13.5\%$$

These estimates for the required return seem much better for Anheuser Busch and Tribune, but the Hilton Hotels estimate may be a little high.

questions

1. Consider an asset that provides the same return no matter what economic state occurs. What would be the standard deviation (or risk) of this asset? Explain. *(LG1)*

2. Why is expected return considered "forward-looking"? What are the challenges for practitioners to utilize expected return? *(LG1)*

3. In 2000, the S&P 500 Index earned −9.1 percent while the T-bill yield was 5.9 percent. Does this mean the market risk premium was negative? Explain. *(LG2)*

4. How might the magnitude of the market risk premium impact people's desire to buy stocks? *(LG2)*

5. Describe how adding a risk-free security to modern portfolio theory allows investors to do better than the efficient frontier. *(LG3)*

6. Show on a graph like Figure 10.2 where a stock with a beta of 1.3 would be located on the security market line. Then show where that stock would be located if it is undervalued. *(LG3)*

7. Consider that you have three stocks in your portfolio and wish to add a fourth. You want to know if the fourth stock will make the portfolio riskier or less risky. Compare and contrast how this would be assessed using standard deviation versus market risk (beta) as the measure of risk. *(LG3)*

8. Describe how different allocations between the risk-free security and the market portfolio can achieve any level of market risk desired. Give examples of a portfolio from a person who is very risk averse and a portfolio for someone who is not so averse to taking risk. *(LG3)*

9. Cisco Systems has a beta of 1.88. Does this mean that you should expect Cisco to earn a return 88 percent higher than the S&P 500 Index return? Explain. *(LG4)*

10. Note from Table 10.2 that some technology-oriented firms (Intel and IBM) in the Dow Jones Industrial Average have high market risk while others (AT&T, Microsoft, and Verizon) have low market risk. How do you explain this? *(LG4)*

11. Find a beta estimate from three different sources for General Electric (GE). Compare these three values. Why might they be different? *(LG4)*

12. If you were to compute beta yourself, what choices would you make regarding the market portfolio, the holding period for the returns (daily, weekly, etc.), and the number of returns? Justify your choices. *(LG4)*

13. Explain how the concept of a positive risk-return relationship breaks down if you can systematically find stocks that are overvalued and undervalued. *(LG5)*

14. Determine what level of market efficiency each event is consistent with:

    a. Immediately after an earnings announcement the stock price jumps and then stays at the new level. *(LG5)*

    b. The CEO buys 50,000 shares of his company and the stock price does not change. *(LG5)*

    c. The stock price immediately jumps when a stock split is announced, but then retraces half of the gain over the next day. *(LG5)*

d. An investor analyzes company quarterly and annual balance sheets and income statements looking for undervalued stocks. The investor earns about the same return as the S&P 500 Index. *(LG5)*

15. Why do most investment scams conducted over the Internet and e-mail involve penny stocks instead of S&P 500 Index stocks? *(LG5)*

16. Describe a stock market bubble. Can a bubble occur in a single stock? *(LG5)*

17. If stock prices are not strong-form efficient, then what might be the price reaction to a firm announcing a stock buyback? Explain. *(LG6)*

18. Compare and contrast the assumptions that need to be made to compute a required return using CAPM and the constant growth rate model. *(LG7)*

19. How should you handle a case where required return computations from CAPM and the constant growth rate model are very different? *(LG7)*

problems

10-1 Expected Return Compute the expected return given these three economic states, their likelihoods, and the potential returns: *(LG1)*

basic problems

ECONOMIC STATE	PROBABILITY	RETURN
Fast growth	0.3	40%
Slow growth	0.5	10
Recession	0.2	−25

10-2 Expected Return Compute the expected return given these three economic states, their likelihoods, and the potential returns: *(LG1)*

ECONOMIC STATE	PROBABILITY	RETURN
Fast growth	0.2	35%
Slow growth	0.6	10
Recession	0.2	−30

10-3 Required Return If the risk-free rate is 6 percent and the risk premium is 5 percent, what is the required return? *(LG2)*

10-4 Required Return If the risk-free rate is 3 percent and the risk premium is 7 percent, what is the required return? *(LG2)*

10-5 Risk Premium The average annual return on the S&P 500 Index from 1986 to 1995 was 15.8 percent. The average annual T-bill yield during the same period was 5.6 percent. What was the market risk premium during these 10 years? *(LG2)*

10-6 Risk Premium The average annual return on the S&P 500 Index from 1996 to 2005 was 10.8 percent. The average annual T-bill yield during the same period was 3.6 percent. What was the market risk premium during these 10 years? *(LG2)*

10-7 CAPM Required Return Hastings Entertainment has a beta of 0.24. If the market return is expected to be 11 percent and the risk-free rate is 4 percent, what is Hastings' required return? *(LG3)*

10-8 **CAPM Required Return** Nanometrics Inc. has a beta of 4.05. If the market return is expected to be 12 percent and the risk-free rate is 4.5 percent, what is Nanometrics' required return? *(LG3)*

10-9 **Company Risk Premium** Netflix, Inc. has a beta of 3.61. If the market return is expected to be 13 percent and the risk-free rate is 6 percent, what is Netflix' risk premium? *(LG3)*

10-10 **Company Risk Premium** Paycheck Inc. has a beta of 0.94. If the market return is expected to be 11 percent and the risk-free rate is 3 percent, what is Paycheck's risk premium? *(LG3)*

10-11 **Portfolio Beta** You have a portfolio with a beta of 1.2. What will be the new portfolio beta if you keep 90 percent of your money in the old portfolio and 10 percent in a stock with a beta of 1.9? *(LG3)*

10-12 **Portfolio Beta** You have a portfolio with a beta of 1.1. What will be the new portfolio beta if you keep 85 percent of your money in the old portfolio and 15 percent in a stock with a beta of 0.5? *(LG3)*

10-13 **Stock Market Bubble** The Nasdaq stock market bubble peaked at 4,816 in 2000. Two and a half years later it had fallen to 1,000. What was the percentage decline? *(LG5)*

10-14 **Stock Market Bubble** The Japanese stock market bubble peaked at 38,916 in 1989. Two and a half years later it had fallen to 15,900. What was the percentage decline? *(LG5)*

10-15 **Required Return** Paccar's current stock price is $73.10 and it is likely to pay a $2.69 dividend next year. Since analysts estimate Paccar will have a 11.2 percent growth rate, what is its required return? *(LG7)*

10-16 **Required Return** Universal Forest's current stock price of Universal Forest is $54.00 and it is likely to pay a $0.23 dividend next year. Since analysts estimate Universal Forest will have a 10.0 percent growth rate, what is its required return? *(LG7)*

intermediate problems

10-17 **Expected Return Risk** For the same economic state probability distribution in problem 10-1, determine the standard deviation of the expected return. *(LG1)*

ECONOMIC STATE	PROBABILITY	RETURN
Fast growth	0.3	40%
Slow growth	0.5	10
Recession	0.2	−25

10-18 **Expected Return Risk** For the same economic state probability distribution in problem 10-2, determine the standard deviation of the expected return. *(LG1)*

ECONOMIC STATE	PROBABILITY	RETURN
Fast growth	0.2	35%
Slow growth	0.6	10
Recession	0.2	−30

10-19 **Under-/Overvalued Stock** A manager believes his firm will earn a 14 percent return next year. His firm has a beta of 1.5, the expected return on the market is 12 percent, and the risk-free rate is 4 percent. Compute the return the firm should earn given its level of risk and determine whether the manager is saying the firm is undervalued or overvalued. *(LG3)*

10-20 **Under-/Overvalued Stock** A manager believes his firm will earn a 14 percent return next year. His firm has a beta of 1.2, the expected return on the market is 11 percent, and the risk-free rate is 5 percent. Compute the return the firm should earn given its level of risk and determine whether the manager is saying the firm is undervalued or overvalued. *(LG3)*

10-21 **Portfolio Beta** You own $5,000 of Olympic Steel stock that has a beta of 2.9. You also own $7,000 of Rent-a-Center (beta = 1.5) and $8,000 of Lincoln Educational (beta = 0.2). What is the beta of your portfolio? *(LG3)*

10-22 **Portfolio Beta** You own $7,000 of Human Genome stock that has a beta of 3.5. You also own $8,000 of Frozen Food Express (beta = 1.6) and $10,000 of Molecular Devices (beta = 0.4). What is the beta of your portfolio? *(LG3)*

advanced
problems

10-23 **Expected Return and Risk** Compute the expected return and standard deviation given these four economic states, their likelihoods, and the potential returns: *(LG1)*

ECONOMIC STATE	PROBABILITY	RETURN
Fast growth	0.30	60%
Slow growth	0.50	13
Recession	0.15	−15
Depression	0.05	45

10-24 **Expected Return and Risk** Compute the expected return and standard deviation given these four economic states, their likelihoods, and the potential returns: *(LG1)*

ECONOMIC STATE	PROBABILITY	RETURN
Fast growth	0.25	50%
Slow growth	0.55	11
Recession	0.15	−15
Depression	0.05	−50

10-25 **Risk Premiums** You own $10,000 of Denny's Corp stock that has a beta of 2.9. You also own $15,000 of Qwest Communications (beta = 1.5) and $15,000 of Southwest Airlines (beta = 0.4). Assume that the market return will be 13 percent and the risk-free rate is 5.5 percent. What is the market risk premium? What is the risk premium of each stock? What is the risk premium of the portfolio? *(LG3)*

10-26 **Risk Premiums** You own $15,000 of Opsware Inc. stock that has a beta of 3.8. You also own $10,000 of Lowe's Companies (beta = 1.6) and $10,000 of New York Times (beta = 0.8). Assume that the market return will be 12 percent and the risk-free rate is 6 percent. What is the market risk premium? What is the risk premium of each stock? What is the risk premium of the portfolio? *(LG3)*

10-27 **Portfolio Beta and Required Return** You hold the positions in the table below. What is the beta of your portfolio? If you expect the market to earn 12 percent and the risk-free rate is 3.5 percent, what is the required return of the portfolio? *(LG3)*

	PRICE	SHARES	BETA
Amazon.com	$40.80	100	3.8
Family Dollar Stores	30.10	150	1.2
McKesson Corp	57.40	75	0.4
Schering-Plough Corp	23.80	200	0.5

10-28 **Portfolio Beta and Required Return** You hold the positions in the table below. What is the beta of your portfolio? If you expect the market to earn 12 percent and the risk-free rate is 3.5 percent, what is the required return of the portfolio? *(LG3)*

	PRICE	SHARES	BETA
Advanced Micro Devices	$ 14.70	200	4.2
FedEx Corp	120.00	50	1.1
Microsoft	28.90	150	0.7
Sara Lee Corp	17.25	200	0.5

10-29 **Required Return** Using the information in the table, compute the required return for each company using both CAPM and the constant-growth model. Compare and discuss the results. Assume that the market portfolio will earn 12 percent and the risk-free rate is 3.5 percent. *(LG3, LG7)*

	PRICE	UPCOMING DIVIDEND	GROWTH	BETA
US Bancorp	$36.55	$1.60	10.0%	0.8
Praxair	64.75	1.12	11.0	0.7
Eastman Kodak	24.95	1.00	4.5	2.0

10-30 **Required Return** Using the information in the table, compute the required return for each company using both CAPM and the constant-growth model. Compare and discuss the results. Assume that the market portfolio will earn 11 percent and the risk-free rate is 4 percent. *(LG3, LG7)*

	PRICE	UPCOMING DIVIDEND	GROWTH	BETA
Estee Lauder	$47.40	$0.60	11.7%	0.75
Kimco Realty	52.10	1.54	8.0	1.3
Nordstrom	5.25	0.50	14.6	2.2

10-31 **Excel Problem** As discussed in the text, beta estimates for one firm will vary depending on various factors such as the time over which the estimation is conducted, the market portfolio proxy, and the return intervals. You will demonstrate this variation using returns for Microsoft.

a. Using all 45 monthly returns for Microsoft and the three stock market indices, compute Microsoft's beta using the S&P 500 Index as the market proxy. Then compute the beta using the DJIA and the Nasdaq indices as the market portfolio proxy. Compare the three beta estimates.

b. Now estimate the beta using only the most recent 30 monthly returns and the S&P 500 Index. Compare the beta estimate to the estimate in part A when using the S&P 500 Index and all 45 monthly returns.

DATE	MSFT	S&P 500	DJIA	NASDAQ	DATE	MSFT	S&P 500	DJIA	NASDAQ
Jun 2007	4.45%	3.07%	4.04%	4.19%	Jul 2005	7.22%	−1.12%	−1.50%	−1.50%
May 2007	−3.98	−1.78	−1.61	−0.05	Jun 2005	3.10	3.60	3.56	6.22
Apr 2007	2.85	3.25	4.32	3.15	May 2005	−3.70	−0.01	−1.84	−0.54
Mar 2007	7.42	4.33	5.74	4.27	Apr 2005	2.28	3.00	2.70	7.63
Feb 2007	−1.07	1.00	0.70	0.23	Mar 2005	4.69	−2.01	−2.96	−3.88
Jan 2007	−8.38	−2.18	−2.80	−1.94	Feb 2005	−3.93	−1.91	−2.44	−2.56
Dec 2006	3.34	1.41	1.27	2.01	Jan 2005	−3.97	1.89	2.63	−0.52
Nov 2006	1.71	1.26	1.97	−0.68	Dec 2004	−1.66	−2.53%	−2.72	−5.20
Oct 2006	2.60	1.65	1.17	2.75	Nov 2004	−0.31	3.25%	3.40	3.75
Sep 2006	4.99	3.15	3.44	4.79	Oct 2004	6.80	3.86%	3.99	6.17
Aug 2006	6.41	2.46	2.62	3.42	Sep 2004	1.17	1.40%	−0.52	4.12
Jul 2006	7.21	2.13	1.75	4.41	Aug 2004	1.31	0.94%	−0.92	3.20
Jun 2006	3.26	0.51	0.32	−3.71	Jul 2004	−3.89	0.23%	0.34	−2.61
May 2006	2.86	0.01	−0.16	−0.31	Jun 2004	−0.28	−3.43%	−2.83	−7.83
Apr 2006	−5.86	−3.09	−1.75	−6.19	May 2004	8.90	1.80%	2.42	3.07
Mar 2006	−11.22	1.22	2.32	−0.74	Apr 2004	0.40	1.21%	−0.36	3.47
Feb 2006	1.25	1.11	1.05	2.56	Mar 2004	4.82	−1.68%	−1.28	−3.71
Jan 2006	−4.21	0.05	1.18	−1.06	Feb 2004	−6.05	−1.64%	−2.14	−1.75
Dec 2005	7.61	2.55	1.37	4.56	Jan 2004	−4.05	1.22%	0.91	−1.76
Nov 2005	−5.50	−0.10	−0.82	−1.23	Dec 2003	1.01	1.73%	0.33	3.13
Oct 2005	8.01	3.52	3.50	5.31	Nov 2003	6.47	5.08%	6.86	2.20
Sep 2005	−0.12	−1.77	−1.22	−1.46	Oct 2003	−1.64	0.71%	−0.19	1.45
Aug 2005	−6.02	0.69	0.83	−0.02					

c. Estimate Microsoft's beta using the quarterly data returns below. Compare the estimate to the ones from parts (a) and (b).

DATE	MSFT	S&P 500
Q2 2007	3.15%	4.53%
Q1 2007	−2.64	3.07
Q4 2006	7.85	4.38
Q3 2006	19.76	7.93
Q2 2006	0.00	−2.59
Q1 2006	−13.90	2.39
Q4 2005	9.84	6.05
Q3 2005	0.64	−1.20
Q2 2005	1.55	6.68
Q1 2005	−3.42	−2.07
Q4 2004	4.70	4.52
Q3 2004	−1.50	2.59
Q2 2004	9.02	−0.50
Q1 2004	−5.52	−2.11
Q4 2003	5.79	7.65

research it! Find a Beta

Using beta as a risk measure has been fully integrated into corporate finance and the investment industry. You can obtain a beta for most companies at many financial Web sites. Sites that list a beta include: Hoovers (in the Market Data section), MSN Money (in the Company Report section), Yahoo! Finance (in the Key Statistics section), and Zacks (follow the Detailed Quote link). Obtain the beta for your favorite company from several different Web sites. Are the values you obtain similar? If they are not, why might they be different? (**hoovers.com, moneycentral.msn.com, finance.yahoo.com, www.zacks.com**)

integrated minicase: AT&T's Beta

When you go on the Web to find a firm's beta, you do not know how recently it was computed, what index was used as a proxy for the market portfolio, or which time series of returns the calculations used. Earlier in this chapter, it was shown that when we went on the Web to find a beta for AT&T, we found the following: Hoovers (1.5), MSN Money (1.52), Yahoo! Finance (0.50), and Zacks (1.52).

An alternative is to compute beta yourself. A common estimation procedure is to use 60 months of return data and to use the S&P 500 Index as the market portfolio. You can obtain price data for a company and for the S&P 500 Index for free from Web sites like Yahoo! Finance. Using monthly prices, you can compute the monthly returns, as $(P_n - P_{n-1}) \div P_{n-1}$. Below are 60 monthly returns for AT&T and the S&P 500 Index. You can use these returns to compute AT&T's beta. A spreadsheet, like Excel, can run a regression (go to Tool menu, select Data Analysis, and then Regression). Select AT&T returns as the y variable and S&P 500 Index return as the x variable. The coefficient for the x variable is the beta estimate. The regression will provide all the statistical information you might like. However, if you only want beta, you can simply use the SLOPE function in Excel. Or, you may have learned to run a regression using statistical software.

DATE	AT&T	S&P 500 INDEX	DATE	AT&T	S&P 500 INDEX	DATE	AT&T	S&P 500 INDEX
Jun 2007	−2.26%	3.07%	Oct 05	4.45%	3.52%	Feb 04	2.22%	−1.64%
May 2007	0.39	−1.78	Sep 05	0.85	−1.77	Jan 04	−5.83	1.22
Apr 2007	6.77	3.25	Aug 05	−0.45	0.69	Dec 03	−1.04	1.73
Mar 2007	−0.90	4.33	Jul 05	−1.54	−1.12	Nov 03	11.95	5.08
Feb 2007	7.14	1.00	Jun 05	4.36	3.60	Oct 03	−2.89	0.71
Jan 2007	−2.22	−2.18	May 05	1.58	−0.01	Sep 03	9.61	5.50
Dec 2006	6.36	1.41	Apr 05	−1.78	3.00	Aug 03	−0.96	−1.19
Nov 2006	5.42	1.26	Mar 05	1.82	−2.01	Jul 03	−3.83	1.79
Oct 2006	−0.97	1.65	Feb 05	−1.51	−1.91	Jun 03	−7.25	1.62
Sep 2006	6.27	3.15	Jan 05	1.25	1.89	May 03	0.38	1.13
Aug 2006	4.59	2.46	Dec 04	−6.60	−2.53	Apr 03	8.97	5.09
Jul 2006	3.81	2.13	Nov 04	2.35	3.25	Mar 03	18.28	8.10
Jun 2006	8.82	0.51	Oct 04	−0.35	3.86	Feb 03	−3.61	0.84
May 2006	7.02	0.01	Sep 04	−1.53	1.40	Jan 03	−14.85	−1.70
Apr 2006	−0.59	−3.09	Aug 04	0.61	0.94	Dec 02	−9.07	−2.74
Mar 2006	−1.86	1.22	Jul 04	1.79	0.23	Nov 02	−4.88	−6.03
Feb 2006	−1.97	1.11	Jun 04	5.86	−3.43	Oct 02	11.08	5.71
Jan 2006	6.29	0.05	May 04	2.32	1.80	Sep 02	29.35	8.64
Dec 2005	7.40	2.55	Apr 04	−4.79	1.21	Aug 02	−18.76	−11.00
Nov 2005	−1.66	−0.10	Mar 04	2.70	−1.68	Jul 02	−10.55	0.49

(continued)

a. Compute AT&T's beta using the above returns.

b. Compare your estimate with the ones found on the Web as listed above.

c. How different will the required returns be using these betas? Compute required return using each beta (assume that the risk-free rate is 5 percent and the market return will be 13 percent).

ANSWERS TO TIME OUT

10-1 Average return is computed using the simple average of historical returns. The expected return is a forward-looking return. However, it is computed using a weighted average (the probabilities) of returns. The returns used in the various economic stages are usually chosen from historical knowledge of how the firm performs in each stage. Thus, both measures use an average of historical returns in one way or another. The historical risk and expected risk are both measured using standard deviation and historical knowledge of returns as well.

10-2 Many people are willing to take market risk because over time they expect to earn a risk premium. This risk premium allows them to build their wealth significantly more than just investing in the risk-free asset. However, because risk is involved, these people should have a long-term focus and recognize that they can lose money in the short term.

10-3 For every point on the efficient frontier (except the market portfolio), you can form a portfolio that has the same level of risk, but a higher expected return through a combination of the market portfolio and the risk-free asset. Thus, the capital market line has a better risk-return trade-off because it has higher return at every level of risk.

10-4 Procter & Gamble is a diversified firm selling consumer goods that are purchased in good economies and bad. Thus, its low beta of 0.61 seems reasonable. Similarly, Altria is a tobacco company whose products also seem recession-proof. The low beta of 0.24 seems fine. At this time, General Motors has been in financial difficulty and has seen shrinking market share. The high and very risky beta of 1.94 seems right. On the other hand, Disney's beta of 0.56 seems too low given how entertainment dollars are spent with the economic cycle. On the other hand, McDonald's beta of 1.67 seems too high.

10-5 No. Weak-form efficiency is a subset of semistrong-form efficiency. Information about market prices and volumes is public and is thus included in the broader definition of public information in the semistrong-form efficiency hypothesis. Therefore, if a market is semistrong-form efficient, it is also weak-form efficient, by definition.

10-6 Consider a case when the market consistently overreacted to bad news announcements. This means that prices would fall too far after the announcement and eventually partially rebound. If this scenario was predictable, an investor could make money by buying stocks after bad news and capturing the price bounce.

10-7 Consider that you obtained money from the bank and had to pay them an 8 percent interest rate. If you invested that money in a project that returned 5 percent to you, then you would not be earning enough to pay back the bank. You need to earn more than 8 percent on your business project in order to be successful. Corporate managers are using the shareholders' equity capital and need to know what return they require. This return is more difficult to estimate than a bank loan. But it helps managers to know what return they must achieve when using the capital to fund business opportunities.

chapter 11:

CALCULATING THE COST OF CAPITAL

Learning Goals

LG1 Grasp the basic intuition behind calculating the cost of capital and its relationship to the investor's required return.

LG2 Use the weighted-average cost of capital (WACC) formula to calculate a project's cost of capital.

LG3 Debate the firm's choices in estimating the appropriate capital component costs of equity, preferred stock, and debt.

LG4 Calculate and justify appropriate weights used for WACC projections.

LG5 Clarify which parts of a firmwide WACC can be used in calculating a project-specific WACC and which parts do not apply.

LG6 Note the trade-offs implicit in using either a firmwide WACC or a divisional cost of capital approach.

LG7 Differentiate between the objective and subjective approaches to computing a divisional cost of capital.

LG8 Denote the impact that flotation costs have on capital budgeting decisions and adjust the WACC to reflect flotation costs.

I n the previous two chapters, we discussed investors' required return given a particular risk profile. In this chapter, we examine the question from the firm's point of view: How much must the firm pay to finance its operations and expansions using debt and equity sources? Firms use a combination of debt and equity sources to fund their operations, projects, and any expansions they may undertake. In Chapter 14, we'll explore the factors that managers consider as they choose the optimal capital structure mix. For now, we'll assume that management has chosen the optimal mix for us, and that it's our job to implement it.

As we've seen in previous chapters, investors face different kinds of risks associated with debt, preferred stock, and equity. As a result, their required rates of return for each debt or equity source differ as well. So as the firm uses a combination of different financing sources, we must calculate the investors' average required rate of

viewpoints

Business Application

MP3 Devices, Inc. is about to launch a new project to create and market a combination MP3 player/video projector. The new project will be funded with 40 percent debt, 10 percent preferred stock, and 50 percent common stock. MP3 Devices currently has 10 million shares of common stock outstanding, selling at $18.75 per share, and expects to pay an annual dividend of $1.35 one year from now, after which future dividends are expected to grow at a constant 6 percent rate. MP3's debt consists of 20-year, 10-percent annual coupon bonds with a face value of $150 million and a market value of $165 million. The company's capital mix also includes 100,000 shares of 10 percent preferred stock selling at par. If MP3 Devices faces a marginal tax rate of 34 percent, what weighted-average cost of capital should it to use as it evaluates this project? **(See solution on p. 376)**

Personal Application

Mackenzie is currently finishing up her B.S. degree and is considering going back to grad school for a master's. She currently has $17,125 in student loans carrying an 8 percent interest rate from her B.S. and estimates that she will need to take out an additional $29,000 in student loans (at the same interest rate) to make it through the master's program she'd like to attend. The IRS allows taxpayers with student loans to deduct the interest on those loans, but only up to a maximum amount of $2,500 per year. Assuming that Mackenzie will face a marginal personal tax rate of 25 percent when she graduates, what will be the average after-tax interest rate that she will be paying on the student loans immediately after she graduates with her master's? **(See solution on p. 376)**

A practice test can be found on the Online Learning Center at
www.mhhe.com/can1e

return. Since firms seldom use equal amounts of debt and equity capital sources, we will need to calculate a *weighted* average, with weights based on the proportion of debt and equity capital used.

One important point about the **component costs** to be used in the firm's computation of the average required rate of return is that dividends paid to either common or preferred stockholders are not tax deductible. Thus paying a certain interest rate to either costs the firm that same interest rate. On the other hand, interest paid to debt holders *is* tax deductible, implying that the firm's effective after-tax out-of-pocket interest cost will be equal to the interest rate paid on debt multiplied by one minus the firm's relevant tax rate.

For example, if a firm pays a 10 percent coupon on $1 million in debt while it is subject to a 35 percent tax rate, then each coupon payment will be equal to .10 × $1,000,000 = $100,000, but that $100,000 in interest, being tax deductible, will reduce the firm's tax bill by .35 × $100,000 = $35,000. So paying $100,000 in interest saves the firm $35,000 in taxes, making the effective after-tax cost of debt equal to $100,000 − $35,000 = $65,000 and the effective after-tax interest rate equal to 10% × (1 − 35%) = 6.5%.

 ## 11.1 The WACC Formula

The average cost per dollar of capital raised is called the **weighted-average cost of capital (WACC)**. We calculate WACC using equation (11-1):

$$\text{WACC} = \frac{E}{E + P + D} i_E + \frac{P}{E + P + D} i_P + \frac{D}{E + P + D} i_D \times (1 - T_C) \qquad \text{(11-1)}$$

where

$$E \quad = \quad \text{the market value of equity used in financing the relevant project or firm.}$$

$$P \quad = \quad \text{the market value of preferred stock used.}$$

$$D \quad = \quad \text{the market value of debt used.}$$

$$i_E \quad = \quad \text{the after-tax cost of equity.}$$

$$i_P \quad = \quad \text{the after-tax cost of preferred stock.}$$

$$i_D \quad = \quad \text{the before-tax cost of debt.}$$

$$T_C \quad = \quad \text{the appropriate corporate tax rate.}$$

Notice that we use weights based on market values rather than book values because market values reflect investors' assessment of what they would be willing to pay for the various types of securities.

Calculating the Component Cost of Equity

We could calculate i_E using the capital asset pricing model:

$$i_E = i_f + \beta_E \big[E(i_M) - i_f \big] \qquad \text{(11-2)}$$

Or we can assume that the equity in question is a constant-growth stock such as the ones we modeled in Chapter 8. Under this assumption, we can solve the constant-growth model for i_E:

$$i_E = \frac{D_1}{P_0} + g \qquad \text{(11-3)}$$

Which way is better? Well, theoretically, they should both give us the same answer, but some pragmatic reasons may dictate why we may prefer one method over the other, depending on the particular situation.

To the extent that β_E estimates *future* systematic risk, but we calculate it based on *historic* systematic risk, we obviously won't want to use the CAPM in situations in which we either don't have sufficient historic observations to estimate β_E (i.e., when the stock is fairly new), or when we suspect that the past level of the stock's systematic (or market) risk might not be a good indicator of the future. On the other hand, the constant-growth model is only going to be appropriate for the limited number of stocks that just happen to expect constant dividend growth. We can try to adjust the model to use it for those stocks without constant dividend growth, but doing so will tend to introduce potentially sizable errors. Remember that our mathematical results are only as good as their underlying assumptions and data. Under CAPM, we may have a data problem; under the constant-growth model, our assumptions may not hold.

Overall, we should expect that the CAPM approach to estimating i_E will apply more accurately in most cases. However, if you do encounter a situation in which the constant-growth model applies, then you can certainly use it. If we are really fortunate and happen to have enough information to use both approaches, then we should probably *use* both, taking an average of the resulting estimates of i_E.[1]

 For interactive versions of this example visit www.mhhe.com/can1e

EXAMPLE 11-1

COST OF EQUITY

 LG2

ADK Industries' common shares sell for $32.75 per share. ADK expects to set their next annual dividend at $1.54 per share. If ADK expects future dividends to grow by 6 percent per year, indefinitely, the current risk-free rate is 3 percent, the expected return on the market is 9 percent, and the stock has a beta of 1.3, what should be firm's cost of equity?

SOLUTION:

The cost of equity using the CAPM will be

$$i_E = i_f + \beta_E\left[E(i_M) - i_f\right]$$

$$= .03 + 1.3[.09 - .03]$$

$$= .1080, \text{ or } 10.80\%$$

The cost of equity using the constant-growth model will be

$$i_E = \frac{D_1}{P_0} + g$$

$$= \frac{\$1.54}{\$32.75} + .06$$

$$= .1070, \text{ or } 10.70\%$$

Our best estimate of ADK's equity would therefore be $\dfrac{10.70\% + 10.80\%}{2} = 10.75\%$.

---

[1]Think of taking such an average as being intuitively the same as diversifying our "portfolio" of data across the two different estimation techniques, thereby reducing the average amount of estimation error.

Calculating the Component Cost of Preferred Stock

As we discussed in Chapter 8, preferred stock represents a special case of the constant-growth model, wherein g equals zero. So we can estimate preferred stocks' component cost using a simplified version of equation 11-3:

$$i_P = \frac{D_1}{P_0} \qquad \text{(11-4)}$$

 EXAMPLE 11-2   For interactive versions of this example visit www.mhhe.com/can1e

LG3 COST OF PREFERRED STOCK

Suppose that ADK also has one million shares of 7 percent preferred stock outstanding, trading at $72 per share. What is ADK's component cost for preferred equity?

SOLUTION:

The cost of the preferred stock will equal

$$i_P = \frac{D_1}{P_0}$$

$$= \frac{\$7}{\$72}$$

$$= .0972, \text{ or } 9.72\%$$

Calculating the Component Cost of Debt

Because of the tax deductibility of debt for the firm, computing the component cost of debt, unlike computing the component costs of equity and preferred stock, actually has two parts. We must estimate the before-tax cost of debt, i_D, and then adjust this figure to convert it to the post-tax residual rate of return.

To estimate i_D, we need to solve for the yield to maturity (YTM) on the firm's existing debt:

$$\text{Solve}\left\{ PV = PMT \times \left[\frac{1 - \frac{1}{(1 + i_D)^N}}{i_D} \right] + \frac{PV}{(1 + i_D)^N} \right\} \text{for } i_D \qquad \text{(11-5)}$$

Then we adjust this result by multiplying by $(1 - T_C)$.

 EXAMPLE 11-3   For interactive versions of this example visit www.mhhe.com/can1e

LG3 COST OF DEBT

ADK has 30,000 20-year, 8 percent annual coupon bonds outstanding. If the bonds currently sell for 97.5 percent of par and the firm pays an average tax rate of 35.92 percent, what will be the before-tax and after-tax component cost for debt?

(continued)

SOLUTION:

The before-tax cost of debt will be the solution to

$$\text{Solve} \left\{ \$975 = \$80 \times \left[\frac{1 - \dfrac{1}{(1+i_D)^{20}}}{i_D} + \frac{\$1000}{(1+i_D)^{20}} \right] \text{for } i_D \right\}$$

which will equal 8.26 percent. Multiplying this by one minus the tax rate will yield the after-tax cost of debt: $8.26\% \times (1 - .3592) = 5.2930\%$.

Choosing the Appropriate Tax Rate for the WACC

The interest paid on debt is tax deductible, but the benefit of that tax deductibility will vary based on the firm's marginal tax rate. The appropriate tax rate to be used in the WACC will be the weighted average of the marginal tax rates that would have been paid on the taxable income shielded by the interest deduction.

For example, if a firm had earnings before interest and taxes (EBIT) of $400,000, taxable interest deductions of $100,000, and faced the corporate tax schedule shown in Table 11.1, then the appropriate tax rate would equal a weighted average of the marginal tax rates from the fourth (i.e., "39%") and fifth ("34%") tax brackets. The weights would be determined by the relative impacts of the brackets in the computation of the post-interest tax bill:

$$\frac{\$35,000}{\$100,000} \times 39\% + \frac{\$65,000}{\$100,000} \times 34\% = 35.75\%$$

 For interactive versions of this example visit www.mhhe.com/can1e

EXAMPLE 11-4

TAX RATE

Suppose that ADK expects EBIT to be approximately $20,000,000 per year for the foreseeable future. Given the 30,000 20-year, 8 percent annual coupon bonds discussed in the previous example, what would the appropriate tax rate be for use in the calculation of the debt component of ADK's WACC?

SOLUTION:

The interest payments on the bonds would total $30,000 \times \$1,000 \times .08 = \$2,400,000$ per year, resulting in earnings before tax (EBT) of $\$20,000,000 - \$2,400,000 = \$17,600,000$.

As taxable income falls from $20,000,000 to $17,600,000 after the firm pays the interest on the bonds $1,666,667, or 69.44 percent, of the $2,400,000 reduction would fall in the highest 35 percent bracket, while the remaining $733,333, or 30.56 percent ($733,333/$2,400,000) would occur in the 38 percent tax bracket, making the weighted average applicable tax rate equal to:

$$T_c = (.6944 \times 35\%) + (.3056 \times 38\%)$$

$$= .3592, \text{ or } 35.92\%$$

TAXABLE INCOME			TAX RATE
$0	–	$50,000	15%
50,001	–	75,000	25
75,001	–	100,000	34
100,001	–	335,000	39
335,001	–	10,000,000	34
10,000,001	–	15,000,000	35
15,000,001	–	18,333,333	38
18,333,334	+		35

Calculating the Weights

When we calculate weights for WACC, we want to ensure that we use relevant market values of equity, preferred stock, and debt. If we're calculating WACC for a firm, then E, P, and D would be the entire market value of each source of capital; if we're calculating WACC for a project, then we would set them equal to the amount of each type used for that particular project.[2]

EXAMPLE 11-5

 For interactive versions of this example visit www.mhhe.com/can1e

 ## CAPITAL STRUCTURE WEIGHTS AND WACC

Let's continue the previous examples. Suppose that ADK has issued 3 million shares of common stock, 1 million shares of preferred stock, and the previously mentioned 30,000 bonds outstanding. What will ADK's WACC be, considering ADK as a firm?

SOLUTION:

Using the securities' prices given in previous examples, ADK's equity, preferred stock, and debt will have the following total market values:

- Equity: 3,000,000 × $32.75 = $98,250,000.
- Preferred stock: 1,000,000 × $72 = $72,000,000.
- Debt: 30,000 × $975 = $29,250,000.

The total combined market value for all three capital sources is $199,500,000. The applicable weights for each capital source will therefore be

$$\text{For common equity}: \frac{E}{E+P+D} = \frac{\$98,250,000}{\$199,500,000} = .4925, \text{ or } 49.25\%$$

$$\text{For preferred stock}: \frac{P}{E+P+D} = \frac{\$72,000,000}{\$199,500,000} = .3609, \text{ or } 36.09\%$$

$$\text{For debt}: \frac{D}{E+P+D} = \frac{\$29,250,000}{\$199,500,000} = .1466, \text{ or } 14.66\%$$

Tying this all in together with the answers from the previous examples, ADK will have a WACC of

$$\text{WACC} = \frac{E}{E+P+D}i_E + \frac{P}{E+P+D}i_P + \frac{D}{E+P+D}i_D \times (1-T_C)$$

$$= (.4925 \times 10.75\%) + (.3609 \times 9.72\%) + (.1466 \times 8.26\% \times [1-.3592])$$

$$= .0958, \text{ or } 9.58\%$$

[2]We'll discuss more about calculating WACC for a project later in the chapter.

11.2 Firm WACC versus Project WACC

So far, we've been defining the WACC as a weighted-average cost across the firm's different financing sources. If we think of a firm as a portfolio of different projects and products, we can also see that the WACC will be a weighted-average cost of capital across the items in that portfolio, too, and will therefore represent the cost of capital for the "typical" project that the firm is currently undertaking. So now the question we need to address is whether our firmwide WACC, calculated above, will also be appropriate to use as management evaluates new proposed projects.

The answer is: It depends. If a new project is similar enough to existing projects, then yes, the firm's WACC can be used as the project's WACC, too. But say that a firm is contemplating undertaking a significantly different project—one far different from any project that the firm is already engaged in. Then we *cannot expect* the firm's overall WACC to appropriately measure the new project's cost of capital. Let your intuition work on this: If the new project is riskier than the firm's existing projects, then it should expect to be "charged" a *higher* cost of capital. If it's safer, then the firm should assign the new project a *lower* cost of capital.

For example, consider a U.S. firm—let's call it GassUp—that currently owns a chain of gas stations. Firm management is considering a new project: opening up a series of gourmet coffee shops. Given the demand for upscale coffee in the United States, as well as the historically volatile oil markets, it's probably difficult to say exactly whether the coffee shops will be *more* or *less* risky than gas stations. We can probably say, though, that the two enterprises will face *different* risks. For example, if the coffee shops are located within the busiest and most stable gas stations—say the ones that lie along freeways—then the firm faces remodeling of existing buildings rather than starting from scratch. Locating the coffee shops within existing structures would likely mean that the risks will be lower than building new stations or new coffee shops.

So, does this mean that GassUp should calculate a heterogeneous WACC for each new project using purely project-specific numbers? Well, not exactly. As we'll discuss below, some inputs to WACC should be project-specific, but others should be consistent with the firmwide values used in calculating a firmwide WACC.

Project Cost Numbers that We Should Take from the Firm

It's tempting to argue that all component inputs for a project-specific WACC should be based on the specific project attributes, but if we created all project-specific numbers, we would be ignoring a fundamental issue pertaining to all bond and preferred stock indenture contracts. Both bonds and preferred stocks create claims on the *firm*, not of any particular group of projects within that firm. Furthermore, debt claims are superior to those of common stockholders. Thus, if the new project *does* significantly increase the firm's overall risk, the increased risk will be borne disproportionately by common stockholders. Debt holders and preferred stockholders will likely face minimal impact on the risk and return that their investments give them, no matter what new project the firm undertakes—even if those claimants own bonds or preferred shares that the firm issued to fund the new project.

For example, suppose GassUp decides to build entirely separate facilities for its coffee shops, which they'll name "Bottoms Up." They partially finance their expansion into coffee shops with debt, and the project turns out to be more like "Bottoms Down"—far less successful than the firm had hoped. Though this would be an unfortunate turn of events for GassUp's shareholders, the firm's creditors would likely still collect their usual interest and dividend payments from GassUp's gross revenues from gas station operations.

Creditors understand that their repayment will likely come from continuing operations and take current cash flows into account when a firm comes seeking funds. For example, if a small firm approaches a bank for a loan to finance an expansion, the bank will normally spend more time analyzing *current* cash flows to determine the probability that they will recoup their loan than it will analyzing the potential new cash flows from the proposed expansion.

Note that this situation holds true only as long as the "new" projects represent fairly small investments compared to ongoing operations. As new projects become *large* relative to ongoing cash-flow producing activities, creditors will have to examine the likelihood of being repaid from the new projects much more closely. New projects, however great their potential, inherently carry more risk than do established current operations. Changes in the proportion of new projects relative to ongoing operations will thus translate into increased risk for the creditor, who will ask for a higher rate of return to offset the risk.

Since most firms tend to grow incrementally, we will assume (unless otherwise indicated) that we're examining situations in which the number of new projects is small relative to ongoing operations. We can therefore assume that using the firm's existing WACC for both debt and preferred stock is appropriate.

Project Cost Numbers that We Should Not Take from the Firm: The Pure Play Approach

Since we've decided not to adjust the firmwide costs of debt or preferred stock for the risk of a project, where *should* we account for the new project risk brought to the firm overall? As with several other questions associated with risk- and profit-sharing that we'll discuss in Chapter 14, the answer lies with the residual claimant: equity.

The firm's risk will obviously change when it takes on a project that's noticeably different from its existing lines of business. Since debt holders and preferred stockholders won't notice this change in risk, the firm spreads the risks that it takes with new projects by transferring most of the risk to the common stockholders.

In response to such a change in the firm's risk profile, the stockholders will adjust their required rate of return to adjust for the new risk level. Absent any alteration to the firm's capital structure,[3] changes in the firm's risk profile are due to differences in the firm's **business risks** based on the mix of the new and existing product lines. The firm's beta will reflect those differences in each product line.

---

[3]In reality, new projects are often financed with different proportions of equity, debt, and preferred stock than were used to fund the firm's existing operations. As we'll discuss in Chapter 14, such a change in capital structure will result in a change in **financial risk**, with increased leverage magnifying β_E.

Obviously, no proposed new project will have a history of previous returns. Without such returns data, neither analysts nor investors can calculate a project-specific beta. But to the extent that we can find other firms engaged in the proposed new line of business, we can use their betas as proxies to estimate the project's risk. Ideally, the other firms would be engaged *only* in the proposed new line of business; such monothemed firms are usually referred to as *pure plays*, with this term also in turn being applied to this approach to estimating a project's beta.

An average of n such **proxy betas** will give us a fairly accurate estimate of what the new project's beta will be.[4]

$$i_E = r_f + \beta_{Avg}\left[E(r_M) - r_f\right]$$

where

$$\beta_{Avg} = \frac{\sum_{j=1}^{n} \beta_j}{n} \qquad \textbf{(11-6)}$$

This average will *be* an estimate, in the strictest statistical sense of the word. You might recall from your statistics classes that we will need to be careful to get as large a sample as possible if we want to get as much statistical power for our estimate as possible. Ideally, we would like to find at least three or four **pure-play proxies** to ensure that we have a large enough sample size to safely make meaningful inferences. In reality, however, two (or even one) proxies might represent a suitable sample if their business line resembles the proposed new project closely enough. In particular, we may want to use betas from industry front-runners, and rely less on betas of any firms that the company really doesn't want to emulate.

What shall we do if we can't find *any* pure-play proxies? Well, in that case, we may want to use firms that, while not *solely* in the same business as the proposed project's venture, have a sizable proportion of revenues from that line. We may then be able to "back out" the impact of their other lines of business from their firm's beta to leave us with a good enough estimate of what the new project's beta might be.

We should also ensure that we use weights based on the *project's* sources of capital, and not necessarily the *firm's* capital structure. If the new project is going to use more or less debt than the firm's existing projects do, then the risk- and reward-sharing are going to vary across the different types of capital (as discussed in Chapter 14), and we will want to recognize this in our WACC computation.

Finally, we need to consider the appropriate corporate tax rate to use in calculating the WACC for a project. That marginal corporate tax rate will be the average marginal tax rate to which the project's cash flows will be subject. Referring back to our previous example about the appropriate marginal average tax rate to use in computing a firm's WACC, assume that the same firm with $400,000 of EBIT from current operations is considering a new project that will increase EBIT by $200,000. Since this $200,000 increase will keep the firm's marginal tax in the fifth bracket of Table 11.1, the appropriate tax rate to compute the project's WACC will simply be 34 percent.

---

[4]As we'll also discuss in Chapter 14, we will be able to take a straight average of the proxy firm's betas as the estimate of our beta only if the capital structures of all the proxies are identical to each other and to that of our proposed new project. If not, we will need to adjust the proxies' estimated betas for differences in capital structures before averaging them. Then we will need to readjust the average beta for our project's capital structure before using the estimate.

To summarize, the component costs and weights to compute a project-specific WACC should be as shown below in equation 11-7, with the source of each part indicated by the appropriate subscript:

$$WACC_{Project} = \frac{E_{Project}}{E_{Project} + P_{Project} + D_{Project}} i_{E,Project}$$

$$+ \frac{P_{Project}}{E_{Project} + P_{Project} + D_{Project}} i_{P,Firm}$$

$$+ \frac{D_{Project}}{E_{Project} + P_{Project} + D_{Project}} i_{D,Firm} \times (1 - T_{C,Project}) \qquad \textbf{(11-7)}$$

EXAMPLE 11-6

 For interactive versions of this example visit www.mhhe.com/can1e

 CALCULATION OF PROJECT WACC

Suppose that Evita's Subs, a local shipyard, is considering opening up a chain of sandwich shops. Evita's capital structure currently consists of 2 million outstanding shares of common stock, selling for $83 per share, and a 50 million dollar bond issue, selling at 103 percent of par. Evita's stock has a beta of 0.72, the expected market risk premium is 7 percent, and the current risk-free rate is 4.5 percent. The bonds pay a 9 percent annual coupon and mature in 20 years. The current operations of the firm produce EBIT of $100 million per year, and the new sandwich operations would add only an expected $12 million per year to that. Also, suppose that Evita's management has done some research on the sandwich shop industry, and discovered that such firms have an average beta of 1.23. If the new project will be funded with 50 percent debt and 50 percent equity, what should be the WACC for this new project?

SOLUTION:

First, note that Evita's doesn't currently have any outstanding preferred stock and doesn't plan on using any to finance the new project, so that makes our job a little simpler. Also note that, though we are given enough information to calculate the firm's current capital structure weights and component cost of equity, we won't need those figures, as this new project differs from the firmwide WACC weights. We already know the capital structure weights for the new project (50 percent debt and 50 percent equity), so we just need to calculate the appropriate component costs.

For equity, the appropriate cost will based upon the average risk of sandwich shops:

$$i_E = r_f + \beta_{E,Project}[E(r_M) - r_f]$$

$$= .0045 + 1.23[.07]$$

$$= .1311, \text{ or } 13.11\%$$

The YTM on the new bonds issued to finance this project will be the same as the YTM on the existing bonds:

$$\text{Solve} \left\{ \$1,030 = \$90 \times \left[\frac{1 - \frac{1}{(1+i_D)^{20}}}{i_D} \right] + \frac{\$1000}{(1+i_D)^{20}} \right\} \text{ for } i_D$$

which gives us an i_D of 8.68%.

(continued)

Finally, the current EBIT already puts the firm in the top 35 percent tax bracket, so the additional EBIT generated by the project will also be taxed at this same marginal 35 percent tax rate. Therefore, the WACC of the new project will be

$$WACC_{Project} = \frac{E_{Project}}{E_{Project} + P_{Project} + D_{Project}} i_{E,Project} + \frac{D_{Project}}{E_{Project} + P_{Project} + D_{Project}} i_{D,Firm} \times (1 - T_{C,Firm})$$

$$= .5 \times .1311 + .5 \times .0868 \times (1 - .35)$$

$$= .0938, \text{ or } 9.38\%$$

CALCULATOR HINTS
N = 20
PV = -1030
PMT = 90
FV = 1000
CPT I = 8.68%

TIME OUT

11-3   For computing a project WACC, why do we take some component costs from the firm, but compute others that are specific for the project being considered?

11-4   It is usually much easier to find proxy firms that are engaged in multiple lines of business than it is to find pure-play proxies. Explain how such firms can be used to estimate the beta for a new project.

11.3 Divisional WACC

Ideally, a firm would calculate a risk-appropriate WACC for every new project under consideration. Pragmatically, doing so isn't always feasible—particularly for large corporations, the managers of which must consider dozens or even hundreds of proposed new projects each year. The costs in terms of time and effort of estimating project-specific WACCs individually for each project are simply prohibitive.

Instead, large firms often take a middle-of-the-road approach to achieve many of the benefits that accrue to project-specific WACC calculations while spending much less time and resources. The key to this approach is to calculate a **divisional WACC**.

Advantages and Disadvantages of a Divisional WACC

To see the advantages and disadvantages of using divisional WACCs, let's first consider the disadvantage of using a firm's WACC to evaluate new, risk-heterogeneous projects. To make things simple, let's assume that we're looking at a firm that uses only equity finance, so that WACC is simply equal to i_E.

Similar to our discussion of the security market line in Chapter 10, required rates of return for projects with varying degrees of risk would lie along the sloped line shown in Figure 11.1. We could then evaluate projects with various degrees of risk based on the relationship between their expected rate of return and the required rate of return for that risk level. As Figure 11.2 shows, using risk-appropriate WACCs, projects A and B would be accepted, since their *expected* rates of return would be higher than their respective *required* rates of return. Projects C and D would be rejected because our simple scheme shows that these projects aren't expected to return enough to cover market required returns, given the projects' riskiness.

However, using a firmwide WACC would result in a comparison of the project's expected rates of return to a single, flat, firmwide cost of capital as Figure 11.3 shows. Using a simple firmwide WACC to evaluate new projects would give an

figure 11.1

Risk-Appropriate WACCs

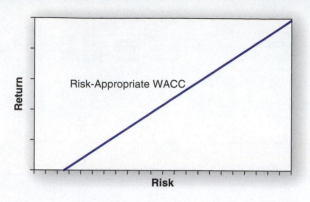

figure 11.2

Sample Projects versus
Risk-Sensitive WACC

figure 11.3

Sample Project versus
Firmwide WACC

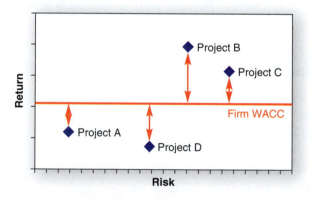

unfair advantage to projects that present more risk than the firm's average beta. Using a firmwide WACC would also work against projects that involved less risk than the firm's average beta. Looking at the same sample projects as before, we see that Project A would now be rejected, while Project C would be accepted.

Using a firmwide WACC in this way, as an inappropriate benchmark for projects of differing risk from the firm's current operations, will result in quite a few incorrect decisions. In fact, the use of a firmwide WACC to evaluate *any* projects with risk-return coordinates lying in the two triangles indicated in Figure 11.4 will result in an incorrect accept/reject decision.

figure 11.4

figure 11.5

If we can divide the firm's existing projects into divisions, where the different divisions proxy for systematically different average project risk levels, then calculating WACCs for each division separately, as Figure 11.5 shows, will greatly reduce the problem of basing decisions on inaccurate results from using firmwide WACC for all projects.

Using divisional WACCs like this will not *eliminate* problems of incorrect acceptance and incorrect rejection as we saw in Figure 11.4, but it will greatly reduce their frequency. Instead of making errors corresponding to the two large triangular areas indicated in Figure 11.4, we will instead have six smaller areas of error shown in Figure 11.6. More acceptance/rejection regions will result in fewer errors.

For example, let's consider our four sample projects from before. We now evaluate them using divisional WACCs as shown in Figure 11.7. We would correctly accept both projects A and B and correctly reject projects C and D.

Subjective versus Objective Approaches to Calculating Divisional WACCs

We can form divisional WACCs subjectively by simply considering the project's risk relative to the firm's existing lines of business. If the project is riskier (safer) than the firm average, adjust the firm WACC upward (downward) to account

figure 11.6

Divisional WACC Errors

figure 11.7

Example Decisions
Using Divisional WACCs

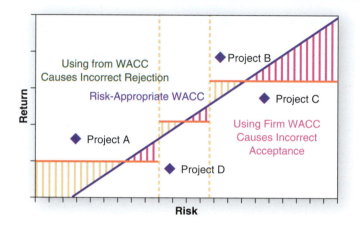

for our subjective opinion of project riskiness. The biggest disadvantage to this approach is that the adjustments are subjective and created just for the project at hand. For example, consider the sample subjective divisional WACCs in Table 11.2. Both the project assignments to the divisions and then the WACC adjustments for the very low risk, low risk, high risk, and very high risk are fairly arbitrary.

An objective approach to calculating divisional WACCs would be to compute the average beta per division, use these figures in the CAPM formula to calculate i_E for each division, and then, in turn, use divisional estimates of i_E to construct divisional WACCs. Though the objective approach would usually be more precise, resulting in fewer incorrect accept/reject decisions, the subjective approach is more frequently used because it is easier to implement.

Subjective Divisional WACCs	table 11.2

RISK LEVEL	DISCOUNT RATE
Very low risk	Firm WACC − 5%
Low risk	Firm WACC − 2%
Same risk as firm	Firm WACC
High risk	Firm WACC + 3%
Very high risk	Firm WACC + 7%

EXAMPLE 11-7

DIVISIONAL COSTS OF CAPITAL

LG7

Assume that BF, Inc., an all-equity firm, has a firmwide WACC of 10 percent, and that the firm is broken into three divisions: Textiles, Accessories, and Miscellaneous. The average Textiles project has a beta of 0.7; the average Accessories project has a beta of 1.3; and the average Miscellaneous project has a beta of 1.1.

The firm is currently considering the projects shown in the table below. Their current approach is to use the firm's WACC to evaluate all projects, but they see the wisdom in adopting a subjective divisional cost of capital approach. Firm management is thus considering a divisional cost of capital scheme in which they will use the firm's WACC for Miscellaneous projects, the firm's WACC minus 1 percent for Textiles projects, and the firm's WACC plus 3 percent for Accessories projects. The current expected return to the market is 12 percent, and the current risk-free rate is 5.75 percent.

For this group of projects, how much better would their accept/reject decisions be if they used this approach rather than if they continued to use the firm's WACC to evaluate all projects? Would switching to an objective divisional cost of capital approach, where the WACC for each division is based on that division's average beta, improve their accept/reject criteria any further?

SOLUTION:

Determine the required rates of return for each project assuming that the firm uses the firm-wide WACC and adds the subjective adjustments to construct divisional WACCs. The objective computation of divisional WACCs using each division's average beta and the i_E computed using each project's specific beta is indicated in the table below. In each case, project acceptances appear in blue print, and project rejections appear in red print.

PROJECT	DIVISION	EXPECTED i_E	BETA
A	$\beta_{Accessories}$	17.00%	1.3
B	$\beta_{Accessories}$	15.00	1.2
C	$\beta_{Miscellaneous}$	13.00	1.3
D	$\beta_{Miscellaneous}$	11.00	0.7
E	$\beta_{Textiles}$	9.00	0.8
F	$\beta_{Textiles}$	7.00	0.5

PROJECT	DIVISION	EXPECTED i_E	BETA	FIRM WACC	SUBJECTIVE i_E	OBJECTIVE i_E	SPECIFIC i_E
A	$\beta_{Accessories}$	17.00%	1.3	10.00%	13.00%	13.88%	13.88%
B	$\beta_{Accessories}$	15.00	1.2	10.00	13.00	13.88	13.25
C	$\beta_{Miscellaneous}$	13.00	1.3	10.00	10.00	12.63	13.88
D	$\beta_{Miscellaneous}$	11.00	0.7	10.00	10.00	12.63	10.13
E	$\beta_{Textiles}$	9.00	0.8	10.00	9.00	10.13	10.75
F	$\beta_{Textiles}$	7.00	0.5	10.00	9.00	10.13	8.88

Using the "Specific i_E" yields the "correct" accept/reject decision; that is, these accept/reject decisions would be generated exactly the same if the firm had the time and resources to compute the i_E on a project-by-project basis. In this particular situation, using the firm WACC as a benchmark for all the projects would result in projects E and F being rejected, since they both will return expected rates less than the firm's 10 percent required rate of return. By comparison to the results using the Specific i_E, both of these rejections are appropriate. We would prefer that the accept/reject criteria took account of risk; that is, both projects be rejected because their expected returns (9 percent and 7 percent, respectively) are less than the required returns (10.75 and 8.88 percent, respectively) based on their specific levels of project risk rather than assuming that both projects carry the same risk as the firm's overall risk.

(continued)

Using the subjectively adjusted approach to calculating i_E results in required rates of return of 13 percent for Accessories projects, 10 percent for Miscellaneous projects, and 9 percent for Textiles projects. The associated accept/reject decisions actually incorrectly accept project E, making the subjectively adjusted WACC approach worse (in this specific example) than simply using the firmwide WACC.

Finally, using the objective approach to constructing divisional costs of capital, along with the three divisions' average betas given above, results in required rates of return for the three divisions of

$$i_E = i_f + \beta_E [E(i_M) - i_f]$$
$$i_{E,Accessories} = .0575 + 1.3[.12 - .0575] = .1388, \text{ or } 13.88\%$$
$$i_{E,Miscellaneous} = .0575 + 1.1[.12 - .0575] = .1263, \text{ or } 12.63\%$$
$$i_{E,Textiles} = .0575 + 0.7[.12 - .0575] = .1013, \text{ or } 10.13\%$$

As the solutions above show, using these divisional cost of capital figures as required rates of return for each project results in correct rejections of projects E and F, but also result in an incorrect rejection of project D and an incorrect acceptance of project C relative to computing i_E on a project-by-project basis.

Overall, using either the objective or subjective approaches to calculating divisional costs of capital will not be as precise as using project-specific WACCs: we will wind up incorrectly accepting and/or rejecting some projects. But this **"costs."** In terms of making incorrect decisions on some of our project choices may be worth it if the projects in question aren't large enough for project-specific calculations to be cost-effective.

TIME OUT

11-5 Divisions of a corporation aren't usually formed based explicitly on differences in risk between the projects in different divisions. Rather, they're normally formed along product-type or geographic differences. Explain how this division scheme may still result in divisions that *do* differ among themselves by average risk. Also explain why calculating divisional WACCs in such a situation will still improve decision making over simply using a firmwide WACC for project acceptance or rejection.

11-6 Explain why, in Example 11-7, using objectively computed divisional WACCS still resulted in an incorrect accept/reject decision for project D.

LG8 # 11.4 Flotation Costs

If a firm uses only retained earnings or other internally generated sources of capital to finance a new project, then the component costs are exactly as discussed above. However, if a firm funds a project by issuing externally generated new capital—additional stock, bonds, and so on—then the firm will also have to pay commissions to the underwriting firm that floats the issue. Component costs will then need to integrate these **flotation costs** to figure project WACCs.

We can approach the commission costs in two basic ways. We can either increase the project's WACC to incorporate the flotation costs' impact as a percentage of WACC, or we can leave the WACC alone and adjust the project's initial investment upwards so as to reflect the "true" cost of the project. Both approaches have advantages and disadvantages. The first approach tends to understate the component cost of new equity, and the latter approach violates the **separation principle** of capital budgeting, which states that the calculations of cash flows should remain independent of financing. We'll discuss the separation principle in the next chapter and so will also put off our discussion of the second approach to handling flotation costs until that time, too.

Adjusting the WACC

The first approach to adjusting for flotation costs involves adjusting the issue price of new securities by subtracting flotation cost, F, to reflect the net security price and then using this net price to calculate the component cost of capital. For equity, this approach is most commonly applied to the constant-growth model:

$$i_E = \frac{D_1}{P_0 - F} + g \qquad\qquad \textbf{(11-8)}$$

If we instead want to apply this approach to the cost of equity obtained from the CAPM formula, we would adjust it upward by an equivalent amount.

 For interactive versions of this example visit www.mhhe.com/can1e

EXAMPLE 11-8

Flotation-Adjusted Cost of Equity

 LG8

Suppose that, as in Example 11-1, ADK Industries' common shares are selling for $32.75 per share, and the company expects to set its next annual dividend at $1.54 per share. All future dividends are expected to grow by 6 percent per year, indefinitely. In addition, let's also suppose that ADK faces a flotation cost of 20 percent on new equity issues. Calculate the flotation-adjusted cost of equity.

SOLUTION:

Twenty percent of $32.75 will be $6.55, so the flotation-adjusted cost of equity will be

$$i_E = \frac{D_1}{P_0 - F} + g$$

$$= \frac{\$1.54}{\$32.75 - \$6.55} + .06$$

$$= .1188, \text{ or } 11.88\%$$

Notice that the result is 1.18 percent above the non-flotation-adjusted cost of equity, 10.70 percent, computed using the constant-growth model in Example 11-1. If we instead wanted to use the CAPM estimate, we would take the non-flotation-adjusted CAPM estimate from the same example, 10.80 percent and add the same differential of 1.18 percent to it to get the flotation-adjusted value:

$$i_E = .1080 + .0118 = .1198, \text{ or } 11.98\%$$

The adjustments for the component costs of preferred stock and debt will be similar:

$$i_P = \frac{D_1}{P_0 - F} \qquad\qquad \textbf{(11-9)}$$

$$\text{Solve}\left\{ PV - F = PMT \times \left[\frac{1 - \dfrac{1}{(1+i_D)^N}}{i_D} \right] + \frac{PV}{(1+i_D)^N} \right\} \text{for } i_D \qquad\qquad \textbf{(11-10)}$$

 TIME OUT

11-7 Why should we expect the flotation costs for debt to be significantly lower than those for equity?

11-8 Explain how we should go about computing the WACC for a project which uses both retained earnings and a new equity issue.

Business Application Solution

MP3 Devices, Inc. faces current component costs of capital equal to:

$$i_E = \frac{D_1}{P_0} + g \qquad\qquad i_P = \frac{D_1}{P_0}$$

$$= \frac{\$1.35}{\$18.75} + .06 \qquad\qquad = \frac{\$10}{\$100}$$

$$= .1320, \text{ or } 13.20\% \qquad = .1000, \text{ or } 10.00\%$$

$$\text{Solve}\left\{\$1,100 = \$100 \times \left[\frac{1 - \dfrac{1}{(1 + i_D)^{20}}}{i_D}\right] + \frac{\$1,000}{(1 + i_D)^{20}}\right\} \text{ for } i_D$$

gives $i_D = .0891$, or 8.91%

CALCULATOR HINTS

N = 20
PV = −1,100
PMT = 100
FV = 1000
CPT I = 8.91%

Using the target capital structure weights, MP3's WACC equals:

$$\text{WACC} = .5 \times 13.20\% + .1 \times 10\% + .4 \times 8.91\% \times (1 - .34)$$

$$= .0995, \text{ or } 9.95\%$$

Personal Application Solution

Mackenzie can expect a total of $17,125 + $29,000 = $46,125 in student loans when she graduates from her master's program. At an 8 percent rate of interest, the yearly interest charges will be $3,690 immediately after she graduates (though they will go down once she starts paying off some of the principal). Since the yearly interest will be more than the allowable $2,500 deduction, we can express her after-tax interest rate as the following weighted average:

$$\text{WACC} = \frac{D_{Nondeductible}}{D_{Nondeductible} + D_{Deductible}} i_D$$

$$+ \frac{D_{Deductible}}{D_{Nondeductible} + D_{Deductible}} i_D \times (1 - T_P)$$

$$= \frac{\$3,690 - \$2,500}{\$3,690} \times 8\% + \frac{\$2,500}{\$3,690} \times 8\% \times (1 - .25)$$

$$= .3225 \times 8\% + .6775 \times 8\% \times .75$$

$$= 6.645\%$$

summary of learning goals

This chapter covers how to incorporate previous chapters' pricing formulas into weighted-average costs of capital calculations. We also discussed situations in which a firmwide WACC is appropriate for valuing a project, and when we need to calculate a project-specific WACC. We also discussed the trade-offs inherent in using divisional WACCs. Finally, we saw that incorporating flotation costs will increase the WACC above the value it would have if the firm was able to raise all funds internally.

www.mhhe.com/can1e

LG1 Grasp the basic intuition behind calculating the cost of capital. When firms use multiple sources of capital, they need to calculate the appropriate interest rate for valuing their firm's cash flows as a weighted average of the capital component costs.

LG2 Use the weighted-average cost of capital (WACC) formula to calculate a firm's cost of capital. The WACC formula uses the after-tax costs of capital to compute the firm's weighted-average cost of debt financing. Since interest on a firm's pure debt is paid out of before-tax income, the yield paid on bonds doesn't really come entirely out of the firm's pockets. If the firm hadn't paid out the interest owed to debt holders, then those funds would have been taxed. So, effectively, the firm only pays out $(1 - T_c)$ times the yield of debt to the debt holders; the government "pays" the remainder, T_c times the yield.

LG3 Debate the firm's choices in estimating capital component costs of equity, preferred stock, and debt. We estimate the component costs of capital using pricing formulas we've seen in previous chapters for equity, preferred stock, and debt, reworked to solve for the appropriate interest rate.

LG4 Calculate and justify appropriate weights used for a WACC projection. Appropriate weights used in calculating a WACC should reflect the relative sizes of the total market capitalizations for each kind of security that the firm issues—debt, preferred stock, and pure equity. Use market values rather than book values to calculate a WACC because market values reflect investors' assessment of what they would be willing to pay for the various types of securities.

LG5 Clarify which parts of a firmwide WACC can be used in calculating a project-specific WACC and which parts do not apply. Any debt or preferred stock that a firm issues, regardless of whether the securities will finance new projects or fund existing operations, are rightfully obligations of the entire firm. Thus, any debt and preferred stock components of capital should use firmwide, not project-specific, WACC figures. Therefore, we

can expect common stockholders to bear the brunt of the risk of new projects. Accordingly, the component cost of equity should reflect the *project* risk as measured by a proxy beta.

LG6 Detail the trade-offs implicit in using a firmwide WACC versus using a divisional cost of capital approach. Since firms evaluate projects continually, managers need a shortcut to avoid calculating project-specific WACCs for every project that they consider. They may use either a firmwide WACC or a divisional WACC instead, but using the shortcuts involves a trade-off between speed and precision. Using firmwide or divisional WACCS means that the firm can calculate many fewer WACCs than they have projects, but doing so will also introduce error into the accept/reject decisions. Decision errors rise further when managers use a single, firmwide WACC for all projects, or when they evaluate projects with significantly different risk than the firm's or division's average risk.

LG7 Differentiate between the objective and subjective approaches to computing a divisional cost of capital. An objective approach to computing a divisional WACC uses the average beta of projects in each division to calculate the WACC. The subjective approach requires only that WACCs for "risky" divisions be adjusted (sometimes arbitrarily so that risky division WACCs will be higher than firm WACCs). Similarly, subjective approaches adjust downward divisional WACCs for relatively safe divisions.

LG8 Denote the impact that flotation costs have on capital budgeting decisions and adjust the WACC to reflect them. Flotation costs increase costs if the firm must rely upon externally raised funds for a project. We adjust the WACC for flotation costs by subtracting the flotation costs from the prices of new securities at issue. Then we use the lower adjusted prices to calculate the respective component costs. Since we reduce the price of the securities but not the size of the expected future cash flows due to capital providers, this approach raises each capital source's effective cost.

chapter equations

11-1 $\quad \text{WACC} = \dfrac{E}{E + P + D}i_E + \dfrac{P}{E + P + D}i_P + \dfrac{D}{E + P + D}i_D \times (1 - T_C)$

11-2 $\quad i_E = i_f + \beta_E[E(i_M) - i_f]$

11-3 $\quad i_E = \dfrac{D_1}{P_0} + g$

11-4 $\quad i_P = \dfrac{D_1}{P_0}$

11-5 $\quad \text{Solve}\left\{ \text{PV} = \text{PMT} \times \left[\dfrac{1 - \dfrac{1}{(1 + i_D)^N}}{i_D} \right] + \dfrac{\text{PV}}{(1 + i_D)^N} \right\} \text{for } i_D$

11-6 $\quad i_E = r_f + \beta_{Avg}[E(r_M) - r_f]$

where

$$\beta_{Avg} = \dfrac{\sum\limits_{j=1}^{n} \beta_j}{n}$$

11-7 $\quad \text{WACC}_{\text{Project}} = \dfrac{E_{\text{Project}}}{E_{\text{Project}} + P_{\text{Project}} + D_{\text{Project}}}i_{E,\text{Project}}$

$\qquad\qquad\qquad + \dfrac{P_{\text{Project}}}{E_{\text{Project}} + P_{\text{Project}} + D_{\text{Project}}}i_{P,\text{Firm}}$

$\qquad\qquad\qquad + \dfrac{D_{\text{Project}}}{E_{\text{Project}} + P_{\text{Project}} + D_{\text{Project}}}i_{D,\text{Firm}} \times (1 - T_{C,\text{Firm}})$

11-8 $\quad i_E = \dfrac{D_1}{P_0 - F} + g$

11-9 $\quad i_P = \dfrac{D_1}{P_0 - F}$

11-10 $\quad \text{Solve}\left\{ \text{PV} - \text{F} = \text{PMT} \times \left[\dfrac{1 - \dfrac{1}{(1 + i_D)^N}}{i_D} \right] + \dfrac{\text{PV}}{(1 + i_D)^N} \right\} \text{for } i_D$

key terms

business risk, The risk of a project arising from the line of business it is in; the variability of a firm's or division's cash flows. (p. 366)

component costs, The individual costs of each type of capital—bonds, preferred stock, and common stock. (p. 360)

divisional WACC, An estimated WACC computed using some sort of proxy for the average equity risk of the projects in a particular division. (p. 369)

financial risk, The risk of a project to equity holders stemming from the use of debt in the financial structure of the firm; refers to the issue of how a firm decides to distribute the business risk between debt and equity holders. (p. 366)

flotation costs, Fees paid by firms to investment banks for issuing new securities. (p. 374)

proxy beta, The beta (a measure of the riskiness) of a firm in a similar line of business as a proposed new project. (p. 367)

separation principle, Theory maintaining that the sources and uses of capital should be decided upon independently. (p. 374)

weighted-average cost of capital (WACC), The weighted average after-tax cost of the capital used by a firm, with weights set equal to the relative percentage of each type of capital used. (p. 360)

self-test problems with solutions

① **Computing Companywide WACC** Sound & Vision Studios (SVS) has 5 million common shares outstanding, which sell for $24 per share. SVS management is expected to set the next annual dividend at $2.25 per share, and investors and analysts expect all future dividends to grow by 8 percent per year, indefinitely. The current risk-free rate is 5.50 percent, the expected return on the market is 11 percent, and the stock has a beta of 2.2. SVS also has 1 million shares of 5 percent preferred stock outstanding, with these shares selling for $44 per share, and 150,000 15-year, 9 percent annual coupon bonds outstanding, currently selling for 112 percent of par. If SVS is in the 35 percent tax bracket, what is the firm's WACC?

LG3, LG4

Solution:

The component cost of equity, i_E, computed using the CAPM, will be equal to

$$.055 + 2.2(.11 - .055) = .1760$$

The component cost of equity computed using the constant-growth model will be equal to:

$$\frac{\$2.25}{\$24.00} + .08 = .1738$$

Absent any guidance concerning which estimate is most appropriate, our best approach is to take the average of the two as i_E:

$$i_E = \frac{.1760 + .1738}{2} = .1749$$

The component cost of preferred stock, i_p, will be equal to:

$$\frac{\$5}{\$44} = .1136$$

The component cost of debt, i_D, will be the solution to:

$$\$1,120 = \$90 \times \left[\frac{1 - \dfrac{1}{(1 + i_D)^{15}}}{i_D} \right] + \frac{\$1000}{(1 + i_D)^{15}} \Rightarrow i_D = .0763$$

www.mhhe.com/can1e

The market values of equity, preferred stock and debt will be

$$E = 5,000,000 \times \$24.00 = \$120,000,000$$
$$P = 1,000,000 \times \$44.00 = \$44,000,000$$
$$D = 150,000 \times \$1,120 = \$168,000,000$$

And we can use these proportions to calculate the weights:

$$\frac{E}{E+P+D} = \frac{\$120,000,000}{\$120,000,000 + \$44,000,000 + \$168,000,000} = .3614$$

$$\frac{P}{E+P+D} = \frac{\$44,000,000}{\$120,000,000 + \$44,000,000 + \$168,000,000} = .1325$$

$$\frac{E}{E+P+D} = \frac{\$168,000,000}{\$120,000,000 + \$44,000,000 + \$168,000,000} = .5060$$

Using the weights, the component costs, and the tax rate, we can calculate the WACC as

$$WACC = .3614 \times 17.49\% + .1325 \times 11.36\% + .5060 \times 7.63\% \times (1 - .35)$$
$$= .1034, \text{ or } 10.34\%$$

LG5

2 **Calculating Project WACC** Ranks Engineering, a civil engineering firm that has historically gotten most of its revenues from the planning and construction of public works projects, is considering starting a new division that will submit architectural designs for private engineering projects, such as designing shopping malls. While the civil engineering industry has a fairly low beta of 0.65, the private design market is a bit riskier, and Ranks has commissioned a study that shows that the average beta in that industry is approximately 1.3. Rank's capital structure currently consists of 1 million outstanding shares of common stock, selling for $37 per share, and a $15 million bond issue, selling at 98 percent of par. The expected market risk premium is 8 percent, and the current risk-free rate is 5.7 percent. The bonds pay an 8 percent annual coupon and mature in 10 years. If the new project will be funded with 70 percent equity and 30 percent debt, what should be the WACC for this new project?

Solution:

The weights to be used in the calculation of the project's WACC will be the 70 percent equity/30 percent debt specified in the problem and will not be based upon the company's existing capital structure.

The component cost of equity, i_E, will use the beta of the new line of business:

$$.057 + 1.3(.08) = .1610$$

The component cost of debt, i_D, will be the solution to

$$\$980 = \$80 \times \left[\frac{1 - \frac{1}{(1 + i_D)^{10}}}{i_D} \right] + \frac{\$1000}{(1 + i_D)^{10}} \Rightarrow i_D = .0830$$

The rise in EBIT from \$8 million to \$10 million will occur entirely in the second 34 percent tax bracket of Table 11.1, so 34 percent will be the appropriate tax rate for computation of the project's WACC, which will be equal to

$$\text{WACC} = .7 \times 16.10\% + .3 \times 8.30\% \times (1 - .34)$$
$$= .1291, \text{ or } 12.9\%$$

3 An all-equity firm is considering the projects shown in the table below. The T-bill rate is 6 percent and the market risk premium is 9 percent. If the firm uses its current WACC of 16.8 percent to evaluate these projects, which project(s), if any, will be incorrectly rejected?

PROJECT	EXPECTED RETURN	BETA
A	8.0%	0.2
B	19.0	1.4
C	13.0	0.8
D	17.0	1.3

Solution:

If the firm uses the current WACC of 16.8 percent to evaluate all projects, projects A and C will be rejected. To determine if these rejections are correct or incorrect, we have to calculate what the projects' risk-specific WACCs should be:

$$\text{WACC}_A = i_{E,A} = .06 + 0.2 \times .09 = .078, \text{ or } 7.8\%$$
$$\text{WACC}_C = i_{E,C} = .06 + 0.8 \times .09 = .132, \text{ or } 13.2\%$$

Based on these numbers, project C *should* be rejected, as its risk-appropriate WACC of 13.2 percent is higher than its expected return of 13 percent. This result indicates that the project is not expected to earn a high enough level of return to compensate for its expected risk.

Project A's risk-appropriate rate of return at 7.8 percent doesn't meet its expected 8 percent return, so it should be rejected. Project A's rejection when using the firmwide WACC is incorrect.

4 **Include impact of flotation costs** Redo ST-1 for a proposed new project in the same line of business as the firm's current operations, but assuming that new equity will have a flotation cost of 15 percent, preferred stock will have a flotation cost of 10 percent, and debt will have a flotation cost of 3 percent.

Solution:

The component cost of equity, i_E, using flotation costs and the constant-growth model, will be

$$\frac{\$2.25}{\$24.00 - (.15 \times \$24.00)} + .08 = .1903$$

Since this is $19.03\% - 17.38\% = 1.65\%$ higher than the calculated number when we ignored flotation costs, we could also adjust the i_E we had previously calculated using the CAPM of 17.60% by adding 1.65% to it, also: $17.60\% + 1.65\% = 19.25\%$, similar to the approach we took in Example 11-8.

Taking an average of the two measures of i_E computed incorporating flotation costs will give us the number we should use in the calculation of the WACC:

$$\frac{.1903 + .1925}{2} = .1914, \text{ or } 19.14\%$$

The component cost of preferred stock, i_P, will equal

$$\frac{\$5}{\$44 - (.1 \times \$44)} = .1263$$

The component cost of debt, i_D, will be the solution to

$$\$1,120(1 - .03) = \$90 \times \left[\frac{1 - \dfrac{1}{(1 + i_D)^{15}}}{i_D} \right] + \frac{\$1000}{(1 + i_D)^{15}} \Rightarrow i_D = .0799$$

No change in the capital structure weights or in the tax rate will occur, so the WACC for the new project will be

$$WACC = .3614 \times 19.14\% + .1325 \times 12.63\% + .5060 \times 7.99\% \times (1 - .35)$$
$$= .1122, \text{ or } 11.22\%$$

questions

1. How would you handle calculating the cost of capital if a firm were planning to issue two different classes of common stock? *(LG1)*

2. Why don't we multiply the cost of preferred stock by 1 minus the tax rate, as we do for debt? *(LG2)*

3. Expressing WACC in terms of i_E, i_P, and i_D, what is the theoretical minimum for the WACC? *(LG2)*

4. Under what situations would you want to use the CAPM approach for estimating the component cost of equity? The constant-growth model? *(LG3)*

5. Could you calculate the component cost of equity for a stock with nonconstant expected growth rate in dividends if you didn't have the information necessary to compute the component cost using the CAPM? Why or why not? *(LG3)*

6. Why do we use market-based weights instead of book-value-based weights when computing the WACC? *(LG4)*

7. Suppose your firm wanted to expand into a new line of business quickly, and that management anticipated that the new line of business would constitute over 80 percent of your firm's operations within three years. If the expansion was going to be financed partially with debt, would it still make sense to use the firm's existing cost of debt, or should you compute a new rate of return for debt based on the new line of business? *(LG5)*

8. Explain why the divisional cost of capital approach may cause problems if new projects are assigned to the wrong division. *(LG6)*

9. When will the subjective approach to forming divisional WACCs be better than using the firmwide WACC to evaluate all projects? *(LG7)*

10. Suppose a new project was going to be financed partially with retained earnings. What flotation costs should you use for retained earnings? *(LG8)*

problems

basic
problems

11-1 **Cost of Equity** Diddy Corp stock has a beta of 1.2, the current risk-free rate is 5 percent, and the expected return on the market is 13.5 percent. What is Diddy's cost of equity? *(LG3)*

11-2 **Cost of Equity** JaiLai Cos. stock has a beta of 1.1, the current risk-free rate is 6.2 percent, and the expected return on the market is 12 percent. What is JaiLai's cost of equity? *(LG3)*

11-3 **Cost of Debt** Oberon Inc. has a $20 million (face value) 10-year bond issue selling for 97 percent of par that pays an annual coupon of 8.25 percent. What would be Oberon's before-tax component cost of debt? *(LG3)*

11-4 **Cost of Debt** KatyDid Clothes has a $150 million (face value) 20-year bond issue selling for 104 percent of par that carries a coupon rate of 11 percent, paid semiannually. What would be Katydid's before-tax component cost of debt? *(LG3)*

11-5 **Cost of Preferred Stock** ILK has preferred stock selling for 97 percent of par that pays an 8 percent annual coupon. What would be ILK's component cost of preferred stock? *(LG3)*

11-6 **Cost of Preferred Stock** Marme Inc. has preferred stock selling for 137 percent of par that pays an 11 percent annual coupon. What would be Marme's component cost of preferred stock? *(LG3)*

11-7 **Weight of Equity** FarCry Industries, a maker of telecommunications equipment, has 2 million shares of common stock outstanding, 1 million shares of preferred stock outstanding, and 10,000 bonds. If the common shares are selling for $27 per share, the preferred shares are selling for $14.50 per share, and the bonds are selling for 98 percent of par, what would be the weight used for equity in the computation of FarCry's WACC? *(LG4)*

11-8 **Weight of Equity** OMG Inc. has 4 million shares of common stock outstanding, 3 million shares of preferred stock outstanding, and 5,000 bonds. If the common shares are selling for $17 per share, the preferred share are selling for $26 per share, and the bonds are selling for 108 percent of par, what would be the weight used for equity in the computation of OMG's WACC? *(LG4)*

11-9 **Weight of Debt** FarCry Industries, a maker of telecommunications equipment, has 2 million shares of common stock outstanding, 1 million shares of preferred stock outstanding, and 10,000 bonds. If the common shares are selling for $27 per share, the preferred shares are selling for $14.50 per share, and the bonds are selling for 98 percent of par, what weight should you use for debt in the computation of FarCry's WACC? *(LG4)*

11-10 **Weight of Debt** OMG Inc. has 4 million shares of common stock outstanding, 3 million shares of preferred stock outstanding, and 5,000 bonds. If the common shares are selling for $17 per share, the preferred share are selling for $26 per share, and the bonds are selling for

108 percent of par, what weight should you use for debt in the computation of OMG's WACC? *(LG4)*

11-11   **Weight of Preferred Stock** FarCry Industries, a maker of telecommunications equipment, has 2 million shares of common stock outstanding, 1 million shares of preferred stock outstanding, and 10,000 bonds. If the common shares sell for $27 per share, the preferred shares sell for $14.50 per share, and the bonds sell for 98 percent of par, what weight should you use for preferred stock in the computation of FarCry's WACC? *(LG4)*

11-12   **Weight of Preferred Stock** OMG Inc. has 4 million shares of common stock outstanding, 3 million shares of preferred stock outstanding, and 5,000 bonds. If the common shares sell for $17 per share, the preferred shares sell for $26 per share, and the bonds sell for 108 percent of par, what weight should you use for preferred stock in the computation of OMG's WACC? *(LG4)*

intermediate
problems

11-13   **WACC** Suppose that TapDance, Inc.'s capital structure features 65 percent equity, 35 percent debt, and that its before-tax cost of debt is 8 percent, while its cost of equity is 13 percent. If the appropriate weighted average tax rate is 34 percent, what will be TapDance's WACC? *(LG2)*

11-14   **WACC** JLP Industries has 6.5 million shares of common stock outstanding with a market price of $14.00 per share. The company also has outstanding preferred stock with a market value of $10 million, and 25,000 bonds outstanding, each with a face value of $1,000 and selling at 90 percent of par value. The cost of equity is 14 percent, the cost of preferred is 10 percent, and the cost of debt is 7.25 percent. If JLP's tax rate is 34 percent, what is the WACC? *(LG2)*

11-15   **WACC** Suppose that JB Cos. has a capital structure of 78 percent equity, 22 percent debt, and that its before-tax cost of debt is 11 percent while its cost of equity is 17 percent. If the appropriate weighted-average tax rate is 25 percent, what will be JB's WACC? *(LG2)*

11-16   **WACC** Suppose that B2B, Inc. has a capital structure of 37 percent equity, 17 percent preferred stock, and 46 percent debt. If the before-tax component costs of equity, preferred stock, and debt are 14.5 percent, 11 percent, and 9.5 percent, respectively, what is B2B's WACC if the firm faces an average tax rate of 30%? *(LG2)*

11-17   **WACC** Suppose that MNINK Industries' capital structure features 63 percent equity, 7 percent preferred stock, and 30 percent debt. If the before-tax component costs of equity, preferred stock, and debt are 11.60 percent, 9.5 percent, and 7 percent, respectively, what is MNINK's WACC if the firm faces an average tax rate of 34%? *(LG2)*

11-18   **WACC** TAFKAP Industries has 3 million shares of stock outstanding selling at $17 per share and an issue of $20 million in 7.5 percent, annual coupon bonds with a maturity of 15 years, selling at 106 percent of par. If TAFKAP's weighted average tax rate is 34 percent and its cost of equity is 14.5 percent, what is TAFKAP's WACC? *(LG3)*

11-19   **WACC** Johnny Cake Ltd. has 10 million shares of stock outstanding selling at $23 per share and an issue of $50 million in 9 percent, annual coupon bonds with a maturity of 17 years, selling at 93.5 percent of par. If Johnny Cake's weighted-average tax rate is 34 percent, its next dividend is expected to be $3 per share, and all future dividends are expected to grow at 6 percent per year, indefinitely, what is its WACC? *(LG3)*

11-20 WACC Weights BetterPie Industries has 3 million shares of common stock outstanding, 2 million shares of preferred stock outstanding, and 10,000 bonds. If the common shares are selling for $47 per share, the preferred shares are selling for $24.50 per share, and the bonds are selling for 99 percent of par, what would be the weights used in the calculation of BetterPie's WACC? *(LG4)*

11-21 Flotation Cost Suppose that Brown-Murphies' common shares sell for $19.50 per share, are expected to set their next annual dividend at $.57 per share, and that all future dividends are expected to grow by 4 percent per year, indefinitely. If Brown-Murphies faces a flotation cost of 13 percent on new equity issues, what will be the flotation-adjusted cost of equity? *(LG8)*

11-22 Flotation Cost A firm is considering a project that will generate perpetual after-tax cash flows of $15,000 per year beginning next year. The project has the same risk as the firm's overall operations and must be financed externally. Equity flotation costs 14 percent and debt issues cost 4 percent on an after-tax basis. The firm's D/E ratio is 0.8. What is the most the firm can pay for the project and still earn its required return? *(LG2)*

11-23 Risk-Free Rate in WACC A firm has 5 million shares of common stock outstanding, each with a market price of $8 per share. It has 25,000 bonds outstanding, each selling for $800. The bonds mature in 10 years, have a coupon rate of 8 percent, and pay coupons semiannually. The firm's equity has a beta of 1.4, and the expected market return is 15 percent. The tax rate is 35 percent and the WACC is 15 percent. Calculate the risk-free rate. *(LG2)*

11-24 Firm-wide vs. Project-Specific WACCs An all-equity firm is considering the projects shown below. The T-bill rate is 4 percent and the market risk premium is 7 percent. If the firm uses its current WACC of 12 percent to evaluate these projects, which project(s), if any, will be incorrectly rejected? *(LG6)*

PROJECT	EXPECTED RETURN	BETA
A	8.0%	0.5
B	19.0	1.2
C	13.0	1.4
D	17.0	1.6

11-25 Firm-wide vs. Project-Specific WACCs An all-equity firm is considering the projects shown below. The T-bill rate is 4 percent and the market risk premium is 7 percent. If the firm uses its current WACC of 12 percent to evaluate these projects, which project(s), if any, will be incorrectly accepted? *(LG6)*

PROJECT	EXPECTED RETURN	BETA
A	8.0%	0.5
B	19.0	1.2
C	13.0	1.4
D	17.0	1.6

11-26 Divisional WACCs Suppose your firm has decided to use a divisional WACC approach to analyze projects. The firm currently has four divisions, A through D, with average betas for each division of 0.6, 1.0, 1.3, and 1.6, respectively. If all current and future projects will be financed with half debt and half equity, and if the current cost of equity (based on an average firm beta of 1.0 and a current risk-free rate of 7 percent) is 13 percent and the after-tax yield on the company's bonds is 8 percent, what will the WACCs be for each division? *(LG7)*

research it! Finding the Before-Tax Cost of Debt, i_D

For component debt costs, we'd like to use the yield to maturity on bonds that resembles the maturity of our potential debt if possible. Let's assume that we want to find a bond issue with approximately 10 years until maturity (as of January 2007) for Sears. Luckily, Sears has quite a few outstanding bond issues to choose from, and we can access the information on these issues on the Yahoo! Finance page.

Go to **http://finance.yahoo.com** and start by clicking on "Investing" and then "Bonds." Then enter Sears in the "Bond Lookup" box and click on "Search." You'll be presented with a list of Sears outstanding bonds sorted in order of decreasing maturity. Once you've identified the bond with the maturity closest to the maturity you want, click on the "Issue" entry and look up the Yield to Maturity.

Your turn: go to the Yahoo! Finance Web site and find the YTM on the bond with a maturity that's as close as possible to 10 years from today's date.

integrated minicase WACC for a New Project

LilyMac Studios, a national chain of photography studios, is considering opening up a chain of coffee shop/art galleries. While the existing operations of the firm have a beta of 1.17, the new chain is expected to have a beta of 0.8.

LilyMac currently has 500,000 shares of common stock outstanding, which are selling for $63.72 per share, and a $10 million bond issue, selling at 104 percent of par. The expected market risk premium is 6 percent, and the current risk-free rate is 5.5 percent. The bonds pay an 8 percent semiannual coupon and mature in 20 years.

The current operations of the firm produce EBIT of $18 million per year, and the chain's operations are expected to add only $25 million per year to that. The new chain will be funded with 65 percent equity and 35 percent debt, and estimated flotation costs are expected to be 12 percent and 5 percent, respectively.

What should be the WACC for the new chain of coffee shops?

ANSWERS TO TIME OUT

11-1 Debt interest is paid out of before-tax earnings, implying that paying $1 in interest really only costs the firm $I \times (1 - T_c)$; common and preferred stock are paid out of after-tax net income, and so don't have a tax shelter effect.

11-2 We would compute the *weighted-average cost* of debt, using the percentage of total market value of each issue as its weight.

11-3 The costs of debt and preferred stock are *firmwide* obligations, not project-specific ones, because *debt holders* and owners of preferred shares can legally expect to be paid back out of the firm's revenues even if the specific project being funded isn't successful.

11-4 We can often "back out" a pure-play beta by adjusting such a firm's beta to offset the impact of the other lines of business. For example, suppose that we are trying to find a proxy beta for a project involving the production of dishwashers. If we can find a potential proxy company with a beta of .75 that makes both dishwashers and air conditioners (and which earns approximately half its revenue from each line of business), and we can elsewhere estimate the average beta of an air-conditioning manufacturer to be, say, .8, then we extrapolate that the beta for the dishwasher division of that company must be the solution to $.75 = (.5 \times .8) + (.5 \times \beta_{Dishwashers})$, or $\beta_{Dishwashers} = .7$.

11-5 Divisions based on either product type or geographic location will also usually proxy for differences in project risk. For example, many large auto manufacturers use divisional breakdowns based on both product types and geography (e.g., "Ford of North America," or "Dodge Truck Division"). Though these divisions are not explicitly targeted at separating projects by risk, selling a new Ford Focus in Europe is obviously going to have different risks than selling the same car in North America due to the differences in competitive environment, consumer tastes, and so on.

11-6 Project D's beta is lower than average for its division, so the objectively computed divisional WACC for its division will still overstate the project's required rate of return versus a project-specific WACC. Holding the project up to too high of a benchmark will cause it to be incorrectly rejected.

11-7 Debt is easier for the underwriter to sell for several reasons. Debt is safer and therefore more attractive to many groups of potential buyers. It also tends to be sold in larger denominations primarily to large financial institutions such as mutual funds, pensions funds, and so on, which requires the underwriter to contact a smaller group of potential buyers than they would have to if assisting in a stock issue.

11-8 We would take a weighted average of the flotation cost for new equity and that of retained earnings (which would be equal to zero), where the weights would be equal to the proportion of each type of equity financing used.

chapter 12:
ESTIMATING CASH FLOWS ON CAPITAL BUDGETING PROJECTS

Learning Goals

LG1 Explain why we use *pro forma* statements to analyze project cash flows.

LG2 Identify which cash flows we can incrementally attribute to a proposed project and which ones we can't.

LG3 Calculate a project's expected cash flows using the free cash flow approach.

LG4 Explain how accelerated depreciation affects project cash flows.

LG5 Calculate free cash flows for replacement equipment.

LG6 Calculate cash flows associated with cost-cutting proposals.

LG7 Explain and demonstrate the EAC approach to choose between alternative cash streams when projects recur.

LG8 Adjust initial project investments to account for flotation costs.

s new capital budgeting projects arise, we must estimate when such projects will require cash flows. Estimating those cash flows isn't difficult, but it *is* complicated. As you look through this chapter's examples, questions, and problems, you'll notice that we have given you a lot more information in these types of problems than we've given you anywhere else in the text. To correctly estimate project cash flows, we need to consider quite a number of factors, such as:

- The particular new product or service's costs and revenues.
- The likely impact that the new service or product will have on the firm's *existing* products' costs and revenues.
- The use of assets or employees already employed by the firm.
- The way to handle charges such as the research and development costs incurred to develop the new product.
- A multitude of other relevant details.

viewpoints

Business Application

Suppose that McDonald's is considering introducing the McTurkey Dinner (MTD). They anticipate that the MTD will have unit sales, prices, and cost figures as shown below for the next five years, after which the firm will retire the MTD. Introducing the MTD will require $7 million in new assets, which will fall into the MACRS five-year class life. McDonald's expects the necessary assets to be worth $2 million in market value at the end of the project life. In addition, the company expects that NWC requirements at the beginning of each year will be approximately 13 percent of the projected sales throughout the coming year. McDonald's uses an 11 percent cost of capital for similar projects and is subject to a 35 percent marginal tax rate. What will be this project's expected cash flows? **(See solution on p. 406)**

Personal Application

Achmed contemplates going back to school part time to get an MBA. He anticipates that it would take him 4 years to get his MBA, and the program would cost $15 thousand per year in books and tuition (payable at the beginning of each year). He also thinks that he would need to get a new laptop (which he was going to buy anyway as a portable gaming system) for $2,500 when he starts the program, and he just paid $250 to take the GMAT. After graduation, Achmed anticipates that he will be able to earn approximately $10,000 more per year with the MBA, and he thinks he'll work for about another 20 years after getting the MBA. What total cash flows should Achmed consider in his decision? **(See solution on p. 406)**

YEAR	ESTIMATED UNIT SALES	ESTIMATED SELLING PRICE PER UNIT	ESTIMATED VARIABLE COST PER UNIT
1	400,000	$7.00	$3.35
2	1,000,000	$7.21	$3.52
3	$1,000,000.00	$7.43	$3.70
4	$1,000,000.00	$7.65	$3.89
5	$ 500,000.00	$7.88	$4.08

A practice test can be found on the Online Learning Center at
www.mhhe.com/can1e

Fortunately, we *do* have a way to work through all of these details systematically. In this chapter, we're going to construct a process which, if we follow it faithfully, will guide us to consider factors such as the ones listed on p. 388. The process of estimating expected future cash flows of a project using only the relevant parts of the balance sheet and income statements is called **pro forma analysis.** The type of *pro forma analysis* of potential projects we'll use will focus on the question, "What will be this project's impact on the firm's total cash flows if we go forward?"

12.1 Sample Project Description

Let's suppose that we're working for a game development company, First Strike Software (FSS). FSS is considering leasing a new plant in Gatlinburg, Tennessee, which they will use to produce copies of their new game "FinProf," a "first-person shooter" game where the player battles aliens invading your local college's finance department.

FSS will price this game at $39.99, and they estimate sales for each of the next three years as shown in Table 12.1. Given buyers' rapidly changing tastes in computer games, they don't expect to be able to sell any more copies after year 3.

Variable costs per game are low ($4.25), and FSS expects fixed costs to total $150,000 per year, including rent. Start-up costs involve $75,000 for a software-duplicating machine, plus an additional $2,000 in shipping and installation costs. For our first stab at analyzing this project, we will assume that the duplicating machine will be straight-line depreciated to $5,000 over the life of the project. We'll expect that machine to bring only $2,000 on the market after we're done using it.

FinProf is an updated version of an older game sold by FSS, MktProf. FSS intends to keep selling MktProf but anticipates that FinProf will decrease sales of MktProf by 2,000 units per year throughout the life of the new game. MktProf sells for $19.99 and has variable costs of $3.50 per unit.

Development costs totaled $150,000 throughout development of the game, and First Strike estimates its NWC requirements at the beginning of each year will be approximately 10 percent of the projected sales during the coming year. First Strike is in the 34 percent tax bracket and uses a discount rate of 15 percent on projects with risk profiles such as this. The relevant question: Should FSS put FinProf into production or not?

12.2 Guiding Principles for Cash Flow Estimation

When we calculate a project's expected cash flows, we must ensure that we cover all **incremental cash flows,** that is, the cash flow changes that we would expect throughout the entire firm as the new project comes on board. Some incremental cash flow effects are fairly obvious. For example, suppose a firm has to buy a new asset to support a new project but would not be buying the asset if the project were not adopted. Clearly, the cash flows from buying the asset are obviously incremental to the project, and we should therefore count them when we

Sample Project Projected Unit Sales	table 12.1
YEAR	**UNIT SALES**
1	15,000
2	27,000
3	5,000

calculate the cash flows associated with that project. But we can hardly expect all incremental cash flows to be so obvious. Other incremental cash flows, as discussed below, are more subtle, and we'll have to watch for them very carefully.

Opportunity Costs

As you likely remember from your microeconomics classes, an **opportunity cost** exists whenever a firm has to choose how to allocate scarce resources. If those resources go into project A, the firm must forgo using them in any other way. Those forgone choices will cost the firm in some way, and we must remember to take account of such opportunity costs in calculating cash flows attributable to project A.

For example, suppose that FSS already owned the piece of software-duplicating machinery discussed above. If the machinery was already being fully utilized by another project within the company, then obviously switching it over to the FinProf game would require that other project to find another source of software duplication. To be fair, the FinProf project should be charged for the use of the machinery.

Even if the machinery wasn't currently being used in any other projects, it could still possibly have an opportunity cost associated with using it in the FinProf project. If FSS could potentially sell the machinery on the open market for $75,000, the company would have to give up that $75,000 in order to use the piece of machinery for the FinProf game. In the end, it wouldn't really matter whether the firm had to buy the asset from outside sources or not: either way, the project will be tying up $75,000 worth of capital, and it should be charged for doing so.

The underlying concept behind charging the project for the opportunity cost of using an asset also has broader implications: overall, we should charge any new project for any assets used by that project as well as any wages and benefits paid to employees working on it. Even if the firm was already employing those people prior to starting work on the new project, they are no longer available to work on any existing projects; and if the firm didn't have any new projects, it could have laid those employees off, saving their wages and benefits.

Sunk Costs

If a firm has already paid an expense or is obligated to pay one in the future, regardless of whether a particular project is undertaken, that expense is a **sunk cost.** A firm should never count sunk costs in project cash flows.

For example, FSS incurred $150,000 in development costs in the example above. Development costs would presumably include items such as the salaries of the game's programmers, market research costs, and so forth. Since we're not told otherwise, we can sensibly assume that FSS will never recoup its development money, even if it decides not to go ahead with publishing the game. Thus those costs are sunk, and FSS wouldn't even consider them as part of its decision about whether to move forward with putting the FinProf game into production.

Substitutionary and Complementary Effects

If a new product or service will either reduce or increase sales, costs, or necessary assets for existing products or services, then those changes are incremental to the project and should rightfully be included in the project cash flows. For example, consider how FSS's FinProf game may affect the existing MktProf game. The gross sales and variable cost figures for the new game might be as shown in Table 12.2.

Gross Sales and Variable Costs for FinProf		table 12.2
YEAR	**SALES**	**VARIABLE COSTS**
1	15,000 × $39.99 = $599,850	15,000 × $4.25 = $63,750
2	27,000 × $39.99 = $1,079,730	27,000 × $4.25 = $114,750
3	5,000 × $39.99 = $199,950	5,000 × $4.25 = $21,250

Net Incremental and Variable Costs for FinProf		table 12.3
YEAR	**SALES**	**VARIABLE COSTS**
1	$599,850 − $39,980 = $559,870	$63,750 − $7,000 = $56,750
2	$1,079,730 − $39,980 = $1,039,750	$114,750 − $7,000 = $107,750
3	$199,950 − $39,980 = $159,970	$21,250 − $7,000 = $14,250

However, FSS also expects the MktProf game to lose yearly sales of 2,000 × $19.99 = $39,980 when FinProf comes aboard. Further, the decrease in sales of MktProf will also result in yearly variable costs of 2,000 × $3.50 = $7,000 per year, so the net incremental sales and variable cost figures for the project will be as shown in Table 12.3.

We see a reduction in both sales and variable costs because FinProf is a partial **substitute** for MktProf. If the new game had been a **complement,** then both sales and variable costs of the existing product would have increased instead.

 ## Stock Dividends and Bond Interest

One final, important note concerning incremental project cash flows: We will never count any **financing costs,** including dividends paid on stock or interest paid on debt, as expenses of the project. The costs of capital are already included as component costs in the weighted average cost of capital (WACC) that we will be using to discount these cash flows in the next chapter. If we were to include them in the cash flow figures as well, we would be double-counting them.

TIME OUT

12-1 Suppose that your manager will be devoting half of her time to a new project, with the other half devoted to currently existing projects. How would you reflect this in your calculation of the incremental cash flows of the project?

12-2 Could a new product have both substitutionary and complementary effects on existing products?

12.3 Total Project Cash Flow

In Chapter 2, we discussed the concept of free cash flow (FCF), which we defined as

$$\text{FCF} = \text{Operating cash flow} - \text{Investment in operating capital} \qquad \text{(12-1)}$$
$$= [\text{EBIT} - \text{Taxes} + \text{Depreciation}]$$
$$- [\Delta\text{Gross fixed assets} + \Delta\text{Net operating working capital}]$$

In this chapter, we're going to use this variable again as a measure of the total amount of available cash flow from a project. However, we'll observe two important differences from how we used it in Chapter 2. First, since we'll be considering potential projects rather than a particular firm's actual, historic activities, the FCF numbers we calculate will be, frankly, guesses—informed guesses, surely, but guesses nonetheless. Since we'll be "calculating" guesses, we'll introduce possible estimation error into our capital budgeting decision statistics, which we'll discuss in the next chapter.

Second, we'll now calculate FCF on potential projects individually, rather than across the firm as a whole as we did in Chapter 2. In some ways, calculating FCF on individual projects will make our job much easier, since we need not worry about estimating an entire set of balance sheets for the firm. Instead, we'll only have to be concerned with the limited subset of pro forma statements necessary to keep track of the assets, expense categories, and so on that a new project will affect. Unfortunately, the elements of that limited set will vary from situation to situation, and the hard part will be identifying which parts of the balance sheets are necessary and which are not.

Calculating Depreciation

Expected depreciation on equipment used during the life of the project will affect both the operating cash flows and the change in gross fixed assets that will occur at the end of the project. Whether an asset is sold or whether it's discarded with any remaining book value, calculating the expected depreciation charges on assets before calculating the FCF components is usually helpful.

For First Strike's proposed FinProf project, the firm will depreciate capital assets such as the software-duplicating machine using the straight-line method to an ending book value of $5,000. To calculate the annual depreciation amount, First Strike will first need to compute the machinery's **depreciable basis.** According to the Internal Revenue Service's (IRS) Publication 946, the depreciable basis for real property is:

- Its cost.
- Amounts paid for items such as sales tax.
- Freight charges.
- Installation and testing fees.

So the depreciable basis for the new project's software-duplicating machine will be the $75,000 purchase price plus the $2,000 shipping and installation cost, for a total depreciable basis of $77,000. Since initially First Strike will depreciate this asset using the most basic form of straight-line depreciation, it will use the following formula to compute depreciation per year:

$$\text{Depreciation} = \frac{\text{Ending book value} - \text{Beginning book value}}{\text{Life of asset}} \quad \text{(12-2)}$$

$$= \frac{\$77,000 - \$5,000}{3}$$

$$= \$24,000 \text{ per year}$$

We'll discuss later in the chapter why this depreciation assumption is far too simple. Other, more-complicated depreciation methods can be much more advantageous to the company. For now, this straight-line depreciation approach will suffice for our initial go at calculating the project's cash flows.

	YEAR 1		YEAR 2		YEAR 3	
Sales of FinProf	$599,850		$1,079,730		$199,950	
Reduced sales of MktProf	39,980		39,980		39,980	
Net incremental sales		$559,870		$1,039,750		$159,970
Variable costs of FinProf	$ 63,750		$ 114,750		$ 21,250	
Reduced variable costs of MktProf	7,000		7,000		7,000	
Net increase in variable costs		56,750		107,750		14,250
Less: Fixed costs		150,000		150,000		150,000
Less: Depreciation		24,000		24,000		24,000
EBIT		329,120		758,000		−28,280
Less: Taxes		111,901		257,720		−9,615
Net income		217,219		500,280		−18,665
Plus: Depreciation		24,000		24,000		24,000
OCF		$ 241,219		$ 524,280		$ 5,335

Calculating Operating Cash Flow

We defined operating cash flow (OCF) in Chapter 2 as *EBIT − Taxes + Depreciation*. We'll still calculate OCF as being mathematically equal to *EBIT − Taxes + Depreciation*. But remember that we'll be constructing the FCF components ourselves instead of taking them off an income statement that someone else has already produced. So we'll usually find it most helpful to conduct this calculation as what we will call a "quasi-income statement" that leaves out some components like interest deductions. (Note that the process of leaving out any interest deduction is exactly in line with our discussion above of not counting interest on debt as an expense of the project, but the resulting financial statement would *not* make an accountant happy). Such a statement is shown in Table 12.4 for First Strike's proposed project. The primary benefit of calculating OCF this way instead of as an algebraic formula is that with this format, we have space to expand subcalculations, such as the impact of FinProf being a partial substitute for the MktProf product.

You may wonder why we treat EBIT as negative for tax purposes in year 3 of the project. Since we are just calculating the cash flows to a single project, we draw upon the conventional approach for handling situations where the project "loses money" (on a taxable-income basis). We would thus assume that the rest of the firm would *make* enough positive taxable income that it would need this project's loss to shelter an equivalent amount of income from the taxing authority. Table 12.4 reflects this by the negative taxes (−$9,615) "paid" during year 3, which is conceptually equal to a tax credit of $9,615.

Calculating Change in Gross Fixed Assets

Gross fixed assets will change in almost every project at both the beginning (when assets are usually purchased) and at the end (when assets are usually sold). First Strike's proposed project is no exception.

Calculating the change in gross fixed assets at the beginning of the project is fairly straightforward—it will simply equal the asset's depreciable basis. So, for FSS's project, we will increase gross fixed assets by $77,000 at time zero.

At the end of a project, the change in gross fixed assets is a little more complicated, because whenever a firm sells any asset, it has to consider the tax consequences of that sale. The IRS treats any sale of assets for more than depreciated book value as taxable gains and any sale for less than book value as taxable losses. In either event, we can calculate the after-tax cash flow (ATCF) from the sale of an asset using the following formula where T_C is the same appropriate corporate tax rate discussed in the previous chapter.

$$\text{ATCF} = \text{Book value} + (\text{Market value} - \text{Book value}) \times (1 - T_C) \qquad \textbf{(12-3)}$$

Since the machinery for FSS's project will be depreciated down to $5,000 but is expected to sell for only $2,000, the ATCF for that asset's sale will equal:

$$\text{ATCF} = \$5,000 + (\$2,000 - \$5,000) \times (1 - .34)$$
$$= \$3,020$$

Note that this formula would work equally well on an asset sold at a gain.

 For interactive versions of this example visit www.mhhe.com/can1e

EXAMPLE 12-1

ATCF FOR AN ASSET SOLD AT A GAIN

Suppose that a firm facing a marginal tax rate of 25 percent sells an asset for $4,000 when its depreciated book value is $2,000. What will be the ATCF from the sale of this asset?

SOLUTION:

The ATCF will equal:

$$\text{ATCF} = \$2,000 + (\$4,000 - \$2,000) \times (1 - .25)$$
$$= \$3,500$$

Calculating Changes in Net Working Capital

We can make several different assumptions concerning the NWC level necessary to support a project. The most straightforward of these would be to simply assume that we add NWC at the beginning of the project and reduce it at the end. This assumption would be valid if the project is expected to have steady sales throughout its life, and in these relatively rare circumstances we will use this assumption.

FSS's proposed project, however, features a more typical product life cycle. Its unit sales will follow an approximate bell-shaped curve. When sales are timed in this way, FSS needs to give a little more thought to exactly when the firm needs to set aside net working capital to support high sales volumes and when it can reduce NWC as sales drop off.

The assumption that First Strike's NWC at any particular time will be a function of the *next* year's sales might seem odd at first glance. But a little thought about how we measure balance sheet numbers (such as NWC) and income statement items (such as sales) will show that, really, this assumption makes a lot of sense. Since income statements (and our quasi-income statement discussed above) measure what happens *during* a period, the sales show up on the statement at time 1, even though they actually start accumulating at the *beginning* of year 1, which is time 0. The balance sheet "snapshots," on the other hand, capture how much capital sits in NWC accounts *at a particular point in time*. Therefore, the

YEAR	0	1	2	3
Level of NWC	$59,985	$107,973	$19,995	$0
$NWC_t - NWC_{t-1}$	$59,985 − $0	$107,973 − $59,985	$19,995 − $107,973	$0 − $19,995
$= \Delta NWC_t$	= $59,985	= $47,988	= −$87,9789,985	= −$19,995

sales figures that appear in time 1 OCF calculation must be supported when they start occurring, at time 0. The time 0 NWC changes need to reflect that activity. Of course, the same argument holds true in general: Any sales figures that appear in a time N OCF calculation need support at the beginning of year N by the NWC level in time N-1 balance sheet.

Since we covered the expected changes in gross fixed assets from a new project in the previous section, we don't even really have to track all of the changes in the balance sheet here. We only need to track the change in net current assets, and any change in NWC is actually measuring exactly the total net effect of changes in gross current assets and current liabilities for this project.

So, we can use the given information for the First Strike project to compute the NWC necessary to support sales throughout the project's life, and then in turn use NWC levels to compute the necessary changes in NWC, as shown in Table 12.5. Notice that the NWC level at each time is simply 10 percent of the following year's sales figures from Table 12.4.

This method for computing changes in NWC levels has several appealing features:

- The changes in NWC at the beginning of a project will always equal the level at time 0, as NWC will be going from a presumed zero level before the project starts up to that new, non-zero level.

- Allowing NWC to vary as a percentage of coming sales like this allows FSS to add NWC during periods when it expects sales to increase (e.g., years 0 and 1 in this example) and to decrease NWC when it expects sales to fall off (e.g., years 2 and 3 in this example). NWC levels fall off the last two years of this project precisely because FSS expects sales to fall off and is adjusting NWC to compensate.

- Finally, one especially nice feature of this approach is that it will always automatically bring NWC back down to a zero level when the project ends. Since sales in the year *after* the project ends are always zero, 10 percent of zero will also be zero. This corresponds to what we would expect to see in the real world: when a project ends, the firm sells off inventory, collects from customers, pays off accounts receivable, and so forth.

Bringing It All Together

Using the numbers that we calculated for OCF, change in gross fixed assets, and change in NWC, First Strike's expected total cash flows from the new project would be as shown in Table 12.6.

Note, in particular, that correct use of the after-tax cash flow from selling the machinery at the end of the project requires that we change the cash flows' sign to negative when we enter it for year 3. Why? Because the ATCF formula shown in equation 12-3 does a little *too* much work for us. It computes cash flow effects of selling the asset, while the formula we're using for FCF wants us to enter the change in fixed assets. Or, to put it another way, cash flow at the end of the project

Total Cash Flows								table 12.6

YEAR	0		1		2		3	
OCF		$ 0		$241,219		$524,280		$ 5,335
FA	$77,000		$ 0		$ 0		−$3,020	
NWC	59,985		47,988		−87,978		−19,995	
Less: IOC		136,985		47,988		−87,978		−23,015
FCF		−$136,985		$193,231		$612,258		$28,350

should go up *because* fixed assets decrease. We subtract that decrease in our FCF = OCF − (ΔFA + ΔNWC) calculation, which has the effect of "subtracting a minus." Eventually, then, we increase the final year's FCF above that which we would have generated by just combining OCF with the cash freed up from decreasing NWC.

TIME OUT

12-3 Explain why an increase in NWC is treated as a cash outflow rather than as an inflow.

12-4 Will OCF typically be larger or smaller than Net Income? Why?

12.4 Accelerated Depreciation and the Half-Year Convention

Our FCF calculation in the previous section was complete, but we used a rather simplistic assumption concerning depreciation to complete the calculation. In reality, the IRS requires that depreciation must be calculated using the half-year convention. The IRS thus requires that all property placed in service during a given period is assumed to be placed in service at the midpoint of that period.[1] By implication, three years of asset life, such as the machinery in the First Strike example, will extend over four calendar years of the firm. Table 12.7 shows an excerpt from the IRS depreciation table for straight-line depreciation using the half-year convention.

The percentage figures denote how much of the asset's depreciable basis may be deducted in each respective firm calendar year. For example, an asset with a depreciable basis of $100,000 falling into the three-year class life would be depreciated $100,000 × 16.67% = $16,670 during the first calendar year the firm owned it, $33,330 during the second and third years of ownership, and another $16,670 during the fourth year of ownership.

The IRS provides guidance on which categories various assets fall into, so it's usually pretty easy to figure out which column to use. For this text, we'll assume that we're always told which class-life category an asset falls under.

Note that the IRS's interpretation of the half-year convention isn't as direct as simply taking one-half of the first year's depreciation and moving it to the end of the asset's life. For example, the column for 3.5-year depreciation shows that such an asset would have 14.29 percent of its value depreciated during the first

---

[1]There are also midmonth and midquarter conventions, which apply in special circumstances. Please refer to IRS Publication 946 for details.

table 12.7

Excerpt of Straight-Line Depreciation Table with Half-Year Convention

			NORMAL RECOVERY PERIOD		
YEAR	2.5	3	3.5	4	5
1	20.00%	16.67%	14.29%	12.50%	10.00%
2	40.00	33.33	28.57	25.00	20.00
3	40.00	33.33	28.57	25.00	20.00
4	0.00	16.67	28.57	25.00	20.00
5	0.00	0.00	0.00	12.50	20.00
6	0.00	0.00	0.00	0.00	10.00

DDB Depreciation with Half-Year Convention   table 12.8

			NORMAL RECOVERY PERIOD			
YEAR	3	5	7	10	15	20
1	33.33%	20.00%	14.29%	10.00	5.00%	3.750%
2	44.45	32.00	24.49	18.00	9.50	7.219
3	14.81	19.20	17.49	14.40	8.55	6.677
4	7.41	11.52	12.49	11.52	7.70	6.177
5	0.00	11.52	8.93	9.22	6.93	5.713
6	0.00	5.76	8.92	7.37	6.23	5.285
7	0.00	0.00	8.93	6.55	5.90	4.888
8	0.00	0.00	4.46	6.55	5.90	4.522
9	0.00	0.00	0.00	6.56	5.91	4.462
10	0.00	0.00	0.00	6.55	5.90	4.461
11	0.00	0.00	0.00	3.28	5.91	4.462
12	0.00	0.00	0.00	0.00	5.90	4.461
13	0.00	0.00	0.00	0.00	5.91	4.462
14	0.00	0.00	0.00	0.00	5.90	4.461
15	0.00	0.00	0.00	0.00	5.91	4.462
16	0.00	0.00	0.00	0.00	2.95	4.461
17	0.00	0.00	0.00	0.00	0.00	4.462
18	0.00	0.00	0.00	0.00	0.00	4.461
19	0.00	0.00	0.00	0.00	0.00	4.462
20	0.00	0.00	0.00	0.00	0.00	4.461
21	0.00	0.00	0.00	0.00	0.00	2.231

year and 28.57 percent during each of the second, third, and fourth years. So, rather than using a formula to compute the depreciation percentage, it's preferable to look the percentages up from the appropriate IRS table. A copy of the entire table for straight-line depreciation using the half-year convention appears as Appendix 12A at the end of this chapter.

MACRS Depreciation Calculation

Though the IRS allows firms to use the straight-line method with the half-year convention to depreciate assets, most businesses probably benefit from using some form of accelerated depreciation. Accelerated depreciation allows firms to receive more of the dollars of depreciation earlier in the asset's life. An example of this is the double-declining-balance (DDB) depreciation method, under which the depreciation rate is double that used in the straight-line method. The IRS also uses the half-year convention with DDB depreciation, so the actual yearly percentages appear in Table 12.8. The IRS allows businesses to take the most advantageous choice between straight-line and DDB depreciation methods under the modified accelerated cost recovery system (MACRS).

Section 179 Deductions

We can accelerate asset expensing even further by expensing it immediately in the year of purchase. The IRS allows most businesses to immediately expense up to $108,000 of property placed in service during each year under what is referred to as a **Section 179 deduction.** The Section 179 deduction is obviously targeted at helping small businesses, so it places a limit on the annual total of deductible property. If the cost of qualifying Section 179 property you put into service in a single tax year exceeds a statutory base of $430,000, then you can't take the full deduction.

For example, consider a manufacturer who completely reequips his facility this year, which costs $437,000. This is $7,000 more than allowed, so he must reduce his eligible deductible limit to $101,000: the current $108,000 expensing limit minus $7,000. Extending this even further, a company that spent $430,00 + $108,000 = $538,000 or more on qualifying Section 179 property would not be able to take the deduction at all, though the firm could depreciate the property using MACRS.

Property eligible for a Section 179 deduction includes:

- Machinery and equipment.
- Furniture and fixtures.
- Most storage facilities.
- Single-purpose agricultural or horticultural structures.
- Off-the-shelf computer software.

Ineligible property includes:

- Buildings and their structural components.
- Income-producing property (investment or rental property).
- Property held by an estate or trust.
- Property acquired by gift or inheritance.
- Property used in a passive activity.
- Property purchased from related parties.
- Property used outside of the United States.

Impact of Accelerated Depreciation

So, let's return to our FSS example and FinProf. Remember that our initial, simplistic view of depreciation had us taking $24,000 per year for each of the three years of the project's life. If the software reproduction machinery fell into the three-year life class, we could instead have taken the following depreciation amounts by using either the straight-line or DDB approaches:

FSS's Yearly Depreciation and Ending Book Values under Alternative Depreciation				table 12.9
	YEAR 1	**YEAR 2**	**YEAR 3**	**ENDING BV**
Straight-line	$77,000 × 16.67% = $12,835.90	$77,000 × 33.33% = $25,664.10	$77,000 × 33.33% = $25,664.10	$12,835.90
DDB	$77,000 × 33.33% = $25,664.10	$77,000 × 44.45% = $34,226.50	$77,000 × 14.81% = $11,403.70	$5,705.70

If First Strike could take advantage of the Section 179 deduction that would probably be the most advantageous way to deduct the cost of the new machinery—it could deduct the entire $77,000 in year 1. If FSS couldn't use a Section 179 deduction, the DDB depreciation available under MACRS would result in the next quickest recovery of the tax breaks associated with the machinery purchase.

TIME OUT

12-5 Explain why, under MACRS, "five-year" depreciation is actually spread over six years, six-year depreciation spreads into seven years, and so forth.

12-6 If the IRS wanted to encourage businesses to invest in certain types of assets, would they put them into shorter or longer MACRS life-class categories?

LG5

12.5 "Special" Cases Aren't Really That Special

As long as we're consistent in using incremental FCF to calculate total project cash flows, we can handle many project types that are habitually viewed as "special" cases requiring extraordinary treatment with some relatively simple revisions to the methods we used for valuing First Strike's proposed new project.

EXAMPLE 12-2

 For interactive versions of this example visit www.mhhe.com/can1e

LG5

REPLACEMENT PROBLEM

Suppose that Just-in-Time Donuts is considering replacing one of its existing ovens. The original oven cost $100,000 when purchased five years ago and has been depreciated by $9,000 per year since then. Just-in-Time thinks that they can sell the old machine for $65,000 if they sell it today, and for $10,000 if they wait another five years until its anticipated life is over. Just-in-Time is considering replacing this oven with a new one, which costs $150,000, partly because the new oven will save them $50,000 in costs per year relative to the old oven. The new oven will be subject to three-year class life DDB depreciation under MACRS, with an anticipated useful life of five years. At the end of the five years, Just-In-Time will abandon the oven as worthless. If Just-in-Time faces a marginal tax rate of 35 percent, what will be the total project cash flows if they replace the oven?

SOLUTION:

If we sell the old oven today for $65,000 when it has a remaining book value of $55,000 ($100,000 purchase price − 5 years of $9,000 per year depreciation), then the ATCF from its sale will equal:

$$\text{ATCF} = \text{Book value} + (\text{Market value} - \text{Book value}) \times (1 - T_c)$$

$$= \$55,000 + (\$65,000 - \$55,000) \times (1 - .40)$$

$$= \$61,000$$

In return for selling the old oven today, however, JIT will have to forgo both the yearly depreciation that the company would have received for it over the next five years and the $10,000 that it could get for selling it at the end of the five years. We must reflect both of these factors in our calculation of incremental FCFs so that we are reckoning the true costs of the project. In addition, switching from the old oven to the new one would apparently alter neither sales nor NWC requirements across the five-year life of the new oven:

(continued)

Year	0		1	2	3	4	5	
Net incremental sales			$0	$0	$0	$0		$0
Net incremental variable costs			−50,000	−50,000	−50,000	−50,000		−50,000
Depreciation on new oven			$49,995	$66,675	$22,215	$11,115	$0	
Foregone depreciation on old oven			−9,000	−9,000	−9,000	−9,000	−9,000	
Less: Incremental depreciation	$0		40,995	57,675	13,215	2,115		−9,000
EBIT	$0		9,005	−7,675	36,785	47,885		59,000
Less: Taxes	$0		3,152	−2,686	12,875	16,760		20,650
"Net income"	$0		5,853	−4,989	23,910	31,125		38,350
Plus: Depreciation	$0		40,995	57,675	13,215	2,115		−9,000
OCF	$0		$46,848	$52,686	$37,125	$33,240		$29,350
ΔFA for new oven	$150,000						$0	
ΔFA for old oven	−$61,000						$10,000	
ΔFA	$89,000		$0	$0	$0	$0	$10,000	
ΔNWC	0		0	0	0	0	0	
Less: Investment in operating capital	$89,000		$0	$0	$0	$0		$10,000
FCF = OCF − IOC	−$89,000		$46,848	$52,686	$37,125	$33,240		$19,350

We usually think that a positive value for ΔFA is associated with the purchase of FA. But note that in this circumstance, the $10,000 for the forgone sale of the old oven at time 5 is *not* an investment in fixed assets, but rather the opportunity cost of not getting to sell the old oven at higher than book value.

 For interactive versions of this example visit www.mhhe.com/can1e

EXAMPLE 12-3

COST-CUTTING PROBLEM

Your company is considering a new computer system that will initially cost $1 million. It will save your firm $300,000 a year in inventory and receivables management costs. The system is expected to last for five years and will be depreciated using three-year MACRS. The firm expects that the system will have a salvage value of $50,000 at the end of year 5. This purchase does not affect net working capital; the marginal tax rate is 34 percent, and the required return is 8 percent. What will be the total project cash flows if this cost-cutting proposal is implemented?

SOLUTION:

Since the new computer falls into the 3-year MACRS category, it will be fully depreciated when the project ends five years from now. As a result, the ATCF from the sale of the computer will be:

$$ATCF = BV + (MV - BV) \times (1 - T_c)$$

$$= \$0 + (\$50,000 - \$0) \times (1 - .34)$$

$$= \$33,000$$

And the FCFs for the cost-cutting proposal will be equal to:

Year	0		1	2	3	4	5	
Net incremental sales			$0	$0	$0	$0		$0
Less: Incremental variable costs			−300,000	−300,000	−300,000	−300,000		−300,000
Less: Incremental depreciation	$0		$333,300	$444,500	$148,100	$74,100		$0
EBIT	$0		−33,300	−144,500	151,900	225,900		300,000
Less: Taxes	$0		−11,322	−49,130	51,646	76,806		102,000
"Net income"	$0		−21,978	−95,370	100,254	149,094		198,000
Plus: Depreciation	$0		333,300	444,500	148,100	74,100		0
OCF	$0		$311,322	$349,130	$248,354	$223,194		$198,000
ΔFA	$1,000,000		$0	$0	$0	$0	−$33,000	
ΔNWC	0		0	0	0	0	0	
Less: Investment in operating capital	$1,000,000		$0	$0	$0	$0		−$33,000
FCF = OCF − IOC	−$1,000,000		$311,322	$349,130	$248,354	$223,194		$231,000

12.6 Choosing between Alternative Assets with Differing Lives: EAC

Suppose a company has decided to go ahead with a project but needs to choose between two alternative assets, wherein:

- Both assets will result in the same sales.
- Both assets may have different costs and recurring expenses.
- Assets will last different lengths of time.
- When the chosen asset wears out, it will be replaced with an identical machine.

In such a situation, the firm can't really compare one iteration of each machine to the other, since they last different lengths of time. The key here is to use the fact that, since the firm will replace each machine with another identical machine when it wears out, it is really being asked to choose between two sets of infinite, but systematically varying, sets of cash flows. To handle such a situation, "smooth out" the variation in each set of cash flows so that each becomes a perpetuity. Then the company can choose between the two machines based on which will generate the highest present value of cash flows.

Since the decision will involve only a subset of a project's cash flows—the purchase of one of a choice of assets—that present value will probably be negative. If the firm were to look at all the benefits deriving from the choice of which asset to use, including expected sales and so forth, the present value of all cash flows would need to be positive for the entire project to be attractive. We will discuss this in much greater depth in the next chapter when we cover the **net present value** (**NPV**) rule for capital budgeting decisions.

The best approach to convert an infinite series of asset purchases into a perpetuity is known as the **equivalent annual cost** (EAC) approach. To compute and use the EACs of two or more alternative assets,

1. Find the sum of the present values of the cash flows (the net present value, or NPV, which we will cover in great detail in the next chapter) for one iteration of A and one iteration of B.

2. Treat each sum as the present value of an annuity with life equal to the life of the respective asset, and solve for each asset's payment.

3. Choose the asset with the highest (i.e., least negative) EAC.

It may seem that we have just done exactly what we said we should not do: compare the cash flows from one machine A to those from one machine B. In fact, the comparison we just did is actually much broader than that, though it will take a little explanation to see.

Visualize the cash flows to the infinitely repeated purchases of machine B (chosen simply because it has a short life, so it will be easier to see multiple iterations on a time line in the following discussion) as shown in Figure 12.1.

figure 12.1

Year	0	1	2	3	4	5	6	
B	–$12,000	–$3,500	–$3,500	–$3,500 –$12,000	–$3,500	–$3,500	–$3,500 –$12,000	
B Total	–$12,000	–$3,500	–$3,500	–$15,500	–$3,500	–$3,500	–$15,500	

Cash Flows of Repeated Purchases of Machine B

 For interactive versions of this example visit www.mhhe.com/can1e

EXAMPLE 12-4

EAC APPROACH

Suppose that your company has won a bid for a new project—painting highway signs for the local highway department. Based on past experience, you're pretty sure that your company will have the contract for the foreseeable future, and now you have to decide whether to use machine A or machine B to paint the signs: machine A costs $20,000, lasts five years, and will generate annual after-tax net expenses of $2,500. Machine B costs $12,000, lasts three years, and will have after-tax net expenses of $3,500 per year. Assume that, in either case, each machine will simply be junked at the end of its useful life, and the firm faces a cost of capital of 12 percent. Which machine should you choose?

SOLUTION:

One iteration of each machine will consist of the sets of cash flows shown below:

YEAR	0	1	2	3	4	5
Machine A CFs	–$20,000	–$2,500	–$2,500	–$2,500	–$2,500	–$2,500
Machine B CFs	–12,000	–3,500	–3,500	–3,500		

The sum of the present values of machine A's cash flows will be

$$\sum_{t=0}^{5}\frac{CF_t}{(1+i)^t}=\frac{CF_0}{(1+i)^0}+\frac{CF_1}{(1+i)^1}+\frac{CF_2}{(1+i)^2}+\frac{CF_3}{(1+i)^3}+\frac{CF_4}{(1+i)^4}+\frac{CF_5}{(1+i)^5}$$

$$=\frac{-\$20,000}{(1.12)^0}+\frac{-\$2,500}{(1.12)^1}+\frac{-\$2,500}{(1.12)^2}+\frac{-\$2,500}{(1.12)^3}+\frac{-\$2,500}{(1.12)^4}+\frac{-\$2,500}{(1.12)^5}$$

$$=-\$29,012$$

Treating this as the present value of a 5-period annuity, setting i to 12 percent, and solving for payment will yield a payment of –$8,048, which is machine A's EAC.

The sum of the present values of machine B's cash flows will be

$$\sum_{t=0}^{3}\frac{CF_t}{(1+i)^t}=\frac{CF_0}{(1+i)^0}+\frac{CF_1}{(1+i)^1}+\frac{CF_2}{(1+i)^2}+\frac{CF_3}{(1+i)^3}$$

$$=\frac{-\$12,000}{(1.12)^0}+\frac{-\$3,500}{(1.12)^1}+\frac{-\$3,500}{(1.12)^2}+\frac{-\$3,500}{(1.12)^3}$$

$$=-\$20,406$$

Treating this as the present value of a three-period annuity, setting i to 12 percent, and solving for payment will yield a payment of –$8,496, which is machine B's EAC.

Since machine A's EAC is less negative than machine B's, your firm should choose machine A.

figure 12.2

Converted Cash Flows
of Repeated Purchases
of Machine B

Year	0	1	2	3	4	5	6
New B	$0	−$8,496	−$8,496	−$8,496			
				$0	−$8,496	−$8,496	−$8,496
							$0
New B Total	$0	−$8,496	−$8,496	−$8,496	−$8,496	−$8,496	−$8,496

Notice that, after the initial purchase of the first machine B, the cash flows exhibit a systematic cycle: −$3,500 for two years, followed by −$15,500 for one year (when the next machine B is purchased), repeating this way forever. This systematic cycle, which we don't have a formula for valuing, makes it necessary to convert these cash flows into a perpetuity, which we *can* value.

When we computed the NPV of one iteration of machine B, we basically "squished" that machine's cash flows down to a single lump sum, and when we treated that as the present value of an annuity and solved for the payments we were effectively taking that same value and spreading it evenly across the life of the first machine B. Furthermore, since subsequent machine B purchases will be identical to this first one, we can visualize doing the exact same thing to *every* machine B's cash flow. Turning each machine B's cash flow into an annuity in this manner has the net effect of turning all the machine B's cash flows into a perpetuity, as shown in Figure 12.2

In the process, we also turn the repeated purchase of machine A into a perpetuity. We *could* calculate the present values of these two perpetuities and then compare them, which is what we're really interested in doing:

$$PV_{\text{Perpetuity of Infinitely Repeated As}} \text{ vs. } PV_{\text{Perpetuity of Infinitely Repeated Bs}}$$

$$\frac{-\$8,048}{.12} \text{ vs. } \frac{-\$8,496}{.12}$$

But do we really need to? No. The relationship between these two present values of the respective perpetuities is really the same as the relationship between their payment amounts[2]—each machine's respective EAC.

TIME OUT

12-9 Explain how the EAC approach turns uneven cash flows for infinitely repeated asset purchases into perpetuities.

12-10 What if two alternative assets would last the same length of time: would the EAC approach still work?

LG8 12.7 Flotation Costs Revisited

In the previous chapter, we talked about how to take account of flotation costs by adjusting the WACC upwards, incorporating flotation costs directly into the issue prices of the securities used to fund projects. Another way that we can

---

[2]Because the two perpetuities have the same interest rate and the same periodicity (i.e., length between payments), the only possible source of difference in their present values would be the respective payment amounts.

account for flotation costs is to adjust the project's initial cash flow so that it will reflect the flotation costs of raising capital for the project as well as the necessary investment in assets.

In this approach, we will

1. Compute the weighted average flotation cost, f_A, using the firm's target capital weights (because the firm will issue securities in these percentages over the long term)

$$f_A = \frac{E}{E+P+D}f_E + \frac{P}{E+P+D}f_P + \frac{D}{E+P+D}f_D \qquad \text{(12-4)}$$

where f_E, f_P, and f_D are the percentage flotation costs for new equity, preferred stock, and debt, respectively.

2. Compute the flotation-adjusted initial investment, CF_0, using

$$\text{Adjusted } CF_0 = \frac{CF_0}{1 - f_A} \qquad \text{(12-5)}$$

 For interactive versions of this example visit www.mhhe.com/can1e

EXAMPLE 12-5

ADJUSTING CF_o FOR FLOTATION COST

 LG8

Your company is considering a project that will cost $1 million. The project will generate after-tax cash flows of $375,000 per year for five years. The WACC is 15 percent and the firm's target D/A ratio is .375. The flotation cost for equity is 5 percent, the flotation cost for debt is 3 percent, and your firm does not plan on issuing any preferred stock within its capital structure. If your firm follows the practice of incorporating flotation costs into the project's initial investment, what will the flotation-adjusted cash flows for this project be?

SOLUTION:

Since the D/A is .375, the E/A ratio will be equal to $1 - .375 = .625$, and the weighted-average flotation cost for the firm will be:

$$f_A = \frac{E}{E+P+D}f_E + \frac{P}{E+P+D}f_P + \frac{D}{E+P+D}f_D$$

$$= (.625 \times 5\%) + (.375 \times 3\%)$$

$$= 4.25\%$$

Using this, the adjusted CF_o for the project will be:

$$\text{Adjusted } CF_o = \frac{CF_o}{1 - f_A}$$

$$= \frac{-\$1,000,000}{1 - .0425}$$

$$= -\$1,044,386.42$$

So the flotation-adjusted cash flows for the project will be:

YEAR	0	1	2	3	4	5
Cash Flow	−$1,044,386.42	$375,000	$375,000	$375,000	$375,000	$375,000

Business Application Solution

Based on the given information, the yearly sales, levels of NWC and resulting changes in NWC for McDonald's will be:

YEAR	YEARLY SALES	YEARLY LEVELS OF NWC	CHANGES IN NWC
0	$ 0	$364,000	$364,000
1	$2,800,000	$937,300	$ 573,300
2	$ 7,210,000	$965,900	$ 28,600
3	$7,430,000	$994,500	$ 28,600
4	$7,650,000	$512,200	−$482,300
5	$3,940,000	$ 0	−$ 512,200

OCF calculations, ΔNWC, and ΔFA for each year are shown below:

Personal Application Solution

Achmed's purchase of a new computer should not be counted as an incremental cash flow to getting an MBA, as he has indicated that he would be getting one anyways. Likewise, the $250 that he paid to take the GMAT is a sunk cost, and should not be counted, either. His tuition payments constitute an annuity due, so his incremental cash flows will equal:

YEARS	0-3	4-23
FCF	−$15,000	$10,000

YEAR	0	1	2	3	4	5
S	0.0000	2.8000	7.2100	7.4300	7.6500	3.9400
−VC	0.0000	−1.3400	−3.5200	−3.7000	−3.8900	−2.0400
−FC	0.0000	−2.0000	−2.0000	−2.0000	−2.0000	−2.0000
−Dep	0.0000	−1.4000	−2.2400	−1.3440	−0.8064	−0.8064
EBIT	0.0000	−1.9400	−0.5500	0.3860	0.9536	−0.9064
−Tax	0.0000	0.6790	0.1925	−0.1351	−0.3338	0.3172
"NI"	0.0000	−1.2610	−0.3575	0.2509	0.6198	−0.5892
+Dep	0.0000	1.4000	2.2400	1.3440	0.8064	0.8064
OCF	0.0000	0.1390	1.8825	1.5949	1.4262	0.2172
− ΔNWC	−0.3640	−0.5733	−0.0286	−0.0286	0.4823	0.5122
−ΔFA	−7.0000	0.0000	0.0000	0.0000	0.0000	0.0000
FCF	−7.3640	−0.4343	1.8539	1.5663	1.9085	0.7294

TIME OUT

12-11 How would you compute the equity flotation cost if a firm were going to use a mixture of retained earnings and new equity to finance a project?

12-12 Why do we divide the initial cash flow by $(1 - f_A)$ instead of multiplying it by $(1 + f_A)$?

summary of learning goals

In this chapter, we discussed how to apply the concept of free cash flow to measure expected cash flows from proposed new projects. The key concept is that only factors that affect a firm's cash flows that are incrementally attributable to the project should be included, but that we must also be comprehensive in finding these incrementally attributable cash flows.

LG1 Use *pro forma* statements to analyze project cash flows. Calculating expected future cash flows for a project is a complex undertaking. Using a systematic approach involving quasi-income statements and other *pro forma* financial statements ensures that our calculations will be careful and methodical.

LG2 Identify which cash flows we can incrementally attribute to a proposed project and which ones we can't. If a particular cash flow effect will take place if the project is undertaken but won't occur if the project is not accepted, then it should be included in the project cash flows.

LG3 Calculate a project's expected cash flows using the free cash flow approach. Free cash flow measures the operating cash flow a project produces minus the necessary investment in operating capital. This concept is as valid for proposed new projects as it is for the firm's current operations.

LG4 Explain how accelerated depreciation affects project cash flows. The IRS allows firms to take the same total depreciation amount on an asset regardless of how quickly the firms take it. Since no one gives you any interest or credit for delaying depreciation, time value of money concepts tell us that sooner is always better.

LG5 Calculate free cash flows for replacement equipment. New projects and replacement projects differ only in that with replacement projects, we must consider not only the incremental cash flows of purchasing a new asset, but also any cash flows that arise in the process of surrendering old equipment before the end of its usable life.

LG6 Calculate cash flows associated with cost-cutting proposals. For cost-cutting proposals, the main benefit comes from cost reductions; often we see no actual change in sales revenues in response to a cost-cutting proposal.

LG7 Demonstrate how we can use the EAC approach to choose between alternative streams of multiple-repeated projects. The EAC approach basically involves taking one iteration of an asset purchase, "squishing it down" to find the present value of all the asset's cash flows at a single point in time, and then spreading them back out "flat"; that is, in the form of an annuity. By conceptualizing doing this for *all* iterations of an infinitely repeated asset purchase, we can turn that infinite series of cash flows into a perpetuity, which we know how to value.

LG8 Adjust initial project investments to account for flotation costs. To adjust an initial investment for flotation costs, we simply divide it by one minus the average percentage flotation cost, which gives us the sum of financial securities we must sell in order to raise enough capital to both fund the project and pay underwriting fees.

chapter equations

12-1   FCF = Operating cash flow − Investment in operating capital

= [EBIT − Taxes + Depreciation]

− [ΔGross fixed assets + ΔNet operating working capital]

12-2 $\text{Depreciation} = \dfrac{\text{Ending book value} - \text{Beginning book value}}{\text{Life of asset}}$

12-3 $\text{ATCF} = \text{Book value} + (\text{Market value} - \text{Book value}) \times (1 - T_C)$

12-4 $f_A = \dfrac{E}{E + P + D} f_E + \dfrac{P}{E + P + D} f_P + \dfrac{D}{E + P + D} f_D$

12-5 $\text{Adjusted } CF_0 = \dfrac{CF_0}{1 - f_A}$

key terms

depreciable basis, An asset's cost plus the amounts you paid for items such as sales tax, freight charges, and installation and testing fees. (p. 393)

financing costs, Interest paid to debt holders or dividends paid to stockholders. (p. 392)

incremental cash flows, Cash flows directly attributable to the adoption of a new project. (p. 390)

opportunity cost, The dollar cost or forgone opportunity of using an asset already owned by the firm, or a person already employed by the firm, in a new project. (p. 391)

pro forma analysis, Process of estimating expected future cash flows of a project using only the relevant parts of the balance sheet and income statements. (p. 390)

Section 179 deduction, A deduction targeted at small businesses that allows them to immediately expense asset purchases up to a certain limit rather than depreciating them over the assets' useful lives. (p. 399)

substitute and complement, Effects that arise from a new product or service either decreasing or increasing sales, respectively, of the firm's existing products and services. (p. 392)

sunk cost, A cost that has already been incurred and cannot be recovered. (p. 391)

self-test problems with solutions

 LG3, LG4

1 **Computing FCF for Expansion Project** The SCFE Co. wants to add a production line. To do this, the company must spend $200,000 to expand its current building and purchase $1.0 million in new equipment. The company anticipates moving locations in five years, and it expects to sell its current building and the new equipment at that time. SCFE estimates that the building expansion will add $80,000 to the price the building can be sold for, and that the equipment will have a market value of $290,000 at that time. The new equipment falls into the MACRS five-year class, and the building improvements fall into the "Non-residential Real Estate" MACRS category.

The new production line is expected to produce 100,000 units per year of a new product, which has a projected sales price of $7.75 per unit and a variable cost of $3.90 a unit. Introducing the new product is expected to cause sales of existing products to decline by $89,000 per year and existing costs to decline by $49,000 per year. Fixed costs of the new line will be $142,000 annually, and the company expects NWC to increase by $1,800,000 when the new line is added.

If the company faces a marginal tax rate of 34 percent, what will be the total expected cash flows for the project?

Solution:

The equipment and the building improvements have to be depreciated separately. The depreciation percentages and the annual dollar depreciation amounts for each year are shown below, along with the remaining book value of both at the end of the project life:

YEAR	1	2	3	4	5	REMAINING BOOK VALUE
Equipment MACRS %	20.00%	32.00%	19.20%	11.52%	11.52%	
Depreciation	$200,000	$320,000	$192,000	$115,200	$115,200	$ 57,600
Improvement MACRS %	3.1746%	3.1746%	3.1746%	3.1746%	3.1746%	
Depreciation	$6,349.20	$6,349.20	$6,349.20	$6,349.20	$6,349.20	$168,254

Calculations of OCF for the five years of the project will be equal to:

	YEAR 1	YEAR 2	YEAR 3	YEAR 4	YEAR 5
Sales	$775,000.00	$775,000.00	$775,000.00	$775,000.00	$775,000.00
Lost sales	89,000.00	89,000.00	89,000.00	89,000.00	89,000.00
VC	390,000.00	390,000.00	390,000.00	390,000.00	390,000.00
FC	142,000.00	142,000.00	142,000.00	142,000.00	142,000.00
Costs	532,000.00	532,000.00	532,000.00	532,000.00	532,000.00
Lost costs	49,000.00	49,000.00	49,000.00	49,000.00	49,000.00
Depreciation	206,349.20	326,349.20	198,349.20	121,549.20	121,549.20
EBIT	−3,349.20	−123,349.20	4,650.80	81,450.80	81,450.80
Taxes	−1,138.73	−41,938.73	1,581.27	27,693.27	27,693.27
NI	−2,210.47	−81,410.47	3,069.53	53,757.53	53,757.53
Depreciation	206,349.20	326,349.20	198,349.20	121,549.20	121,549.20
OCF	$204,138.73	$244,938.73	$201,418.73	$175,306.73	$175,306.73

The ATCF from the sale of the two assets will be equal to:

$$ATCF_{Equipment} = \$57,600 + (\$290,000 - \$57,600)(1 - .34)$$
$$= \$210,984.00$$
$$ATCF_{Improvements} = \$168,254 + (\$80,000 - \$168,254)(1 - .34)$$
$$= \$110,006.36$$

The levels and changes in NWC will be equal to:

Level of NWC	$1,800,000	$1,800,000	$1,800,000	$1,800,000	$1,800,000	$0
Change in NWC	1,800,000	0	0	0	0	−1,800,000

So the total cash flows for the project will be equal to:

	YEAR 0	YEAR 1	YEAR 2	YEAR 3	YEAR 4	YEAR 5
OCF		$204,138.73	$244,938.73	$201,418.73	$175,306.73	$ 175,306.73
Change in fixed assets	$1,000,000					−210,984.00
	200,000					−110,006.36
Change in NWC	1,800,000	0.00	0.00	0.00	0.00	−1,800,000.00
Total CF	−$2,800,000	$204,138.73	$244,938.73	$201,418.73	$175,306.73	$2,186,290.73

2 **Computing FCF for Cost-Cutting Proposal** Your firm is considering the purchase of a new air conditioning unit at a cost of $50,000. It will be straight-line depreciated to zero over the next five years. At that time, you expect that the unit can be sold for a salvage value of $20,000. This air conditioner is more energy efficient than the one it's replacing, so you anticipate saving $2,000 annually in electricity costs. You also anticipate that your workers will be more productive in a cool environment, and you expect to be able to reduce overtime costs by $20,000 per year. If all applicable tax rates are 35 percent, what will be the expected cash flows associated with the purchase of the new air conditioner?

Solution:

	YEAR 0	YEAR 1	YEAR 2	YEAR 3	YEAR 4	YEAR 5
Sales	$ 0.00	$ 0.00	$ 0.00	$ 0.00	$ 0.00	$ 0.00
− Variable costs	0.00	0.00	0.00	0.00	0.00	0.00
− Fixed costs	0.00	22,000.00	22,000.00	22,000.00	22,000.00	22,000.00
− Depreciation	0.00	−5,000.00	−10,000.00	−10,000.00	−10,000.00	−10,000.00
EBIT	0.00	17,000.00	12,000.00	12,000.00	12,000.00	12,000.00
− Taxes	0.00	−5,950.00	−4,200.00	−4,200.00	−4,200.00	−4,200.00
Net income	0.00	11,050.00	7,800.00	7,800.00	7,800.00	7,800.00
+ Depreciation	0.00	5,000.00	10,000.00	10,000.00	10,000.00	10,000.00
OCF	0.00	16,050.00	17,800.00	17,800.00	17,800.00	17,800.00
−ΔNWC	0.00	0.00	0.00	0.00	0.00	0.00
−ΔFA	−50,000.00	0.00	0.00	0.00	0.00	14,750.00
Total Cash Flow	−$50,000.00	$ 16,050.00	$ 17,800.00	$ 17,800.00	$ 17,800.00	$ 32,550.00

3 **Using EAC** Dumb & Dumber Development Company has two mutually exclusive investment projects to evaluate. Assume both projects can be repeated indefinitely. The following cash flows are associated with each project:

YEAR	PROJECT A CASH FLOW	PROJECT B CASH FLOW
0	−$100,000	−$70,000
1	20,000	30,000
2	50,000	30,000
3	50,000	30,000
4	70,000	45,000
5	−	10,000

The project types are equally risky and the firm's cost of capital is 10 percent. Which project should the firm chose?

Solution:

Using the EAC approach:

$$NPVA = \$44,880.8142$$

Solving for the EAC PMT for A:

$$N = 4$$
$$I/Y = 10$$
$$PV = \$44,880.8142$$
$$[CPT]\ PMT = \$14,158.5865$$
$$NPVB = 41,550.3785$$

Solving for the EAC PMT for B:

$$N = 5$$
$$I/Y = 10$$
$$PV = \$41{,}550.3785$$
$$[CPT]\ PMT = \$10{,}960.8852$$

Which do you choose? A, because $14,158.5865 > $10,960.8852.

questions

1. How is the *pro forma* statement we used in this chapter for computing OCF different from an accountant's income statement? *(LG1)*

2. Suppose you paid your old college finance professor to evaluate a project for you. If you would pay him regardless of your decision concerning whether to proceed with the project, should his fee for evaluating the project be included in the project's incremental cash flows? *(LG2)*

3. Why does a decrease in NWC result in a cash inflow to the firm? *(LG3)*

4. Everything else held constant, would you rather depreciate a project with straight-line depreciation or with DDB? *(LG4)*

5. Everything else held constant, would you rather depreciate a project with DDB depreciation or deduct it under a Section 179 deduction? *(LG4)*

6. In a replacement problem, would we ever see changes in NWC? *(LG5)*

7. In a replacement problem, will incremental net depreciation always be less than the gross depreciation on the new piece of equipment? *(LG5)*

8. In a cost-cutting proposal, what might cause you to sometimes have negative EBIT? *(LG6)*

9. How many TVM formulas do you use every time you calculate EAC for a project? *(LG7)*

10. Will an increase in flotation costs increase or decrease the initial cash flow for a project? *(LG8)*

problems

basic problems

12-1 **After-tax Cash Flow from Sale of Assets** Suppose you sell a fixed asset for $109,000 when its book value is $129,000. If your company's marginal tax rate is 39 percent, what will be the effect on cash flows of this sale (i.e., what will be the after-tax cash flow of this sale)? *(LG3)*

12-2 **PV of Depreciation Tax Benefits** Your company is considering a new project that will require $1 million of new equipment at the start of the project. The equipment will have a depreciable life of 10 years and will be depreciated to a book value of $150,000 using straight-line depreciation. The cost of capital is 13 percent, and the firm's tax rate is 34 percent. Estimate the present value of the tax benefits from depreciation. *(LG4)*

12-3 **EAC Approach** You are trying to pick the least-expensive car for your new delivery service. You have two choices: the Scion xA, which will cost $14,000 to purchase and which will have OCF of −$1,200 annually throughout the vehicle's expected life of three years as a delivery vehicle; and the Toyota Prius, which will cost $20,000 to purchase and which will have OCF of −$650 annually throughout that vehicle's expected four-year life. Both cars will be worthless at the end of their life. If you intend to replace whichever type of car you choose with the same thing when its life runs out, again and again out into the foreseeable future, and if your business has a cost of capital of 12 percent, which one should you choose? *(LG7)*

12-4 **EAC Approach** You are evaluating two different cookie-baking ovens. The Pillsbury 707 costs $57,000, has a five-year life, and has an annual OCF (after tax) of −$10,000 per year. The Keebler CookieMunster costs $90,000, has a seven-year life, and has an annual OCF (after tax) of −$8,000 per year. If your discount rate is 12 percent, what is each machine's EAC? *(LG8)*

12-5 **EAC Approach** You are considering the purchase of one of two machines used in your manufacturing plant. Machine A has a life of two years, costs $80 initially, and then $125 per year in maintenance costs. Machine B costs $150 initially, has a life of three years, and requires $100 in annual maintenance costs. Either machine must be replaced at the end of its life with an equivalent machine. Which is the better machine for the firm? The discount rate is 12 percent and the tax rate is zero. *(LG8)*

intermediate
problems

12-6 **Project Cash Flows** KADS, Inc. has spent $400,000 on research to develop a new computer game. The firm is planning to spend $200,000 on a machine to produce the new game. Shipping and installation costs of the machine will be capitalized and depreciated; they total $50,000. The machine has an expected life of three years, a $75,000 estimated resale value, and falls under the MACRS 7-year class life. Revenue from the new game is expected to be $600,000 per year, with costs of $250,000 per year. The firm has a tax rate of 35 percent, an opportunity cost of capital of 15 percent, and it expects net working capital to increase by $100,000 at the beginning of the project. What will the cash flows for this project be? *(LG3)*

12-7 **Depreciation Tax Shield** Your firm needs a computerized machine tool lathe which costs $50,000 and requires $12,000 in maintenance for each year of its three-year life. After three years, this machine will be replaced. The machine falls into the MACRS three-year class life category. Assume a tax rate of 35 percent and a discount rate of 12 percent. Calculate the depreciation tax shield for this project in year 3. *(LG4)*

12-8 **After-tax Cash Flow from Sale of Assets** If the lathe in the previous problem can be sold for $5,000 at the end of year 3, what is the after-tax salvage value? *(LG4)*

12-9 **Project Cash Flows** You have been asked by the president of your company to evaluate the proposed acquisition of a new special-purpose truck for $60,000. The truck falls into the MACRS three-year class, and it will be sold after three years for $20,000. Use of the truck will require an increase in NWC (spare parts inventory) of $2,000. The truck will have no effect on revenues, but it is expected to save the firm $20,000 per year in before-tax operating costs, mainly labor. The firm's marginal tax rate is 40 percent. What will the cash flows for this project be? *(LG6)*

12-10 Change in NWC You are evaluating a project for The Tiff-any golf club, guaranteed to correct that nasty slice. You estimate the sales price of The Tiff-any to be $400 per unit and sales volume to be 1,000 units in year 1; 1,500 units in year 2; and 1,325 units in year 3. The project has a three-year life. Variable costs amount to $225 per unit and fixed costs are $100,000 per year. The project requires an initial investment of $165,000 in assets, which will be depreciated straight-line to zero over the three-year project life. The actual market value of these assets at the end of year 3 is expected to be $35,000. NWC requirements at the beginning of each year will be approximately 20 percent of the projected sales during the coming year. The tax rate is 34 percent and the required return on the project is 10 percent. What change in NWC occurs at the end of year 1? *(LG3)*

12-11 Operating Cash Flow Continuing the previous problem, what is the operating cash flow for the project in year 2? *(LG3)*

12-12 Project Cash Flows You are evaluating a project for The Ultimate recreational tennis racket, guaranteed to correct that wimpy backhand. You estimate the sales price of The Ultimate to be $400 per unit and sales volume to be 1,000 units in year 1; 1,250 units in year 2; and 1,325 units in year 3. The project has a three-year life. Variable costs amount to $225 per unit and fixed costs are $100,000 per year. The project requires an initial investment of $165,000 in assets, which will be depreciated straight-line to zero over the three-year project life. The actual market value of these assets at the end of year 3 is expected to be $35,000. NWC requirements at the beginning of each year will be approximately 20 percent of the projected sales during the coming year. The tax rate is 34 percent and the required return on the project is 10 percent. What will the cash flows for this project be? *(LG3)*

12-13 Project Cash Flows Mom's Cookies Inc. is considering the purchase of a new cookie oven. The original cost of the old oven was $30,000; it is now five years old, and it has a current market value of $13,333.33. The old oven is being depreciated over a 10-year life toward a zero estimated salvage value on a straight-line basis, resulting in a current book value of $15,000 and an annual depreciation expense of $3,000. The old oven can be used for six more years but has no market value after its depreciable life is over. Management is contemplating the purchase of a new oven whose cost is $25,000 and whose estimated salvage value is zero. Expected before-tax cash savings from the new oven are $4,000 a year over its full MACRS depreciable life. Depreciation is computed using MACRS over a five-year life, and the cost of capital is 10 percent. Assume a 40 percent tax rate. What will the cash flows for this project be? *(LG5)*

research it! Looking up Information on Section 179 Deduction

Go to the IRS's Web site at **www.irs.gov** and search for information on Section 179 deductions for the current tax year.

What is the maximum Section 179 deduction for the current tax year?

integrated minicase: Project Cash Flows

Your company, Dawgs "R" Us, is evaluating a new project involving the purchase of a new oven to bake your hotdog buns. If purchased, the new oven will replace your existing oven, which was purchased seven years ago for a total installed price of $1 million.

You have been depreciating the old oven on a straight-line basis over its expected life of 15 years to an ending book value of $250,000, even though you expect it to be worthless at the end of that 15-year period. The new oven will cost $2 million and will fall into the MACRS five-year depreciation class life. If you purchase the new oven, you expect it to last for eight years. At the end of those eight years, you expect to be able to sell it for $100,000. (Note that both of the ovens, old and new, therefore have an effective remaining life of eight years at the time of your analysis.) If you do purchase the new oven, you estimate that you can sell the old one for its current book value at the same time.

The advantages of the new oven are two-fold: not only do you expect it to reduce the before-tax costs on your current baking operations by $75,000 per year, but you will also be able to produce new types of buns. The sales of the new buns are expected to bring your company $200,000 per year throughout the eight-year life of the new oven, while associated costs of the new buns are only expected to be $80,000 per year.

Since the new oven will allow you to sell these new products, you anticipate that NWC will have to increase immediately by $20,000 upon purchase of the new oven. It will then remain at that increased level throughout the life of the new oven to sustain the new, higher level of operations.

Your company uses a required rate of return of 12 percent for such projects, and your incremental tax rate is 34 percent. What will be the total cash flows for this project?

ANSWERS TO TIME OUT

12-1 You should charge half of her salary and benefits to the new project, and the other half to the existing projects.

12-2 Sure. For example, think about a restaurant chain adding a new item to their menu: say, gourmet coffee. To the extent that some customers who would have bought their current drinks will replace that selection with the new coffee, the coffee is a substitute for those drinks; but, assuming that the coffee will attract some "new" customers, ones who wouldn't have come into the restaurant otherwise, and that those new customers will also buy some of your existing pastry products, then the new coffee is a complement for the pastries.

12-3 Even though we're explicitly keeping track of the level of NWC, what we're really concerned with is the inflow or outflow of cash arising from changes to that level. When we increase NWC, we have to buy inventory, make sales on credit, or tie up cash flow in the form of physical cash, all of which use up cash flow.

12-4 As long as we have any depreciation, OCF will be larger than Net Income because it reflects the fact that depreciation is not a real expense.

(continued)

ANSWERS TO TIME OUT (concluded)

12-5 Because of the half-year convention, the IRS only allows us to take one-half of the first year's life of the asset during the first calendar year we own it. This, in turn, implies that we will still have the last half of the fifth year of the asset's life to take during the sixth year that we own it, and so forth.

12-6 They would encourage investment in certain types of assets by putting them into shorter life-class categories. Since the IRS gives you the same total amount of depreciation regardless of how long the length of depreciable life allowed, the present value of the total tax shields from the depreciation of an asset will be higher if you get to take the depreciation quicker.

12-7 Although a positive investment in operating capital would normally be associated with a purchase of fixed assets, here the positive value was generated by the forgone sale of the old assets: since we sold them at the beginning of the replacement project, we had to give up selling them at the end.

12-8 No. As long as the tax rate is less than 100 percent, the present value of the depreciation tax shields will always be less than the present value of the costs of those assets, implying that net cash flows for such a project would have to be, on average across the life of the project, negative.

12-9 It does so by turning each individual asset purchase not only into an annuity, but into an annuity that is perfectly aligned with the annuities of the identical assets purchased before and after it so as to form a perpetuity.

12-10 Sure. Since the EAC is calculated as the equivalent cost per year, it doesn't matter if both projects have the same or differing lives.

12-11 Since retained earnings do not have a flotation cost, the average equity flotation cost would simply be a weighted average (where the weights are the relative proportions of retained earnings and new equity) of the flotation cost of the new equity and zero. For example, if a firm was going to use one-third retained earnings and two-thirds new equity, and new equity had a flotation cost of 5 percent, then the weighted average flotation cost of equity would be $1/3 \times 0 + 2/3 \times 5\% = 3.33\%$.

12-12 Multiplying by $(1 + f_A)$ would give us the flotation expense on the initial cash flow itself, but it would not give us the "flotation cost on the flotation cost." If we want to raise both the money needed for a project and the money needed to cover the flotation costs, both entirely from the sale of new securities, we will have to keep in mind that the underwriter will charge us a fee on *all* of the money. Dividing by $(1 - f_A)$ handles this. For example, if we wanted to raise $1 million to buy new assets, and the underwriter was going to charge us a weighted average flotation cost of 5 percent, then we would actually have to sell $1,000,000/ (1 - .05) = $1,052,631.58 worth of securities, giving $52,631.58 of the proceeds to the underwriter for their fee in order to be able to keep the $1 million we needed.

www.mhhe.com/can1e

415

appendix 12A
MACRS DEPRECIATION TABLES

MACRS Depreciation

YEAR			NORMAL RECOVERY PERIOD				REAL ESTATE RESIDENTIAL	REAL ESTATE NONRESIDENTIAL	
	3	**5**	**7**	**10**	**15**	**20**	**27.5**	**31.5**	**39**
1	33.33%	20.00%	14.29%	10.00%	5.00%	3.750%	3.485%	3.0420%	2.461%
2	44.45	32.00	24.49	18.00	9.50	7.219	3.636	3.1750	2.564
3	14.81	19.20	17.49	14.40	8.55	6.677	3.636	3.1750	2.564
4	7.41	11.52	12.49	11.52	7.70	6.177	3.636	3.1750	2.564
5	0.00	11.52	8.93	9.22	6.93	5.713	3.636	3.1750	2.564
6	0.00	5.76	8.92	7.37	6.23	5.285	3.636	3.1750	2.564
7	0.00	0.00	8.93	6.55	5.90	4.888	3.636	3.1750	2.564
8	0.00	0.00	4.46	6.55	5.90	4.522	3.636	3.1750	2.564
9	0.00	0.00	0.00	6.56	5.91	4.462	3.636	3.1740	2.564
10	0.00	0.00	0.00	6.55	5.90	4.461	3.637	3.1750	2.564
11	0.00	0.00	0.00	3.28	5.91	4.462	3.636	3.1740	2.564
12	0.00	0.00	0.00	0.00	5.90	4.461	3.637	3.1750	2.564
13	0.00	0.00	0.00	0.00	5.91	4.462	3.636	3.1740	2.564
14	0.00	0.00	0.00	0.00	5.90	4.461	3.637	3.1750	2.564
15	0.00	0.00	0.00	0.00	5.91	4.462	3.636	3.1740	2.564
16	0.00	0.00	0.00	0.00	2.95	4.461	3.637	3.1750	2.564
17	0.00	0.00	0.00	0.00	0.00	4.462	3.636	3.1740	2.564
18	0.00	0.00	0.00	0.00	0.00	4.461	3.637	3.1750	2.564
19	0.00	0.00	0.00	0.00	0.00	4.462	3.636	3.1740	2.564
20	0.00	0.00	0.00	0.00	0.00	4.461	3.637	3.1750	2.564
21	0.00	0.00	0.00	0.00	0.00	2.231	3.636	3.1740	2.564
22	0.00	0.00	0.00	0.00	0.00	0.00	3.637	3.1750	2.564
23	0.00	0.00	0.00	0.00	0.00	0.00	3.636	3.1740	2.564
24	0.00	0.00	0.00	0.00	0.00	0.00	3.637	3.1750	2.564
25	0.00	0.00	0.00	0.00	0.00	0.00	3.636	3.1740	2.564
26	0.00	0.00	0.00	0.00	0.00	0.00	3.637	3.1750	2.564
27	0.00	0.00	0.00	0.00	0.00	0.00	3.636	3.1740	2.564
28	0.00	0.00	0.00	0.00	0.00	0.00	1.970	3.1750	2.564
29	0.00	0.00	0.00	0.00	0.00	0.00	0.00	3.1740	2.564
30	0.00	0.00	0.00	0.00	0.00	0.00	0.00	3.1750	2.564
31	0.00	0.00	0.00	0.00	0.00	0.00	0.00	3.1740	2.564
32	0.00	0.00	0.00	0.00	0.00	0.00	0.00	1.7200	2.564
33	0.00	0.00	0.00	0.00	0.00	0.00	0.00	0.00	2.564
34	0.00	0.00	0.00	0.00	0.00	0.00	0.00	0.00	2.564
35	0.00	0.00	0.00	0.00	0.00	0.00	0.00	0.00	2.564
36	0.00	0.00	0.00	0.00	0.00	0.00	0.00	0.00	2.564
37	0.00	0.00	0.00	0.00	0.00	0.00	0.00	0.00	2.564
38	0.00	0.00	0.00	0.00	0.00	0.00	0.00	0.00	2.564
39	0.00	0.00	0.00	0.00	0.00	0.00	0.00	0.00	2.564
40	0.00	0.00	0.00	0.00	0.00	0.00	0.00	0.00	0.107
41	0.00	0.00	0.00	0.00	0.00	0.00	0.00	0.00	0.000

SL Depreciation

NORMAL RECOVERY PERIOD

YEAR	2.5	3	3.5	4	5	6	6.5	7	7.5	8	8.5	9
1	20.00%	16.67%	14.29%	12.50%	10.00%	8.33%	7.69%	7.14%	6.67%	6.25%	5.88%	5.56%
2	40.00	33.33	28.57	25.00	20.00	16.67	15.39	14.29	13.33	12.50	11.77	11.11
3	40.00	33.33	28.57	25.00	20.00	16.67	15.38	14.29	13.33	12.50	11.76	11.11
4	0.00	16.67	28.57	25.00	20.00	16.67	15.39	14.28	13.33	12.50	11.77	11.11
5	0.00	0.00	0.00	12.50	20.00	16.66	15.38	14.29	13.34	12.50	11.76	11.11
6	0.00	0.00	0.00	0.00	10.00	16.67	15.39	14.28	13.33	12.50	11.77	11.11
7	0.00	0.00	0.00	0.00	0.00	8.33	15.38	14.29	13.34	12.50	11.76	11.11
8	0.00	0.00	0.00	0.00	0.00	0.00	0.00	7.14	13.33	12.50	11.77	11.11
9	0.00	0.00	0.00	0.00	0.00	0.00	0.00	0.00	0.00	6.25	11.76	11.11
10	0.00	0.00	0.00	0.00	0.00	0.00	0.00	0.00	0.00	0.00	0.00	5.56
11	0.00	0.00	0.00	0.00	0.00	0.00	0.00	0.00	0.00	0.00	0.00	0.00
12	0.00	0.00	0.00	0.00	0.00	0.00	0.00	0.00	0.00	0.00	0.00	0.00
13	0.00	0.00	0.00	0.00	0.00	0.00	0.00	0.00	0.00	0.00	0.00	0.00
14	0.00	0.00	0.00	0.00	0.00	0.00	0.00	0.00	0.00	0.00	0.00	0.00
15	0.00	0.00	0.00	0.00	0.00	0.00	0.00	0.00	0.00	0.00	0.00	0.00
16	0.00	0.00	0.00	0.00	0.00	0.00	0.00	0.00	0.00	0.00	0.00	0.00
17	0.00	0.00	0.00	0.00	0.00	0.00	0.00	0.00	0.00	0.00	0.00	0.00
18	0.00	0.00	0.00	0.00	0.00	0.00	0.00	0.00	0.00	0.00	0.00	0.00
19	0.00	0.00	0.00	0.00	0.00	0.00	0.00	0.00	0.00	0.00	0.00	0.00
20	0.00	0.00	0.00	0.00	0.00	0.00	0.00	0.00	0.00	0.00	0.00	0.00
21	0.00	0.00	0.00	0.00	0.00	0.00	0.00	0.00	0.00	0.00	0.00	0.00
22	0.00	0.00	0.00	0.00	0.00	0.00	0.00	0.00	0.00	0.00	0.00	0.00
23	0.00	0.00	0.00	0.00	0.00	0.00	0.00	0.00	0.00	0.00	0.00	0.00
24	0.00	0.00	0.00	0.00	0.00	0.00	0.00	0.00	0.00	0.00	0.00	0.00
25	0.00	0.00	0.00	0.00	0.00	0.00	0.00	0.00	0.00	0.00	0.00	0.00
26	0.00	0.00	0.00	0.00	0.00	0.00	0.00	0.00	0.00	0.00	0.00	0.00
27	0.00	0.00	0.00	0.00	0.00	0.00	0.00	0.00	0.00	0.00	0.00	0.00
28	0.00	0.00	0.00	0.00	0.00	0.00	0.00	0.00	0.00	0.00	0.00	0.00
29	0.00	0.00	0.00	0.00	0.00	0.00	0.00	0.00	0.00	0.00	0.00	0.00
30	0.00	0.00	0.00	0.00	0.00	0.00	0.00	0.00	0.00	0.00	0.00	0.00
31	0.00	0.00	0.00	0.00	0.00	0.00	0.00	0.00	0.00	0.00	0.00	0.00
32	0.00	0.00	0.00	0.00	0.00	0.00	0.00	0.00	0.00	0.00	0.00	0.00
33	0.00	0.00	0.00	0.00	0.00	0.00	0.00	0.00	0.00	0.00	0.00	0.00
34	0.00	0.00	0.00	0.00	0.00	0.00	0.00	0.00	0.00	0.00	0.00	0.00
35	0.00	0.00	0.00	0.00	0.00	0.00	0.00	0.00	0.00	0.00	0.00	0.00
36	0.00	0.00	0.00	0.00	0.00	0.00	0.00	0.00	0.00	0.00	0.00	0.00
37	0.00	0.00	0.00	0.00	0.00	0.00	0.00	0.00	0.00	0.00	0.00	0.00
38	0.00	0.00	0.00	0.00	0.00	0.00	0.00	0.00	0.00	0.00	0.00	0.00
39	0.00	0.00	0.00	0.00	0.00	0.00	0.00	0.00	0.00	0.00	0.00	0.00
40	0.00	0.00	0.00	0.00	0.00	0.00	0.00	0.00	0.00	0.00	0.00	0.00
41	0.00	0.00	0.00	0.00	0.00	0.00	0.00	0.00	0.00	0.00	0.00	0.00
42	0.00	0.00	0.00	0.00	0.00	0.00	0.00	0.00	0.00	0.00	0.00	0.00
43	0.00	0.00	0.00	0.00	0.00	0.00	0.00	0.00	0.00	0.00	0.00	0.00
44	0.00	0.00	0.00	0.00	0.00	0.00	0.00	0.00	0.00	0.00	0.00	0.00
45	0.00	0.00	0.00	0.00	0.00	0.00	0.00	0.00	0.00	0.00	0.00	0.00
46	0.00	0.00	0.00	0.00	0.00	0.00	0.00	0.00	0.00	0.00	0.00	0.00
47	0.00	0.00	0.00	0.00	0.00	0.00	0.00	0.00	0.00	0.00	0.00	0.00
48	0.00	0.00	0.00	0.00	0.00	0.00	0.00	0.00	0.00	0.00	0.00	0.00
49	0.00	0.00	0.00	0.00	0.00	0.00	0.00	0.00	0.00	0.00	0.00	0.00
50	0.00	0.00	0.00	0.00	0.00	0.00	0.00	0.00	0.00	0.00	0.00	0.00
51	0.00	0.00	0.00	0.00	0.00	0.00	0.00	0.00	0.00	0.00	0.00	0.00
52	0.00	0.00	0.00	0.00	0.00	0.00	0.00	0.00	0.00	0.00	0.00	0.00

SL Depreciation

NORMAL RECOVERY PERIOD

YEAR	9.5	10	10.5	11	11.5	12	12.5	13	13.5	14	15	16	16.5
1	5.26%	5.00%	4.76%	4.55%	4.35%	4.17%	4.00%	3.85%	3.70%	3.57%	3.33%	3.13%	3.03%
2	10.53	10.00	9.52	9.09	8.70	8.33	8.00	7.69	7.41	7.14	6.67	6.25	6.06
3	10.53	10.00	9.52	9.09	8.70	8.33	8.00	7.69	7.41	7.14	6.67	6.25	6.06
4	10.53	10.00	9.53	9.09	8.69	8.33	8.00	7.69	7.41	7.14	6.67	6.25	6.06
5	10.52	10.00	9.52	9.09	8.70	8.33	8.00	7.69	7.41	7.14	6.67	6.25	6.06
6	10.53	10.00	9.53	9.09	8.69	8.33	8.00	7.69	7.41	7.14	6.67	6.25	6.06
7	10.52	10.00	9.52	9.09	8.70	8.34	8.00	7.69	7.41	7.14	6.67	6.25	6.06
8	10.53	10.00	9.53	9.09	8.69	8.33	8.00	7.69	7.41	7.15	6.66	6.25	6.06
9	10.52	10.00	9.52	9.09	8.70	8.34	8.00	7.69	7.41	7.14	6.67	6.25	6.06
10	10.53	10.00	9.53	9.09	8.69	8.33	8.00	7.70	7.40	7.15	6.66	6.25	6.06
11	0.00	5.00	9.52	9.09	8.70	8.34	8.00	7.69	7.41	7.14	6.67	6.25	6.06
12	0.00	0.00	0.00	4.55	8.69	8.33	8.00	7.70	7.40	7.15	6.66	6.25	6.06
13	0.00	0.00	0.00	0.00	0.00	4.17	8.00	7.69	7.41	7.14	6.67	6.25	6.06
14	0.00	0.00	0.00	0.00	0.00	0.00	0.00	3.85	7.40	7.15	6.66	6.25	6.06
15	0.00	0.00	0.00	0.00	0.00	0.00	0.00	0.00	0.00	3.57	6.67	6.25	6.06
16	0.00	0.00	0.00	0.00	0.00	0.00	0.00	0.00	0.00	0.00	3.33	6.25	6.06
17	0.00	0.00	0.00	0.00	0.00	0.00	0.00	0.00	0.00	0.00	3.12	6.07
18	0.00	0.00	0.00	0.00	0.00	0.00	0.00	0.00	0.00	0.00	0.00	0.00	0.00
19	0.00	0.00	0.00	0.00	0.00	0.00	0.00	0.00	0.00	0.00	0.00	0.00	0.00
20	0.00	0.00	0.00	0.00	0.00	0.00	0.00	0.00	0.00	0.00	0.00	0.00	0.00
21	0.00	0.00	0.00	0.00	0.00	0.00	0.00	0.00	0.00	0.00	0.00	0.00	0.00
22	0.00	0.00	0.00	0.00	0.00	0.00	0.00	0.00	0.00	0.00	0.00	0.00	0.00
23	0.00	0.00	0.00	0.00	0.00	0.00	0.00	0.00	0.00	0.00	0.00	0.00	0.00
24	0.00	0.00	0.00	0.00	0.00	0.00	0.00	0.00	0.00	0.00	0.00	0.00	0.00
25	0.00	0.00	0.00	0.00	0.00	0.00	0.00	0.00	0.00	0.00	0.00	0.00	0.00
26	0.00	0.00	0.00	0.00	0.00	0.00	0.00	0.00	0.00	0.00	0.00	0.00	0.00
27	0.00	0.00	0.00	0.00	0.00	0.00	0.00	0.00	0.00	0.00	0.00	0.00	0.00
28	0.00	0.00	0.00	0.00	0.00	0.00	0.00	0.00	0.00	0.00	0.00	0.00	0.00
29	0.00	0.00	0.00	0.00	0.00	0.00	0.00	0.00	0.00	0.00	0.00	0.00	0.00
30	0.00	0.00	0.00	0.00	0.00	0.00	0.00	0.00	0.00	0.00	0.00	0.00	0.00
31	0.00	0.00	0.00	0.00	0.00	0.00	0.00	0.00	0.00	0.00	0.00	0.00	0.00
32	0.00	0.00	0.00	0.00	0.00	0.00	0.00	0.00	0.00	0.00	0.00	0.00	0.00
33	0.00	0.00	0.00	0.00	0.00	0.00	0.00	0.00	0.00	0.00	0.00	0.00	0.00
34	0.00	0.00	0.00	0.00	0.00	0.00	0.00	0.00	0.00	0.00	0.00	0.00	0.00
35	0.00	0.00	0.00	0.00	0.00	0.00	0.00	0.00	0.00	0.00	0.00	0.00	0.00
36	0.00	0.00	0.00	0.00	0.00	0.00	0.00	0.00	0.00	0.00	0.00	0.00	0.00
37	0.00	0.00	0.00	0.00	0.00	0.00	0.00	0.00	0.00	0.00	0.00	0.00	0.00
38	0.00	0.00	0.00	0.00	0.00	0.00	0.00	0.00	0.00	0.00	0.00	0.00	0.00
39	0.00	0.00	0.00	0.00	0.00	0.00	0.00	0.00	0.00	0.00	0.00	0.00	0.00
40	0.00	0.00	0.00	0.00	0.00	0.00	0.00	0.00	0.00	0.00	0.00	0.00	0.00
41	0.00	0.00	0.00	0.00	0.00	0.00	0.00	0.00	0.00	0.00	0.00	0.00	0.00
42	0.00	0.00	0.00	0.00	0.00	0.00	0.00	0.00	0.00	0.00	0.00	0.00	0.00
43	0.00	0.00	0.00	0.00	0.00	0.00	0.00	0.00	0.00	0.00	0.00	0.00	0.00
44	0.00	0.00	0.00	0.00	0.00	0.00	0.00	0.00	0.00	0.00	0.00	0.00	0.00
45	0.00	0.00	0.00	0.00	0.00	0.00	0.00	0.00	0.00	0.00	0.00	0.00	0.00
46	0.00	0.00	0.00	0.00	0.00	0.00	0.00	0.00	0.00	0.00	0.00	0.00	0.00
47	0.00	0.00	0.00	0.00	0.00	0.00	0.00	0.00	0.00	0.00	0.00	0.00	0.00
48	0.00	0.00	0.00	0.00	0.00	0.00	0.00	0.00	0.00	0.00	0.00	0.00	0.00
49	0.00	0.00	0.00	0.00	0.00	0.00	0.00	0.00	0.00	0.00	0.00	0.00	0.00
50	0.00	0.00	0.00	0.00	0.00	0.00	0.00	0.00	0.00	0.00	0.00	0.00	0.00
51	0.00	0.00	0.00	0.00	0.00	0.00	0.00	0.00	0.00	0.00	0.00	0.00	0.00
52	0.00	0.00	0.00	0.00	0.00	0.00	0.00	0.00	0.00	0.00	0.00	0.00	0.00

SL Depreciation

NORMAL RECOVERY PERIOD

YEAR	17	18	19	20	22	24	25	26.5	28	30	35	40	45	50
1	2.94%	2.78%	2.63%	2.50%	2.273%	2.083%	2.00%	1.887%	1.786%	1.667%	1.429%	1.25%	1.111%	1.00%
2	5.88	5.56	5.26	5.00	4.545	4.167	4.00	3.774	3.571	3.333	2.857	2.50	2.222	2.00
3	5.88	5.56	5.26	5.00	4.545	4.167	4.00	3.774	3.571	3.333	2.857	2.50	2.222	2.00
4	5.88	5.55	5.26	5.00	4.545	4.167	4.00	3.774	3.571	3.333	2.857	2.50	2.222	2.00
5	5.88	5.56	5.26	5.00	4.546	4.167	4.00	3.774	3.571	3.333	2.857	2.50	2.222	2.00
6	5.88	5.55	5.26	5.00	4.545	4.167	4.00	3.774	3.571	3.333	2.857	2.50	2.222	2.00
7	5.88	5.56	5.26	5.00	4.546	4.167	4.00	3.773	3.572	3.333	2.857	2.50	2.222	2.00
8	5.88	5.55	5.26	5.00	4.545	4.167	4.00	3.774	3.572	3.333	2.857	2.50	2.222	2.00
9	5.88	5.56	5.27	5.00	4.546	4.167	4.00	3.773	3.572	3.333	2.857	2.50	2.222	2.00
10	5.88	5.55	5.26	5.00	4.545	4.167	4.00	3.774	3.571	3.333	2.857	2.50	2.222	2.00
11	5.89	5.56	5.27	5.00	4.546	4.166	4.00	3.773	3.572	3.333	2.857	2.50	2.222	2.00
12	5.88	5.55	5.26	5.00	4.545	4.167	4.00	3.774	3.571	3.333	2.857	2.50	2.222	2.00
13	5.89	5.56	5.27	5.00	4.546	4.166	4.00	3.773	3.572	3.334	2.857	2.50	2.222	2.00
14	5.88	5.55	5.26	5.00	4.545	4.167	4.00	3.773	3.571	3.333	2.857	2.50	2.222	2.00
15	5.89	5.56	5.27	5.00	4.546	4.166	4.00	3.774	3.572	3.334	2.857	2.50	2.222	2.00
16	5.88	5.55	5.26	5.00	4.545	4.167	4.00	3.773	3.571	3.333	2.857	2.50	2.222	2.00
17	5.89	5.56	5.27	5.00	4.546	4.166	4.00	3.774	3.572	3.334	2.857	2.50	2.222	2.00
18	2.94	5.55	5.26	5.00	4.545	4.167	4.00	3.773	3.571	3.333	2.857	2.50	2.222	2.00
19	0.00	2.78	5.27	5.00	4.546	4.166	4.00	3.774	3.572	3.334	2.857	2.50	2.222	2.00
20	0.00	0.00	2.63	5.00	4.545	4.167	4.00	3.773	3.571	3.333	2.857	2.50	2.222	2.00
21	0.00	0.00	0.00	2.50	4.546	4.166	4.00	3.774	3.572	3.334	2.857	2.50	2.222	2.00
22	0.00	0.00	0.00	0.00	4.545	4.167	4.00	3.773	3.571	3.333	2.857	2.50	2.222	2.00
23	0.00	0.00	0.00	0.00	2.273	4.166	4.00	3.774	3.572	3.334	2.857	2.50	2.222	2.00
24	0.00	0.00	0.00	0.00	0.000	4.167	4.00	3.773	3.571	3.333	2.857	2.50	2.222	2.00
25	0.00	0.00	0.00	0.00	0.000	2.083	4.00	3.774	3.572	3.334	2.857	2.50	2.222	2.00
26	0.00	0.00	0.00	0.00	0.000	0.000	2.00	3.773	3.571	3.333	2.857	2.50	2.222	2.00
27	0.00	0.00	0.00	0.00	0.000	0.000	0.00	3.774	3.572	3.334	2.857	2.50	2.223	2.00
28	0.00	0.00	0.00	0.00	0.000	0.000	0.00	0.000	3.571	3.333	2.858	2.50	2.222	2.00
29	0.00	0.00	0.00	0.00	0.000	0.000	0.00	0.000	1.786	3.334	2.857	2.50	2.223	2.00
30	0.00	0.00	0.00	0.00	0.000	0.000	0.00	0.000	0.000	3.333	2.858	2.50	2.222	2.00
31	0.00	0.00	0.00	0.00	0.000	0.000	0.00	0.000	0.000	1.667	2.857	2.50	2.223	2.00
32	0.00	0.00	0.00	0.00	0.000	0.000	0.00	0.000	0.000	0.000	2.858	2.50	2.222	2.00
33	0.00	0.00	0.00	0.00	0.000	0.000	0.00	0.000	0.000	0.000	2.857	2.50	2.223	2.00
34	0.00	0.00	0.00	0.00	0.000	0.000	0.00	0.000	0.000	0.000	2.858	2.50	2.222	2.00
35	0.00	0.00	0.00	0.00	0.000	0.000	0.00	0.000	0.000	0.000	2.857	2.50	2.223	2.00
36	0.00	0.00	0.00	0.00	0.000	0.000	0.00	0.000	0.000	0.000	1.429	2.50	2.222	2.00
37	0.00	0.00	0.00	0.00	0.000	0.000	0.00	0.000	0.000	0.000	0.000	2.50	2.223	2.00
38	0.00	0.00	0.00	0.00	0.000	0.000	0.00	0.000	0.000	0.000	0.000	2.50	2.222	2.00
39	0.00	0.00	0.00	0.00	0.000	0.000	0.00	0.000	0.000	0.000	0.000	2.50	2.223	2.00
40	0.00	0.00	0.00	0.00	0.000	0.000	0.00	0.000	0.000	0.000	0.000	2.50	2.222	2.00
41	0.00	0.00	0.00	0.00	0.000	0.000	0.00	0.000	0.000	0.000	0.000	1.25	2.223	2.00
42	0.00	0.00	0.00	0.00	0.000	0.000	0.00	0.000	0.000	0.000	0.000	0.00	2.222	2.00
43	0.00	0.00	0.00	0.00	0.000	0.000	0.00	0.000	0.000	0.000	0.000	0.00	2.223	2.00
44	0.00	0.00	0.00	0.00	0.000	0.000	0.00	0.000	0.000	0.000	0.000	0.00	2.222	2.00
45	0.00	0.00	0.00	0.00	0.000	0.000	0.00	0.000	0.000	0.000	0.000	0.00	2.223	2.00
46	0.00	0.00	0.00	0.00	0.000	0.000	0.00	0.000	0.000	0.000	0.000	0.00	1.111	2.00
47	0.00	0.00	0.00	0.00	0.000	0.000	0.00	0.000	0.000	0.000	0.000	0.00	0.000	2.00
48	0.00	0.00	0.00	0.00	0.000	0.000	0.00	0.000	0.000	0.000	0.000	0.00	0.000	2.00
49	0.00	0.00	0.00	0.00	0.000	0.000	0.00	0.000	0.000	0.000	0.000	0.00	0.000	2.00
50	0.00	0.00	0.00	0.00	0.000	0.000	0.00	0.000	0.000	0.000	0.000	0.00	0.000	2.00
51	0.00	0.00	0.00	0.00	0.000	0.000	0.00	0.000	0.000	0.000	0.000	0.00	0.000	1.00
52	0.00	0.00	0.00	0.00	0.000	0.000	0.00	0.000	0.000	0.000	0.000	0.00	0.000	0.00

chapter 13:

WEIGHING NET PRESENT VALUE AND OTHER CAPITAL BUDGETING CRITERIA

Learning Goals

LG1 Develop intuition to understand the logic underlying capital budgeting decision techniques.

LG2 Calculate and use the net present value (NPV) method for evaluating capital investment opportunities.

LG3 Calculate and use the payback (PB) and discounted payback (DPB) methods for valuing capital investment opportunities.

LG4 Calculate and use the internal rate of return (IRR) and the modified internal rate of return (MIRR) methods for evaluating capital investment opportunities; understand which problems associated with IRR that MIRR can and cannot correct.

LG5 Use NPV profiles to reconcile sources of conflict between NPV and IRR methods.

LG6 Compute and use the profitability index (PI).

Once you've calculated the cost of capital for a project and estimated its cash flows, deciding whether or not to invest in that project basically boils down to asking the question "Is the project worth its projected future value?" To answer this question, we will, not surprisingly, turn once again to the time value of money (TVM) formulas we used to value stocks, bonds, loans, and other marketable securities in Chapters 7 and 8. But first, a caveat: Though the *mechanics* of using the TVM formulas will be the same, the *intuition* underlying our analysis of investment criteria is very different. You will recall that we used the pricing equations for stocks, bonds, and other instruments with an emphasis on equations that had "=" signs. We will see here that most capital budgeting decision rules that we will encounter will have ">" or "<" signs. This difference arises because marketable securities are *financial* assets that trade in competitive financial markets, while capital budgeting projects usually involve the purchase of *real* assets, which typically trade in much less

viewpoints

Business Application

ADK Industries, a startup firm in the "online social networking" industry, has run into capacity constraints with their Internet bandwidth provider. ADK management is considering building their own dedicated Web server farm at a cost of $5 million. In return, the firm expects that the increased bandwidth will generate higher demand for their services, resulting in increased cash flows of $1.2 million in the first year, $1.6 million in the second year, $2.3 million in the third year, and $2.8 million in the fourth year, for a total of $7.9 million over the next four years. At that point, the firm will scrap the server farm as obsolete. If ADK estimates that its target rate of return on such projects is 14 percent, should ADK go ahead with the project? **(See solution on p. 442)**

Personal Application

Letitia Tyler is considering some improvements to her house. The work will take six months to complete, and the contractor has asked for payments of $5,000 at the start, $5,000 after three months, and another $10,000 upon completion. Letitia plans to sell the house in approximately three years and estimates that the work will increase the selling price of her house by approximately $30,000 from its current estimated market price of $124,000. If she must borrow money to pay for the improvements from the bank at an APR (based upon monthly compounding) of 9 percent, should she have the improvements done? **(See solution on p. 442)**

A practice test can be found on the Online Learning Center at
www.mhhe.com/can1e

competitive markets. Real assets are considerably less liquid than are financial assets, and firms purchase real assets in the form of capital equipment to create value for their customers. As a result, projects and purchases that involve capital equipment typically convey at least some monopoly power (and the associated monopolistic profits) to the firm purchasing them and adopting them for long-term use. In fact, the reason for the inequality signs in the capital budgeting decision rules we'll be examining is that, rather than looking for projects that are worth "enough," we seek projects that are worth "more than enough." That is, capital budgeting equations seek projects that offer more return than they should (sometimes called *economic profits*), even after taking into account their associated risk.

 ## 13.1 The Set of Capital Budgeting Techniques

So, now we are going to apply what we've learned in the preceding two chapters about the cost of capital and cash flows that result from capital budgeting decisions to choose the projects that most deserve the scarce capital—that is, to determine which projects promise the best returns to the company. No one can perfectly predict the future, so these techniques are, by their very nature, accompanied by uncertainty. That said, commonly used capital budgeting techniques include:

- NPV (net present value).
- PB (payback).
- DPB (discounted payback).
- IRR (internal rate of return).
- MIRR (modified internal rate of return).
- PI (profitability index).

As we discuss each of these techniques in this chapter, we will find that, while the net present value (NPV) technique is the preferred one for most project evaluations, various situations arise in which you might wish to use one of the other decision rules, either in lieu of NPV or in conjunction with it. For example, a company or person faced with a time constraint to repay the initial capital for a project might well be more worried about a project's payback (PB) statistic, while a firm facing capital constraints might prefer to use one of the interest-rate-based decision statistics, such as the profitability index (PI), to prioritize their project choices. We will discuss the contexts for choosing one technique over another throughout the chapter.

 ## 13.2 The Choice of Decision Statistic Format

In general, three factors drive the choice of which decision rule(s) to use:

1. The desired format or units of measurement for the decision statistic.
2. Whether the project's cash flows are **normal** or non-normal.
3. Whether the firm is considering the project independently of other projects, or whether its project selection will be *mutually exclusive.*

We will discuss the impact of non-normal cash flows and the problems faced in using some of the techniques to choose between mutually exclusive projects as they become relevant, but the first factor, the desired decision statistic format, deserves some attention before we start.

Decision Statistic Formats

Managers tend to focus on three general measurement units for financial decisions: currency, time, and rate of return. Of these three types, rate-based statistics usually pose the most problems.[1] Unfortunately, managers also usually prefer the seemingly concrete nature of rate-based statistics, presumably because they can then easily compare the "earned" rate of return constructed by these decision rules with the "borrowing" rates that potential lenders and the capital markets are currently quoting.

Both the popularity and the problems associated with rate-of-return-based decision rules stem from a common source: the ability to conceptualize rate relationships. The "expected rate of return per dollar invested" provides an appealingly tangible measure of a project's anticipated viability, but computing this measurement involves summarizing the relationship between cash inflows and cash outflows across the project's lifetime through the use of a ratio. Any time we use a ratio to create a summary statistic, some (crucial) information is lost along the way. In particular, though rate-based decision statistics tell us the rate of return *per dollar invested*, they don't reflect the *amount* of the investment on which that return is based. This omission will sometimes cause those rate-based decision statistics to incorrectly prefer projects with lower dollar returns, as we'll see in our discussion of IRR, MIRR, and PI.

13.3 Processing Capital Budgeting Decisions

For all of our decision techniques, we need to identify how to calculate a *decision statistic;* decide on an appropriate *benchmark* for comparing the calculated statistic with; and define what relationship between the two will dictate project acceptance. When we consider one project at a time, or when we examine each of a group of independent projects, capital budgeting techniques involve two-step decision processes:

1. Compute the statistic.
2. Compare the computed statistic with the benchmark to decide whether to accept or reject the project.

However, when we deal with mutually exclusive projects, we will need to add a new step in the middle of the process:

1. Compute the statistic for each project.
2. *Have a "runoff" between the mutually exclusive projects, choosing the one with the best statistic.*
3. Compare the computed statistic from the runoff winner with the benchmark to decide whether to accept or reject.

As we'll see, the presence of this runoff step for mutually exclusive projects, as well as its placement, will create problems when we use decision statistics that either ignore or summarize critical information in the first step.

13.4 Net Present Value

LG1

At its heart, **net present value (NPV)** represents the "purest" of capital budgeting rules, measuring exactly the value we are interested in: the amount of wealth increase we expect from accepting a project. As we cover in more detail below,

---

[1]This is true particularly when dealing with mutually exclusive projects; please see below.

the NPV method measures this expected wealth increase by computing the difference between the present values of a project's cash inflows and outflows. Since this calculation includes the necessary capital expenditures and other startup costs of the project as cash outflows, a positive value indicates that the project is desirable—that it more than covers all of the necessary resource costs to do the project.

 ## NPV Statistic

We actually already know how to calculate the NPV statistic. In fact, we use a very similar approach in developing bond and stock pricing equations. The NPV statistic is simply the sum of all the cash flows' present values:

$$NPV = \frac{CF_0}{(1+i)^0} + \frac{CF_1}{(1+i)^1} + \cdots + \frac{CF_N}{(1+i)^N} \tag{13-1}$$
$$= \sum_{n=0}^{N} \frac{CF_n}{(1+i)^n}$$

 ## NPV Benchmark

NPV analysis includes all of the cash flows—both inflows and outflows. This inclusion implies that any required investment in the project is already factored

---

EXAMPLE 13-1

 For interactive versions of this example visit www.mhhe.com/can1e

NPV FOR A NORMAL SET OF CASH FLOWS

A company is evaluating a project with the set of normal cash flows using a risk-appropriate discount rate of 12 percent as shown in Table 13.1. Compute the NPV to determine whether the company should undertake the project.

Sample Project with Normal Cash Flows						table 13.1
YEAR	0	1	2	3	4	5
Cash Flow	−$10,000	$2,500	$3,500	$5,000	$4,000	$2,000

SOLUTION:

CALCULATOR
−$10,000	[CF0]
$ 2,500	[CF1]
$ 3,500	[CF2]
$ 5,000	[CF3]
$ 4,000	[CF4]
$ 2,000	[CF5]
	NPV
12%	[I]
[CPT]	[NPV] = $2,258.15

The NPV statistic for this project will be:

$$NPV = \frac{-\$10,000}{(1.12)^0} + \frac{\$2,500}{(1.12)^1} + \frac{\$3,500}{(1.12)^2} + \frac{\$5,000}{(1.12)^3} + \frac{\$4,000}{(12.1)^4} + \frac{\$2,000}{(1.12)^5}$$

$$= \$2,258.15 > 0$$

The NPV decision will be to *accept* the project.

When you first start calculating NPV, it is easy to miss its deeper meaning. A relatively small NPV, such as the $2,258.15 figure in this example, raises the question of whether $2,258.15 is "worth it," in this sense: Will the project cover the opportunity cost of using the $10,000 of necessary capital? The point, of course, is that the $2,258.15 is above and beyond the recovery of that opportunity cost, so, *yes, it's worth it.*

MATH COACH

USING A FINANCIAL CALCULATOR—PART 2

The TVM worksheet present in most financial calculators has been fine, so far, for the types of TVM problems we've been solving. Sometimes we had to use the worksheet two or three times for a single problem, but that was usually because we needed an intermediate calculation to input into another TVM equation.

In this chapter, we will generally be using simpler TVM equations (i.e., PV and FV), but we'll find ourselves having to use them repeatedly, making only small variations in inputs over and over again within the same problem. We're also going to run up against the problem of cash flow inconsistencies in most projects. If you thought the cash flows of stocks jumped around a lot, wait until you see what project cash flows do! If we stick with the TVM worksheet, these inconsistent cash flows will be a problem for us. If we want to solve for a "common" i or N value, the TVM worksheet won't let us enter multiple cash flows unless we're solving an annuity problem. (The one notable exception to this has been when we used the TVM worksheet to simultaneously solve the annuity/lump sum problems that arise with bonds. If you recall, those problems require agreement between the inputs to the annuity and the lump sum problems. This kind of agreement is highly unlikely to occur in other circumstances.)

Luckily, most financial calculators also have built-in worksheets specifically designed for computing NPV in problems with multiple nonconstant cash flows. In many cases, they will also calculate most of the other decision rule statistics that we're going to be discussing.

To make calculator worksheets as flexible as possible, they are usually divided into two parts: one for input, which we'll refer to as the CF (for cash flow) worksheet, and one or more for calculating decision statistics. We'll go over the conventions concerning the CF worksheet here. We'll wait to cover the conventions of the various decision rules until we discuss them.

The CF worksheet is usually designed to handle inputting sets of multiple cash flows as quickly as possible. As a result, it normally consists of two sets of variables or cells—one for the cash flows and one to hold a set of frequency counts for the cash flows, so that we can tell it we have seven $1,500 cash flows in a row instead of having to enter $1,500 seven times.

Using the frequency counts to reduce the number of inputs is handy, but you must take care. Frequency counts are only good for embedded annuities of identical cash flows. You have to ensure that you don't mistake another kind of cash flow for an annuity.

Also, using frequency counts will usually affect the way that the calculator counts time periods. As an example, let's talk about how we would put the set of cash flows shown here into a CF worksheet:

To designate which particular value we'll place into each particular cash flow cell in this worksheet, we'll note the value and the cell identifier, such as CF0, CF1, and so forth. We'll do the same for the frequency cells, using F1, F2, etc., to identify which CF cell the frequency cell goes with. (Note that, in most calculators, CF0 is treated as a unique value with an unalterable frequency of 1; we're going to make the same assumption here so you'll never see a listing for F0. For this sample timeline, our inputs would be:

−$800	[CF0]		
$150	[CF1]	1	[F1]
$200	[CF2]	1	[F2]
$0	[CF3]	1	[F3]
$150	[CF4]	3	[F4]
$75	[CF5]	2	[F5]

Then, on the NPV worksheet, you would simply need to enter the interest rate and solve for the NPV:

10%	[I]
[CPT]	[NPV] = −$144.61

Note a few important things about this example:

1. We had to manually enter a value of $0 for CF3: If we hadn't, the calculator wouldn't have known about it and would have implicitly assumed that CF4 came one period after CF2.

2. Once we use a frequency cell for one cash flow, all numbering on any subsequent cash flows that we enter into the calculator is going to be messed up, at least from our point of view. For instance, the first $75 isn't what we would call "CF5," is it? We'd call it "CF7" because it comes at time period 7; but calculators usually treat CF5 as "the fifth set of cash flows," so we'll just have to try to do the same to be consistent.

3. If we really don't need to use frequency cells, we will usually just leave them out of the guidance instructions in this chapter to save space.

in, so any NPV greater than zero represents value *above and beyond* that investment. Accordingly, the NPV decision rule is:

$$\text{Accept project if NPV} > 0$$
$$\text{Reject project if NPV} < 0$$

(13-2)

EXAMPLE 13-2

 For interactive versions of this example visit www.mhhe.com/can1e

 NPV FOR A NON-NORMAL SET OF CASH FLOWS

Note that the NPV rule works equally well with non-normal cash flows, such as those for the project shown in Table 13.2. Compute the NPV for this project to determine whether it should be accepted.

Sample Project with Non-Normal Cash Flows						table 13.2
YEAR	**0**	**1**	**2**	**3**	**4**	**5**
Cash Flow	$5,000	−$10,000	−$3,000	$5,000	$4,000	$2,000

CALCULATOR
$ 5,000	[CF0]
−$10,000	[CF1]
−$ 3,000	[CF2]
$ 5,000	[CF3]
$ 4,000	[CF4]
$ 2,000	[CF5]
	NPV
12%	[I]
[CPT]	[NPV]
	= $915.67

SOLUTION:

Once again assuming a 12 percent discount rate, the NPV statistic will be:

$$NPV = \frac{\$5,000}{(1.12)^0} + \frac{-\$10,000}{(1.12)^1} + \frac{-\$3,000}{(1.12)^2} + \frac{\$5,000}{(1.12)^3} + \frac{\$4,000}{(12.1)^4} + \frac{\$2,000}{(1.12)^5}$$

$$= \$915.67 > 0$$

Based on this NPV, the project should be accepted.

 ## NPV Strengths and Weaknesses

One strength of the NPV rule is that the statistic is *not* a ratio as with the rate-based decision statistics. It works equally well for independent projects as it does for choosing among mutually exclusive projects. In the latter case, the mutually exclusive project with the highest NPV should add the most wealth to the firm, and so management should accept it over any competing projects.

Unfortunately, this ability to choose among projects stems from exactly what gives it its greatest weakness: the format of the statistic. Since the NPV statistic is a dollar figure, it accurately reflects the net effect of any differences in timing or scale of two projects' expected cash flows. It thus allows comparisons of two projects' NPV statistics to fully incorporate those differences. However, this same currency format often results in confusion for uninformed decision-makers: managers not completely familiar with how the NPV statistic works often insist on comparing the NPV to the *cost* of the project, not understanding that the cost is already incorporated into the NPV.

TIME OUT

13-1 Why is a project's cost *not* an appropriate benchmark for its NPV?

13-2 Assuming that it's fairly priced, what should be the NPV of a purchase decision on a corporate bond?

13.5 Payback and Discounted Payback

Both the payback and discounted payback rules carry great emotional appeal: if we assume that we are borrowing money to finance a new project, both techniques answer slightly different versions of the question, "How long is it going to take us to recoup our costs?"

So it would seem that these techniques use the same reasoning that banks and other lenders employ when they examine a potential borrower's finances to determine the probability of repayment. While at first this seems like a fairly simple question, it can actually lead to some rather sophisticated insight concerning a project's potential. For example, a project that lasts seven years but is slated to repay its initial investment within the first two years is obviously a stronger candidate than a project that also repays in two years but is slated to last only three years, assuming that the two projects are expected to have the same yearly cash flows once payback is achieved.

Payback Statistic

The **payback** statistic remains very popular because it's easy to compute. All we have to do is keep a running subtotal of the cumulative sum of the cash flows up to the point that this sum exactly offsets the initial investment. That is, PB is determined by using this formula:

$$0 = \sum_{n=0}^{PB} CF_n \qquad \text{(13-3)}$$

Notice that this computation demands a couple of strong assumptions:

1. The whole concept of payback rests on the assumption that cash flows are normal, with all outflows occurring at the beginning of the project's life, so that we can think of the PB statistic as a type of recovery period for that initial investment. This implies that payback would be meaningless for a set of non-normal cash flows. If, for example, a project required an infusion of cash after it started, such as the cash outflows shown at times 1 and 2 in Table 13.2, we could not calculate a payback statistic.

2. Note that PB will not be very likely to occur in an exact, round number of periods, so we will need to make another assumption concerning how cash inflows occur *during* the course of a year. The usual approach to handling this condition is to assume that cash flows arrive smoothly throughout each period, allowing us to count out the months and days to estimate the exact payback statistic.

Payback Benchmark

The payback method shows an additional weakness in that its benchmark must be exogenously specified: that is, it's not always the same value, nor is it determined by the required rate of return or any other input variable. Ideally, the maximum allowable PB for a project should be set based on some relevant external constraint, such as the number of periods until capital providers need their money back, or the time available until a project would violate a bond issue's protective covenants. As you might suspect, in real life managers often indicate the maximum allowable payback—that is, set the exogenous specification—arbitrarily.

Let's assume that we've been told that the maximum allowable payback for this project is three years. With this decision rule, we want to accept projects that show a calculated statistic less than the benchmark of three years:

Accept project if calculated payback < Maximum allowable payback
Reject project if calculated payback > Maximum allowable payback

(13-4)

Since our calculated payback is 2.8 (computed in Example 13-3) and the maximum allowable payback is three years, we should accept the project according to the payback rule.

EXAMPLE 13-3

 For interactive versions of this example visit www.mhhe.com/can1e

 PAYBACK CALCULATION

Consider the sample project introduced in Table 13.1. To calculate this project's payback, we would first calculate the cumulative cash flows until they went from negative to positive, using the information in Table 13.3:

Payback Calculation on Sample Project with Normal Cash Flows						**table 13.3**

YEAR	0	1	2	3	4	5
Cash Flow	−$10,000	$2,500	$3,500	$5,000	$4,000	$2,000
Cumulative Cash Flow	−10,000	−7,500	−4,000	1,000		

SOLUTION:

CALCULATOR	
−$10,000	[CF0]
$ 2,500	[CF1]I
$ 3,500	[CF2]
$ 5,000	[CF3]
$ 4,000	[CF4]
$ 2,000	[CF5]
	NPV
12%	[I]
[CPT]	[PB] = 2.80

From this first step, we know that payback occurs somewhere between periods 2 and 3. To determine the exact statistic, we note that, if the magnitude of the last negative cumulative cash flow represents how much cash flow we *need* during year 3 to achieve payback, then the marginal cash flow for year 3 represents how much we will *get* over the course of the entire third year. By linear interpolation, our exact statistic is therefore where we start (year 2) plus what we need (the absolute value of the last negative cumulative cash flow, −$4,000) over what we're going to get during that year:

$$PB = 2 + \frac{\$4,000}{\$5,000} = 2.8 \text{ years}$$

 ## Discounted Payback Statistic

Yet another problem that arises when we use the payback technique is that it does not recognize or incorporate the time value of money. To compensate for this exclusion, we often calculate the **discounted payback (DPB)** statistic instead, using the following formula:

$$0 = \sum_{n=0}^{DPB} \frac{CF_n}{(1 + i)^n}$$

(13-5)

Notice that all we're doing here is summing the *present values* of the cash flows until we get a cumulative sum of zero, instead of summing the cash flows themselves as we did for the PB statistic. Other than that, we follow all the steps in the computation of DPB just as we did for the PB statistic.

Discounted Payback Benchmark

LG3

We may be tempted to assume that we should simply use the same maximum allowable payback benchmark for DPB that we used for PB. If we did so, then we would obviously have to reject this project, since its calculated DPB is 3.5581 years versus a stated maximum allowable time of only three years. However, we should be very cautious about applying the same benchmark to DPB that we did to PB. To see why, recall that payback calculations only make sense when applied to normal cash flows, so we would assume that we'll be dealing with normal cash flows here. But think about *which* cash flows are affected when we switch from calculating payback to discounted payback: Only the ones in the future will fall to lower values, because the present value of the time 0 cash flow will always be the same as its nominal value. And, if the future cash flows are all positive and the initial cash flow is negative, then it is only the positive cash flows that will be affected by switching to cumulative present value for DPB.

 For interactive versions of this example visit www.mhhe.com/can1e

EXAMPLE 13-4

DISCOUNTED PAYBACK CALCULATION

LG3

Consider the same project from Example 13-3. To calculate this project's discounted payback, we would first need to calculate the PV of each cash flow separately. Assuming the same 12 percent interest rate used when we calculated the NPV of this project, we would calculate these values as shown in Table 13.4.

Discounted Payback Calculation: Present Values of Cash Flows						**table 13.4**
YEAR	**0**	**1**	**2**	**3**	**4**	**5**
Cash Flow	−$10,000.00	$2,500.00	$3,500.00	$5,000.00	$4,000.00	$2,000.00
Cash Flow Present Value	−10,000.00	2,232.14	2,790.18	3,558.90	2,542.07	1,134.85

In Table 13.5 we calculate the cumulative present value of the cash flows until they switch from negative to positive:

Discounted Payback Calculation on Sample Project with Normal Cash Flows						**table 13.5**
YEAR	**0**	**1**	**2**	**3**	**4**	**5**
Cash Flow	−$10,000.00	$2,500.00	$3,500.00	$5,000.00	$4,000.00	$2,000.00
Cash Flow Present Value	−10,000.00	2,232.14	2,790.18	3,558.90	2,542.07	1,134.85
Cumulative Cash Flow PV	−10,000.00	−7,767.86	−4,977.68	−1,418.78	1,123.29	

CALCULATOR	
−$10,000	[CF0]
$ 2,500	[CF1]
$ 3,500	[CF2]
$ 5,000	[CF3]
$ 4,000	[CF4]
$ 2,000	[CF5]
	NPV
12%	[I]
[CPT]	[DPB] = 3.56

SOLUTION:

As before, we can stop once the cumulative values go from negative to positive. In this case, linear interpolation will give us a DPB statistic of:

$$DPB = 3 + \frac{\$1,418.78}{\$2,542.07} = 3.5581 \text{ years}$$

In other words, we would expect the calculated DPB statistic to always be larger than the "regular" PB statistic because DPB incorporates the interest you must pay until you reach the benchmark. Said another way, DPB will always take longer to achieve payback if you're "chipping away" at the same-sized initial cash outflow with the present values of a bunch of positive cash inflows rather than their simple nominal values. Therefore, it probably isn't fair to hold the DPB statistic up to the same benchmark we use for the PB statistic.

What benchmark should we use? Well, as with PB, management will set the DPB maximum allowable payback exogenously and, once again, often arbitrarily. Let's assume that we're told that senior management has set the maximum allowable payback for DPB as 3.5 years.

Accept project if calculated DPB < Maximum allowable discounted payback
Reject project if calculated DPB > Maximum allowable discounted payback

(13-6)

Since our calculated DPB is 3.5581 years and the maximum allowable amount is 3.5 years, we should reject the project.

Payback and Discounted Payback Strengths and Weaknesses

A common criticism of PB is that it doesn't account for the time value of money; the use of PV formulas in computing DPB compensates for TVM. But DPB isn't intended to really replace PB, but rather to complement it, providing additional information to analyze capital budgeting decisions.

For example, if we consider a typical, normal payback statistic based on a set of cash flows as a loan problem in which the company borrows the money for the initial investment and then pays it off over time, then PB will intuitively equal the amount of time necessary to repay just principal on the loan, and DPB will indicate the time necessary to repay principal plus interest.

Both PB and DPB have yet another serious flaw. Both decision statistics completely ignore any cash flows that accrue *after* the project reaches its respective type of payback benchmark. Ignoring this vital information can have serious implications when managers choose between two mutually exclusive projects that have very similar paybacks, but very different cash flows after payback is achieved.

EXAMPLE 13-5

 For interactive versions of this example visit www.mhhe.com/can1e

 ### PAYBACK CALCULATION FOR ALTERNATIVE PROJECT

Consider once again the sample project shown in Table 13.1. As we calculated in Example 13-3, that project has a PB statistic of 2.8 years. Now, compare that project to the one shown in Table 13.6:

Payback Calculation on Alternative Sample Project with Normal Cash Flows						table 13.6
YEAR	**0**	**1**	**2**	**3**	**4**	**5**
Cash Flow	−$10,000	$2,500	$3,500	$4,000	$104,000	$102,000
Cash Flow Present Value	−10,000	−7,500	−4,000			

(continued)

SOLUTION:

This project would have a slightly higher PB statistic of 3.0. Given that it still achieves payback in exactly the maximum allowable three years, it should be highly favored over the first project due to the large positive cash flows that will accrue in the later years. But managers who ignore this aspect of the PB rule and who focus only on the PB statistics of these two projects will likely incorrectly choose the first project due to its lower PB statistic.

Note that NPV will *not* suffer from this problem. Since the NPV statistic takes all of a project's cash flows into account, there aren't "remaining" cash flows to get left out of the statistic as there are with PB and DPB.

TIME OUT

13-3 Which should we expect to be larger: a project's payback statistic, or its discounted payback statistic?

13-4 Suppose a project has a discounted payback equal to its termination date. What will be the project's NPV?

13.6 Internal Rate of Return and Modified Internal Rate of Return

 LG1

The **internal rate of return (IRR)** technique is, by far, the most popular rate-based capital budgeting technique. The main reason for its popularity is that, if you are considering a project with normal cash flows that is independent of other projects, the IRR statistic will give exactly the same accept/reject decision as the NPV rule does.

However, IRR runs into a lot of problems if project cash flows are not normal, or if you are using this statistic to decide among mutually exclusive projects. As we'll show below, while we can correct for the non-normal cash flows, all rate-based decision statistics will exhibit problems with deciding among mutually exclusive projects.

 For interactive versions of this example visit www.mhhe.com/can1e

EXAMPLE 13-6

IRR Calculation

 LG4

Looking once again at our sample set of normal cash flows from Table 13.1, IRR will be the solution to:

$$0 = \frac{-\$10,000}{(1+IRR)^0} + \frac{\$2,500}{(1+IRR)^1} + \frac{\$3,500}{(1+IRR)^2} + \frac{\$3,500}{(1+IRR)^3} + \frac{\$4,000}{(1+IRR)^4} + \frac{\$2,000}{(1+IRR)^5}$$

$IRR = .2062$, or 20.62%

CALCULATOR	
−$10,000	[CF0]
$ 2,500	[CF1]
$ 3,500	[CF2]
$ 5,000	[CF3]
$ 4,000	[CF4]
$ 2,000	[CF5]
	IRR
[CPT]	[IRR]
	= 20.61%

Internal Rate of Return Statistic

To solve for the IRR statistic, we simply solve the NPV formula for the interest rate that will make NPV equal zero:

$$0 = \sum_{n=0}^{N} \frac{CF_n}{(1 + IRR)^n} \qquad \text{(13-7)}$$

Unfortunately, we cannot solve directly for the interest rate that will set NPV equal to zero. We either have to use trial-and-error to determine the appropriate rate, or we have to rely on a calculator or computer, both of which use much the same approach.

Internal Rate of Return Benchmark

Once we calculate the IRR, we must then compare the decision statistic to the relevant cost of capital for the project—the average rate of return necessary to pay back the project's capital providers, given the risk that the project represents:

> Accept project if IRR > Cost of capital
> Reject project if IRR < Cost of capital $\qquad$ **(13-8)**

At this point, you may find yourself getting a little confused about which rate is *the* interest rate. The IRR statistic will equal the expected rate of return, which incorporates risk (as probabilities). We'll compare that expected rate of return to the cost of capital, which is often called the required rate of return. Up until this chapter, we've been using all of these phrases interchangeably for "*the*" interest rate. We have fudged a bit because stocks, bonds, and all other types of *financial* assets trade in relatively liquid, competitive financial markets. In such an environment, it makes sense to assume that we're not going to be able to earn any "extra" return or economic profit above and beyond what's appropriate for the amount of risk we're bearing.

Remember, though, that in this chapter, we're no longer talking about *financial* assets, but *real* assets such as land, factories with inventories, and production lines. These types of assets don't generally trade in perfectly competitive markets. Instead, they trade in quite illiquid markets in which an individual or a firm can gain at least some amount of market or monopoly power by virtue of technological, legal, or marketing expertise.

We noted this difference at the beginning of this chapter when we differentiated between formulas for financial assets such as stocks and bonds and the equations we're using in this chapter to value projects. The formulas we used to value stocks and bonds use "=" signs because those assets trade in nearly perfectly competitive markets, where what you get is (approximately, at least) equal to what you paid for it. Here, on the other hand, we examine situations in which companies seek to choose projects that are worth *more* than what they pay for them—leaving room for economic profit. That's why all of these capital budgeting rules use ">" and "<" signs.

So, when we deal with physical asset projects, we have to expect that two different rates of return will arise. The best way to think of these two rates is as the *expected* rate of return (IRR), and the *required* rate of return (*i*). We only want to invest in projects where the rate we expect to get (IRR) is larger than the rate investors require (*i*) based on the project's expected return, including risk.[2]

---

[2]As explained in earlier chapters, by definition the expected rate of return incorporates risk.

figure 13.1

NPV Profile for Sample
Normal Cash Flows

Problems with Internal Rate of Return

As we mentioned above, IRR will give the same accept/reject decision as NPV if two conditions hold true:

1. The project has normal cash flows.
2. We are evaluating the project independently of other projects—that is, we aren't considering mutually exclusive projects.

To see the problems that arise if these conditions do *not* hold, we'll make use of a tool called the **NPV profile.** This is simply a graph of a project's NPV as a function of possible capital costs. The NPV profile for our sample project with normal cash flows from Table 13.1. appears as Figure 13.1.

As you can see, the NPV profile for this normal set of cash flows slopes downward. As we noted above concerning the relationship between the PB and DPB statistics, increasing values of *i* with a normal set of cash flows affect the present value of positive cash flows, but not that of negative cash flows. All sets of normal cash flows will therefore share this general, downward-sloping shape.

Note that IRR appears on this graph as the intersection of the NPV profile with the *x*-axis (horizontal)—the intersection will represent the interest rate where NPV equals exactly zero. With normal cash flows such as these, the constant downward slope of the NPV profile dictates that only one such intersection will exist for each project.

TIME OUT

13-5 Is it possible for the NPV profile of a finite set of normal set of cash flows to never cross the X-axis?

13-6 Suppose a normal set of cash flows has an IRR equal to zero. Would NPV accept or reject such a project?

IRR and NPV Profiles with Non-normal Cash Flows

But let's revisit what happens to the NPV profile if cash flows are *not* normal. The NPV profile will not necessarily slope continually downward and thus may cross over the *x*-axis at more than one interest rate. In this case we may find more than

figure 13.2

NPV Profile for Sample
Non-Normal Cash Flows

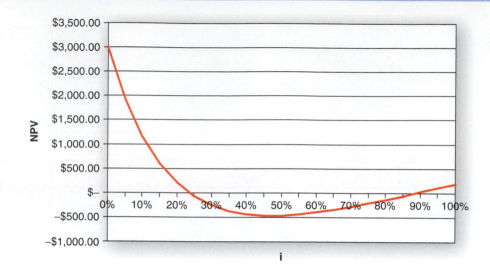

one valid IRR for which NPV equals precisely zero. An example of such an NPV profile, constructed from the cash flows in Table 13.2, appears in Figure 13.2.

In this instance, the project shows two valid IRRs: one at 23.62 percent and another at 88.62 percent. Which of these two should we use as "the" statistic? Well, it depends on what the firm pays as the actual cost of capital. If the firm pays 12 percent for capital, then using either of these two IRR values would generate a correct "accept" decision, as the project *does* have a positive NPV at $i = 12$ percent. But what if the firm paid a relatively high cost of capital, say, for example, 30 percent? Then the IRR rule would have us accept the project if we used the higher value (88.62 percent) as the project's statistic, but reject it if we used the lower IRR (23.62 percent). Of course, since the project generates a negative NPV if i is 30 percent, we would actually want to reject the project.

Using the IRR technique requires a bit more complicated analysis if we come across more than one valid IRR. Perhaps the best thing to do in such a situation is to simply use a decision statistic other than IRR on projects with non-normal cash flows.

If you (or, more likely, upper management) insist on using IRR with non-normal cash flows, you're going to need to use some trial and error to find all the possible IRRs. It will help to know how many there might possibly be. According to the Rule of Signs,[3] we can end up with no more different positive IRRs than the number of sign changes in the cash flows—that is, inflows to outflows or outflows to inflows. Since our non-normal cash flows set shows two sign changes (one change from positive to negative and one change from negative to positive), we know that the two IRRs we have found constitute the entire possible set.

Luckily we can solve IRR's problems associated with non-normal cash flows, using the modified internal rate of return (MIRR), which also accounts for another problem associated with IRR, that of an unrealistic reinvestment rate assumption.

Differing Reinvestment Rate Assumptions of NPV and IRR

In addition to the problems associated with non-normal cash flows and handling mutually exclusive projects discussed above, IRR also has a different assumption than NPV concerning what we do with the cash inflows once we get them back. IRR implies that any cash inflows will be reinvested in another project with the

---

[3]First described by René Descartes in his 1637 manuscript *La Geometrie*.

same earning power as the first project, while NPV assumes that cash inflows will be reinvested at the cost of capital, *i*.

Which assumption is more reasonable? NPV's is because one way to "earn" the cost of capital is to pay back your capital investors. IRR's assumption doesn't make sense. Assuming that this project beat out a bunch of other projects at step 2 of the decision process, it must have had the highest possible IRR among all the alternatives, right? But now that the cash flows are rolling in, we find another project with the same, highest possible rate of return? Seems like a little too much to expect, doesn't it? Who is ever that lucky all the time?

Modified Internal Rate of Return Statistic

LG4

The name **modified internal rate of return** is a little misleading. We are going to calculate IRR the same way as we did before, but we're going to *modify* the set of cash flows to account for the cost of capital before we calculate IRR. We first use the cost of capital to "move" all the negative cash flows to the initial project start date (i.e., time 0) and all the positive cash inflows to the project termination date—and only *then* will we use the regular steps to calculate IRR.

EXAMPLE 13-7

For interactive versions of this example visit www.mhhe.com/can1e

MIRR Calculation

Turning once again to the sample non-normal project cash flows in Table 13.2, and assuming that the firm still faces a cost of capital of 12 percent, we convert the cash flows as shown in Table 13.7.

MIRR Cash Flow Adjustments for Sample Project with Non-Normal Cash Flows						table 13.7
YEAR	**0**	**1**	**2**	**3**	**4**	**5**
Cash flow	$5,000.00	−$10,000.00	−$3,000.00	$5,000.00	$4,000.00	$2,000.00
Present value (if negative)		−8,928.57	−2,391.58			
Sum of PV	−11,320.15					
Future value (if positive)	8,811.71			6,272.00	4,480.00	2,000.00
Sum of FV						21,563.71
Modified CFs	−11,320.15					21,563.71

SOLUTION:

With this new set of modified cash flows, the (M)IRR is:

$$0 = \frac{-\$11,320.15}{(1+IRR)^0} + \frac{\$21,563.71}{(1+IRR)^5}$$

IRR = .1376, or 13.76%

Since our (M)IRR decision statistic exceeds the 12 percent cost of capital, we would accept the project under the MIRR method, which uses the same benchmark as the IRR rule. Notice that, regardless of how many possible IRRs a project may have, it will only ever have *one* possible MIRR. When you take a bunch of cash flows and convert them into two cash flows, one negative and one positive, you will only ever see one change in sign.

CALCULATOR	
$ 5,000	[CF0]
−$10,000	[CF1]
−$ 3,000	[CF2]
$ 5,000	[CF3]
$ 4,000	[CF4]
$ 2,000	[CF5]
	IRR
12%	[I]
12%	[RI]
[CPT]	[MOD = 13.76%]

YEAR	0	1	2	3	4	5
Sample Mutually Exclusive Projects						**table 13.8**
Project A Cash Flows	$800	$600	$500	$400	$ 0	$200
Project B Cash Flows	−$400	$250	$200	$250	$50	$100

IRRs, MIRRs, and NPV Profiles with Mutually Exclusive Projects

As we have noted above, even if we use the MIRR method for a project with non-normal cash flows we can still run into problems if we try to use IRR or MIRR to choose between mutually exclusive projects.

Two or more projects are **mutually exclusive** if management can accept one, the other, or neither, but not both, projects. As discussed below, if we compare two mutually exclusive projects using a rate-based decision statistic, problems can arise if the projects' cash flows exhibit differences in *scale* or *timing* (i.e., the size of the initial investment in each project). Over time, a "large" project that earns a slightly lower rate of return may be a better choice for the firm than a "small" project that earns a higher rate, but we will see that the rate-based decision techniques don't do well in choosing between these types of alternative projects.

What makes two or more projects mutually exclusive? Generally, mutually exclusive projects either share a common asset or target a common market, but the firm can only spare resources for one of them, or the market may only accept one product. Consider the prototypical example of mutually exclusive projects: a landowner owns two plots of land on either side of a river that people want to cross, and she is considering either building a bridge or operating a ferry for that purpose.

First, let's assume enough land on each lot to provide space for bridge footings or for pier pilings, but not for both. In this case, the two plots of land represent assets that the two projects can't share, which is the first factor making the bridge and the ferry mutually exclusive projects.

Second, even if the land provided enough room to build both ferry landing piers and bridge footings, it stands to reason that no one would take the ferry if they could simply drive across the bridge—so the two projects' inability to share a potential target market provides a second reason why the projects are mutually exclusive.

To see the problems associated with choosing between two manually exclusive projects using a rate-based decision statistic, let's suppose that we face a choice between two mutually exclusive projects with the cash flows shown in Table 13.8.

Calculating the NPVs for these two projects across a range of possible rates as shown in Table 13.9 will yield the NPV profiles shown in Figure 13.3.

As you can see approximately (and calculate precisely), A's IRR equals 32.88 percent and B's equals 40.59 percent. You'll also notice that the two NPV profiles cross each other in the first quadrant, and that intersection is exactly what is going to cause problems for us as we try to apply an IRR decision rule.

To see why, recall our discussion of the three-step decision process necessary for mutually exclusive projects, and go through that process for both NPV and IRR using a couple of not-so-arbitrary interest rates.

First, let's suppose that the project would be subject to a 30 percent cost of capital. In that case, as per Table 13.10, the NPV for project A would be $29.47 and the NPV for project B would be $68.88. This means that project B would win the runoff. Since its NPV is greater than zero, the NPV decision rule would have us also accept project B.

NPV Profiles — table 13.9

i	NPV A	NPV B
0.00%	$540.00	$450.00
2.00	487.66	409.68
4.00	439.15	372.48
6.00	394.07	338.08
8.00	352.09	306.22
10.00	312.91	276.63
12.00	276.27	249.12
14.00	241.92	223.48
16.00	209.67	199.54
18.00	179.33	177.16
20.00	150.75	156.20
22.00	123.76	136.54
24.00	98.25	118.07
26.00	74.10	100.69
28.00	51.21	84.32
30.00	29.47	68.88
32.00	8.80	54.30
34.00	−10.86	40.51
36.00	−29.61	27.45
38.00	−47.49	15.07
40.00	−64.56	3.33

Decision Process for Projects A and B at $i = 30\%$ — table 13.10

NPV

1. Compute the statistic for each project.

$NPV_A = \$29.47$
$NPV_B = \$68.88$

2. Have a runoff between the mutually exclusive projects, choosing the one with the best statistic.

$NPV_B > NPV_A$

3. Compare the computed statistic for the winner of the runoff to the benchmark to decide whether to accept or reject.

$\mathbf{NPV_B > 0}$

IRR

1. Compute the statistic for each project.

$IRR_A = 32.88\%$
$IRR_B = 40.59\%$

2. Have a runoff between the mutually exclusive projects, choosing the one with the best statistic.

$IRR_B > IRR_A$

3. Compare the computed statistic for the winner of the runoff to the benchmark to decide whether to accept or reject.

$\mathbf{IRR_B > 30\%}$

figure 13.3

NPV Profiles for Sample Mutually Exclusive Projects

NPV

1. Compute the statistic for each project.　　　　　　　　$NPV_A = \$312.91$

　　　　　　　　　　　　　　　　　　　　　　　　　　$NPV_B = \$276.63$

2. Have a runoff between the mutually exclusive projects, choosing the one with the best statistic.　　　　　　　　$NPV_A > NPV_B$

3. Compare the computed statistic for the winner of the runoff to the benchmark to decide whether to accept or reject.　　　　**$NPV_A > 0$**

IRR

1. Compute the statistic for each project.　　　　　　　　$IRR_A = 32.88\%$

　　　　　　　　　　　　　　　　　　　　　　　　　　$IRR_B = 40.59\%$

2. Have a runoff between the mutually exclusive projects, choosing the one with the best statistic.　　　　　　　　$IRR_B > IRR_A$

3. Compare the computed statistic for the winner of the runoff to the benchmark to decide whether to accept or reject.　　　　**$IRR_B > 30\%$**

Likewise, if we were using IRR in the same situation, project B's IRR of 40.59 percent would win the runoff over project A's IRR of 32.88 percent. But since 40.59 percent is greater than the 30 percent cost of capital, IRR would also have us accept project B. These results appear in Table 13.10 on the previous page.

Now let's see what happens if the cost of capital is, say, 10 percent. In that case, as per Table 13.9, the NPV for project A would be $312.91 and the NPV for project B would be $276.63. This means that project A would now win the runoff and, ultimately, would be accepted under the NPV statistic as well.

However, if we were using IRR in the same situation, project B's IRR of 40.59 percent would *still* win the runoff over project A's IRR of 32.88 percent, and, since 40.59 percent is greater than the 30 percent cost of capital, IRR would continue to have us accept project B. These results are summarized in Table 13.11.

Why is IRR still choosing project B, despite the 30 percent cost of capital? Well, IRR's refusal to "change its mind"[4] arises from a combination of how we calculate the statistic and how we use it in the three-step decision process. Think about it this way: The NPV statistic includes the cost of capital in its calculation, so when we get to the runoff, NPV is able to make an **interest-rate-cognizant** decision. IRR does not incorporate the cost of capital in calculating its statistic. Therefore, when it reaches step two it will always be comparing the same two IRRs for two particular projects, no matter what the cost of capital is.

The implication here is that, for any interest rate to the right of where the two NPV profiles cross, NPV and IRR will make the same accept/reject decision. For rates to the left of the crossover point, NPV will choose the right project but IRR will chose the wrong project. So, since it's sort of important, how do we calculate the rate at which the two NPV profiles cross? Well, we mathematically manipulate each NPV profile until one comes as close to the x-axis as possible, and then figure out the rate at which they cross each other as the IRR of the other project.

It sounds complicated, but it really isn't. All we have to do is subtract one project's cash flows from those of the other, period by period, to get a new set of cash flows that show the differences between the original two projects' cash flows, and then find the IRR of these differences. The values for the cash flows

---

[4]You'll sometimes hear this phenomenon referred to as IRR being "myopic," which is the technical name for nearsightedness.

Difference in Cash Flows—Sample Mutually Exclusive Projects						**table 13.12**

YEAR	0	1	2	3	4	5
Project A Cash Flows	−$800	$600	$500	$ 40	$ 0	$200
Project B Cash Flows	−400	250	200	250	50	100
A-B	−400	350	300	−210	−50	100

NPV Profile, A-B	**table 13.13**

i	NPV, A-B
0.00%	$ 90.00
2.00	77.98
4.00	66.67
6.00	55.99
8.00	45.88
10.00	36.28
12.00	27.15
14.00	18.45
16.00	10.13
18.00	2.17
20.00	−5.45
22.00	−12.77
24.00	−19.81
26.00	−26.59
28.00	−33.12
30.00	−39.41
32.00	−45.49
34.00	−51.37
36.00	−57.06
38.00	−62.56
40.00	−67.89

figure 13.4

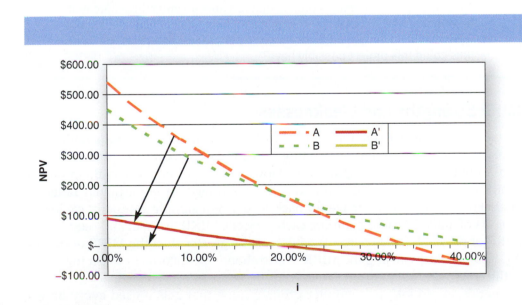

Translated NPV Profiles

of "A-B," the calculated values for the NPV profile of these differences, and the resulting translated NPV profiles (note that A′ will be equal to "A-B," while B′ will be the new, translated, *x*-axis) appear in Table 13.12, Table 13.13, and Figure 13.4.

The crossover rate will be equal to the IRR of the "A-B" cash flows:

$$0 = \frac{-\$400}{(1 + IRR)^0} + \frac{\$350}{(1 + IRR)^1} + \frac{\$300}{(1 + IRR)^2} + \frac{-\$210}{(1 + IRR)^3}$$
$$+ \frac{-\$50}{(1 + IRR)^4} + \frac{\$100}{(1 + IRR)^5}$$

$$IRR = .1856, \text{ or } 18.56\%$$

So now, IRR will give us the correct answer for these two projects if i is greater than 18.56 percent, and will choose exactly the wrong project if i is less than 18.56 percent.

You may have noticed that the set of "A-B" cash flows is *not* normal. How, then, can we feel comfortable using IRR to calculate "the" crossover rate given that we've previously decided not to use IRR with non-normal cash flows? Well, this is a special case: we knew that the two original projects' cash flows *were* normal. So we intuitively understood that their NPV profiles, while not exactly straight lines, at least sloped downward continually. So, if two "almost straight" lines do cross, they're probably only going to cross once. That is, we expect only one solution to the IRR problem for the "A-B" differences in cash flows.

Also notice that we only have to worry about IRR giving incorrect decisions if the NPV profiles cross in the so-called "first quadrant" of the graph. If they cross outside this quadrant at a rate higher than both projects' IRRs, then we don't have to worry about problems with IRR choosing the wrong project. Any cost of capital high enough for IRR to reject the project at the third step of the IRR decision process will also result in a negative NPV.[5]

TIME OUT

13-7 Suppose two projects with normal cash flows, X and Y, have exactly the same required initial investment, but X has a longer payback. Can we say anything about X's IRR versus that of Y?

13-8 Assume you're evaluating a project that requires an initial investment of $5,000 at time zero, then another investment of $4,000 in one year, after which it will have cash inflows of $3,000 per year for five years. How many IRRs could this project possibly have?

 LG5 ## MIRR Strengths and Weaknesses

As we have constructed it, the MIRR statistic explicitly corrects IRR's faulty and unreasonable reinvestment rate assumption, implicitly fixing any problems with non-normal cash flows along the way. However, it does not correct the problem of IRR choosing the wrong mutually exclusive project for a particular range of rates. For example, even if we go back to the two sample mutually exclusive projects of Table 13.8 and compute each project's MIRR, we will still see that the MIRR of project B (23.39 percent) will *always* be greater than the MIRR of project A (18.85 percent), causing the MIRR to also choose the incorrect project to the left of the crossover rate.

LG1 There's an old joke in computer programming that gets reused every time a major software product is revised: "That's not a bug, it's a feature!" Well, this

---

[5]Actually, in such cases the IRR rule will still choose the wrong project at step 2 of the decision process, the runoff, but the last step of the decision process, the comparison with the benchmark, will save us. The wrong project may be chosen at the runoff, but if they're both bad projects, they'll be rejected anyway.

Sample Mutually Exclusive Projects							table 13.14
YEAR	**0**	**1**	**2**	**3**	**4**	**5**	
Project A Cash Flows	−$800	$600	$500	$400	$ 0	$200	
Project B Cash Flows	−400	250	200	250	50	100	

"problem" we're experiencing with IRR and MIRR, as well as NPV, truly *is* a feature. It's a feature of all rate-based decision statistics: They tend to focus on the rate of return *per dollar invested* at the expense of ignoring *how many* dollars are getting invested in each project. IRR and MIRR chose project B all the time because, even though it sometimes had a lower NPV, it was always earning a higher rate of return *per dollar invested*.

What causes this confusion? The two cash flows differ in timing and scale. Looking back at the cash flows associated with our two mutually exclusive projects again (shown again in Table 13.14) we see that project B only costs half as much as project A.

This, together with the fact that project B's cash flows tend to be front-end loaded in terms of percentage of total cash flows, relative to project A's, gives project B a "flatter," less steeply sloped, indifference curve. This, in turn, results in a higher NPV for project B when rates are relatively high.

TIME OUT

13-9 For a project with normal cash flows, what would you expect the relationship to be between its IRR and its MIRR?

13-10 Describe how you would go about calculating the IRR of perpetuity.

13.7 Profitability Index

Another popular rate-based decision technique is the **profitability index (PI)**. PI is based upon NPV, so its results will more closely resemble NPV than will IRR or PB/DPB. PI takes a project's NPV and standardizes it by simply dividing by the project's initial investment. The result: We get a decision statistic that measures "bang per buck invested." Such a measure comes in handy when the firm faces resource constraints concerning how much capital is available for new projects.

Profitability Index Statistic

The mathematics of computing the PI are straightforward:

$$PI = \frac{NPV}{CF_0} \qquad \text{(13-9)}$$

For interactive versions of this example visit www.mhhe.com/can1e **EXAMPLE** 13-8

CALCULATION OF PROFITABILITY INDEX

Turning yet again to the sample project cash flows in Table 13.1, the PI for that project will be:

$$PI = \frac{\$2,258.15}{\$10,000} = 22.58\%$$

Business Application Solution

ADK's project will have an NPV of:

$$NPV = \frac{-\$5m}{(1.14)^0} + \frac{\$1.2m}{(1.14)^1} + \frac{\$1.6m}{(1.14)^2}$$
$$+ \frac{\$2.3m}{(1.14)^3} + \frac{\$2.8m}{(1.14)^4}$$
$$= \$494,038.89 > 0$$

and an IRR of:

$$NPV = \frac{-\$5m}{(1 + IRR)^0} + \frac{\$1.2m}{(1 + IRR)^1} + \frac{\$1.6m}{(1 + IRR)^2}$$
$$+ \frac{\$2.3m}{(1 + IRR)^3} + \frac{\$2.8m}{(1 + IRR)^4}$$
$$IRR = 18.09\% > 14\%$$

Both the NPV and IRR support accepting the project.

We could also calculate MIRR (16.72%) and PI (9.88%), and these would provide additional support for accepting the project.

Finally, though we are not given maximum allowable payback or discounted payback, values of 2.96 and 3.70, respectively, those statistics would seem to be in an acceptable range, too.

Personal Application Solution

First, we should note that, since cash flows occur every three months, we need to convert the APR of 9 percent to an APR:

$$i_{qtr} = \left(1 + \frac{.09}{12}\right)^3 - 1 = .0227$$

With these types of cash flows, our choice of decision rules is limited to NPV, MIRR, or PI; we can't use either payback rule or IRR because of the non-normality.

The NPV of this project will be:

$$NPV = \frac{-\$5,000}{(1.0227)^0} + \frac{-\$5,000}{(1.0227)^1}$$
$$+ \frac{-\$10,000}{(1.0227)^2} + \frac{\$30,000}{(1.0227)^4}$$
$$= -\$347.02 < 0$$

This NPV indicates that the project just isn't worth it.

 LG6

Profitability Index Benchmark

Though we might be tempted to assume that, like IRR and MIRR, we should compare the PI to the cost of capital, such is not the case. Remember that the NPV already includes the necessary investment, so any PI above zero is "found money" or the present value of expected economic profits. In this case, the PI of 22.58 percent is telling us that the project will, roughly speaking, earn the equivalent of a 22.58 percent return on the initial investment of $10,000 above and beyond the return necessary to repay the initial cost.

> **TIME OUT**
>
> **13-11** There is another version of the PI that uses the present value of just the future cash flows as its numerator instead of the NPV. How would you expect that version's benchmark to change from the version of PI we initially discussed?
>
> **13-12** Suppose you have a project whose payback is equal to its termination date. What can you say for sure about its PI? (*Hint:* what will the project's NPV be?)

summary of learning goals

In this chapter, we apply time value of money (TVM) concepts to project valuation. While the mathematics here are very similar to those used in the valuation of stocks, bonds and loans, the underlying intuition in valuing capital equipment projects is very different. In project valuation, the main goal is to find projects that convey enough monopoly power to the acquirer that they are worth more than they cost, even taking into account the cost of capital.

Of the capital budgeting techniques we've discussed, NPV is the hands-down winner, working equally well with normal or non-normal cash flows and with independent or mutually exclusive projects. However, the NPV decision technique uses a statistic denominated in currency, which may not be the only pertinent unit of measurement if the firm faces time or resource constraints. In such situations, the additional capital budgeting techniques may provide valuable supplementary guidance in deciding whether to accept a project or not.

A summary of the relevant attributes and strengths and weaknesses of the various capital budgeting techniques is shown below in Table 13.15:

Strengths and Weaknesses of Capital Budgeting Techniques					table 13.15
TECHNIQUE	**UNIT OF MEASUREMENT**	**SUITABLE FOR NON-NORMAL CASH FLOWS**	**SUITABLE FOR CHOOSING BETWEEN MUTUALLY EXCLUSIVE PROJECTS**	**USEFUL FOR FIRMS FACING TIME CONSTRAINTS**	**USEFUL FOR FIRMS FACING CAPITAL CONSTRAINTS**
NPV	Currency	Y	Y	N	Y
Payback	Time	N	N	Y	N
Discounted Payback	Time	N	N	Y	N
IRR	Interest Rate	N	N	N	Y
MIRR	Interest Rate	Y	N	N	Y
Profitability Index	Interest Rate	Y	N	N	Y

As we can see, NPV does tend to be the most useful technique, but the others also have their place, particularly for firms facing either time or capital constraints.

Recent surveys of practitioners concerning which capital budgeting techniques they use in practice tend to support this idea, showing NPV to be the most commonly used technique, and that practitioners often use NPV in conjunction with one of the other techniques when making decisions.

However, the choice of such other techniques indicates that practitioners tend to favor the conceptually simpler techniques over the more complicated ones. For example, a recent survey by Ryan and Ryan of firms in the Fortune 1000 indicates that, after NPV, IRR and regular Payback are next most often used, with discounted payback, profitability index, and modified IRR being used the least. Their results are summarized in Table 13.16.

CAPITAL BUDGETING TECHNIQUE	USAGE INDICATED BY RESPONDENTS				
	ALWAYS	OFTEN	SOMETIMES	RARELY	NEVER
Net Present Value	49.8%	35.3%	10.9%	3.0%	1.0%
Internal Rate of Return	44.6%	32.2%	15.3%	6.4%	1.5%
Payback	19.4%	33.2%	21.9%	16.8%	8.7%
Discounted Payback	15.5%	22.2%	19.1%	21.1%	22.2%
Profitability Index	5.9%	15.5%	22.5%	21.9%	34.2%
Modified IRR	2.2%	7.1%	12.6%	27.9%	50.3%

LG1 **Understand the intuition behind capital budgeting decision techniques.** All capital budgeting techniques attempt to achieve the same thing, but they render different measurement units. Not only do they use different measurement units, but almost all of them exclude some crucial information and may thus give incorrect, inconclusive, or misleading answers.

This kind of "blurry" information with which to make decisions is especially evident when using rate-based decision rules to choose between or among mutually exclusive projects. Rate-based statistics represent summary cash flows, and those summaries tend to lose two important details: the investment size and cash inflows that occur after the rather arbitrary testing period.

LG2 **Calculate and use net present value (NPV).** NPV is the best decision rule we have. This technique handles normal or non-normal cash flows and independent or mutually exclusive projects equally well. Corporate decision-makers do, however, need to understand TVM principles thoroughly if they are to calculate decision statistics and then to comprehend exactly what the statistics say or don't say.

LG3 **Calculate and use payback (PB) and discounted payback (DPB).** The payback technique tells us how long it will take the firm to earn back the money invested in a project. Discounted payback tells managers how long it will take to earn back the money invested plus interest at market rates. Management can compute either statistic fairly easily, so PB and DPB remain very popular techniques today. The techniques are particularly useful when firms face time constraints in repaying investors. Managers who are not quite as

comfortable with TVM principles also feel more comfortable with PB and DPB techniques. Neither method accounts for cash flows that occur after payback. Both methods are subject to managers' sometimes arbitrary maximum payback periods as their benchmarks. Another way to describe these benchmarks is that they are exogenously specified.

LG4 **Calculate, use, and note the deficiencies that the internal rate of return (IRR) and the modified internal rate of return (MIRR) techniques offer.** Managers find both IRR and the MIRR methods intuitively appealing, measuring what is best thought of as the "expected" rate of return to be earned from investing in a project. Unfortunately, the basic IRR statistic becomes unreliable when dealing with non-normal cash flows. The method also chooses precisely the wrong project when it's used to compare mutually exclusive projects with marked differences in timing and/or scale of their cash flows. Third, IRR embodies a rather unreasonable assumption about the rate at which cash inflows from the project can be reinvested.

The MIRR decision rule explicitly alters IRR's reinvestment rate assumption, implicitly curing any problems associated non-normal cash flows along the way. But, as a rate-based decision rule, it still suffers from invalidity when it's used to choose between or among mutually exclusive projects.

LG5 **Learn now to use NPV profiles to demonstrate the sources of conflict between NPV and IRR decision rules.** The main discrepancy between the NPV choice and the IRR's/MIRR's choice between mutually exclusive projects arises because of rate-based decision statistic attributes, which place undue preference for shorter-term, smaller projects rather than longer-term, larger scale

www.mhhe.com/can1e

projects that might really give the firm a leg up. Since at times a rate-based decision metric is *desirable* but not necessarily appropriate, we need to be able to explain exactly why the project with the largest IRR isn't necessarily the best project.

LG6 **Compute and use the profitability index (PI).** We presented a simple version of the profitability index (PI) that is a simple arithmetic

transformation of the NPV into a rate-based decision statistic. Its one important attribute is that, unlike the other rate-based statistics discussed in this chapter, it measures the *excess* return—the amount above and beyond the cost of capital for a project, rather than the gross return. Consequently, its appropriate benchmark is zero or anything larger than zero rather than the cost of capital.

chapter equations

13-1 NPV Statistic

$$NPV = \frac{CF_0}{(1+i)^0} + \frac{CF_1}{(1+i)^1} + \cdots + \frac{CF_N}{(1+i)^N}$$

$$= \sum_{n=0}^{N} \frac{CF_n}{(1+i)^n}$$

13-2 NPV Decision Rule

Accept project if $NPV > 0$

Reject project if $NPV < 0$

13-3 Payback Statistic is the solution to:

$$0 = \sum_{n=0}^{PB} CF_n$$

13-4 Payback Decision Rule

Accept project if calculated payback $\leq$ Maximum allowable payback

Reject project if calculated payback $>$ Maximum allowable payback

13-5 Discounted Payback Statistic is the solution to:

$$0 = \sum_{n=0}^{DPB} \frac{CF_n}{(1+i)^n}$$

13-6 Discounted Payback Decision Rule

Accept project if calculated DPB $\leq$ Maximum allowable discounted payback

Reject project if calculated DPB $>$ Maximum allowable discounted payback

13-7 IRR Statistic is the solution to:

$$0 = \sum_{n=0}^{N} \frac{CF_n}{(1+IRR)^n}$$

13-8 IRR Decision Rule

Accept project if IRR $\geq$ Cost of capital

Reject project if IRR $<$ Cost of capital

13-9 Profitability Index Statistic

$$PI = \frac{NPV}{CF_0}$$

key terms

discounted payback (DPB), A capital budgeting method that generates decision rules and associated metrics that choose projects based on how quickly they return their initial investment plus interest. (p. 428)

interest-rate cognizant, Including the cost of capital calculation into decision-making process. (p. 438)

internal rate of return (IRR), A capital budgeting technique that generates decision rules and associated metrics for choosing projects based on the implicit expected geometric average of a project's rate of return. (p. 431)

modified internal rate of return (MIRR), A capital budgeting method that converts a project's cash flows using a more consistent reinvestment rate prior to applying the IRR decision rule. (p. 435)

mutually exclusive projects, Groups or pairs of projects where you can accept one but not all. (p. 436)

net present value (NPV), A technique that generates a decision rule and associated metric for choosing projects based on the total discounted value of their cash flows. (p. 423)

NPV profile, A graph of a project's NPV as a function of the cost of capital. (p. 433)

normal cash flows, A set of cash flows where all the initial cash flows are negative and all subsequent ones are either zero or positive. (p. 422)

payback (PB), A capital budgeting technique that generates decision rules and associated metrics for choosing projects based on how quickly they return their initial investment. (p. 427)

profitability index (PI), A decision rule and associated methodology for converting the NPV statistic into a rate-based metric. (p. 441)

self-test problem with solution

1   Assume you are evaluating the two mutually exclusive projects, the cash flows of which appear to the right, and that your company uses a cost of capital of 8 percent to evaluate projects such as these.

TIME	PROJECT A CASH FLOW	PROJECT B CASH FLOW
0	−$650	−$700
1	100	300
2	250	−200
3	250	550
4	200	200
5	100	80

a. Calculate the payback of Project A.

b. Calculate the discounted payback of Project A.

c. Calculate the IRR of Project A.

d. Calculate the MIRR of Project B.

e. At which rate do these project's NPV profiles cross?

f. Using the NPV method and assuming a cost of capital of 8 percent, which of these projects should be accepted?

Solution:

a. Calculate the payback of Project A.

YEAR	0	1	2	3	4	5
Cash Flow	−$650	$100	$250	$250	$200	$100
Cumulative Cash Flow	−650	−550	−300	−50	−150	

$$PB = 3 + \frac{50}{200} = 3.25$$

b. Calculate the discounted payback of Project A.

YEAR	0	1	2	3	4	5
Cash Flow	$650.00	$100.00	$250.00	$250.00	$200.00	$100.00
Cash Flow Present Value	−650.00	92.59	214.33	198.46	147.01	
Cumulative Cash Flow PV	−650.00	−557.41	−343.07	−144.61	2.39	

$$DPB = 3 + \frac{144.61}{147.01} = 3.98$$

c. Calculate the IRR of Project A.

$$0 = \frac{-\$650}{(1 + IRR)^0} + \frac{\$100}{(1 + IRR)^1} + \frac{\$250}{(1 + IRR)^2} + \frac{\$250}{(1 + IRR)^3}$$
$$+ \frac{\$200}{(1 + IRR)^4} + \frac{\$100}{(1 + IRR)^5}$$

$$IRR = .1202, \text{ or } 12.02\%$$

d. Calculate the MIRR of Project B.

YEAR	0	1	2	3	4	5
Cash Flow	$700.00	$300.00	−$200.00	$550.00	$200.00	$ 80.00
Present Value (if negative)	−700.00		−171.47			
Sum of PV	−871.47					
Future Value (if positive)		408.15		641.52	216.00	80.00
Sum of FV						1,345.67
Modified CFs	−871.47					1,345.67

With this new set of modified cash flows, the (M)IRR is:

$$0 = \frac{-\$871.47}{(1 + IRR)^0} + \frac{\$1,345.67}{(1 + IRR)^5}$$

$$IRR = .0908, \text{ or } 9.08\%$$

447

e. At which rate do these projects' NPV profiles cross?

YEAR	0	1	2	3	4	5
Project A Cash Flows	−$650	$100	$250	$250	$200	$100
Project B Cash Flows	−700	300	−200	550	200	80
A−B	−50	−200	450	−300	0	20

$$0 = \frac{\$50}{(1+IRR)^0} + \frac{-\$200}{(1+IRR)^1} + \frac{\$450}{(1+IRR)^2} + \frac{-\$300}{(1+IRR)^3}$$
$$+ \frac{\$0}{(1+IRR)^4} + \frac{\$20}{(1+IRR)^5}$$
$$IRR = -.1266, \text{ or } -12.66\%$$

Note: This is outside the first quadrant.

f. Using the NPV method and assuming a cost of capital of 8 percent, which of these mutually exclusive projects should the firm accept?

$$NPV_A = \frac{\$650}{(1.08)^0} + \frac{\$100}{(1.08)^1} + \frac{\$250}{(1.08)^2} + \frac{\$250}{(1.08)^3} + \frac{\$200}{(1.08)^4} + \frac{\$100}{(1.08)^5} = \$70.45$$

$$NPV_B = \frac{-\$700}{(1.08)^0} + \frac{\$300}{(1.08)^1} + \frac{-\$200}{(1.08)^2} + \frac{\$550}{(1.08)^3} + \frac{\$200}{(1.08)^4} + \frac{\$80}{(1.08)^5} = \$44.37$$

$NPV_A > NPV_B$, so Project A should be accepted.

questions

1. Is the set of cash flows depicted below normal or non-normal? Explain. *(LG1)*

TIME	0	1	2	3	4	5
Cash Flow	−$100	−$50	−$80	$0	$100	$100

2. Derive an accept/reject rule for IRR similar to equation 13-8 that would make the correct decision on cash flows that are non-normal, but which always have one large positive cash flow at time zero followed by a series of negative cash flows. *(LG1)*

TIME	0	1	2	3	4	5
Cash Flow	+	−	−	−	−	−

3. Is it possible for a company to initiate two products that target the same market and are *not* mutually exclusive? *(LG1)*

4. Suppose that your company used "APV," or "All-the-Present, Value-Except-CF_v," to analyze capital budgeting projects. What would this rule's benchmark value be? *(LG2)*

5. Under what circumstances could payback and discounted payback be equal? *(LG3)*

6. Could a project's MIRR ever *exceed* its IRR? *(LG4)*

7. If you had two mutually exclusive, normal-cash-flow projects whose NPV profiles crossed at all points, for which range of interest rates would IRR give the right accept/reject answer? *(LG5)*

8. Suppose a company wanted to double their firm's value with the next round of capital budgeting project decisions. To what would they set the PI benchmark to make this goal? *(LG6)*

9. Suppose a company faced different borrowing and lending rates: How would this range change the way that you would compute the MIRR statistic? *(LG4)*

problems

13-1 **NPV with Normal Cash Flows** Compute the NPV for Project M and accept or reject the project with the cash flows shown below if the appropriate cost of capital is 8 percent. *(LG2)*

basic
problems

Project M

TIME	0	1	2	3	4	5
Cash Flow	−$1,000	$350	$480	$520	$300	$100

13-2 **NPV with Normal Cash Flows** Compute the NPV statistic for Project Y and tell whether the firm should accept or reject the project with the cash flows shown below if the appropriate cost of capital is 12 percent. *(LG2)*

Project Y

TIME	0	1	2	3	4
Cash Flow	−$11,000	$3,350	$4,180	$1,520	$300

13-3 **NPV with Non-normal Cash Flows** Compute the NPV statistic for Project U and recommend whether the firm should accept or reject the project with the cash flows shown below if the appropriate cost of capital is 10 percent. *(LG2)*

Project U

TIME	0	1	2	3	4	5
Cash Flow	−$1,000	$350	$1,480	−$520	$300	−$100

13-4 **NPV with Normal Cash Flows** Compute the payback statistic for Project A and recommend whether the firm should accept or reject the project

with the cash flows shown below if the appropriate cost of capital is
8 percent and the maximum allowable payback is four years. (LG3)

Project A						
TIME	**0**	**1**	**2**	**3**	**4**	**5**
Cash Flow	−$1,000	$350	$480	$520	$300	$100

13-5 **Payback** Compute the payback statistic for Project B and decide whether
the firm should accept or reject the project with the cash flows shown
below if the appropriate cost of capital is 12 percent and the maximum
allowable payback is three years. (LG3)

Project B						
TIME	**0**	**1**	**2**	**3**	**4**	**5**
Cash Flow	−$11,000	$3,350	$4,180	$1,520	$0	$1,000

13-6 **Discounted Payback** Compute the discounted payback statistic for Project
C and recommend whether the firm should accept or reject the project
with the cash flows shown below if the appropriate cost of capital is 8 percent and the maximum allowable discounted payback is three years. (LG3)

Project C						
TIME	**0**	**1**	**2**	**3**	**4**	**5**
Cash Flow	−$1,000	$350	$480	$520	$300	$100

13-7 **Discounted Payback** Compute the discounted payback statistic for Project D and recommend whether the firm should accept or reject the project
with the cash flows shown below if the appropriate cost of capital is 12 percent and the maximum allowable discounted payback is four years. (LG3)

Project D						
TIME	**0**	**1**	**2**	**3**	**4**	**5**
Cash Flow	$11,000	$3,350	$4,180	$1,520	$0	$1,000

13-8 **IRR** Compute the IRR statistic for Project E and note whether the firm
should accept or reject the project with the cash flows shown below if the
appropriate cost of capital is 8 percent. (LG4)

Project E						
TIME	**0**	**1**	**2**	**3**	**4**	**5**
Cash Flow	−$1,000	$350	$480	$520	$300	$100

13-9 **IRR** Compute the IRR statistic for project F and note whether the firm
should accept or reject the project with the cash flows shown below if the
appropriate cost of capital is 12 percent. (LG4)

Project F

TIME	0	1	2	3	4
Cash Flow	−$11,000	$3,350	$4,180	$1,520	$2,000

13-10 **IRR** Compute the IRR statistic for Project G and note whether the firm should accept or reject the project with the cash flows shown below if the appropriate cost of capital is 10 percent. *(LG4)*

Project G

TIME	0	1	2	3	4	5
Cash Flow	−$1,000	$350	$1,480	−$520	$300	−$100

13-11 **MIRR** Compute the MIRR statistic for Project H and note whether to accept or reject the project with the cash flows shown below if the appropriate cost of capital is 8 percent. *(LG4)*

Project H

TIME	0	1	2	3	4	5
Cash Flow	−$1,000	$350	$480	$520	$300	$100

13-12 **MIRR** Compute the MIRR statistic for Project I and tell whether to accept or reject the project with the cash flows shown below if the appropriate cost of capital is 12 percent. *(LG4)*

Project I

TIME	0	1	2	3	4
Cash Flow	−$11,000	$3,350	$4,180	$1,520	$2,000

13-13 **MIRR** Compute the MIRR statistic for Project J and advise whether to accept or reject the project with the cash flows shown below if the appropriate cost of capital is 10 percent. *(LG4)*

Project J

TIME	0	1	2	3	4	5
Cash Flow	−$1,000	$350	$1,480	−$520	$300	−$100

13-14 **PI** Compute the PI statistic for Project Z and advise the firm whether to accept or reject the project with the cash flows shown below if the appropriate cost of capital is 8 percent. *(LG6)*

Project Z

TIME	0	1	2	3	4	5
Cash Flow	−$1,000	$350	$480	$520	$300	$100

13-15 **PI** Compute the PI statistic for Project Q and tell whether you would accept or reject the project with the cash flows shown below if the appropriate cost of capital is 12 percent. *(LG6)*

Project Q					
TIME	0	1	2	3	4
Cash Flow	−$11,000	$3,350	$4,180	$1,520	$2,000

13-16 **PI** Compute the PI statistic for Project LL and decide whether to accept or reject the project with the cash flows shown below if the appropriate cost of capital is 10 percent. *(LG6)*

Project LL						
TIME	0	1	2	3	4	5
Cash Flow	−$1,000	$350	$1,480	−$520	$300	−$100

13-17 **Multiple IRRs** How many possible IRRs could you find for the following set of cash flows? *(LG1)*

TIME	0	1	2	3	4
Cash Flow	−$11,000	$3,350	$4,180	$1,520	$2,000

13-18 **Multiple IRRs** How many possible IRRs could you find for the following set of cash flows? *(LG1)*

TIME	0	1	2	3	4
Cash Flow	−$11,000	−$39,350	$440,180	$217,520	−$2,000

intermediate problems

Use this information to answer the next six questions. If a particular decision method should not be used, indicate why.
Suppose your firm is considering investing in a project with the cash flows shown below, that the required rate of return on projects of this risk class is 8 percent, and that the maximum allowable payback and discounted payback statistics for the project are 3.5 and 4.5 years, respectively.

TIME	0	1	2	3	4	5	6
Cash Flow	−$5,000	$1,200	$1,400	$1,600	$1,600	$1,400	$1,200

13-19 **Payback** Use the payback decision rule to evaluate this project; should it be accepted or rejected? *(LG3)*

13-20 Discounted Payback Use the discounted payback decision rule to evaluate this project; should it be accepted or rejected? *(LG3)*

13-21 IRR Use the IRR decision rule to evaluate this project; should it be accepted or rejected? *(LG4)*

13-22 MIRR Use the MIRR decision rule to evaluate this project; should it be accepted or rejected? *(LG4)*

13-23 NPV Use the NPV decision rule to evaluate this project; should it be accepted or rejected? *(LG2)*

13-24 PI Use the PI decision rule to evaluate this project; should it be accepted or rejected? *(LG6)*

Use this information to answer the next 6 questions. If you should not use a particular decision technique, indicate why.

Suppose your firm is considering investing in a project with the cash flows shown below, that the required rate of return on projects of this risk class is 11 percent, and that the maximum allowable payback and discounted payback statistics for your company are 3 and 3.5 years, respectively.

TIME	0	1	2	3	4	5
Cash Flow	−$235,000	$65,800	$84,000	$141,000	$122,000	$81,200

13-25 Payback Use the payback decision rule to evaluate this project; should it be accepted or rejected? *(LG3)*

13-26 Discounted Payback Use the discounted payback decision rule to evaluate this project; should it be accepted or rejected? *(LG3)*

13-27 IRR Use the IRR decision rule to evaluate this project; should it be accepted or rejected? *(LG4)*

13-28 MIRR Use the MIRR decision rule to evaluate this project; should it be accepted or rejected? *(LG4)*

13-29 NPV Use the NPV decision rule to evaluate this project; should it be accepted or rejected? *(LG2)*

13-30 PI Use the PI decision rule to evaluate this project; should it be accepted or rejected? *(LG6)*

Use the project cash flows for the two mutually exclusive projects shown below to answer the following 4 questions.

TIME	PROJECT A CASH FLOW	PROJECT B CASH FLOW
0	−$725	−$850
1	$100	$200
2	$250	$200
3	$250	$200
4	$200	$200
5	$100	$200
6	$100	$200
7	$100	$200

13-31 NPV Profiles Graph the NPV profiles for both projects on a common chart, making sure that you identify all of the "crucial" points. *(LG5)*

13-32 IRR Applicability For what range of possible interest rates would you want to use IRR to choose between these two projects? For what range of rates would you NOT want to use IRR? *(LG5)*

13-33 Multiple IRRs Construct an NPV profile and determine EXACTLY how many nonnegative IRRs you can find for the following set of cash flows: *(LG5)*

TIME	0	1	2	3	4	5	6	7
Cash Flow	−200	400	150	−100	−100	−300	200	−300

13-34 Multiple IRRs Construct an NPV profile and determine EXACTLY how many nonnegative IRRs you can find for the following set of cash flows: *(LG5)*

TIME	0	1	2	3	4	5	6	7
Cash Flow	−150	275	150	−100	300	−300	200	−300

research it! Business Valuation

The capital budgeting decision techniques that we've discussed all have strengths and weaknesses, but they do comprise the most popular rules for valuing projects. Valuing entire businesses, on the other hand, requires that some adjustments be made to various pieces of these methodologies. For example, one alternative to NPV used quite frequently for valuing firms is called Adjusted Present Value (APV).

To explore these alternative decision rules, do a Web search on Google (**www.google.com**) for APV and answer the following questions:

1. What is APV, and how does it differ from NPV?

2. What other business valuation models seem to be popular?

integrated minicase Project Valuation

Suppose your firm is considering investing in a project with the cash flows shown on the next page, that the required rate of return on projects of this risk class is 11 percent, and that the maximum allowable payback and discounted payback statistics for your company are 3 and 3.5 years, respectively.

(continued)

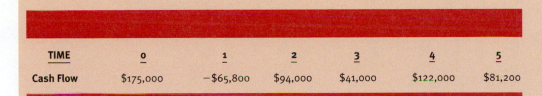

TIME	0	1	2	3	4	5
Cash Flow	$175,000	−$65,800	$94,000	$41,000	$122,000	$81,200

Using every one of the capital budgeting decision methods discussed in this chapter, evaluate this project, indicating whether each decision rule would call for acceptance or rejection of the project.

ANSWERS TO TIME OUT

13-1   Because the cost is already included in the NPV; using it as the benchmark, also, would involve double-counting it.

13-2   It should be equal to zero, because the cost of the bond to the purchaser should be exactly equal to the sum of the present values of the coupons and the face value.

13-3   Given that we are only going to be calculating for projects with normal sets of cash flows, the discounted payback will always be large, as it will take longer for the present values of the future, positive cash flows to sum to the initial cost than it will for the cash flows themselves to do so.

13-4   If the discounted payback is equal to the end of the project, then the project's NPV will be equal to zero, as the cumulative present value of all cash flows at the end of the project is equal to the NPV.

13-5   No: if the cash flows are normal, some large interest rate has to exist at which the size of the present value of the future, positive cash flows becomes less than the initial, negative cash flow.

13-6   It should reject: such a project would have the sums of the positive cash flows equal to the negative, initial cash flow, which would have to result in a negative NPV under any positive interest rate.

13-7   The project with the longer payback will have the lower IRR, as its cash flows will, on average, be later than the other project's.

13-8   Only one, because there is only one change in sign of the cash flows: from negative to positive between years 1 and 2.

13-9   The MIRR should be less than the IRR due to MIRR using a lower reinvestment rate assumption.

13-10 You would solve the perpetuity formula for the interest rate by dividing the cash flow by the initial cost.

13-11 It would use a benchmark of 1 instead of zero.

13-12 It will have a PI and an NPV of zero.

chapter 14:
ASSESSING LONG-TERM DEBT, EQUITY, AND CAPITAL STRUCTURE

Learning Goals

LG1 Differentiate between active and passive changes to capital structure.

LG2 Demonstrate why finance professionals refer to debt as "leverage" in firms' capital structures.

LG3 Show how the firm apportions risk and return amongst stockholders and bondholders in a "perfect world."

LG4 Describe how optimal capital structure changes when we relax the assumption of no corporate taxation—at which point the optimal capital structure becomes one in which "The More Debt, the Better" applies.

LG5 Demonstrate how individual shareholders can mimic or reverse firm capital structure changes by borrowing and lending on their own account.

LG6 Calculate the EBIT and EPS levels at which shareholders will become indifferent about the choice between two alternative capital structures.

LG7 Describe how the firm's choice of optimal capital structure changes if we allow for the possibility of bankruptcy.

LG8 Argue whether real-world business practices seem to reflect the theoretical basis for firms' choices of optimal capital structure.

So far, we've assumed that a firm's **capital structure**—the mix of debt and equity that a firm uses to finance its operations—is either already given or is irrelevant to the decisions we've been making. Though we might appropriately use this assumption in the very short term, firms can and do change their capital structures in the longer term, so we need to analyze factors that affect the firm's decision to change its funding mix.

As we'll see, two main factors come into play: (1) whether debt interest payments are tax deductible and (2) how increased debt might affect the likelihood of the firm either going bankrupt or entering into **financial distress** (i.e., approaching

viewpoints

Business Application

Suppose that Kieran has decided that it's time to take her photography business, currently run on an all-equity basis, and leverage it so that it's funded with 50 percent debt. The business currently has $30 thousand worth of assets and pays 15 percent tax on gross income. Kieran has in hand a bank quote at an interest rate of 9.5 percent on an interest-only loan. As long as Kieran doesn't anticipate any chance that the firm won't be able to cover the required interest payments on the loan, or that the bank won't renew the loan at the end of its term, what economic benefits will accrue to Kieran by re-leveraging the firm? **(See solution on p. 478)**

Personal Application

Gunter has just graduated college and started a new job. He's thinking about buying a townhouse for $150,000, but doesn't have a down payment. His bank has offered to lend him 80 percent of the money—a 30-year mortgage at a rate of 5.875%. Further, the bank will lend Gunter the other $30,000 through a home equity loan at a rate of 7.90%. If he accepts the bank's offer, what weighted-average after-tax interest rate will Gunter pay for the purchase of the townhouse? **(See solution on p. 478)**

bankruptcy). Financial managers carefully choose a capital structure that sets these two factors' marginal effects equal to one another. By doing so, they simultaneously maximize firm value and minimize any new project's financing costs.

14.1 Active versus Passive Capital Structure Changes

In theory, firms seeking to change their capital structure could take one of two approaches. They could immediately sell additional claims of one type of capital and use the proceeds to retire other kinds of claims. We will refer to this kind of approach as **active management**. The second way that firms could change their capital structure would be more passive: they could wait until the firm required additional capital to cover capital budgeting needs and then sell more of the type of claims they wish to increase in their capital structure.

For example, suppose that Kennemore Corp. currently has $10 million in assets, financed entirely with equity. The firm has decided to switch to a 50 percent debt/50 percent equity structure. With *active* capital structure management, they would sell $5 million of debt and use the proceeds to retire half of the equity. Thus Kennemore will wind up with $5 million of debt and $5 million of equity today. With passive capital structure management, they would attempt to fund the next $10 million of assets for future projects entirely with debt, winding up with $10 million of debt and $10 million of equity at some point in the future.

We sometimes call active capital structure management *restructuring*. If the firm wishes to dramatically change its capital structure in a relatively short period of time, restructuring is preferable, both from the firm's point of view and from financial analysts' perspective. The downside to restructuring, however, is costs. The firm will need to pay at least one "extra" set of flotation costs associated with selling additional securities of the type of capital it wishes to increase. It might also have to pay additional costs associated with retiring the type of capital it wishes to reduce, such as having to pay a call premium on bonds retired early.

Which approach—active or passive—is better? It depends on:

- How quickly the firm is growing.
- How much the firm faces in flotation costs under the active management approach.
- How strongly and how quickly the firm wishes to change the capital structure.

In general, for businesses that expect to add significant assets in the near future (either due to growth or due to replacing existing assets), the passive management approach works best. Such firms will be able to alter their structure relatively quickly without incurring the additional costs of active management.

TIME OUT

14-1 Which strategy, active or passive capital structure management, would make the process of changing the firm's capital structure a longer-term proposition? Why?

14-2 Suppose that a firm was simultaneously evaluating the addition of a new capital budgeting project and a proposed capital structure change: should the old capital structure or the proposed new capital structure be used in determining the WACC for the new project?

Having said that, in this chapter we focus on active capital structure management. This focus will allow us to examine the benefits of a proposed capital structure change without having to winnow out the additional impacts of capital budgeting decisions. Passive capital structure management must account for capital budgeting as the firm increases its capital on an as-needed basis.

14.2 Capital Structure Theory: The Effect of Financial Leverage

In finance, we refer to using debt within a firm's capital structure as **leverage.** Why? Because just as a physical lever magnifies force in one direction and movement in another, debt magnifies both the potential expected return to equity as well as the variability around that expected return. To see why it does so, we first need to tie up some theoretical loose ends.

Modigliani and Miller's "Perfect World"

The basic tool for examining various variables' effects on the firm's choice of optimal capital structure is the **Modigliani–Miller (M&M) theorem,** named after its authors, Franco Modigliani and Merton Miller, who completed the theorem in 1958. The full development of the M&M theorem starts with a "perfect world," one that features:

- No taxes.
- No chance of bankruptcy.
- Perfectly efficient markets.
- Symmetric information sets for all participants.

In this perfect world, the M&M theorem's two main propositions are:

Proposition I (perfect world): $V_L = V_U$ **(14-1)**

where

V_U is the value of an unleveraged, or all-equity-financed, firm.

V_L is the value of a leveraged firm (i.e., one whose capital structure contains debt).

Proposition II (perfect world): $i_E = i_{E,0} + \dfrac{D}{E}(i_{E,0} - i_D)$ **(14-2)**

where

$i_{E,0}$ is the cost of capital for an all-equity firm.

i_E and i_D are the costs of equity and debt in a leveraged firm.

Both of these propositions reflect a common underlying intuition, which we sometimes refer to as the **capital structure irrelevance assertion.** Merton Miller, in his testimony in Glendale Federal Bank's lawsuit against the U.S. government in December 1997, probably put it best:

> I have a simple explanation [for the first Modigliani-Miller proposition]. It's after the ball game, and the pizza man comes up to Yogi Berra and he says, 'Yogi, how do you want me to cut this pizza, into quarters?' Yogi says, 'No, cut it into eight

pieces, I'm feeling hungry tonight.' Now when I tell that story the usual reaction is, 'And you mean to say that they gave you a [Nobel] prize for that?'

THE EFFECT OF LEVERAGE ON THE COST OF EQUITY

Even Proposition II, which explicitly deals with the cost increase of equity capital as a function of the firm's D/E ratio, stems from this same argument of capital structure irrelevance. To see this, we need to combine a couple of observations from earlier chapters with a new bit of information:

1. First, think back to our previous discussion of WACC in Chapter 11. From this, we should realize that WACC will have to be equal to $i_{E,0}$ for an all-equity firm, as equity will be the only component cost of capital with any weight in the WACC:

$$\text{WACC} = \frac{E}{E + 0}i_{E,0} + \frac{0}{E + D}i_D \times (1 - T_C)$$
$$= i_{E,0} \text{ for an all-equity firm}$$

2. Second, we need to think back to the IRR rule discussed in Chapter 13. If firms will only accept projects for which the expected rate of return is at least as large as the required, or target, rate of return, then we can think of the WACC not only as the *average* rate that the firm will *pay* to capital providers but also as the minimum average expected rate of return on the firm's asset investments that must be *earned* if the firm wants to be able to pay back the capital providers.

$$IRR \geq i_{E,0} \Rightarrow i_{E,0} = \text{min acceptable expected rate of return}$$

3. Finally, we need to address the question of what will happen to a firm's WACC in M&M's perfect world as the capital structure changes. Irving Fisher's seminal work on the theory of investment[1] included the **separation principle,** which states that, with a well-functioning capital market, the firm's capital budgeting decisions are separate from its capital structure decisions. That is, *what you do* with the money and *where you get it* are two distinctly separate decisions. So changing the firm's capital structure in our perfect world should not affect the group of projects chosen, or the minimum acceptable rate of return dictated by those projects' lower boundary of expected returns.

$$\text{WACC} = i_{E,0} \,\forall\, \frac{D}{E}$$

Putting all of this together with a simplified[2] version of the formula for WACC from Chapter 11 allows us to solve the WACC formula for i_E:

---

[1]See Irving Fisher, *The Theory of Interest, as Determined by Impatience to Spend Income and Opportunity to Invest It* (New York: Macmillan, 1930).

[2]The two simplifications that we've made are that we can use the before-tax cost of debt instead of the after-tax cost (as we're operating in a world without taxes for right now), and we've left out any consideration of preferred stock so as to make our analysis a little more succinct. Given preferred stock's aspect as a hybrid form of debt and equity, leaving it in wouldn't really add any intuition to the discussion below, but would instead merely make it needlessly more complex.

$$\text{WACC} = \frac{E}{E+D}i_E + \frac{D}{E+D}i_D$$

$$i_{E,0} = \frac{E}{E+D}i_E + \frac{D}{E+D}i_D$$

$$\Rightarrow$$

$$i_E = \frac{E+D}{E}\left[i_{E,0} - \frac{D}{E+D}i_D\right]$$

$$= \frac{E+D}{E}i_{E,0} - \left(\frac{E+D}{E} \times \frac{D}{E+D}\right)i_D$$

$$= \left(\frac{E}{E} + \frac{D}{E}\right)i_{E,0} - \frac{D}{E}i_D$$

$$= i_{E,0} + \frac{D}{E}i_{E,0} - \frac{D}{E}i_D$$

$$i_E = i_{E,0} + \frac{D}{E}(i_{E,0} - i_D) \qquad\qquad \textbf{(14-3)}$$

This derivation shows that the firm's cost of equity increases with the use of debt in the capital structure. But the fact that WACC, $i_{E,0}$, is constant in the D/E ratio implies that a positive relationship between the cost of equity capital and the use of debt in the capital structure is solely due to reapportioning the expected rate of return to the firm's assets among claimholders. It does not imply any addition or subtraction of the total amount of return available. That is, the cost of equity goes up as the amount of debt increases, but the WACC stays the same.

THE EFFECT OF LEVERAGE ON THE WACC Since debt is cheaper than equity, the firm uses less expensive equity and more relatively cheap debt at a rate that just offsets the effect on WACC of the increased cost of equity. This leads us to what we will call Proposition IIa, which M&M's theorem implies (but to which we don't usually refer so formally):

$$\text{Proposition IIa (perfect world): WACC} = i_{E,0} = \frac{E}{E+D}i_E + \frac{D}{E+D}i_D \qquad \textbf{(14-4)}$$

$$\text{which will be constant in } \frac{D}{E}$$

To see why this should hold true, let's take Merton Miller's analogy of a pizza pie and extend it to a cake, dividing up two layers among a group of people on the TV show *Survivor*. If you've ever seen this show, you're probably aware that it consists of following the day-to-day activities of groups of people "stranded" in some exotic locale with very few resources. The survivors usually have access to some plentiful staple food source, but the participants all get rather sick of this plain fare after the first couple of weeks. Periodic infusions of small delicacies, either as prizes in a game or simply to stave off a rebellion, go a long way towards making the winners more satisfied with their participation.

Assume that one such group has been given the task of eating a two-layered cake. If it's a cake that everyone likes, then the most basic logical distribution of the finished product would be to give each person a proportionate share of the cake. However, show producers are rarely nice enough to just drop off delicacies for no reason at all. So let's assume that, while one layer of this cake *is* filled with some savory delight that everyone likes, the other layer is filled with exotic cockroaches, which all group members loathe, albeit to different degrees. Furthermore, let's assume that the show's producers have dictated that the group must finish off the entire cake in a certain amount of time, or someone will be "kicked off the island."

You can see that this situation might prompt the group to make some very interesting allotment decisions concerning who gets to/has to eat how much of the cake. The group might decide that the people who agree to take more of the cockroach layer get a larger, proportionate share of the enjoyable layer, too. Or the group may decide that people who eat a slight majority of the disgusting layer get virtually *all* of the enjoyable layer.

These two allocation schemes correspond exactly to the situation seen in all-equity and mixed debt/equity capital structures, respectively. If we logically assume that all humans are risk averse, then any financial claim against a firm comes with some of the layer that everyone wants—returns. But any financial claim will also come with some less desirable layer that everyone loathes—risks. In an all-equity firm, the equity holders share the firm's expected return and expected risk in strictly proportional amounts. Someone who has put in one-fourth of the equity, thereby buying one-fourth of the firm's shares, can in return expect to receive one-fourth of the firm's returns on its assets. That investor has at risk the money paid for those shares. Someone who put in twice as much money would expect twice as much in return, but would also run the risk of losing twice as much money, and so forth.

In a firm that employs a mixture of debt and equity, however, the parties have implicitly agreed to a disproportionate sharing of the risk and return layers of the firm. The debt holders have put in a certain portion of the firm's capital and thereby expect exactly the return (and the return of their capital) as spelled out in the bond indenture. Their expected returns will never change; they'll get exactly what they signed up for, with no business risk on the line. The equity holders, in accepting for themselves a residual claim on the company's future proceeds, have agreed to accept more than their fair share of the risk layer—they take on both business and financial risk. In return, they also expect a disproportionately large share of the expected return layer.

This is what we're seeing in equation 14-3. The reason that i_E increases in D/E is to compensate stockholders for bearing more and more residual risk as the number of stockholders declines.

EXAMPLE 14-1

 For interactive versions of this example visit www.mhhe.com/can1e

 ### IMPACT ON EXPECTED RETURN AND VOLATILITY OF INCREASING LEVERAGE IN A PERFECT WORLD

Suppose we are in M&M's perfect world, and we have a firm with $100 million in assets, currently financed entirely with equity. Equity is worth $100 per share, and book value of equity is equal to market value of equity.[3] Also, let's assume that the firm's expected EBIT values depend on which state of the economy occurs this year, with the possible values of EBIT and their associated probabilities as shown below:

STATE	RECESSION	AVERAGE	BOOM
Probability of state	.2	.6	.2
Expect EBIT in state	$10 million	$25 million	$35 million

The firm is considering switching to either a 30-percent or 60-percent debt capital structure and has determined that it would have to pay an 8 percent yield on perpetual debt in either

(continued)

[3]Please note that this assumption is made purely to simplify the math. Having the market and book values of equity differ would add to the complexity of this example, but wouldn't change the basic intuition.

event.[4] What will be the effect on expected EPS and the volatility of that EPS if they stay with their current capital structure or switch to either of the two proposed structures?

SOLUTION:

If the firm stays with their all-equity structure, they will have $100 million/$100 = 1 million shares outstanding, and the EPS under each state of nature will be:

STATE	RECESSION	AVERAGE	BOOM
EBIT	$10,000,000	$25,000,000	$35,000,000
− Interest	0	0	0
EBT	10,000,000	25,000,000	35,000,000
− Taxes	0	0	0
Net income	$10,000,000	$25,000,000	$35,000,000
EPS	$ 10.00	$ 25.00	$ 35.00

The expected EPS and standard deviation of the EPS will be:

$$E(EPS) = .2 \times \$10.00 + .6 \times \$25.00 + .2 \times \$35.00 = \$24.00$$

$$\sigma_{EPS} = \sqrt{.2(\$10.00 - \$24.00) + .6(\$25.00 - \$24.00) + .2(\$35.00 - \$24.00)} = \$8.00$$

If the firm refinances 30 percent of the capital by selling $30 million in debt and uses the proceeds to retire $30 million in equity, the interest on the debt will amount to .08 × $30 million = $2.4 million, and the firm will have $70 million/$100 = 700,000 shares outstanding, and the EPS under each state of nature will be:

STATE	RECESSION	AVERAGE	BOOM
EBIT	$10,000,000	$25,000,000	$35,000,000
− Interest	2,400,000	2,400,000	2,400,000
EBT	7,600,000	22,600,000	32,600,000
− Taxes	0	0	0
Net income	$ 7,600,000	$22,600,000	$32,600,000
EPS	$ 10.86	$ 32.29	$ 46.57

The expected EPS and standard deviation of the EPS will be:

$$E(EPS) = .2 \times \$10.86 + .6 \times \$32.29 + .2 \times \$46.57 = \$30.86$$

$$\sigma_{EPS} = \sqrt{.2(\$10.86 - \$30.86) + .6(\$32.29 - \$30.86) + .2(\$46.57 - \$30.86)} = \$11.43$$

If the firm refinances 60 percent of the capital by selling $60 million in debt and using the proceeds to retire $60 million in equity, the interest on the debt will amount to .08 × $60 million = $4.8 million, and it will have $40 million/$100 = 400,000 shares outstanding, and the EPS under each state of nature will be:

STATE	RECESSION	AVERAGE	BOOM
EBIT	$10,000,000	$25,000,000	$35,000,000
− Interest	4,800,000	4,800,000	4,800,000
EBT	5,200,000	20,200,000	30,200,000
− Taxes	0	0	0
Net income	$ 5,200,000	$22,200,000	$30,200,000
EPS	$ 13.00	$ 50.50	$ 75.50

(continued)

[4]This assumption is also made to simplify the calculations. We could consider a situation in which debt had a finite maturity, but to the extent that a firm would want to stick with a particular capital structure, any retirement of debt would have to be perfectly offset with an equivalent issue of new debt, which would add much numerical complexity of the example, but nothing to the intuition.

The expected EPS and standard deviation of the EPS will be:

$$E(EPS) = .2 \times \$13.00 + .6 \times \$50.50 + .2 \times \$75.50 = \$48.00$$

$$\sigma_{EPS} = \sqrt{.2(\$13.00 - \$48.00) + .6(\$50.50 - \$48.00) + .2(\$75.50 - \$48.00)} = \$20.00$$

As this example shows, increasing the amount of debt in the capital structure will increase the expected EPS level, but it will also increase the variation—also known as risk—that we can expect around that expected EPS. This basic intuition is driven by the fact that stockholders hold the residual claim to earnings. Thus they bear more of the business risk, also known as the state-of-nature-induced volatility, than debt holders do. In fact, as long as EBIT is large enough to ensure that debt holders receive their promised interest payments even in the worst state of nature, and even under all three levels of debt considered in this problem, equity holders bear *all* of the risk once debt is introduced into a firm's capital structure.

 ## M&M with Corporate Taxes

The value of the M&M theorem doesn't really lie in the wisdom of their two propositions, which are driven by the very unrealistic set of "perfect world" assumptions listed above. Instead, the value lies in examining what happens to these two propositions when we relax the unrealistic assumptions and move closer to what we see in real life.

For example, if we slightly relax the assumptions above and allow ourselves to assume that corporations are taxed and that corporate debt is perpetual and tax deductible, then the main propositions of the M&M theorem become[5]

$$\text{Proposition I (with corporate taxes): } V_L = V_U + DT_C \tag{14-5}$$

where

V_U is the value of an unlevered firm.

V_L is the value of a levered firm.

D is the level of perpetual firm debt.

T_C is the applicable coporate tax rate.

$$\text{Proposition II (with corporate taxes): } i_E = i_{E,0} + \frac{D}{E}(i_{E,0} - i_D) \times (1 - T_C) \tag{14-6}$$

where

$i_{E,0}$ is the cost of capital of capital for an all-equity firm.

i_E and i_D are the costs of equity and debt in a leveraged firm.

$$\text{Proposition IIa (with corporate taxes): } WACC = \frac{E}{E+D}i_E + \frac{D}{E+D}i_D(1-T_C) \tag{14-7}$$

which will be decreasing in $\dfrac{D}{E}$

[5]The assumption of perpetual debt makes the mathematical expressions for Propositions I and II concise: with perpetual debt, the present value of the tax shields to interest on debt are the present value of the perpetuity, $PV = [(D \times i_D) \times T_C]/i_D$, which simplifies to DT_C.

We often refer to this situation as the "The More Debt, the Better" condition. Under this condition implied by M&M, the firm's value forever increases (and the WACC forever decreases) as the firm takes on larger and larger amounts of debt, as implied in Proposition I above.

Note how a relatively minor change in our assumptions has dramatically altered the firm's suggested capital structure strategy. In the perfect world, capital structure didn't matter, so the firm was free to choose whichever level of debt it preferred. In this slightly more realistic world with corporate taxes, managers can maximize the firm's value by taking on as much debt as possible. Thus the firm should try to be as close to 100 percent debt-financed as possible.

What caused this change in optimal strategy? It's not so much that we've added taxation, but that we've added it *differentially*: any money paid out to stockholders is taxable, so that a dollar paid in dividends actually means removing $1.00/(1-T_C)$ in company earnings. On the other hand, paying a dollar in interest to service debt carries no equivalent tax "surcharge."

However, though adding corporate taxes to our environment changes the firm's optimal strategy, it doesn't really change the effect that an increase in leverage has on the stockholders' expected returns and the volatility of those returns.

 For interactive versions of this example visit www.mhhe.com/can1e

EXAMPLE 14-2

IMPACT OF LEVERAGE ON SHAREHOLDERS' EXPECTED RETURN AND VOLATILITY WITH CORPORATE TAXES

Reexamine the situation we described in Example 14-1. Now suppose that the firm faces a 35 percent tax rate; what will be the effect on expected EPS and the volatility of that EPS if the firm stays with its current capital structure or switches to either of the two proposed structures?

SOLUTION:

If the firm stays with its all-equity structure, it will have $100 million/$100 = 1 million shares outstanding, and the EPS under each state of nature will be:

STATE	RECESSION	AVERAGE	BOOM
EBIT	$10,000,000	$25,000,000	$35,000,000
− Interest	0	0	0
EBT	10,000,000	25,000,000	35,000,000
− Taxes (@35%)	3,500,000	8,750,000	12,250,000
Net income	$ 6,500,000	$16,250,000	$22,750,000
EPS	$ 6.50	$ 16.25	$ 22.75

The expected EPS and standard deviation of the EPS will be:

$$E(EPS) = .2 \times \$6.50 + .6 \times \$16.25 + .2 \times \$22.75 = \$15.60$$

$$\sigma_{EPS} = \sqrt{.2(\$6.50 - \$15.60) + .6(\$16.25 - \$15.60) + .2(\$22.75 - \$15.60)} = \$5.20$$

If the firm refinances 30 percent of the capital by selling $30 million in debt and using the proceeds to retire $30 million in equity, the interest on the debt will amount to .08 × $30 million = $2.4 million, and the firm will have $70 million/$100 = 700,000 shares outstanding, and the EPS under each state of nature will be:

(continued)

STATE	RECESSION	AVERAGE	BOOM
EBIT	$10,000,000	$25,000,000	$35,000,000
− Interest	2,400,000	2,400,000	2,400,000
EBT	7,600,000	22,600,000	32,600,000
− Taxes (@35%)	2,660,000	7,910,000	11,410,000
Net income	$ 4,940,000	$14,690,000	$ 21,190,000
EPS	$ 7.06	$ 20.99	$ 30.27

The expected EPS and standard deviation of the EPS will be:

$$E(EPS) = .2 \times \$7.06 + .6 \times \$20.99 + .2 \times \$30.27 = \$20.06$$

$$\sigma_{EPS} = \sqrt{.2(\$7.06 - \$20.06) + .6(\$20.99 - \$20.06) + .2(\$30.27 - \$20.06)} = \$7.43$$

If the firm refinances 60 percent of the capital by selling $60 million in debt and using the proceeds to retire $60 million in equity, the interest on the debt will amount to .08 × $60 million = $4.8 million, and the firm will have $40 million/$100 = 400,000 shares outstanding, and the EPS under each state of nature will be

STATE	RECESSION	AVERAGE	BOOM
EBIT	$10,000,000	$25,000,000	$35,000,000
− Interest	4,800,000	4,800,000	4,800,000
EBT	5,200,000	20,200,000	30,200,000
− Taxes (@35%)	1,820,000	7,070,000	10,570,000
Net income	$ 3,380,000	$13,130,000	$ 19,630,000
EPS	$ 8.45	$ 32.83	$ 49.08

The expected EPS and standard deviation of the EPS will be:

$$E(EPS) = .2 \times \$8.45 + .6 \times \$32.83 + .2 \times \$49.08 = \$31.20$$

$$\sigma_{EPS} = \sqrt{.2(\$8.45 - \$31.20) + .6(\$32.83 - \$31.20) + .2(\$49.08 - \$31.20)} = \$13.00$$

To summarize, the expected EPS and volatility in EPS for the three different proposed capital structures in Examples 14-1 and 14-2 are shown in Table 14.1. As we can see, adding corporate taxes to the mix reduces both the level and volatility of EPS, but increasing leverage still magnifies the expected EPS and its volatility.

A casual glance at the two versions of Proposition I that we've encountered so far, the one in equation 14-1 for the perfect world and the one in equation 14-5 for the world with corporate taxes, would probably lead one to believe that it's better to be a leveraged firm in a world with taxes: after all, $V_L = V_U + DT_C$ sounds like a good deal compared to $V_L = V_U$, right? Well, not really: We have to remember that V_U in a world with taxes is going to be less than V_U in a world without taxes, so the equations for V_L in these two versions of Proposition I really aren't comparable.

The Choice to Re-leverage

In both of the worlds we've talked about so far, we've seen that increasing the amount of firm debt increases both the expected cash flows to equity holders and the volatility of those cash flows. Considering our discussion of the CAPM and the SML back in Chapter 10, we should probably be wondering what happens to

Expected EPS and Volatility in EPS in Examples 14-1 and 14-2			table 14.1		
E(EPS)	**0% DEBT**		**30% DEBT**		**60% DEBT**
Perfect world	$24.00		$30.86		$48.00
With corporate taxes	15.60		20.06		31.20
EPS S.D.	**0% DEBT**		**30% DEBT**		**60% DEBT**
Perfect world	$ 8.00		$11.43		$20.00
With corporate taxes	5.20		7.43		13.00

For interactive versions of this example visit www.mhhe.com/can1e

EXAMPLE 14-3

UNDOING A CHANGE IN LEVERAGE

For example, let's suppose that an investor originally owned 100 shares in the unleveraged firm that we started with in Example 14-2, but that the firm switched to the proposed 30 percent debt level in its capital structure. How could the investors change their holdings so that they could return to exactly the same combination of expected return and risk that they had before the change?

SOLUTION:

Owning 100 shares in the original unleveraged firm, the shareholder would expect to receive total earnings of $650, $1,625, or $2,275 on those 100 shares, depending on the state of the economy that occurred:

STATE	RECESSION	AVERAGE	BOOM
EBIT	$10,000,000.00	$25,000,000.00	$35,000,000.00
− Interest	0	0	0
EBT	10,000,000.00	25,000,000.00	35,000,000.00
−Taxes (@35%)	3,500,000.00	8,750,000.00	12,250,000.00
Net income	$ 6,500,000.00	$16,250,000.00	$22,750,000.00
EPS	$ 6.50	$ 16.25	$ 22.75
Average EPS	$ 15.60		
EPS S.D.	$ 5.20		
Shareholder earnings	$ 650.00	$ 1,625.00	$ 2,275.00
Average earnings	$ 1,560.00		
Earnings S.D.	$ 520.00		

Once the firm re-leveraged, that same shareholder would face a stream of earnings that would be, on average, higher than before, but also more volatile:

STATE	RECESSION	AVERAGE	BOOM
EBIT	$10,000,000.00	$25,000,000.00	$35,000,000.00
−Interest	$ 2,400,000.00	$ 2,400,000.00	$ 2,400,000.00
−Taxes (@35%)	$ 2,660,000.00	$ 7,910,000.00	11,410,000.00
EPS	$ 7.06	$ 20.99	$ 30.27
EPS S.D.	$ 7.43		
Shareholder earnings	$ 705.71	$ 2,098.57	$ 3,027.14
Average earnings	$ 2,005.71		
Earnings S.D.	$ 742.86		

(continued)

To undo the firm's "leveraging up" move, the shareholder would need to "leverage down." That is, since the firm borrowed 30 percent of its capital structure, shareholders would need to lend 30 percent of their own personal investment portfolios to counter that borrowing. To do so, they would sell 30 of their 100 shares, which would yield $30 \times \$100$ per share = $3,000. They would then turn around and invest this $3,000 in the firm's bonds. The bonds would earn a before-tax return of $\$3,000 \times .08 = \$240$ per year, or $\$240 \times (1 - .35) = \$156$ per year after taxes. Combining these after-tax earnings with the after-tax earnings on the 70 shares of stock they still owned would give them the exact same distribution of total earnings they would have earned if the firm hadn't leveraged up:

STATE	RECESSION	AVERAGE	BOOM
After-tax earnings on 3 bonds	$156	$ 156	$ 156
After-tax earnings on 70 shares	494	1,469	2,119
Total after-tax earnings	650	1,625	2,275

the firm's investors if it decides to change its capital structure. If they were happiest with the mix of risk and expected return the firm was offering before, are they going to be upset if they are "booted" off their optimal mix to something that has a different mixture of risk and expected return?

So far, the answer is no. Remember that the worlds we've been working in so far assume perfectly efficient capital markets, implying that any investors who were unhappy with a change in the firm's capital structure would be able to costlessly undo any changes inflicted upon them.

EXAMPLE 14-4

 For interactive versions of this example visit www.mhhe.com/can1e

 ### EXCEEDING THE FIRM'S LEVERAGE

Assume that the firm in the previous example decided not to add debt to its capital structure, but one of its investors, who currently owns 50 shares in the company, has decided that she would like to have the same risk/expected return combination that she would have had if the firm had adopted a capital structure that was 60 percent debt. What could this investor do?

SOLUTION:

Since she currently owns 50 shares in the unleveraged firm, her "starting" wealth will be equal to $50 \times \$100 = \$5,000$, and she is facing a distribution of total earnings per period, dependent on the state of the economy, that look like this:

STATE	RECESSION	AVERAGE	BOOM
EBIT	$10,000,000	$25,000,000	$35,000,000
−Interest	0	0	0
EBT	10,000,000	25,000,000	35,000,000
−Taxes (@35%)	3,500,000	8,750,000	12,250,000
Net income	$ 6,500,000	$16,250,000	$22,750,000
EPS	$ 6.50	$ 16.25	$ 22.75
Average EPS	$ 15.60		
EPS S.D.	$ 5.20		
Shareholder earnings	$ 325.00	$ 812.50	$ 1,137.50
Average earnings	$ 780.00		
Earnings S.D.	$ 260.00		

(continued)

She would rather have a distribution that looks like this:

STATE	RECESSION	AVERAGE	BOOM
EBIT	$10,000,000	$25,000,000	$35,000,000
−Interest	4,800,000	4,800,000	4,800,000
EBT	5,200,000	20,200,000	30,200,000
−Taxes (@35%)	1,820,000	7,070,000	10,570,000
Net income	$ 3,380,000	$ 13,130,000	$19,630,000
EPS	$ 8.45	$ 32.83	$ 49.08
Average EPS	$ 31.20		
EPS S.D.	$ 13.00		
Shareholder earnings	$ 422.50	$ 1,641.25	$ 2,453.75
Average earnings	$ 1,560.00		
Earnings S.D.	$ 650.00		

To replicate this distribution of earnings across the possible states of the economy, she will need to borrow enough money, B, so that the borrowed money will be 60 percent of the total amount and that her initial capital will be 1 − .60 = 40% of the total amount she will invest in the stock:

$$\$5,000 = .4(\$5,000 + B)$$

$$\frac{\$5,000}{.4} - \$5,000 = B$$

$$\$12,500 - \$5,000 = B$$

$$\$7,500 = B$$

If she follows this strategy, borrowing $7,500 and putting the entire $12,500 into the stock of the nonleveraged firm, then she will have to pay .08 × $7,500 = $390 in interest no matter what the state of the economy is, and her distribution of net payoffs will be exactly the same as if she had been able to buy shares in a leveraged firm:

STATE	RECESSION	AVERAGE	BOOM
After-tax payments on $7,500 loan	−$390.00	−$ 390.00	−$ 390.00
After-tax earnings on 125 shares	$812.50	$2,031.25	$2,843.75
Total after-tax earnings	$422.50	$1,641.25	$2,453.75

Note that investors could also leverage themselves *more* than the firm if they wished to. All they would have to do is to borrow enough money and invest it in stock along with the money they started with, so that the ratio of borrowed money to their initial money was set equal to the D/E ratio that they wished the firm had chosen.

Break-Even EBIT and EBIT Expectations

The last few examples have had us examining what we expect the distribution of EPS to look like, given a particular choice of capital structure. It's also possible that to analyze this issue "backwards," solving for a particular expected EPS level would make investors indifferent between two proposed capital structures. To do so, we simply need to express EPS for each capital structure as a function of EBIT, set the two EPS expressions equal to one another, and then solve for the EBIT level that will solve the equality, called the **break-even EBIT.**

LEVERAGED BUYOUTS (LBOS)

One of the most extreme examples of firm re-leveraging occurs when someone uses a firm's debt capacity to buy out the majority of the firm's equity holders. Such a *leveraged buyout* is designed to allow the acquirer to gain control of a firm without having to commit a lot of capital.

A typical LBO uses a ratio of 70 percent debt to 30 percent equity, although debt can reach as high as 90 percent to 95 percent of the target company's total capitalization. In fact, when LBOs first became popular back in the 1960s, they were originally known as *bootstrap* transactions, a reference to the expression "pulling yourself up by your own bootstraps," which reflected the general consensus that the firm was, more or less, paying for its own acquisition.

 want to know more? **Key Words to Search for Updates:** See "syndicated loan," "Management buyout," and LBO.

EXAMPLE 14-5

 For interactive versions of this example visit www.mhhe.com/can1e

 ## CALCULATING BREAK-EVEN EBIT

Calculate the break-even EBIT between the all-equity and 30-percent-debt capital structures for the firm used in the previous examples.

SOLUTION:

Remember that the formula for EPS is net income divided by the number of shares, and that, for an all-equity firm, EBIT will be the same as EBT. Then EPS for the all-equity firm can be written as:

$$EPS_{All-equity} = \frac{EBIT(1-T_c)}{\text{Number of shares}}$$

$$= \frac{EBIT(1-.35)}{1,000,000}$$

For the capital structure with 30-percent debt, EPS can be expressed as:

$$EPS_{30\%\,Debt} = \frac{(EBIT - \text{Interest})(1-T_c)}{\text{Number of shares}}$$

$$= \frac{(EBIT - \$2,400,000)(1-.35)}{700,000}$$

Setting these two equations equal to one another and solving for EBIT will give us the break-even EBIT:

$$EPS_{30\%\,Debt} = EPS_{All-equity}$$

$$\frac{(EBIT - \$2,400,000)(1-.35)}{700,000} = \frac{EBIT(1-.35)}{1,000,000}$$

$$\frac{.65EBIT - \$1,560,000}{700,000} = \frac{.65EBIT}{1,000,000}$$

$$650,000EBIT - \$1,560,000,000,000 = 455,000EBIT$$

$$195,000EBIT = \$1,560,000,000,000$$

$$EBIT = \frac{\$1,560,000,000,000}{195,000}$$

$$EBIT = \$8,000,000$$

(continued)

To show that this level of EBIT really will set EPS equal for the two alternative capital structures, we can compute the two EPS figures and compare:

$$EPS_{All-equity} = \frac{EBIT(1-.35)}{1,000,000}$$

$$= \frac{\$8,000,000(1-.35)}{1,000,000}$$

$$= \$5.20$$

vs.

$$EPS_{30\% Debt} = \frac{(EBIT - \$2,400,000)(1-.35)}{700,000}$$

$$= \frac{(\$8,000,000 - \$2,400,000)(1-.35)}{700,000}$$

$$= \$5.20$$

TIME OUT

14-3 Why does the optimal capital structure shift from "debt doesn't matter" to "the more debt, the better" when we add corporate taxation to our assumptions?

14-4 If a firm increases its leverage and one of its shareholders doesn't like the EPS impact of the change, how can the firm undo the effects of the change?

14.3 M&M with Corporate Taxes and Bankruptcy

We can relax the final M&M unrealistic assumption by allowing for the possibility that the firm may go bankrupt. By doing this, we imply that the firm's debt holders will have to allow for the possibility that they might not receive everything they've been promised. In this more realistic type of situation, bondholders will be asked to bear some firm risk. Debt holders will thus ask for a little more compensation than they would if our "perfect world" assumptions held true.

As discussed below, it turns out that a firm needn't actually go bankrupt for the costs of financial distress to start affecting firm value.

Types of Bankruptcies in the United States

The United States' Bankruptcy Code allows for two types of bankruptcy for which most businesses can file. We generally refer to the two types by the chapter of that code that describes the procedure for each—**Chapter 7** and **Chapter 11** bankruptcies.

Chapter 7 bankruptcy involves a business liquidation. When the firm files for Chapter 7, it must immediately cease operations, and the bankruptcy court will very quickly appoint a trustee whose primary responsibility will be to sell the firm's assets and use the proceeds to pay off as many claimants as possible.

These claimants are paid according to the absolute priority rule in the following order:

1. *Secured lenders,* including bondholders where the bonds give them liens on specific assets.

2. *Lawyers,* primarily those handling the bankruptcy for the company.

3. *Employees.*
4. *Government.*
5. *Unsecured debt holders.*
6. *Equity holders.*

Depending on the size and number of claims above them, unsecured debt holders (such as those who hold debentures) rarely receive all the money owed them in a Chapter 7 liquidation. Stockholders seldom receive much at all.

A Chapter 11 bankruptcy, on the other hand, involves an attempt to allow the firm to reorganize the business under court supervision. When a firm files for Chapter 11, it is allowed to remain in operation, but its creditors must refrain from contacting the company about due debts except through the bankruptcy court. This explains why you will sometimes hear a Chapter 11 filing referred to as the company seeking *protection*.

Once a company files for Chapter 11, all of its creditors must register with the bankruptcy court and may file informational briefs concerning their preferences for the form that the firm reorganization will take. The court will consider this input and will try to come up with a reorganized capital structure for the firm that follows the guidelines in Section 507 of the bankruptcy code. In general, such reorganizations usually involve maintaining (in some form) any higher claimants' stake in the firm, but it is not unusual for the process to result in a reorganization plan that involves canceling unsecured debt.

Within a period of a few months to several years, companies that file for Chapter 11 may "emerge" from bankruptcy if a proposed reorganization plan gains approval by a sufficient majority[6] of the firm's debt holders. The firm may also find their bankruptcy converted to a Chapter 7 filing if the court feels that the firm is not viable, or if a sufficient majority of the firm's debt holders can't agree on a reorganization plan.

Costs of Financial Distress

A firm filing for bankruptcy will most certainly incur some substantial costs, such as fees to lawyers, consultants, and accountants, in addition to the reorganization or restructuring costs. However, a long list of costs is incurred if a firm even *gets close* to bankruptcy—a situation called *financial distress*.

When firms come close to bankruptcy (or if they are *perceived* as being close to bankruptcy), many groups start treating those troubled firms differently:

- Customers may be leery of buying from them, especially if buyers are concerned about post-sales support.

- Suppliers will be concerned about selling to the firm, particularly on credit, so sellers will start to tighten the credit terms they offer the firm.

- Other firms will be less likely to offer the firm valuable partnering opportunities, decreasing the number of wealth-enhancing projects the firm might be able to choose from.

- The firm's better employees may decide to look elsewhere for jobs, resulting in a loss of efficiency in the firm's operations.

---

[6]Proposed reorganization plans must meet with approval of two-thirds of outstanding claimants in terms of dollars due and one-half of claimants by numbers.

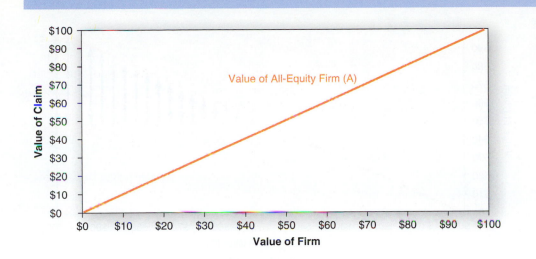

figure 14.1

Total Value of Equity in an All-Equity Firm

figure 14.2

Value of Bondholders' Claim Against Firm

EQUITY AS A CALL OPTION ON THE VALUE OF THE FIRM   If the firm gets close enough to bankruptcy that the equity market value is close to worthless, even the equity holders may start treating the firm differently. To see why, let's envision what the payoff diagram for equity in a leveraged firm looks like.

In an all-equity firm, the total value of equity will simply equal the firm value. Thus if we graph the value of the equity holders' claims against the firm, value will simply be a 45-degree line, as illustrated in Figure 14.1.

However, if we allow debt holders into the firm, the bondholders' claims will take precedence over those of equity holders, up to the amount of promised repayment. So the *debt holders'* claims will be equal to that shown by the yellow line in Figure 14.2. In such a situation, the equity holders will receive a residual claim, equal to the amount left over after debt holders have been paid. The size of this claim is represented by the area highlighted in Figure 14.3.

figure 14.3

Residual Value of Equity in Firm

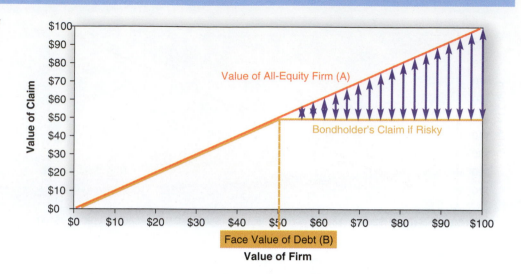

figure 14.4

Stockholders' Claim with Debt in the Firm

Taking the absolute magnitude of this portion of the equity holders' claim, along with the minimum equity value of zero implied by equity's limited liability attribute, the payoff to the entire claim of the equity holders will appear as shown in Figure 14.4.

As you can see, the size of the equity holders' claim if the firm were not leveraged would be divided into two parts—a debt holders' portion and an equity holders' portion—if the firm became leveraged. This payoff diagram is interesting because this payoff diagram for equity holders looks exactly like the payoff to someone who owns a **long position** on a **call option.** A call option is a contract that gives the owner the right, but not the obligation, to purchase an underlying asset at a certain price. In this case, the equity in a leveraged firm has the right to "buy" the firm back from the debt holders by paying them an amount, B, that the debt holders are due under the debt contract.

THE OVERINVESTMENT AND UNDERINVESTMENT PROBLEMS
More important, equity actually represents a very special case of a long call position, one in which the call owners (the equity holders) presumably also have some control over the potential value of the underlying asset through their choice of investment projects between now and when the debt is due.

figure 14.5

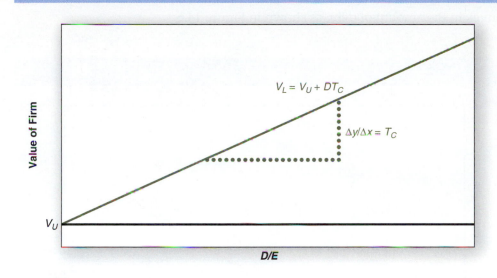

Envision a leveraged firm that has assets with a current value of exactly ($B − $1,000,000), all currently held in cash. Also assume that the firm has one more chance to invest in a project before $B are due to the debt holders, and that management is trying to choose between two projects, both of which will cost the entire ($B − $1,000,000) stock of cash. Project X will return $B with no risk. Project Y will return ($B + $5,000,000) with a probability of 1 percent and $0 with a probability of 99 percent.

Ignoring TVM, project X's NPV will be $B − ($B − $1,000,000) = $1,000,000, while project Y's expected NPV will be .01 × [($B + $5,000,000) − ($B − $1,000,000)] + .99 × [$0 − ($B − $1,000,000)] = $60,000 − .99 × ($B−$1,000,000). As long as $B is greater than $60,606.06 (which seems likely, given that project X is offering a risk-free return of $1,000,000), project X's NPV will be greater than project Y's expected NPV, and we would expect the firm to chose project X, right?

Wrong: if stockholders have their way, the firm will choose project Y every time. Why? Because on the slim chance that it pays off, they will have $5 million above what they need to pay to the debt holders. In the very probable event that the project fails to return any money, thereby losing the entire investment. . . . well, it wasn't like the equity holders were ever going to get any of that money, anyway, because they would just have had to pay it out to the debt holders if they hadn't invested it in this project.

We call this tendency on stockholders' part in leveraged firms—where equity is close to being worthless—to invest in arguably bad projects "gambling with other people's money" or, more formally, the **overinvestment problem.** Equity holders' associated decision not to invest in the safe project X—because the resulting increase in wealth from ($B − $1,000,000) to $B would simply go to the debt holders—the **underinvestment problem.**

The Value of the Firm with Taxes *and* Bankruptcy

We modeled the functional relationship between the impact of debt on firm value and the tax rate in the previous section under the assumption that debt was perpetual. This impact of debt on firm value represents a fairly well-known, linear relationship, with the slope being equal to the tax rate, as shown in Figure 14.5.

The relationship between the amount of debt and the expected costs of bankruptcy or financial distress is not as well known. We've discussed some of the factors that we believe can reasonably affect this relationship. In light of that discussion, we're going to assume that the relationship between the amount of debt and the expected costs of bankruptcy or financial distress is nonlinear and convex in the amount of debt, as shown in Figure 14.6.

figure 14.6

Financial Distress Costs as a Function of D/E

So let's combine the linearly increasing benefits to debt created by the interest tax shield with nonlinearly increasing costs to debt posed by the potential costs of financial distress. Doing so, we will eventually come to a point where we're increasing the D/E ratio of the firm beyond which the marginal costs of financial distress starts to outweigh the marginal benefits of the interest tax shield. Such a situation is shown in Figure 14.7.

Exactly which D/E level will be optimal for a particular firm will depend on both the firm's tax rate and how quickly the potential costs of financial distress increase as a function of debt. For example, a firm with a very low marginal tax rate would have the financial distress costs offsetting the tax deductibility of

figure 14.7

Value of Leveraged Firm: Taxes and Bankruptcy

interest very quickly (i.e., at a low level of D/E), while a firm with a large debt capacity/high marginal tax rate would find a higher level of D/E optimal.

In this world (as opposed to M&M's ideal world), we can write a version of M&M's Proposition I as long as we're willing to be rather vague about the functional relationship between debt and the costs of financial distress, However, we really can't formulate an analogous form of Proposition II because doing so would require us to come up with a more specific function of the costs of financial distress than we're capable of.

Proposition I (with corporate taxes and bankruptcy):

$$V_L = V_U + DT_C - PV \text{ (costs of financial distress)} \tag{14-8}$$

where

V_U is the value of an unlevered firm.

V_L is the value of a levered firm.

D is the level of perpetual firm debt.

T_C is the applicable corporate tax rate.

If we could write a nice, concise functional form for Proposition II in this world, it would still have i_E increasing in the D/E ratio. But the rate of increase would be nonlinear since, as the amount of debt in the firm got larger and larger, making the probability/costs of bankruptcy increasingly higher, the debt holders would have to bear some of that risk.

Likewise, a form of Proposition IIa would have the WACC decreasing up until the optimal debt level was achieved, but increasing past that point. In effect, the WACC would initially be decreasing as the firm switched from the "expensive" capital (i.e., equity) to the "cheap" capital (debt). But in this world the debt wouldn't stay cheap but would itself get more and more expensive as the firm used more of it because the debt holders would ask for a higher and higher rate of return to compensate them for the increasingly higher chance of bankruptcy. Past the optimal debt level, it would just be too expensive to use more of it.

TIME OUT

14-5 What causes the overinvestment problem discussed in this section?

14-6 If the bondholders of a firm in financial distress felt that they could recoup more of their investment by renegotiating their claims with the firm and allowing it to continue to operate, what type of bankruptcy would they probably push for?

14.4 Capital Structure Theory versus Reality

Optimal Theoretical Capital Structure

Based on our discussions of M&M's theory of optimal capital structure, we can't develop a closed-end formula that will definitively tell us how much debt a particular firm should have in its capital structure, but we can come up with a list of factors that should affect firms' capital structures:

- Firms facing relatively high tax rates should make more use of debt.
- Firms with stable, predictable income streams will be able to worry less about unexpected fluctuations in income driving the company into financial distress and hence should also be able to make more use of debt than would otherwise be the case.

Business Application Solution

If she re-leverages, Kieran will be financing 50 percent of the assets, or $15,000, with debt. The tax savings per year will be equal to:

$$\$15,000 \times .095 \times .15 = \$213.75$$

And the present value of those tax savings, assuming that they continue on indefinitely, will be:

$$\frac{\$213.75}{.095} = \$2,250$$

Personal Application Solution

Since both the first mortgage and the home-equity loan would be tax deductible under current IRS guidelines, Gunter's weighted-average after-tax interest rate will be equal to $.8 \times 5.875\% \times (1-.35) + .2 \times 7.90\% \times (1-.35) = 4.082\%$.

Figure 14.8

Average D/E Ratios for Major Sectors of U.S. Economy

Source: *Yahoo!* http://biz. yahoo.com/p/sectors.html

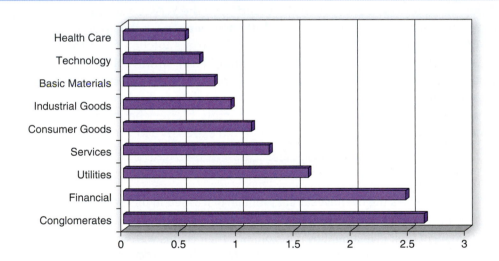

Observed Capital Structures

Though debt levels vary, the general levels of debt we see across segments of our economy do tend to follow these rough rules. As shown in Figure 14.8, the sectors of the U.S. economy with the lowest D/E ratios—health care and technology—both tend to have quite variable income streams, and the sectors with the highest D/E ratios—utilities, financial, and conglomerates—tend to have high, stable income streams.

TIME OUT

14-7 What effect is the "graying of America" (i.e., the approach of the baby boomers to retirement age) likely to have on debt ratios in the health care industry? Why?

14-8 Explain why utility companies tend to have fairly high debt ratios.

summary of learning goals

This chapter has explored the concept of the firm's optimal capital structure. While we were not able to construct a closed-form equation to tell us exactly how much debt a particular firm should take on, we were able to identify the attributes of the firm that should affect such a decision.

LG1 **Differentiate between active and passive changes to capital structure.** When firms wish to change their capital structure, they will often do so gradually by raising capital for new projects gradually to minimize underwriting costs. This passive approach is in contrast with the firm actively selling one type of financial claim (usually debt) and using the proceeds to retire another type of capital (usually equity).

LG2 **Demonstrate why finance professionals refer to debt as "leverage" in firms' capital structures.** Debt in the firm's capital structure magnifies both the potential earning power of equity and its volatility or risk.

LG3 **Show how the firm apportions risk and return among stockholders and bondholders in a "perfect world."** In such a world, the entire "layers" of risk and return are split between the equity holders and the debt holders, but they're not split proportionately. Equity holders, in agreeing to take more than their fair share of the risk of the firm, also get a disproportionately large portion of the return, too.

LG4 **Describe how optimal capital structure changes when we relax the assumption of no corporate taxation—at which point the optimal capital structure becomes one in which "The More Debt, the Better" applies.** With corporate taxation, the tax-deductibility of the interest payments to debt holders means that such payments are partially subsidized by the taxing authority, making them more attractive. Since we have not yet relaxed the assumption of no chance of bankruptcy, this attractiveness applies no matter how much debt is used, so a capital structure that is as close as possible to all-debt will maximize the subsidy and minimize the firm's WACC.

LG5 **Demonstrate how individual shareholders can mimic or reverse firm capital structure changes by borrowing and lending on their own account for investing in that firm's shares.** Individual shareholders can choose to borrow part of their investment in the firm's stock if they wish to increase their own personal leverage, or they can choose to lend part of their personal wealth if they wish to reduce their personal leverage.

LG6 **Calculate the EBIT and EPS levels at which shareholders will become indifferent about the choice between two alternative capital structures.** We can calculate the break-even EBIT by setting EPS as a function of the firm's EBIT at two different capital structures equal to one another and then solving for the level of EBIT that makes this equality hold.

LG7 **Describe how the firm's choice of optimal capital structure changes if we allow for the possibility of bankruptcy.** Once we relax the "no possibility of bankruptcy" assumption from M&M's perfect world, increasing the firm's debt level increases both this probability and the expected costs of financial distress. Past a certain level of debt, increasing the debt further will cause the expected costs of financial distress to increase more than will the benefits of the tax-deductibility of interest.

LG8 **Argue whether the theoretical basis for firms' choices of optimal capital structure seem to reflect real-world business practices.** As observed from real data, firms that have higher chances of financial distress tend to use less debt, while those firms for whom the tax benefits are substantial tend to use more. This more or less confirms the theory derived from M&M's work.

chapter equations

14-1 Proposition I (perfect world): $V_L = V_U$

14-2 Proposition II (perfect world): $i_E = i_{E,0} + \dfrac{D}{E}(i_{E,0} - i_D)$

14-3 $i_E = i_{E,0} + \dfrac{D}{E}(i_{E,0} - i_D)$

14-4 Proposition IIa (perfect world): $WACC = i_{E,0} = \dfrac{E}{E+D}i_E + \dfrac{D}{E+D}i_D$

14-5 Proposition I (with corporate taxes): $V_L = V_U + DT_C$

14-6 Proposition II (with corporate taxes): $i_E = i_{E,0} + \dfrac{D}{E}(i_{E,0} - i_D) \times (1 - T_C)$

14-7 Proposition IIa (with corporate taxes):

$$WACC = \frac{E}{E+D}i_E + \frac{D}{E+D}i_D(1 - T_C)$$

14-8 Proposition I (with corporate taxes and bankruptcy): $V_L = V_U + DT_C - PV$ (costs of financial distress)

key terms

active capital structure management, The policy of selling one type of claim (debt or equity) explicitly to retire the other type. (p. 458)

break-even EBIT, The level of EBIT at which EPS will be equal for two different capital structures. (p. 469)

call option, A derivative instrument that grants the holder the right, but not the obligation, to buy the underlying asset at some prespecified price for a finite length of time. (p. 474)

capital structure, The mixture of debt and equity used to finance the firm's operations. (p. 456)

capital structure irrelevance assertion, Another name for the Modigliani-Miller theorem. (p. 459)

Chapter 7 bankruptcy, Form of bankruptcy in which the firm is liquidated, with the assets sold off to satisfy the claims of the capital providers. (p. 471)

Chapter 11 bankruptcy, Form of bankruptcy in which the firm seeks to reorganize, restructuring debt claims to remain viable. (p. 471)

financial distress, The condition in which a firm is near bankruptcy. (p. 456)

leverage, Another name for debt in the capital structure. (p. 459)

long position, The position of buying and owning a particular security, which will show a profit if the security increases in value. (p. 474)

Modigliani–Miller (M&M) theorem, In an efficient market without taxes and bankruptcy costs, the value of a firm does not depend upon the firm's capital structure. (p. 459)

overinvestment problem, A situation that arises when a firm's equity is close to worthless, equity holders will prefer to invest in overly risky projects with a small chance of success rather than simply paying debt holders their regularly scheduled payments. (p. 475)

passive capital structure management, The policy of changing the capital structure gradually over time by funding new capital projects disproportionately with the type of capital you want to increase in the capital structure. (p. 459)

separation principle, The assumption that decisions about *which* projects to fund are separate from the decisions about *how* to fund them. (p. 460)

underinvestment problem, The situation that arises when a firm's equity is close to worthless, equity holders will prefer not to invest in safe projects. (p. 475)

self-test problems with solutions

1 **Computing Expected Return and Standard Deviation in a Perfect World**
ILKD, Inc., doesn't face any taxes or chance of bankruptcy and has $500 million in assets, currently financed entirely with equity. Equity is worth $80 per share, and book value of equity is equal to market value of equity. Also, let's assume that the firm's expected values for EBIT depend on which state of the economy occurs this year, with the possible values of EBIT and their associated probabilities as shown below:

LG2, LG3

STATE	RECESSION	AVERAGE	BOOM
Probability of state	.15	.55	.30
Expect EBIT in state	$2 million	$15 million	$25 million

The firm is considering switching to a 30-percent debt capital structure and has determined that they would have to pay a 10 percent yield on perpetual debt whether or not they change their capital structure. What will be the effect on expected EPS and the volatility of that EPS if they switch to the proposed capital structure?

Solution:

Expected values of and standard deviations of EPS will be as shown below:

EPS WITHOUT DEBT

STATEW	RECESSION	AVERAGE	BOOM
EBIT	$2,000,000	$15,000,000	$25,000,000
− Interest	0	0	0
EBT	2,000,000	15,000,000	25,000,000
− Taxes	0	0	0
Net income	$2,000,000	$15,000,000	$25,000,000
EPS	$ 3.20	$ 24.00	$ 40.00
EPS S.D.	$ 11.78		

EPS WITH 30% DEBT

STATE	RECESSION	AVERAGE	BOOM
EBIT	$2,000,000	$15,000,000	$25,000,000
− Interest	1,500,000	1,500,000	1,500,000
EBT	500,000	13,500,000	23,500,000
− Taxes	0	0	0
Net income	$ 500,000	$13,500,000	$23,500,000
EPS	$ 1.14	$ 30.86	$ 53.71
Average EPS	$ 33.26		
EPS S.D.	$ 16.83		

As expected, the expected EPS is larger if the firm is leveraged, but so is the standard deviation of EPS.

2 **Impact of Leverage on Expected Return and Volatility with Corporate Taxes** Reexamine the situation described in Problem ST-1, but now suppose that the firm faces a 34 percent tax rate. What will be the effect on expected EPS and the volatility of that EPS if the firm stays with its current capital structure or switches to either of the two proposed structures?

LG4

www.mhhe.com/can1e

481

Solution:

The expected values and standard deviations for EPS will be as shown below:

EPS WITHOUT DEBT

STATE	RECESSION	AVERAGE	BOOM
EBIT	$2,000,000.00	$15,000,000.00	$25,000,000.00
− Interest	0	0	0
EBT	2,000,000.00	15,000,000.00	25,000,000.00
− Taxes (@34%)	680,000.00	5,100,000.00	8,500,000.00
Net income	$ 1,320,000.00	$ 9,900,000.00	$ 16,500,000.00
EPS	$ 2.11	$ 15.84	$ 26.40.00
Average EPS	$ 16.95		
EPS S.D.	$ 7.78		

EPS WITH 30% DEBT

STATE	RECESSION	AVERAGE	BOOM
EBIT	$2,000,000.00	$15,000,000.00	$25,000,000.00
− Interest	1,500,000.00	1,500,000.00	1,500,000.00
EBT	500,000.00	13,500,000.00	23,500,000.00
− Taxes (@34%)	170,000.00	4,590,000.00	7,990,000.00
Net income	$ 330,000.00	$ 8,910,000.00	$ 15,510,000.00
EPS	$ 0.75	$ 20.37	$ 35.45
Average EPS	$ 21.95		
EPS S.D.	$ 11.11		

(3) **Undoing a Change in Leverage** Let's suppose that investors originally owned 100 shares each in the unleveraged firm that we started with in ST-2, but that the firm switched to the proposed 30 percent debt level in its capital structure. How could the investors change their holdings to return themselves to exactly the same combination of expected return and risk that they had before the change?

Solution:

Owning 100 shares in the original, unleveraged firm, the shareholders would expect to receive total earnings of $211.20, $1,584.00, or $2,640.00 on those 100 shares, depending on the state of the economy that occurred.

EPS WITHOUT DEBT

STATE	RECESSION	AVERAGE	BOOM
EBIT	$2,000,000.00	$15,000,000.00	$25,000,000.00
− Interest	0	0	0
EBT	2,000,000.00	15,000,000.00	25,000,000.00
− Taxes (@35%)	680,000.00	5,100,000.00	8,500,000.00
Net income	$ 1,320,000.00	$ 9,900,000.00	$ 16,500,000.00
EPS	$ 2.11	$ 15.84	$ 26.40
Average EPS	$ 16.95		
EPS S.D.	$ 7.78		
Shareholder earnings	$ 211.20	$ 1,584.00	$ 2,640.00
Average earnings	$ 1,694.88		
Earnings S.D.	$ 777.77		

Once the firm re-leveraged, those same shareholders would face a stream of earnings that would be, on average, higher than before, but also more volatile:

EPS WITH 30% DEBT

STATE	RECESSION	AVERAGE	BOOM
EBIT	$2,000,000.00	$15,000,000.00	$25,000,000.00
−Interest	1,500,000.00	1,500,000.00	1,500,000.00
EBT	500,000.00	13,500,000.00	23,500,000.00
−Taxes (@35%)	170,000.00	4,590,000.00	7,990,000.00
Net income	$ 330,000.00	$ 8,910,000.00	$ 15,510,000.00
EPS	$ 0.75	$ 20.37	$ 35.45
Average EPS	$ 21.95		
EPS S.D.	$ 11.11		
Shareholder earnings	$ 75.43	$ 2,036.57	$ 3,545.14
Average earnings	$ 2,194.97		
Earnings S.D.	$ 1,111.11		

To undo the firm "leveraging up," the shareholders would need to "leverage down"; that is, since the firm borrowed 30 percent of its capital structure, the shareholders would need to lend 30 percent of their own personal investment portfolio to counter that out. To do so, they would sell 30 out of their 100 shares, which would yield 30 × $80 per share = $2,400. They would then turn around and invest this $2,400 in the firm's bonds, which would earn a before-tax return of $2,400 × .10 = $240 per year, or $240 × (1−.34) = $158.40 per year after taxes. Combining these after-tax earnings with the after-tax earnings on the 70 shares of stock they still owned would give them the exact same distribution of total earnings they would have earned if the firm hadn't leveraged up.

After-tax earnings on $2,400 invested in bonds	$158.40	$ 158.40	$ 158.40
After-tax earnings on 70 shares	$ 52.80	$1,425.60	$2,481.60
Total after-tax earnings	$ 211.20	$1,584.00	$2,640.00

4 **Calculating Break-Even EBIT:** Calculate the break-even EBIT between the all-equity and 30-percent-debt capital structures for the firm used in the previous problems.

LG6

Solution:

EPS for the all-equity firm can be written as:

$$EPS_{All-equity} = \frac{EBIT(1 - T_C)}{\#\,of\,shares}$$
$$= \frac{EBIT(1 - .34)}{625,000}$$

For the capital structure with 30-percent debt, EPS can be expressed as:

$$EPS_{30\%\,Debt} = \frac{(EBIT - Interest)(1 - T_C)}{\#\,of\,shares}$$
$$= \frac{(EBIT - \$1,500,000)(1 - .34)}{437,500}$$

Setting these two equations equal to one another and solving for EBIT will give us the break-even EBIT:

$$EPS_{30\%Debt} = EPS_{All-equity}$$

$$\frac{(EBIT - \$1{,}500{,}000)(1 - .34)}{437{,}500} = \frac{EBIT(1 - .34)}{625{,}000}$$

$$\frac{.66EBIT - \$990{,}000}{437{,}500} = \frac{.66EBIT}{625{,}000}$$

$$412{,}500EBIT - \$618{,}750{,}000{,}000 = 288{,}750EBIT$$

$$123{,}750EBIT = \$618{,}750{,}000{,}000$$

$$EBIT = \frac{\$618{,}750{,}000{,}000}{123{,}750}$$

$$EBIT = \$5{,}000{,}000$$

questions

1. How will passive and active capital structure changes differ? *(LG1)*

2. Why is debt often referred to as *leverage* in finance? *(LG2)*

3. In M&M's perfect world, will the debt holders ever bear any of the risk of the firm? *(LG3)*

4. Why does allowing for the existence of corporate taxation cause firms to prefer the maximum amount of debt possible? *(LG4)*

5. If a firm increased the amount of debt in its capital structure, but a shareholder wanted to switch back to the mixture of expected return and risk she had before the switch, how would she go about doing so? *(LG5)*

6. If an investor wanted to reduce the risk of a levered stock in their portfolio, how could they go about doing so while still retaining shares in the company? *(LG5)*

7. Suppose you were the financial manager for a firm and were considering a proposed increase in the amount of debt in the firm's capital structure. If you thought the firm was going to consistently earn a level of EBIT above its break-even level of EBIT (based on the current and proposed new capital structures) would this cause you to prefer leveraging the firm up or staying at your current capital structure? *(LG6)*

8. Explain why, in a world with both corporate taxes and the chance of bankruptcy, a small firm with volatile EBIT is unlikely to have much debt. *(LG7)*

9. If the U.S. government completely eliminated taxation at the corporate level, how would this influence the capital structures of firms in a world with bankruptcy? *(LG7)*

10. Would you expect a utility company to have high or low debt levels? Why? *(LG8)*

problems

basic problems

14-1 Capital Structure Weights Suppose that Lil John Industries' equity is currently selling for $37 per share and that there are 2 million shares outstanding. If the firm also has 50,000 bonds outstanding, which are selling at 103 percent of par, what are the firm's current capital structure weights? *(LG3)*

14-2 Restructuring Strategy In the previous problem, suppose that Lil John was considering an active change to its capital structure so that the firm would have a D/E of 1.4. Which type of security (stocks or bonds) would Lil John need to sell to accomplish this, and how much would it have to sell? *(LG1)*

14-3 Capital Structure Weights Suppose that Papa Bell Inc.'s equity is currently selling for $55 per share, with 4 million shares outstanding. If the firm also has 7,000 bonds outstanding, which are selling at 94 percent of par, what are the firm's current capital structure weights? *(LG3)*

14-4 Restructuring Strategy In the previous problem, suppose that Papa Bell was considering an active change to its capital structure so as to have a D/E of .4. Which type of security (stocks or bonds) would it need to sell to accomplish this, and how much would it have to sell? *(LG1)*

intermediate problems

14-5 Expected EPS after Leveraging Daddi Mac, Inc., doesn't face any taxes and has $350 million in assets, currently financed entirely with equity. Equity is worth $37 per share, and book value of equity is equal to market value of equity. Also, let's assume that the firm's expected values for EBIT depend on which state of the economy occurs this year, with the possible values of EBIT and their associated probabilities as shown below:

STATE	RECESSION	AVERAGE	BOOM
Probability of state	.25	.55	.20
Expect EBIT in state	$5 million	$10 million	$17 million

The firm is considering switching to a 20 percent debt capital structure and has determined that they would have to pay an 8 percent yield on perpetual debt in either event. What will be the level of expected EPS if they switch to the proposed capital structure? *(LG3)*

14-6 Standard Deviation in EPS after Leveraging Daddi Mac, Inc., doesn't face any taxes and has $350 million in assets, currently financed entirely with equity. Equity is worth $37 per share, and book value of equity is equal to market value of equity. Also, let's assume that the firm's expected values for EBIT are dependent on which state of the economy occurs this year, with the possible values of EBIT and their associated probabilities as shown below:

STATE	RECESSION	AVERAGE	BOOM
Probability of state	.25	.55	.20
Expect EBIT in state	$5 million	$10 million	$17 million

The firm is considering switching to a 20 percent debt capital structure, and has determined that they would have to pay an 8 percent yield on perpetual debt regardless of whether they change their capital structure. If the firm faces a 35 percent tax rate, what will be the standard deviation in EPS if they switch to the proposed capital structure? *(LG3)*

14-7   **Break-even EBIT** Continuing the previous problem, what will be the break-even level of EBIT? *(LG6)*

14-8   **Expected EPS after Leveraging** HiLo, Inc., doesn't face any taxes and has $100 million in assets, currently financed entirely with equity. Equity is worth $7 per share, and book value of equity is equal to market value of equity. Also, let's assume that the firm's expected values for EBIT depend on which state of the economy occurs this year, with the possible values of EBIT and their associated probabilities as shown below:

STATE	PESSIMISTIC	OPTIMISTIC
Probability of state	.45	.55
Expect EBIT in state	$5 million	$19 million

The firm is considering switching to a 40 percent debt capital structure and has determined that it would have to pay a 12 percent yield on perpetual debt in either event. If it faces a tax rate of 34 percent, what will be the level of expected EPS if it switches to the proposed capital structure? *(LG3)*

14-9   **Standard Deviation in EPS after Leveraging** HiLo, Inc., doesn't face any taxes and has $100 million in assets, currently financed entirely with equity. Equity is worth $7 per share, and book value of equity is equal to market value of equity. Also, let's assume that the firm's expected values for EBIT depend on which state of the economy occurs this year, with the possible values of EBIT and their associated probabilities as shown below:

STATE	PESSIMISTIC	OPTIMISTIC
Probability of state	.45	.55
Expect EBIT in state	$5 million	$19 million

The firm is considering switching to a 40 percent debt capital structure and has determined that it would have to pay a 12 percent yield on perpetual debt in either event. If it faces a tax rate of 34 percent, what will be the standard deviation in EPS if it switches to the proposed capital structure? *(LG3)*

14-10   **Break-even EBIT** Continuing the previous problem, what will be the break-even level of EBIT? *(LG6)*

14-11   **Expected EPS after Leveraging with Taxes** NoNuns Cos. has a 25 percent tax rate and has $350 million in assets, currently financed entirely with equity. Equity is worth $37 per share, and book value of equity is equal to market value of equity. Also, let's assume that the firm's expected values for EBIT depend on which state of the economy occurs

advanced
problems

this year, with the possible values of EBIT and their associated probabilities as shown below:

STATE	RECESSION	AVERAGE	BOOM
Probability of state	.25	.55	.20
Expect EBIT in state	$5 million	$10 million	$17 million

The firm is considering switching to a 20 percent debt capital structure and has determined that they would have to pay an 8 percent yield on perpetual debt in either event. What will be the level of expected EPS if it switches to the proposed capital structure? *(LG4)*

14-12 Standard Deviation in EPS after Leveraging with Taxes NoNuns Cos. has a 25 percent tax rate and has $350 million in assets, currently financed entirely with equity. Equity is worth $37 per share, and book value of equity is equal to market value of equity. Also, let's assume that the firm's expected values for EBIT depend on which state of the economy occurs this year, with the possible values of EBIT and their associated probabilities as shown below:

STATE	RECESSION	AVERAGE	BOOM
Probability of state	.25	.55	.20
Expect EBIT in state	$5 million	$10 million	$17 million

The firm is considering switching to a 20 percent debt capital structure and has determined that it would have to pay an 8 percent yield on perpetual debt in either event. What will be the standard deviation in EPS if the firm switches to the proposed capital structure? *(LG4)*

14-13 Break-even EBIT with Taxes Continuing the previous problem, what will be the break-even level of EBIT? *(LG6)*

14-14 Expected EPS after Leveraging with Taxes GTB, Inc., has a 34 percent tax rate and has $100 million in assets, currently financed entirely with equity. Equity is worth $7 per share, and book value of equity is equal to market value of equity. Also, let's assume that the firm's expected values for EBIT depend on which state of the economy occurs this year, with the possible values of EBIT and their associated probabilities as shown below:

STATE	PESSIMISTIC	OPTIMISTIC
Probability of state	.45	.55
Expect EBIT in state	$5 million	$19 million

The firm is considering switching to a 40 percent debt capital structure and has determined that they would have to pay a 12 percent yield on perpetual debt in either event. What will be the level of expected EPS if it switches to the proposed capital structure? *(LG4)*

14-15 **Standard Deviation in EPS after Leveraging with Taxes** GTB, Inc., has a 34 percent tax rate and has $100 million in assets, currently financed entirely with equity. Equity is worth $7 per share, and book value of equity is equal to market value of equity. Also, let's assume that the firm's expected values for EBIT depend on which state of the economy occurs this year, with the possible values of EBIT and their associated probabilities as shown below:

STATE	PESSIMISTIC	OPTIMISTIC
Probability of state	.45	.55
Expect EBIT in state	$5 million	$19 million

The firm is considering switching to a 40 percent debt capital structure and has determined that they would have to pay a 12 percent yield on perpetual debt in either event. What will be the standard deviation in EPS if it switches to the proposed capital structure? *(LG4)*

14-16 **Break-even EBIT with Taxes** Continuing the previous problem, what will be the break-even level of EBIT? *(LG6)*

research it! Investigating Firms' Debt Ratios

Go to the Yahoo! Industry Center at **http://biz.yahoo.com/ic/,** choose an industry from among the "Top Industries" listed in the left column, and choose three of the leading firms for that industry.

What are these firms' debt ratios? Investigate each firm's background to try to determine whether the factors we discussed in this chapter are driving any differences in the amount of debt that they each have in their capital structures.

integrated minicase: Change in Equity Ownership

The CEO of JJJ, Inc., owns 27 percent of his currently all-equity-financed firm worth $100 million. He has proposed splitting off one of the divisions (worth $25 million) of his company to let it operate as an independent firm. Existing shareholders will not get shares in the new firm; instead, the new firm is expected to raise $25 million through an IPO, the proceeds from which are to be used to repurchase shares in JJJ.

Assuming that the CEO does not participate in the stock buyback, what will his percentage ownership be after the division is split off?

ANSWERS TO TIME OUT

14-1 Passive capital management would take longer, as the firm would have to wait until new capital budgeting projects required funds before altering the capital structure.

14-2 The new capital structure should be used. As pointed out in Chapter 11, new projects should be evaluated using the capital structure that will actually be used to fund them.

14-3 With interest on debt being tax deductible, the government essentially picks up part of the tab for debt. This makes it even cheaper, so firms maximize their use of debt so as to maximize the interest tax shield.

14-4 The firm can unleverage, or lend, part of its portfolio.

14-5 When stockholders' equity stake is close to worthless, they can gamble on risky projects without any risk to themselves but with the opportunity of regaining some value if such projects earn a high rate of return. Given this, they will tend to actually prefer such projects in this type of situation.

14-6 They would prefer a Chapter 11 reorganization.

14-7 Given that the health care industry will likely experience higher, more stable revenues and profits, we should expect that the industry will be able to support higher debt ratios.

14-8 Utility companies have fairly high debt ratios because they have relatively high, stable cash flows, both due to the nature of their product and due to the barriers to entry represented by the large initial capital investment necessary to build a power plant and a power distribution infrastructure.

chapter 15:

SHARING FIRM WEALTH: DIVIDENDS, SHARE REPURCHASES, AND OTHER PAYOUTS

 Learning Goals

LG1 Identify general factors that affect a firm's payout policies.

LG2 Discuss how investors' preferences regarding differential tax rates and differential timing can guide the firm's policies on the distribution of dividends and capital gains.

LG3 Define the information effect and the clientele effect and explain corporate control issues that affect investors' preferences for dividends versus capital gains.

LG4 Articulate reasons why firms seem to prefer keeping ordinary dividends constant at a relatively low rate and then periodically distributing extraordinary dividends occasionally when they feel a less pressing need to retain earnings.

LG5 Detail cash dividend payment procedures and explain the effect that these procedures have on the stock price path.

LG6 Differentiate between a stock dividend's impact on the firm's books and a stock split's impact on the books.

LG7 Note the advantages and disadvantages of a firm's stock repurchases.

 Thus far, we've examined the firm's investment and financing decisions. Both kinds of decisions are vitally important for the firm to achieve its primary goal: maximizing shareholder wealth. But few shareholders would be satisfied with maximized share value if they didn't get to participate in the increased share value. The firm also needs to get that wealth back into shareholders' pockets. That's what this chapter is all about.

In a theoretically perfect world without any taxes, or where all of the firm's cash disbursements were taxed equally (whether capital gains, regular interest payments, or dividends), distributing capital to shareholders would be a simple proposition. It

viewpoints

Business Application

Suppose that SWV Corp. has consistently followed the pure residual dividend policy in the past, but is considering switching to a "smoothed" residual dividend policy, where dividends would be set at a level that management feels they could comfortably maintain for the foreseeable future. If SWV does have a considerable amount of excess cash, it will consider either issuing an extraordinary dividend or buying back some of its stock. What would be the probable impact on the firm's stock price if they do adopt this new policy? **(See solution on p. 504)**

Personal Application

Assume that personal tax rates on dividends and capital gains have shifted back such that the rate on dividends is significantly higher than that on capital gains. Marc is considering buying stock to put into his Roth IRA, a type of retirement account allowed under U.S. tax law that allows individuals to deposit funds into an account up to a certain maximum each year. Contributions are taxed before they are deposited, but all deposits plus any earnings can be withdrawn tax-free after the individual reaches the age of 59 1/2. Marc is interested in two stocks. One pays returns primarily as a dividend yield, and the other returns primarily a capital gains yield. If he can't buy both stocks under the annual contribution limit, which should he choose for his Roth IRA? **(See solution on p. 504)**

A practice test can be found on the Online Learning Center at
www.mhhe.com/can1e

would be based entirely upon the firm's available opportunities for investment in prospective projects. In the real world, though, it's not so straightforward. As we'll discuss below, the U.S. government treats dividends and interest payments differently than it does capital gains for individual tax returns. Further, potentially varying personal tax rates throughout a shareholder's investment horizon dictate that firms will have to consider bondholder and shareholder preferences when the firms design their payout strategies.

 ## 15.1 Dividends versus Capital Gains

We can see the basic choice between a firm paying out money in the form of a cash dividend or using the money to repurchase shares of stock by examining the formula for a constant-growth stock we used in Chapter 8:

$$P_0 = \frac{D_1}{i - g} \tag{15-1}$$

You will recall from Chapter 8 that the amount of the next dividend, D_1, links to the capital gains rate, g, through the dividend payout ratio, defined as

$$\text{Dividend payout ratio} = \frac{\text{Dividends}}{\text{Net income}} \tag{15-2}$$

Firms that pay out a relatively high percentage of current earnings will have fewer retained earnings, and hence less capital to fund future growth in earnings and dividends. The opposite is also true: firms that hold onto retained earnings won't have much left with which to pay dividends and interest payments. Assuming that the capital markets to which firms turn to raise capital are competitive, firms should only retain earnings to the extent that they can invest those funds in projects that will earn at least as high a rate of return as the rate that investors could earn by taking the same money and investing it in other firms with similar risk profiles.

Dividend Irrelevance Theory

The idea that it does not matter whether a firm pays dividends or not derives from another Modigliani and Miller Theorem. This theory is referred to, appropriately enough, as the **dividend irrelevance theorem.** As with their theory about capital structure irrelevance discussed in the last chapter, the dividend irrelevance theorem is set in a perfect world, one that features:

- No taxes.
- No transaction costs (including trading commissions).
- Perfectly efficient markets.
- Completely rational investors.

In such an environment, M&M show that the decision to pay or not to pay dividends doesn't matter. If a firm pays dividends, doing so will simply reduce the value of each share by the amount paid in dividends. If shareowners don't want the value of their shares reduced by dividends, they can simply turn around and buy additional shares in the company with the dividend proceeds. Doing so will keep the total amount of wealth they have invested in the firm constant. Similarly, if a firm chooses not to pay dividends, but investors wish that the firm would pay out regularly, then they can simply sell enough shares to reap the same dollars of income that they would have gotten if the firm had paid dividends.

Of course, just as with the capital structure irrelevance theorems, relaxing the "no taxes" assumption substantially changes the implications concerning optimal firm dividend policy. Until fairly recently, the capital gains tax rate was substantially lower than was the tax rate on dividends, which were taxed as normal income. This inequality led some firms to prefer to pay out lower dividends/retain higher levels of earnings than probably would have been the case otherwise.

However, the **Jobs and Growth Tax Relief Reconciliation Act (JGTRRA)** of 2003 (Public Law 108-27) changed the general tax rate applicable to net capital gains for individuals to 15 percent or 5 percent (depending on the taxpayer's total taxable income). The new capital gains rates also apply to most dividends paid from domestic corporations and certain qualified foreign corporations. The upshot: Investors find that dividends are much more attractive relative to capital gains than they have been in the past, when dividends were taxed at a higher rate than capital gains income.

For most investors, this equalization of the tax rates on capital gains and dividends has moved the real world *closer* to the concept of dividend irrelevance embodied in M&M's perfect world, but additional factors might give investors strong preferences for or against dividends.

Why Some Investors Favor Dividends

Gordon and Lintner proposed one of the strongest arguments for dividends, sometimes referred to as the **bird-in-the-hand theory.** This theory argues that dividends that the firm has committed to pay are less risky (and hence more attractive) to risk-averse investors than are potential future capital gains. Allowing the firm to retain "extra" earnings increases the risk that the firm will spend those earnings on non-value-maximizing investments.

M&M refer to this argument as the *bird-in-the-hand fallacy,* claiming that many, if not most, investors will reinvest their dividends in the same or similar firms anyway. Further, the long-run riskiness of the firm's cash flows to investors is determined only by the riskiness of the firm's asset cash flows and not by its dividend payout policy.

Why Some Investors Favor Capital Gains

Even though tax rates on capital gains and dividends are currently very similar, one important tax-based reason suggests why some investors might prefer capital gains. The two approaches differ in terms of how much choice investors have when they're obligated to pay taxes.

When a firm pays out dividends, all stockholders share in the dividend distribution. All must pay taxes on those dividends as income in that tax period. The firm may instead retain earnings, consequently causing share price to increase over what it would have been if the firm had paid dividends. Only shareholders who want the equivalent of a dividend will sell shares of stock, thereby incurring the obligation to pay capital gains taxes.

Investors who don't need or want any cash will not sell their stock and they therefore will not incur any obligation to pay taxes on capital gains until they choose to do so. Note that this ability to "time" tax assessments will be especially attractive for investors who expect their capital gains tax rate to decline over time. Not only will these investors be able to push the tax bill off into later in the future, they may also be able to reduce the total tax in doing so.

TIME OUT

15-1 Why should increasing a firm's dividend payout ratio cause the future dividend growth rate to decrease?

15-2 Would dividends truly be irrelevant in a more realistic world that features trading costs?

15.2 Other Dividend Policy Issues

Risks, taxation, and cash flow timing, which we discussed in the previous section, are all fairly tangible. Managers must consider some additional factors in setting the firm's optimal dividend payout policy.

The Information Effect

Managers hate to cut dividends—and investors hate to have them cut, so firms do not do so except in very dire circumstances. Along the same lines, managers will hesitate to raise dividends unless they feel that the firm can maintain dividends at the new, higher level for the foreseeable future. Because of management's hesitation to ever cut dividends, if a firm announces an increase in the next dividend, analysts often see such announcements as a very positive signal concerning the firm's performance and its expected future cash flow levels.

The Clientele Effect

The **clientele effect** refers to the fact that, in real life, investors do *not* have identical desires about the taxability and timing of firm payouts. Different groups of investors, or clienteles, will be attracted to different firms based on those firms' varying payout policies.

When firms set their dividend policies, shareholders who desire that particular mix of dividend policy attributes invest in the firms with dividend policies that match. If firms then change their dividend policy, the investors who desired the previous policy will sell their shares to reinvest in another firm with a policy closer to that which they desire. New investors who were previously uninterested in the stock may be attracted to it because of the policy change.

If we assume that investors face no transaction fees for buying or selling stock, and that unlimited demand exists for both old and new dividend policies, then a firm changing its policy in this manner would not see any effect on its stock price. However, investors *do* incur transaction fees for trading shares, and some evidence suggests that changes in tax laws or in the macroeconomic environment result in a demand shift from one dividend policy type to another. If demand for a certain dividend policy increases enough, then a firm changing to that dividend policy might actually see its demand for its stock increase enough to positively affect its stock price, even though investors will have to pay transaction fees to switch into the stock.

For example, Microsoft's September 2003 announcement that it would double its dividend was particularly well received. The dividend change occurred approximately four months after JGTRRA made dividends more attractive for most investors.

Corporate Control Issues

While the clientele effect implies a rather passive role for shareholders—one in which they are either forced to accept a company's dividend policy or leave to look for one more to their liking—firms that have shareholders with significant stakes in the firm may actually find those shareholders *dictating* the dividend payout policy. For example, in Germany, where banks are allowed to have sizable equity investments in firms to which they lend, recent studies[1] show that bank-controlled firms pay out lower dividends and are much more likely to omit dividends than any other type of firm.

Similar research also shows this tendency in closely held corporations, where owners have historically sought to avoid double taxation by leaving the profits in the corporation as accumulated earnings.[2] As long as the firm can justify accumulating earnings as necessary to the business's reasonable needs, such as funding a possible expansion or similar activity, then shareholders will have at least some latitude in determining when they wish to pay the earnings out.

TIME OUT

15-3 What type of clientele would you expect to prefer dividends over capital gains? Why?

15-4 When might raising a firm's dividend payout ratio be seen as a negative signal?

15.3 Real-World Dividend Policy

Taking into account all of the factors noted above, it would still seem intuitive that the firm's basic dividend policy should be to pay out as dividends any cash flow that is surplus after the firm has invested in all available positive net present value projects:

$$\text{Dividends} = \text{Net income}$$
$$-\text{Retained earnings necessary to fund positive NPV projects}$$

(15-3)

The Residual Dividend Model

We generally refer to this dividend policy approach as the **residual dividend model,** or the *free cash flow theory of dividends.* Though we would expect that the firm might respond to the factors discussed above and thence to deviate somewhat from this ideal, the current low tax rates on dividends would seem to be a prime environment for it to apply.

However, the residual dividend model doesn't really seem to explain the observed dividend policies of real-world companies. Most companies pay relatively consistent dividends from one year to the next, and managers seem to prefer paying a steadily increasing dividend rather than paying a dividend that fluctuates dramatically from one year to the next. For example, consider the recent dividends and EPS figures for General Electric Co. (GE) shown in Figure 15.1.

GE has very consistently kept the dividend for all four quarters of each year constant, raising the dividend smoothly from year to year, but EPS has been quite volatile throughout this time period. Many companies follow an approach similar

---

[1]See, for example, Luis Correia da Silva, et al., *Dividend Policy and Corporate Governance.* (New York: Oxford University Press, 2004).

[2]In fact, many recent tax court cases related to closely held C corporations involve the nonpayment of sufficient dividends relative to profits, which subjects the C corporation to the accumulated earnings tax.

figure 15.1

General Electric Company's Recent Dividend and EPS History

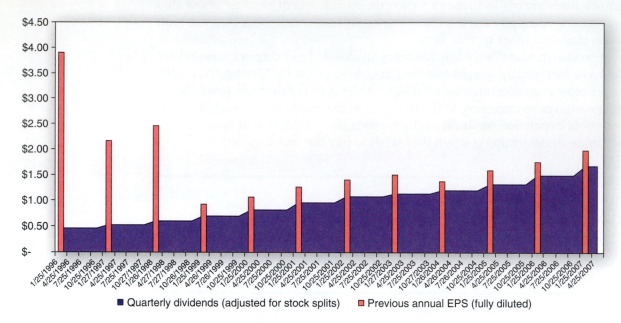

■ Quarterly dividends (adjusted for stock splits)   ■ Previous annual EPS (fully diluted)

to GE's. The general consensus about why firms follow this approach seems to be that management at these firms feel that their investors value dependability and stability in their personal dividend streams more than investors resent the burden that such a strategy places on the firm's cash flows.

Paying a constant yet steadily increasing dividend *does* impose a burden on the firm, for several different reasons. For exmple, firms in this situation quite commonly find themselves simultaneously issuing new equity (and paying the associated underwriting fees for doing so) and paying dividends to existing equity holders.

Probably the most compelling reason that most firms have for paying a consistent dividend like this is that most investors are very risk averse, so they actually prefer a slightly lower, consistent dividend stream than one that is, on average, higher but more volatile.

Extraordinary Dividends

To minimize the burden of stable dividends, some firms divide dividends into two classes: ordinary and extraordinary. By setting the ordinary dividends relatively low, the firm signals the minimum expected payout level that investors can count on. Because the ordinary dividends are set fairly low, the firms supplement small payments with periodic extraordinary dividends, such as those shown for Bassett Furniture in Figure 15.2.

The firm gains at least one advantage from this strategy. During periods when the firm really needs retained earnings for various projects, the firm simply forgoes the extraordinary dividend but continues to pay the ordinary one.

TIME OUT

15-5   What would prompt a firm like GE to start paying out a much higher percentage of its earnings as dividends?

15-6   Would extraordinary dividends be more likely to be used by a firm with cyclical sales or by one with stable sales?

MICROSOFT'S EXTRAORDINARY DIVIDEND

In 2004, Microsoft amassed a cash balance of nearly $60 billion. It then announced that it would pay out more than $32 billion of that war chest as a one-time, extraordinary dividend. This was one of the largest extraordinary dividend payments in history and came about because of a confluence of several different factors.

First, Microsoft had been enjoying monopoly-like profits on its software products for quite a few years, which allowed it to amass a large amount of cash. Second, the JGTRRA had just been passed, making the payment of such a large dividend less burdensome to investors from a tax standpoint. Third, Microsoft's opportunities for new products, and hence the need for capital investment in new projects, didn't seem to be keeping up with the accumulation of cash.

 want to know more? **Key Words to Search for Updates: See the article "Microsoft Announces Payouts to Investors" on www.washingtonpost.com.**

---

figure 15.2

Recent Dividend History for Bassett Furniture

(Bar chart titled "Recent Dividend History for Bassett Furniture" showing regular dividends and extra dividends from Mar-81 to Mar-07, with y-axis from $- to $0.45. Legend: Regular dividend, Extra dividend.)

15.4 Dividend Payment Logistics

LG5

Technically, dividends do not become firm obligations until the firm declares them. The firm must allow itself some lead time between announcing the dividend and actually paying it. The firm must also allow time to determine the owner of record for each share as well as provide processing time between determining owners of record and actually mailing the checks. These different tasks require corporations to establish a definitive set of dates associated with paying out a dividend:

- The declaration date.
- The ex-dividend date.

- The record date.
- The payment date.

Payment Procedures

The board of directors announces its intention to pay a dividend on the **declaration date.** On the declaration date, that specific dividend becomes a firm liability, and the company records that liability on its book accordingly. On the declaration date, the Board will also announce a date of record and a payment date.

The **ex-dividend date** is the first day that the shares will trade without the dividend attached. Prior to that date, anyone purchasing a share of the firm's stock can claim the right to receive the dividend. So the stock is said to trade *cum dividend* (or, with dividend) until the ex-dividend date; subsequent to the ex-dividend date, anyone purchasing the share will purchase the share ex-dividend and can no longer claim the right to the dividend. On the **record date,** the firm will look on its books to find the registered owners of record so that they can start addressing payments. The record date is usually set at least a couple of business days after the ex-dividend date to allow time for shares purchased before the ex-dividend date to be properly registered.[3] The firm sends dividends out on the **payment date.**

Effect of Dividends on Stock Prices

You will recall from Chapter 8, a stock share's price should equal the present value of its expected future dividends. If dividends were paid as a continuous, steady stream at every instant through time, then we wouldn't expect dividend payment procedures to have much impact on the stock's price. But the fact that firms pay dividends as discrete cash flows received at certain intervals implies that the price of a share of stock will appreciate as the next, and every subsequent, dividend get closer, and then fall precipitously once that dividend no longer accompanies the stock.

For example, consider a stock that's expected to pay a $1.00 per year dividend forever and that the next dividend is expected exactly one year from now. If the appropriate rate of return on this share of stock is 10 percent, then the stock price should simply be set as the present value of the perpetuity:

$$P_0 = \frac{D}{i} \tag{15-4}$$
$$= \frac{\$1}{.1}$$
$$= \$10$$

Now, to see what's going to happen as we get closer to the dividend payment date, let's express this as the sum of the present value of the next dividend (D_1) and the present value of the perpetuity of all subsequent dividends (starting with D_2):

$$P_0 = \frac{D_1}{1+i} + \left(\frac{D_2}{i} \times \frac{1}{1+i} \right) \tag{15-5}$$

[3]In most countries, registration is essentially automatic for shares purchased before the ex-dividend date, so the likelihood of someone who bought the shares prior to the ex-dividend date not receiving the dividend they're due is pretty small.

We can also express the lump sum portions of this formula in terms of a daily interest rate so that we can examine what happens as the number of days until the next dividend payment approaches zero:

$$
\begin{aligned}
P_0 &= \frac{D_1}{\left(1 + i_{daily}\right)^n} + \left(\frac{D_2}{i_{yearly}} \times \frac{1}{\left(1 + i_{daily}\right)^n}\right) \tag{15-6}\\
&= \frac{\$1}{(1 + .000261)^{365}} + \left(\frac{\$1}{.10} \times \frac{1}{(1 + .000261)^{365}}\right)\\
&= \$.9091 + \$9.0909\\
&= \$10
\end{aligned}
$$

Note that the daily interest rate in this problem can be computed as shown in Chapter 5:

$$
\begin{aligned}
i_{daily} &= \sqrt[365]{1.10} - 1 \tag{15-7}\\
&= .000261
\end{aligned}
$$

As the number of days until the next dividend decreases, the present value will increase. For example, when there are only 200 days left, the present value will become:

$$
\begin{aligned}
P_0 &= \frac{D_1}{\left(1 + i_{daily}\right)^n} + \left(\frac{D_2}{i_{yearly}} \times \frac{1}{\left(1 + i_{daily}\right)^n}\right)\\
&= \frac{\$1}{(1 + .000261)^{200}} + \left(\frac{\$1}{.10} \times \frac{1}{(1 + .000261)^{200}}\right)\\
&= \$.9491 + \$9.4912\\
&= \$10.44
\end{aligned}
$$

If we temporarily ignore the difference between the ex-dividend date and the payment date, then the present value upon payment will become:

$$
\begin{aligned}
P_0 &= \frac{D_1}{\left(1 + i_{daily}\right)^n} + \left(\frac{D_2}{i_{yearly}} \times \frac{1}{\left(1 + i_{daily}\right)^n}\right)\\
&= \frac{\$1}{(1 + .000261)^0} + \left(\frac{\$1}{.10} \times \frac{1}{(1 + .000261)^0}\right)\\
&= \$1 + \$10\\
&= \$11
\end{aligned}
$$

This pattern in the present value of the dividends leading up to the next dividend is shown in Figure 15.3.

After that next dividend has been paid, the stock once again becomes a perpetuity for which the next cash flow is one year away, so the price will immediately fall back to $10. This process of a buildup in price followed by a precipitous drop once the next dividend is paid will continue through time as shown in Figure 15.4.

Adding back in the gap between the ex-dividend date and the payment date causes the present value both to peak at a lower value (the present value of $11 on the ex-dividend date instead of the explicit value of the $11 on the payment

figure 15.3

Price-Path of Stock
Approaching Dividend
Payment

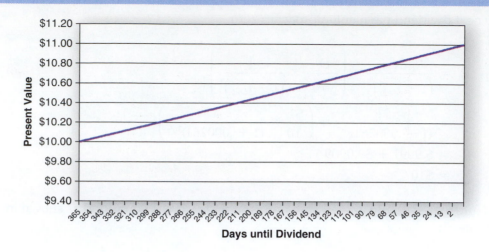

figure 15.4

Price Pattern in
Response to Repeated
Dividends

date itself). Then the present value falls a little further after the ex-dividend date.
For example, taking the hypothetical stock discussed above and further assuming a 30-day gap between the ex-dividend date and the payment date, the price
will hit its highest value one day before the ex-dividend day:

$$P_0 = \frac{D_1}{\left(1 + i_{daily}\right)^n} + \left(\frac{D_2}{i_{yearly}} \times \frac{1}{\left(1 + i_{daily}\right)^n}\right)$$

$$= \frac{\$1}{(1 + .000261)^{31}} + \left(\frac{\$1}{.10} \times \frac{1}{(1 + .000261)^{31}}\right) = \$.9919 + \$9.9194 = \$10.91$$

After the stock goes ex-dividend, the first dividend to be received will then be
D_2, which will still be $365 + 30 = 395$ days away at that point, so the price will
drop to:

$$P_0 = \left(\frac{\$1}{.10} \times \frac{1}{(1 + .000261)^{30}}\right) = \$9.9220$$

figure 15.5

This will cause the price path of the stock to follow the red path shown in Figure 15.5.

Though this example has been a little simplistic, the basic intuition—that stock prices should increase as the next dividend approaches and then fall by the present value of that dividend once the stock goes ex-dividend—has been shown repeatedly.

TIME OUT

15-7 Most firms set the ex-dividend date one month in advance of the payment date. Why?

15-8 Suppose that the gap between the ex-dividend date and the payment date was eliminated. What effect would you expect that to have on the pattern of stock prices leading up to the dividend payment?

15.5 Stock Dividends and Stock Splits

In addition to disbursing cash through the dividend payment system as described above, firms may also distribute additional shares of stock through either a **stock dividend** or a **stock split.** Though the mechanics and accounting treatments of these two approaches are different, they both have the end result of increasing the number of shares outstanding without changing the total market value of owner's equity. So either a stock dividend or a stock split will decrease the stock price.

Stock Dividends

When they wish to distribute a stock dividend, the company performs a pro-rata distribution of additional shares of stock to the current owners of the stock. For example, a 20 percent stock dividend would increase the number of shares held by each stockholder by 20 percent, so an investor who owned 100 shares before the dividend would own 120 afterwards. For accounting purposes, the fair market value of these shares is transferred from retained earnings to the Common Stock and Additional Paid-In Capital accounts, meaning that no change occurs in the share's par value.

Stock Splits

In a stock split, the company exchanges new shares for old shares in the firm. A split usually involves converting each old share into more than one new share, which increases the shares outstanding. Sometimes you will also hear of "reverse" stock splits, in which stockholders trade in multiple shares for fewer new shares. For example, if you owned 250 shares in a firm and they announced a 2-for-1 stock split, you would receive 2 × 250 = 500 new shares of stock. If, instead, they announced a 1-for-5 reverse split, you would receive 250/5 = 50 new shares once you turned in your original 250 shares (likely held in street name).

Although a stock split will alter the par value of a firm's stock on the company's books, it will not cause any shift in money among the owner's equity accounts.

Effect of Splits and Stock Dividends on Stock Prices

The purpose of either a stock dividend or stock split is to lower (or, in the case of a reverse split, raise) the share's market price proportionately. For example, in a 3-for-1 split, you should expect to see the post-split shares trading at approximately one-third of the presplit price.

Why do firms do this? The general consensus seems to be that firms like to have their shares trade in a particular price range. If their share price moves outside that range, then the firms split their shares or announce a stock dividend to move their share price back into the desired range. Given investors' preference to trade in "round lots" (i.e., in increments of 100 shares), as well as the fact that many brokers' commission schedules encourage trading in round lots, this strategy of keeping the price within a certain range may not be a bad one. If typical investors invest in "chunks" of $10,000 or less, then they'll find it more cost-effective to buy 100 shares of a $75 stock (100 × $75 = $7,500) rather than investing in an odd lot of a $150 stock.

15.6 Stock Repurchases

Firms sometimes use another method to return capital to shareholders: They engage in a stock **repurchase** or **buyback.** In the U.S., the most common method to do so is through an open-market stock repurchase. In such a repurchase, the firm simply buys shares of its own stock on the stock market just like any other investor. The firm may or may not publicly announce their intention to buy back shares, but any such announcement is not binding. Open market repurchases can span months or even years, allowing the firm to choose to repurchase only when the price is within a particular range or when they feel the advantages outweigh the disadvantages.

Prior to 1981, all repurchases were carried out using a **fixed-price tender offer.** Such an offer is announced publicly and specifies in advance a single purchase price, the number of shares sought, and the duration of the offer. The offer may allow tendered shares to be withdrawn prior to the offer's expiration date and may also be made conditional upon receiving tender offers for a minimum acceptable number of shares. If the number of shares tendered exceeds the number sought, then the company usually purchases shares from those tendered on a *pro rata* basis. For example, if a company is seeking to repurchase 1 million shares of stock but shareholders offer 2 million shares, then it would buy half of the offered shares from each seller. If the number of shares tendered is less than the number sought, then the company might choose to extend the offer's expiration date.

Since 1981, firms have been increasingly using an alternative form of tender offer, the Dutch auction share repurchase. A Dutch auction offer specifies a price range within which the shares will ultimately be purchased and the number of shares desired by the company, and shareholders are invited to offer their shares for sale at any price within that stated range. At the close of the auction, the firm then analyzes all submitted sale offers to choose the lowest purchase price that allows the firm to buy the number of shares it is seeking. The firm pays that price to all investors who tendered at or below that price but does not purchase any shares that are offered at higher prices. If too few shares are tendered, then the firm either cancels the offer (provided it had been made conditional on a minimum acceptance), or it buys back all tendered shares at the maximum price bid by the shareholders who chose to participate in the auction.

Dutch auction share repurchases have increased in popularity for several reasons. First, the Dutch auction process relies on the company's shareholders to value the stock rather than an independent valuation assessment. To the extent that such valuations are often inaccurate or result in an offer price that the shareholders find unsatisfactory, this seems to be a more efficient, market-driven approach to coming up with a bid price. Second, the Dutch auction process offers at least the possibility that the firm will pay less than the maximum price of the specified range, implying that the stock is less likely to be overvalued in the offer. Finally, since Dutch auctions increase the uncertainty concerning the final price at which a repurchase may take place, they tend to discourage arbitrageurs, who often drive up the price in fixed-price tender offers, from participating.

Advantages of Repurchases

Under tax structures in which capital gains rates are significantly less than dividend tax rate, repurchases can offer the firm a very efficient way to return money to shareholders. Even if capital gains aren't preferentially taxed relative to dividends, shareholders' choice of whether to participate in a buyback implies that capital gains taxes can be deferred until the shareholder wishes to incur them.

Stock repurchases offer another advantage in that, unlike with dividends, reductions in or cessations of repurchase programs don't seem to be perceived as a negative informational signal in the same way that reduced dividends are. So starting a buyback program doesn't imply the same kind of long-term commitment on the firm's part that increasing the dividend would.

Finally, though the cessation of a repurchase program isn't perceived negatively, the announcement of the *initiation* of a stock repurchase program *is* usually viewed as a *positive* signal. The reasoning here: if management, who knows the firm's prospects better than anyone, thinks that the shares are worth buying, then the stock is probably underpriced.

Disadvantages of Repurchases

As you might suspect, repurchases also pose several potential disadvantages. First, that very same positive informational effect that a share repurchase announcement gives may actually be a double-edged sword. Say a shareholder sells shares to the firm in a repurchase. Subsequently, the shareholder finds out that management had information about good future prospects for the firm that wasn't publicly announced prior to the repurchase. Such a situation will make the firm vulnerable to litigation.

A stock repurchase announcement may even be viewed as a negative signal if investors perceive the repurchase as a signal that the firm doesn't have enough attractive capital budgeting projects available to use the cash used for the

viewpoints REVISITED

Business Application Solution

If SWV does adopt the new payout policy, they should probably expect their stock price to benefit (i.e., go up) because of it. Since investors are risk averse, they will value the increased certainty in the "promised" dividend.

To the extent that they can disburse any extra funds in a stock repurchase instead of an extraordinary dividend, SWV should probably be able to benefit the stock price even more by doing so.

Personal Application Solution

Marc should think in terms of leaving the stock for which he will face the lowest tax rate for gains outside the Roth account, which means that he should put the high-dividend-yield stock in the Roth.

---

repurchase. Even if the announcement is perceived as a positive signal, that isn't necessarily a good thing if it results in the firm paying more for the shares than they're worth. Doing so will result in share dilution, which basically involves a transfer of wealth from the shareholders staying in the firm (i.e., those not tendering their shares) to those leaving it.

Finally, the IRS may impose penalties on the firm if tax authorities can show that the repurchase was performed primarily to avoid dividend taxation. This possibility makes the attractiveness/legality of using a repurchase in lieu of a cash dividend questionable.

Effect of Repurchases on Stock Prices

A large body of evidence supports the idea that, on average, the advantages of share repurchases outweigh the disadvantages. For example, Josef Lakonishok and Theo Vermaelen[4] have shown that repurchasing companies experience economically and statistically significant abnormal returns in the two years after the repurchase. The upward price drift seems to be mainly caused by the behavior of the small firms in their sample.

TIME OUT

15-9 If the par value of stock might represent a superior claim in the event of bankruptcy, would stockholders profit more from a stock dividend or stock split? Why?

15-10 Explain why shareholders who do not participate in a firm's stock repurchase will normally see a concentration of their equity stake.

[4]See Josef Lakonishok and Theo Vermaelen, "Anomalous Price Behavior around Repurchase Tender Offers," *The Journal of Finance* 45, no. 2 (June 3 1990), pp. 455–477.

summary of learning goals

In this chapter, we've explored major factors affecting the firm's decisions about how much cash to pay out to shareholders and what form this payout should take. We've seen that tax considerations stemming from differential taxation of dividends and capital gains must be a significant consideration in these decisions. Firms should also be concerned with the signaling aspect of changes in the firm's dividend stream. Finally, managers must remain conscious of their investors' timing preferences.

LG1 **Identify general factors that affect a firm's payout policies.** Factors include the impact of differential investor tax rates on dividends and capital gains, information effects of changes to a firm's dividend policy, the shareholders' preference for a particular payout policy, and the impact on corporate control issues of a change in the firm's dividend payout policy.

LG2 **Discuss how investors' preferences regarding differential tax rates and differential timing can guide the firm's policies on the distribution of dividends and capital gains.** Capital gains are normally taxed at a lower rate than are dividends for the firm's investors. Investors may choose to some extent when they incur capital gains taxes but don't have that freedom with dividends. Both of these factors tend to make capital gains the preferred method for firms to disseminate excess cash. However, some regulatory restrictions against doing so too often will tend to mitigate this tendency.

LG3 **Define the information effect, the clientele effect, and corporate control issues that affect investors' preferences for dividends versus capital gains.** Dividends act as signals, not just of management's opinion concerning the firm's short-term prospects, but also of the firm's perceived ability to maintain that level of dividends for the foreseeable future. So a relatively small change in a firm's dividend payout can have a relatively large impact on the stock price. Similarly, investors will find it relatively expensive to change their investments due to a change in the company's payout policy, so firms will tend to exhibit "inertia" with regards to their payout policy, if for no other reason than to placate the clientele that they've managed to attract while using past and current payout policies.

LG4 **Articulate reasons why firms seem to prefer keeping ordinary dividends constant at a relatively low rate and then periodically distributing** extraordinary dividends occasionally when they feel a less pressing need to retain earnings. Analysts tend to see dividend changes as signals about persistent changes in the firm's future prospects. Therefore, managers are loathe to either lower dividends or to increase them unless they are fairly confident that the new level can be sustained into the foreseeable future. The residual dividend policy lets managers commit to a fairly conservative dividend payout policy in that they don't raise the "normal" dividend without very good cause, but they can and do issue extraordinary dividends to share occasional "windfalls" with equity holders without fear of such extraordinary dividends committing them to continued higher payouts in the future.

LG5 **Detail cash dividend payment procedures and explain the effect that these procedures have on the stock price path.** Firms delay between the last date that a dividend accompanies a share of stock (i.e., the day before the ex-dividend date) and the actual payment date. Because of this delay, stock prices will get larger and larger as the front end of the infinite stream of dividends approaches, but will peak and decline on the ex-dividend date by the present value of the dividend.

LG6 **Differentiate between a stock dividend's impact on the firm's books and a stock split's impact on the books.** Stock dividends involve a transfer from the retained earnings account into the common shares and additional paid-in-capital accounts but don't cause any change in par value per share. Stock splits do not involve a transfer of funds between any of the company's bookkeeping accounts, but the increase in the number of shares dictates that the amounts in each account must be shared over a new, different number of shares than was previously the case, so a stock split does change both the par value and book value per share.

www.mhhe.com/can1e

Note the advantages and disadvantages of a firm's stock repurchases. The primary advantage of a stock repurchase arises when capital gains are taxed at a significantly lower rate than dividends, while the primary disadvantage of a repurchase stock is the potential for the dilution of existing owners' value if the firm pays too much for the repurchased shares.

chapter equations

15-1 $P_0 = \dfrac{D_1}{i - g}$

15-2   Dividend payout ratio $= \dfrac{\text{Dividends}}{\text{Net income}}$

15-3   Dividends = Net income − Retained earnings necessary to fund positive NPV projects

15-4 $P_0 = \dfrac{D}{i}$

15-5 $P_0 = \dfrac{D_1}{1 + i} + \left(\dfrac{D_2}{i} \times \dfrac{1}{1 + i} \right)$

15-6 $P_0 = \dfrac{D_1}{\left(1 + i_{daily}\right)^n} + \left(\dfrac{D_2}{i_{yearly}} \times \dfrac{1}{\left(1 + i_{daily}\right)^n} \right)$

15-7 $i_{daily} = \sqrt[365]{1 + i_{yearly}} - 1$

key terms

bird-in-the-hand theory, The argument that receiving a dividend today is preferable to letting management have the chance to spend or waste the money between now and the future. (p. 493)

clientele effect, The tendency of investors to find a payout policy that they prefer and stick with it. (p. 494)

declaration date, The date the board of directors announces its intention to pay a dividend. (p. 498)

dividend irrelevance theorem, A theorem showing that, in M&M's perfect world, it doesn't matter if a firm pays out funds through dividends or capital gains. (p. 492)

ex-dividend date, The first day that shares will trade without the purchaser receiving an upcoming dividend. (p. 498)

fixed-price tender offer, A repurchase offer specifying a single purchase price. (p. 502)

free cash flow theory of dividends, Another name for the residual dividend model. (p. 495)

Jobs and Growth Tax Relief Reconciliation Act, A 2003 law that lowered the rate on both dividends and capital gains for individual investors in most situations. (p. 493)

payment date, The actual date that a dividend will be sent out. (p. 498)

record date, The day that the firm will determine the owner-of-record for the purposes of an upcoming dividend payment. (p. 498)

repurchase or buyback, The firm buys back shares of its own stock. (p. 502)

residual dividend model, The policy of a firm paying out only funds that are left over after all positive-NPV projects are funded. (p. 495)

stock dividend, A pro-rata distribution of additional shares of stock to the current owners of the stock. (p. 501)

stock split, An exchange of existing shares for a different (usually large) number of "new" shares,

with proportionately different par and market values. (p. 501)

self-test problems with solutions

① Computing Pattern of Stock Prices Due to Dividend Payments Stone Woof Beds is expected to pay a dividend of $2.25 per year, indefinitely. If the appropriate rate of return on this stock is 12 percent per year, and the stock consistently goes ex-dividend 25 days before dividend payment date, what will be the expected minimum and maximum prices in light of the dividend payment logistics?

LG5

Solution:

The daily interest rate will be equal to:

$$i_{daily} = \sqrt[365]{1.12} - 1$$
$$= .000311$$

As with the example in the chapter, the stock will hit its highest value one day before its ex-dividend date:

$$P_0 = \frac{D_1}{\left(1 + i_{daily}\right)^n} + \left(\frac{D_2}{i_{yearly}} \times \frac{1}{\left(1 + i_{daily}\right)^n}\right)$$

$$= \frac{\$2.25}{(1 + .000311)^{26}} + \left(\frac{\$2.25}{.12} \times \frac{1}{(1 + .000311)^{26}}\right)$$

$$= \$2.2319 + \$18.5992 = \$20.83$$

and it will hit its lowest value on the ex-dividend date:

$$P_0 = \frac{D_1}{\left(1 + i_{daily}\right)^n} + \left(\frac{D_2}{i_{yearly}} \times \frac{1}{\left(1 + i_{daily}\right)^n}\right)$$

$$= \frac{\$2.25}{(1 + .000311)^{390}} + \left(\frac{\$2.25}{.12} \times \frac{1}{(1 + .000311)^{390}}\right)$$

$$= \$1.9930 + \$16.6086 = \$18.60$$

② Calculating shares in a stock split. You own 300 shares in a firm that are selling for $20 per share. The firm has just announced a 5-for-4 stock split. How many shares will you have after the split, and what do you expect them to be selling for?

LG6

Solution:

You should wind up with $300 \times \frac{5}{4} = 375$ shares, and each share should sell for

$\$20 \times \frac{4}{5} = \$16$.

www.mhhe.com/can1e

507

questions

1. Why might a firm's investors wish to delay receiving cash from the firm? *(LG1)*

2. Why might the government actually want the capital gains tax rate to be lower than the dividend tax rate? *(LG2)*

3. What condition would have to be necessary in order for the riskiness of the firm's cash flows to investors to be affected by the firm's dividend payout policy? *(LG2)*

4. Explain how an announced increase in a firm's dividend payout might be perceived as either a good or a bad information signal. *(LG3)*

5. We talked about how a firm might attract a different clientele in switching dividend payout policies. Might a particular clientele change its preference for dividends vs. capital gains through no action of the firm? Explain. *(LG3)*

6. Suppose that federal banking regulators in the United States announced that they are going to allow banks to take on significant equity investments in firms to which they have lent. What would you expect, on average, to happen to those firms' dividend payout ratios over time? *(LG4)*

7. If a firm follows the modified residual dividend model discussed in this chapter, are extraordinary dividends paid out of residual net income? *(LG4)*

8. Suppose a firm announces a new dividend amount every year with the first quarterly dividend declaration, but never explicitly states that the dividend will be continued for the other three quarters of the year. However, in the past the firm has always continued the first quarter's dividend into the other three quarters of the year. How much would you expect this firm's share price to react when it announced the new, first-quarter dividend at the beginning of a new year? *(LG4)*

9. Could the record date ever be before the ex-dividend date? Why or why not? *(LG5)*

10. Suppose a firm managed to consistently lower the length of time between the ex-dividend date and the payment date. On average, how would this affect firm stock price? *(LG5)*

11. If a firm announces a dividend decrease, would you expect the stock price to go down more or less than the present value of that decrease? Why? *(LG5)*

12. How big of a stock dividend would a firm have to announce for the stock price to be affected as much as it would through a 3-for-1 stock split? *(LG6)*

13. Why might a firm announce a reverse stock split? *(LG6)*

14. Would it be possible for a firm to announce a "reverse stock dividend"? *(LG6)*

15. Why might firms prefer to conduct stock repurchases though open-market operations rather than through fixed-price tender offers? *(LG7)*

problems

basic
    problems

15-1 **Payout Ratio** Suppose a firm pays total dividends of $500,000 out of net income of $2 million. What would the firm's payout ratio be? *(LG2)*

15-2 **Total Dividend Amount** Suppose a firm has a retention ratio of 35 percent and net income of $5 million. How much does it pay out in dividends? *(LG2)*

15-3 **Dividend per Share** Suppose a firm has a retention ratio of 40 percent, net income of $17 million, and 10 million shares outstanding. What would be the dividend per share paid out on the firm's stock? *(LG2)*

15-4 **Stock Dividend Effects** If a firm has retained earnings of $3 million, a common shares account of $5 million, and additional paid-in capital of $10 million, how would these accounts change in response to a 10 percent stock dividend? *(LG6)*

intermediate
    problems

15-5 **Extraordinary Dividend** JBK Inc. normally pays a quarterly dividend. The last such dividend paid was $2.50, all future quarterly dividends are expected to grow at 5 percent, and the firm faces a required rate of return on equity of 11 percent. If the firm just announced that the next dividend will be an extraordinary dividend of $17 per share that is not expected to affect any other future dividends, what should the stock price be? *(LG4)*

15-6 **Extraordinary Dividend** MMK Cos. normally pays an annual dividend. The last such dividend paid was $2.25, all future dividends are expect to grow at a rate of 7 percent per year, and the firm faces a required rate of return on equity of 13 percent. If the firm just announced that the next dividend will be an extraordinary dividend of $25 per share that is not expected to affect any other future dividends, what should the stock price be? *(LG4)*

15-7 **Effects of Dividends on Stock Prices** Gen Corp. is expected to pay a dividend of $3.50 per year indefinitely. If the appropriate rate of return on this stock is 11 percent per year, and the stock consistently goes ex-dividend 35 days before dividend payment date, what will be the expected minimum and maximum prices in light of the dividend payment logistics? *(LG5)*

advanced
    problems

15-8 **Dividends versus Capital Gains** Show mathematically that, with a tax rate on both dividends and capital gains of 5 percent, it doesn't matter whether earnings are paid out as dividends or kept in the firm. *(LG2)*

15-9 **Dividends Set Annually** Suppose that a firm always announces a yearly dividend at the end of the first quarter of the year but then pays the dividend out as four equal quarterly payments. If the next such annual dividend has been announced as $4, it is exactly one quarter until the first quarterly dividend from that $4, the effective annual required rate of return on the company's stock is 13 percent, and all future annual dividends are expected to grow at 3 percent per year indefinitely, how much will this stock be worth? *(LG4)*

15-10 **Change in Lead Time of Dividend Announcement** Everything else held constant, if a firm announces that it will double the length of time between its ex-dividend date and its payment date, what should be the effect on stock price? *(LG5)*

research it! Identifying a Firm's Dividend Policy

Go to Ford Motor Company's Investor Relations Web site and download their dividend history from **www.corporate-ir.net/ireye/ir_site.zhtml?ticker=F& script=11909&layout=-6&item_id='96topresent.htm.** Adjust the dividends for stock splits and graph them: identify any trends in dividends you see. Does Ford seem to follow a residual dividend policy or another policy?

integrated minicase Investor Perceptions of Dividend Growth

Your firm currently pays a quarterly dividend of $1.35. You are planning on doubling this dividend but then keeping it flat for the next three years, after which it is expected to increase at the industry standard rate of 4 percent per year indefinitely. Your required rate of return on your company's stock is 12.5 percent, and the last $1.35 dividend was just paid.

What will be the time value of money impact on your stock price if investors are fully informed concerning your future intentions for all dividends? What will be the present value of all expected future dividends if you don't tell the investors that you will be keeping the quarterly dividend constant for the first three years, and they assume after the fifth coming dividend that dividends will remain at $2.70 indefinitely?

ANSWERS TO TIME OUT (concluded)

15-5 In general, a firm would increase its payout ratio if earnings became more stable or if commitments on earnings (such as future investments in projects) decrease.

15-6 A firm with cyclical sales would be more likely to use extraordinary dividends, as it would be unwilling to commit to a higher, fixed dividend amount.

15-7 A firm sets the ex-dividend date one month in advance of the dividend payment date so as to give itself plenty of time to determine the owner of record for each share and to provide ample processing time between determining owners of record and actually mailing the checks.

15-8 Stock prices would peak higher, following the blue path shown in Figure 15.5.

15-9 It would be more to stockholders' advantage for the firm to pay a stock dividend, as this would give shareholders more shares while keeping the par value of each share constant.

15-10 The shareholders who do not participate will see their equity stake stay more-or-less constant on a dollar basis, but that constant dollar amount will represent a larger proportion of the firm's equity due to the shareholders who do participate, taking their money out of the firm.

chapter 16:
ISSUING CAPITAL AND THE INVESTMENT BANKING PROCESS

 Learning Goals

LG1 Evaluate different methods for small firms to get funding.

LG2 Appreciate what venture capital is and the role it plays in encouraging entrepreneurship.

LG3 Differentiate among sources of capital funding for public firms.

LG4 Trace the process by which securities are underwritten.

Firms finance their existing and new assets with capital. Some capital used to finance assets comes from retained earnings—the profits that firms retain and reinvest. In addition, firms use debt financing (borrowed funds, usually loans or bonds) and equity financing (ownership shares that the firm sells). A firm will choose its preferred type of capital funding depending upon its size, its stage in its life cycle, and, as a related issue, its prospects for future growth.

In this chapter, we describe the decisions that firms face when they raise capital. We first look at small firms in their early operating stages. Small firms that are just getting started depend mainly on banks and venture capital firms for their capital funding. We then look at the process of going public, as well as publicly traded firms' subsequent issues of debt and equity. Then we describe the types of securities that public firms issue and explore the role that investment banks play in the process. As we go through the chapter, note how important financial institutions become in raising capital funds to finance a firm's assets. For example, banks and venture capital firms (firms that purchase equity interests in firms that give the venture capitalists the same rights and privileges associated with equity investments made by the firm's other owners) provide short- and medium-term financing to small and newer firms, while investment banks assist publicly traded funds to arrange new securities issues.

viewpoints

Business Application

ADK Industries, a publicly traded firm in the "online social networking" industry, is considering building its own dedicated Web server firm at a cost of $5 million. The firm currently has $20 million of assets on its balance sheet, financed with $6 million in debt and $14 million in equity. Firm managers are considering options about how to finance the $5 million. What types of issues do managers need to consider as they make their decisions? **(See solution on p. 528)**

Personal Application

After spending several years raising her children, Marge Upton has decided to reopen her bicycle repair shop. Prior to the time off, Marge operated a successful bicycle repair business in her hometown. Marge remained involved in civic activities while she was raising her children and has maintained her relations with local bankers and other business people. To get the business up and running again, Marge will need to rent a building for the repair shop and purchase equipment and supplies. She estimates that she will need $25,000 to get started. Marge has $5,000 in savings to invest in the business. She also has friends and relatives who will invest another $5,000. What can Marge do to get the remaining funds needed to reopen her bicycle repair shop? **(See solution on p. 528)**

A practice test can be found on the Online Learning Center at
www.mhhe.com/can1e

16.1 Sources of Capital for New and Small Firms

Most new and small firms finance their business assets by borrowing funds from private or public sources. Private capital fund suppliers fall into two basic categories: suppliers of debt financing and suppliers of equity financing. Debt financing includes capital funds borrowed from personal savings, friends or relatives, financial institutions such as commercial bank loans, or venture capitalists. Equity financing includes capital funds invested by venture capitalists. Public sources of capital include debt and equity financing provided by government agencies such as the U.S. Small Business Administration (SBA).

Debt Financing

Debt financing includes personal capital (the firm owners' own savings or loans from friends and relatives) or external capital (loans from banks or venture capitalists). Most new businesses use personal capital. So often, the firm's owners' personal wealth ties directly to the firm's success. However, almost all new and small business owners must borrow capital from external sources. Most external capital providers require that a significant percentage of the firm owners' funds be invested in the business. This investment serves as a signal to capital providers that the firm's owners, with a lot at stake, will work hard to make the firm succeed. Hard work generally increases the probability that the loan will be paid back in full.

BANK LOANS Most new and small firms rely on bank loans as a major part of their capital funding. Figure 16.1 shows that bank loans, including mortgages, represent between 62 and 75 percent of debt financing and between 19 and 29 percent of total financing in non-publicly traded firms from 1975 through 2007.

Commercial banks find small-business loans to be complicated and risky propositions because the bank is frequently asked to assume the credit risk of an individual whose business cash flows require considerable analysis, often with incomplete accounting information available to the credit officer. The payoff for these loans is also small, by definition, because loan principal amounts are usually small. A $50,000 loan with 3 percent interest spread over the cost of funds provides only $1,500 of gross revenues before loan loss provisions, monitoring costs, and allocation of overheads. Low profitability has caused many banks to build small-business scoring models similar to, but more sophisticated than, those used for mortgage loans and consumer credit. Small business models often combine computer-based financial analysis of borrower financial statements with behavioral analysis of the owner of the new and/or small business.

Midmarket business firms also rely heavily on banks for their capital needs. Although definitions of midmarket firms vary, they typically have sales revenues from $5 million to $100 million a year and have a recognizable corporate structure (unlike many small businesses). However, midmarket firms are not publicly traded. Thus, they do not have ready access to deep, liquid capital markets (as do large corporations). Midmarket firms require credit analysis different from the kinds of analysis used for new or small businesses because, while still assessing the character of the firm's management, the main focus is on the business itself.

The credit process begins with a loan officer gathering information on the firm. Having gathered information about the firm, the loan officer will decide whether it is worthwhile to pursue the new business, given the firm's needs, the bank's credit policies, the current economy, and the competitive lending environment. If loan officers decide that midmarket firms are worth the investment, they structure and price agreements as laid out in the bank's credit-granting policy.

figure 16.1

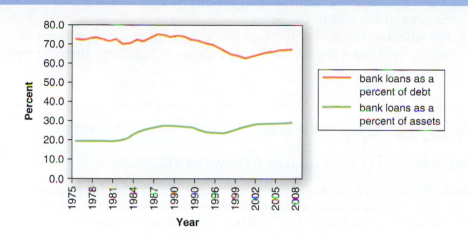

The bank's credit-granting policy will include several areas of analysis, including cash flow analysis, ratio analysis, and financial statement comparisons (as described in Chapters 2 and 3). At any time in this process, conditions could change or new information could be revealed, significantly changing the firm's situation and forcing the account officer to begin the process again.

Once the firm owners and loan officer tentatively agree on a loan, the loan officer must obtain internal approval from the bank's credit risk management team. Generally, even for the smallest midmarket credit, at least two officers must approve a new loan customer. Larger credit requests must be presented formally (either in hard copy or through a computer network) to a credit approval officer and/or committee before they can be signed.

Having reviewed the financial and other applicant conditions, the bank can include loan covenants (similar to bond covenants discussed in Chapter 6) as a part of the loan agreement. Loan covenants reduce the bank's risk of granting and carrying the loan. Covenants can include a variety of conditions, such as ratio maintenance at or within stated ranges or key-person insurance policies on employees critical to the business' success.

Typically, the firm's credit needs will change from time to time. A growing firm will have expanding credit needs. A firm moving into the international arena will need foreign exchange. Even if the credit agreements offered do not change, bank loan officers review the firm's credit needs annually to ensure that the firm complies with the original credit agreement terms. Banks typically wish to maintain close contact with new and small firms to meet their ongoing financial service requirements—both credit and noncredit—so that the relationship will develop into a permanent, mutually beneficial one as the firm grows.

Loan Commitments   In the old days, businesses would borrow **spot loans,** in which the firm would receive the funds as soon as the bank approved the loan. These days, most business loans are made as firms **"take down"** (or borrow against) pre-negotiated lines of credit or loan commitments. Banks make **loan commitment agreements**—contractual commitments to loan the firm a certain maximum amount (say, $10 million)—at given interest rate terms (say, 12 percent). The loan commitment agreement also defines the length of time over which the borrower may take down this loan. In return for making the loan commitment, the bank may charge an **up-front (or facility) fee** of, say, 1/8 of 1 percent of the commitment size, or $12,500 in this example. In addition, the bank must stand ready to supply the full $10 million at any time over the commitment period—for example, one year. Meanwhile, the firm has a valuable option to take down any amount between $0 and $10 million. The bank may also charge the borrower a **back-end** (or **commitment**) **fee** on any unused balances on the commitment line at the end of the period. In this example, if the firm takes down only $8 million in funds over the year and the fee on *unused* commitments is ¼ percent, the firm must pay an additional expense of ¼ percent times $2 million, or $5,000.

EXAMPLE 16-1

 For interactive versions of this example visit www.mhhe.com/can1e

CALCULATING FEES ON A LOAN COMMITMENT

Calculate the total fees a firm would have to pay if its bank offers the firm the following loan commitment: A loan commitment of $1,000,000 with an up-front fee of 1 percent and a back-end fee of 50 basis points (0.5 percent). The take down on the loan is 85 percent.

SOLUTION:

$$
\begin{aligned}
\text{Up-front fee} &= \$1,000,000 \times 0.0100 &&= \$10,000 \\
\text{Back-end fee} &= \$1,000,000 \times 0.0050 \times 0.15 &&= \underline{750} \\
\text{Total} &&&= \$10,750
\end{aligned}
$$

Fixed versus Floating Rate Loans   Banks make loans (both spot loans and loan commitments) available to firms at either (1) fixed interest rates as fixed-rate loan commitments or (2) floating (or variable) rates as variable-rate loans. With **fixed-rate loans,** the firm makes fixed interest payments over the life of the loan. With **variable-rate loans** the loan's interest rate (and thus the interest payments the firm must make) changes over the loan life. A floating rate is set at a fixed spread over a prevailing benchmark rate, such as a Treasury-bill rate, the federal funds rate, or a prime rate. If the benchmark rate rises during the loan period, so does the firm's loan cost. The floating interest rate is specified in the loan contract. The spread is also stated in the loan contract; the bank sets the spread as a function of the firm's credit risk and the owners' credit history.

SMALL BUSINESS ADMINISTRATION   The U.S. Congress created the Small Business Administration (SBA) on July 30, 1953, to "aid, counsel, assist and protect, insofar as is possible, the interests of small business concerns." For qualified new and small firms that cannot obtain long-term financing on reasonable terms from banks or other financial institutions, the SBA offers a basic loan guarantee program. Through this program, the SBA can guarantee up to $750,000 (representing 70 to 90 percent of the loan value) at an interest rate not to exceed 2.75 percent more than the prime lending rate. Maturities on these loans can extend up to 10 years for working-capital loans and 25 years for fixed-asset loans.

While the SBA's primary function is to guarantee loans made to new and small businesses by private financial institutions (such as banks), the SBA offers direct loan programs as well. The SBA's Certified Development Company Loan Program provides long-term, fixed-rate capital funding to small businesses that use the funds to purchase real estate, machinery, or equipment for expansion or modernization. Private, nonprofit corporations called *certified development companies* offer these loans to contribute to communities' or regions' economic development. The SBA funds the loans via a 100 percent SBA-guaranteed debenture and a bank generally secures the loans. SBA loans require an investment of at least 10 percent owner equity. The SBA's Microloan Loan Program provides up to $35,000 in short-term loans to small businesses to fund working-capital purchases. Through this program the SBA makes or guarantees a loan to a bank, which then makes the microloan to the firm. The bank also provides the fledgling firm with management and technical assistance.

Equity Financing and Expertise

New and small firms have difficulty obtaining debt financing from banks because banks are generally not willing or able to make loans to new companies with no assets and little or no business history. In these cases, new and small firms often turn to venture capital firms to get capital financing as well as advice. **Venture capital** is a professionally managed pool of money used to finance new and often high-risk firms. Venture capital is generally provided by investment institutions or private individuals willing to back an untried company and its managers in return for an equity investment in the firm.

Venture capital firms do not make outright loans. Rather, they purchase equity interests in firms that give the venture capitalists the same rights and privileges associated with equity investments made by the firm's other owners. As equity holders, venture capital firms are *not* generally passive investors. Rather, they provide valuable expertise to the firm's managers and sometimes even help in recruiting senior managers for the firm. They also generally expect to be kept fully informed about the firm's operations, any problems, and whether all firm owners' joint goals are being met.

Many types of venture capital firms have sprung up, especially since 1980. **Institutional venture capital firms'** sole purpose is to find and fund the most promising new firms. Private-sector institutional venture capital firms include venture capital limited partnerships (that are established by professional venture capital firms, acting as general partners in the firm: organizing and managing the firm and eventually liquidating their equity investment); financial venture capital firms (subsidiaries of banks); and corporate venture capital firms (subsidiaries of nonfinancial corporations that generally specialize in making start-up investments in high-tech firms). Limited partner venture capital firms dominate the industry.

In addition to private sector institutional venture capital firms, the federal government, through the SBA, operates Small Business Investment Companies (SBICs). SBICs are privately organized venture capital firms licensed by the SBA to make equity investments (as well as loans) to entrepreneurs for start-up activities and expansions. As federally sponsored entities, SBICs rely on their unique opportunity to obtain investment funds from the U.S. Treasury at very low rates relative to private-sector institutional venture capital firms. In contrast to institutional venture capital firms, **angel venture capitalists** (or **angels**) are wealthy individuals who make equity investments. Angel venture capitalists have invested much more in new and small firms than institutional venture capital firms have.

Venture capital firms receive many unsolicited proposals of funding from new and small firms. The venture capital firms reject the majority of these requests. Venture capital firms look for two things in making their decisions to invest in a firm. The first is a high return. Venture capital firms are willing to invest in high-risk new and small firms. However, they require high levels of returns (sometimes as high as 700 percent within five to seven years) to take on these risks. The second is an easy exit. Venture capital firms realize a profit on their investments by eventually selling their firm interests. They want a quick and easy exit opportunity when it comes time to sell. Basically, venture capital firms provide equity funds to new, unproven, and young firms. This willingness separates venture capital firms from commercial banks and investment firms, which prefer to invest in existing, financially secure businesses.

TIME OUT

16-1 What sources of debt financing are available to new and small firms?

16-2 What is a venture capital firm?

The Choice to Go Public

If they succeed, at some point new and small firms grow such that they need more capital than they can raise on their own and do not want or need to pay to get additional funds from banks and venture capitalists. At this point, the firm decides to make an **initial public offering (IPO)** of stock. That is, the firm allows its equity, some of which was held privately by managers and venture capital investors, to be *publicly* traded in stock markets for the first time. The Finance at Work reading highlights the unusually large number of IPOs seen in the first half of 2006.

The technical details associated with the sale of public stock appear below. However, in making the decision to go from a private to a public firm, managers must consider the benefits versus the costs of doing so. As mentioned above, a major benefit of going public is that the firm will have a new, larger pool of equity capital than is available from any previous source (bank or venture capitalist). This new equity allows a firm to undertake new and profitable investment opportunities that it could not undertake as a private firm. The market provides a market value for the firm's common stock, which is really a readily available measure of firm performance (another advantage of going public). Such a transparent measure of firm performance can attract even more stockholders and can provide a tool that can be used to reward firm managers (i.e., through stock or option payments as part of compensation packages). Finally, as private firms, managers generally must invest much of their personal wealth and human capital in the firm. From Chapters 9 and 10, we know that this results in a poorly diversified portfolio for the firm's original owners. By going public, the original owners can reallocate their personal wealth away from the firm and into more diversified portfolios.

However, some significant costs are attached to the decision to become a public firm. First and foremost is the direct financial cost of an IPO. Cash expenses associated with an IPO (e.g., legal services, printing) can total $1 million. These expenses must be paid regardless of whether the IPO succeeds or not. Additionally, underwriters charge a discount (on average about 7 percent) to sell the stock and IPOs are typically underpriced (on average about 15 percent) to ensure a successful sale. Thus, a significant amount of the issue proceeds do not actually become available to the newly public firm.

Add to these financial costs a substantial demand for time from the firm's owners during the IPO process. That is, the firm's owners and top managers must spend a significant amount of time with the investment bankers to discuss all aspects of the firm and with major potential stockholders before the IPO is completed. These time demands grow even more significantly as the offering date approaches.

Finally, throughout the IPO process, managers must disclose firm details that may be valuable to competitors. Further, as a public firm, shareholders have the right to a great deal of information about the firm. The release of this information to stockholders also releases it to competitors.

THE IPO POP: FILINGS SURGE AMID RUSH TO TAP RISING MARKET

A raft of new companies filed for stock offerings in the U.S.—no fewer than 10 registered with the Securities and Exchange Commission on Friday, the highest daily number since 2000. "People have been asking, with the market as high as it is, why aren't there more companies rushing to go public? Well, apparently there are now," says Ben Holmes, publisher of Morningnotes.com, a research firm that tracks stock issuance.

The average number of IPOs filed with the SEC is 1.3 a day over the past 12 months, according to deal tracker Dealogic, so Friday's output stands out. The last time more than 10 were filed in a single day was in March 2000, when the

tech-stock bubble was about to burst. Friday was the end of an especially active week for IPO filings. There were 19 deals—the busiest week for IPO registrations so far this year, says Dealogic.

"Clearly, the volume of transactions filed last week is of a magnitude that we haven't seen since 2000 and is indicative of underwriters' and issuers' posture toward the market," says Suzanne Skipper, head of equity capital markets at Merriman Curhan Ford & Co.

Source: Lynn Cowan, "The IPO Pop: Filings Surge Amid Rush to Tap Rising Market," *The Wall Street Journal*, May 16, 2006, p. C4.

 want to know more? **Key Words to Search for Updates: IPOs, stock sales, stock markets**

16.2 Public Firms' Capital Sources

In contrast to small and new firms that can only get capital funding from mainly private sources, public firms raise the majority of their capital funds from public debt and equity markets. Public firms raise large amounts of short-term debt in the money market, primarily as commercial paper. Further, public firms raise long-term capital by issuing securities in the public debt and equity markets.

Debt Financing

Public firms or corporations obtain debt financing to meet their capital needs in two major ways: commercial paper and corporate bonds. As we noted in Chapter 8, both of these types of debt financing trade in the financial markets. Commercial paper is short-term debt sold and traded in the money markets, while long-term debt is sold and traded in the capital markets.

COMMERCIAL PAPER **Commercial paper** is an unsecured short-term promissory note issued by a public firm to raise short-term cash, often to finance working-capital requirements. Commercial paper is the largest (in terms of dollar value outstanding) of the money market instruments, with $1,860.9 billion outstanding as of 2008. One reason that so much commercial paper is outstanding is that companies with strong credit ratings can generally borrow money at a lower interest rate by issuing commercial paper than by directly borrowing (via loans) from banks. Indeed, although business loans were the major asset on bank balance sheets between 1965 and 1990, they have dropped in importance since 1990. This trend reflects the growth of the commercial paper market.

Figure 16.2 illustrates the difference between commercial paper rates and the prime rate for borrowing from banks from 1973 through 2008. Notice that in the late 1990s, as the U.S. economy thrived and default risk on the highest quality borrowers decreased, the spread between the prime rate and the commercial paper rate increased.

figure 16.2

Commercial Paper and
Prime Rates

figure 16.3

Direct versus Dealer
Placements of
Commercial Paper

Trading Process for Commercial Paper   Commercial paper is sold to investors either directly (about 20 percent of all issues in 2008—see Figure 16.3), using the issuers' own sales force (e.g., GMAC), or indirectly through brokers and dealers (about 80 percent of all issues in 2008), such as commercial banks and investment banks underwriting the issues (see below). Commercial paper underwritten and issued through brokers and dealers is more expensive to the issuer, usually increasing the cost of the issue by 1/10 to 1/8 of a percent, reflecting an underwriting cost. In return, the dealer guarantees the sale of the whole issue. To help achieve this goal, the dealer contacts prospective buyers of the commercial paper, determines the appropriate discount rate on the commercial paper, and relays any special requests in terms of specific quantities and maturities to the issuer. If a potential investor (such as a money market mutual fund) issues commercial paper through a dealer and makes a request at the beginning of the day for a particular maturity, the request is often completed by the end of the day.

When a firm issues commercial paper directly to a buyer, the company saves the cost of the dealer (and the underwriting services) but must find appropriate investors and determine the appropriate discount rate that will place the complete paper issue. When the firm decides how much commercial paper it wants to issue, it posts offering rates to potential buyers based on its own estimates of investor demand. The firm then monitors the flow of money during the day and adjusts its commercial paper rates depending on investor demand.

Because commercial paper is unsecured debt, the issuing company's credit rating is of particular importance in determining how marketable a commercial paper issue will be. Credit ratings provide potential investors with information regarding the ability of the issuing firm to repay the borrowed funds as promised and to compare the commercial paper issues of different companies. Several credit rating firms rate commercial paper issues (e.g., Standard & Poor's, Moody's, and Fitch ICBA, Inc.). Standard & Poor's rates commercial paper from A-1 for highest quality issues to D for lowest quality issues, while Moody's rates commercial paper from P-1 for highest quality issues to "not rated" for lowest quality issues. Virtually all companies that issue commercial paper obtain ratings from at least one rating services company, and most obtain two rating evaluations. The better the credit rating on a commercial paper issue, the lower the interest rate (or discount from par) on the issue.

Commercial paper issuers with lower than prime credit ratings often back their commercial paper issues with lines of credit from commercial banks. In these cases, banks agree to make the promised payment on the commercial paper if the issuer cannot pay off the debt at maturity. Thus, a letter of credit backing commercial paper effectively substitutes the credit rating of the issuing firm with the credit rating of the bank. This reduces the paper purchasers' risk and results in a lower interest rate (and higher credit rating) on the commercial paper. In other cases, the issuing firm arranges a line of credit with a bank (a loan commitment) and draws on this line if it has insufficient funds to repay the commercial paper issue at maturity.

LONG-TERM DEBT   As Chapter 6 described in detail, corporate bonds are long-term debt securities issued by public corporations ($10,581.8 billion outstanding in 2007; approximately 55 percent of all outstanding long-term bonds). The minimum denomination on publicly traded corporate bonds is $1,000, and coupon-paying corporate bonds generally pay interest semiannually.

The Trading Process for Corporate Bonds   The initial or primary sale of corporate bond issues occurs either through a public offering, using an investment bank serving as a security underwriter, or through a private placement to a small group of investors (often financial institutions). Generally, when a firm issues bonds to the public, many investment banks are interested in underwriting the bonds. The bonds can generally be sold in a national market. Total dollar volume of new debt issues was $6,633.6 billion in 2007, down from $7,122.6 billion in 2006. Table 16.1 lists the activity of the top 10 bond underwriters in 2007. Most bonds issued by smaller firms are underwritten by small regional investment banks located in the immediate area of the municipal issuer (e.g., Bernardi Securities located in Chicago). The high cost of gathering information about smaller corporate bond issuers limits smaller investors' interest in the sales of these issues.

Most often, corporate bonds are offered publicly through investment banking firms as underwriters. Normally, the investment bank facilitates this transaction using a **firm commitment underwriting,** illustrated in Figure 16.4. The investment bank guarantees the firm a price for newly issued bonds by buying

MANAGER	AMOUNT	2007 MARKET SHARE	NUMBER OF DEALS	2006 MARKET SHARE
Citigroup	$ 546.5	8.2%	1,431	8.7%
JP Morgan	476.3	7.2	1,294	6.6
Deutsche Bank AG	429.7	6.5	1,197	6.7
Merrill Lynch	370.8	5.6	1,169	5.8
Lehman Brothers	365.6	5.5	855	6.2
Morgan Stanley	361.2	5.5	1,055	5.8
Barclays Capital	349.4	5.3	946	5.3
Goldman Sachs	286.5	4.3	672	4.6
Royal Bank of Scotland Group	282.2	4.3	787	4.6
Banc of America Securities	276.5	4.2	726	4.4
Top ten total	$3,744.9	56.6	10,132	58.7
Industry total	$6,633.6	100.0	17,865	$7,122.6

Top Underwriters of Global Debt (in billions of dollars)   table 16.1

Source: Thomson Financial Web site 2008. **www.tfibcm.com**

figure 16.4

Firm Commitment Underwriting of a Corporate Bond Issue

the whole issue at a fixed price (the bid price) from the bond-issuing firm at a discount from par. The investment bank then seeks to resell these securities to investors at a higher price (the offer price). As a result, the investment bank takes a risk that it may not be able to resell the securities to investors at a higher price. This may occur if a firm's bond value suddenly falls due to an unexpected change in interest rates or negative information being released about the issuing firm. If this occurs, the investment bank takes a loss on its security underwriting. However, the bond *issuer* is protected by being able to sell the whole issue.

The investment bank can purchase the bonds through competitive bidding against other investment bankers or by directly negotiating with the issuer. In a **competitive sale,** the bond-issuing firm invites bids from a number of underwriters. The investment bank that submits the highest bid to the bond issuer wins the bid. The underwriter may use a syndicate of other underwriters and investment banks to distribute (sell) the issue to the public. With a **negotiated sale,** a single investment bank obtains the exclusive right to originate, underwrite, and distribute the new bonds through a one-on-one negotiation process. With a negotiated sale, the investment bank provides the origination and advising services to the issuers.

Some corporate securities are offered on a **best efforts underwriting** basis, in which the underwriter does not guarantee a firm price to the issuer (as with a firm commitment offering). Here, the underwriter acts more as a placing or distribution agent for a fee. Unlike a firm commitment underwriting, with a best efforts underwriting, the investment bank incurs no risk of mispricing the security since it simply seeks to sell the securities at the best market price it can get for the issuing firm.

In a private placement, a public firm (sometimes with an investment bank's help) seeks to find a large institutional buyer or group of buyers (usually less than 10) to purchase the whole issue. To protect smaller individual investors against a lack of disclosure, the Security and Exchange Act of 1934 requires publicly traded securities to be registered with the Securities and Exchange Commission (SEC). Private placements, on the other hand, can be unregistered and can only be resold to large, financially sophisticated investors. These large investors supposedly possess the resources and expertise to analyze a security's risk.

Privately placed bonds (and stocks) have traditionally been among the most illiquid securities in the bond market, with only the very largest financial institutions or institutional investors being able or willing to buy and hold them without an active secondary market. In April 1990, however, the Securities and Exchange Commission (SEC) amended its Regulation 144A. The amendment allowed large investors to begin trading privately placed securities among themselves even though, in general, privately placed securities do not satisfy the stringent disclosure and informational requirements that the SEC imposes on approved publicly registered issues. Rule 144A private placements may now be underwritten by investment banks on a firm commitment basis. Of the total $844.9 billion in private debt and equity placements in the first two quarters of 2007, $769.1 billion (91 percent) were Rule 144A placements. Citigroup was the lead underwriter of Rule 144A debt placements over this period (underwriting $91.1 billion, 11.9 percent of the total placements).

The SEC defined "large investors" as those with assets of $100 million or more—which excludes all but the very wealthiest household savers. We might well ask how long this size restriction will remain. As they become more sophisticated and information acquisition costs fall, savers will increasingly demand access to the private placement market. In such a world, savers would have a choice not only between the secondary securities from financial institutions and the primary securities publicly offered by public firms, but also between publicly offered (registered) securities and privately offered (unregistered) securities.

The secondary market for corporate bonds is thin (i.e., trades are relatively infrequent). Thin trading is mainly a result of a lack of information on bond issuers, as well as special features (such as covenants) that are built into those bonds' contracts. Information on corporate bond issuers (particularly smaller firms) is generally more costly to obtain and evaluate, although this is in part offset by bond rating agencies (see Chapter 6).

Equity Financing

Public firms can also issue corporate stock or equity as another major source of capital financing. As Chapter 7 described in detail, corporate stock represents ownership shares in the public corporation. In exchange for funds, the firm gives the stockholders ownership rights in the firm, as well as cash flows in the form of dividends. Further, common stockholders have voting privileges on major issues in the firm, such as the election of the board of directors, which oversees the day-to-day operations of the firm.

Before a corporation can issue common stock, a majority of both the board of directors and the firm's existing common stockholders must authorize the sale of shares. In the 1990s, the market value of corporate stock outstanding increased faster than any other type of financial security. From 1994 through 2000, stock values increased over 200 percent, from $6,333.3 billion to $19,522.8 billion outstanding. A slow U.S. economy saw market values fall to a low of $11,900.5 billion at the end of 2002, but by 2007 stock market values had rebounded to $22,445.0 billion.

THE TRADING PROCESS FOR CORPORATE EQUITY Primary markets are markets in which corporations raise funds through *new* stock issues. Initial investors (fund suppliers) buy new stock securities in exchange for funds

figure 16.5

Primary Market Stock Transaction

Top Underwriters of Global Equity (in billions of dollars)				table 16.2
MANAGER	**AMOUNT**	**2007 MARKET SHARE**	**NUMBER OF DEALS**	**2006 MARKET SHARE**
UBS	$ 81.2	9.3%	365	8.3%
JP Morgan	77.8	8.9	312	6.5
Citigroup	71.1	8.1	309	8.5
Goldman Sachs	70.6	8.1	233	9.7
Morgan Stanley	64.7	7.4	271	8.0
Merrill Lynch	60.6	6.9	260	7.6
Credit Suisse	54.6	6.2	235	5.9
Deutsche Bank AG	52.2	6.0	214	4.9
Lehman Brothers	29.4	3.4	153	3.8
China International Capital	20.2	2.3	12	1.6
Top ten total	$582.4	66.6	2,364	64.8
Industry total	$876.3	100.0	4,388	$719.5

Source: Thomson Financial Web site 2008. **www.tfibcm.com**

(money) that the issuer (user of funds) needs. A primary market sale may be a first-time issue by a private firm going public (i.e., an IPO). Alternatively, a primary market sale may be a seasoned offering, in which the firm already has shares of the stock trading in the secondary markets. In both cases, the issuer receives the sale proceeds and the primary market investors receive the securities.

As illustrated in Figure 16.5, most primary securities market transactions go through investment banks (e.g., Goldman Sachs or Morgan Stanley), which serve as intermediaries between the issuing firms (fund users) and ultimate investors (fund suppliers). Total dollar volume of new equity issues was $876.3 billion in 2007, up from $719.5 billion in 2005. Table 16.2 lists the activity of the top 10 equity underwriters in 2007.

As with the primary sales of bonds (discussed above), investment banks can conduct a primary sale of stock using a firm commitment underwriting, in which investment banks guarantee a price for newly issued securities to the issuing corporation by buying the whole issue at a fixed price, or on a best efforts underwriting basis, in which the underwriter does not guarantee a price to the issuer but rather acts more as a placing or distribution agent. In a firm commitment underwriting, the investment bank purchases stock from the issuing firm for a guaranteed price (called the **net proceeds**) and resells them to investors at a higher price (called the **gross proceeds**). The difference between the gross proceeds and the net proceeds on an issue (called the **underwriter's spread**) is compensation for the expenses and risks incurred by the investment bank. In the 2000s, underwriter's gross spread on first-time equity issues (i.e., private firms going public—the initial public offering, or IPO) averaged 7.65 percent and

figure 16.6

Tombstone
Announcement

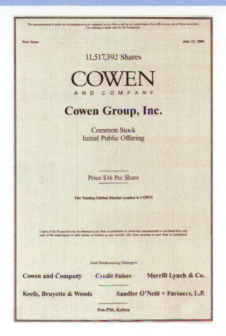

This announcement is under no circumstances to be construed as an offer to sell or as a solicitation of an offer to buy any of these securities. The offering is made only by the Prospectus.

New Issue   July 12, 2006

11,517,392 Shares

COWEN
AND COMPANY

Cowen Group, Inc.

Common Stock
Initial Public Offering

Price $16 Per Share

The Nasdaq Global Market symbol is COWN

Copies of the Prospectus may be obtained in any State or jurisdiction in which this announcement is circulated from only such of the undersigned or other dealers or brokers as may lawfully offer these securities in such State or jurisdiction.

Joint Bookrunning Managers

Cowen and Company   Credit Suisse   Merrill Lynch & Co.

Keefe, Bruyette & Woods   Sandler O'Neill + Partners, L.P.

Fox-Pitt, Kelton

 For interactive versions of this example visit www.mhhe.com/can1e

EXAMPLE 16-2

CALCULATING COSTS OF ISSUING STOCK

Renee's, Inc. needs to raise $100 million to finance firm expansion. In discussions with its investment bank, Renee's learns that the bankers recommend a gross proceeds price of $40 per share, and they will charge an underwriter's spread of 6.5 percent of the gross price. Calculate the net proceeds to Renee's from the sale of stock. How many shares of stock will Renee's need to sell in order to receive the $100 million they need?

SOLUTION:

Net proceeds = Gross proceeds − Underwriter's spread

$$= \$40 - (.065 \times \$40) = \$37.40$$

Funds needed = $100 million = $37.40 × Number of shares sold

Number of shares sold = $100 million/$37.40 = 2,673,797 shares

on seasoned equity issues (i.e., publicly traded firms issuing additional shares) averaged 5.67 percent.

Often, investment banks will bring in a number of other investment banks to help sell and distribute a new security issue. Such a group of sellers is called a **syndicate.** For example, the tombstone in Figure 16.6 announcing the initial public offering of 11,517,392 million shares of common stock in Cowen and Company lists the syndicate of six investment banks involved in the initial issue. The investment banks are listed according to their degree of participation in new share sales. The lead bank(s) in the syndicate (Cowen and Company, Credit Suisse,

figure 16.7

Getting Shares of Stock
to the Investing Public

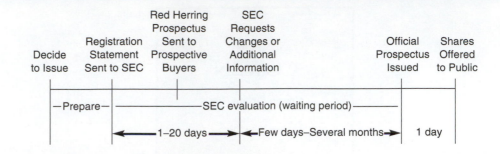

and Merrill Lynch), who directly negotiate with the issuing firm on behalf of the syndicate, are called the **originating house(s).** Once an issue is arranged and its terms set, each syndicate member is assigned a given number of shares in the issue for which it is responsible for selling. Shares of stock issued through a syndicate of investment banks spread the risk associated with the stock sale among several investment banks. A syndicate also results in a larger pool of potential outside investors, widening the scope of the investor base and increasing the probability of a successful sale.

Just as with primary sales of corporate bond issues, firms may initially issue corporate stocks through public sales (wherein the stock issue is offered to the general investing public). New stock issues may also be sold by private placement (wherein stock is sold privately to a limited number of large investors). In a public sale of stock, once the issuing firm and the investment bank have agreed on the stock issue details, the investment bank must get SEC approval in accordance with the Securities and Exchange Act of 1934. Stock registration can be a lengthy process. We illustrate the process in Figure 16.7. The process starts with the preparation of the registration statement to be filed with the SEC. The registration statement includes:

- Information about the issuing firm's business.
- The key provisions and features of the security to be issued.
- The risks involved with the security.
- Managements' background.

The focus of the registration statement is to fully disclose information about the firm and the securities issued to the public at large. At the same time that the issuing firm and its investment bank prepare the registration statement to be filed with the SEC, they must also prepare a preliminary version of the public offering's prospectus called the **red herring prospectus.** The red herring prospectus is similar to the registration statement, but is distributed to potential equity buyers. Once the SEC registers the issue, the red herring prospectus is replaced with the official or final prospectus.

After the firm submits the registration statement, the SEC has 20 days to request additional information or changes to the registration statement. This review period is called the waiting period, during which the SEC works through the new security issue approval process. First-time or infrequent issuers can sometimes wait up to several months for SEC registration, especially if the SEC

figure 16.8

Getting Shelf Registrations to the Investing Public

keeps requesting additional information and revised red herring prospectuses. However, companies that know the registration process well can generally obtain registration in a few days.

Once the SEC is satisfied with the registration statement, it registers the issue. At this point, the issuing firm (along with its investment bankers) sets the final share selling price, prints the official **prospectus** describing the issue, and sends it to all potential buyers of the issue. Upon issuance of the prospectus (generally the day following SEC registration), the firm may sell the shares.

To reduce registration time and costs, yet still protect the public by requiring issuers to disclose information about the firm and the security to be issued, the SEC passed a rule in 1982 allowing for "shelf registration." As illustrated in Figure 16.8, **shelf registration** allows firms that plan to offer multiple issues of stock over a two-year period to submit one registration statement as described above (called a *master registration statement*). The registration statement summarizes the firm's financing plans for the two-year period. Thus, the securities are shelved for up to two years until the firm is ready to issue them. Once the issuer and its investment bank decide to issue shares during the two-year shelf registration period, they prepare and file a short-form statement with the SEC. Upon SEC approval, the shares can be priced and offered to the public usually within one or two days of deciding to take the shares "off the shelf."

Thus, shelf registration allows a firm to get stocks into the market quickly (e.g., in one or two days) if the firm feels conditions (especially the price they can get for the new stock) are right, without the time lag generally associated with full SEC registration. For example, in July 2006, Alamo Group, Inc. announced a public offering of 2.3 million shares of its common stock under its shelf registration filed with the SEC. UBS Investment Bank led the underwriting of shares that were sold just days after this announcement.

TIME OUT

16-3 What sources of debt financing are available to public firms?

16-4 What is the difference between a public firm's commercial paper and its long-term debt?

Business Application Solution

As a publicly traded firm, the managers of ADK Industries need to consider several factors as they decide how to finance the $5 million needed for firm expansion. The first issue managers must consider is whether to finance the $5 million with debt, equity, or a combination of the two forms of capital. Public firms obtain debt financing in two major ways: commercial paper and corporate bonds. Commercial paper underwritten and issued through brokers and dealers can be expensive to the issuer, usually increasing the cost of the issue by 1/10 to 1/8 of a percent, reflecting an underwriting cost. In return, the dealer guarantees the sale of the whole issue. The initial or primary corporate bond issue sales occur either through a public offering, using an investment bank serving as a security underwriter, or through a private placement to small groups of investors. ADK Industries could also raise their capital by selling corporate stock or equity. In a public sale of stock, once the issuing firm and the investment bank have agreed on the details of the stock issue, the investment bank must get SEC approval in accordance with the Securities and Exchange Act of 1934.

Personal Application Solution

Marge Upton has to consider several issues as she seeks to find the $15,000 she needs to reopen her bicycle repair shop. Marge will want to consider borrowing funds from private or public sources. Private debt financing includes capital funds borrowed from personal savings, friends or relatives, financial institutions such as commercial bank loans, or venture capitalists. Private equity financing includes capital funds invested by venture capitalists. Public sources of capital include debt and equity financing provided by government agencies such as the U.S. Small Business Administration (SBA).

summary of learning goals

This chapter presented an overview of the decisions firms face when they raise capital. The chapter noted the important role that financial institutions play in this process.

LG1 **Evaluate different methods for small firms to get funding.** Most new and small firms finance their assets by borrowing funds from private or public sources. Private debt financing includes capital funds borrowed from personal savings, friends or relatives, financial institutions such as commercial bank loans, or venture capitalists. Private equity financing includes capital funds invested by venture capitalists. Public sources of capital include debt and equity financing provided by government agencies such as the U.S. Small Business Administration.

LG2 **Appreciate what venture capital is and the role it plays in encouraging entrepreneurship.** Venture capital is a professionally managed pool of money used to finance new and often high-risk firms. Venture capital is generally provided by investment institutions or private individuals willing to back an untried company and its managers in return for an equity investment in the firm.

LG3 **Differentiate among sources of capital funding for public firms.** The initial or primary sale of corporate bond issues occurs either through a public offering, or a private placement. In a

public offering, an investment bank facilitates this transfer using a firm commitment underwriting. The investment bank guarantees the firm a price for newly issued bonds by buying the whole issue at a fixed price from the bond-issuing firm. The investment bank then seeks to resell these securities to investors at a higher price.

LG4 **Trace the process by which securities are underwritten.** Public firms raise the majority of their capital funds from the public debt and equity markets. Public firms raise large amounts of short-term debt in the money market, primarily in the form of commercial paper. Further, public firms raise long-term capital by issuing securities in the public debt and equity markets.

key terms

angel venture capitalists (or **angels**), Wealthy individuals who make equity investments. (p. 517)

back-end (or **commitment**) **fee,** A fee charged by a bank on any unused balances of a loan commitment line at the end of the loan commitment period. (p. 516)

best efforts underwriting, A security issue in which the underwriter does not guarantee a firm price to the issuer (as with a firm commitment offering) and acts more as a placing or distribution agent for a fee. (p. 522)

commercial paper, An unsecured short-term promissory note issued by a public firm to raise short-term cash, often to finance working capital requirements. (p. 519)

competitive sale, A sale of securities in which the issuing firm invites bids from a number of underwriters. The investment bank that submits the highest bid to the issuer wins the bid. The winning bid underwriter then distributes (sells) the issue to the public. (p. 522)

firm commitment underwriting, A security issue in which the investment bank guarantees the issuer a price for newly issued securities by buying the whole issue at a fixed price from the security issuer (the bid price). The investment bank then seeks to resell the securities to investors at a higher price (the offer price). (p. 521)

fixed-rate loan, A loan on which the interest payments the firm must make can not change over the life of the loan. (p. 516)

gross proceeds, The higher price at which the investment bank resells the stock to investors in a firm commitment underwriting. (p. 524)

initial public offerings (IPOs), A first-time issue of stock by a private firm going public (e.g., allowing its equity, some of which was held privately by managers and venture capital investors, to be *publicly* traded in stock markets for the first time). (p. 518)

institutional venture capital firms, Business entities whose sole purpose is to find and fund the most promising new firms. (p. 517)

loan commitment agreement, A contractual commitment by a bank to loan a firm a certain maximum amount at given interest rate terms for a stated length of time over which the firm has the option to take down this loan. (p. 515)

negotiated sale, A sale of securities in which the investment bank obtains the exclusive right to originate, underwrite, and distribute the new securities through a one-on-one negotiation process. With a negotiated sale, the investment bank provides the origination and advising services to the issuers. (p. 522)

net proceeds, The guaranteed price the investment bank purchases the stock from the issuing firm in a firm commitment underwriting. (p. 524)

originating house(s), The lead bank(s) in a syndicate, who directly negotiate with the issuing firm on behalf of the syndicate. (p. 526)

primary markets, Markets in which corporations raise funds through *new* issues of securities. (p. 523)

prospectus, Official document in which the issuing firm (along with its investment bankers) sets the final selling price on the securities and describes the issue. (p. 527)

red herring prospectus, A preliminary registration statement filed with the SEC. (p. 526)

shelf registration, A method of registering securities that allows firms that plan to offer multiple issues of the security over a two-year period to submit one registration statement. (p. 527)

spot loan, A loan in which the firm receives the funds as soon as the loan is approved. (p. 515)

syndicate, The group of investment banks used to help sell and distribute a new security issue. (p. 525)

take down, Borrowing against a line of credit or loan commitment. (p. 515)

underwriter's spread, The difference between the gross proceeds and the net proceeds. (p. 524)

up-front (or facility) fee, A fee charged by a bank for making funds available through a loan commitment. (p. 515)

variable-rate loan, A loan on which the interest rate on the loan (and thus the interest payments the firm must make) can change over the life of the loan. (p. 516)

venture capital, A professionally managed pool of money used to finance new and often high-risk firms. (p. 517)

self-test problems with solutions

1 **Calculating Fees on a Loan Commitment** Sandy's Bed and Breakfast has been approved for a $125,000 loan commitment from its local bank. The bank has offered the following terms: term = 1 year, up-front fee = 45 basis points, back-end fee = 65 basis points, and rate on the loan = 8.25%. Sandy's expects to immediately take down $110,000 and no more during the year unless there is some unforeseen need. Calculate the total interest and fees Sandy's Bed and Breakfast can expect to pay on this loan commitment.

Solution:

$$
\begin{aligned}
\text{Up-front fee} &= \$125{,}000 \times 0.0045 & &= \$\ \ \ 562.50 \\
\text{Back-end fee} &= (\$125{,}000 - \$110{,}000) \times 0.0065 &= & \ \ \ \ \ 97.50 \\
\text{Interest} &= \$110{,}000 \times .0825 & &= \ \ 9{,}075.00 \\
\text{Total} & & &= \$9{,}735.00
\end{aligned}
$$

2 **Calculating Costs of Issuing Stock** Jerry's Bait & Tackle Corp. recently went public with an initial public offering of 3.75 million shares of stock. The underwriter used a firm commitment offering in which the net proceeds were $13.875 per share and the underwriter's spread was 7.5 percent of the gross proceeds. Jerry's also paid legal and other administrative costs of $850,000 for the IPO. Calculate the gross proceeds and the total funds received by Jerry's Bait & Tackle Corp. from the sale of the 3.75 million shares of stock.

Solution:

$$
\begin{aligned}
\text{Net proceeds} = \$13.875 &= \text{Gross proceeds} - \text{Underwriter's spread} \\
&= \text{Gross proceeds} - (.075 \times \text{Gross proceeds}) \\
&= (1 - .075) \times \text{Gross proceeds} \\
\text{Gross proceeds} &= \$13.875/(1 - .075) = \$15.00
\end{aligned}
$$

Total funds received by Jerry's Bait & Tackle = ($13.875 × 3,750,000) − $850,000 = $51,181,250

questions

1. Describe the various sources of capital funding available to new and small firms. *(LG1)*

2. What process do banks use to evaluate bank loans to small versus mid-market business firms? *(LG1)*

3. What is the difference between a spot loan and a loan commitment? *(LG1)*

4. Why do banks charge up-front fees and back-end fees on loan commitments? *(LG1)*

5. What is the difference between a fixed-rate and a floating-rate loan? *(LG1)*

6. What types of programs does the Small Business Administration offer to new and small businesses? Under what conditions would a new or small firm use each program? *(LG1)*

7. What is venture capital? *(LG2)*

8. What are the different types of venture capital firms? How do institutional venture capital firms differ from angel venture capital firms? *(LG2)*

9. What are the advantages and disadvantages to a new or small firm of getting capital funding from a venture capital firm? *(LG2)*

10. As a new or small firm considers going public what must the owners consider? *(LG1)*

11. Describe the various sources of capital funding available to public firms. *(LG3)*

12. What is the difference between a direct and an indirect placement of commercial paper? *(LG3)*

13. Can a public firm with a lower-than-prime credit rating issue commercial paper? *(LG3)*

14. How does a best efforts underwriting differ from a firm commitment underwriting? If you operated a company issuing stock for the first time, which type of underwriting would you prefer? Why might you still choose the alternative? *(LG4)*

15. How does a competitive sale of securities differ from a negotiated sale? Which type of underwriting would you prefer? Why might you still choose the alternative? *(LG4)*

16. How does a public offering of debt or equity securities issued by a public firm differ from a private placement? *(LG4)*

17. What are the net proceeds, gross proceeds, and underwriter's spread? How does each affect the funds received by a public firm when debt or equity securities are issued? *(LG4)*

18. Why would an investment bank use a syndicate to assist in underwriting debt or equity securities? *(LG4)*

19. What is the difference between a prospectus and a red herring prospectus? *(LG4)*

20. What is a shelf registration? Why would a public firm want to issue securities using a shelf registration? *(LG4)*

problems

www.mhhe.com/can1e

basic problems

16-1 Calculating Fees on a Loan Commitment You have approached your local bank for a start-up loan commitment for $250,000 needed to open a computer repair store. You have requested that the term of the loan be one year. Your bank has offered you the following terms: size of loan commitment = $250,000, term = 1 year, up-front fee = 50 basis points, back-end fee = 75 basis points. If you take down 80 percent of the total loan commitment, calculate the total fees you have paid on this loan commitment. *(LG1)*

16-2 Calculating Fees on a Loan Commitment Calculate the total fees a firm would have to pay when its bank offers the firm the following loan commitment: A loan commitment of $2,500,000 with an up-front fee of 75 basis points and a back-end fee of 25 basis points. The take down on the loan is 50 percent. *(LG1)*

16-3 Calculating Costs of Issuing Stock Husker's Tuxedo's, Inc. needs to raise $250 million to finance its plan for nationwide expansion. In discussions with its investment bank, Husker's learns that the bankers recommend an offer price (or gross price) of $35 per share and they will charge an underwriter's spread of $1.75 per share. Calculate the net proceeds to Husker's from the sale of stock. How many shares of stock will Husker's need to sell in order to receive the $250 million they need? *(LG4)*

16-4 Calculating Costs of Issuing Stock Don's Captain Morgan, Inc. needs to raise $12.5 million to finance plant expansion. In discussions with its investment bank, Don's learns that the bankers recommend an offer price (or gross proceeds) of $15 per share and Don's will receive $14 per share. Calculate the underwriter's spread on the issue. How many shares of stock will Don's need to sell in order to receive the $250 million they need? *(LG4)*

16-5 Calculating Costs of Issuing Debt KellyGirl's Golf Games, Inc., with the help of its investment bank recently issued $43.125 million of new debt. The offer price (and face value) on the debt was $1,000 per bond and the underwriter's spread was 7 percent of the gross proceeds. Calculate the amount of capital funding KellyGirl's Golf Games, Inc. raised through this debt offering. *(LG4)*

16-6 Calculating Costs of Issuing Debt Bailey's Dog Pens, Inc., with the help of its investment bank, recently issued $112,500,000 of new debt. The offer price on the debt was $1,000 per bond and the underwriter's spread was 5 percent of the gross proceeds. Calculate the amount of capital funding Bailey's Dog Pens, Inc. raised through this bond issue. *(LG4)*

intermediate problems

16-7 Calculating Fees on a Loan Commitment You have approached your local bank for a start-up loan commitment for $250,000 needed to open a computer repair store. You have requested that the term of the loan be one year. Your bank has offered you the following terms: size of loan commitment = $250,000, term = 1 year, up-front fee = 50 basis points, back-end fee = 75 basis points, and rate on the loan = 8%. If you immediately take down $150,000 and no more during the year, calculate the total interest and fees you have paid on this loan commitment. *(LG1)*

16-8 **Calculating Fees on a Loan Commitment** Casey's One Stop has been approved for a $75,000 loan commitment from its local bank. The bank has offered the following terms: term = 1 year, up-front fee = 85 basis points, back-end fee = 35 basis points, and rate on the loan = 7.75%. Casey's expects to immediately take down $70,000 and no more during the year unless there is some unforeseen need. Calculate the total interest and fees Casey's One Stop can expect to pay on this loan commitment. *(LG1)*

16-9 **Calculating Costs of Issuing Debt** Sipe's Paint and Wallpaper, Inc. needs to raise $1 million to finance plant expansion. In discussions with its investment bank, Sipe's learns that the bankers recommend a debt issue with a gross proceeds of $1,000 per bond and they will charge an underwriter's spread of 6.5 percent of the gross proceeds. How many bonds will Sipe's Paint and Wallpaper need to sell in order to receive the $1 million they need? *(LG4)*

16-10 **Calculating Costs of Issuing Debt** Renee's Boutique, Inc. needs to raise $100 million to finance firm expansion. In discussions with its investment bank, Renee's learns that the bankers recommend a debt issue with an offer price of $1,000 per bond and they will charge an underwriter's spread of 5 percent of the gross price. Calculate the net proceeds to Renee's from the sale of the debt. How many bonds will Renee's Boutique need to sell in order to receive the $100 million they need? *(LG4)*

16-11 **Calculating Costs of Issuing Stock** KellyGirl's Golf Games, Inc., with the help of its investment bank, recently issued 2.5 million shares of new stock. The offer price on the stock was $20.50 per share and KellyGirl's received a total of $48,687,500 through this stock offering. Calculate the net proceeds and the underwriter's spread on the stock offering. What percentage of the gross price is the investment bank charging KellyGirl's for underwriting the stock issue? *(LG4)*

16-12 **Calculating Costs of Issuing Stock** Bailey's Dog Pens, Inc., with the help of its investment bank, recently issued 5 million shares of new stock. The offer price on the stock was $12.50 per share and Bailey's received a total of $57.5 million from the stock offering. Calculate the net proceeds and the underwriter's spread charged by the underwriter to Bailey's Dog Pens, Inc. What percentage of the gross proceeds is the investment bank charging Bailey's Dog Pens for underwriting the stock issue? *(LG4)*

16-13 **Calculating Costs of Issuing Stock** Zimba Technology Corp. recently went public with an initial public offering of 2.5 million shares of stock. The underwriter used a firm commitment offering in which the net proceeds was $8.05 per share and the underwriter's spread was 8 percent of the gross proceeds. Zimba also paid legal and other administrative costs of $250,000 for the IPO. Calculate the gross proceeds and the total funds received by Zimba from the sale of the 2.5 million shares of stock. *(LG4)*

16-14 **Calculating Costs of Issuing Stock** Howett Pockett, Inc. plans to issue 10 million new shares of its stock. In discussions with its investment bank, Howett Pocket learns that the bankers recommend a net proceed of $19.90 per share and they will charge an underwriter's spread of 5.5 percent of the gross proceeds. In addition, Howett Pockett must pay $2 million in legal and other administrative expenses for the seasoned stock offering. Calculate the gross proceeds and the total funds received by Howett Pockett from the sale of the 10 million shares of stock. *(LG4)*

16-15 Calculating Fees on a Loan Commitment During the last year you have had a loan commitment from your bank to fund inventory purchases for your small business. The total line available was $500,000, of which you took down $400,000. It is now the end of the loan commitment period and your bank had you pay the back-end fees. You have misplaced the paperwork that listed the terms of the commitment, but you know you paid total fees (this does not include any interest paid to borrow the $400,000) of $3,250 on this loan commitment. You remember that the up-front fee was 50 basis points. Calculate the back-end fee on this loan commitment. *(LG1)*

16-16 Calculating Fees on a Loan Commitment During the last year you have had a loan commitment from your bank to fund working capital for your business. The total line available was $10 million, of which you took down $8 million. It is now the end of the loan commitment period and your bank had you pay the back-end fees. You have misplaced the paperwork that listed the terms of the commitment, but you know you paid total fees (this does not include any interest paid to borrow the $8 million) of $42,650 on this loan commitment. You remember that the back-end fee was 75 basis points. Calculate the front-end fee on this loan commitment. *(LG1)*

16-17 Calculating Costs of Issuing Stock Sipe's Paint and Wallpaper, Inc. needs to raise $1 million to finance plant expansion. In discussions with its investment bank, Sipe's learns that the bankers recommend a gross price of $25 per share and that 45,000 shares of stock be sold. If the net proceeds on the stock sale leaves Sipe's with $1 million, calculate the underwriter's spread on the stock issue. *(LG4)*

16-18 Calculating Costs of Issuing Stock Renee's Boutique, Inc. needs to raise $99.75 million to finance firm expansion. In discussions with its investment bank, Renee's learns that the bankers recommend an offer price of $35 per share and that 3 million shares of stock be sold. If the net proceeds on the stock sale leaves Renee's with $99.75 million, calculate the underwriter's spread on the stock issue. *(LG4)*

16-19 Calculating Costs of Issuing Stock Hughes Technology Corp. recently went public with an initial public offering in which they received a total of $60 million in new capital funding. The underwriter used a firm commitment offering in which the offer price was $10 and the underwriter's spread was $0.75. Hughes also paid legal and other administrative costs of $1,050,000 for the IPO. Calculate the number of shares issued through this IPO. *(LG4)*

16-20 Calculating Costs of Issuing Stock Howett Pockett, Inc. needs to raise $20 million in new capital funding from a seasoned equity offering. In discussions with its investment bank, Howett Pockett learns that the bankers recommend a gross price of $15.50 per share and they will charge an underwriter's spread of $1.50 percent of the gross price. In addition, Howett Pockett must pay $1 million in legal and other administrative expenses for the seasoned stock offering. Calculate the number of shares of stock that Howett Pockett will need to sell to raise the $20 million. *(LG4)*

research it! Underwriters

Go to the Thomson Financial—Investment Banking and Capital Markets Group Web site at **www.thomsonreuters.com/business_units/financial/league_tables** and find the latest information available for debt and equity securities underwriting. Go to the first date (the most recent information) listed under Debt and Equity and click on "Equity Capital Markets Review." This will download a file onto your computer that will contain the most recent information on top underwriters for equity securities. Go back and repeat the last step, clicking on "Debt Capital Markets Review." What is the most recent dollar value of global debt and equity underwritten by investment banks? Who are the top underwriters of debt and equity? How have the top writers' market shares changed in the last year?

integrated minicase: Capital Funding in a Public Firm

Nuran Security Systems, Inc. needs to raise $150,000,000 for asset expansion. As it raises the capital funding, Nuran wants to maintain its current debt ratio of 60 percent. Nuran has been approved for a loan commitment from its local bank. The bank has offered the following terms: term = 1 year, up-front fee = 60 basis points, back-end fee = 90 basis points. Nuran expects it will take down 90 percent of the loan commitment.

Nuran's will also issue new shares of stock to support this asset growth. Nuran's investment bank will use a firm commitment offering in which the net proceeds are $23.875 per share and the underwriter's spread was 7 percent of the gross proceeds. Nuran Security Systems will also pay legal and other administrative costs of $750,000 for the stock issue.

Calculate the amount of debt and equity funding Nuran Security Systems will need to keep its current debt ratio constant and the number of shares of stock the firm must issue to raise the needed stock. What can Nuran Security Systems, Inc. expect to pay for fees on this loan commitment and stock issue?

ANSWERS TO TIME OUT

16-1 Most new and small firms finance their business assets by borrowing funds from private or public sources. Private capital fund suppliers fall into two basic categories: suppliers of debt financing and suppliers of equity financing. Debt financing includes capital funds borrowed from personal savings, friends or relatives, financial institutions such as commercial bank loans, or venture capitalists. Equity financing includes capital funds invested

(continued)

ANSWERS TO TIME OUT   (concluded)

by venture capitalists. Public sources of capital include debt and equity financing provided by government agencies such as the U.S. Small Business Administration (SBA).

16-2   Venture capital is a professionally managed pool of money used to finance new and often high-risk firms.

16-3   In contrast to small and new firms that can only get capital funding from mainly private sources, public firms raise the majority of their capital funds from public debt and equity markets. Public firms raise large amounts of short-term debt in the money market, primarily as commercial paper. Further, public firms raise long-term capital by issuing securities in the public debt and equity markets.

16-4   Commercial paper is short-term debt sold and traded in the money markets, while long-term debt is sold and traded in the capital markets.

chapter 17:

ADDRESSING WORKING CAPITAL POLICIES AND MANAGING SHORT-TERM ASSETS AND LIABILITIES

Learning Goals

LG1 Set overall objectives of a good working capital policy.

LG2 Discuss how net working capital serves the firm.

LG3 Calculate and use the firm's operating cycle and cash cycle to discover how much funding for current assets the firm has to find.

LG4 Model the optimal trade-off between carrying costs and shortage costs that dictates the firm's current asset investment.

LG5 Compare the flexible and restrictive approaches to financing current assets.

LG6 Differentiate among sources of short-term financing available for funding current assets.

LG7 Justify the firm's need to hold cash.

LG8 Use the Baumol and Miller-Orr models for determining cash policy.

LG9 Identify sources of float and show how to control float for the firm's disbursement and collection functions.

LG10 Investigate why firms have excess cash and identify their choices about what to do with it.

LG11 Draw the connection between the firm's credit terms and collection policy and the amount of capital the firm has invested in accounts receivable.

In this chapter, we want to focus on the major trade-off implicit in funding net working capital. By and large, the trade-off involves comparing how much it costs the firm to carry an investment in current assets with the **shortage costs** associated with the firm's not having enough cash, inventory, or accounts receivable.

viewpoints

Business Application

Chewbacca Manufacturing expects sales of $32 million next year. CM's cost of goods sold normally runs at 55 percent of sales; inventory requirements are usually 10 percent of annual sales; the average accounts receivable balance is one-sixth of annual sales; and the average accounts payable balance is 5 percent of sales. If all sales are on credit, what will Chewbacca's level of net working capital and its cash cycle be? **(See solution on p. 558)**

Personal Application

Wanda has saved enough money to go back to grad school. She is planning to put the money in a money market account where it will earn 3.50 percent. If she anticipates slowly drawing the money out over the course of her time in grad school at a constant rate of $25,000 per year, but is charged a commission of $9.95 every time she sells shares, how much should she take out of the mutual fund at a time? **(See solution on p. 558)**

A practice test can be found on the Online Learning Center at
www.mhhe.com/can1e

As we'll see, the firm's ideal solution to providing net working capital would be to get someone else to foot the bill. Though this may be a valid approach to fund *some* of the firm's current assets, it's usually difficult to get someone else to cover the *entire* amount of net working capital necessary to run the firm efficiently. We will, however, discuss how to shift those costs elsewhere as much as possible in this chapter by covering the following topics:

1. How to determine the optimal amount of investment in current assets.
2. How to measure the portion of current assets that the firm is responsible for funding.
3. How to choose the source of funding for that portion of current assets.

 ## 17.1 Revisiting the Balance-Sheet Model of the Firm

Remember our discussion of the balance sheet in Chapter 2:

The Basic Balance Sheet		table 17.1
TOTAL ASSETS		**TOTAL LIABILITIES AND EQUITY**
Current assets:	net working capital	Current liabilities:
Cash and marketable securities		Accrued wages and taxes
Accounts receivable		Accounts payable
Inventory		Notes payable
Fixed assets:		Long-term debt
Gross plant and equipment		Stockholders' equity:
Less: Depreciation		Preferred stock
Net plant and equipment		Common stock and paid-in surplus
Other long-term assets		Retained earnings

Earlier in the book, we discussed the fact that the current assets, while the most liquid, are also usually less profitable than fixed assets. This explains why some managers like to think of net working capital as *"the net amount of current assets that the firm has to fund, above and beyond those that someone else funds for them."*

To put it bluntly, net working capital is a necessary evil: most firms can't sell finished goods without inventory to display, or without offering to sell to customers on credit, and so forth. Therefore, those firms incur costs associated with keeping inventory on hand and with selling to customers on credit.

But just because a firm has to fund *some* net working capital doesn't mean that it should fund all of it or even a large portion of it. Instead, the firm should, to the best of its ability, ensure that the marginal benefit of each dollar tied up in net working capital equals the marginal **opportunity cost** of not having that dollar invested in positive-NPV fixed assets.

TIME OUT

17-1 Why might a firm's creditors *not* think of net working capital as a necessary evil, but rather as a good thing?

17-2 If demand for a firm's products suddenly slows down so that inventory increases while sales decrease, how will the firm's needs for net working capital react?

17.2 Tracing Cash and Net Working Capital

To trace cash flows through the firm's operations, we must measure the **operating cycle**—the time necessary to acquire raw materials, turn them into finished goods, sell them, and receive payment for them—as well as the firm's **cash cycle.**

Let's think of net working capital as the portion of current assets that the firm must fund (above and beyond those assets funded by current liabilities). Then we can similarly think of the firm's cash cycle as the portion of the operating cycle that the firm must finance.

The Operating Cycle

To measure the firm's operating cycle, we need to turn to some of the ratios that we discussed in Chapter 3:

$$\text{Operating cycle} = \text{Days' sales in inventory} + \text{Average collection period} \quad \textbf{(17-1)}$$

$$= \frac{\text{Inventory} \times 365}{\text{Cost of goods sold}} + \frac{\text{Accounts receivable} \times 365}{\text{Credit sales}}$$

 For interactive versions of this example visit www.mhhe.com/can1e

EXAMPLE 17-1

CALCULATION OF OPERATING CYCLE

Suppose that MMK Industries has annual sales of $1 million, cost of goods sold of $650,000, average inventories of $116,000, and average accounts receivable of $150,000. Assuming that all MMK's sales are on credit, what will be the firm's operating cycle?

SOLUTION:

The operating cycle will be equal to

$$\text{Operating cycle} = \frac{\text{Inventory} \times 365}{\text{Cost of goods sold}} + \frac{\text{Accounts receivable} \times 365}{\text{Credit sales}}$$

$$= \frac{\$116,000 \times 365}{\$650,000} + \frac{\$150,000 \times 365}{\$1,000,000}$$

$$= 65.14 \text{ days} + 54.75 \text{ days}$$

$$= 119.89 \text{ days}$$

So it will take MKK almost 120 days from the time they receive raw materials to produce, market, sell, and collect the cash for their finished goods.

The Cash Cycle

The firm's cash cycle will simply be the operating cycle minus the average payment period as shown in Figure 17.1:

$$\text{Cash cycle} = \text{Operating cycle} - \text{Average payment period} \quad \textbf{(17-2)}$$

$$= \text{Operating cycle} - \frac{\text{Accounts payable} \times 365}{\text{Cost of good sold}}$$

KAIZEN (改善)

Kaizen is a Japanese approach to productivity improvement that aims to eliminate waste through just-in-time delivery, standardized work and equipment, and so on. The five basic elements of kaizen are:

1. Teamwork
2. Personal discipline
3. Improved morale
4. Quality circles
5. Suggestions for improvement

Studies show that the kaizen approach can reduce (sometimes dramatically) net working capital requirements, with businesses adopting the approach reporting reductions in finished-goods and in-process inventory of anywhere from 10 to 30 percent.

(!) want to know more? **Key Words to Search for Updates: See the article, "Off the shelf: low inventories drove down working capital last year. But will that continue as the economy improves?" at www.cfo.com.**

figure 17.1

Relationship between Operating and Cash Cycles

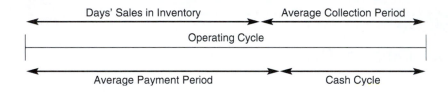

EXAMPLE 17-2

For interactive versions of this example visit www.mhhe.com/can1e

 CALCULATION OF CASH CYCLE

Extending the previous example, assume that MMK's average accounts payable balance is $120,000. What will be the firm's cash cycle?

 SOLUTION:

The cash cycle will be equal to

$$\text{Cash cycle} = \text{Operating cycle} - \frac{\text{Accounts payable} \times 365}{\text{Cost of good sold}}$$

$$= 119.89 \text{ days} - \frac{\$120,000 \times 365}{\$650,000}$$

$$= 119.89 \text{ days} - 67.38 \text{ days}$$

$$= 52.50 \text{ days}$$

Note that, even though it will take MKK almost 120 days to turn their raw materials into cash, the cash cycle indicates that they will only have to foot the bill for their production cycle for 52.50 days of that time. This is the crux of managing the firm's operating and cash cycles: Minimize the number of days that the firm has to pay for its production cycle.

TIME OUT

17-3 How will a firm affect its operating cycle if it can reduce inventory on hand?

17-4 When we compare two firms, will the one with the longer cash cycle tend to have more or less net working capital requirements than the one with a shorter cash cycle, everything held equal? Why?

17.3 Some Aspects of Short-Term Financial Policy

In the last section, we derived the cash cycle by first determining the operating cycle and then subtracting the payment cycle. This derivation suggests two obvious ways that firms can reduce their net working capital needs.

1. They can manage their need for current assets.
2. They can seek to obtain as many current liabilities as economically feasible to fund the current assets that they do need.

The Size of the Current Assets Investment

Choosing the optimal level of investment in each current asset type involves a trade-off between carrying costs and shortage costs.

Carrying costs are associated with having current assets and fall into two general categories:.

1. The opportunity costs associated with having capital tied up in current assets instead of more productive fixed assets.
2. Explicit costs necessary to maintain the value of the current assets.

For example, a car dealer who purchases used vehicles and keeps them in inventory would incur the opportunity cost of not being able to invest the money paid for the used vehicles in a more lucrative opportunity, such as new cars when an exciting new hybrid come out. Our car dealer will also have to pay rental or lease payments on the piece of property where the used cars are on display and any maintenance costs necessary to keep the cars ready to sell.

Shortage costs are the costs associated with not having enough current assets and can include opportunity costs such as sales lost due to not having enough inventory on hand, as well as any explicit transaction fees paid to replenish the particular type of current asset. . . . For example, consider a camera shop that has a reorder policy to only reorder particular lenses from their supplier if a customer comes in asking for them, and even then to only order one at a time. In today's business environment, most customers who are seeking an item want it *now*. If that item is out of stock at one store, the customer will probably turn around and order it from someone else over the Internet, resulting in lost sales to the store. If, in addition, we assume that the store pays a shipping fee for every order placed—or if they get quantity discounts if they order in bulk—then their policy will probably result in higher shipping fees. The store may also face higher costs of goods sold than it would if they ordered in quantity.

Carrying costs will increase, and shortage costs will decrease, as the firm buys more of any particular asset. Therefore, firms should ideally try to choose the level of each current asset and the associated replenishment policy so that the marginal carrying and shortage costs are equal, which will result in the lowest total cost. This level is identified as CA* in Figure 17.2.

figure 17.2

Carrying and Shortage
Costs

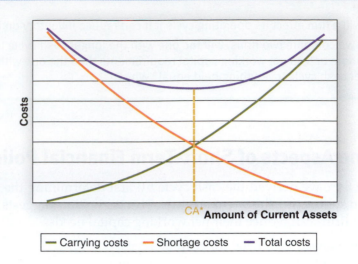

Amount of Current Assets

— Carrying costs — Shortage costs — Total costs

figure 17.3

Components of Current
Assets

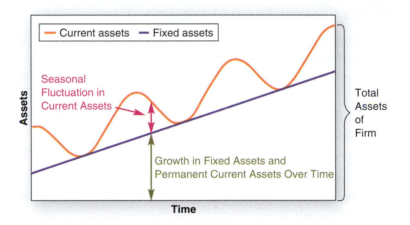

Alternative Financing Policies for Current Assets

LG5

In a perfect world, a firm would use long-term debt and equity to finance long-term (i.e., fixed) assets and short-term debt to finance current assets. Such an approach would allow the firm to maturity-match assets with their corresponding liabilities, resulting in a low or nonexistent level for net working capital. As we've previously discussed, in the real world, net working capital is usually positive for most firms. The implication: at least some portion of current assets must be financed with long-term debt, equity, or a mixture of both.

Assuming that most firms can expect to have some steady, stable need for current assets throughout their calendar year and additional demand for current assets that fluctuates on some seasonal cycle, a growing firm's total demand for assets would resemble that shown in Figure 17.3.

So, a firm in such a situation faces the basic question of whether it should finance the peaks or the valleys of total asset demand (or somewhere in between) using long-term financing. Figure 17.4, Figure 17.5, and Figure 17.6 illustrate some of these choices.

We usually refer to the decision to finance the peaks of asset demand with long-term debt and equity, shown in Figure 17.4, as a *flexible financing policy*. It

figure 17.4

figure 17.5

figure 17.6

provides the firm with a surplus of cash and marketable securities most of the time—except during peak asset demand.

On the opposite side of the continuum, we refer to a decision to finance the troughs or valleys of asset demand with long-term debt and equity, shown in Figure 17.5, as a *restrictive financing policy*. Under this policy, the firm will have to seek short-term financing for all peak demand fluctuations for current assets, as well as for in-between demand situations. In some ways, this policy is the most "conservative"; on the other hand, it's also the least convenient for the firm, as it involves seeking some level of short-term financing almost all of the time.

A third choice is to follow a *compromise financing policy*, wherein the firm finances the seasonally adjusted average level of asset demand with long-term debt and equity. The firm uses both short-term financing and short-term investing as needed. Figure 17.6 illustrates such a policy. Which approach works best? As is the case with almost all working capital decisions, it depends on several factors:

- Current and future expected interest rate levels. If we expect rates to rise in the future, the firm may want to lock in fixed rates for a longer time by shifting towards a flexible financing policy. With falling rates, the opposite would of course hold true.

- The spread between short- and long-term rates. Long-term borrowing usually costs more than short-term financing, but the "gap" (called the *spread*) between the two terms may be historically small or large, encouraging firms to shift to a more restrictive or flexible policy, respectively.

- Alternative financing availability and costs, discussed below. Firms with easy and sustained access to alternative sources will want to shift towards more restrictive policies.

TIME OUT

17-5 Suppose that the gap between short-term rates and long-term rates increases. Would firms tend to shift more towards flexible current asset financing policies, or towards more restrictive policies?

17-6 If a firm offers longer credit terms to its customers, what will happen to its carrying costs?

 ## 17.4 The Short-Term Financial Plan

Firms that follow any financing policy other than a flexible financing plan will find themselves forced to seek short-term financing at times. Depending on their industry, they may find themselves using either unsecured loans, secured loans, or other sources of short-term financing.

Unsecured Loans

For most businesses—particularly smaller ones—the most common way to cover a short-term financing need is to apply at a bank for a commercial loan. The company may expect to need such short-term loans repeatedly in the future—perhaps because they're following a restrictive financing policy but face seasonal fluctuations in asset demand, as discussed above. If the bank deems the firm creditworthy enough, the bank will usually grant the firm a *line of credit*, upon which the firm can draw and then pay off repeatedly as the firm goes through those seasonal fluctuations.

Fees for lines of credit can be both explicit (usually taking the form of an interest rate equal to the bank's prime lending rate plus a small premium) and implicit (as a compensating balance requirement and/or a bank's up-front commitment fee). A **compensating balance** is a percentage of the borrowed money (usually 5 to 10 percent) that the bank requires the firm to keep on deposit in the firm's bank accounts. In return, the bank agrees to lend money to the firm.[1]

Commitment fees, if charged, are usually calculated as a flat percentage of the credit line. But banks also charge commitment fees based on the portion of the line of credit "taken down" (i.e., used by the firm) or even of the portion *not* taken down. The amount of fees the bank charges for a line of credit and their type will depend on whether the bank is trying to encourage the use of the line of credit or not.

Secured Loans

Asset-based loans are short-term loans secured by a company's assets. Secured loans carry lower interest rates than unsecured loans, so it is usually in the firm's best interest to provide security (or collateral) when it can. Though real estate, accounts receivable, inventory, and equipment are all sometimes used to back asset-based loans, most firms seeking such a loan to finance seasonal fluctuations in current assets will typically prefer to use inventory or accounts receivable as security for the loan, as they won't wish to encumber long-term assets such as real estate or equipment.

Accounts receivable can either be sold outright to a factor or assigned. A **factor** is an entity who will buy accounts receivable on a discounted basis before they are due, with the spread between the discounted price and the receivable's face value providing the factor with expected compensation for both the time value of money and for the expected level of defaults among the accounts receivable. **Assignment** is a process whereby the firm borrows money from another entity, providing them in return with both a lien on the accounts receivable as well as the right of **recourse** (i.e., the legal right to hold the firm responsible for payment of the debt if the accounts receivable debtors do not repay as promised).

Firms can also use their inventory as collateral for an inventory loan, a secured short-term loan used to purchase that inventory. Inventory loans include blanket inventory liens, trust receipts, and field warehousing financing. The major difference between the three lies with the question of who owns and keeps the inventory in question:

- Under a blanket inventory lien, the lender gets a lien against all the firm's inventory, but the firm retains ownership and possession.

- When the borrower holds the inventory in trust for the lender, with any proceed from the sale of the inventory being the property of that lender, the document acknowledging this loan commitment is referred to as the *trust receipt*.

- In field warehousing financing, a public warehouse company takes possession and supervises the inventory for the lender.

---

[1]If you're sitting there wondering why the bank doesn't just lend only 95 percent or 90 percent of the money, instead of lending it all and then asking for part of it back, the answer has to do with bank regulations. Though it's too complicated to go into great detail, the simple answer is that bank regulators see a difference between a $900,000 loan and a $1,000,000 loan with a 10 percent compensating balance requirement, though they may sound the same to us.

Other Sources

Two other primary sources of short-term financing are commercial paper issues and financing through banker's acceptances. Commercial paper, which we explored in depth in Chapter 16, is a money-market security, issued by large banks and medium-to-large corporations, that matures in nine months or less. Since these issues have such short durations, and since firms use the proceeds only for current transactions, commercial paper (or simply *paper*) is exempt from registering as a security with the SEC. The corresponding lack of paperwork and regulations to issue short-term debt, along with the fact that commercial paper is usually issued only by firms with very high credit rankings, makes commercial paper cheaper than using a bank line of credit.

A **banker's acceptance** (or **B.A.**) is a short-term promissory note issued by a corporation, bearing the unconditional guarantee (*acceptance*) of a major bank. The bank guarantee makes them very safe, and the rates are usually roughly equivalent to those charged on commercial paper.

TIME OUT

17-7 If its bank started charging fees to a firm based upon the portion of a line of credit not taken down, how would the firm's financing policy for current assets likely change? Why would a bank take such a stance?

17-8 If a firm starts selling its accounts receivable to a factor, how will the firm's cash cycle change?

17.5 Cash Management

One confusing distinction in this class is the difference between a *cash flow* and a *cash account*. Cash flows, which we've discussed in a number of contexts within this book, such as estimating cash flows for proposed new projects in Chapter 12, is a good thing. A cash account, on the other hand, is a current asset account just like all the other current asset accounts we've been discussing, and it has exactly the same attributes of high liquidity and low profitability that inventory and accounts receivable accounts have. Sure, cash may be a bit more liquid than inventory or money tied up in accounts receivable, but it's not really any more profitable.[2]

Reasons for Holding Cash

A firm may keep part of its capital tied up in cash for three primary reasons:

1. **Transaction facilitation** Firms need cash to pay employees' wages, taxes, suppliers' bills, interest on debts, and stock dividends. Though the firm will have cash coming in from day-to-day operations and any financing activities, the inflows and outflows are not usually perfectly synchronized, so the firm will need to keep enough cash on hand to meet reasonable transaction demands.

---

[2]Most students realize that cash held in the form of currency doesn't earn any interest, but they're usually surprised to learn that, by law, corporate checking accounts at commercial banks are not allowed to earn interest, either. Though firms find legal ways around that restriction, we'll leave that discussion to a more advanced text on financial institutions.

2. **Compensating balances:** As we previously discussed, firms must often keep a certain percentage of borrowed funds in their checking accounts with their lending institution. Since lenders are exempt from paying interest on corporate checking accounts, compensating balances become a cheap source of funds for the lender and represent opportunity costs for borrowing firms.

3. **Investment opportunities:** In some industries, investment opportunities come and go very quickly. Sometimes, this happens even too quickly for the firm to arrange a loan or seek other financing, so having excess cash on hand may allow the firm to take advantage of investment opportunities that would otherwise be impossible to transact.

To determine how much cash to keep on hand, firms must trade off the opportunity costs associated with holding too much cash against the shortage costs of not holding enough. The two standard models for calculating the trade-offs are the Baumol Model and the Miller-Orr Model.

TIME OUT

17-9 In what types of industries would firms need more cash on hand for transaction facilitation? In what industries might firms need less?

17-10 If a firm is going to take a loan with a bank that has a compensating balance requirement, how does that affect the amount of money the firm must borrow?

Determining the Target Cash Balance: The Baumol Model

William Baumol developed[3] the first model designed to minimize the sum of the opportunity costs associated with holding cash and the trading costs associated with converting other assets to cash. Baumol's model is intuitively appealing, and analysts still use it in industries for which cash outflows are fairly predictable. For other industries, its use is more problematic due to the model's rather unrealistic assumptions:

- The model assumes that the firm has a constant, perfectly predictable disbursement rate for cash. In reality, disbursement rates are much more variable and unpredictable.

- The model assumes that no cash will come in during the period in question. Since most firms hope to make more money than they pay out, and usually have cash inflows at all times, this assumption is obviously at odds with what we usually see.

- The model doesn't allow for any **safety stock** of extra cash to buffer the firm against unexpectedly high demand for cash.

In Baumol's model, cash is assumed to start from a **replenishment level,** C, and then decline smoothly to a value of zero. When cash declines to zero, it can be immediately replenished by selling another C worth of marketable securities, for which the firm has to pay a trading cost of F.

Thus the model implies that cash levels will follow a cyclical pattern throughout the year. For example, if a firm sells $20,000 worth of marketable securities

[3]See W. S. Baumol, "The Transactions Demand for Cash: An Inventory Theoretic Approach," *Quarterly Journal of Economics* 66, no. 4 (November 1952), pp. 545–556.

figure 17.7

Cash Flow Patterns of
the Baumol Model

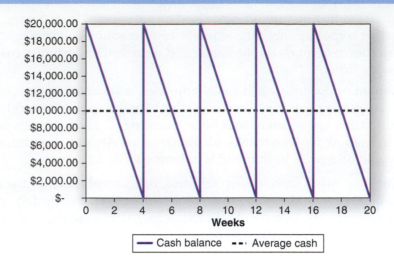

each time it needs to replenish cash and disburses $5,000 in cash each week, then
the cash balance would cycle every four weeks, as shown in Figure 17.7.

Notice another implication of the cash being disbursed at a constant rate. The
average cash level should equal one-half of the replenishment level, C/2. If the
firm can earn an interest rate i on marketable securities, then keeping an average
cash balance of C/2 will impose an opportunity cost on the firm of

$$\text{Opportunity cost} = \frac{C}{2} \times i \tag{17-3}$$

If we also assume that a particular firm faces an annual demand for cash of T,
then the firm will need to sell marketable securities T/C times during the year,
incurring in the process annual trading costs of

$$\text{Trading cost} = \frac{T}{C} \times F \tag{17-4}$$

EXAMPLE 17-3

 For interactive versions of this example visit www.mhhe.com/can1e

 OPTIMAL CASH REPLENISHMENT UNDER BAUMOL MODEL

Suppose that AFS Industries faces an annual demand for cash of $2 million, incurs transac-
tion costs of $150 every time they sell marketable securities, and can earn 6 percent on their
marketable securities. What will be their optimal cash replenishment level?

SOLUTION:

The optimal cash replenishment level will be:

$$C^* = \sqrt{2TF/i}$$

$$= \sqrt{2(\$2,000,000)(\$150)/.06}$$

$$= \$100,000$$

The firm's total annual costs associated with their cash management policy will therefore be:

$$\text{Total cost} = \frac{C}{2} \times i + \frac{T}{C} \times F \qquad \textbf{(17-5)}$$

Solving this for the value of C that minimizes annual costs, C^*, yields:

$$C^* = \sqrt{2TF/i} \qquad \textbf{(17-6)}$$

Determining the Target Cash Balance: The Miller-Orr Model

The Miller-Orr Model[4] takes a different approach to calculating the optimal cash management strategy. It assumes that the distribution of daily net cash flows is normally distributed and allows for both cash inflows and outflows. This model bases its computations on information about:

- The lower control limit, L.
- The trading cost for marketable securities per transaction, F.
- The standard deviation in net daily cash flows, σ.
- The daily interest rate on marketable securities, i_{day}.

Using their model, Miller and Orr show that the optimal cash return point, Z^*, and upper limit for cash balances, H^*, are equal to:

$$Z^* = \sqrt[3]{3F\sigma^2/4i_{day}} + L \qquad \textbf{(17-7)}$$

$$H^* = 3Z^* - 2L \qquad \textbf{(17-8)}$$

Note that the firm determines L, and that the firm can set it to a non-zero number to recognize the use of safety stock.

The optimal cash return point, Z^*, is analogous to the replenishment level, C^*, in Baumol's model, but with one key difference. Since Baumol's model only allowed for cash disbursements, C^* was always "replenished to" from a level of zero. In the Miller-Orr model, Z^* will be the replenishment level to which cash is replenished when the cash level hits L, but it will also be the return level that cash is brought back *down* to when cash hits H^*.

 For interactive versions of this example visit www.mhhe.com/can1e

EXAMPLE 17-4

CALCULATION OF OPTIMAL RETURN POINT AND UPPER LIMIT FOR MILLER-ORR MODEL

Suppose that Dandy Candy, Inc., would like to maintain its cash account at a minimum level of $100,000, but expects the standard deviation in net daily cash flows to be $5,000; the effective annual rate on marketable securities will be 8 percent per year, and the trading cost per sale or purchase of marketable securities will be $200 per transaction. What will be Dandy Candy's optimal cash return point and upper limit?

(continued)

---

[4]See M.H. Miller and D. Orr, "A Model of the Demand for Money by Firms," *Quarterly Journal of Economics* 80, no. 3 (August 1966), pp. 413–435.

The daily interest rate on marketable securities will equal:

$$i_{day} = \sqrt[365]{1.10} - 1 = .000211$$

And the optimal cash return point and upper limit will equal:

$$Z^* = \sqrt[3]{3F\sigma^2/4i_{day}} + L$$

$$= \sqrt[3]{3(\$200)(\$5,000)^2/(4 \times .000211)} + \$100,000$$

$$= \$126,101.72$$

$$H^* = 3Z^* - 2L$$

$$= \$178,305.16$$

As Figure 17.8 shows, the firm will reduce cash to \$126,101.72 by buying marketable securities when the cash balance gets up to \$178,305.16, and it will increase cash to \$126,101.72 by selling marketable securities when the cash balance gets down to \$100,000.

Other Factors Influencing the Target Cash Balance

Even the Miller-Orr model, the more realistic of the two models because it deals with both cash inflows and outflows, still ignores fundamental factors that influence firms' cash management practices. First, firms also have the option of borrowing short-term to meet unexpected demands for cash. Though the short-term borrowing rate faced by the firm is likely to be more expensive than the opportunity cost incurred by selling marketable securities[5], this isn't necessarily the comparison that matters. If the probability of an unexpected demand for cash causing a firm to borrow in the short term is low enough, or if the amount of interest to be earned by investing in longer-term securities is sufficiently higher than that to be earned on marketable securities, then it might be worth it for the firm to risk occasionally paying a relatively high interest rate on short-term borrowing if it can earn a substantially higher return by investing the funds that would have been tied up in marketable securities in something more lucrative.

Second, the authors of both models developed their ideas when buying and selling marketable securities was a relatively expensive and time-consuming proposition. The costs and delays of trading securities have fallen dramatically since the advent of the Internet. The cost has fallen so much that many large firms habitually use all or the majority of their available cash to purchase overnight securities. If trading costs are low enough that it makes sense for the firm to incur at least two sets of trading costs each day—one for selling enough marketable securities in the morning to make it through the day, and another for purchasing marketable securities at the end of the business day—then it's also probable that any unforeseen demand for cash *during* the day can probably be met fairly cheaply by selling marketable securities as needed. Or, put another way, the transactions costs associated with trading securities have fallen so dramatically relative to the opportunity costs of not having cash invested in marketable securities that keeping any "extra" money idle in cash just doesn't make sense.

---

[5]To see why, go down to your local bank or savings and loan and see which is higher: the rate they pay on savings accounts or the rate they charge on short-term borrowing.

figure 17.8

Finally, both models ignore the fact that many firms must keep compensating balances in their deposit accounts as part of borrowing agreements with their banks. If the compensating balance requirement was a constant amount or percentage, then we could adjust the Miller-Orr model so that *L* included the compensating balance, but many firms must only keep a certain minimum compensating balance *on average*. This implies that an unforeseen demand for cash that causes a firm's deposit account to temporarily dip below the minimum compensating balance can be offset by keeping a corresponding amount of excess cash in the account in a later period. Even the more modern Miller-Orr Model doesn't allow for that.

TIME OUT

17-11 What effect does increasing the standard deviation in daily cash flows have on the cash return point in the Miller-Orr model?

17-12 If you were asked to adjust the Baumol model to reflect the need to keep a minimum cash balance, how would you go about doing so?

17.6 Float Control: Managing the Collection and Disbursement of Cash

The economic definition of cash includes undeposited checks, but as we all know, an undeposited check isn't really as liquid as the same amount of cash sitting inside your checking account. So another component of a good cash management policy involves making sure that checks clear in a timely manner.

Accelerating Collections

The period of time between when a check is written and when it clears and is deposited is referred to as **float.** The checks sent to a firm experience three different types of collection float:

1. Mail float is the length of time that checks are en route to the firm, either through the postal system or through some sort of electronic transfer.

figure 17.9

Components of
Collection Float

| Mail Float | In-house Processing Float | Availability Float |

Collection Float

2. In-house processing float is the length of time that it takes the firm to process and deposit check payments from its customers once they've been received.

3. Availability float is the length of time necessary for a check to clear through the banking system once it's been deposited.

Together, these three types of float span the entire length of time between when a customer first sends in a payment and when the firm receives cash into its account.

Several different techniques can help firms reduce collection float:

- A lockbox system is a collection of geographically dispersed post office boxes, each maintained for the firm by a bank local to the respective box. For firms with hundreds or thousands of customers spread across a large region, the ideal situation is to have enough locations so that no customer is more than a couple of hundred miles from one of the firm's post office boxes. Having customers send their payments to the closest post office box, and then having the local bank pick up and handle the payment processing several times a day, the firm can reduce both mail float and in-house processing float.

- Concentration banking accelerates cash collections from customers by having funds sent to several geographically situated regional banks and then transferred to a main concentration account in another bank. The funds can be transferred through depository transfer checks and electronic transfers.

- Wire transfers are the fastest way of transmitting money from a local bank into the concentration bank. Banks within the United States utilize the Society for Worldwide Interbank Financial Telecommunication (SWIFT) system to make payments to banks in countries outside of the United States. Bank-to-bank transfers conducted within the United States take place over the Fedwire system, which uses the Federal Reserve System and its assignment of bank routing numbers.

Delaying Disbursements

Disbursement float is the delay between the firm sending out a payment and the money being taken out of the firm's bank account. Two legal ways to increase disbursement float involve keeping the cash available to the firm until the very last moment:

- A **zero-balance account** is a checking account that the firm sets up so that the bank agrees to automatically transfer funds from an interest-bearing account to pay off any checks presented. Since zero-balance accounts never contain excess cash, they represent one way that firms can get around regulations against corporations having interest-bearing checking accounts.

- **Drafts** resemble checks, but differ in that they are payable by the firm issuing them rather than payable by a bank. When a draft is sent to the firm's bank for payment, the bank must present the draft to the firm *before* disbursing the funds.

CULTURAL DIFFERENCES IN PREFERENCES FOR PAYING BILLS

Japan's Postal Savings Bank, the world's largest bank, has long been used as an example of the efficiencies available to both individuals and businesses of electronic transactions. Electronic transactions are instantaneous transactions that use security authentication rather than conventional check-clearing processes to transfer funds from a buyer to the seller.

However, in 2006, one of the Nikkei trade papers summarized the results of a survey among Japanese women regarding payment methods used for Internet shopping. Not surprisingly, the vast majority (56%) of respondents purchasing goods over the Internet reported that they used credit cards for their transactions. However, the distribution of the rest of the responses illustrates a vast difference between alternative payment pipelines that American and Japanese consumers use.

For example, 17.6 percent of Japanese respondents ordered online, then paid in cash at their local convenience store; 13.1 percent paid COD when the mailman delivered the goods; and 4.3 percent paid using electronic transfers from their post office savings accounts.

What implications does this have for the money management policies of firms doing business in Japan? Well, given that a far larger percentage of Americans probably pay for their online purchases with credit cards, and that the alternative methods of payment listed above could be expected to have different clearing times than do payments received through a merchant's credit card account, it's something that firms seeking to do business in Japan should consider.

 want to know more? **Key Words to Search for Updates:** See the entry "Marketing Tip: Payment Methods" on the Japan Marketing News blog at www.japanmarketing-news.com/consumer_industry_data/index.html.

Ethical and Legal Questions

Using collected cash before actually receiving it, or continuing to use disbursed cash after you've sent a check out, can earn your firm higher returns, but this practice is illegal. The most extreme form of taking illegal advantage of disbursement float is a practice called *check kiting*, which, defined, is any sort of fraud that involves drawing out money from a bank account with insufficient funds to cover the check.

The Check Clearing for the 21st Century Act, which allows for transmitting electronic images of checks rather than the physical paper checks themselves, is expected to greatly reduce the incidence of check kiting by substantially shortening the time required for a check to be cleared from one bank to another.

 TIME OUT

17-13 In Japan, many consumers pay their bills by electronic deduction from their checking accounts instead of using paper checks. What effect do you think this has on the collection float of Japanese firms versus that of American firms?

17-14 What's the difference between a lockbox system and concentration banking?

17.7 Investing Idle Cash

As both the Baumol and Miller-Orr models imply, firms habitually move cash into and out of marketable securities in order to partially offset the opportunity costs of having capital tied up in current assets. Most large firms will manage their marketable securities investments themselves. Smaller firms will typically invest through an independently managed money-market fund or by letting their bank transfer all available excess funds at the end of each business day into a sweep account, which will then be invested on their behalf.

Why Firms Have Surplus Cash

Firms tend to have surplus cash available either due to seasonal fluctuations in their cash flow patterns, or in preparation for planned expenditures. Seasonal fluctuations in the amount of cash on hand can occur either as a result of cyclical sales or cyclical purchases of raw materials. For example, a firm that produces swimming pool accessories will obviously experience higher sales from spring through late fall, and a firm that distributes fresh vegetables purchased on the spot market will have higher cash outflows during the harvest season.

Firm's cash balances may also temporarily increase immediately prior to a planned expenditure, either because the company has been "saving up" for the expenditure, or because they issued stocks or bonds in advance of the expenditure but need someplace to "park" the funds until they're needed.

What to Do with Surplus Cash

As mentioned both in Chapter 16 and this chapter, firms usually put surplus cash into money-market securities. As discussed in Chapter 16, these include Treasury bills, federal funds and repurchase agreements, commercial paper, negotiable certificates of deposit, and banker's acceptances.

TIME OUT

17-15 Should a firm with nonseasonal cash flows that doesn't have any good prospective investments keep excess cash on hand? Why or why not?

17-16 Suppose a firm has a temporary surplus of cash meant to fund an upcoming expansion project. Why might it not wish to invest these funds in capital-market (as opposed to money-market) securities?

 ## 17.8 Credit Management

As is the case with the firm's cash management policy, the firm's optimal credit policy will trade off the opportunity cost of lost sales (if the firm does not grant credit or is too conservative in terms of the credit it does grant) against the carrying costs associated with funding the accounts receivable plus the expected costs of default on the accounts receivable.

Credit Policy: Terms of the Sale

As a minimum, the **credit terms** of sales usually contain at least the credit period, the cash discount, and a description of the type of credit instrument. The credit period is the maturity of the credit that the firm is willing to extend, which varies based on attributes of the goods being sold and the customer purchasing the goods. For example, perishable goods will usually carry a lower credit period, regardless of who is purchasing them. Creditworthy, established customers will probably be given better credit terms than customers the firm hasn't dealt with before.

To encourage early repayment, firms will often offer a percentage discount if the bill is paid within a certain time period. For example, a firm that quotes a customer terms of "2/10, net 30" is offering them the choice between paying the entire bill within 30 days or taking a 2 percent discount off the invoiced price if they pay within 10 days.

For most trade credit, the invoice is the only type of credit instrument involved. When the customer signs a copy upon receipt of the goods, the customer makes an implicit promise to pay under the terms listed on the invoice. If a firm wishes for a customer to make a more explicit acknowledgement of its ability and obligation to pay, a firm can ask the customer to sign a promissory note upon delivery of the goods or to furnish a commercial draft or banker's acceptance in advance of the delivery of the goods.

Credit Analysis

Before granting a customer credit, the firm may wish to engage in **credit analysis.** Such analysis involves a systematic determination of the potential borrower's ability and willingness to pay for the goods being provided on credit. A thorough credit analysis will look at the potential borrower's past record and its present and forecasted future financial condition, which generally involves examining the "five C's":

1. **Capacity:** Ensure that borrower has the legal and economic capacity to borrow.

2. **Character:** Refers to borrower's reputation and hence desire to settle debt obligations.

3. **Capital:** Having its own capital at risk makes it more likely that the borrower will repay as promised.

4. **Collateral:** Collateral that can be seized and sold, with the proceeds being used to pay the firm in the event of bankruptcy by the borrower, also makes it more likely that the customer will repay as promised.

5. **Conditions:** Any economic conditions that may affect the borrower's ability to repay the loan should also be taken into account.

Collection Policy

The firm's collection policy is aimed at collecting past-due debts from customers. The usual procedure for collecting follows a typical path of:

1. Send one or more delinquency letters informing the customer of the past-due status of the account, asking them to contact the firm to discuss alternative means of repayment and pointing out what legal recourse the firm has.

2. Initiate telephone calls conveying the same information as above.

3. Employ a collection agency.

4. Take legal action against the customer if all else fails.

To monitor and control this process, firms use a tool called an *aging schedule,* which stratifies a firm's accounts receivable by the age of each account. For example, a firm that offers terms of 2/10, net 60 to its customers might want to measure the age of A/R using the categories shown in Table 17.2.

Such an aging schedule would allow the firm to see what percentage of its customers are still eligible to take the discount (i.e., those in the "0–10 days" category), how many are past due by less than 30 days (i.e., those in the "61–90 days"

viewpoints REVISITED

Business Application Solution

Chewbacca's operating cycle will be equal to

$$\text{Operating cycle} = \frac{.1 \times 365}{.55} + \frac{.1667 \times 365}{1}$$

$$= 127.197 \text{ days}$$

Their cash cycle will be equal to

$$\text{Cash cycle} = 127.197 - \frac{.05 \times 365}{.55}$$

$$= 94.0152 \text{ days}$$

Absent any other information about current assets or current liabilities, Chewbacca's net working capital will be

$$(.10 + .1667 - .05) \times \$32 \text{ million} = \$6,934,000$$

Personal Application Solution

Since Wanda will be drawing out the money smoothly from the account, she can use the Baumol model to determine the optimal replenishment level for her personal stock of cash:

$$C^* = \sqrt{2(\$25,000)(\$9.95)/.035}$$

$$= \$3,770.18$$

Sample Aging Schedule	table 17.2

AGE BRACKET	PERCENTAGE OF AR IN BRACKET
0–10 days	10%
11–30 days	35
31–60 days	45
61–90 days	7
Over 90 days	3
	100

category), and how many are over 30 days past due (i.e., those in the "Over 90 days" category).

Firms often link their collection policies to their aging schedules. For example, the customers in the table above that fall into the "61–90 days" category might be sent a delinquency letter, while those in the "Over 90 days" category might be phoned.

TIME OUT

17-17 Why do firms offer customers discounts for paying early?

17-18 Should a firm always turn far-overdue bills from customers over to a collection agency or sue the customers? Why or why not?

summary of learning goals

In this chapter, we have discussed the firm's working capital policy, focusing on how we can determine the optimal amount to be invested in current assets, the portion of that amount to be provided by the firm, and sources of funding for that portion.

LG1 **Set overall objectives of a good working capital policy.** A good working capital policy has the firm providing enough net working capital, but not too much.

LG2 **Discuss how net working capital serves the firm.** Net working capital measures the portion of current assets that are not funded by current liabilities, but which must be funded by other sources of capital.

LG3 **Calculate and use the firm's operating cycle and cash cycle to discover how much funding for current assets the firm has to find.** The cash cycle is basically the operating cycle minus the average payment period.

LG4 **Model the optimal trade-off between carrying costs and shortage costs that dictates the firm's current asset investment.** Ideally, the firm will have just enough current assets so that the marginal carrying costs and marginal shortage costs are equal, thereby minimizing total cost.

LG5 **Compare the flexible and restrictive approaches to financing current assets.** A flexible financing policy has the firm funding short-term fluctuations in the amount of current assets with long-term debt; a restrictive policy has the firm funding those fluctuations with short-term debt.

LG6 **Differentiate among sources of short-term financing available for funding current assets.** The firm can use unsecured loans, secure loans, commercial paper, or banker's acceptances.

LG7 **Justify the firm's need to hold cash.** The three main reasons for holding cash are to facilitate transactions, to provide for compensating balance for loan agreements, and to take advantage of short-lived investment opportunities.

LG8 **Use the Baumol and Miller-Orr models for determining cash policy.** The Baumol model was designed to help determine a firm's cash policy under conditions of certain cash demand, while the Miller-Orr model is designed for conditions of stochastic cash demand.

LG9 **Identify sources of float and show how to control float for the firm's disbursement and collection functions.** Float arises due to delays involved in physically sending or receiving a payment, processing it in the receiving firm, and because of the delays imposed by the check-clearing process. To the extent that it is legally and ethically possible, firms will attempt to increase disbursement float and reduce collection float so as to reduce the amount of cash they have to keep on hand.

LG10 **Investigate why firms have excess cash and identify their choices about what to do with it.** Firms tend to have excess cash available either due to seasonal fluctuations in their cash flows or in preparation for a planned major expenditure.

LG11 **Draw the connection between the firm's credit terms and collection policy and the amount of capital the firm has invested in accounts receivable.** The more generously the firm grants credit, the more its customers will take advantage of that generosity and the longer the firm will have to pay for producing and selling their product without collecting any money for it, so generous credit terms will result in the firm requiring a larger investment in net working capital than would otherwise be the case.

chapter equations

17-1 Operating Cycle = Days' Sales in Inventory + Average Collection Period

$$= \frac{\text{Inventory} \times 365}{\text{Cost of Goods Sold}} + \frac{\text{Accounts Receivable} \times 365}{\text{Credit Sales}}$$

17-2 Cash Cycle = Operating Cycle − Average Payment Period

$$= \text{Operating Cycle} - \frac{\text{Accounts Payable} \times 365}{\text{Cost of Good Sold}}$$

17-3 $\text{Opportunity Cost} = \dfrac{C}{2} \times i$

17-4 $\text{Trading Cost} = \dfrac{T}{C} \times F$

17-5 $\text{Total Cost} = \dfrac{C}{2} \times i + \dfrac{T}{C} \times F$

17-6 $C^* = \sqrt{2TF/i}$

17-7 $Z^* = \sqrt[3]{3F\sigma^2/4i_{day}} + L$

17-8 $H^* = 3Z^* - 2L$

key terms

asset-based loans, Short-term loans secured by a company's assets. (p. 547)

assignment, a process whereby the firm borrows money from another entity, providing them in return with both a lien on the accounts receivable as well as the right of **recourse.** (p. 547)

banker's acceptance, a short-term promissory note issued by a corporation, bearing the unconditional guarantee (*acceptance*) of a major bank. (p. 548)

carrying costs, the opportunity costs associated with having capital tied up in current assets instead of more productive fixed assets and explicit costs necessary to maintain the value of the current assets. (p. 543)

cash cycle, The operating cycle minus the average payment period. (p. 541)

commercial paper, A money-market security, issued by large banks and medium-to-large corporations, that matures in nine months or less. (p. 548)

compensating balance, Amount of money required to be kept in a firm's deposit accounts with a lender as per agreed to in a lending arrangement. (p. 547)

credit analysis, A systematic determination of a borrower's ability and willingness to repay a potential loan. (p. 557)

credit terms, A listing of the credit period, the cash discount, and the type of credit instrument to be used. (p. 556)

draft, Similar to a check, but payable by the issuing firm rather than by its bank. (p. 554)

float, The period of time between when a payment is sent out and when the money is actually received by the collecting firm. (p. 553)

opportunity cost, The cost or forgone opportunity of using an asset already in use by the firm, or a person already employed by the firm, in a new project. (p. 540)

recourse (p. 547)

replenishment level, The level to which the cash account is "refilled" when marketable securities are sold to recapitalize it. (p. 549) safety stock, Excess amounts of a current asset kept on hand to meet unexpected shocks in demand. (p. 549)

shortage costs (p. 538)

transaction facilitation, The use of cash to pay employee's wages, taxes, suppliers' bills, interest on debts and dividends on stock. (p. 548)

zero-balance account, A corporate checking account which keeps a zero balance, automatically transferring in just enough funds to cover any checks received on the account from another interest-bearing account. (p. 554)

self-test problems with solutions

1 **Computing Operating Cycle and Cash Cycle** Your firm currently has an operating cycle of 73 days. You are analyzing some operational changes that are expected to decrease the average collection period by five days and decrease the days' sales in inventory by three days. The average payment period is expected to decrease by 10 days. If all of these changes are adopted, what will your firm's new operating cycle be?

Solution:

Since the operating cycle is equal to days' sales in inventory plus the average collection period, the operating cycle of the firm will decrease to $73 - 5 - 3 = 65$ days. The change in the average payment period has no effect on the operating cycle.

2 **Minimizing Carrying and Shortage Costs** Suppose that your firm is seeking a five-year, amortizing $500,000 loan with annual payments and your bank is offering you the choice between a $600,000 loan with a $100,000 compensating balance and a $500,000 loan without a compensating balance. If the interest rate on the $500,000 loan is 9 percent, how low would the interest rate on the loan with the compensating balance have to be in order for you to choose it?

Solution:

The payments on the $500,000 loan would be equal to $128,546.23. To pay less on the $600,000 loan, you would have to have an interest rate lower than 2.34 percent.

3 **Flexible versus Restrictive Financing** If your firm faces a long-term borrowing rate of 8 percent, a short-term borrowing rate of 10 percent, can earn 7 percent when investing marketable securities, and needs to fund $3 million in permanent current assets and $1 million in seasonal current assets (for six months out of the year), what would be the cost difference between using a flexible and a restrictive financing policy?

Solution:

Under either policy, you will be funding the $3 million in permanent current assets with long-term debt, so you can ignore this as an incremental difference between the two policies. If you use long-term debt, you will be paying $1 million × 8 percent = $80,000 per year in interest, but earning $1 million × 7 percent × .5 = $35,000 in interest for the half year that you get to invest the money in marketable securities, for a net cost of $80,000 − $35,000 = $45,000 for the flexible financing policy. With the restrictive financing policy, you will be paying $1 million × 10 percent × .5 = $50,000 per year, so your net costs will be lower if you follow the flexible financing policy.

4 Baumol Model Suppose that Overton, Inc., faces an annual demand for cash of $17 million, incurs transaction costs of $200 every time they sell marketable securities, and can earn 7.3 percent on their marketable securities. What will be their optimal cash replenishment level?

Solution:

The optimal cash replenishment level will be:

$$C^* = \sqrt{2TF/i}$$
$$= \sqrt{2(\$17,000,000)(\$200)/.073}$$
$$= \$305,205.97$$

5 Miller-Orr Model GenCo would like to maintain its cash account at a minimum level of $250,000, but management expects the standard deviation in net daily cash flows to be $15,000, the effective annual rate on marketable securities to be 5 percent per year, and the trading cost per sale or purchase of marketable securities to be $110 per transaction. What will be Genco's optimal cash return point and upper limit?

Solution:

The daily interest rate on marketable securities will be equal to:

$$i_{day} = \sqrt[365]{1.05} - 1 = .000134$$

And the optimal cash return point and upper limit will be equal to:

$$Z^* = \sqrt[3]{3F\sigma^2/4i_{day}} + L$$
$$= \sqrt[3]{3(\$110)(\$15,000)^2/(4 \times .000134)} + \$250,000$$
$$= \$301,783.25$$
$$H^* = 3(\$301,783.25) - 2(\$250,000)$$
$$= \$405,349.76$$

6 Float Calculation AFS, Inc. estimates that it takes, on average, three days for their customers' payments to reach them, two days for the payments to be processed and deposited by AFS's bookkeeping department, and three more days for the check to clear once they're deposited. What is AFS's collection float?

Solution:

The collection float will be 3 + 2 + 3 = 8 days.

7 Aging Schedule OTK Sports has constructed the aging schedule shown in the table below. If the company offers terms of 2/10, net 30 to its customers, and if its collection policy is to send a letter on bills more than 30 days overdue and to call on bills more than 60 days overdue, how many letters will it need to print?

AGE BRACKET	NUMBER OF CUSTOMERS IN BRACKET
0–10 days	25
11–30 days	78
31–60 days	17
61–90 days	3
Over 90 days	1

Solution:

They will need to print 17 letters.

questions

1. Is it possible for a firm to have negative net working capital? How? *(LG1)*

2. Would it be possible for a decision to deny credit to your customers to be value maximizing? How? *(LG1)*

3. Which of the following will result in an increase in net working capital? *(LG2)*

   a. An increase in cash.

   b. A decrease in accounts payable.

   c. An increase in notes payable.

   d. A decrease in accounts receivable.

   e. An increase in inventory.

4. Would it be possible for a firm to have a negative cash cycle? How? *(LG3)*

5. If a firm's inventory turnover ratio increases, what will happen to the firm's operating cycle? *(LG3)*

6. If a firm's inventory turnover ratio increases, what will happen to the firm's cash cycle? *(LG3)*

7. Everything else held constant, will an increase in the amount of inventory on hand increase or decrease the firm's profitability? *(LG4)*

8. Would a firm ever use short-term debt to finance permanent current assets? Why or why not? *(LG5)*

9. Suppose that short-term borrowing actually becomes more expensive than long-term borrowing: How would this affect the firm's choice between a flexible financing policy and a restrictive policy? *(LG5)*

10. If asset-backed loans are cheaper than unsecured loans, what is the disadvantage to the firm in using an asset-backed loan? *(LG6)*

11. Is an increase in the cash account a source of funds or a use of funds? *(LG7)*

12. What will be the carrying cost associated with a compensating balance requirement? *(LG7)*

13. What will be the shortage cost associated with a compensating balance requirement? *(LG7)*

14. What would be the shortage costs associated with a restaurant not having enough cash on hand to make change? *(LG7)*

15. If a firm needs to keep a minimum cash balance on hand and faces both cash inflows and outflows, which of the cash management models discussed in this chapter would be more appropriate for them to use? *(LG8)*

16. What effect will increase the trading costs associated with selling marketable securities have on the optimal replenishment level in the Baumol model? Why? *(LG8)*

17. What effect will an increase in the standard deviation of daily cash flows have on the return point in the Miller-Orr model? Why? *(LG8)*

18. Could a firm ever have negative collection float? Why or why not? *(LG9)*

19. Could a firm ever have negative disbursement float? Why or why not? *(LG9)*

20. Would a draft have availability float? Why or why not? *(LG9)*

21. From our discussion of capital markets elsewhere in this book, why would you expect a firm to have a time delay between raising funds to finance a project and the expenditure of those funds on that project? *(LG9)*

22. What purpose does a discount on credit terms serve? What is the cost of such a discount to the offering firm? *(LG9)*

problems

basic problems

17-1 **Net Working Capital Requirements** JohnBoy Industries has a cash balance of $45,000; accounts payable of $125,000; inventory of $175,000; accounts receivable of $210,000; notes payable of $120,000; and accrued wages and taxes of $37,000. How much net working capital does the firm need to fund? *(LG2)*

17-2 **Net Working Capital Requirements** Dandee Lions, Inc. has a cash balance of $105,000; accounts payable of $220,000; inventory of $203,000; accounts receivable of $319,000; notes payable of $65,000, and accrued wages and taxes of $75,000. How much net working capital does the firm need to fund? *(LG2)*

17-3 **Days' Sales in Inventory** Dabble, Inc. has sales of $980,000 and cost of goods sold of $640,000. The firm had a beginning inventory of $36,000 and an ending inventory of $46,000. What is the length of the days' sales in inventory? *(LG3)*

17-4 **Average Payment Period** If a firm has a cash cycle of 73 days and an operating cycle of 127 days, what is its average payment period? *(LG3)*

17-5 **Payables Turnover** If a firm has a cash cycle of 73 days and an operating cycle of 127 days, what is its payables turnover? *(LG3)*

17-6 **Average Payment Period** If a firm has a cash cycle of 45 days and an operating cycle of 77 days, what is its average payment period? *(LG3)*

17-7 **Payables Turnover** If a firm has a cash cycle of 45 days and an operating cycle of 77 days, what is its payables turnover? *(LG3)*

17-8 **Compensating Balance** Would it be worth it to incur a compensating balance of $10,000 in order to get a 1 percent lower interest rate on a one-year, pure discount loan of $225,000? *(LG7)*

17-9 **Compensating Balance** Would it be worth it to incur a compensating balance of $5,000 in order to get a .65 percent lower interest rate on a two-year, pure discount loan of $150,000? *(LG7)*

17-10 **Collection Float** CM Enterprises estimates that it takes, on average, five days for its customers' payments to reach them, one day for the payments to be processed and deposited by its bookkeeping department, and two more days for the check to clear once it's deposited. What is their collection float? *(LG9)*

17-11 **Collection Float** Smelpank, Inc., estimates that it takes, on average, four days for its customers' payments to reach them, three days for the payments to be processed and deposited by its bookkeeping department, and three more days for the check to clear once it's deposited. What is their collection float? *(LG9)*

17-12 Days' Sales in Inventory B&B Cos. has sales of $732,000 and cost of goods sold of $347,000. The firm had a beginning inventory of $48,000 and an ending inventory of $34,000. What is the length of the days' sales in inventory? *(LG3)*

intermediate problems

17-13 Operating Cycle Suppose that Dunn Industries has annual sales of $2.3 million, cost of goods sold of $1,650,000, average inventories of $1,116,000, and average accounts receivable of $750,000. Assuming that all of Dunn's sales are on credit, what will be the firm's operating cycle? *(LG3)*

17-14 Operating Cycle Suppose that LilyMac Photography has annual sales of $230,000, cost of goods sold of $165,000, average inventories of $4,500, and average accounts receivable of $25,000. Assuming that all of LilyMac's sales are on credit, what will be the firm's operating cycle? *(LG3)*

17-15 Cash Cycle Suppose that LilyMac Photography has annual sales of $230,000; cost of goods sold of $165,000; average inventories of $4,500; average accounts receivable of $25,000, and an average accounts payable balance of $7,000. Assuming that all of LilyMac's sales are on credit, what will be the firm's cash cycle? *(LG3)*

17-16 Compensating Balance Interest Rate Suppose your firm is seeking a seven-year, amortizing $800,000 loan with annual payments and your bank is offering you the choice between an $850,000 loan with a $50,000 compensating balance and an $800,000 loan without a compensating balance. If the interest rate on the $800,000 loan is 8.5 percent, how low would the interest rate on the loan with the compensating balance have to be in order for you to choose it? *(LG4)*

17-17 Compensating Balance Interest Rate Suppose your firm is seeking a three-year, amortizing $200,000 loan with annual payments and your bank is offering you the choice between a $205,000 loan with a $5,000 compensating balance and a $200,000 loan without a compensating balance. If the interest rate on the $200,000 loan is 9.8 percent, how low would the interest rate on the loan with the compensating balance have to be in order for you to choose it? *(LG4)*

17-18 Optimal Cash Replenishment Level Rose Axels faces a smooth annual demand for cash of $5 million; incurs transaction costs of $225 every time they sell marketable securities, and can earn 4.3 percent on their marketable securities. What will be their optimal cash replenishment level? *(LG8)*

17-19 Optimal Cash Replenishment Level Watkins Resources faces a smooth annual demand for cash of $1.5 million; incurs transaction costs of $75 every time it sells marketable securities, and can earn 3.7 percent on their marketable securities. What will be their optimal cash replenishment level? *(LG8)*

advanced problems

17-20 Optimal Cash Return Point HotFoot Shoes would like to maintain its cash account at a minimum level of $25,000, but expect the standard deviation in net daily cash flows to be $2,000; the effective annual rate on marketable securities to be 6.5 percent per year; and the trading cost per sale or purchase of marketable securities to be $200 per transaction. What will be their optimal cash return point? *(LG8)*

17-21 Optimal Upper Cash Limit HotFoot Shoes would like to maintain their cash account at a minimum level of $25,000; but expect the standard deviation in net daily cash flows to be $2,000; the effective annual rate on marketable securities to be 6.5 percent per year, and the trading cost per sale or purchase of marketable securities to be $200 per transaction. What will be their optimal upper cash limit? *(LG8)*

17-22 **Optimal Cash Return Point** Veggie Burgers, Inc., would like to maintain its cash account at a minimum level of $245,000; but expect the standard deviation in net daily cash flows to be $12,000; the effective annual rate on marketable securities to be 4.7 percent per year; and the trading cost per sale or purchase of marketable securities to be $27.50 per transaction. What will be its optimal cash return point? *(LG8)*

17-23 **Optimal Upper Cash Limit** Veggie Burgers, Inc., would like to maintain its cash account at a minimum level of $245,000; but expect the standard deviation in net daily cash flows to be $12,000; the effective annual rate on marketable securities to be 4.7 percent per year; and the trading cost per sale or purchase of marketable securities to be $27.50 per transaction. What will be its optimal upper cash limit? *(LG8)*

research it! Looking Up Information on a Firm's Cash Cycle

Go to the SEC's Edgar site at **www.sec.gov/edgar.shtml** and download the latest annual (10-K) report for the firm of your choice. Use the financial statements in the report to calculate the firm's cash cycle.

integrated minicase   Line of Credit

Your bank offers you a $140,000 line of credit with an interest rate of 2.30 percent per quarter. The loan agreement also requires that 7 percent of the unused portion of the credit line be deposited in a non-interest-bearing account as a compensating balance. Your short-term investments are paying 1.55 percent per quarter.

1. What is your effective annual interest rate if you borrow the whole $40,000 for the entire year?
2. What will be the carrying cost in this problem?
3. What will be the shortage cost in this problem?

ANSWERS TO TIME OUT

17-1 A creditor might think of net working capital as a buffer, in that it represents the amount of short-term capital slated to come in to the firm above and beyond the amount that the creditor is owed. The larger the amount of the net working capital is, the greater is the chance that the creditor will get paid back.

17-2 Everything else held constant, we would normally expect net working capital to increase in such a situation: inventory would increase and accounts receivable might also increase if the firm offered better credit terms to try and stimulate sales.

(continued)

17-3 Reducing inventory on hand would reduce days' sales in inventory, which would cause the operating cycle to decrease.

17-4 The firm with a longer cash cycle will tend to have more net working capital requirements, as the firm will have to fund current assets for a longer period of time.

17-5 As the relative cost of long-term debt increased, firms would tend to shift towards more restrictive policies.

17-6 Carrying costs will increase, because the firm will have to fund a longer collection cycle.

17-7 The firm would be less likely to ask for an excessive amount when it requested a line of credit, implying that the firm's use of such a line of credit would tend to decrease slightly. A bank might adopt such a policy if it wanted to encourage firms to ask for only as much credit as they intended to use.

17-8 Since the firm would not have to wait on collection of the accounts receivable, the cash cycle would decrease.

17-9 Retail firms, which involve a lot of customer transactions, will probably need more cash on hand; industries where direct customer interaction is rare, such as utilities, would need less.

17-10 The firm will need to borrow more money than it really needs, so that both its needs and the compensating balance requirement are met.

17-11 It will cause the cash return point to increase.

17-12 Add the minimum cash balance to C^*.

17-13 Since mail float will be eliminated, collection float should decrease.

17-14 In a lockbox system, customer's payments are physically collected close to them, but not necessarily processed close to them; in concentration banking, both the physical collection and much of the processing takes place close to the customer, speeding up the firm's receipt of funds.

17-15 No, they shouldn't keep excess cash on hand, as it is costing the firm interest to raise the money but they're not earning any interest on spare cash that's just sitting around.

17-16 Investing money in long-term, capital market funds could expose the firm to the risk that the invested principle might be worth less when the firm needs the money. For example, if a firm bought bonds that were longer-term than its time horizon for investing in an expansion project, it could see its investment value go down if interest rates went up.

17-17 If customers pay early, the firm's cash cycle is shortened.

17-18 Not necessarily. If the amount due is small enough, it probably isn't worth pursuing the overdue bill. However, if a collection agency is willing to work for a percentage of the amount recovered, the firm might as well turn collection over to the agency regardless of the size involved because there is no out-of-pocket cost to the firm.

chapter 18:

CONSIDERING INTERNATIONAL ASPECTS OF CORPORATE FINANCE

 Learning Goals

LG1 Gauge the dynamics of the global economy and recognize potential international opportunities.

LG2 Recognize patterns of increasing capital involvement as the firm seeks to expand business internationally.

LG3 Compute currency exchanges.

LG4 Recognize situations that evoke exchange rate risk and develop tools to manage exchange rate risks.

LG5 Apply theories of how interest rates and inflation influence forward exchange rates and future spot rates.

LG6 Anticipate political risks when investing internationally.

LG7 As a financial manager, plan to work through capital budgeting issues for international investments.

We work and live today in a global business and financial environment. Consider Starbucks Coffee Company. Starbucks operates in 37 countries, including the United States, its home country. Starbucks buys coffee beans from countries all over the world. To provide the exotic blends that their customers have come to expect, company employees travel to many of these countries with agriculturally based, small economies, like Colombia, Ethiopia, Guatemala, Kenya, Papua New Guinea, Yemen, and so on. After blending and processing, the coffee is then sold in stores (on virtually any corner) in large economy countries like the United States, Australia, Canada, China, Germany, United Kingdom, to name a few.

Consider the financial transactions that Starbucks must process to enable these business activities. Financial managers need to assess the risks of investing in property and buildings in less-developed countries. They must plan for currency exchange between

viewpoints

Business Application

A firm's CEO is investigating the possibility of building its first overseas production facility. As the financial manager, Andres must report on the financial risks involved with building a factory in Mexico.

Because the firm has experienced only domestic operations to date, the managers aren't familiar with the potential problems that conducting international operations entail. Andres must educate the other managers not only about these potential problems, but also about the additional steps in their capital budgeting process to account for the international aspects of this project. What topics does Andres need to address with the management team? **(See solution on p. 586)**

Personal Application

Juliana is studying at a U.S. university and has been accepted into a study abroad program for a semester in Switzerland. This program will begin in six months. She has been advised that she will probably spend $10,000 during the semester abroad.

Juliana will need to convert her dollars to Swiss francs (Switzerland is not a member of the EU and does not use the euro as its currency, in keeping with the country's traditional neutrality). How many francs will her $10,000 purchase and should she buy them now, or wait for six months? Has she any other strategies to keep her costs as low as possible? **(See solution on p. 586)**

A practice test can be found on the Online Learning Center at
www.mhhe.com/can1e

the U.S. dollar and foreign currencies—no small feat today with the large changes in the value of the dollar—to pay for labor, beans, and capital investments in other countries and return shareholder profits in U.S. dollars. Exchange rates between currencies change over time. Such fluctuations can change the value of foreign investments and future cash flows. Especially today, managers must plan to counteract exchange rate uncertainty or risk. Starbucks uses techniques like hedging to reduce these risks.

In general, we can say that all of the typical opportunities and risks we've discussed so far are magnified and complicated in the global environment. In this chapter, we'll describe these complications and provide background and tools to help address them.

18.1 Global Business

International Opportunities

The United States has the largest economy in the world. Table 18.1 shows many other very large economies too. In fact, some large economies are experiencing faster growth rates than the United States. While the U.S. economy grows at a level close to the world average rate, countries like China, India, and South Korea have a lot of catching up to do—they have been experiencing much faster growth. It's no wonder that firms around the world are interested in the opportunities these developing economies represent.

How does a business decide how best to operate in the global economy? Most firms start out slowly, minimizing their risk should something not work out. The most basic level of participation is to either import foreign goods, export goods overseas, or both. Figure 18.1 shows that the U.S. actively imports and exports many goods. Canada (31.5%), Mexico (18.3%), Japan (8.2%), and China (7.5%) are the United States' favorite export destinations. In a different order—Canada (23.1%), China (22.0%), Mexico (15.1%), and Japan (11.3%)—the same four nations provide the United States with the most imports. In 2006, the United States imported $576 billion more in products from these countries than it exported. The figure shows why there is so much interest in China—trade with China represents nearly half of this overall trade imbalance.

Two factors that affect the trading activity between countries are restrictions on the kinds of products that may enter a country and tariffs charged for transporting goods across borders. To protect domestic firms (often agricultural businesses) from foreign competition, some countries' governments pass laws restricting trade. Such laws may prohibit or limit importation of certain products or place a tax, or tariff, on imported goods. Trade barriers enacted by one country often lead to retaliatory barriers by other countries, so that both countries face about the same restrictions. The resultant trade war usually harms all economies involved.

To facilitate trade between countries, several international trade agreements have been enacted in the past two decades. Trade agreements seek to reduce, or even eliminate, trade restrictions and tariffs to ease trade between the countries. For example, in 1988, Canada and the United States agreed to form a free-trade zone for unrestricted trade. In 1994, they expanded the free-trade zone to include Mexico in the **North American Free Trade Agreement (NAFTA).** In 2003 and 2004 respectively, the United States signed a bilateral trade pact with Chile and a regional deal with Costa Rica, the Dominican Republic, El Salvador, Guatemala, Honduras, and Nicaragua, known as the **Central American Free Trade Agreement.** South American countries created their own free trade zone called the **Mercosur** (Argentina, Brazil, Paraguay, Uruguay, and Venezuela) starting in 1998.

COUNTRY	2006 GDP ($ BILLIONS)	AVERAGE ANNUAL GDP GROWTH (%) 1990–2000	AVERAGE ANNUAL GDP GROWTH (%) 2000–2006
United States	$13,202	3.5%	2.9%
Japan	4,340	1.3	1.6
Germany	2,907	1.8	1.4
China	2,668	10.6	9.5
United Kingdom	2,345	2.7	2.5
France	2,231	2.0	2.0
Italy	1,845	1.6	1.2
Canada	1,251	3.1	3.0
Spain	1,224	2.6	3.4
Brazil	1,068	2.9	2.8
Russia	987	−4.7	6.8
India	906	6.0	6.8
South Korea	888	5.8	5.2
Mexico	839	3.1	2.9
Australia	768	3.9	2.9
Netherlands	658	2.9	1.4
Belgium	392	2.1	2.0
Sweden	385	2.2	2.8
Switzerland	380	1.0	1.6
Austria	322	2.4	1.9
Average	**1,980**	**2.8**	**3.2**

Source: Word Development Indicators 2007, World Bank

figure 18.1

Exports from and Imports to the United States by Country, 2006

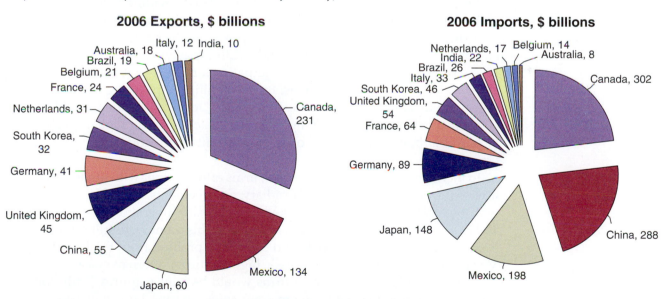

Source: US Department of Commerce: Bureau of Economic Analysis

Other regions of the world have also formed trading zones or are in the process of doing so. One of the largest, oldest, and most important is the **European Union (EU).** The current 27 members include the original Western Europe countries (except Switzerland) and, more recently, Eastern Europe countries such as the Czech Republic, Hungary and Poland (added in 2004), and Bulgaria and Romania (added in 2007). The EU creates an open marketplace where goods and services can easily cross borders. Taken together, the EU rivals the United States' economic power. In addition to this economic cooperation between European countries, many of the countries have formed a monetary union. Fifteen countries use a single currency called the *euro* (€). The euro was created on January 1, 1999, but was not available as coins and notes until 2002. The former country currencies, like the French franc and the German mark, are no longer legal tender. The newest members of the EU have also agreed to change their currency to the euro. This changeover occurs between 2008 and 2011, depending on the country.

In addition to free-trade zones, international organizations promote and facilitate unrestricted trade globally. For example, the **World Trade Organization** (located in Geneva, Switzerland) has 151 country signatories. Its goals are to increase international trade by promoting lower trade barriers and providing a platform for negotiations and disputes. Also, the **International Monetary Fund (IMF),** an organization of 185 countries (located in Washington, D.C.), monitors currency exchange, examines financial stability, and watches the overall global financial system.

 ## Corporate Expansion into Other Countries

Seattle, Washington, coffee giant Starbucks provides an illustration of how firms evolve from doing business locally or domestically to expanding their operations across nations and, eventually, overseas. Firms typically become involved internationally in steps, and companies show different levels of international involvement.

Probably the lowest level of involvement is the simple import and export operation. Say that Starbucks simply bought coffee beans from farmers in other countries, that is, they imported coffee beans. Indeed, this was exactly what Starbucks' mission was at its founding in 1971. After processing the imported beans in the United States, the three founders focused on providing fellow coffee lovers in the Seattle area with the best coffee available. At this stage in its development, the company risked only the hazards of importing the beans. By 1981, Starbucks had expanded to four coffee shops and a coffee roasting plant outside of Seattle. Likewise, many firms expand into international markets with simple, relatively low-risk import/export operations. But remaining simple import/export operations with this low involvement level seems to "leave money on the table"—that is, companies miss out on serving potential customers with higher levels of service. In Starbucks' case, they could glean profits from coffee lovers across the United States.

To increase the level of involvement, firms often partner with other firms using licenses, franchising, or sales subsidiary arrangements. Starbucks did exactly that. By 1991, Starbucks had worked out licensing operations in U.S. airports and began selling mail-order coffee. Its risks at this point were still minimal—the licensees took on all of the risk, and Starbucks profited from the licensing fees. Many firms follow this same low-risk, higher return pattern overseas.

The next logical step for most firms would be joint ventures, with domestic companies partnering with foreign companies, sharing both the risks and the profits. By 1987, Starbucks had plans in place for 125 coffee stores in Vancouver, Portland, and Chicago—up from 17 stores. In 1992, Starbucks went public with an initial public offering (IPO) and started growing quickly. By 1997, the company had 10 times as many stores as it had had when it went public and had expanded into Japan and Singapore in addition to opening more stores in the United States. Moving into new countries quickly meant that the firm had to leave foreign operations to local managers via joint ventures. Starbucks had started courting customers across the world, selling various blended coffee beans

figure 18.2

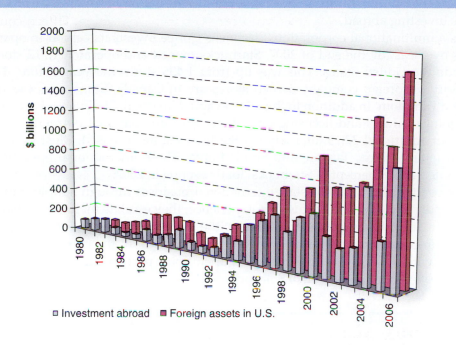

☐ Investment abroad ■ Foreign assets in U.S.

as well as the beverages themselves. By doing so, the coffee giant risked its own capital for a chance of much greater profits. They chose their locations carefully, in politically stable, relatively wealthy countries.

The last stage of international operations involves direct capital involvement. Starbucks embarked upon this stage in Japan and Singapore—operating directly in foreign countries by opening and operating stores itself. In this case, Starbucks faces all the risks of operating a business in the foreign country, but also reaps all the potential rewards. In summary, firms can expand internationally through several methods that require increasingly higher participation in capital at risk and potential for profits. These levels are:

- Import/export
- Partnering
  - Sales subsidiary
  - Licensing/franchising
  - Joint venture
- Direct ownership

Multinational corporations (MNC) invest their capital for direct ownership of asset to produce products and services in multiple countries. For example, Starbucks now owns and operates over 3,000 stores in 37 locations. Companies like Nike find it less expensive to manufacture their product in low labor-cost countries like China and Vietnam. In other cases, companies have found that it is more efficient to manufacture the products they sell within the countries where they want to sell those products. For example, Toyota announced plans to invest $830 million to open (in 2009) its eighth car assembly plant in North America. Some of these multinational corporations often become truly global firms, producing and selling many products all over the world.

The capital spent to run overseas operations is called **foreign direct investment.** The direct investment of U.S. firms abroad and the investment of foreign firms in the United States have substantially increased recently. Figure 18.2 shows the direct investment each year since 1980. With all of the political talk about U.S.

jobs being outsourced overseas, you may be surprised to see that direct foreign investment by foreign firms into the United States is higher than that of U.S. firms investing abroad.

As a multinational corporation, Starbucks Coffee invests its capital in operations overseas. By the end of 2007, Starbucks owned and operated 1,712 stores outside the United States. This was up from 1,435 stores the year before. The majority of foreign company-owned stores are in Canada, Singapore, and the United Kingdom. In addition to this direct capital invested, Starbucks also enters into joint ventures and licensing operations with international partners. There were an additional 2,615 international Starbucks stores licensed. Most of these are in Japan, China, Taiwan, and South Korea. These international operations accounted for 18 percent of Starbucks' total revenue in 2007.

It's common for firms to start international business through simple import and export operations. As firms gain experience, they escalate their international commitment through partnering. Finally, the firms gain enough knowledge to make direct ownership investments in other countries. In the end, many firms end up with a variety of import/export operations, partnership arrangements, and direct ownership—just like Starbucks has!

TIME OUT

18-1 What motivates the governments of countries to create free-trade zones?

18-2 What does the large amount of FDI coming into the United States mean for U.S. workers?

18.2 Foreign Currency Exchange

The first challenge that managers face when they seek to conduct business internationally is that different countries, or monetary unions, use different currencies. Selling products internationally requires conversion of one currency into another. The foreign exchange (or forex) market, by which traders convert one foreign currency into another, is one of the largest financial markets in the world. Currency trading entails no specific physical location; instead, it's an over-the-counter market whose main participants are commercial and investment banks, and foreign exchange dealers and brokers around the world. They communicate using electronic networks. Any firm's bank, or experts within the firm, can access this market to exchange one currency for another.

 ### Exchange Rates

To buy products internationally, a U.S. firm must buy foreign currency with U.S. dollars. We call the price of one currency in terms of another an **exchange rate.** If we're exchanging one currency for another immediately, we participate in a **spot transaction.** Table 18.2 shows quotes from the exchange market. A currency's price can appear in either domestic currency units or foreign currency units. An **indirect quote** lists the amount of foreign currency it takes to buy one unit of domestic currency. Table 18.2 shows that on this day in January 2008, it cost 106.085 Japanese yen to purchase one U.S. dollar. It also cost 0.6924 euros to buy one dollar, denoted as $1 = €0.6924. A **direct quote** expresses the exchange rate as the amount of domestic currency needed to buy one unit of foreign currency. So Table 18.2 also shows that one yen will purchase 0.00943 U.S. dollars. One euro buys 1.444 dollars, denoted as €1 = $1.444. Note that a direct quote is simply the inverse of an indirect quote: Direct quote = 1 ÷ Indirect quote.

U.S. $1 WILL BUY	INDIRECT QUOTE
Yen, ¥	106.085
Euro, €	0.6924
Canada, $	1.0322
United Kingdom, £	0.5145
Australian, $	1.163
Swiss Franc	1.1095

1 OF THE FOLLOWING WILL BUY	DIRECT QUOTE
Yen, ¥	$0.00943
Euro, €	$1.444
Canada, $	$0.969
United Kingdom, £	$1.943
Australian, $	$0.860
Swiss Franc	$0.901

Data Source: **http://finance.yahoo.com/currency**

 For interactive versions of this example visit www.mhhe.com/can1e   **EXAMPLE** 18-1

EXCHANGING CURRENCY

Erin has been invited to go on a ski vacation in Canada over the holiday break. She figures that she will need 1,500 Canadian dollars for the trip. How many U.S. dollars does Erin need to convert to Canadian dollars?

SOLUTION:

Using the currency exchange rates in Table 18.2, observe that US$1 = CA$1.0322. Therefore, Erin will need US$1,453 as shown:

$$CA\$1,500 \times \frac{US\$1}{CA\$1.0322} = US\$1,453$$

Of course, some U.S. firms may want to exchange two non-dollar currencies. So cross-currency quotes are useful. Table 18.3 shows the **cross rates** on this day in January 2008. The table shows that ¥1 = €0.00653 and €1 = ¥153.2132. Again, all of these rates are inverses of each other. If an exchange rate quote between two currencies isn't available, you can derive it as a cross rate through two exchange rates with a third currency. For example, the direct quote exchange rate between U.S. dollars and euros is €1 = $1.444 and between U.S. dollars and yen is ¥1 = $0.00943. We can then compute the cross rate between yen and euros as

$$\frac{€1}{\$1.444} \times \frac{\$0.00943}{¥1} = \frac{€0.00653}{¥1}$$

MATH COACH

Converting Currency

When you're determining how much of one currency results from a sum of another currency, it may get confusing which exchange rate quote to use (direct or indirect) and how to use it. You can use either quote. The trick is to make sure the right currency label is cancelled out, to leave the desired currency label. See that in the example above, Erin is using the indirect quote. She places the desired currency in the numerator and the currency to be converted in the denominator so that CA$ can be cancelled out, leaving US$. She could have solved the problem using the direct quote, CA$1 = US$0.969. All she needed to do was to make sure that her desired currency is in the numerator and the other is in the denominator, like:

$$CA\$1,500 \times \frac{US\$0.969}{CA\$1} = US\$1,453$$

	YEN, ¥	EURO, €	CANADA, $	U.K., £	AUSTRALIAN, $	SWISS FRANC
1 Yen, ¥	1	0.00653	0.00973	0.00485	0.010963	0.010459
1 Euro, €	153.2132	1	1.4908	0.7431	1.6797	1.6025
1 Canada, $	102.7756	0.6708	1	0.4985	1.1267	1.0749
1 United Kingdom, £	206.1708	1.3456	2.006	1	2.2602	2.1564
1 Australian, $	91.2171	0.5954	0.8875	0.4424	1	0.954
1 Swiss Franc	95.6108	0.624	0.9303	0.4637	1.0482	1

The result, ¥1 = €0.00653, is the cross rate shown in Table 18.3.

In fact, some people intentionally look for exchange rate mispricings by comparing direct quote exchange rates between two currencies with cross rates determined through a third currency. If direct quotes and cross rates differ, **arbitrage**—a form of buying low and selling high—is possible. For example, suppose that the yen-to-euro exchange rate was ¥1 = €0.00655. Obviously, this rate is higher than the cross rate of ¥1 = €0.00653, so a profitable arbitrage exists. To earn the profit, make the three simultaneous trades:

1. Trade $1,000,000 for ¥106,044,538.70 (= $1,000,000 × ¥1 ÷ $0.00943).
2. Trade ¥106,044,538.70 for €694,591.73 (= ¥106,044,538.70 × €0.00655 ÷ ¥1).
3. Trade €694,591.73 for $1,002,990.46 (= €694,591.73 × $1.444 ÷ €1).

Notice that the beginning $1 million has become $1,002,990.46. Because the exchange rate is mispriced, a trader made a $2,990.46 profit! Because three exchange rates are necessary to profit from a mispricing, this process is sometimes called *triangular* arbitrage and a person doing it is called an **arbitrageur**.

 ## Exchange Rate Risk

Corporations easily exchange one currency for another. The problem that firms face is that exchange rates change over time. Consider a company that invests $100 million in projects in Europe when the exchange rate to euros was €1 = $1.15. The company would be investing €86.96 million (= $100 × €1 ÷ $1.15). Say that two years later, the investment had increased by 10 percent to €95.65 million. But when the company sells the projects and converts the euros back to dollars, it finds that the exchange rate changed unfavorably to €1 = $0.85. The exchange to dollars results in $81.3 million (= €95.65 × $0.85 ÷ €1). Even though the investment earned a 10 percent return in the foreign market, the company lost money on it because the exchange rate moved in the wrong direction. Specifically, the loss was due to the 26 percent decline [(= $1.15 − $0.85) ÷ $1.15] in the value of the euro. The potential for exchange rates to change (unfavorably) over time is called **exchange rate risk.**

The exchange rates between most major world currencies have a **freely floating regime.** That is, the exchange rates are free to change according to supply and demand for the currencies. Governments sometimes try to influence exchange rates by buying or selling their currency to change supply or demand. Such an attempt to manipulate the exchange rate through the currency exchange market indicates a **managed-floating regime.**

The dramatic dollar/euro exchange rate change shown in the Figure 18.3 actually occurred in January of 1999 and 2001. Right after the decline in the value of the euro, the euro's value rallied strongly. In two and half years, the euro's value increased by nearly 50 percent. This large change in the exchange rate significantly affected importing, exporting, and foreign direct investment. When it

EXCHANGING CURRENCY FOR YOUR TRIP

One ramification of a global economy is that many people travel to foreign countries for business or pleasure. How do you get foreign currency for your trip? Currency exchange rates vary from place to place and day to day. You can find exchange bureaus at airports and banks. You can even exchange currency in the lobby of your five-star hotel! But retail exchange services are costly. You will find that where and how you exchange currency can make a big difference in how much you'll have to spend.

You'll get the best exchange rate if you let your bank make your transactions for you. Banks frequently participate in the currency exchange market and earn the best exchange rates. Your bank converts the currency for you when you use your credit card or ATM card in a foreign country. The cost of using credit cards issued in the United States to make purchases internationally has risen in recent years because some banks have added a *currency-conversion fee* of up to 2 percent. Credit card companies charge this fee in addition to the standard 1 percent fee that they charge for foreign purchases. Credit cards should work well for most purchases.

But you will still need cash for the little things like taxis, tips, and a coffee at Starbucks. ATM networks have proliferated globally, so you can use your ATM or debit card to get foreign currency almost anywhere in the world. But again, be aware of the fees. Some banks charge 1 to 3 percent of the withdrawal as a conversion fee for foreign ATM use. Others impose a flat fee of up to $5 per withdrawal. Check your bank's Web site to find out which ATM brands are in your bank's network and how much your bank will charge you for transactions.

Even with fees imposed on credit card and ATM use, they are still a better deal than the exchange bureaus found at airports and hotels. A 2005 *Consumer Reports* survey of transaction costs found that converting dollars into euros at an exchange bureau cost 10 percent more than using a Visa with a 3 percent conversion fee. Exchanging dollars at a five-star hotel costs even more! It's good to know the exchange rate before you leave so that you will know whether you are getting ripped-off or not!

 want to know more? **Key Words to Search for Updates: exchange rates, currency-conversion fee**

---

takes more dollars to buy a foreign currency than it did before, we say that the dollar is *weakening.* If it takes fewer dollars to buy the foreign currency then the dollar is *strengthening.* The euro remains strong today, especially relative to the dollar.

In some cases, a government fixes, or *pegs,* its currency's value to another currency. For nearly seven years, China's currency was pegged at 8.28 yuan to the U.S. dollar. Then, on July 21, 2005, China changed its exchange rate to a **fixed peg arrangement** to a basket of world currencies. This change effectively meant that the new rate became 8.11 yuan per U.S. dollar. The People's Republic of China stated that the foreign currency basket is dominated by the U.S. dollar, euro, Japanese yen, and South Korean won, with a smaller proportion made up of the British pound, Thai baht, Russian ruble, Australian dollar, Canadian dollar, and Singapore dollar. Since China changed its pegging standard, the yuan has strengthened to 6.945 yuan per dollar (May 30, 2008).

The Forward Exchange Rate and Hedging

Financial managers can manage exchange rate risk to some extent by using **forward exchange rates.** While spot exchange rates hold for transactions occurring right now, traders quote forward rates for transactions to be completed in 30, 90, or 180 days. Companies can negotiate an exchange rate in advance for currency that they will exchange months in the future. Table 18.4 shows spot and forward rates for converting Swiss francs and U.K. pounds sterling to U.S. dollars. The

figure 18.3

Number of U.S. Dollars to Purchase 1 Euro, Exchange Rates January 1999 to January 2008

Data Source: Board of Governors of the Federal Reserve System

Spot and Forward Exchange Rates, January 17, 2008	table 18.4

EXCHANGE RATE PER US$1	
Switzerland franc spot rate	1.0997
1-month forward	1.0983
3-months forward	1.0961
6-months forward	1.0939
U.K. pound spot rate	0.5076
1-month forward	0.5083
3-months forward	0.5096
6-months forward	0.5120

Source: *The Wall Street Journal*

table shows that over the next six months, you would be able to buy fewer Swiss francs with one dollar than you could today. The spot rate is US$1 = 1.0997 francs and the six-month forward rate is US$1 = 1.0939 francs. In this circumstance, we say that the forward Swiss franc is selling at a **premium** to the spot rate. The opposite is occurring with the exchange for U.K. pounds sterling. One dollar will buy more pounds in the forward market, so we say that the forward pound is selling at a **discount** to the spot rate.

Financial managers implement **hedging** strategies to reduce exchange rate risks. First, they can minimize the amount of foreign currency that the firm needs to exchange. For example, consider a case in which money is borrowed in the United States, converted to euros, and invested in Europe. As the project earns cash flows each year, the cash flows are converted back to dollars to pay interest and principal on the loan. An alternative is to borrow euros with a loan from a European bank. Then the loan can be repaid with the project cash flows without currency exchange. A second strategy is to lock in the exchange rates by negotiating currency trades that will occur in the future using forward rates. Last, financial derivative securities can be used for hedging. To hedge currency risks, companies use **futures** contracts, **options,** and **currency swaps.**

Starbucks operates on a large scale in Canada, the United Kingdom, and Japan, and thus has large exchange rate exposure risk. To manage these risks, Starbucks implements all three strategies mentioned on the previous page:

1. It has acquired Japanese yen-denominated bank loans to support Japanese operations.

2. It has forward rate contracts in yen, the Canadian dollar, and the pound to hedge its investments and exchange rate exposures in Starbucks Japan and the Canadian and U.K. subsidiaries.

3. It claims in its annual report that it "may engage in transactions involving various derivative instruments, with maturities generally not exceeding five years, to hedge assets, liabilities, revenues and purchases denominated in foreign currencies."

 For interactive versions of this example visit www.mhhe.com/can1e

EXAMPLE 18-2

CURRENCY EXCHANGE RISK

LG4

Starbucks Coffee begins some international activities by entering into partnership agreements with companies already operating in the country. Sometimes, Starbucks purchases 100 percent ownership of the foreign business. For example, in early 2007, Starbucks announced a deal to purchase 18 percent of Marinopolus Romania B.V., a coffee business in Romania. Although they did not announce the specifics of the deal, imagine negotiating a $20 million deal with a Romanian firm when the Romanian currency, the leu, is under distress. In fact, a new leu replaced the old one in late 2006. The old leu required 3,333 to exchange for one dollar. The new leu needs only 2.57 per dollar. If Starbucks invests $20 million in Romania, how many new lei (plural of leu) are they investing? If the exchange rate changes to 3.15, how much value has Starbucks' investment lost?

SOLUTION:

$20 million will purchase 51.4 million lei (= $20 million × 2.57 lei/$). If the exchange rate changes, then the 51.4 million lei will be worth only $16.3 million (= 51.4 million lei ÷ 3.15 lei/$). This weakening of the leu would cause an 18.5 percent reduction in the value of the investment in Romania.

Interest Rate Parity

LG5

Why do spot exchange rates and forward rates differ? Table 18.4 shows that forward rates can be either higher or lower then the spot rate. What factors affect the forward rate? The answer lies in comparing interest rates in the two countries. Say that you hear about an interest rate available in another country—say South Africa—that is higher than any available in your country, the United States. If you want to earn the higher rate for six months, you would need to convert your dollars to South African rand at the spot rate, earn the high return and then convert the money back to your own currency in six months. In order to lock in your future exchange rate and thus your profit, you could use a forward rate contract. As long as the forward rate is the same as the spot rate, you would earn a higher interest rate on the South African investment than is available domestically.

Unfortunately, the financial markets have already thought this one through. The concept of **interest rate parity** suggests that the forward rate will be such that the total return earned (interest rate and changes in exchange rate) will be the same between the two countries. In other words, the difference between the spot and forward rates arises precisely because of the difference in the interest rates available in the two countries. If i_d is the interest rate available in your home (domestic) country and i_f is the rate in the foreign country, then the interest rate parity relationship is expressed as

$$\frac{\text{Forward exchange rate}}{\text{Spot exchange rate}} = \frac{(1 + i_d)}{(1 + i_f)}$$

(18-1)

The forex market requires that both the forward and spot rates be expressed as direct quotes. That means the amount of domestic currency received per unit of foreign currency. Consider that the U.S. risk-free rate is 4.9 percent and in South Africa it is 5.25 percent. While we always express interest rates in annualized terms, the actual investment problem and thus our equation requires us to express the interest rates for the same period as the forward exchange rate.

The spot and forward rates in Table 18.4 are indirect quotes. The direct quote for the South Africa spot rate would be 1.970 (= 1 ÷ 0.5076) and for the six-month forward rate 1.953 (= 1 ÷ 0.5120). Given interest rate parity, what should the forward rate be? Use a six-month interest rate for the United States of 2.91 percent and for the United Kingdom of 3.81 percent. Rearranging equation 18–1 means that the forward rate should be

$$\frac{1 + 0.0291}{1 + 0.0381} \times 1.970 = 1.9529$$

This result is within the rounding error of the actual forward rate. Note how the equation implies that when the foreign interest rate is higher, then the forward rate will indicate a weakening of the foreign currency. When the foreign interest rate is lower than the domestic rate, the forward exchange rate will indicate a strengthening of the foreign currency. Thus, the difference in spot and forward rates is directly a result of the difference in interest rate in the two countries. If the forward rate is not consistent with interest rate parity, then an arbitrage is possible. Arbitrageurs could (1) borrow in one low-rate country, (2) exchange the money to another currency and deposit it to earn the higher rate, (3) enter into a forward rate contract to guarantee the future exchange rate, and at the end (4) repay the loan. The money left over would be the arbitrage profit.

 ## Purchasing Power Parity (PPP) and Future Exchange Rates

Interest rate parity describes why spot and forward rates differ. But why do exchange rates change over time—even from one day to the next? Why has the exchange rate between two major currencies like the dollar and euro changed so much, as shown in Figure 18.3? In short, the answer is inflation. The concept of **purchasing power parity (PPP)** illustrates how inflation causes exchange rates to change.

The idea of purchasing power parity stems from a concept known as the **law of one price.** Essentially, the law of one price dictates that identical products should have the same price, adjusted for currency exchange, no matter where in the world they sell. The law of one price seems reasonable when we consider an item like an ounce of gold. Denote the price in the domestic country as P_d and the price in the foreign country is P_f. Then the PPP relationship is shown as

$$P_d = P_f \times \text{Spot rate}$$

(18-2)

THE YEN CARRY TRADE

In early 2007, a concern about the ramifications of a large-scale unwinding of the "yen carry trade" hit the financial press around the world. What is this trade and how might it affect world economies and stock markets?

The yen carry trade strategy supposes that an investor borrows money in Japan, which has had an annual interest rate of around 0.50 percent for years. The trader then converts the borrowed yen into U.S. dollars or U.K. pounds and invests the proceeds at a higher fixed interest rate or even in the stock market. As an example, say that a trader borrows 100 million yen from a Japanese bank, converts the funds into US$845,237, and buys a U.S. bond for this amount. Assume that the U.S. bond pays 5 percent. The trader stands to make a profit of 4.5 percent (= 5% − 0.5%), or $38,036, in one year as long as the exchange rate between the countries does not change. Since the trader originally borrowed the Japanese yen and thus did not even use his own money, why not borrow even more? In fact, many traders used borrowed Japanese yen to buy stocks in companies around the world.

So, how much total money have global traders borrowed in the yen carry trade? No one really knows. Experts estimate that figure at anywhere from $85 billion to hundreds of billions of dollars. The big risk in this strategy is the uncertainty of future exchange rates. Purchasing power parity suggests that the difference in interest rates between Japan and the United States arises from different inflation rates. Indeed, Japan has been suffering from deflation, or negative inflation rates, while the U.S. inflation rate has been in the low single digits. So IRP would predict that the U.S. dollar's value will fall relative to the Japanese yen's value, thereby wiping out the profit of this strategy. However, the yen/dollar has been relatively stable over the past decade, averaging ¥117 per dollar and mostly deviating by only 10 percent in either direction.

But recently, the U.S. dollar has started weakening against the yen. If all the yen carry traders rush to unwind their positions by selling their stocks and bonds to convert to yen and pay off their debt, significant pressure could be put on stock prices, interest rates, and exchange rates.

 want to know more? **Key Words to Search for Updates:** yen carry trade, yen dollar exchange rate

Note that we must denote the spot rate as the amount of domestic currency exchanged for one unit of foreign currency. So, if gold is selling in the United States for $855 per ounce and Table 18.2 shows that $1.943 = £1, then gold should sell for £440.04 (= $855 ÷ $1.943/£) in the United Kingdom. If gold sold for only £435 per ounce, then you could buy gold in the United Kingdom and sell it in the United States for a profit, acting as an arbitrageur. Large players in the gold market are very happy to make a profit through buying in one market and selling in another. Their buying in the United Kingdom will boost the price and their selling in the United States will apply downward pressure on prices, thus moving prices to the appropriate levels as shown in PPP. In this way, opportunities for arbitrage eliminate different prices and ensure that the law of one price holds.

PPP may not hold exactly because of transaction costs that may include shipping, insurance, trading costs, and so on. Trade restrictions and tariffs may also inhibit the law of one price. Finally, many products and services are not reasonably transportable, so the law of one price may not apply. For example, you may not expect the law of one price to hold for a haircut in London as it would in a small Midwestern town in the United States.

So, even though the PPP doesn't work perfectly, the concept can illustrate why exchange rates can—must—change over time. Imagine that the price level of goods did not change in the United States, but the overall price index increased by 10 percent in Argentina. This is one way of saying that the inflation rate was zero in the United States and 10 percent in Argentina. In order for PPP to hold at the end of the year, the current spot exchange rate of 1 peso = $0.322 would have to change by the end of the year, or arbitrage becomes possible. Since inflation in Argentina was 10 percent higher than in the United States, then the peso must decrease in value (purchasing power) by 10 percent in order for PPP to hold. This relationship is shown in the *relative* form of the PPP equation. The new exchange rate will be

$$\text{Expected exchange rate} = \text{Current spot rate}$$

Expected exchange rate (domestic amount per unit of foreign currency) = Current spot rate (domestic amount per unit of foreign currency)

$$\times \ (1 + \text{Domestic inflation rate} - \text{Foreign inflation rate})$$
(18-3)

Using this relative PPP equation, we expect the Argentinean peso exchange rate at the end of the year to be $0.290 (= $0.322 × {1 + 0 − 0.10}). If inflation in Argentina went even higher, its currency would depreciate further. Of course, many other factors could change worldwide in the course of the year to impact both exchange rates in either or both countries. Further, PPP adjustments don't take place on a particular day at the end of the year. Rather, the forex and other markets adjust minute-by-minute to take new information into account. However, because it takes all current information about the future into account, we consider the relative PPP estimate to be the best forecast of future exchange rates between countries.

Interest rate parity describes the relationship between the current spot rate and the forward rate. Purchasing power parity describes how the current spot rate will likely change in the future. Your intuition likely tells you that the two parity concepts are related. Chapter 8 shows how expected inflation is one component of a country's current and future interest rates. High interest rates tend to go with and to predict high inflation. So both the forward rate from interest rate parity and the expected future spot rate from PPP should be consistent in indicating either a weakening or strengthening of a particular country's currency.

EXAMPLE 18-3   For interactive versions of this example visit www.mhhe.com/can1e

 EXPECTED EXCHANGE RATES

You know that your firm will want to convert 25 million Brazilian real to U.S. dollars in six months. The current exchange rate is $0.4766 = 1 real. The inflation rates in Brazil and in the United States are expected to be 7 percent and 3.5 percent, respectively. You need to estimate the likely exchange rate in six months and how many dollars your firm will likely realize in the transaction.

SOLUTION:

Inflation is stated in annual terms, so you will have to use six-month values of 3.5 percent and 1.75 percent for Brazil and the United States. Using the relative form of PPP, compute that the expected exchange rate is:

$$\$0.4766 \times (1 + 0.0175 - 0.035) = \$0.4683 \text{ per real.}$$

If this turns out to be the spot rate in six months, then the 25 million real will be exchanged for $11.7 million (= 25 million real × $0.4683/real). Thus, your firm will want to use some kind of exchange risk management tool to lock in a better real-to-dollar value. What might your firm do to protect itself from foreign exchange risk?

TIME OUT

18-3 Why is currency exchange risky for a multinational firm? What can be done to reduce the risk?

18-4 Describe how arbitrage works and how it reinforces the relationship between exchange rates and cross rates.

18-5 Explain why currency exchange rates change over time and how to forecast those changes.

18.3 Political Risks

MNCs face uncertainty in addition to foreign currency risks. These firms also face uncertainty about foreign and domestic government actions. **Political risk** refers to the possibility that a country's political decisions or events will adversely affect the business climate so that the MNCs' investment might fall in value or even completely lose its value.

Sometimes governments change suddenly and violently. A new government typically will not honor the agreements and policies of the former government unless the country or government will profit handsomely for doing so. Although revolution is an extreme case of a change in government, even publicly elected governments may change at each election. In a two-party system like the one in the United States, one administration may create certain trade, tax, and labor policies and the next administration may change those policies. Some political risks to the assets and cash flows of MNCs are:

- Government seizure of a company's assets in the country.

- Expropriation with minimal compensation (the government demanding specific cash flows).

- Enactment of new taxation.

- Limiting or blocking the conversion of local currency to the MNC's domestic currency.

Consider how quickly a country can change from foreign-investment-friendly to hostile. Venezuela has immense oil reserves. For many years Venezuela did not have the capital to fully develop these resources. Consequently, the country entered into service contracts with numerous foreign oil companies to invest in and operate Venezuela's oil fields. In the 1990s, several dozen foreign companies participated in the Venezuelan oil sector at the government's invitation. But Venezuela's hospitality towards foreign companies did not last long. In the past few years, the Venezuelan government under Hugo Chavez has sought to force the renegotiation of contracts and nationalized (seized) entire companies. Venezuela also began nationalizing companies in vitally important industries, including the energy and telecommunications industries. In the Spring of 2007, Verizon (ticker: VZ) was forced to sell its stake in CANTV to the Venezuelan government for $572 million—about $100 million less than a previously agreed-to sale price that was awaiting Venezuelan regulatory approval. Similar nationalization movements are taking place in Bolivia and Ecuador. In May 2006, Evo Morales, the recently elected president of Bolivia, announced plans to nationalize the country's oil and gas industry. He also announced that his government planned to nationalize companies in other industries and to implement new tax measures aimed at foreign companies. We await any moves by Ecuadorian President Rafael Correa Delgado in a similar direction.

figure 18.4

Political Stability and
Control of Corruption
Rankings, World Bank
2005

Source: Daniel Kaufmann, Aart
Kraay, and Massimo Mastruzzi
(September 2006), "Governance
Matters V: Governance Indica-
tors for 1996–2005" World Bank
Policy Research Working Paper,
and "A Decade of Measuring the
Quality of Governance," **www.
govindicators.org,** September
2006.

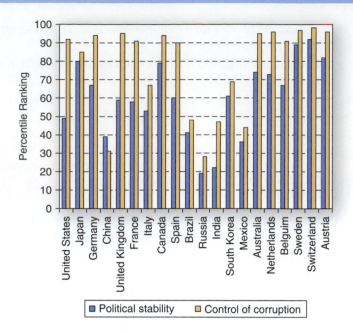

Some countries seem to require payments to various government officials as a condition of doing business in the country. While some countries consider such payments simply part of doing business, the Western world considers such practices corrupt and illegal. This corruption and bribery is banned by the agreement signed by countries in the World Trade Organization. Nevertheless, it likely still occurs, especially in smaller, less developed countries. Each year, the World Bank reports on various country governance indicators. Figure 18.4 shows the percentile ranking of the *political stability* indicator and the *control of corruption* indicator. Political stability measures the likelihood of government destabilization or significant policy change. A higher-ranking indicates a more stable government. A higher control of corruption ranking means the bribery and other forms of corruption are minimal. The countries in the figure are in the same order as the size of their economy (as shown in Table 18.1). Of these countries, Switzerland has both the highest political stability and firmest control of corruption rankings, while Russia has the lowest rankings.

Companies can minimize the impact of political risk. Remember that acquiring the capital from inside the foreign country can reduce the need for currency exchange. Similarly, using local financing may reduce losses from a confiscation of assets. If the assets are seized by the government, then the company can refuse to pay back the financing obtained within the country. Another strategy is to purchase country risk insurance from private insurance companies or from the U.S. government sponsored Overseas Private Investment Corporation. Some political risks must be borne by the MNCs as a cost of doing business internationally. Presumably, the opportunities are valuable enough to take these risks.

TIME OUT

18-6 Give some examples of how an MNC can lose assets or cash flow because of political risk.

18-7 Describe some strategies for dealing with political risk.

18.4 International Capital Budgeting

Great business opportunities arise globally every day. But we have also demonstrated that the opportunities come with significant financial and political risks when the firm does business internationally. Financial managers can use strategies like hedging to minimize some of these risks. Managers need to look at global opportunities with their eyes wide open, recognizing all of the potential risks as well as the opportunities for above-average profits as they evaluate foreign opportunities.

Managers may begin their evaluation of possible foreign projects with regular capital budgeting processes, but the global component adds several complications. Recall that assessing the net present value of a project requires that we estimate the value of future cash flows and that we establish a discount rate that's consistent with project risk. Estimating future cash flows is difficult in a domestic analysis, so we can only imagine the problems with estimating direct and indirect costs and future revenues in unfamiliar territory. We should also use a high discount rate that will account for the added exchange and political risk that the project may incur.

Note that the cash flows of a foreign project will be in the foreign currency, while the discount rate is usually evaluated from the domestic country perspective. A financial manager has two alternative methods for resolving this problem. First, all incremental cash flows can be converted to the domestic currency, which requires exchange rate estimates for each year. We estimate the exchange rate from estimates of how the spot rate will change using PPP. Once the cash flows have been translated into the domestic currency, the regular NPV computation can proceed. The second possibility is to convert the domestic discount rate to an equivalent rate in the foreign country. You would need to use different discount rates in two countries because the two countries will likely experience different inflation rates, which affects PPP. So analysts will have to adjust the discount rate by the difference in the inflation rates between the two countries. The resulting NPV will be denoted in the foreign currency and should be converted back into the domestic currency using the current spot rate. Since both methods rely on some inflation rate estimates, they should produce the same NPV.

TIME OUT

18-8 Explain why the two methods for applying the NPV analysis in an international context should produce the same result.

Business Application Solution

Andres should discuss the dynamics of foreign currency exchange. The current spot rate between the dollar and the Mexican peso is $1 = 11.13 pesos. However, the exchange rate has been volatile over the past five years and has varied from 9 pesos to the dollar to 11.5 pesos to the dollar. Thus, managers should know how a weakening or strengthening dollar will affect the value of the assets invested in Mexico and the cash flow earned from those operations.

The managers should also be aware of the political risks that could impact investment in Mexico. Mexico does not rate highly in political stability or control of corruption (see Figure 18.4), but political policy decisions in the United States can also impact the trade and investment between the two countries.

Andres must account for the increased risks of this project by increasing the discount rate in the NPV analysis. Also, he will have to estimate the future exchange rates in order to translate future cash flows in pesos to dollars.

Personal Application Solution

Juliana can see from Table 18.4 that the exchange rate between the Swiss franc and the U.S. dollar is $1 = 1.0997 francs. Therefore, if she buys the currency now, she will receive 10,997 francs (=$10,000 × 1.0997 francs/$).

Juliana can also see from the six-month forward rate that the dollar is expected to weaken compared to the Swiss franc. Therefore, she may be tempted to exchange the currency now. However, the interest rate parity concept suggests that she will likely end up with the same amount of francs in six months if she either buys the francs now and deposits them in a Swiss bank to earn interest, or keeps the $10,000 deposited in a U.S. bank and exchanges for francs in six months. Therefore, she should do whichever is more convenient for her.

summary of learning goals

International business opportunities have substantially increased over the past few decades. Multinational corporations like Starbucks can produce and sell products in whichever countries maximize their firms' values. In this chapter, we've explored the risks associated with international business operations and how to ameliorate those risks.

LG1 **Gauge the dynamics of the global economy and recognize potential international opportunities.** Many large economies in the world trade extensively among themselves. In addition, many smaller developing economies provide investment and trading opportunities. Although the United States has the largest economy by far, the combined economies of the European countries in the European Union creates a marketplace nearly as big as the United States. Other trading zones have also formed in other parts of the world. These zones voluntarily reduce trading restrictions and tariffs. The World Trade Organization and the International Monetary Fund also promote free trade globally.

LG2 **Recognize patterns of increasing capital involvement as the firm seeks to expand business internationally.** Firms typically take a step-by-step approach to expanding their business overseas, taking on increasing risks with each step they take. The low risk (but low reward) approach is simple importing and exporting. Domestic firms can also partner with in-country firms through sales subsidiaries, licensing arrangements, and joint ventures. The MNC invests capital directly into projects in multiple countries. This foreign direct investment in the United States by foreign MNCs has reached a trillion dollars annually the last few years. U.S. MNCs invested less then half of that into foreign countries recently.

LG3 **Compute currency exchanges.** To buy and sell products internationally, you will need to exchange one currency for another to pay for foreign goods. The direct quote spot currency exchange rate determines how much of your domestic currency you will need for each unit of the foreign currency. You can also determine the cross rate between two foreign currencies if you know the two exchange rates between the domestic currency and each foreign currency. If the relationship between the currency exchange rates and cross rate between the three currencies does not hold, then triangular arbitrage may be possible.

LG4 **Recognize situations that evoke exchange rate risk and develop tools to manage exchange rate risks.** Currency exchange rates change over time. This is a financial risk for firms doing business overseas because the firms are exposed to the risk that future foreign or domestic cash flows will be adversely affected by a drastic change in exchange rates. Most currency exchange rates either freely float over time or are managed by a government via a pegging system. When it takes more dollars over time to buy a unit of foreign currency, the dollar is said to be weakening. If fewer dollars will buy a unit of foreign currency, then the dollar is strengthening.

Financial managers can cope with the exchange rate risk through forming contracts in the forward market or through hedging in the derivative markets. In addition, managers can minimize the need for exchanging currencies by obtaining capital within the country that the investment is to be made.

LG5 **Apply theories of how interest rates and inflation influence forward exchange rates and future spot rates.** The relationship between the spot rate and the forward exchange rate is established by the level of interest rates in the two countries as specified by interest rate parity. An expected change in the spot exchange rates is described by purchasing power parity. It shows the difference in expected inflation rates between the two countries, which determines the exchange rates. The country with the higher inflation rate will see a weakening of its currency.

LG6 **Anticipate political risks when investing internationally.** Governments can suddenly change in terms of who has power and in terms of political ideology. New governments may make new and different demands on international firms' assets and cash flows invested in the country. This political risk can also occur when stable governments change trade restrictions, tariffs, taxes, and other trade policies. Some political risks can be managed through country risk insurance and through raising capital within the country the firm is operating.

LG7 **As a financial manager, plan to work through capital budgeting issues for international investments.** The presence of exchange rate risk and political risk increase the overall risk of investing in new projects in foreign countries. Financial managers need to adjust for this increased risk by evaluating projects using higher discount rates in the NPV analysis. For capital budgeting, either future foreign currency cash flows need to be converted to domestic currency or the discount rate needs to be translated from the domestic country to the foreign country.

chapter equations

18-1 $\dfrac{\text{Forward exchange rate}}{\text{Spot exchange rate}} = \dfrac{(1 + i_d)}{(1 + i_f)}$

18-2 $P_d = P_f \times \text{Spot rate}$

$$\text{Expected exchange rate} = \text{Current spot rate}$$

(domestic amount per
unit of foreign currency)

(domestic amount per
unit of foreign currency)

$$\times\ (1 + \text{Domestic inflation rate} - \text{Foreign inflation rate})$$

key terms

arbitrage, The practice of simultaneously purchasing and selling an asset in different forms or markets to take advantage of an imbalance in price. (p. 576)

arbitrageur, A trader who engages in arbitrage. (p. 576)

Central American Free Trade Agreement, A free trade agreement between the Central American countries and the Dominican Republic. (p. 570)

cross rates, The currency exchange rate between two foreign currencies, each of which are not the currency of the domestic country. (p. 575)

currency swap, A foreign exchange agreement to exchange a given amount of one currency for another and then later return the original amounts swapped. (p. 578)

direct quote, The amount of domestic currency it takes to buy one unit of foreign currency. (p. 574)

discount, The case when the forward rate indicates a weaker currency over the spot rate. (p. 578)

European Union (EU), A political and economic union of 27 European countries. (p. 571)

exchange rate, Specifies how much one currency is worth in terms of the other. (p. 574)

exchange rate risk, The possibility that the spot currency exchange rate will change and reduce the value of foreign assets and cash flows. (p. 576)

fixed peg arrangement, An exchange rate regime where a currency's price is fixed to the value of another currency or to a basket of other currencies. (p. 577)

foreign direct investment, A long-term investment of capital in a business operation located in an economy other than that in which the company is based. (p. 573)

forward exchange rate, A contractual arrangement that states the exchange rate to be used at a future exchange date. (p. 577)

freely floating regime, An exchange rate regime where the currency is completely determined by the foreign-exchange market through supply and demand. (p. 576)

futures, A standardized contract traded in a futures exchange market designed to buy (or sell) the underlying asset at a specific price on a certain future date. (p. 578)

hedging, A strategy used to minimize exposure to an unwanted business or financial risk, while still allowing the business to profit. (p. 578)

indirect quote, The amount of foreign currency it takes to buy one unit of domestic currency. (p. 574)

interest rate parity, A theory that the difference in interest rates between two countries is equal to the difference between the forward currency exchange rate and the spot exchange rate. (p. 579)

International Monetary Fund (IMF), An international organization that monitors exchange rates and balance of payments, and oversees the global financial system. (p. 572)

law of one price, An economic principle that states all identical goods in different markets must have the same price. (p. 580)

managed-floating regime, An exchange rate regime where the country's central bank allows its currency price to float freely between an upper and lower bound and may buy or sell large amounts of it in order to provide price support or resistance. (p. 576)

Mercosur, The Southern Common Market of South America. (p. 570)

multinational corporation (MNC), A company that operates production and/or sales facilities in multiple countries. (p. 573)

North American Free Trade Agreement (NAFTA), The trading block consisting of Canada, Mexico, and the United States. (p. 570)

option, A standardized contract in which the buyer has the right (but not the obligation) to buy (or sell) an asset at a set price by a future date. (p. 578)

political risk, The possibility that changes in the business environment will occur that reduce the profitability of doing business in that country. (p. 583)

premium, The case when the forward rate indicates a stronger currency over the spot rate. (p. 578) purchasing power parity (PPP), A theory relating the expected adjustment needed in the future spot exchange rate between countries to the inflation rate in each economy. (p. 580)

spot transaction, An exchange of one currency for another today. (p. 574)

World Trade Organization (WTO), An international organization that deals with international trade rules and helps settle disputes between its member governments. (p. 572)

self-test problems with solutions

1 **Exchange Rate Risk** Your firm has invested $150 million in projects in Europe and $250 million in Japan. The current spot exchange rates are $1 = €0.7623 and $1 = ¥118.04. Consider that over this year, these investments appreciate by 10 percent each, as measured in the foreign currency. However, the spot rates also change to $1 = €0.7563 and $1 = ¥124.66. You need to determine the value of the projects in dollars and their appreciation for the year.

Solution:

First compute the starting values of the projects in Europe and Japan:

In Europe: $150 million × €0.7623/$= €114.345 million
In Japan: $250 million × ¥118.04/$= ¥29,510 million

Next, compute the value after the 10 percent appreciation:

In Europe: €114.345 million × (1 + 0.1) = €125.780 million
In Japan: ¥29,510 million × (1 + 0.1) = ¥32,461 million

Last, compute the dollar value using the new spot rates:

In Europe: €125.780 million ÷ €0.7563/$= $166.31 million
In Japan: ¥32,461 million ÷ ¥124.66/$= $260.4 million

Note that while both project values increased 10 percent in their own markets, the change in exchange rates made the value changes 10.9 percent [= ($166.31 − $150) ÷ $150] in Europe and 4.2 percent [= (260.4 − $250) ÷ $250] in Japan.

2 **Interest Rate Parity Arbitrage** You believe that you have found a small mispricing between the spot exchange rate and the forward rate between the Japanese yen and the British pound. Consider the following information:

Spot rate: £1 = ¥229.02
6-month forward rate: £1 = ¥227.01
Interest rate in Japan: 0.5%
Interest rate in the United Kingdom: 5.25%

You want to verify that a mispricing exists and determine the profit (in pounds) of a £10 million arbitrage.

Solution:

You can use the interest rate parity equation 18-1 to verify a mispricing in the forward rate. First, you need to convert these exchange rates and interest rate for use in the equation. From the perspective of the British pound, these are indirect quotes and need to be direct quotes. Also, the forward rate is for six months, thus a six-month interest rate must be used. The recomputed exchange rates and interest rates are

Direct quote spot rate: ¥1 = £0.004366
Direct quote 6-month forward rate: ¥1 = £0.004405

6-month interest rate in Japan: 0.25%
6-month interest rate in the United Kingdom: 2.625%

Given the current spot rate and interest rates, the forward rate should be

$$\text{Forward rate} = \frac{1 + 0.02625}{1 + 0.0025} \times 0.004366 = 0.004469 \text{ £/¥}$$

Since this is different from the forward rate quote, an arbitrage is possible. You want to borrow enough Japanese yen to deposit £10 million. So, you should conduct the following trades:

- Borrow ¥2,290 million (= £10 million ÷ 0.004366 ¥/£) at the annual 0.5 percent interest rate

- Convert the yen to £10 million and make a deposit to earn a 5.25 percent rate

- Enter into a forward contract for the amount that will be owed, ¥2,295.7 million (= ¥2,290 million × 1.0025)

After six months:

- The deposit will result in £10.262 million (= £10 million × 1.02625)

- Convert £10.113 million (= ¥2,295.7 million × 0.004405 £/¥) into yen using the forward contract to repay the loan

- You keep the difference of £149,000 (= £10.262 million − £10.113 million)

questions

1. What do global organizations like the World Trade Organization and the International Monetary Fund do? *(LG1)*

2. What is the purpose of trading zones? What are some of the most important for world trade? *(LG1)*

3. Explain how a country's import trade limitations and tariffs influence MNC's foreign direct investment. *(LG1)*

4. What are the risks of foreign direct investment into the United States? What does new FDI into the United States mean for firms already operating in that industry in the United States? *(LG2)*

5. Describe the similarities and the differences of exchange rate/cross rate arbitrage and spot rate/forward rate arbitrage. *(LG3, LG5)*

6. What is meant when it is said that the U.S. dollar is strengthening? How would it impact your vacation abroad and foreign visitors to the United States? *(LG4)*

7. Describe the difference between a forward rate selling at a discount and selling at a premium. If the spot rate between the U.S. dollar and the Brazilian real is $1 = 2.0875 real and the three-month forward rate is $1 = 2.1025 real, is the forward real selling at a discount or a premium? *(LG4)*

8. What is meant by hedging exchange rate risk and what are some ways it is done? *(LG4)*

9. What are the advantages of borrowing money in the country you plan to invest it in? *(LG4, LG6)*

10. If a Sony television costs $500 in the United States, what do you think it should cost in Japan? What are some reasons that your price might not be right? *(LG5)*

11. What happens to a country's currency over time when it has a high inflation rate? What will that mean for the country's exports and imports? *(LG5)*

12. What forces are at work that cause the price of wheat per bushel to be the same in most every country of the world? *(LG5)*

13. If the spot exchange rate between the U.S. dollar and the Singapore dollar is $1 = SG$1.5266 and the three-month expected exchange rate is $1 = SG$1.5305, then what is the expected inflation relationship between the two countries? *(LG5)*

14. Over the past decade, China has acquired hundreds of billions of U.S. dollars because of the trade imbalance between the two countries. They have used many of these dollars to purchase U.S. Treasury bonds. What would likely happen to the dollar's value, and interest rates and inflation in the United States, if China decided to suddenly sell the Treasury bonds and exchange the dollars for other currencies? *(LG5)*

15. Can a U.S. firm experience political risk problems in its overseas projects because of the U.S. government? Give examples. *(LG6)*

16. Give some examples of the financial complications that occur when evaluating a capital budgeting project in a foreign country. *(LG7)*

problems

basic problems

18-1 **Exchange Rate Quote** Convert each of the following direct quotes to dollar indirect quotes *(LG3)*:

    a. 1 Danish Krone = $0.1761

    b. 1 Indian Rupee = $0.02268

    c. 1 Israeli Shekel = $0.2381

18-2 **Exchange Rate Quote** Convert each of the following direct quotes to dollar indirect quotes *(LG3)*:

    a. 1 Korean Won = $0.001056

    b. 1 Malaysian Ringgit = $0.2854

    c. 1 Thai Baht = $0.03046

18-3 **Exchange Rate Quote** Convert each of the following indirect quotes to dollar direct quotes *(LG3)*:

    a. $1 = 16,005 Vietnam Dong

    b. $1 = 2,149.6 Venezuelan Bolivar

    c. $1 = 7.3523 South African Rand

18-4 **Exchange Rate Quote** Convert each of the following indirect quotes to dollar direct quotes *(LG3)*:

    a. $1 = 3.7487 Saudi Arabian Riyal

    b. $1 = 48.450 Philippine Peso

    c. $1 = 0.5381 Latvian Lat

18-5 **Currency Exchange** Compute the amount of each foreign currency that can be purchased for $500,000 *(LG3)*:

    a. 1 Danish Krone = $0.1761

    b. 1 Indian Rupee = $0.02268

    c. 1 Israeli Shekel = $0.2381

18-6 **Currency Exchange** Compute the amount of each foreign currency that can be purchased for $1,000,000 *(LG3)*:

    a. 1 Korean Won = $0.001056

    b. 1 Malaysian Ringgit = $0.2854

    c. 1 Thai Baht = $0.03046

18-7 **Currency Exchange** Compute the number of dollars that can be bought with 2 million of each foreign currency units *(LG3)*:

    a. $1 = 16,005 Vietnam Dong

    b. $1 = 2,149.6 Venezuelan Bolivar

    c. $1 = 7.3523 South African Rand

18-8 **Currency Exchange** Compute the number of dollars that can be bought with 1 million of each foreign currency units *(LG3)*:

    a. $1 = 3.7487 Saudi Arabian Riyal

    b. $1 = 48.450 Philippine Peso

    c. $1 = 0.5381 Latvian Lat

18-9 **Law of One Price** If the price of silver in England is £6.71 per ounce, what is the expected price of silver in the United States if the spot exchange rate is $1 = £0.5173? *(LG5)*

18-10 **Law of One Price** If the price of copper in Europe is €2.12 per ounce, what is the expected price of copper in the United States if the spot exchange rate is $1 = €0.7623? *(LG5)*

18-11 **Discount Rates** A financial manager has determined that the appropriate discount rate for a foreign project is 14 percent. However, that discount rate applies in the United States using dollars. What discount rate should be used in the foreign country using the foreign currency? The inflation rate in the United States and in the foreign country is expected to be 4 percent and 7 percent, respectively. *(LG7)*

18-12 **Discount Rates** A financial manager has determined that the appropriate discount rate for a foreign project is 16 percent. However, that discount rate applies in the United States using dollars. What discount rate should the manager use in the foreign country using the foreign currency? The inflation rate in the United States and in the foreign country is expected to be 5 percent and 4 percent, respectively. *(LG7)*

intermediate problems

18-13 **Cross Rate** Given these two exchange rates, $1 = 11.13 Mexican pesos and $1 = €0.7623, compute the cross rate between the Mexican peso and the euro. State this exchange rate in pesos and in euros. *(LG3)*

18-14 **Cross Rate** Given these two exchange rates, $1 = 1.2825 Australian dollars and $1 = £0.5173, compute the cross rate between the Australian dollars and the pound. State this exchange rate in Australian dollars and in pounds. *(LG3)*

18-15 **Exchange Rate Risk** In 1997, many East Asian currencies suddenly and dramatically devalued. What is the percentage change in value of a $50 million investment in Indonesia when the exchange rate changes from $1 = 2,000 rupiah to $1 = 10,000 rupiah? *(LG4)*

18-16 **Exchange Rate Risk** The Russian financial crisis of 1998 caused its currency to be dramatically devalued. What is the percentage change in value of a $100 million investment in Russia when the exchange rate changes from $1 = 6 rubles to $1 = 21 rubles? *(LG4)*

18-17 **Interest Rate Parity** The spot rate between the U.S. dollar and the New Zealand dollar is $1 = NZD1.4425. If the interest rate in the United States is 6 percent and in New Zealand is 4 percent, then what should be the three-month forward exchange rate? *(LG5)*

18-18 **Interest Rate Parity** The spot rate between the U.S. dollar and the Taiwan dollar is $1 = TWD32.348. If the interest rate in the United States is 5 percent and in Taiwan is 3 percent, then what should be the one-month forward exchange rate? *(LG5)*

18-19 **Purchasing Power Parity** The current spot rate between the U.S. dollar and the Swedish krona is $1 = 7.0958 krona. If the inflation rate in the United States is 4 percent and in Sweden is 1 percent, then what is the expected spot rate in one year? *(LG6)*

18-20 **Purchasing Power Parity** The current spot rate between the U.S. dollar and the Netherland Antilles Guilder is $1 = 1.78 Guilder. If the inflation rate in the United States is 3 percent and in the Netherland Antilles is 7 percent, then what is the expected spot rate in one year? *(LG6)*

advanced problems

18-21 **Exchange Rate Risk** A U.S. firm is expecting cash flows of 20 million Mexican pesos and 35 million Indian rupees. The current spot exchange rates are: $1 = 11.722 pesos and $1 = 45.204 rupees. If these cash flows are not received for one year and the expected spot rates at that time will be $1 = 11.118 pesos and $1 = 44.075 rupees, then what is the difference in dollars received that was caused by the delay? *(LG4)*

18-22 **Exchange Rate Risk** A U.S. firm is expecting to pay cash flows of 15 million Egyptian pounds and 25 million Qatar rials. The current spot exchange rates are: $1 = 5.725 pounds and $1 = 3.639 rials. If these cash flows are delayed one year and the expected spot rates at that time will be $1 = 5.892 pounds and $1 = 3.988 rials, what is the difference in dollars paid that was caused by the delay? *(LG4)*

18-23 **Triangular Arbitrage** The U.S. dollar spot exchange rate with the Canadian dollar is $1 = CA$1.18. The U.S. dollar and Swiss Franc exchange rate is $1 = 1.219 francs. If the cross rate between the franc and Canadian dollar is 1 franc = CA$0.9750 then show that an arbitrage is possible. What positions should be taken to profit from the mispricing? *(LG3)*

18-24 **Triangular Arbitrage** The U.S. dollar spot exchange rate with the Australian dollar is $1 = AU$1.2697. The U.S. dollar and Euro exchange rate is $1 = €0.7559. If the cross rate between the Euro and Australian dollar is €1 = AU$1.598 then show that an arbitrage is possible. What positions should be taken to profit from the mispricing? *(LG3)*

18-25 **Spreadsheet Problem** Below are the Consumer Price Index inflation rates each year for the United States and Japan. Also shown is the spot exchange rate for the beginning of each year.

a. Using PPP (equation 18-3), compute what the one year forward exchange rate should be each year.

b. Compare the forward rates computed in part (a) to the actual exchange rate at the beginning of the next year. How well does PPP predict the future exchange rate? Is it biased too high, too low, or about right?

YEAR	BEGINNING OF YEAR EXCHANGE RATE (YEN PER $)	US CPI INFLATION RATE	JAPAN CPI INFLATION RATE
1990	146.25	6.1	3.1
1991	134.60	3.1	3.3
1992	124.50	2.9	1.6
1993	125.40	2.8	1.1
1994	112.50	2.7	0.5
1995	100.52	2.5	−0.3
1996	103.92	3.3	0.0
1997	115.49	1.7	1.6
1998	132.40	1.6	0.7
1999	112.15	2.7	−0.4
2000	101.70	3.4	−0.9
2001	114.73	1.6	−0.9
2002	132.02	2.4	−1.1
2003	119.86	1.9	−0.3
2004	106.95	3.3	0.0
2005	102.83	3.4	−0.4
2006	116.34	2.5	0.3
2007	118.83	4.1	−0.4
2008	109.70		

research it! Find Currency Exchange Rates

Currency spot exchange rates are widely available on the Web. For example, at Yahoo! Finance (**http://finance.yahoo.com/currency**) you can find the exchange rates between more than 150 currencies. The calculator the site provides computes the amount of one currency resulting from converting money in another currency. You can also see a graph of the desired exchange rate for a history of up to five years. Daily and monthly historical data for the dollar exchange rates are available at the Federal Reserve Web site (**http://research.stlouisfed.org/ fred2/**). Many of the exchange rate data are available for more than 30 years. See how exchange rates have changed over the years.

integrated minicase: Assessing Exchange Rate Risk

Imagine that you are a financial manager of a multinational corporation, like Starbucks Coffee, in charge of determining the impact of exchange rate changes on the firm. Changes in currency exchange affect both the balance sheet and the

(continued)

income statement. The balance sheet impact occurs when the value of international assets are translated to U.S. dollars. The values of those assets change as the exchange rate changes. The value of costs, revenue, and profit also are impacted on the income statement because of exchange rate risk. Consider that your firm has the following investments in coffee bean production and processing:

COUNTRY	VALUE ($ MILLIONS)
Columbia	$ 75
Kenya	100
Papua New Guinea	80

The expense of all the labor, production, and beans will require the following exchanges to the foreign currency:

COUNTRY	CASH FLOW (MILLIONS)
Columbia	78,180 pesos
Kenya	3,200 shilling
Papua New Guinea	100 kina

Your firm has also invested in store facilities to sell the coffee products. The countries and the value of the investments are

COUNTRY	VALUE (MILLIONS)
Canada	$200
Japan	$100
United Kingdom	$150

The net profit from these countries next year is projected to be

COUNTRY	CASH FLOW (MILLIONS)
Canada	CA$80
Japan	¥7,200
United Kingdom	£30

Current spot exchange rates are

$1 = 2,204.5 Columbian pesos

$1 = 69.480 Kenyan shilling

$1 = 3.0189 Papua New Guinea kina

$1 = 1.1690 Canadian dollar

(continued)

$1 = 117.04$ Japanese yen

$1 = 0.5182$ British pound

Your task is to determine the following:

a. What is the impact on the value of the international assets and the cash flow if the dollar were to devalue by 10 percent against each currency (one at a time)?

b. What is the overall impact of a 10 percent dollar devaluation against every currency?

c. What is the impact on the value of the international assets and the cash flow if the dollar were to strengthen by 10 percent against each currency (one at a time)?

d. What is the overall impact of a 10 percent strengthening against every currency?

e. What can be done to hedge this risk?

ANSWERS TO TIME OUT

18-1 Free-trade zones are motivated by the idea that when trade between multiple countries is unencumbered by tariffs, restrictions, and quotas, then more trade will occur. An increase in trade benefits all countries involved. Thus, the wealth of all countries increases in a free-trade zone. This free trade is only perceived as fair when the same laws (labor, pollution, etc.) apply to all countries involved.

18-2 Capital that flows into the United States winds itself through the economy and increases the investment in new business projects, factories, technology, and so on. In short, capital coming into the United States will lead to more jobs for U.S. workers. In addition, capital usually buys factories and technology, so those jobs will be higher-quality ones.

18-3 Multinational firms make investments in foreign countries. One risk is that the value of these investments changes as the exchange rates between the home countries and the foreign countries change. A second risk involves the payment and receipt of cash flows. In business, payment and receipt of cash flows is contracted for the future. But the value of those payments can change before they are made because of the change in exchange rates. To reduce the risks, firms can hedge their investments and cash flows through contracts in the forward markets, futures, options, and currency swaps.

18-4 Arbitrage seeks to find two different avenues to buy and sell the same assets at different prices. When arbitrageurs find this case to occur, they buy the low price assets and sell the high price asset to capture the difference as profit. For currency exchange rates, an arbitrage opportunity exists when the price of U.S. to a foreign currency is different from the price through a third currency using cross rates. The buying of the low priced exchange rate and the selling of the high price rate causes prices to adjust so that the opportunity disappears.

18-5 The difference in interest rates and inflation between two countries drives the changes in the exchange rate between the currencies. The difference in interest rates impacts the forward exchange rates. This can be seen through

(continued)

the interest rate parity equation. When inflation differs between to countries, the change in prices of goods directly leads to changes in the exchange rate as seen in the purchasing power parity equation. These changes can be forecasted using estimates of inflation and interest rates, and the forward rate.

18-6 Multinational companies can lose assets invested in a country when civil war breaks out and those assets get destroyed. Assets can also be lost when the government decides to seize the firm's assets. Cash flow of the firm can be reduced when the government enacts new taxes, new tariffs, or limits the conversion of the local currency into the MNC's home country currency.

18-7 MNC's should acquire some capital from within the countries they operate. This will allow for less currency exchange to be needed because some of the capital to be repaid will be done so within the foreign countries. In addition, governments may be less likely to seize assets when those assets are partially owned by local investors. In addition, insurance can be purchased to protect against some political risks.

18-8 The NPV method requires cash flows and a discount rate. Whether the cash flows are in domestic currency or in the foreign currency, they are equivalent if they are converted using the PPP equation in the future and estimates of future inflation. The discount rates will also be equivalent if they are adjusted by the inflation rates too. Since both the cash flows and the discount rates are equivalent in the two currencies, the NPV analysis conducted in each currency will provide the same outcome.

chapter 19:

MANAGING MERGERS AND ACQUISITIONS AND FINANCIAL DISTRESS

Learning Goals

LG1 Differentiate among types of and address motives for mergers and acquisitions.

LG2 Mathematically value mergers.

LG3 Suggest methods by which a firm can informally resolve severe financial distress.

LG4 Differentiate between Chapter 7 and Chapter 11 bankruptcy.

LG5 Build and use statistical models to predict bankruptcy.

You may recall that as we discussed various organizational structures in Chapter 1, we stated that one advantage of corporate organization is that the expected life of a corporation can be unlimited. But no corporation can expect to go on forever despite all circumstances. In this chapter, we look at two situations that may cause corporations to cease to exist—mergers and acquisitions or financial distress.

First, we look at mergers and acquisitions, in which two firms combine assets, liabilities, and equity. Figure 19.1 shows the total value of mergers and acquisitions between 1990 and 2007. For most of this period, the mergers and acquisitions business boomed as firms sought to combine with like firms to make the most of their economic clout. Total dollar volume (measured by market value of the target firm; i.e., the transaction value) of domestic mergers and acquisitions increased from less than $200 billion in 1990 to $1.83 *trillion* in 2000. Nevertheless, as the U.S. economy experienced falling economic activity in the early 2000s, merger and acquisition activity fell 53 percent in 2001 to $819 billion. Domestic M&A activity bottomed out at $458 billion in 2002 before recovering to $1.59 trillion in 2003.

We will then look at a second way that firms cease to exist—through financial distress. In the most extreme cases of financial distress, firms go out of business and another firm buys their assets or everything is liquidated to pay off creditors and, possibly, the firms' stockholders. Indeed, in the summer of 2002, stock markets reacted quite negatively to several large corporate scandals and firm failures such as Enron, Global Crossings, United Airlines, and WorldCom. However, financial distress can

viewpoints

Business Application

BSW Corporation has approached MHM Production, Inc. for a possible merger. The cash flows of the two firms currently total $25.5 million ($20 million from BSW and $5.5 million from MHM) and are growing at 3 percent annually (for both firms). Managers of BSW estimate that, because of synergies, the merged firm's cash flows would increase by $6 million for the first six years following the merger. After the first six years, they expect incremental cash flows to be $2 million annually. BSW Corp.'s management expects the WACC for the merged firms over the foreseeable future to be 9 percent. Managers of MHM Production, Inc. are asking $900 million for the firm. Should BSW Corporation acquire MHM Production, Inc. at this price? **(See solution on p. 620)**

Personal Application

James Upton holds $25,000 in subordinated debentures of Jaylon's Jazz Music Production, Inc. The firm has just announced that it will file Chapter 7 bankruptcy. The firm's assets had a book value of $500,000. The liquidated assets produced $250,000. Administrative expenses associated with the bankruptcy, unpaid wages, employee benefits, and taxes total $10,000. The firm has debt owed to secured creditors of $175,000, accounts payable of $25,000, notes payable to banks of $120,000, and total subordinated debt outstanding of $100,000. How much of the total $25,000 in subordinated debentures in Jaylon's Jazz Music Production, Inc. can James Upton expect to recover? **(See solution on p. 620)**

A practice test can be found on the Online Learning Center at
www.mhhe.com/can1e

figure 19.1

Total Values of Mergers and Acquisitions Managed by Invest Banks, 1990–2007 (in billions of dollars)

Source: Thomson Reuters Financial Web site, **www.thomsonreuters.com/ business_units/financial/ league_tables**

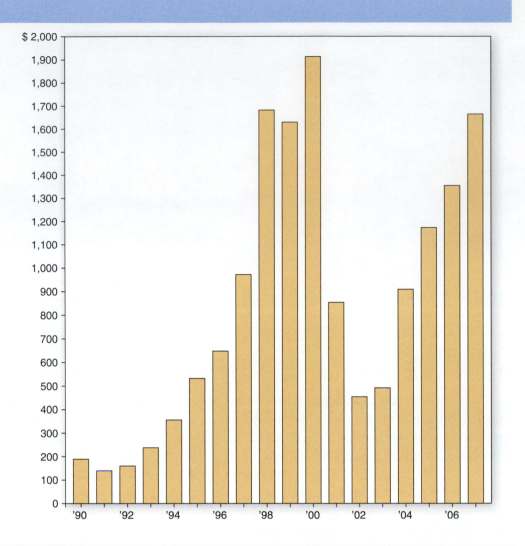

figure 19.2

Default Rates on Outstanding Debt

Source: Author's research.

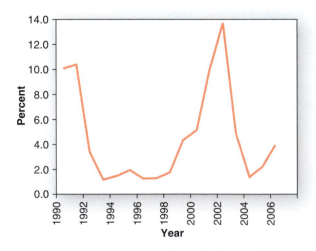

involve much less devastating circumstances, consisting of events like a manufacturing plant fire that stops production for a week. Firms can usually recover quickly from these types of financially distressing events. Figure 19.2 shows defaulted debt issues—the definition of financial distress—as a percent of all debt outstanding from 1990 through 2006.

BIDDER	TARGET	PRICE OFFERED	YEAR ANNOUNCED
Pfizer, Inc.	Warner-Lambert Co.	$116,705.4m.	1999
America Online, Inc.	Time Warner, Inc.	101,002.5m.	2000
Exxon Corp.	Mobil Corp.	81,429.8m.	1988
SBC Communications, Inc.	Ameritech Corp.	75,233.5m.	1998
Vodafone Group PLC – UK	AirTouch Communications, Inc.	62,768.0m.	1999
Bell Atlantic Corp.	GTE Corp.	60,489.9m.	1998
J.P. Morgan Chase	Bank One Corp.	57,614.9m.	2004
Blackstone Group	Equity Office Properties Trust	36,000.0m.	2006
Monsanto Co.	Pharmacia & Upjohn, Inc.	30,752.7m.	1999
Sprint	NEXTEL Communications	28,449.0m.	2004

Source: Author's research.

19.1 Mergers and Acquisitions

A **merger** is a transaction in which two firms combine to form a single firm. An **acquisition** is the purchase of one firm by another. Despite these two distinct definitions, the two terms, mergers and acquisitions, are often used interchangeably. From the definition of acquisition above, we can see a clear distinction between the buyer (or bidder firm) and the seller (or target firm). Likewise, but perhaps a bit less clear, in mergers we can classify the acquiring firm (the bidder, who initiates the transaction) and the seller (or target, who receives the offer). Typically, in a merger or acquisition the acquiring firm retains its identity, while the target firm ceases to exist. A **consolidation** is another type of merger in which an entirely new firm is created. A consolidation absorbs both the bidder and target firms into this new firm and the old firms cease to exist as separate entities. Table 19.1 lists the largest mergers as of 2007.

Types of Mergers

The general expression *merger and acquisition* encompasses many specific types of financial combinations. For example, a **horizontal merger** combines two companies in the same industry, such as the merger between J.P. Morgan Chase[1] (itself a product of a 2000 merger when Chase Manhattan Corp. acquired J.P. Morgan & Co.) and Bank One listed in Table 19.1. A **market extension merger,** a type of horizontal merger, combines two firms that sell the same products in different market areas. As we will discuss below, forming a larger firm may create beneficial economies of scale. The impact on an industry of a horizontal merger of two small competitors is generally minimal. However, the horizontal merger of two industry leaders, such as J.P. Morgan Chase and Bank One, can restrict competition within the firms' industry. Federal Trade Commission (FTC) regulators (a branch of the Justice Department) scrutinize any merger that involves industry leaders for any negative impact on the industry before the merger is approved. Horizontal mergers are regulated by the government for possible negative effects on competition. They decrease the number of firms in an industry, possibly making it easier for the industry members to go into cartels for monopoly profits.

[1]Chase Manhattan Corporation kept the J.P. Morgan name because of its prestige—John Pierpont Morgan (1837–1913) was the most influential American banker of the 19th and early 20th century. Morgan bailed out the U.S. Treasury on more than one occasion.

A **vertical merger** combines a firm with a supplier or distributor, such as the merger of Barnes & Noble (the nation's largest book retailer) and Ingram Book Group (the nation's largest book wholesaler). Vertical mergers occur between firms in different stages of production operation for many reasons such as avoidance of fixed costs, the elimination of costs of searching for prices, contracting, payment collection, communication, advertising and coordination, and better planning for inventory.

A **conglomerate merger** combines two companies that have no related products or markets. For example, in 2001 Tyco International, which among other things produces residential and commercial alarm systems, purchased C.R. Bard, a medical equipment maker. Conglomerate mergers were very popular in the 1960s and 1970s. The motive for these mergers comes from portfolio theory. That is, the merger combines two companies that operate in businesses so different that if an event has a negative effect on one business, the other business and the overall cash flows of the firm will be minimally affected. Thus, these mergers are intended to make earnings and cash flows less volatile. However, it turned out that many conglomerate mergers resulted in decreased market values and were dismantled in the 1980s and 1990s. This type of merger is seen infrequently in the 2000s.

A **product extension merger** is a combination of firms that sell different, but somewhat related, products. For example, the merger of Citicorp and Travelers Group to form Citigroup combined two types of financial institutions: a commercial bank and an insurance company. Product extension mergers are something of a hybrid classification: crossing a horizontal merger and a conglomerate merger. That is, these mergers are not horizontal in that they do not combine firms that compete directly for business customers for a single product, and they are not conglomerate mergers in that they do not combine firms in two completely different lines of business. Rather, the firms involved in a product extension merger produce different products and sell them with greater success to the already common set of customers that the two separate companies share.

 ## Motives for Mergers and Acquisitions

The main motivation for a merger or acquisition is **synergy,** the working together of the two firms to produce a combined value that is greater than the sum of their individual values. Thus, managers merge firms so as to maximize the value of the firms to the shareholders. The sources of value enhancing synergy in a merger come from four areas: revenue enhancement, cost reduction, tax considerations, and lower cost of capital. However, there are also some non-value-maximizing motives behind a merger. These include managers' personal incentives that may destroy firm value and the misallocation of capital between the merged firms.

REVENUE ENHANCEMENT   The revenue synergies argument has three dimensions. First, acquiring a firm in a growing market may enhance revenues. For example, while the merger of J.P. Morgan and Chase Manhattan to form J.P. Morgan Chase was estimated to produce a cost savings of $1.5 billion, the CEOs of both companies stated that the success of the merger was pinned on revenue growth. The merger combined J.P. Morgan's greater array of products with Chase's broad client base. The merger added substantially to many businesses (such as equity underwriting and asset management) that Chase had been trying to build on its own through smaller deals and gave it a bigger presence in Europe where investment and corporate banking were fast-growing businesses. When J.P. Morgan Chase then acquired Bank One, analysts praised the combination as one that offered revenue growth potential, the result of the combination of two different business models as well as expense reduction.

Second, the acquiring firm's revenue stream may become more stable if the asset and liability portfolio of the target institution exhibits credit, interest rate, and liquidity risk characteristics that differ from those of the acquirer. Indeed, managers often cite diversification as the reason for a merger, stating that diversification of risk helps to stabilize the firm's earnings, which benefits owners. For example, real estate loan portfolios of commercial banks have shown very strong cycles. Specifically, in the early 2000s, U.S. subprime real estate declined in value, while high grade mortgages did not. Thus, a diversified real estate portfolio (including both subprime and high grade mortgages), and consequently, the cash and revenue streams of the merged banks, may be far less risky than one in which both acquirer and target specialize in a single type of mortgage.

Third, expanding into markets that are less than fully competitive offers an opportunity for revenue enhancement. That is, firms may be able to identify and expand geographically into those markets in which *economic rents* potentially exist, but in which regulators will not view such entry as potentially anticompetitive. Indeed, to the extent that geographic expansions are viewed as enhancing a firm's monopoly power by generating excessive rents, regulators may act to prevent a merger unless it produces potential efficiency gains that cannot be reasonably achieved by other means. In recent years, the ultimate enforcement of antimonopoly laws and guidelines has fallen to the U.S. Department of Justice. In particular, the Department of Justice has established guidelines regarding the acceptability or unacceptability of acquisitions based on the potential increase in concentration in the market in which an acquisition takes place with the cost-efficiency exception just noted.

COST REDUCTION   A reason frequently given for a merger is the potential cost synergies that may result from economies of scale, economies of scope, or managerial efficiency sources (often called *X-efficiencies* because they are difficult to specify in a quantitative fashion).

Economies of Scale   As firms become larger through a merger, the increase in size allows for the reduction or elimination of overlapping resources. If these cuts lower the firm's operating costs of production, merged firms may have an **economy of scale** advantage over smaller firms. Economies of scale imply that the unit or average cost of producing goods and services falls as the size of the firm expands.

Examples of mergers that are intended to take advantage of economies of scale are those by Exxon Corporation and Mobil Corporation. With a larger production base, the oil companies were able to gain greater economies of scale as they were able to pursue new policies in upstream exploration and production of oil. As a result, the ExxonMobil merger was expected to save $2.8 billion in costs over a period of three years. A second example is the merger of Bell Atlantic and GTE. This merger produced cost synergies totaling $2 billion within three years of completion. The cost cuts were principally related to economies of scale for purchasing equipment for data communications, wireless, and telecommunications.

Figure 19.3 depicts economies of scale for three firms of different size. The average cost of production is:

$$AC_i = \frac{TC_i}{S_i} \qquad\qquad \textbf{(19-1)}$$

where

AC_i = Average costs of the ith firm

TC_i = Total costs of the ith firm

S_i = Size of the firm measured by sales

figure 19.3

Economies of Scale in
Mergers

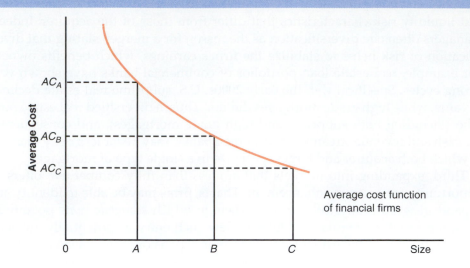

The average production cost to the largest (merged) firm in Figure 19.3 (size C) is lower than the cost to smaller (nonmerged) firms B and A. This means that at any given price for the firm's products, firm C can make a higher profit than either B or A. Alternatively, firm C can undercut B and A in price and potentially gain a larger market share. For example, AOL's acquisition of Time Warner was billed as a cost-savings acquisition. Because of overlapping savings from lower overhead, technical costs, and marketing expenses, the firms said they expected $1 billion in cost savings during the first year. In the framework of Figure 19.3, AOL, firm A, might be operating at AC_A and Time Warner might be represented as firm B operating at AC_B. Savings on overhead, technology, and marketing would lower the average costs for the combined (larger) firm to point C in Figure 19.3, operating at AC_C.

The long-term implication of economies of scale for a firm is that the larger and most cost-efficient firms will drive out smaller, less cost-efficient firms, leading to increased large-firm dominance and concentration in production. Such an implication is reinforced if time-related operating improvements increasingly benefit large firms more than small firms. For example, satellite technology and supercomputers, in which enormous operating or technological advances are being made, may be available to only the largest firms in an industry. The effect of improving operations over time, which is biased toward larger projects, is to shift the AC curve downward over time but with a larger downward shift for large, merged firms; see Figure 19.4. AC_1 is the hypothetical AC curve prior to cost-reducing innovations. AC_2 reflects the cost-lowering effects of technology and consolidation on firms of all sizes but with the greatest benefit accruing to those of the largest size.

Economies of Scope The simple economy of scale concept ignores these inter-relationships among products and the "jointness" in the costs of producing them. In particular, merged firms' abilities to generate synergistic cost savings through the joint use of inputs in producing multiple products are called **economies of scope** as opposed to economies of scale.

The mergers and acquisitions in the banking industry in recent years (a result of the loosening of federal regulations) provide numerous examples of attempts to take advantage of economies of scope. For example, in 1997 Travelers Group acquired Salomon Brothers for $9 billion. Then in 1998 Travelers and Citicorp announced an $83 billion merger. Travelers' chairman, Sanford I. Weill, decided

figure 19.4

to build the largest financial services company in the United States. Travelers had long been involved in the insurance and mutual fund business before the acquisition of Salomon (it already owned Smith Barney), but it had lacked foreign influence and recognition as well as respect on Wall Street. The Salomon Brothers acquisition and the Citicorp merger were attempts to alleviate these deficiencies. Another example is Lincoln National Corp. (an Indiana-based insurance company), which is attempting to become one of the nation's premier sellers of life insurance, annuities, mutual funds, and 401(k) retirement plans through a series of acquisitions of firms such as Delaware Management Holdings (for $510 million) and Voyageur Fund Management (for $70 million), both mutual fund companies. Technology played a particularly large role in Lincoln National's plans as it committed major resources to technology purchases needed to support late night calls from mutual fund, 401(k), and variable annuity customers who expect to be able to make investment selections 24 hours a day.

Mergers may allow two firms to jointly use their input resources such as capital and labor to produce a set of goods or services at a lower cost than if the two firms operated independently of one another. Specifically, let X_1 and X_2 be two products; each is produced by one firm as a specialized producer. That is, firm A produces only X_1, but no X_2, and firm B produces only X_2, but no X_1. The average cost functions (AC) of these firms are:

$$AC_A[X_1, 0] \text{ and } AC_B[0, X_2]$$

Economies of scope exist if these firms merge and jointly produce X_1 and X_2, resulting in:

$$AC_{A+B}[X_1, X_2] < AC_A[X_1, 0] + AC_B[0, X_2] \tag{19-2}$$

That is, the cost of joint production via cost synergies is less than the separate and independent production of these services.

Formally, if AC_{FS} is the total average cost of a nonspecialized firm, economies of scope would imply that:

$$AC_{FS} < TAC \tag{19-3}$$

That is, the average cost to jointly produce goods or services may be less than the average cost to produce these products separately.

CALCULATION OF AVERAGE COSTS WITH ECONOMIES OF SCOPE

Let TC_l be a specialized firm's total cost to produce Internet services to retail customers. Suppose that the total operating costs of producing these services (TC_l) is $2.5 million for a sales volume (S_l) of $10 million. Thus, the average cost (AC_l) of Internet service for the firm is

$$AC_l = \frac{TC_l}{S_l} = \frac{\$2,500,000}{\$10,000,000} = .25 = 25\%$$

At the same time, a specialized cable network provider is selling its service to the same retail customer. The firm's total cost (TC_c) to run the operation is $500,000 for $1 million in sales ($S_c$).

$$AC_c = \frac{TC_c}{S_c} = \frac{\$500,000}{\$1,000,000} = .5 = 50\%$$

Consequently, the total average cost (TAC) for the Internet provider to produce Internet services and the cable network firm to produce cable TV is:

$$TAC = \frac{\$3,000,000}{\$11,000,000} = .27 = 27\%$$

Suppose, instead, that a single firm acting as a provider of Internet and cable TV services (IC) produced both $10 million of Internet services and $1 million cable programming (i.e., $S_{IC} = \$11,000,000$). For the single firm to provide both Internet and cable services requires very similar overhead and marketing services. Further, common technologies in the Internet and cable service production functions suggest that a single firm, simultaneously (or jointly) producing both Internet and cable services at a total cost TC_{IC}, should be able to do this at a lower average cost than could the specialized firms that separately produce these services. That is, the single firm should be able to produce the $11,000,000 ($S_{IC}$) of financial services at a lower cost (say $TC_{IC} = \$2,550,000$) than should two specialized firms.

$$AC_{IC} = \frac{TC_{IC}}{S_{IC}} = \frac{\$2,550,000}{\$11,000,000} = 23.18\% < 27.27\%$$

X-efficiencies   **X-efficiencies** are those cost savings not directly due to economies of scope or economies of scale. As such, they are usually attributed to superior management skills and other difficult-to-measure managerial factors. For example, a change in management can cause the value of merged firms to be greater than the sum of the value of the two individual firms. New, better managers may be able to force necessary cuts or realign the firm's operations where incumbent managers were not. The motive for these acquisitions does not come from the combining of the two firms. Rather, the merger is the mechanism which allows new managers to replace old inefficient managers. To date, the explicit identification of what composes these efficiencies remains to be established in the empirical finance literature.

TAX CONSIDERATIONS   Tax considerations have been the motive for many mergers. Tax gains with an acquisition can result from the ability to use net operating losses to reduce taxes, tax gains from unused debt capacity, and tax gains from the use of surplus funds.

Tax Gains from Net Operating Losses Profitable firms in a high tax bracket can merger with a firm with large accumulated tax losses. When the firms merge, losses of the unprofitable firm can be used to offset taxes of the profitable firm rather than being carried forward and used in the future to offset possible profits.

Tax Gains from Unused Debt Capacity Tax savings arise when mergers result in an increase in debt. Mergers typically result in increased leverage for the merged firm. As discussed in Chapter 14, because interest on debt is tax deductible, firms experience a tax gain with the increased leverage after a merger. Of course, remember that the increased leverage increases firm value only if the marginal tax benefit from additional debt is greater than or equal to the marginal increase in the financial distress costs from the additional debt. This is true if the merged firm is better diversified than the two independent firms and the cost of financial distress is less for the merged firm.

Tax Gains from Surplus Funds Mergers can reduce taxes by disposing of surplus cash. That is, if a firm has free cash flow (i.e., the firm has cash available after all taxes have been paid and after all positive net present value projects have been purchased), it has several ways to use this free cash flow. It could pay extra dividends, invest in marketable securities, repurchase its stock, or acquire another firm. However, an extra dividend will increase the income tax paid by some of the firm's stockholders. Marketable securities, while a reasonable short-term use of funds, earn a rate of return less than that required by the firm's stockholders. Like a cash dividend, a stock repurchase can result in a capital gain and more tax payments for stockholders. However, when the firm makes an acquisition with surplus cash it avoids these problems.

LOWERING THE COST OF CAPITAL A merger can often result in a lower cost of capital because the costs of issuing securities are subject to economies of scale. However, diversification resulting from a merger also results in a lower cost of capital. That is, stabilization of earnings can make the debt of the merged firm less risky than that of the two independent firms. As a result, lenders demand a lower interest rate on the debt of the merged firm.

MANAGERS' PERSONAL INCENTIVES Unfortunately, business decisions are sometimes based on managers' personal incentives rather than on economic analysis. Managers expand through mergers to get personal benefits from building and managing large corporations. Academic research has documented this motive, finding that mergers are often positively related to sales and asset growth and do not always result in increased stock prices. For example, in order to build corporate empires from which they get personal benefits, managers use free cash flows to acquire a firm that may have a negative net present value. This is particularly true for poorly monitored managers who merge to maximize their corporation's asset size because managers' compensation is based on firm size. Likewise, unmonitored managers can try to build corporate empires through the pursuit of negative NPV mergers to entrench themselves. That is, because of its greater size and the managers' supposed expertise in managing the large company, managers make themselves indispensable to the firm. Finally, some managers overestimate their own managerial abilities and merge with the belief that they can manage the takeover target better than the target's current management. Acquiring managers then overbid for the target and fail to realize the gains expected from the merger in the post-merger period. Thus, the stock price and stockholders' wealth fall.

MISALLOCATION OF CAPITAL If managers of the merged firm use the merger to transfer resources between the two firms to subsidize negative NPV projects that would otherwise be rejected, a merger destroys value. This occurs if the firm's managers are reluctant to cut jobs or have other reasons to keep a losing business in operation.

 ## Valuing a Merger

The net present value (NPV) or discounted cash flow (DCF) method discussed in Chapter 13 is the most accurate and reliable tool used to evaluate whether a merger will be a profitable one. The NPV method allows bidder and target firm managers to predict pro forma cash flows of the merged firm. These forecasted cash flows are then discounted to a present value based on the merged firm's weighted average cost of capital (WACC) to determine the merged firm's present value. Finally, the present value of the merged firm is compared with the asking price of the target firm to determine whether the merger is profitable.

The valuation process starts with estimates of the expected future cash flows and the WACC for the bidder and target firms' cash flows. Managers then must value the synergies resulting from the merger. This requires estimates of the cash flows generated by synergies. To simplify the analysis managers generally assume that some synergies are more certain while others are less predictable. For example, synergies resulting from tax savings or fixed cost reductions are easier to predict, while those related to increased sales or reductions in production costs are less certain.

EXAMPLE 19-2

For interactive versions of this example visit www.mhhe.com/can1e

CALCULATING THE NET PRESENT VALUE OF A MERGER

The cash flows of a firm considering a merger bid currently are growing at 4 percent annually. Managers estimate that because of synergies the merged firm's cash flows will increase by an additional 5 percent for the first five years following the merger. After the first five years, incremental cash flows are expected to grow at a rate of 3 percent annually. The WACC for the merged firms over the foreseeable future is expected to be 10 percent. Managers of the target firm are asking a price of $70 million for the firm. Is this merger a positive NPV project for the bidding firm?

SOLUTION:

Table 19.2 shows the projected incremental cash flow for bidder firm for the first five years after the merger. After the first five years, cash flows will grow at a rate of 3 percent. Thus, the value of cash flows after year 5 can be looked at as a constant growth problem similar to that used to value stocks, in Chapter 7. That is, managers first calculate the value of the firm's incremental cash flows received after year 5 at the end of year 5 (the end of the super-normal growth period) as:

$$\text{Value of incremental cash flows received after year 5} = \frac{\text{Incremental cash flow in year 6}}{(\text{WACC} - \text{Growth rate}) \text{ in cash flows after year 5}}$$

$$= \frac{\$7.2\text{m.}(1+.03)}{(.10-.03)} = \$105.9\text{m. as of the end of year 5}$$

(continued)

	CURRENT 2008	2009	2010	2011	2012	2013
Net sales (all credit)	$ 67.5					
Less: Cost of goods sold	35.7					
Gross profits	31.8					
Less: Depreciation	7.5					
EBIT	24.3					
Less: Taxes	9.5					
Earnings after taxes	14.8					
Plus: Depreciation	7.5					
Cash flow with no merger	$ 22.3	$22.3(1.04)	$22.3(1.04)^2	$22.3(1.04)^3	$22.3(1.04)^4	$22.3(1.04)^5
		= $23.2	= $24.1	= $25.1	= $26.1	= $26.1
Cash flow with merger		22.3(1.09)	22.3(1.09)^2	22.3(1.09)^3	22.3(1.09)^4	22.3(1.09)^5
		= $24.3	= $26.5	= $28.9	= $31.5	= $34.3
Incremental cash flows		$1.1	$2.4	$3.8	$5.4	$7.2

To find the present value of the total incremental cash flows, managers next discount the projected incremental cash flows by the WACC as follows:

$$\text{Present value of incremental cash flows from the merger} = \frac{\$1.1m.}{(1.10)^1} + \frac{\$2.4m.}{(1.10)^2} + \frac{\$3.8m.}{(1.10)^3} + \frac{\$5.4m.}{(1.10)^4} + \frac{\$7.2m.}{(1.10)^5} + \frac{\$105.9m.}{(1.10)^5}$$

$$= \$79.8m.$$

Finally, the NPV of the merger is calculated by subtracting the price of the target firm from the present value of the cash flows from the merger:

$$NPV = \$79.8\,m. - \$70\,m. = \$9.8\,m.$$

This merger would be beneficial for the stockholders of the bidder firm. Their wealth would increase by $9.8 million as a result of the merger

TIME OUT

19-1   What is the difference between a vertical merger and a horizontal merger?

19-2   What are economies of scale and scope?

19.2 Financial Distress

Types and Causes of Financial Distress

A firm in financial distress can mean many things. At the extreme, **business failure** is a type of financial distress in which a firm no longer stays in business. However, financial distress does not automatically mean the end of the firm. Other levels of financial distress exist as well. For example, **economic failure** is a type of financial distress in which the return on a firm's assets is less then the firm's cost of capital. Thus, the firm is not earning enough on its assets to pay the fund suppliers their promised payments. **Technical insolvency** is a type of financial distress in which a firm's operating cash flows are not sufficient to pay its liabilities as they come due. In both cases, the firm can continue as a going concern and even eventually a thriving firm. However, if not addressed, these types of financial distress can lead to dividend cuts, plant closings, layoffs. and eventually, a possible business failure or merger or acquisition by another firm.

Financial distress can be the result of one or several factors, some of which are firm specific, while others are more market specific. A firm's financial leverage can cause financial distress. Large amounts of debt, such as bonds and loans, increase the firm's interest charges and pose a significant claim on its cash flows. Relatively low debt-to-equity ratios may not significantly impact the probability of debt repayment. Yet beyond some point, the risk of financial distress increases, as does the probability of some loss of interest or principal for the firm's creditors.

As with leverage, a highly volatile earnings stream increases the probability that a firm cannot meet its fixed interest and principal charges for any capital structure and thus will experience financial distress. Volatility in earnings can be the result of production issues (such as input price volatility or volatility in the availability of inputs) or sales issues (such as changing needs of the firm's customers or reduced creditworthiness of the firm's customers).

Another firm-specific factor that can cause financial distress is bad or poor management. For example, management may not be skilled at production, marketing, finance or the building of an effective organization. Further, management may fail to put credible and sensible accounting, budgeting, and control systems in place. Finally, the firm may lose one or a few key players on which production or management depended.

Market-specific factors such as fluctuations in the business cycle can cause financial distress in a firm as well. For example, during recessions, firms in the consumer durable goods sector that produce autos, refrigerators, or houses do poorly compared to those in the nondurable goods sector producing foods and clothing. People cut back on luxuries during a recession but are less likely to cut back on necessities such as food. Thus, firms in the consumer durable goods sectors of the economy are especially prone to financial distress. Likewise, the level of interest rates can cause financial distress. High interest rates indicate restrictive monetary policy actions by the Federal Reserve. High interest rate levels may encourage firms to take excessive risks, thus increasing the probability of financial distress.

The challenge for the manager and creditors of a financially distressed firm is to decide whether the situation is temporary and the firm can recover over the long run, or whether the problem is permanent and endangers the firm's existence. Further, the managers and/or creditors must decide whether the situation can be handled with an informal resolution of the financial distress or a formal filing of bankruptcy.

Informal Resolutions of Financial Distress

Informal resolutions of financial distress include the voluntary restructuring of debt agreements or the complete liquidation of the firm's assets. When financial distress appears to be temporary, the firm's creditors will generally work to restructure the firm to help it recover and reestablish itself as a viable entity. If, however, it is determined that the firm cannot recover from the financial distress, the firm and its creditors may agree to a liquidation of the firm's assets.

RESTRUCTURING A FIRM'S DEBT AGREEMENTS   If financial distress in a firm is judged to be temporary, the firm and its creditors will generally agree to restructure the firm. That is, the creditors and the firm will restructure the debt agreements. In this case, the firm arranges a voluntary settlement or **workout** with its creditors. By keeping the firm alive through a workout, the creditors can continue to receive payments from the firm. Restructuring typically takes the form of an extension and/or a composition. An **extension** is an arrangement in which the firm's creditors postpone the dates of the required interest and/or principal payments. With an extension, eventually creditors receive their promised payments in full. Creditors will agree to an extension rather than force a firm to file for bankruptcy if the expected payoff from this voluntary negotiation is higher than their expected payoff after legal bankruptcy proceedings. In a **composition,** creditors voluntarily reduce their claims on the firm, receiving only a partial payment for their claims. This is accomplished by reducing the principal amount or the interest rate on the debt, or by taking equity in exchange for debt.

INFORMAL LIQUIDATION OF A FIRM'S ASSETS After examining a firm's situation, it is also possible that the firm's creditors determine that the only acceptable course of action is to liquidate the firm. **Liquidation** results in the termination of the firm as a going concern. In a voluntary liquidation, the firm's assets are sold or liquidated and any proceeds go to pay off the firm's creditors. The goal of the voluntary liquidation is to recover the maximum amount through the sale of the firm's assets per dollar owed. An **assignment** is a type of informal liquidation that generally yields the firm's creditors a larger amount than they would get through formal bankruptcy liquidation. An assignment passes the liquidation of the firm's assets to a third party that is designated as the **assignee** or **trustee.** The assignee liquidates the firm's assets through a private sale or a public auction. The assignee then distributes any proceeds from the sale to the firms' creditors and stockholders (if any funds are left after all creditors are paid). Once all assets are sold and creditors are paid the proceeds, the assignee has the creditors sign a release acknowledging the full settlement of the claim.

Assignments are most feasible for small firms or firms whose situation is not too complex. This method of resolving financial distress saves all parties in terms of time, legal formality, and expense compared to liquidation in a formal bankruptcy court proceeding. For example, an assignee is more flexible in its ability to sell assets than a federal bankruptcy trustee. Thus, asset sales can take place faster, before plant and equipment or inventory becomes obsolete or ruined. However, an assignment does not necessarily result in a full and legal discharge of all the firm's liabilities and does not protect the firm's creditors against fraud. These problems are resolved only by formal liquidation in bankruptcy.

Federal Bankruptcy Laws

If a firm in financial distress cannot agree on an informal restructuring or liquidation with its creditors, the creditors can force the firm into bankruptcy. Likewise, a firm can voluntarily file for bankruptcy protection with a federal court. Like informal resolutions of financial distress, bankruptcy can result in either a restructuring (or reorganization) or a liquidation of the firm. Table 19.3 lists the biggest bankruptcies of U.S. based firms through 2007. Note some of these, like WorldCom and Global Crossings, received substantial attention in the press and resulted in several changes in U.S. corporate law.

The Bankruptcy Reform Act of 1978 is the governing bankruptcy legislation in the United States. The two key parts of this law for firms in financial distress are Chapters 7 and 11, which cover bankruptcy liquidation and reorganization of a failing firm. Chapter 11 outlines the process for reorganization of a failing firm. The goal of a **Chapter 11** proceeding is to plan a reorganization of the corporation with some provision for repayment to the firm's creditors. The Chapter 11

		table 19.3

Largest U.S. Bankruptcies — table 19.3

FIRM	BANKRUPTCY DATE	TOTAL ASSETS PREBANKRUPTCY
WordCom, Inc.	07/21/2002	$103,914 m.
Enron Corp.	12/02/2001	63,392 m.
Conseco, Inc.	12/18/2002	61,392 m.
Texaco, Inc.	04/12/1987	35,892 m.
Refco Inc.	10/17/2005	33,333 m.
Global Crossing Ltd.	01/28/2002	30,185 m.
Pacific Gas and Electric Co.	04/06/2001	29,770 m.
Calpine Corp.	12/20/2005	27,216 m.
New Century Financial	04/02/2007	26.147 m.
UAL Corp.	12/9/02002	25,197 m.
Delta Air Lines, Inc.	09/14/2005	21,801 m.
Mirant Corp.	07/14/2003	19,415 m.
American Home Mortgage	08/06/2007	18.828 m.
Delphi Corp.	10/08/2005	16,593 m.
Kmart Corp.	01/22/2002	14,630 m.
FINOVA Group, Inc.	03/07/2001	14,050 m.
Northwest Airlines Corp.	09/14/2005	14,042 m.

Source: BankruptcyData.com Web site 2007. **www.BankruptcyData.com**

reorganization process allows a firm in temporary financial distress to continue operating while the creditors' claims are settled using a collective procedure. **Chapter 7** outlines the process to be followed for liquidating a failed firm. Chapter 7 is generally only used if it has been determined that reorganization under Chapter 11 is infeasible.

When a firm files for bankruptcy with a federal court it is officially considered to be bankrupt. At this point, a collective legal procedure begins in which all claims against the firm are resolved. These formal proceedings are designed to protect both the failed firm and its creditors. Specifically, at this time, bankruptcy law takes precedence over commercial and tax laws that normally govern firms. Thus, individual creditors are prohibited from beginning or proceeding with lawsuits against the firm. Further, if the situation is considered to be temporary, the firm may use the time during the bankruptcy proceedings to solve its cash flow problems without fear of asset seizure by its creditors. On the other hand, if the firm is truly bankrupt in the sense that its liabilities exceed its assets, the creditors can use bankruptcy procedures to stop the firm's managers from continuing to operate, lose more money, and thus deplete assets that should go to creditors. Bankruptcy law allows for and even encourages negotiations between a firm, its creditors, and its stockholders.

REORGANIZATION PROCEDURES IN BANKRUPTCY

The procedures for corporate reorganization under Chapter 11 include several steps. First, a firm must voluntarily file a reorganization petition or the firm's creditors can file an involuntary petition of reorganization under Chapter 11 in a federal bankruptcy court. With an involuntary reorganization, three or more creditors (or one creditor if there are fewer than 12 total creditors) of the firm can file a petition alleging that the corporation is not paying its debts. Next, a federal judge reviews the petition. If the petition is approved, a time for filing proof of claims of creditors and shareholders is set and the corporation is given 120 days to submit a reorganization plan. At this point, the firm, now the debtor in possession (DIP) of the firm's assets, continues to run the business. However, creditor committees are appointed by the court to represent the creditors' interests.

Within the stated time period, the firm must submit its reorganization plan to the court. The key section of the plan generally involves the firm's capital

FRIENDLIER SKIES: AIRLINE'S LEAVING BANKRUPTCY WITH LESS BAGGAGE, BRIGHTER FUTURE, CEO TILTON SAYS

When United Airlines went bankrupt December 9, 2002, CEO Glenn Tilton went to O'Hare International Airport to assure customers that the airline would survive—that this wasn't only Chapter 11, but Chapter 1. Today, Tilton and other airline executives will go to O'Hare and other airports to thank employees for taking $4 billion in pay and benefit cuts while improving customer service as the carrier struggled through its three-year rebirth. . .

United will exit the industry's biggest bankruptcy today, and begin trading on the Nasdaq on Thursday. Compared to the airline that sought protection from creditors in 2002, the new United is carrying $13 billion less in debt, $7 billion less in annual costs, and operates in a more disciplined way that Tilton believes will make it competitive. . .

Bill Brandt, a bankruptcy consultant in Chicago, said he doesn't see that United has a cost advantage over other carriers. "Yes, they've got their costs down, but American and Continental got their costs down, too," Brandt said. "American's still treating its workers with dignity," he added. Workers at American Airlines, which narrowly escaped bankruptcy,

kept their defined-benefit pension plans. United unloaded those liabilities onto a federal agency, slashing payouts for many workers. . .

Management is coming out of bankruptcy with big financial rewards tied to how United is valued. The top 400 managers will receive 8 percent of new United stock, which amounts to about $152 million if United is valued at $1.9 billion. Tilton alone could get $15 million—more if the stock becomes more valuable. The stock incentive awards vest after four years . . . He noted that within days of the bankruptcy exit, United employees will receive shares worth more than $2 billion, based on recent claims trading at 20 cents on the dollar. United employees see the airline's exit as a relief, though not a cause for elation, according to flight attendants' union spokeswoman Sara Nelson Dela Cruz. "After all we've been through, it's a little difficult to celebrate," Dela Cruz said. "There have been so many dramatic changes in flight attendants' lives."

Source: Mary Wisniewski, *The Wall Street Journal,* February 1, 2006, p. 192.

 want to know more? Key Words to Search for Updates: **bankruptcy, United Airlines**

structure. As stated above, financial distress generally results from the firm's inability to pay its debt. Thus with a reorganization, the firm's capital structure is generally restructured to reduce the debt obligations. Along with a determination of the new capital structure, the firm must outline a plan for payment of the remaining and new debt securities and for exchanging any outstanding debt for new securities.

Under the Bankruptcy Reform Act of 1978, creditors and stockholders are separated into groups, or classes, with similar priority claims on the assets of the firm. Creditors with substantially the same priority claim are placed in the same class to ensure that they receive similar treatment under the reorganization plan. Senior debt holders, with higher legal priority, are generally paid in full before junior debt holders can receive any payment. Common stockholders are the last to receive any payment or new securities and often receive nothing. Each class of claimants votes to accept or reject the reorganization plan. A class of creditors accepts the plan if two-thirds of the class in dollar amount and one-half the class in number vote for approval. After the creditors have voted to accept the reorganization plan, it is confirmed by the bankruptcy courts. Once approved by all parties, any payments or exchange of securities written into the plan are made.

Chapter 11 bankruptcy does not always mean that a firm survives. Successful firms use the period of reorganization bankruptcy to cut costs, renegotiate contracts, remove debt from their balance sheets, and eventually emerge from bankruptcy. Indeed, Chapter 11 businesses sometimes end up with competitive advantages over competitors thanks to their ability to restructure the company. The Finance at Work selection discusses some of the issues associated with the Chapter 11 bankruptcy and eventual exit from bankruptcy by United Airlines.

A new method of reorganization that combines the informal workout and the formal Chapter 11 reorganization is a **prepackaged bankruptcy.** In a prepackaged bankruptcy the firm and its creditors agree to a private reorganization outside the formal bankruptcy process. After the private reorganization is arranged or prepackaged, the firm files for formal Chapter 11 bankruptcy. Prepackaged bankruptcies are attractive in that they shorten and simplify the bankruptcy process. This means they can save the firm money in the form of legal and other fees and often generate more funds available for the creditors. Further, prepackaged bankruptcies generally result in less disruption to the firm's business and less damage to its goodwill. For example, in March 2006, Oneida Ltd. filed a prepackaged bankruptcy. The deal slashed the firm's debt by about $100 million and Oneida emerged from bankruptcy in 90 days.

LIQUIDATION PROCEDURES IN BANKRUPTCY　If a firm is too financially distressed to be reorganized, it is liquidated via a Chapter 7 bankruptcy. A firm is liquidated once the bankruptcy courts determine that reorganization is not feasible. At this point, the judge appoints a trustee-in-bankruptcy to take over the firm's property and protect the creditors' interests. The trustee is responsible for liquidating the firm's assets, examining the creditors' claims, keeping records, disbursing funds, furnishing information to involved parties as requested, and making final reports on the liquidation. Bankruptcy courts have established a specific priority of claims in a liquidation or an absolute priority rule. Specifically, the distribution of the funds from asset liquidation occurs according to the following priority of claims:

1. Property taxes past due.
2. Claims of secured creditors, who receive the proceeds from the sale of specific collateral as stated in a lien or mortgage.
3. Administrative expenses associated with the bankruptcy proceedings.
4. Unpaid expenses incurred after the filing of the bankruptcy petition but before the trustee is appointed.
5. Wages due to employees in the 90 days immediately preceding the start of the bankruptcy proceedings (limited to $2,000 per employee).
6. Unpaid employee benefit plan contributions that should have been paid in the six months prior to the bankruptcy filing (limited to $2,000 per employee).
7. Unsecured customer claims (limited to $900 per customer).
8. Taxes due to federal, state, and other governmental agencies.
9. Unsecured creditor claims including any unsatisfied amounts of secured creditors' claims.
10. Preferred stockholders (up to the par value of the preferred stock).
11. Common stockholders receive any remaining funds.

Distributions to priority and secured creditors must be paid in full before unsecured creditors receive any funds from asset liquidation. If, after the priority and secured creditors are paid in full, there are insufficient funds to pay the unsecured creditors in full, funds remaining are distributed on a pro rata basis. Further, as funds are distributed to unsecured creditors, senior status unsecured creditors must be paid in full before subordinate creditors receive any funds.

Predicting Bankruptcy

Managers, creditors, and stockholders can use many models to predict bank-ruptcy. These vary from relatively qualitative to highly quantitative models. These models are not mutually exclusive. A manager or creditor may use more than one model to reach a borrowing and/or lending decision. Indeed, a great deal of time and effort has recently been expended by financial institutions in

---

 For interactive versions of this example visit www.mhhe.com/can1e

EXAMPLE 19-3

CALCULATING CREDITOR AND STOCKHOLDER PAYOFFS IN A CHAPTER 7 BANKRUPTCY

Lucky Dog, Inc. declared bankruptcy on August 20, 2010 through a Chapter 7 filing. Lucky Dog's balance sheet at the time of the bankruptcy filing is listed below.

LUCKY DOG, INC.
Balance Sheet as of August 20, 2010
(in millions of dollars)

Assets		Liabilities and Equity	
Current assets:		Current liabilities:	
Cash and marketable securities	$ 42	Accrued wages (1,500 employees)	$ 4
		Unpaid employee benefits	2
Accounts receivable	110	Unsecured customer deposits	1
Inventory	177	Accrued taxes	8
Total	329	Accounts payable	55
		Notes payable to banks	136
Fixed assets:		Total	206
Gross plant and equipment	670	Long-term debt:	
Less: Depreciation	84	First mortgage	100
Net plant and equipment	586	Subordinate debentures	209
		Total	309
		Stockholders' equity:	
		Preferred stock (2.5 million shares)	6
		Common stock and paid-in surplus (20 million shares)	64
		Retained earnings	33
		Total	40
Total assets	$915	Total liabilities and equity	$915

The accrued wages were earned within the last 90 days prior to filing for bankruptcy. The unpaid employee benefits were due in the six months prior to the filing for bankruptcy. The unsecured customer deposits are for less than $900 each. Lucky Dog, Inc. has no prop-erty taxes past due. The first mortgage is secured against the fixed assets of the firm. The debentures are subordinate to the notes payable to banks. The liquidation of the firm's cur-rent assets produced $140 million and of the firm's fixed assets produced $275 million for a total of only $415 million in funds to distribute to the creditors and stockholders of the firm.

The administrative expenses associated with the bankruptcy totaled $0.75 million and unpaid expenses incurred after the filing of the bankruptcy petition but before the trustee was appointed totaled $0.25 million. Show how the trustee will distribute the $415 million of funds among Lucky Dog's creditors and stockholders.

(continued)

The distribution of the $415 million of funds is as follows:

Proceeds from liquidation of assets:	$415.00m.
Administrative expenses associated with the bankruptcy proceedings	0.75m.
Unpaid expenses incurred after the filing of the bankruptcy petition but before the trustee is appointed	0.25m.
Wages due to employees (1,500 employees x $2,000 maximum)	3.00m.
Unpaid employee benefit plan contributions	2.00m.
Unsecured customer claims	1.00m.
Taxes due to federal, state, and other governmental agencies	8.00m.
Funds available for secured creditors:	$400.00m.
First mortgage	100.00m.
Funds available for unsecured creditors:	$300.00m.

Note that the employees received only $3 million of the $4 million, or 75 percent, of the wages due to them. This is because payment of wages due are capped at $2,000 per employee. The remaining $300 million is distributed to the unsecured creditors on a pro rata basis, with senior creditors paid in full before subordinate creditors. The following table shows the distribution to unsecured creditors:

UNSECURED CREDITORS	AMOUNT	SETTLEMENT AT 75%[a]	DISTRIBUTION AFTER SUBORDINATE ADJUSTMENT	PERCENT OF CLAIM RECEIVED
Accounts payable	$ 55m.	$ 41.25m.	$ 41.25m.	75.00%
Notes payable to banks	136m.	102.00m.	136.00m.[b]	100.00
Subordinate debentures	209m.	156.75m.	122.75m.[b]	58.73
Total	$400m.	$300.00m.	$300.00m.	

[a] $300 million is available to pay $400 million in unsecured creditors. Thus, the pro rata settlement rate is $300m./$400m. = 75%.

[b] Notes payable to banks must be paid in full before subordinate debenture holders can be paid anything. Thus, $34 million ($136m. − $102m.) of the original settlement amount is moved from subordinate debentures to notes payable to banks; subordinate debenture holders receive only $122.75 million ($156.75m. − $34m.) or 58.73 percent of the amount owed to them.

building highly technical bankruptcy risk evaluation models. We discuss just a few of the models, so-called credit-scoring models, here.

Credit-scoring models are quantitative models that use data on observed firm characteristics either to sort firms into different bankruptcy risk classes or to calculate the probability of bankruptcy. These models use past data, such as financial ratios, as inputs to explain repayment experiences on old debt. The relative importance of the factors used to explain past repayment performance then forecasts repayment performance on new debt. By selecting and combining different economic and financial firm characteristics, managers or creditors may be able to:

1. Numerically establish which factors are important in explaining bankruptcy risk.
2. Evaluate the relative degree or importance of these factors.
3. Improve the pricing of bankruptcy risk.
4. Screen high-risk firms.

The primary benefit from credit scoring is that creditors can more accurately predict a firm's performance without having to use more resources. With an average accuracy rate of 85 percent, the use of these models means fewer defaults and write-offs for lenders.[2] Indeed, many commercial credit grantors are implementing credit-scoring models as a way to come in accordance with the Sarbanes-Oxley Act of 2002, which sets guidelines for corporate governance in several areas, including risk management and control assessment.

To use credit-scoring models, managers and creditors must identify objective economic and financial measures of risk for any particular class of borrower. For corporate debt, cash flow information and financial ratios such as the debt-to-equity ratio are usually key factors. After data are identified, a statistical technique quantifies or scores the bankruptcy risk probability or classification. Credit-scoring models include three broad types: (1) linear discriminant models, (2) linear probability models, and (3) logit models.

LINEAR DISCRIMINANT MODELS Linear discriminant models divide firms into high or low bankruptcy risk classes based on their observed financial characteristics (X_j). A widely used discriminant model is the *Z-score* model developed by Edward Altman.[3] The indicator variable Z is an overall measure of a firm's bankruptcy risk classification. This classification, in turn, depends on the values of various financial ratios of the firm (X_j) and the weighted importance of these ratios based on the observed experience of bankrupt versus nonbankrupt firms derived from a discriminant analysis model.

Altman's credit-scoring model takes the following form:

$$Z = 1.2X_1 + 1.4X_2 + 3.3X_3 + 0.6X_4 + 1.0X_5 \qquad \text{(19-4)}$$

where

X_1 = Net working capital/Total assets

X_2 = Retained earnings/Total assets

X_3 = Earnings before interest and taxes/Total assets

X_4 = Market value of equity/Book value of long-term debt

X_5 = Sales/Total assets ratio

The lower (higher) the value of Z, the higher (lower) is a firm's bankruptcy risk classification. Specifically, a *Z-score* of less than 1.81 indicates high risk of bankruptcy within the next year, a *Z-score* of greater than 2.99 indicates low risk of bankruptcy within the next year, and a *Z-score* between 1.81 and 2.99 is indeterminate.

Use of the *Z-score* model to make credit risk evaluations has a number of problems. The first problem is that this model usually discriminates only between two extreme cases of firm behavior: bankruptcy and no bankruptcy. In the real world various gradations of bankruptcy risk exist, from nonpayment or delay of interest payments (nonperforming assets) to outright default on all promised interest and principal payments. This problem suggests that a more accurate or finely calibrated sorting among firms may require defining more classes in the scoring model.

The second problem is that there is no obvious economic reason to expect that the weights in the Z-score model—or, more generally, the weights in any credit-scoring model—will be constant over any but very short periods. The same concern also applies to the scoring model's explanatory variables (X_j). Specifically, due to changing financial and market conditions, other firm-specific financial ratios may come to be increasingly relevant in explaining bankruptcy risk.

---

[2]See "Credit Scoring Heats Up," *Collections and Credit Risk,* September 2003, p. 34.

[3]E. I. Altman, "Managing the Commercial Lending Process," in *Handbook of Banking Strategy,* ed. R. C. Aspinwall and R. A. Eisenbeis (New York: John Wiley & Sons, 1985), pp. 473–510.

EXAMPLE 19-4

For interactive versions of this example visit www.mhhe.com/can1e

CALCULATION OF ALTMAN'S Z-SCORE

Suppose that the financial ratios of a potential borrowing firm took the following values:

$$X_1 = .2$$

$$X_2 = 0$$

$$X_3 = -.20$$

$$X_4 = .10$$

$$X_5 = 2.0$$

The ratio X_2 is zero and X_3 is negative, indicating that the firm has had negative earnings or losses in recent periods. Also, X_4 indicates that the firm is highly leveraged. However, the net working capital ratio (X_1) and the sales/total assets ratio (X_5) indicate that the firm is reasonably liquid and is maintaining its sales volume. The Z-score provides an overall score or indicator of the firm's credit risk since it combines and weights these five factors according to their past importance in explaining borrower default.

SOLUTION:

For the borrower in question:

$$Z = 1.2(.2) + 1.4(0) + 3.3(-.20) + 0.6(.10) + 1.0(2.0)$$

$$Z = 0.24 + 0 - .66 + 0.06 + 2.0$$

$$Z = 1.64$$

According to the Altman's Z-score, this firm should be placed in the high bankruptcy risk class. A creditor should not lend to this firm until it improves its financial condition.

The third problem is that these models ignore important, hard-to-quantify factors that may play a crucial role in the bankruptcy/no-bankruptcy decision. For example, the reputation of the firm and the managers' backgrounds could be important firm-specific characteristics, as could macro factors such as the phase of the business cycle. Credit-scoring models often ignore these variables. Moreover, traditional credit-scoring models rarely use publicly available information, such as the prices of the outstanding public debt and equity of the borrower.

A fourth problem relates to the availability of bankruptcy records. Currently, no centralized, publicly available database on defaulted loans or bankruptcies for proprietary or other reasons exists. Some task forces by consortiums of commercial banks and consulting firms are currently seeking to construct such databases, but it may well be many years before they are fully developed. This constrains the ability of many creditors to use credit-scoring models for larger business loans.

LINEAR PROBABILITY MODELS AND LOGIT MODELS While linear discriminant models divide firms into high or low bankruptcy risk classes, **linear probability** and **logit models** produce a value for the expected probability of bankruptcy. That is, factors explaining past repayment performance (or bankruptcy) can be used to assess the probability of future bankruptcy, called the *probability of default (PD)* in these models.

Briefly, these models divide firms into two groups: those that defaulted (or declared bankruptcy) over some past period of time (*PD = 1*) and those that did not default (or declare bankruptcy) over that period ($PD = 0$). They then relate these observations by linear regression to a set of j causal variables (X_{ij}) that reflect financial information about the ith firm, such as leverage or earnings. The models take the following form:

$$PD_i = \sum_{j=1}^{n} \beta_j X_{ij} + \text{error}$$

where β_j is the estimated weight of the jth variable (for example, the debt ratio) in explaining past defaults.

These variables (β_j), derived from past experience, can then be used to find default (or bankruptcy) probabilities (PD) on future debt instruments.

While linear probability models are straight forward as long as current financial information is available on a firm, their major weakness is that the estimated

---

 For interactive versions of this example visit www.mhhe.com/can1e

EXAMPLE 19-5

CALCULATION OF BANKRUPTCY PROBABILITY USING LINEAR PROBABILITY MODELS

Suppose a linear probability model you have developed finds there are two factors influencing the past bankruptcy behavior of firms: the debt-to-equity ratio and the sales-to-total assets ratio. Based on past bankruptcy experience, the linear probability model is estimated as:

$$PD_i = .5 \, (\text{debt/equity}) + .1 \, (\text{sales/total assets})$$

SOLUTION:

A firm you are thinking of lending to has a debt-to-equity ratio of 30 percent and a sales-to-asset ratio of 2.0. Its expected probability of default, or bankruptcy, is estimated as:

$$PD_i = .5 \, (.30) + .1 \, (2.0) = .35 \text{ or } 35 \text{ percent}$$

---

probabilities of bankruptcy can lie outside the interval of 0 to 1. The logit model overcomes this weakness by restricting the estimated range of bankruptcy probabilities from the linear regression model to lie between 0 and 1.[4]

TIME OUT

19-3 What is the difference between a restructuring (or reorganization) and a liquidation of a financially distressed firm?

19-4 What is the Altman's *Z-score*?

---

[4]Essentially this is done by plugging the estimated value of PD_i from the linear probability model (in our example, $PD_i = .35$) into the following formula:

$$F(PD_i) = \frac{1}{1 + e^{-PD_i}}$$

where e is the exponential (equal to 2.718) and $F(PD_i)$ is the logistically transformed value of PD_i. In our example

$$F(PD_i) = \frac{1}{1 + e^{-.35}} = .5866, \text{ or } 58.66\%$$

viewpoints REVISITED

Business Application Solution

MHM Production, Inc. is asking a price of $90 million to be purchased by BSW Corporation. The cash flows of two firms currently total $25.5 million ($20 million form BSW and $5.5 million from MHM)and are growing at 3 percent annually. Managers at BSW estimate that because of synergies, the merged firm's cash flows will increase by $6 million (for a total of $11.5 million increase in cash flows for BSW) for the first six years following the merger. After the first six years incremental cash flows are expected to be $2 million (for a total increase of $7.5 million). Thus, the value of incremental cash flows after year 6 can be looked at as a perpetuity problem. The WACC for the

(continued)

Personal Application Solution

James Upton holds $25,000 in subordinate debentures of Jaylon's Jazz Music Production, Inc. The firm has just announced that it is going to file Chapter 7 bankruptcy. The firm's assets had a book value of $500,000. The liquidation of the assets produced $250,000. Administrative expenses associated with the bankruptcy, unpaid wages, employee benefits, and taxes total $10,000. The firm has debt owed to secured creditors of $175,000, accounts payable of $25,000, notes payable to banks of $120,000, and total subordinate debt outstanding of $100,000.

The distribution of the $250,000 of funds is as follows:

Proceeds from liquidation of assets:	$250,000
Administrative expenses associated with the bankruptcy proceedings, wages due to employees, unpaid employee benefit plan contributions, taxes due to federal, state, and other governmental agencies	10,000
Funds available for secured creditors:	240,000
Payments to secured creditors	175,000
Funds available for unsecured creditors:	$ 65,000

The remaining $65,000 is distributed to the unsecured creditors on a pro rata basis, with senior creditors paid in full before subordinate creditors. Thus

UNSECURED CREDITORS	AMOUNT	SETTLEMENT AT 26.53%[a]	DISTRIBUTION AFTER SUBORDINATE ADJUSTMENT	PERCENT OF CLAIM RECEIVED
Accounts payable	$ 25,000	$ 6,632.65	$ 6,632.65	26.53%
Notes payable to banks	120.000	31,836.74	58,367.35[b]	48.64
Subordinate debentures	100,000	26,530.61	0.00[b]	0.00
Total	$245,000	$245,000.00	$65,000.00	

[a] $65,000 is available to pay $245,000 in unsecured creditors. Thus, the pro rata settlement rata is $65,000/$245,000 = 26.53%.

[b] Notes payable to banks must be paid in full before subordinate debenture holders can be paid anything. Thus, the $26,530.61 of the original settlement amount assigned to the subordinate debenture holders is moved to notes payable to banks; subordinate debenture holders receive none of the amount owed to them.

Business Application Solution (concluded)

merged firms is 9 percent. Thus, first calculate the value of the incremental firm's cash flows received after year 6 as:

Value of incremental cash flows
received after year 6

$$= \frac{\text{Annual incremental cash flows 7}}{\text{WACC}}$$

$$= \frac{\$7.5 \text{ m.}}{.09}$$

$$= \$83.33 \text{ m. as of the end of year 6}$$

To find the present value of the total incremental cash flows to BSW Corp., managers next discount the projected cash flows by the WACC as follows:

Present value of incremental cash flows
from the merger

$$= \frac{\$11.5\text{m.}}{(1.09)^1} + \frac{\$11.5\text{m.}}{(1.09)^2} + \frac{\$11.5\text{m.}}{(1.09)^3}$$

$$+ \frac{\$11.5\text{m.}}{(1.09)^4} + \frac{\$11.5\text{m.}}{(1.09)^5} + \frac{\$11.5\text{m.}}{(1.09)^6}$$

$$+ \frac{\$83.33\text{m.}}{(1.09)^6} = \$101.28 \text{ m.}$$

Finally, the NPV of the merger is calculated by subtracting the price of the MHM from the present value of the cash flows from the merger.

$$\text{NPV} = \$101.28 \text{ m.} - \$90 \text{ m.} = \$11.28\text{m.}$$

This merger would be beneficial for the stockholders of BSW Production, Inc. Their wealth would increase by $11.28 million as a result of the merger.

summary of learning goals

LG1 **Differentiate among types of and address motives mergers and acquisitions** A merger is a transaction in which two firms combine to form a single firm. An acquisition is the purchase of one firm by another. Despite these two distinct definitions, the two terms, mergers and acquisitions, are often used interchangeably. A consolidation is a type of merger in which an entirely new firm is created. A horizontal merger combines two companies in the same industry. A vertical merger combines a firm with a supplier or distributor. A conglomerate merger combines two companies that have no related products or markets. A product extension merger is a combination of firms that sell different, but somewhat related products.

LG2 **Mathematically value mergers** The net present value (NPV) or discounted cash flow (DCF) method is the most accurate and reliable tool used to evaluate whether a merger will be a profitable one. The NPV method allows bidder and target firm managers to predict pro forma cash flows of the merged firm. The valuation process starts with estimates of the expected future cash flows and the WACC for the bidder and target firm's cash flows. Managers then must value the synergies resulting from the merger. This requires estimates of the cash flows generated by synergies. These forecasted cash flows are then discounted to a present value based on the firm's weighted average cost of capital (WACC) to determine the merged firm's present

www.mhhe.com/can1e

value. Finally, the present value of the merged firm is compared with the asking price of the target firm to determine whether the merger is profitable.

LG3 **Suggest different methods by which a firm can informally resolve severe financial distress.** Informal resolutions of financial distress include the voluntary restructuring of debt agreements or the complete liquidation of the firm's assets. When financial distress appears to be temporary, the firm's creditors will generally work to restructure the firm to help it recover and reestablish itself as a viable entity. If, however, it is determined that the firm cannot recover from the financial distress, the firm and its creditors may agree to a liquidation of the firm's assets.

LG4 **Differentiate between a Chapter 7 and a Chapter 11 bankruptcy.** The Bankruptcy Reform Act of 1978 is the governing bankruptcy legislation in the U.S. The two key parts of this law for firms in financial distress are Chapters 7 and 11, which cover bankruptcy liquidation and reorganization of a failing firm. Chapter 11 outlines the process for reorganization of a failing firm. The goal of a Chapter 11 proceeding is to plan a reorganization of the corporation with some provision for repayment to the firm's creditors. The Chapter 11 reorganization process allows a firm in temporary financial distress to continue operating while the creditors' claims are settled using a collective procedure. Chapter 7 outlines the process to be followed for liquidating a failed firm. Chapter 7 is generally only used if it has been determined that reorganization under Chapter 11 is infeasible.

LG5 **Build and use statistical models to predict bankruptcy.** Credit-scoring models are quantitative models that use data on observed firm characteristics either to sort firms into different bankruptcy risk classes or to calculate the probability of bankruptcy. These models use past data, such as financial ratios, as inputs to explain repayment experiences on old debt. The relative importance of the factors used to explain past repayment performance then forecasts repayment performance on new debt. By selecting and combining different economic and financial firm characteristics, managers or creditors may be able to: (1) numerically establish which factors are important in explaining bankruptcy risk; (2) evaluate the relative degree or importance of these factors; (3) improve the pricing of bankruptcy risk; and (4) screen high-risk firms. The primary benefit from credit scoring is that creditors can more accurately predict a firm's performance without having to use more resources.

chapter equations

19-1 $AC_i = \dfrac{TC_i}{S_i}$

19-2 $AC_{A+B}[X_1, X_2] < AC_A[X_1, 0] + AC_B[0, X_2]$

19-3 $AC_{FS} < TAC$

19-4 $Z = 1.2X_1 + 1.4X_2 + 3.3X_3 + 0.6X_4 + 1.0X_5$

key terms

acquisition, The purchase of one firm by another. (p. 601)

assignee or **trustee,** The assignee liquidates the firm's assets through a private sale or a public auction and then distributes any proceeds from the sale to the firms' creditors and stockholders. (p. 611)

assignment, A voluntary liquidation proceeding that passes the liquidation of the firm's assets to a third party that is designated as the assignee or trustee. (p. 611)

business failure, A type of financial distress in which a firm no longer stays in business. (p. 609)

Chapter 7, A formal bankruptcy proceeding which outlines the process to be followed for liquidating a failed firm. (p. 612)

Chapter 11, A formal bankruptcy proceeding involving the reorganization of the corporation with some provision for repayment to the firm's creditors. (p. 611)

composition, An agreement in which creditors voluntarily reduce their claims on the firm, receiving only a partial payment for their claims, by reducing the principal amount or the interest rate on the debt, or by taking equity in exchange for debt. (p. 611)

conglomerate merger, A merger that combines two firms that have no related products or markets. (p. 602)

consolidation, A type of merger in which an entirely new firm is created. Both the bidder and target firms are absorbed into this new firm and cease to exist as separate entities. (p. 601)

credit-scoring models, Quantitative models that use data on observed firm characteristics either to sort firms into different bankruptcy risk classes or to calculate the probability of bankruptcy. (p. 616)

economic failure, A type of financial distress in which the return on a firm's assets is less then the firm's cost of capital. (p. 609)

economies of scale, Merged firm has an advantage over smaller firms if cuts associated with the merger lower the firm's operating costs of production. (p. 603)

economies of scope, Merged firm's ability to generate synergistic cost savings through the joint use of inputs in producing multiple products. (p. 604)

extension, An arrangement in which the firm's creditors postpone the dates of the required interest and/or principal payments. (p. 611)

horizontal merger, The merger of two companies in the same industry. (p. 601)

linear probability and **logit models,** Models that produce a value for the expected probability of bankruptcy. (p. 618)

liquidation, The termination of the firm as a going concern in which assets are sold or liquidated and any proceeds go to pay off the firm's creditors. (p. 611)

market extension merger, A type of horizontal merger that combines tow firms that sell the same products in different market areas. (p. 601)

merger, A transaction in which two firms combine to form a single firm. (p. 601)

prepackaged bankruptcy, A bankruptcy in which the firm and its creditors agree to a private reorganization outside the formal bankruptcy process. After the private reorganization is arranged or prepackaged, the firm files for formal Chapter 11 bankruptcy. (p. 614)

product extension merger, A merger that combines two firms that sell different, but somewhat related products. (p. 602)

synergy, The value of the combined firms is greater than the sum of the value of the two firms individually. (p. 602)

technical insolvency, A type of financial distress in which a firm's operating cash flows are not sufficient to pay its liabilities as they come due. (p. 609)

vertical merger, A combination of a firm with a supplier or distributor. (p. 602)

workout, A voluntary settlement in which a firm's creditors will arrange with the firm to help it recover and reestablish itself as a viable entity. (p. 611)

X-efficiencies, Cost savings not directly due to economies of scope or economies of scale. (p. 606)

self-test problems with solutions

1 **Valuation of a Merger** Tater Bug, Inc. is asking a price of $58 million to be purchased by BSW Corporation. The two firms currently have cumulative total cash flows of $8.5 million ($5.5 million from BSW and $3 million from Tater Bug) which are growing at 2 percent annually (for both fims). Managers at BSW estimate that, because of synergies, the merged firm's cash flows will increase by an additional 4 percent for the first four years following the merger. After the first four years, incremental cash flows will grow at a rate of 2 percent.

The WACC for the merged firms is 9 percent. Calculate the NPV of the merger. Should BSW Corporation agree to acquire Tater Bug for the asking price of $58 million?

Solution:

The incremental cash flows for the first four years after the merger are:

Year after merger	1	2	3	4
Cash flow with merger	$8.5m.(1.06) = $9.01m.	$8.5m.(1.06)^2 = $9.55m.	$8.5m.(1.06)^3 = $10.12m.	$8.5m.(1.06)^4 = $10.73m.
Cash flow with merger	$5.5m.(1.02) = $5.61m.	$5.5m.(1.02)^2 = $5.72m.	$5.5m.(1.02)^3 = $5.83m.	$5.5m.(1.02)^4 = $5.95m.
Incremental cash flows	$3.40m.	$3.83m.	$4.29m.	$4.78m.

The value of incremental cash flows after year 4 is:

$$\frac{\text{Value of incremental cash flows}}{\text{received after year 4 at end of year 4}} = \frac{\text{Incremental cash flow in year 5}}{\text{WACC} - \text{growth rate in cash flows after year 4}}$$

$$= \frac{\$4.78m.(1 + .02)}{(.09 - .02)} = \$69.62 \text{ m.}$$

To find the present value of the total incremental cash flows, managers next discount the projected cash flows by the WACC as follows:

$$\frac{\text{Present value of cash flows}}{\text{from the merger}} = \frac{\$3.40m.}{(1.09)^1} + \frac{\$3.83m.}{(1.09)^2} + \frac{\$4.29m.}{(1.09)^3} + \frac{\$4.78m.}{(1.09)^4}$$

$$+ \frac{\$69.62m.}{(1.09)^4} = \$62.36 \text{ m.}$$

Finally, the NPV of the merger is calculated by subtracting the price of the target firm from the present value of the incremental cash flows from the merger.

$$\text{NPV} = \$62.36 \text{ m.} - \$58 \text{ m.} = \$4.36m.$$

This merger would be beneficial for the stockholders of the bidder firm. Their wealth would increase by $3.45 million as a result of the merger.

 2 **Calculating Bankruptcy Class** Suppose that the financial ratios of a potential borrowing firm took the following values:

X_1 = Net working capital/Total assets = .15
X_2 = Retained earnings/Total assets = .10
X_3 = Earnings before interest and taxes/Total assets = .12
X_4 = Market value of equity/Book value of long-term debt = .80
X_5 = Sales/Total assets ratio = 1.9

Calculate and interpret the Altman's Z-score for this firm.

Solution:

For the borrower in question

$$Z = 1.2(.15) + 1.4(.1) + 3.3(.12) + 0.6(.80) + 1.0(1.9)$$
$$Z = 0.18 + 0.14 + 0.396 + 0.48 + 1.9$$
$$Z = 3.096$$

According to the Altman's *Z-score*, this firm should be placed in the low bankruptcy risk class. A creditor should lend to this firm with a high probability that the investment will be paid back as promised.

questions

1. Describe the difference between a merger and an acquisition. *(LG1)*

2. Describe the difference between a horizontal merger and a vertical merger. *(LG1)*

3. Classify each of the following as a horizontal merger, a vertical merger, a market extension merger, a conglomerate merger, or a product extension merger. *(LG1)*

    a. Wal-Mart acquires Kmart.

    b. Kroger grocery stores acquires Bunny Bread.

    c. Schnucks grocery stores headquartered in St. Louis and operating in the Midwest acquires FoodLand headquartered and operating in Hawaii.

    d. Bank of America acquires Aflac.

    e. Ford Motors buys the St. Louis Rams.

4. What is synergy and how does it apply to mergers? *(LG1)*

5. Describe the three dimensions of revenue synergies that may be achieved in a merger. *(LG1)*

6. What is the difference between economies of scope and economies of scale? Can two firms involved in a merger benefit from both economies of scale and economies of scope? *(LG1)*

7. How can managers' personal incentives result in value-destroying mergers and acquisitions? *(LG1)*

8. Why is NPV valuation an appropriate tool to use in the evaluation of a merger target? *(LG2)*

9. What is the difference between business failure, economic failure, and technical insolvency? *(LG3)*

10. A firm is experiencing a temporary period of financial distress as the result of a hurricane that has hit its local area. Because many of the firm's customers have been severely hurt by the hurricane, they are unable to pay their debts to the firm. This stoppage of cash inflows has left the firm temporarily unable to pay its own bills. What options do the firm's creditors have with respect to getting paid? *(LG3)*

11. What is the job of the trustee in an informal liquidation of a firm's assets? *(LG3)*

12. What is the difference between a Chapter 11 and a Chapter 7 bankruptcy? *(LG4)*

13. Does a Chapter 7 bankruptcy increase the probability that creditors will be paid in full more so than a Chapter 11 bankruptcy? *(LG4)*

14. What is the order of payment to a firm's creditors in a Chapter 7 bankruptcy? *(LG4)*

15. To what extent are employees of a bankrupt firm paid their wages and benefits due? *(LG4)*

16. What is a credit-scoring model? *(LG5)*

17. What is the difference between a linear discriminant and a linear probability credit-scoring model? *(LG5)*

18. A firm has an Altman's *Z-score* of 1.76. What does this mean? *(LG5)*

19. The Altman's *Z-score* model has several weaknesses. What are they? *(LG5)*

20. A linear probability model you have developed finds that a firm has a PD of .16. What does this mean? *(LG5)*

problems

19-1 **Calculation of Average Costs with Economies of Scope** Peter's TV Supplies is considering a merger with Jan's Radio Supply Stores. Peter's total operating costs of producing services are $250,000 for a sales volume (S_p) of $4.5 million. Jan's total operating costs of producing services are $50,000 for a sales volume (S_J) of $550,000. *(LG2)*

   a. Calculate the average cost of production for the two firms.

   b. If the two firms merge, calculate the total average cost (*TAC*) for the merged firm assuming no synergies.

   c. Suppose, instead, that synergies in the production process result in a cost of production for the merged firms totaling $270,000 for a sales volume of $5,050,000. Calculate the total average cost (*TAC*) for the merged firm.

19-2 **Calculation of Average Costs with Economies of Scope** Cindy's Computer Corp. is considering a merger with Bobby's Hard Drive, Inc. Cindy's total operating costs of producing services are $2 million for a sales volume (S_C) of $10 million. Bobby's total operating costs of producing services are $1.5 million for a sales volume (S_B) of $5 million. *(LG2)*

   a. Calculate the average cost of production for the two firms.

   b. If the two firms merge, calculate the total average cost (*TAC*) for the merged firm assuming no synergies.

   c. Suppose, instead, that synergies in the production process result in a cost of production for the merged firms totaling $3.1 million for a sales volume of $15 million. Calculate the total average cost (*TAC*) for the merged firm.

19-3 **Calculation of Altman's Z-Score** Suppose that the financial ratios of a potential borrowing firm took the following values: X_1 = Net working capital/Total assets = .10, X_2 = Retained earnings/Total assets = .20,

X_3 = Earnings before interest and taxes/Total assets = .22, X_4 = Market value of equity/Book value of long-term debt = .60, X_5 = Sales/Total assets ratio = 0.9. Calculate and interpret the Altman's Z-score for this firm. *(LG5)*

19-4 **Calculation of Altman's Z-Score** Suppose that the financial ratios of a potential borrowing firm took the following values: X_1 = Net working capital/Total assets = .25, X_2 = Retained earnings/Total assets = .35, X_3 = Earnings before interest and taxes/Total assets = .46, X_4 = Market value of equity/Book value of long-term debt = 1.20, X_5 = Sales/Total assets ratio = 2.9. Calculate and interpret the Altman's Z-score for this firm. *(LG5)*

19-5 **Calculation of Bankruptcy Probability** Suppose a linear probability model you have developed finds there are two factors influencing the past bankruptcy behavior of firms: the debt ratio and the profit margin. Based on past bankruptcy experience, the linear probability model is estimated as:

$$PD_i = .15 \,(\text{debt ratio}) + .1 \,(\text{profit margin})$$

A firm you are thinking of lending to has a debt ratio of 45 percent and a profit margin of 6 percent. Calculate the firm's expected probability of default, or bankruptcy. *(LG5)*

19-6 **Calculation of Bankruptcy Probability** A linear probability model you have developed finds there are two factors influencing the past bankruptcy behavior of firms: the equity multiplier and the total asset turnover ratio. Based on past bankruptcy experience, the linear probability model is estimated as

$$PD_i = .02 \,(\text{equity multiplier}) + .01 \,(\text{total asset turnover})$$

A firm you are thinking of lending to has an equity multiplier of 2.5 times and a total asset turnover ratio of 2.0. Calculate the firm's expected probability of default, or bankruptcy. *(LG5)*

intermediate problems

19-7 **Calculation of Average Costs with Economies of Scope** George's Dry Cleaning is considering a merger with Weezzie's Laundry Supply Stores. George's total operating costs of producing services are $550,000 for sales volume of (S_G) $4.5 million. Weezzie's total operating costs of producing services are $185,000 for a sales volume (S_W) of $2 million. *(LG2)*

 a. Calculate the average cost of production for the two firms.

 b. For a sales volume of $6.5 million, calculate the reduction in production costs the merged firms need to experience such that the total average cost *(TAC)* for the merged firms is equal to 10 percent.

19-8 **Calculation of Average Costs with Economies of Scope** Jenny's Day Care is considering a merger with Lionel's Diaper Manufacturers. Jenny's total operating costs of producing services are $350,000 for sales volume (S_J) of $1.4 million. Lionel's total operating costs of producing services are $200,000 for a sales volume (S_L) of $800,000. *(LG2)*

 a. Calculate the average cost of production for the two firms.

 b. For a sales volume of $2.2 million, calculate the reduction in production costs the merged firms need to experience such that the total average cost *(TAC)* for the merged firms is equal to 20 percent.

www.mhhe.com/can1e

19-9 **Valuation of a Merger** Stubborn Motors, Inc. is asking a price of $35 million to be purchased by Rubber Tire Motor Corp. The two firms currently have cumulative total cash flows of $6 million ($4 million from Rubber Tire and $2 million from Stubborn Motors) that are growing at 1 percent annually (for both firms). Managers estimate that, because of synergies, the merged firm's cash flows will increase by an additional 4 percent for the first four years following the merger. After the first four years, incremental cash flows will grow at a rate of 1 percent annually. The WACC for the merged firms is 10 percent. Calculate the NPV of the merger. Should Rubber Tire Motor Corporation agree to acquire Stubborn Motors for the asking price of $35 million? *(LG2)*

19-10 **Valuation of a Merger** You own stock in Make-UP-Artists, Inc., which has just made a bid of $32 million to purchase MHM Corporation. The two firms currently have cumulative total cash flows of $12.5 million, ($10 million from Make-UP-Artists and $2.5 million from MHM) which are growing at 2 percent annually (for both firms). Managers estimate that, because of synergies, the merged firm's cash flows will increase by an additional 3 percent for the first five years following the merger. After the first five years, incremental cash flows will grow at a rate of 2 percent annually. The merged firms are expected to have a beta = 1.3, the risk free rate is 4.5 percent, and the market risk premium is currently 6.5 percent. Calculate the NPV of the merger. Will you vote in favor of the merger? *(LG2)*

19-11 **Calculating Creditor and Stockholder Payoffs in a Chapter 7 Bankruptcy** You own $25,000 in subordinated debt of Local Crossings, Inc., which declared bankruptcy on May 15, 2009, through a Chapter 7 filing. Local Crossings' balance sheet at the time of the bankruptcy filing is listed below.

LOCAL CROSSINGS, INC.
Balance Sheet as of May 15, 2009
(in millions of dollars)

Assets		Liabilities and Equity	
Current assets:		Current liabilities:	
Cash and marketable securities	$ 406	Accrued wages (1,500 employees)	$ 50
Accounts receivable	978	Unpaid employee benefits	40
Inventory	1,038	Unsecured customer deposits	20
Total	2,422	Accrued taxes	350
		Accounts payable	841
		Notes payable to banks	1,518
		Total	2,819
Fixed assets:		Long-term debt:	
Gross plant and equipment	7,253	First mortgage	1,200
Less: Depreciation	1,050	Subordinate debentures	2,018
Net plant and equipment	6,203	Total	3,218
		Stockholders' equity:	
		Preferred stock (2.5 million shares)	100
		Common stock and paid-in surplus (20 million shares)	1,500
		Retained earnings	988
		Total	2,588
Total assets	$8,625	Total liabilities and equity	$8,625

The accrued wages were earned within the last 90 days prior to filing for bankruptcy. The unpaid employee benefits were due in the 6 months prior to the filing for bankruptcy. The unsecured customer deposits are for less than $900 each. Local Crossings, Inc. has no property taxes past due. The first mortgage is secured against the fixed assets of the firm. The debentures are subordinate to the notes payable to banks. The liquidation of the firm's current assets produced $1,298 million and of the firm's fixed assets produced $3,552 million for a total of only $4,850 million in funds to distribute to the creditors and stockholders of the firm.

The administrative expenses associated with the bankruptcy totaled $15 million and unpaid expenses incurred after the filing of the bankruptcy petition but before the trustee was appointed totaled $10 million. Show how the trustee will distribute the $4,850 million of funds among the Local Crossings' creditors and stockholders. How much of the $25,000 debt you own will you recover? (LG4)

19-12 Calculating Creditor and Stockholder Payoffs in a Chapter 7 Bankruptcy WorldGone, Inc. declared bankruptcy on September 25, 2009, through a Chapter 7 filing. WorldGone's balance sheet at the time of the bankruptcy filing is listed below.

WORLDGONE, INC.
Balance Sheet as of September 25, 2009
(in millions of dollars)

Assets		Liabilities and Equity	
Current assets:		**Current liabilities:**	
Cash and marketable securities	$ 263	Accrued wages (1,500 employees)	$ 40
Accounts receivable	1,428	Unpaid employee benefits	30
Inventory	2,100	Unsecured customer deposits	59
Total	3,791	Accrued taxes	225
		Accounts payable	711
		Notes payable to banks	1,975
Fixed assets:		Total	3,040
Gross plant and equipment	7,752	**Long-term debt:**	
Less: Depreciation	1,248	First mortgage	1,232
Net plant and equipment	6,504	Subordinate debentures	2,214
		Total	3,652
		Stockholders' equity:	
		Preferred stock (2.5 million shares)	100
		Common stock and paid-in surplus (20 million shares)	2,500
		Retained earnings	1,003
		Total	3,603
Total assets	$10,295	Total liabilities and equity	$10,295

The accrued wages were earned within the last 90 days prior to filing for bankruptcy. The unpaid employee benefits were due in the 6 months prior to the filing for bankruptcy. The unsecured customer deposits are for less than $900 each. WorldGone, Inc. has no property taxes past due. The first mortgage is secured against the fixed assets of the firm. The debentures are subordinate to the notes payable to banks. The liquidation of the firm's current assets produced $2,477 million and of the firm's fixed assets produced $5,068 million for a total of only $7,545 million in funds to distribute to the creditors and stockholders of the firm.

The administrative expenses associated with the bankruptcy totaled $25 million and unpaid expenses incurred after the filing of the bankruptcy petition but before the trustee was appointed totaled $10 million. Show how the trustee will distribute the $7,545 million of funds among the WorldGone's creditors and stockholders. *(LG4)*

19-13 **Calculation of Altman's Z-Score:** Use the following financial statements for Lake of Egypt Marina to calculate and interpret the Altman's *Z-score* for this firm. *(LG5)*

LAKE OF EGYPT MARINA, INC.
Balance Sheet as of December 31, 2009 and 2010
(in millions of dollars)

Assets	2009	2010	Liabilities and Equity	2009	2010
Current assets:			Current liabilities:		
Cash and marketable securities	$ 65	$ 75	Accrued wages and taxes	$ 43	$ 40
Accounts receivable	110	115	Accounts payable	80	90
Inventory	190	200	Notes payable	70	80
Total	365	390	Total	193	210
Fixed assets:			Long-term debt:	280	300
Gross plant and equipment	471	580	Stockholders' equity:		
Less: Depreciation	100	110	Preferred stock (5 million shares)	5	5
Net plant and equipment	371	470	Common stock and paid-in surplus (65 million shares)	65	65
Other long-term assets	49	50	Retained earnings	242	330
Total	420	520	Total	312	400
Total assets	$785	$910	Total liabilities and equity	$785	$910

LAKE OF EGYPT MARINA, INC.
Income Statement for Years Ending December 31, 2009 and 2010
(in millions of dollars)

	2009	2010
Net sales (all credit)	$ 432	$ 515
Less: Cost of goods sold	200	260
Gross profits	232	255
Less: Depreciation	20	22
Earnings before interest and taxes (EBIT)	212	233
Less: Interest	30	33
Earnings before taxes (EBT)	182	200
Less: Taxes	55	57
Net income	$ 127	$ 143
Less: Preferred stock dividends	$ 5	$ 5
Net income available to common stockholders	$ 122	$ 138
Less: Common stock dividends	65	65
Addition to retained earnings	$ 57	$ 73
Per (common) share data:		
Earnings per share (EPS)	$ 1.877	$ 2.123
Dividends per share (DPS)	$ 1.000	$ 1.000
Book value per share (BVPS)	$ 4.723	$ 6.077
Market value (price) per share (MVPS)	$12.550	$14.750

19-14 **Calculation of Altman's Z-Score:** Use the following financial statements for Garners' Platoon Mental Health Care, Inc. to calculate and interpret the Altman's *Z-score* for this firm. *(LG5)*

GARNERS' PLATOON MENTAL HEALTH CARE, INC.
Balance Sheet as of December 31, 2010
(in millions of dollars)

Assets		Liabilities and Equity	
Current assets:		Current liabilities:	
Cash and marketable securities	$ 421	Accrued wages and taxes	$ 316
Accounts receivable	1,109	Accounts payable	867
Inventory	1,760	Notes payable	872
Total	3,290	Total	$2,055
Fixed assets:		Long-term debt:	3,090
Gross plant and equipment	5,812	Stockholders' equity:	
Less: Depreciation	840	Preferred stock (25 million shares)	60
Net plant and equipment	4,972	Common stock and paid-in surplus (200 million shares)	637
Other long-term assets	892	Retained earnings	3,312
Total	5,864	Total	4,009
Total assets	$9,154	Total liabilities and equity	$9,154

GARNERS' PLATOON MENTAL HEALTH CARE, INC.
Income Statement for Years Ending December 31, 2010
(in millions of dollars)

Net sales (all credit)	$ 4,980
Less: Cost of goods sold	2,371
Gross profits	2,609
Less: Depreciation	200
Earnings before interest and taxes (EBIT)	2,409
Less: Interest	315
Earnings before taxes (EBT)	2,094
Less: Taxes	767
Net income	$ 1,327
Less: Preferred stock dividends	$ 60
Net income available to common stockholders	$ 1,267
Less: Common stock dividends	395
Addition to retained earnings	$ 872
Per (common) share data:	
Earnings per share (EPS)	$ 6.335
Dividends per share (DPS)	$ 1.975
Book value per share (BVPS)	$ 19.745
Market value (price) per share (MVPS)	$26.850

19-15 **Calculation of Bankruptcy Probability** Suppose a linear probability model you have developed finds there are two factors influencing the past bankruptcy behavior of firms: the debt ratio and the profit margin. Based on past bankruptcy experience, the linear probability model is estimated as

$$PD_i = .15 \text{ (debt ratio)} + .5 \text{ (profit margin)}$$

You know a particular firm has a debt ratio of 55 percent and a probability of default of 12 percent. Calculate the firm's profit margin. *(LG5)*

19-16 Calculation of Bankruptcy Probability A linear probability model you have developed finds there are two factors influencing the past bankruptcy behavior of firms: the equity multiplier and the total asset turnover ratio. Based on past bankruptcy experience, the linear probability model is estimated as

$$PD_i = .02 \text{ (equity multiplier)} + .01 \text{ (total asset turnover)}$$

A firm has an equity multiplier of 1.8 times and a probability of default of 5 percent. Calculate the firm's total asset turnover ratio. *(LG5)*

advanced problems

19-17 Economies of Scope A survey of a local market has provided the following average cost data: Johnson Construction Corp. (JCC) has assets of $3 million and an average cost of 20 percent. Anderson Architects (AA) has assets of $4 million and an average cost of 30 percent. Cole Home Builders (CHB) has assets of $4 million and an average cost of 25 percent. For each firm, average costs are measured as a proportion of assets. JCC is planning to acquire AA and CHB with the expectation of reducing overall average costs by eliminating the duplication of services.

  a. What should the average cost after the acquisition be for JCC to justify this merger? *(LG1)*

  b. If JCC plans to reduce operating costs by $500,000 after the merger, what will the average cost be for the new firm? *(LG1)*

19-18 Economies of Scope A survey of a national market has provided the following average cost data: Jackson County Construction (JCC) has assets of $1.5 million and an average cost of 30 percent. Arkansas Architects (AA) has assets of $1 million and an average cost of 25 percent. Colorado Home Builders (CHB) has assets of $750,000 and an average cost of 15 percent. For each firm, average costs are measured as a proportion of assets. JCC is planning to acquire AA and CHB with the expectation of reducing overall average costs by eliminating the duplication of services.

  a. What should the average cost after the acquisition be for JCC to justify this merger? *(LG1)*

  b. If JCC plans to reduce operating costs by $250,000 after the merger, what will the average cost be for the new firm? *(LG1)*

19-19 Valuation of a Merger The managers of BSW, Inc. have approached KCMP about a possible merger. KCMP Corp. is asking a price of $72 million to be purchased by BSW Inc. The two firms currently have cumulative total cash flows of $12 million ($6 million from each firm) that are growing at 2 percent annually (for both firms). Managers estimate that, because of synergies, the merged firm's cash flows will increase by an additional 3 percent for the first two years following the merger, but are uncertain of the incremental cash flows in year three after the merger. After the first three years, managers have estimated that these incremental cash flows will be $1.2 million annually. The WACC for the merged firms is 10 percent. Calculate the minimum incremental cash flow needed in year three after the merger such that BSW, Inc. would see this merger as a positive NPV project. *(LG3)*

19-20 **Valuation of a Merger** The managers of State Bank have been approached by City Bank about a possible merger. State Bank is asking a price of $205 million to be purchased by City Bank. The two firms currently have cumulative total cash flows of $30 million ($15 million from each firm) that are growing at 1 percent annually (for both firms). Managers estimate that because of synergies the merged firm's cash flows will increase by an additional 6 percent for the first two years following the merger but are uncertain of the incremental cash flow in year three following the merger. After the first three years, managers have estimated that incrementel cash flows will by $1 million annually. The WACC for the merged firms is 8 percent. Calculate the minimum incremental cash flow needed in year three after the merger such that City Bank would see this merger as a positive NPV project. *(LG3)*

19-21 **Calculating the Probability of Bankruptcy** A linear probability model you have developed finds there are two factors influencing the past bankruptcy behavior of firms: the debt-to-equity ratio and the sales-to-total assets ratio. Based on past bankruptcy experience, the linear probability model is estimated as

$$PD_i = .5\,(\text{debt/equity}) + .01\,(\text{sales/total assets})$$

A firm you are thinking of lending to has a sales-to-asset ratio of 2.0 and its expected probability of default, or bankruptcy, is estimated to be 8 percent. Calculate the firm's debt ratio. *(LG5)*

19-22 **Calculating the Probability of Bankruptcy** A linear probability model you have developed finds there are two factors influencing the past bankruptcy behavior of firms: the debt-to-equity ratio and the profit margin. Based on past bankruptcy experience, the linear probability model is estimated as

$$PD_i = .1\,(\text{debt/equity}) - 1.5\,(\text{profit margin})$$

A firm you are thinking of lending to has a debt-to-equity ratio of 125 percent and its expected probability of default, or bankruptcy, is estimated to be 5 percent. If sales are $1 million, calculate the firm's net income. *(LG5)*

research it! Mergers and Acquisitions

Go to the Thomson Financial—Investment Banking and Capital Markets Group Web site at **www.thomsonreuters.com/financial/league_tables** and find the latest information available for the dollar value of mergers and acquisition activity using the following steps. Click on "Mergers & Acquisition (XQ20XX)". Click on "Global M&A Financial." This will download a file on to your computer that will contain the most recent information on merger and acquisition activity. What is the most recent dollar value of global merger and acquisition activity undertaken? Who are the top advisors on these merger and acquisition deals? How has the top advisor market share changed in the last year?

integrated minicase:

Disaster Airlines is a firm in severe financial distress. The firm can no longer pay its bills on time and it is far behind on payments to its banks and long-term debt holders. The firm has decided to either be purchased by another air carrier or liquidate its assets and close. The managers have approached Altruistic Airlines about being acquired. After examining Disaster's financial statements, looking at the routes owned by Disaster, and looking at the condition of the fixed assets, Altruistic Airlines has offered to pay the stockholders of Disaster Airlines $8 million to be acquired. Disaster Airlines covers flights to both areas in which Altruistic already flies, but also has routes in areas into which Altruistic is interested in expanding. As part of the analysis Altruistic determined that the additional cash flows resulting from the acquisition would total $500,000 this year and would grow at a rate of 4 percent for the next three years. After this time the cash flows would grow at a rate of 2 percent annually. The WACC of Altruistic Airlines would be 8 percent after the merger.

If, instead, Disaster Airlines decides to liquidate its assets, it will pay off its debt and give any remaining funds to the firm's stockholders. Disaster Airlines' balance sheet is listed below.

DISASTER AIRLINES, INC.
Balance Sheet as of June 25, 2008
(in millions of dollars)

Assets		Liabilities and Equity	
Current assets:		**Current liabilities:**	
Cash and marketable securities	$ 63	Accrued wages (1,500 employees)	$ 4
Accounts receivable	28	Unpaid employee benefits	3
Inventory	100	Unsecured customer deposits	6
Total	191	Accrued taxes	22
		Accounts payable	157
		Notes payable to banks	211
Fixed assets:		Total	403
Gross plant and equipment	1,152	**Long-term debt:**	
Less: Depreciation	248	First mortgage	160
Net plant and equipment	904	Subordinate debentures	412
		Total	572
		Stockholders' equity:	
		Common stock and paid-in surplus (20 million shares)	20
		Retained earnings	100
		Total	120
Total assets	$1,095	Total liabilities and equity	$1,095

The accrued wages were earned within the last 90 days prior to filing for bankruptcy. The unpaid employee benefits were due in the six months prior to the filing for bankruptcy. The unsecured customer deposits are for less than $900 each. Disaster Airlines has no property taxes past due. The first mortgage is secured against the fixed assets of the firm. The debentures are subordinate to the notes payable to banks. The liquidation of the firm's current assets produced

(continued)

$186 million and of the firm's fixed assets produced $800 million for a total of only $986 million in funds to distribute to the creditors and stockholders of the firm. The administrative expenses associated with the bankruptcy totaled $1 million and unpaid expenses incurred after the filing of the bankruptcy petition but before the trustee was appointed totaled $5 million.

Show which method of dissolution, an acquisition by Altruistic Airlines or a liquidation of assets, is more beneficial for the creditors and stockholders of Disaster Airlines and the stockholders of Altruistic Airlines.

ANSWERS TO TIME OUT

19-1 A vertical merger combines a firm with a supplier or distributor. Vertical mergers occur between firms in different stages of production operation for many reasons such as avoidance of fixed costs, the elimination of costs of searching for prices, contracting, payment collection, communication, advertising and coordination, and better planning for inventory. A horizontal merger combines two companies in the same industry.

19-2 With economies of scale, a merged firm has an advantage over smaller firms if cuts associated with the merger lower the firm's operating costs of production. With economies of scope, merged firms are able to generate synergistic cost savings through the joint use of inputs in producing multiple products.

19-3 Chapter 11 outlines the process for reorganization of a failing firm. The goal of a Chapter 11 proceeding is to plan a reorganization of the corporation with some provision for repayment to the firm's creditors. The Chapter 11 reorganization process allows a firm in temporary financial distress to continue operating while the creditors' claims are settled using a collective procedure. Chapter 7 outlines the process to be followed for liquidating a failed firm. Liquidation results in the termination of the firm as a going concern. If a firm is too financially distressed to be reorganized, it is liquidated via a Chapter 7 bankruptcy. A firm is liquidated once the bankruptcy courts determine that reorganization is not feasible.

19-4 A widely used discriminant model is the Z-score model developed by Edward Altman. The indicator variable Z is an overall measure of a firm's bankruptcy risk classification. This classification, in turn, depends on the values of various financial ratios of the firm (X_j) and the weighted importance of these ratios based on the observed experience of bankrupt versus nonbankrupt firms derived from a discriminant analysis model. The lower (higher) the value of Z, the higher (lower) is a firm's bankruptcy risk classification. Specifically, a Z-score of less than 1.81 indicates high risk of bankruptcy within the next year, a Z-score of greater than 2.99 indicates low risk of bankruptcy within the next year, and a Z-score between 1.81 and 2.99 is indeterminate.

appendix A Present Value and Future Value Tables

INTEREST RATE PER YEAR

NUMBER OF YEARS	1%	2%	3%	4%	5%	6%	7%	8%	9%	10%	11%	12%	13%	14%	15%
1	1.0100	1.0200	1.0300	1.0400	1.0500	1.0600	1.0700	1.0800	1.0900	1.1000	1.1100	1.1200	1.1300	1.1400	1.1500
2	1.0201	1.0404	1.0609	1.0816	1.1025	1.1236	1.1449	1.1664	1.1881	1.2100	1.2321	1.2544	1.2769	1.2996	1.3225
3	1.0303	1.0612	1.0927	1.1249	1.1576	1.1910	1.2250	1.2597	1.2950	1.3310	1.3676	1.4049	1.4429	1.4815	1.5209
4	1.0406	1.0824	1.1255	1.1699	1.2155	1.2625	1.3108	1.3605	1.4116	1.4641	1.5181	1.5735	1.6305	1.6890	1.7490
5	1.0510	1.1041	1.1593	1.2167	1.2763	1.3382	1.4026	1.4693	1.5386	1.6105	1.6851	1.7623	1.8424	1.9254	2.0114
6	1.0615	1.1262	1.1941	1.2653	1.3401	1.4185	1.5007	1.5869	1.6771	1.7716	1.8704	1.9738	2.0820	2.1950	2.3131
7	1.0721	1.1487	1.2299	1.3159	1.4071	1.5036	1.6058	1.7138	1.8280	1.9487	2.0762	2.2107	2.3526	2.5023	2.6600
8	1.0829	1.1717	1.2668	1.3686	1.4775	1.5938	1.7182	1.8509	1.9926	2.1436	2.3045	2.4760	2.6584	2.8526	3.0590
9	1.0937	1.1951	1.3048	1.4233	1.5513	1.6895	1.8385	1.9990	2.1719	2.3579	2.5580	2.7731	3.0040	3.2519	3.5179
10	1.1046	1.2190	1.3439	1.4802	1.6289	1.7908	1.9672	2.1589	2.3674	2.5937	2.8394	3.1058	3.3946	3.7072	4.0456
11	1.1157	1.2434	1.3842	1.5395	1.7103	1.8983	2.1049	2.3316	2.5804	2.8531	3.1518	3.4785	3.8359	4.2262	4.6524
12	1.1268	1.2682	1.4258	1.6010	1.7959	2.0122	2.2522	2.5182	2.8127	3.1384	3.4985	3.8960	4.3345	4.8179	5.3503
13	1.1381	1.2936	1.4685	1.6651	1.8856	2.1329	2.4098	2.7196	3.0658	3.4523	3.8833	4.3635	4.8980	5.4924	6.1528
14	1.1495	1.3195	1.5126	1.7317	1.9799	2.2609	2.5785	2.9372	3.3417	3.7975	4.3104	4.8871	5.5348	6.2613	7.0757
15	1.1610	1.3459	1.5580	1.8009	2.0789	2.3966	2.7590	3.1722	3.6425	4.1772	4.7846	5.4736	6.2543	7.1379	8.1371
16	1.1726	1.3728	1.6047	1.8730	2.1829	2.5404	2.9522	3.4259	3.9703	4.5950	5.3109	6.1304	7.0673	8.1372	9.3576
17	1.1843	1.4002	1.6528	1.9479	2.2920	2.6928	3.1588	3.7000	4.3276	5.0545	5.8951	6.8660	7.9861	9.2765	10.7613
18	1.1961	1.4282	1.7024	2.0258	2.4066	2.8543	3.3799	3.9960	4.7171	5.5599	6.5436	7.6900	9.0243	10.5752	12.3755
19	1.2081	1.4568	1.7535	2.1068	2.5270	3.0256	3.6165	4.3157	5.1417	6.1159	7.2633	8.6128	10.1974	12.0557	14.2318
20	1.2202	1.4859	1.8061	2.1911	2.6533	3.2071	3.8697	4.6610	5.6044	6.7275	8.0623	9.6463	11.5231	13.7435	16.3665

INTEREST RATE PER YEAR

NUMBER OF YEARS	16%	17%	18%	19%	20%	21%	22%	23%	24%	25%	26%	27%	28%	29%	30%
1	1.1600	1.1700	1.1800	1.1900	1.2000	1.2100	1.2200	1.2300	1.2400	1.2500	1.2600	1.2700	1.2800	1.2900	1.3000
2	1.3456	1.3689	1.3924	1.4161	1.4400	1.4641	1.4884	1.5129	1.5376	1.5625	1.5876	1.6129	1.6384	1.6641	1.6900
3	1.5609	1.6016	1.6430	1.6852	1.7280	1.7716	1.8158	1.8609	1.9066	1.9531	2.0004	2.0484	2.0972	2.1467	2.1970
4	1.8106	1.8739	1.9388	2.0053	2.0736	2.1436	2.2153	2.2889	2.3642	2.4414	2.5205	2.6014	2.6844	2.7692	2.8561
5	2.1003	2.1924	2.2878	2.3864	2.4883	2.5937	2.7027	2.8153	2.9316	3.0518	3.1758	3.3038	3.4360	3.5723	3.7129
6	2.4364	2.5652	2.6996	2.8398	2.9860	3.1384	3.2973	3.4628	3.6352	3.8147	4.0015	4.1959	4.3980	4.6083	4.8268
7	2.8262	3.0012	3.1855	3.3793	3.5832	3.7975	4.0227	4.2593	4.5077	4.7684	5.0419	5.3288	5.6295	5.9447	6.2749
8	3.2784	3.5115	3.7589	4.0214	4.2998	4.5950	4.9077	5.2389	5.5895	5.9605	6.3528	6.7675	7.2058	7.6686	8.1573
9	3.8030	4.1084	4.4355	4.7854	5.1598	5.5599	5.9874	6.4439	6.9310	7.4506	8.0045	8.5948	9.2234	9.8925	10.6045
10	4.4114	4.8068	5.2338	5.6947	6.1917	6.7275	7.3046	7.9259	8.5944	9.3132	10.0857	10.9153	11.8059	12.7614	13.7858
11	5.1173	5.6240	6.1759	6.7767	7.4301	8.1403	8.9117	9.7489	10.6571	11.6415	12.7080	13.8625	15.1116	16.4622	17.9216
12	5.9360	6.5801	7.2876	8.0642	8.9161	9.8497	10.8722	11.9912	13.2148	14.5519	16.0120	17.6053	19.3428	21.2362	23.2981
13	6.8858	7.6987	8.5994	9.5964	10.6993	11.9182	13.2641	14.7491	16.3863	18.1899	20.1752	22.3588	24.7588	27.3947	30.2875
14	7.9875	9.0075	10.1472	11.4198	12.8392	14.4210	16.1822	18.1414	20.3191	22.7374	25.4207	28.3957	31.6913	35.3391	39.3738
15	9.2655	10.5387	11.9737	13.5895	15.4070	17.4494	19.7423	22.3140	25.1956	28.4217	32.0301	36.0625	40.5648	45.5875	51.1859
16	10.7480	12.3303	14.1290	16.1715	18.4884	21.1138	24.0856	27.4462	31.2426	35.5271	40.3579	45.7994	51.9230	58.8079	66.5417
17	12.4677	14.4265	16.6722	19.2441	22.1861	25.5477	29.3844	33.7588	38.7408	44.4089	50.8510	58.1652	66.4614	75.8621	86.5042
18	14.4625	16.8790	19.6733	22.9005	26.6233	30.9127	35.8490	41.5233	48.0386	55.5112	64.0722	73.8698	85.0706	97.8622	112.4554
19	16.7765	19.7484	23.2144	27.2516	31.9480	37.4043	43.7358	51.0737	59.5679	69.3889	80.7310	93.8147	108.8904	126.2422	146.1920
20	19.4608	23.1056	27.3930	32.4294	38.3376	45.2593	53.3576	62.8206	73.8641	86.7362	101.7211	119.1446	139.3797	162.8524	190.0496

INTEREST RATE PER YEAR

NUMBER OF YEARS	1%	2%	3%	4%	5%	6%	7%	8%	9%	10%	11%	12%	13%	14%	15%
1	0.9901	0.9804	0.9709	0.9615	0.9524	0.9434	0.9346	0.9259	0.9174	0.9091	0.9009	0.8929	0.8850	0.8772	0.8696
2	0.9803	0.9612	0.9426	0.9246	0.9070	0.8900	0.8734	0.8573	0.8417	0.8264	0.8116	0.7972	0.7831	0.7695	0.7561
3	0.9706	0.9423	0.9151	0.8890	0.8638	0.8396	0.8163	0.7938	0.7722	0.7513	0.7312	0.7118	0.6931	0.6750	0.6575
4	0.9610	0.9238	0.8885	0.8548	0.8227	0.7921	0.7629	0.7350	0.7084	0.6830	0.6587	0.6355	0.6133	0.5921	0.5718
5	0.9515	0.9057	0.8626	0.8219	0.7835	0.7473	0.7130	0.6806	0.6499	0.6209	0.5935	0.5674	0.5428	0.5194	0.4972
6	0.9420	0.8880	0.8375	0.7903	0.7462	0.7050	0.6663	0.6302	0.5963	0.5645	0.5346	0.5066	0.4803	0.4556	0.4323
7	0.9327	0.8706	0.8131	0.7599	0.7107	0.6651	0.6227	0.5835	0.5470	0.5132	0.4817	0.4523	0.4251	0.3996	0.3759
8	0.9235	0.8535	0.7894	0.7307	0.6768	0.6274	0.5820	0.5403	0.5019	0.4665	0.4339	0.4039	0.3762	0.3506	0.3269
9	0.9143	0.8368	0.7664	0.7026	0.6446	0.5919	0.5439	0.5002	0.4604	0.4241	0.3909	0.3606	0.3329	0.3075	0.2843
10	0.9053	0.8203	0.7441	0.6756	0.6139	0.5584	0.5083	0.4632	0.4224	0.3855	0.3522	0.3220	0.2946	0.2697	0.2472
11	0.8963	0.8043	0.7224	0.6496	0.5847	0.5268	0.4751	0.4289	0.3875	0.3505	0.3173	0.2875	0.2607	0.2366	0.2149
12	0.8874	0.7885	0.7014	0.6246	0.5568	0.4970	0.4440	0.3971	0.3555	0.3186	0.2858	0.2567	0.2307	0.2076	0.1869
13	0.8787	0.7730	0.6810	0.6006	0.5303	0.4688	0.4150	0.3677	0.3262	0.2897	0.2575	0.2292	0.2042	0.1821	0.1625
14	0.8700	0.7579	0.6611	0.5775	0.5051	0.4423	0.3878	0.3405	0.2992	0.2633	0.2320	0.2046	0.1807	0.1597	0.1413
15	0.8613	0.7430	0.6419	0.5553	0.4810	0.4173	0.3624	0.3152	0.2745	0.2394	0.2090	0.1827	0.1599	0.1401	0.1229
16	0.8528	0.7284	0.6232	0.5339	0.4581	0.3936	0.3387	0.2919	0.2519	0.2176	0.1883	0.1631	0.1415	0.1229	0.1069
17	0.8444	0.7142	0.6050	0.5134	0.4363	0.3714	0.3166	0.2703	0.2311	0.1978	0.1696	0.1456	0.1252	0.1078	0.0929
18	0.8360	0.7002	0.5874	0.4936	0.4155	0.3503	0.2959	0.2502	0.2120	0.1799	0.1528	0.1300	0.1108	0.0946	0.0808
19	0.8277	0.6864	0.5703	0.4746	0.3957	0.3305	0.2765	0.2317	0.1945	0.1635	0.1377	0.1161	0.0981	0.0829	0.0703
20	0.8195	0.6730	0.5537	0.4564	0.3769	0.3118	0.2584	0.2145	0.1784	0.1486	0.1240	0.1037	0.0868	0.0728	0.0611

INTEREST RATE PER YEAR

NUMBER OF YEARS	16%	17%	18%	19%	20%	21%	22%	23%	24%	25%	26%	27%	28%	29%	30%
1	0.8621	0.8547	0.8475	0.8403	0.8333	0.8264	0.8197	0.8130	0.8065	0.8000	0.7937	0.7874	0.7813	0.7752	0.7692
2	0.7432	0.7305	0.7182	0.7062	0.6944	0.6830	0.6719	0.6610	0.6504	0.6400	0.6299	0.6200	0.6104	0.6009	0.5917
3	0.6407	0.6244	0.6086	0.5934	0.5787	0.5645	0.5507	0.5374	0.5245	0.5120	0.4999	0.4882	0.4768	0.4658	0.4552
4	0.5523	0.5337	0.5158	0.4987	0.4823	0.4665	0.4514	0.4369	0.4230	0.4096	0.3968	0.3844	0.3725	0.3611	0.3501
5	0.4761	0.4561	0.4371	0.4190	0.4019	0.3855	0.3700	0.3552	0.3411	0.3277	0.3149	0.3027	0.2910	0.2799	0.2693
6	0.4104	0.3898	0.3704	0.3521	0.3349	0.3186	0.3033	0.2888	0.2751	0.2621	0.2499	0.2383	0.2274	0.2170	0.2072
7	0.3538	0.3332	0.3139	0.2959	0.2791	0.2633	0.2486	0.2348	0.2218	0.2097	0.1983	0.1877	0.1776	0.1682	0.1594
8	0.3050	0.2848	0.2660	0.2487	0.2326	0.2176	0.2038	0.1909	0.1789	0.1678	0.1574	0.1478	0.1388	0.1304	0.1226
9	0.2630	0.2434	0.2255	0.2090	0.1938	0.1799	0.1670	0.1552	0.1443	0.1342	0.1249	0.1164	0.1084	0.1011	0.0943
10	0.2267	0.2080	0.1911	0.1756	0.1615	0.1486	0.1369	0.1262	0.1164	0.1074	0.0992	0.0916	0.0847	0.0784	0.0725
11	0.1954	0.1778	0.1619	0.1476	0.1346	0.1228	0.1122	0.1026	0.0938	0.0859	0.0787	0.0721	0.0662	0.0607	0.0558
12	0.1685	0.1520	0.1372	0.1240	0.1122	0.1015	0.0920	0.0834	0.0757	0.0687	0.0625	0.0568	0.0517	0.0471	0.0429
13	0.1452	0.1299	0.1163	0.1042	0.0935	0.0839	0.0754	0.0678	0.0610	0.0550	0.0496	0.0447	0.0404	0.0365	0.0330
14	0.1252	0.1110	0.0985	0.0876	0.0779	0.0693	0.0618	0.0551	0.0492	0.0440	0.0393	0.0352	0.0316	0.0283	0.0254
15	0.1079	0.0949	0.0835	0.0736	0.0649	0.0573	0.0507	0.0448	0.0397	0.0352	0.0312	0.0277	0.0247	0.0219	0.0195
16	0.0930	0.0811	0.0708	0.0618	0.0541	0.0474	0.0415	0.0364	0.0320	0.0281	0.0248	0.0218	0.0193	0.0170	0.0150
17	0.0802	0.0693	0.0600	0.0520	0.0451	0.0391	0.0340	0.0296	0.0258	0.0225	0.0197	0.0172	0.0150	0.0132	0.0116
18	0.0691	0.0592	0.0508	0.0437	0.0376	0.0323	0.0279	0.0241	0.0208	0.0180	0.0156	0.0135	0.0118	0.0102	0.0089
19	0.0596	0.0506	0.0431	0.0367	0.0313	0.0267	0.0229	0.0196	0.0168	0.0144	0.0124	0.0107	0.0092	0.0079	0.0068
20	0.0514	0.0433	0.0365	0.0308	0.0261	0.0221	0.0187	0.0159	0.0135	0.0115	0.0098	0.0084	0.0072	0.0061	0.0053

Annuity table: Present value of $1 per year for each of N years = $1/i - 1/[i(1 + i)^N]$ appendix table a–3

INTEREST RATE PER YEAR

NUMBER OF YEARS	1%	2%	3%	4%	5%	6%	7%	8%	9%	10%	11%	12%	13%	14%	15%
1	0.9901	0.9804	0.9709	0.9615	0.9524	0.9434	0.9346	0.9259	0.9174	0.9091	0.9009	0.8929	0.8850	0.8772	0.8696
2	1.9704	1.9416	1.9135	1.8861	1.8594	1.8334	1.8080	1.7833	1.7591	1.7355	1.7125	1.6901	1.6681	1.6467	1.6257
3	2.9410	2.8839	2.8286	2.7751	2.7232	2.6730	2.6243	2.5771	2.5313	2.4869	2.4437	2.4018	2.3612	2.3216	2.2832
4	3.9020	3.8077	3.7171	3.6299	3.5460	3.4651	3.3872	3.3121	3.2397	3.1699	3.1024	3.0373	2.9745	2.9137	2.8550
5	4.8534	4.7135	4.5797	4.4518	4.3295	4.2124	4.1002	3.9927	3.8897	3.7908	3.6959	3.6048	3.5172	3.4331	3.3522
6	5.7955	5.6014	5.4172	5.2421	5.0757	4.9173	4.7665	4.6229	4.4859	4.3553	4.2305	4.1114	3.9975	3.8887	3.7845
7	6.7282	6.4720	6.2303	6.0021	5.7864	5.5824	5.3893	5.2064	5.0330	4.8684	4.7122	4.5638	4.4226	4.2883	4.1604
8	7.6517	7.3255	7.0197	6.7327	6.4632	6.2098	5.9713	5.7466	5.5348	5.3349	5.1461	4.9676	4.7988	4.6389	4.4873
9	8.5660	8.1622	7.7861	7.4353	7.1078	6.8017	6.5152	6.2469	5.9952	5.7590	5.5370	5.3282	5.1317	4.9464	4.7716
10	9.4713	8.9826	8.5302	8.1109	7.7217	7.3601	7.0236	6.7101	6.4177	6.1446	5.8892	5.6502	5.4262	5.2161	5.0188
11	10.3676	9.7868	9.2526	8.7605	8.3064	7.8869	7.4987	7.1390	6.8052	6.4951	6.2065	5.9377	5.6869	5.4527	5.2337
12	11.2551	10.5753	9.9540	9.3851	8.8633	8.3838	7.9427	7.5361	7.1607	6.8137	6.4924	6.1944	5.9176	5.6603	5.4206
13	12.1337	11.3484	10.6350	9.9856	9.3936	8.8527	8.3577	7.9038	7.4869	7.1034	6.7499	6.4235	6.1218	5.8424	5.5831
14	13.0037	12.1062	11.2961	10.5631	9.8986	9.2950	8.7455	8.2442	7.7862	7.3667	6.9819	6.6282	6.3025	6.0021	5.7245
15	13.8651	12.8493	11.9379	11.1184	10.3797	9.7122	9.1079	8.5595	8.0607	7.6061	7.1909	6.8109	6.4624	6.1422	5.8474
16	14.7179	13.5777	12.5611	11.6523	10.8378	10.1059	9.4466	8.8514	8.3126	7.8237	7.3792	6.9740	6.6039	6.2651	5.9542
17	15.5623	14.2919	13.1661	12.1657	11.2741	10.4773	9.7632	9.1216	8.5436	8.0216	7.5488	7.1196	6.7291	6.3729	6.0472
18	16.3983	14.9920	13.7535	12.6593	11.6896	10.8276	10.0591	9.3719	8.7556	8.2014	7.7016	7.2497	6.8399	6.4674	6.1280
19	17.2260	15.6785	14.3238	13.1339	12.0853	11.1581	10.3356	9.6036	8.9501	8.3649	7.8393	7.3658	6.9380	6.5504	6.1982
20	18.0456	16.3514	14.8775	13.5903	12.4622	11.4699	10.5940	9.8181	9.1285	8.5136	7.9633	7.4694	7.0248	6.6231	6.2593

INTEREST RATE PER YEAR

NUMBER OF YEARS	16%	17%	18%	19%	20%	21%	22%	23%	24%	25%	26%	27%	28%	29%	30%
1	0.8621	0.8547	0.8475	0.8403	0.8333	0.8264	0.8197	0.8130	0.8065	0.8000	0.7937	0.7874	0.7813	0.7752	0.7692
2	1.6052	1.5852	1.5656	1.5465	1.5278	1.5095	1.4915	1.4740	1.4568	1.4400	1.4235	1.4074	1.3916	1.3761	1.3609
3	2.2459	2.2096	2.1743	2.1399	2.1065	2.0739	2.0422	2.0114	1.9813	1.9520	1.9234	1.8956	1.8684	1.8420	1.8161
4	2.7982	2.7432	2.6901	2.6386	2.5887	2.5404	2.4936	2.4483	2.4043	2.3616	2.3202	2.2800	2.2410	2.2031	2.1662
5	3.2743	3.1993	3.1272	3.0576	2.9906	2.9260	2.8636	2.8035	2.7454	2.6893	2.6351	2.5827	2.5320	2.4830	2.4356
6	3.6847	3.5892	3.4976	3.4098	3.3255	3.2446	3.1669	3.0923	3.0205	2.9514	2.8850	2.8210	2.7594	2.7000	2.6427
7	4.0386	3.9224	3.8115	3.7057	3.6046	3.5079	3.4155	3.3270	3.2423	3.1611	3.0833	3.0087	2.9370	2.8682	2.8021
8	4.3436	4.2072	4.0776	3.9544	3.8372	3.7256	3.6193	3.5179	3.4212	3.3289	3.2407	3.1564	3.0758	2.9986	2.9247
9	4.6065	4.4506	4.3030	4.1633	4.0310	3.9054	3.7863	3.6731	3.5655	3.4631	3.3657	3.2728	3.1842	3.0997	3.0190
10	4.8332	4.6586	4.4941	4.3389	4.1925	4.0541	3.9232	3.7993	3.6819	3.5705	3.4648	3.3644	3.2689	3.1781	3.0915
11	5.0286	4.8364	4.6560	4.4865	4.3271	4.1769	4.0354	3.9018	3.7757	3.6564	3.5435	3.4365	3.3351	3.2388	3.1473
12	5.1971	4.9884	4.7932	4.6105	4.4392	4.2784	4.1274	3.9852	3.8514	3.7251	3.6059	3.4933	3.3868	3.2859	3.1903
13	5.3423	5.1183	4.9095	4.7147	4.5327	4.3624	4.2028	4.0530	3.9124	3.7801	3.6555	3.5381	3.4272	3.3224	3.2233
14	5.4675	5.2293	5.0081	4.8023	4.6106	4.4317	4.2646	4.1082	3.9616	3.8241	3.6949	3.5733	3.4587	3.3507	3.2487
15	5.5755	5.3242	5.0916	4.8759	4.6755	4.4890	4.3152	4.1530	4.0013	3.8593	3.7261	3.6010	3.4834	3.3726	3.2682
16	5.6685	5.4053	5.1624	4.9377	4.7296	4.5364	4.3567	4.1894	4.0333	3.8874	3.7509	3.6228	3.5026	3.3896	3.2832
17	5.7487	5.4746	5.2223	4.9897	4.7746	4.5755	4.3908	4.2190	4.0591	3.9099	3.7705	3.6400	3.5177	3.4028	3.2948
18	5.8178	5.5339	5.2732	5.0333	4.8122	4.6079	4.4187	4.2431	4.0799	3.9279	3.7861	3.6536	3.5294	3.4130	3.3037
19	5.8775	5.5845	5.3162	5.0700	4.8435	4.6346	4.4415	4.2627	4.0967	3.9424	3.7985	3.6642	3.5386	3.4210	3.3105
20	5.9288	5.6278	5.3527	5.1009	4.8696	4.6567	4.4603	4.2786	4.1103	3.9539	3.8083	3.6726	3.5458	3.4271	3.3158

INTEREST RATE PER YEAR

NUMBER OF YEARS	1%	2%	3%	4%	5%	6%	7%	8%	9%	10%	11%	12%	13%	14%	15%
1	1.0000	1.0000	1.0000	1.0000	1.0000	1.0000	1.0000	1.0000	1.0000	1.0000	1.0000	1.0000	1.0000	1.0000	1.0000
2	2.0100	2.0200	2.0300	2.0400	2.0500	2.0600	2.0700	2.0800	2.0900	2.1000	2.1100	2.1200	2.1300	2.1400	2.1500
3	3.0301	3.0604	3.0909	3.1216	3.1525	3.1836	3.2149	3.2464	3.2781	3.3100	3.3421	3.3744	3.4069	3.4396	3.4725
4	4.0604	4.1216	4.1836	4.2465	4.3101	4.3746	4.4399	4.5061	4.5731	4.6410	4.7097	4.7793	4.8498	4.9211	4.9934
5	5.1010	5.2040	5.3091	5.4163	5.5256	5.6371	5.7507	5.8666	5.9847	6.1051	6.2278	6.3528	6.4803	6.6101	6.7424
6	6.1520	6.3081	6.4684	6.6330	6.8019	6.9753	7.1533	7.3359	7.5233	7.7156	7.9129	8.1152	8.3227	8.5355	8.7537
7	7.2135	7.4343	7.6625	7.8983	8.1420	8.3938	8.6540	8.9228	9.2004	9.4872	9.7833	10.0890	10.4047	10.7305	11.0668
8	8.2857	8.5830	8.8923	9.2142	9.5491	9.8975	10.2598	10.6366	11.0285	11.4359	11.8594	12.2997	12.7573	13.2328	13.7268
9	9.3685	9.7546	10.1591	10.5828	11.0266	11.4913	11.9780	12.4876	13.0210	13.5795	14.1640	14.7757	15.4157	16.0853	16.7858
10	10.4622	10.9497	11.4639	12.0061	12.5779	13.1808	13.8164	14.4866	15.1929	15.9374	16.7220	17.5487	18.4197	19.3373	20.3037
11	11.5668	12.1687	12.8078	13.4864	14.2068	14.9716	15.7836	16.6455	17.5603	18.5312	19.5614	20.6546	21.8143	23.0445	24.3493
12	12.6825	13.4121	14.1920	15.0258	15.9171	16.8699	17.8885	18.9771	20.1407	21.3843	22.7132	24.1331	25.6502	27.2707	29.0017
13	13.8093	14.6803	15.6178	16.6268	17.7130	18.8821	20.1406	21.4953	22.9534	24.5227	26.2116	28.0291	29.9847	32.0887	34.3519
14	14.9474	15.9739	17.0863	18.2919	19.5986	21.0151	22.5505	24.2149	26.0192	27.9750	30.0949	32.3926	34.8827	37.5811	40.5047
15	16.0969	17.2934	18.5989	20.0236	21.5786	23.2760	25.1290	27.1521	29.3609	31.7725	34.4054	37.2797	40.4175	43.8424	47.5804
16	17.2579	18.6393	20.1569	21.8245	23.6575	25.6725	27.8881	30.3243	33.0034	35.9497	39.1899	42.7533	46.6717	50.9804	55.7175
17	18.4304	20.0121	21.7616	23.6975	25.8404	28.2129	30.8402	33.7502	36.9737	40.5447	44.5008	48.8837	53.7391	59.1176	65.0751
18	19.6147	21.4123	23.4144	25.6454	28.1324	30.9057	33.9990	37.4502	41.3013	45.5992	50.3959	55.7497	61.7251	68.3941	75.8364
19	20.8109	22.8406	25.1169	27.6712	30.5390	33.7600	37.3790	41.4463	46.0185	51.1591	56.9395	63.4397	70.7494	78.9692	88.2118
20	22.0190	24.2974	26.8704	29.7781	33.0660	36.7856	40.9955	45.7620	51.1601	57.2750	64.2028	72.0524	80.9468	91.0249	102.4436

INTEREST RATE PER YEAR

NUMBER OF YEARS	16%	17%	18%	19%	20%	21%	22%	23%	24%	25%	26%	27%	28%	29%	30%
1	1.0000	1.0000	1.0000	1.0000	1.0000	1.0000	1.0000	1.0000	1.0000	1.0000	1.0000	1.0000	1.0000	1.0000	1.0000
2	2.1600	2.1700	2.1800	2.1900	2.2000	2.2100	2.2200	2.2300	2.2400	2.2500	2.2600	2.2700	2.2800	2.2900	2.3000
3	3.5056	3.5389	3.5724	3.6061	3.6400	3.6741	3.7084	3.7429	3.7776	3.8125	3.8476	3.8829	3.9184	3.9541	3.9900
4	5.0665	5.1405	5.2154	5.2913	5.3680	5.4457	5.5242	5.6038	5.6842	5.7656	5.8480	5.9313	6.0156	6.1008	6.1870
5	6.8771	7.0144	7.1542	7.2966	7.4416	7.5892	7.7396	7.8926	8.0484	8.2070	8.3684	8.5327	8.6999	8.8700	9.0431
6	8.9775	9.2068	9.4420	9.6830	9.9299	10.1830	10.4423	10.7079	10.9801	11.2588	11.5442	11.8366	12.1359	12.4423	12.7560
7	11.4139	11.7720	12.1415	12.5227	12.9159	13.3214	13.7396	14.1708	14.6153	15.0735	15.5458	16.0324	16.5339	17.0506	17.5828
8	14.2401	14.7733	15.3270	15.9020	16.4991	17.1189	17.7623	18.4300	19.1229	19.8419	20.5876	21.3612	22.1634	22.9953	23.8577
9	17.5185	18.2847	19.0859	19.9234	20.7989	21.7139	22.6700	23.6690	24.7125	25.8023	26.9404	28.1287	29.3692	30.6639	32.0150
10	21.3215	22.3931	23.5213	24.7089	25.9587	27.2738	28.6574	30.1128	31.6434	33.2529	34.9449	36.7235	38.5926	40.5564	42.6195
11	25.7329	27.1999	28.7551	30.4035	32.1504	34.0013	35.9620	38.0388	40.2379	42.5661	45.0306	47.6388	50.3985	53.3178	56.4053
12	30.8502	32.8239	34.9311	37.1802	39.5805	42.1416	44.8737	47.7877	50.8950	54.2077	57.7386	61.5013	65.5100	69.7800	74.3270
13	36.7862	39.4040	42.2187	45.2445	48.4966	51.9913	55.7459	59.7788	64.1097	68.7596	73.7506	79.1066	84.8529	91.0161	97.6250
14	43.6720	47.1027	50.8180	54.8409	59.1959	63.9095	69.0100	74.5280	80.4961	86.9495	93.9258	101.4654	109.6117	118.4108	127.9125
15	51.6595	56.1101	60.9653	66.2607	72.0351	78.3305	85.1922	92.6694	100.8151	109.6868	119.3465	129.8611	141.3029	153.7500	167.2863
16	60.9250	66.6488	72.9390	79.8502	87.4421	95.7799	104.9345	114.9834	126.0108	138.1085	151.3766	165.9236	181.8677	199.3374	218.4722
17	71.6730	78.9792	87.0680	96.0218	105.9306	116.8937	129.0201	142.4295	157.2534	173.6357	191.7345	211.7230	233.7907	258.1453	285.0139
18	84.1407	93.4056	103.7403	115.2659	128.1167	142.4413	158.4045	176.1883	195.9942	218.0446	242.5855	269.8882	300.2521	334.0074	371.5180
19	98.6032	110.2846	123.4135	138.1664	154.7400	173.3540	194.2535	217.7116	244.0328	273.5558	306.6577	343.7580	385.3227	431.8696	483.9734
20	115.3797	130.0329	146.6280	165.4180	186.6880	210.7584	237.9893	268.7853	303.6006	342.9447	387.3887	437.5726	494.2131	558.1118	630.1655

appendix B Selected Answers to End of Chapter Problems

Chapter 2:

2-1. $1,800,000

2-5. Income taxes = $78,800

Average tax rate = 32.16%

Marginal tax rate = 39%

2-9. Operating cash flow = $50m.

Investment in operating capital = $40m.

Free cash flow = $10m.

2-13. Inventory = $2.5m.

Depreciation = $2.0m.

2-17. $6,650,000

2-21. Net cash flow from operating activities = $17

Net cash flow from investing activities = −$18

Net cash flow from financing activities = $1

Net change in cash and marketable securities = $0

2-25. $295m.

2-29. $17.910m.

Chapter 3:

3-1. Current ratio = 1.9474 times

Quick ratio = 0.84211 times

Cash ratio = 0.21053 times

3-5. $14.29m.

3-9. Book value per share = $3.50

Earnings per share = $0.70

Market-to-book ratio = 2.57 times

PE ratio = 12.86 times

3-13. 8.11%

3-17. $11.43m.

3-21. 12.22%

3-25. $1,518,750

Chapter 4

4-3. $545

4-7. $424.68

4-11. $1020.87

4-15. ≈ 10.3 years

4-19. 13.33%

4-23. $500 today because PV = $482.61

4-27. $1,538.62

4-31. 13 years, 6.5 months

4-35. −25% (first year return), 33.33% (second year return needed)

4-39. $3,944.31

Chapter 5

5-3. $2,992.36

5-7. $1,944.83

5-11. $7,052.50

5-15. 11.57%

5-19. $629,148.01

5-23. $67,662.70

5-27. $3,903.98, $2,372.88

5-31. 7.93%

5-35. $634.06, $208.33 with $25,000 owed at the end.

5-39. $3,677.99

5-45. $501.56

5-49. $877.97, $1,204.89

Combined Chapters 4 and 5 Problems

4&5-1 $1,081,284.33

4&5-5 $2,715.08, $119.11

4&5-9 $1,394.02

Chapter 6

6-3. 88 years and 6 months

6-7. $15.63, 1,136.46

6-11. $278.23

6-15. 4.86%

6-19. $27.48, 2.60%

6-23. $1,032.99, premium bond

6-27. 6.57%

6-31. ETY=6.72%, take the muni bond

6-35. $−2.90, −0.26%

6-39. $−104.22, −11.13%

Chapter 7

7-3. $5,452.95

7-7. $1,980.00

7-11. $38.89

7-15. $62.74

7-19. $66.00

7-23. $15.94

7-27. $49.87

7-31. $22.40, 33.93%

7-35. $47.21

Chapter 8

8-1. 8.35%

8-5. $_1R_1 = 6\%$

$_1R_2 = 6.499\%$

$_1R_3 = 6.832\%$

$_1R_4 = 7.085\%$

8-9. a. 0.00%

b. 0.20%

8-13. 0.1536%

8-17. 8.15%

8-21. 9.04%

Chapter 9

9-3. Idol Staff, Rail Haul, and then Poker-R-Us

9-7. Portfolio Yellow dominates Portfolio Blue

9-11. 1.63%

9-15. 4.31%

9-19. combine Sport Garb and Thumb Devices

9-23. 1.15%

9-27. 105 of Alaska Air, 117 of Best Buy, 528 of Ford Motor

9-31.

	ESTEE LAUDER	LOWE'S COMPANIES
Ave =	30.30%	22.77%
StDev =	17.22%	22.65%
CoV =	0.568318	0.994799

Estee Lauder was better

Chapter 10

10-3. 11%

10-7. 5.68%

10-11. 1.27

10-15. 14.88%
10-19. 16%, over-valued
10-23. 20%, 29.99%
10-27. 1.42, 15.5%

Chapter 11

11-3. 8.71%
11-7. 68.97%
11-11. 18.52%
11-15. 15.08%
11-19. 16.92%
11-23. 5.52%

Chapter 12

12-3. The Scion xA, because it has an EAC of −$7,028.89.
12-7. $2,591.75
12-11. $125,948.13

Chapter 13

13-3. NPV = $293.45; the project should be accepted.
13-7. The NPV for this project is negative, so discounted payback never occurs.
13-11. MIRR = 16.12%; since MIRR exceeds the 8 percent cost of capital, we would accept the project.
13-15. PI = −21.12%; the project should be rejected.
13-19. Payback = 3.5 years, which is equal to the maximum allowable payback, so this project should be accepted.
13-23. NPV = $1,466.58, so the project should be accepted.
13-27. IRR = 28.79%, so the project should be accepted.
13-31. Since the two NPV profiles shown below do not cross in the first quadrant, the only crucial points are the two projects' IRRs: IRR$_A$ = 13% and IRR$_B$ = 14.29%.

NPV Profiles

13-35. Shown below, there appear to be only two.

NPV Profiles

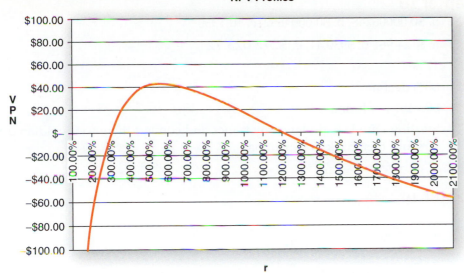

Chapter 14

14-3. 97.10% equity and 2.90% debt.

14-7. $28,000,011

14-11. $0.45

14-15. $0.53

Chapter 15

15-3. $1.02

15-7. The price will be $34.96 right before the ex-dividend date and $31.50 once it goes ex-dividend.

Chapter 16

16-1. Up-front fee   = $1,250
      Back-end fee   =   375
      Total   = $1,625

16-5. $43.125 million − $3,018,750 = $40,106,250

16-9. Number of bonds = $1,069,519/$1,000 = 1,069.519 *or* 1,070

16-13. Gross proceeds = $8.05/(1 − .08) = $8.75

16-17. Underwriter's spread = $125,000/45,000 = $2.78

Chapter 17

17-1. $148,000.

17-5. 365/54 = 6.7593

17-9. Only if the rate is less than −60.03%. Since this is not likely to happen, it isn't worth it.

17-13. 365.8945

17-17. 8.41% or lower

17-21. $70,450.07

Chapter 18

18-3. a. $0.00006248, b. $0.0004652, c. $0.1360

18-7. a. $124.96 , b. $930.41, c. $272,023.72

18-11. 17%

18-15. 80% decline

18-19. $0.1451 per krona

18-23. Starting with U.S. dollars, buy francs and convert them to Canadian dollars and then back to U.S. dollars.

Chapter 19

19-1. a. $$AC_{Peter} = \frac{\$250,000}{\$4,500,000} = .05556 = 5.556\%$$

$$AC_{Jan} = \frac{\$50,000}{\$550,000} = .09091 = 9.091\%$$

b. $$AC_{PeterJan} = \frac{\$300,000}{\$5,050,000} = .05941 = 5.941\%$$

c. $$AC_{PeterJan} = \frac{\$270,000}{\$5,050,000} = .05347 = 5.347\%$$

19-5. PD_i = .15 (.45) + .1 (.06) = .0735 or 7.35%

19-9. NPV = $32.41m. − $25m. = −$2.59m.

This merger would not be beneficial for the stockholders of the bidder firm. Their wealth would decrease by $5.31 million as a result of the merger.

19-13. According to the Altman's Z-score, this firm should be placed in the low bankruptcy risk class.

19-17. a. The average cost after merger = $2,800,000/$11,000,000 = 25.45%. If Johnson Construction can lower its average costs to less than 25.45%, it should go ahead with the merger.

b. The average cost after merger = $2,300,000/$11,000,000 = 20.91%.

19-21. 10.71%

index

a

Accelerated depreciation, 397–400
Accounting function; *see also* Financial statements
  financial function compared, 9
  GAAP, 32–33, 39, 42, 45–46
Accounts payable management, 73
Accounts payable turnover ratio, 73
Accounts receivable, 556–558
Accounts receivable management, 72–73, 547
Accounts receivable turnover ratio, 72–73
Acid-test ratio, 70
ACP (average collection period), 72–73
Acquisitions, 601
Active capital structure management, 458
Actual inflation rate, 268
After-tax cash flow (ATCF), 395
Agency bonds, 184–185
Agency problem, 15–16
Agency relationship, 15
Agency theory, 15–19
Agents, 15
Aging schedule, 557–558
Alamo Group, Inc., 527
Altman, Edward, 617–618
Amaranth Hedge Fund, 338
American Airlines, 613
American Bankers Association, 264
American Stock Exchange (AMEX), 221, 257
Amortization schedules, 159–160
Amortized loans, 158–163
Analyst estimates, 17, 233, 239
Analyzing annuity cash flows; *see* Annuity cash flow analysis
Analyzing financial statements; *see* Financial statements
Analyzing single cash flows; *see* Single cash flow analysis
Angel investors, 11
Angel venture capitalists (angels), 517
AngioDynamics Inc., 256
Announcements and news, 340–341, 494, 498, 502–504
Annual percentage rate (APR), 155–157
Annuities, 143, 152–154
Annuity cash flow analysis
  annuity loans, 157–163
  compounding frequency, 154–157
  future value of multiple cash flows, 142–147
  introduction, 140–142
  ordinary annuities versus annuities due, 152–154
  present value of multiple cash flows, 148–152

Annuity due, 152–154
Annuity loans, 157–163
AOL, 604
APP (average payment period), 73
Apple Inc., 19, 218
APR (annual percentage rate), 155–157
Arbitrage, 576
Arbitrageurs, 576
Ask price, 225
Aspinwall, R. C., 617n
Asset-backed securities, 185
Asset-based loans, 547
Asset class performance, 298–299
Asset class risk, 302–303
Asset management ratios, 72–76
Asset pricing, 331, 338
Assets
  current, 30, 540–541, 543–546
  definition, 30
  financial, 9, 420–422, 432
  fixed, 30–31, 394–395, 540
  ratio analysis, 72–76
  real, 9, 420–422, 432
Asset transformers, 265–266
Assignees, 611
Assignment, 547, 611
ATCF (after-tax cash flow), 395
Auctions, Dutch, 503
Auditors, 17
Average collection period (ACP), 72–73
Average payment period (APP), 73
Average returns, 297–298, 329
Average tax rate, 36

b

Back-end fees, 516
Balance sheet, 30–33, 540
Banker's acceptance (B.A.), 548
Bank loans, 514–516, 546–548
Bank of New York, 309, 310–311
Bank One, 601, 602
Bankruptcy
  costs, 472–475
  firm valuation, 475–477
  predicting, 615–619
  types, 471–472, 611–614
Barnes & Noble, 602
Barry, Norman, 201n
Basic earnings power (BEP) ratio, 79–80
Bassett Furniture, 496
Baumol, William, 549
Baumol Model, 549–551
Bearer bonds, 181
Behavioral finance, 341–343
Bell Atlantic, 603

Benartzi, Shlomo, 306n
BEP (basic earnings power) ratio, 79–80
Bernardi Securities, 521
Berra, Yogi, 459–460
Best efforts underwriting, 522
Beta
  concerns about, 337–339
  definition and overview, 333–334
  finding, 337
  portfolio, 336
  proxy, 367
  security market line and, 334–336
Bid, 225
Bird-in-the-hand theory, 493
Blinder, Meyer, 339
Board of directors, 17
Bolivia, 583
Bondholders
  claims of, 32, 38, 473–474
  investment overview, 178–180
  underinvestment problem, 474–475
Bond interest, 180–181, 392
Bond markets, 178, 180–187, 202–204
Bond prices, 181, 185–187, 189–193
Bond ratings, 199–200
Bonds; *see also* Debt; Leverage
  calling, 195–196
  characteristics, 180–181
  credit risk, 199–202, 269–270
  definition, 180
  introduction, 178–180
  issuers, 182–183
  liquidity risk, 271
  quotes, 185–187
  special provisions, 271
  term to maturity, 271–274
Bond valuation
  bond prices and interest rate risk, 190–192
  bond prices and term structure of interest rates, 192–193
  present value of bond cash flows, 187–189
Bond yields
  current, 193–194
  municipal bonds, 196–197
  summarizing, 198
  yield to call, 195–196
  yield to maturity, 194–195
Book value, 32–33
Book value per share (BVPS), 35
Bootstrap transactions, 470
Brandt, Bill, 613
Break-even EBIT, 469–471
Bristol-Myers Squibb, 297
Brokers, 221
Budgeting; *see* Capital budgeting; Project cash flows

Business failure, 609
Business organization, 11–14
Business ownership, 218
Business risk, 366
Buyback of stock, 502–504
Buy-side analysts, 233
BVPS (book value per share), 35

C

Call features, 180
Call options, 473–474
Call premium, 180
Campbell, John Y., 306n
CANTV, 583
Capital asset pricing model (CAPM), 331–332, 335–336, 360–361
Capital budgeting; *see also* Internal rate of return; Net present value; Project cash flows
    decision statistic formats, 422–423
    international strategies, 585
    introduction, 420–422
    modified internal rate of return, 435–441
    mutually-exclusive projects, 422
    of mutually-exclusive projects, 436–440
    normal/non-normal cash flows, 422, 433–434
    payback and discounted payback, 427–431
    processing decisions, 423
    profitability index, 441–442
    techniques, 422
Capital financing; *see also* Working capital management
    debt, 514–517, 519–523
    equity, 517–519, 523–527
    initial public offerings, 518–519
    introduction, 512
    new and small firm sources, 514–519
    public firm sources, 519–527
Capital intensity ratio, 74
Capital market efficiency, 339–343
Capital market instruments, 259–260
Capital market line (CML), 332–333
Capital markets, 259
Capital structure; *see also* Equity; Leverage
    active versus passive changes in, 458–459
    break-even EBIT, 469–471
    definition, 32, 38, 77, 456
    M&M in a perfect world, 459–464
    M&M with corporate taxes, 464–466
    M&M with corporate taxes and bankruptcy, 471–477
    re-leveraging choices, 466–469
    theory versus reality, 477–478
Capital structure irrelevance assertion, 459
CAPM (capital asset pricing model), 331–332, 335–336, 360–361
Carroll, Archie B., 26n
Carrying costs, 543–544
Cash accounts, 548
Cash coverage ratio, 77
Cash cycle, 541–542
Cash flows; *see also* Annuity cash flow analysis; Project cash flows; Single cash flow analysis
    after-tax, 395
    cash accounts compared with, 548
    definition, 2, 6f
    of financial institutions, 20f
    from financing activities, 40–42
    free, 42–43, 392–393
    future value of, 142–147
    incremental, 390–391

interest rates and, 112
    from investing activities, 40–41
    normal/non-normal, 422, 433–434
    from operations, 40–41
    present value of, 148–152, 187–189
    statement of cash flows, 39–43
    stock valuation and, 227–229
Cash management; *see also* Working capital management
    Baumol Model, 549–551
    Miller-Orr Model, 551–553
    other influences, 552–553
    strategies, 548–549
Cash ratio, 70
Cash replenishment, 549–551
Caterpillar, 240f
Central American Free Trade Agreement, 570
CEOs (chief executive officers), 16
Certified development companies, 516–517
CFOs (chief financial officers), 9
Chapter 7 bankruptcy, 471–472, 612, 614–616
Chapter 11 bankruptcy, 471–472, 611–614
Charles Schwab, 257
Chase Manhattan Corp., 601, 602
Chavez, Hugo, 583
Check Clearing for the 21st Century Act, 555
Check kiting, 555
Chen, Steve, 13
Chief executive officers (CEOs), 16
Chief financial officers (CFOs), 9
China, 577
Citicorp, 602, 604–605
Citigroup, 309, 523, 602
Clientele effect, 494
Closely held corporations, 495
CML (capital market line), 332–333
The Coca-Cola Company, 227–233, 237–238, 261
Coefficient of variation (CoV), 303
Coldwater Creek, 46
Collection policies, 553–554, 557–558
Comizio, Jerry, 264
Commercial banks, 263t, 514, 548n
Commercial paper, 519–521, 548
Commitment fees, 516, 547
Common-size financial statements, 86–87
Common stock, 220, 366; *see also* Equity
Common stock and paid-in surplus, 30
Compensating balance, 547, 549
Competitive sale, 522
Complement and substitution, 391–392
Composition, 611
Compounding
    definition and overview, 113–114
    at different interest rates over time, 116–119
    frequency of, 154–157
    power of, 114–116
    Rule of 72, 123–124, 126t
Compromise financing policy, 545–546
Conglomerate mergers, 602
Consolidations, 601
Consols, 152
Constant growth model
    cost of equity using, 360–361, 375
    definition and overview, 230
    dividends versus capital gains, 492
    preferred stock and, 230–232
    required return using, 343–344
Continental Airlines, 613
Convertible bonds, 271
Corporate bonds, 182, 200, 270, 521–523
Corporate finance; *see* Capital financing; International corporate finance
Corporate governance, 16–17

Corporate income taxes, 35–38
Corporate wealth-sharing
    clientele effect, 494
    corporate control issues, 494–495
    dividend payment logistics, 497–501
    dividends versus capital gains, 492–493
    information effect, 494
    introduction, 490–492
    real-world dividend policies, 495–497
    stock dividends and stock splits, 501–502
    stock repurchases, 502–504
Corporations, 12
Correa Delgado, Rafael, 583
Correia da Silva, Luis, 495n
Correlation, 309
Cost of capital, 358–360; *see also* Weighted-average cost of capital
Cost of debt, 362–363, 375
Cost of equity, 360–361, 375, 460–461
Cost of preferred stock, 362, 375, 405
Costs
    bankruptcy, 472–475
    carrying, 543–544
    economy of scale and, 603–605
    economy of scope and, 604–606
    equivalent annual, 402–404
    financing, 392, 515–516, 547
    flotation, 374–375, 404–405
    historical, 32–33
    opportunity, 391, 543, 549–550
    shortage, 543–544
    sunk, 391
    total, 543–544, 551
    trading, 550
Coupon rate, 181
CoV (coefficient of variation), 303
Coverage ratios, 77–78
Cowan, Lynn, 519n
Cowen and Company, 525
C.R. Bard, 602
Credit analysis, 557
Credit analysts, 17
Credit management, 556–558
Credit risk, 199–202, 269–270
Credit risk premium, 270
Credit-scoring models, 616–619
Credit Suisse, 526
Cross rates, 575–576
Cross-sectional analysis, 88–89
Cum dividend, 498
Currency exchange rate, 574–577, 580–582
Currency exchange risk, 261–262, 576–577, 579
Currency swaps, 578–579
Current assets, 30, 540–541, 543–546
Current liabilities, 30
Current ratio, 70
Current yield, 193–194
Customer credit, 556–558

d

Days' sales in inventory ratio, 72
DCF (discounted cash flow), 228–229, 608–609
DDB (double-declining-balance) depreciation method, 398
Dealers, 222
Dealogic, 519
Debentures, 200
Debt; *see also* Bonds; Financial distress; Leverage
    component cost of, 362–363, 375
    default rates, 600f

firmwide versus project-specific WACC, 365–366
flotation-adjusted, 375, 404–405
M&M with corporate taxes and, 464–466
M&M with corporate taxes and bankruptcy, 471–477
project cash flows and, 392
Debt financing
    bank loans, 514–516, 546–548
    commercial paper, 519–521, 548
    corporate bonds, 521–523
    equity financing versus, 32, 38, 76–77
    for public firms, 519–523
Debt holders; see Bondholders
Debt management ratios, 76–79
Debt ratio, 76
Debt-to-equity ratio, 76
Decision statistic formats, 422–423
Declaration date, 498
Default risk, 199–202, 269–270
Default risk premium, 270
Defined benefit plans, 10
Defined contribution plans, 10
Dela Cruz, Sara Nelson, 613
Delaware Management Holdings, 605
Delegated monitors, 265
Depreciable basis, 393
Depreciation
    accelerated, 397–400
    calculating, 393
    half-year convention, 397–400
    on income statement, 39–40
    MACRS, 31, 398, 416–422
    Section 179 deductions, 399
    on statement of cash flows, 39–40
Derivative securities, 261–262
Descartes, René, 434n
Direct quotes, 574
Direct transfers, 262
Disbursement float, 554–555
Discount, 578
Discount bonds, 186
Discounted cash flow (DCF), 228–229, 608–609
Discounted payback, 428–431
Discounting, 119–122, 148
Discount rate, 120
Disney, 19, 304, 309, 310–311
Diversifiable risk, 304
Diversification
    definition and overview, 302, 304–305
    international, 310
    modern portfolio theory, 305–311, 332
Dividend discount models, 229–230
Dividend irrelevance theorem, 492–493
Dividend payout ratio, 79–80, 492
Dividends
    capital gains versus, 492–493
    clientele effect, 494
    common stock, 34, 37–38, 79, 220
    corporate control issues, 494–495
    extraordinary, 496–497
    information effect, 494
    payment logistics, 497–501
    preferred stock, 230–232
    project cash flows and, 392
    residual dividend model, 495–496
    stock price effects, 498–501
    valuation methods
        cash flow and, 227–229
        constant growth model, 230–232
        dividend discount model, 229–230
        expected return and, 232–233
        P/E model, 236–240
        variable-growth techniques, 233–236
        zero-growth model, 230–232
Dividends per share (DPS), 34
Dividend yield, 231

Divisional WACC, 369–374
Dollar return, 296
Dollar strength and weakness, 576–577
Double-declining-balance (DDB) depreciation method, 398
Double taxation, 12
Dow, Charles H., 223
Dow Jones Industrial Average (DJIA), 223–225, 237–238, 334–335, 342
DPS (dividends per share), 34
Drafts, 554
DuPont analysis system, 83–86
Dutch auctions, 503

e

EAC (equivalent annual cost), 402–404
EAR (effective annual rate), 155–157
Earnings before interest and taxes (EBIT), 34, 469–471
Earnings before taxes (EBT), 34
Earnings management, 45–46
Earnings per share (EPS)
    break-even EBIT and EBIT expectations, 469–471
    with corporate taxes, 465–467
    definition and equation, 34
    in a perfect world, 462–464
    re-leveraging effects, 467–469
EBIT (earnings before interest and taxes), 34, 469–471
EBT (earnings before taxes), 34
Economic failure, 609
Economic profits, 422
Economic rents, 603
Economy of scale, 603–605
Economy of scope, 604–606
EE savings bonds, 184
Effective annual rate (EAR), 155–157
Efficient frontier, 307
Efficient market, 339
Efficient market hypothesis (EMH), 340–341
Efficient portfolios, 306–308
Einstein, Albert, 114, 123
Eisenbeis, R. A., 617n
Employee stock option plans (ESOPs), 16
Enron, 18n, 45, 598
EPS; see Earnings per share
Equations
    accounts payable turnover, 73
    accounts receivable turnover, 72–73
    after-tax cash flow, 395
    amortized loan payments, 158
    annual cost, 551
    assets, 30
    average collection period, 72–73
    average cost of joint production, 605–606
    average cost of production, 603
    average payment period, 73
    average return, 297
    average tax rate, 36
    balance sheet, 30
    basic earnings power ratio, 79
    Baumol Model, 550–551
    beta, 334n
    bond price, 194, 195
    book value per share, 35
    break-even EBIT, 470–471
    callable bond price, 195
    capital intensity ratio, 74
    cash coverage ratio, 77
    cash cycle, 541–542
    cash ratio, 70
    coefficient of variation, 303
    constant growth model, 230, 343, 360, 492

cost of debt, 362, 375
cost of equity, 360, 375
cost of preferred stock, 362, 375
coverage ratios, 77
credit-scoring models, 617–619
current ratio, 70
daily interest rate, 499
days' sales in inventory, 72
debt ratio, 76
debt-to-equity ratio, 76
default risk premium, 270
depreciation, 393
discounted payback decision rule, 430
discounted payback statistic, 428
discounting multiple and varying cash flows, 148
dividend discount models, 229, 230
dividend effect on stock price, 498–501
dividend payout ratio, 79, 492
dividends, 495
dividends per share, 34
dollar return, 296
DuPont analysis, 83
earnings per share, 34
economies of scale, 603
economies of scope, 605–606
effective annual rate, 156
equity multiplier ratio, 76
expected return, 232, 329
Fisher Effect, 268
fixed asset turnover ratio, 74
fixed-charge coverage ratio, 77
flotation-adjusted costs, 375, 405
free cash flow, 42, 392
FV in n periods, 118
FV in n years, 114
FV in one year, 113
FV of a continuously compounded deposit, 155n
FV of an annuity, 143
FV of an annuity due, 153
FV of multiple and varying cash flows, 142
growth valuation model, 235
inflation rate, 268
interest rate, 125n, 268, 270, 274–278, 280
interest rate parity, 580
internal growth rate, 87
inventory turnover ratio, 72
IRR decision rule, 432
IRR minimum acceptable expected rate of return, 460
IRR statistic, 432
linear discriminant model, 617–618
linear probability model, 618–619
liquidity premium theory, 277–278
logit models, 618–619
market-to-book ratio, 81
market value per share, 35
Miller-Orr Model, 551–552
nominal interest rate, 268
NPV decision rule, 426
NPV statistic, 424
number of periods, 126n
number of periods in an annuity, 161n
operating cycle, 541
opportunity cost, 550
optimal cash return point, 551
payback decision rule, 428
payback statistic, 427
P/E ratio, 81, 237
percentage return, 296
portfolio beta, 336
portfolio return, 311
probability of default, 618–619
profitability index statistic, 441
profit margin, 79
project-specific WACC, 368

Equations—*Cont.*
Proposition I (perfect world), 459
Proposition I (with corporate taxes), 464
Proposition I (with taxes and bankruptcy), 477
Proposition II (perfect world), 459
Proposition II (with corporate taxes), 464
Proposition IIa (perfect world), 461
Proposition IIa (with corporate taxes), 464
proxy beta, 367
purchasing power parity, 580, 582
PV of an annuity, 149
PV of an annuity due, 154
PV of a perpetuity, 152, 498–501
PV of a stock, 227, 492, 498–501
PV of a stock over *n* years, 228
PV of a stock's cash flow, 228
PV of bond cash flows, 188
PV of cash flow made in *n* years, 120
PV of next period's cash flow, 120
PV with different discount rates, 122
quick ratio, 70
real interest rate, 268
required return, 330, 335, 343
retention ratio, 87
return on assets, 79, 83
return on equity, 79, 83
Rule of 72, 123
sales to working capital, 74
security risk, 274
standard deviation, 300, 329
stock future price, 239
stock value, 227, 492, 498–501
sustainable growth rate, 87
taxable equivalent yield, 197
times interest earned, 77
total assets turnover ratio, 74
total cost, 551
total risk, 304
trading cost, 550
two-stage growth valuation model, 235
unbiased expectations theory, 275–276
upper limit for cash balances, 551
variable growth rate stock, 235
weighted-average cost of capital, 360, 460–461
weighted-average flotation cost, 405
yield curves, 276–279
Z-score model, 617–618
Equipment trust certificates, 200
Equity
as call option on firm's value, 473–474
cost of, 360–361, 375, 460–461
definition and overview, 11, 218, 220
firm's value with taxes and bankruptcy, 475–477
flotation costs, 375, 404–405
overinvestment/underinvestment problems, 474–475
project risk and, 366
shareholders', 30
Equity financing
debt versus, 32, 38, 76–77
for new and small firms, 517–519
for public firms, 523–527
Equity multiplier ratio, 76
Equivalent annual cost (EAC), 402–404
ESOPs (employee stock option plans), 16
Ethics in financial management, 18–19, 555
European Union (EU), 571–572
Euros, 572, 576–577, 578f
Exchange rate, 574–577, 580–582
Exchange rate risk, 261–262, 576–577, 579
Ex-dividend date, 498
Executive compensation, 18
Executive stock options, 343
Existing shares, 15
Exogenous specification, 427

Expected inflation rate, 268
Expected return
definition and equation, 328–329
IRR minimum, 460
leverage and shareholders' expectations, 465–466
in a perfect world, 462–464
required rate versus, 432
risk and, 302–303, 328–331
standard deviation and, 328–330
in stock valuation, 232–233
Exports and imports, 570–571
Extension, 611
Extraordinary dividends, 496–497
Exxon Corporation, 603
ExxonMobil, 603

f

Facility fees, 515
Factors, 547
Fad investments, 125
"Fallen angels," 201, 202
Fannie Mae (FNMA), 184
FCF (free cash flow), 42–43, 392–393
FDIC (Federal Deposit Insurance Corp.), 264
Federal Home Loan Mortgage Corporation (FHLMC), 184, 256
Federal National Mortgage Association (FNMA), 184
Federal Trade Commission (FTC), 601
Fees; *see* Costs
Fiduciary, 18
Finance; *see also* Capital financing; Financial management; Financial statements; International corporate finance; Project cash flows
application and theory for decision-making, 8–9
in business and life, 4–9
definition, 2, 4–6
in other business functions, 10
in personal life, 10
subareas of, 6–8
Finance companies, 263t
Financial analysts, 17, 233, 239
Financial assets, 9, 420–422, 432
Financial calculators, 117, 425
Financial distress
bankruptcy laws, 471–472, 611–614
bankruptcy predictions, 615–619
capital structure and, 456–458
costs of, 472–475
informal resolutions of, 610–611
introduction, 598–600
types and causes, 609–610
Financial function, 9–11
Financial institutions, 7–8, 20f, 262–266; *see also* Financial markets
Financial leverage, 32, 333, 459; *see also* Leverage
Financial management
agency theory, 15–19
in business and life, 4–9
business organization, 11–14
chief financial officers, 9
definition, 2, 6–7
firm goals, 14–15
function of, 9–11
short-term plans, 546–548
short-term policies, 543–546
Financial managers, 9, 343–344
Financial markets; *see also* Financial institutions; Interest rates; Stock markets

bonds, 178, 180–187, 202–204
definition, 4, 7–9, 256
derivative securities, 261–262
efficiency of, 339–343
foreign exchange, 261
introduction, 254
money markets versus capital markets, 258–260
participants, 4–5, 20
primary versus secondary markets, 256–258
real markets compared with, 9
Financial risk, 366n
Financial statements
analyzing
asset management ratios, 72–76
cautions, 45–46, 89–90
debt management ratios, 76–79
DuPont analysis, 83–86
internal and sustainable growth rates, 87–88
introduction, 68–70
liquidity ratios, 70–71
market value ratios, 81–82
profitability ratios, 79–81
spreading the financial statements, 86–87
time series and cross-sectional analysis, 88–89
characteristics
balance sheets, 30–33, 540
definition and overview, 28
income statements, 34–38
statement of cash flows, 39–43
statement of retained earnings, 44–45
Financing costs, 392
Financing options, 32, 76–77; *see also* Capital financing
"FinProf" game; *see* Project cash flows
Firm commitment underwriting, 521–522
Firm goals, 14–15
Firm-specific risk, 304
Firmwide WACC
divisional WACC versus, 369–374
project WACC versus, 365–369
First Albany Capital, 256
First Strike Software (FSS); *see* Project cash flows
Fisher Effect, 268–269
Fisher, Irving, 268, 460
Fitch ICBA, Inc., 199, 521
Five Cs of credit analysis, 557
Fixed assets, 30–31, 540
Fixed asset turnover ratio, 74
Fixed-charge coverage ratio, 77
Fixed-income securities, 180
Fixed peg arrangement, 577
Fixed-price tender offers, 502–504
Fixed-rate loans, 516
Flexible financing policy, 544–546
Float, 553–555
Floating-rate loans, 516
Flotation costs, 374–375, 404–405
FNMA (Federal National Mortgage Association), 184
Foreign currency
exchange rate risk, 261–262, 576–577, 579
exchange rates, 574–577, 580–582
forward exchange rates and hedging, 577–579
interest rate parity, 579–580, 582
purchasing power parity, 580–582
Foreign direct investment, 573–574
Foreign exchange markets, 261
Foreign exchange risk, 261–262, 576–577, 579
Foreign trade, 570–572; *see also* International corporate finance
Formulas; *see* Equations

Forward exchange rate, 280, 577–580
Forward P/E ratio, 238
Forward rate, 280, 577–580
401(k) plans, 10
Freddie Mac (FHLMC), 184, 256
Free cash flow (FCF), 42–43, 392–393
Free cash flow theory of dividends, 495–496
Freely floating regime, 576
FSS (First Strike Software); *see* Project
    cash flows
FTC (Federal Trade Commission), 601
Futures contracts, 578–579
Future value (FV); *see also* Annuity cash
    flow analysis; Single cash flow
    analysis
    of an annuity due, 153
    compounding and, 113–119, 155n
    definition, 112
    of level cash flows, 143–144
    of multiple and varying cash
      flows, 142–143
    of multiple annuities, 144–147
    in multiple periods, 113–119
    present value and, 122–124
    in single period, 113

g

GDP (gross domestic product), 571t
General Electric Company, 304, 309, 495–496
Generally Accepted Accounting Principles
    (GAAP), 32–33, 39, 42, 45–46
General partners, 13
General partnerships, 12
Ginnie Mae (GNMA), 256
Glass-Steagall Act, 264
Global business; *see* International
    corporate finance
Global Crossings, 598, 611
GMAC, 520
GNMA (Government National Mortgage
    Association), 256
Goldman Sachs, 256, 524
Gold prices, 342
Google, 13, 218, 256
Gordon growth model, 230
Gordon, Myron J., 230, 493
Government National Mortgage
    Association (GNMA), 256
Gross domestic product (GDP), 571t
Gross fixed assets, 394–395
Gross proceeds, 524
Gross profit, 34
Growth stocks, 233
GTE, 603

h

Half-year convention, 397–400
Hedge funds, 338
Hedging, 261–262, 577–579
High-yield bonds, 199–202
Historical cost, 32–33
Historical returns, 237–238, 296–299
Historical risks, 299–303
Holmes, Ben, 519
Horizontal mergers, 601
Hurley, Chad, 13
Hybrid organizations, 13

i

IBM, 304, 307, 309, 311
IMF (International Monetary Fund), 572

Imports and exports, 570–571
Income statement, 34–38
Increasing the discount rate, 190
Incremental cash flows, 390–391
Indenture agreement, 180
Indirect quotes, 574
Indirect transfer, 265
Individual retirement accounts (IRAs), 10
Inflation, 183, 268
Inflow, 112
Information and market efficiency, 340–341
Information effect, 494
Ingram Book Group, 602
Initial public offerings (IPOs), 256,
    518–519, 523–527
Institutional venture capital firms, 517
Insurance companies, 263t
Interest and dividends paid by
    corporations, 38
Interest and dividends received by
    corporations, 37
Interest-rate-cognizant decisions, 438
Interest rate parity, 579–580, 582
Interest rate risk, 190–192
Interest rates
    cash flow and, 112
    compounding and, 116–119
    computing, 124–126, 157–158
    daily, 499
    default risk and, 269–270
    definition, 112
    equations, 125n, 268, 270,
      274–278, 280
    factors influencing, 266–267, 274
    forecasting, 280
    inflation and, 268
    key rates (1972–2007), 267f
    liquidity risk and, 271
    nominal, 266, 268–269
    rate of return compared with, 124n
    real, 268–269
    simple, 114
    special provisions or covenants, 271
    term structure of, 192–193, 271–274
    term to maturity and, 271–274
    theories, 274–279
Intermediaries, 20
Internal growth rate, 87–88
Internal rate of return (IRR)
    benchmark, 432–433
    definition and calculation, 431
    leverage effect on cost of equity, 460
    modified, 435–441
    of mutually-exclusive projects, 436–440
    non-normal cash flows and, 433–434
    problems with, 433
    reinvestment rate assumptions, 434–435
    statistic, 432
Internal Revenue Service (IRS), 17, 393,
    394–395, 397–399
International corporate finance
    capital budgeting, 585
    foreign currency
      exchange rate, 574–577, 580–582
      exchange rate risk, 261–262,
        576–577, 579
      forward exchange rates and hedging,
        577–579
      interest rate parity, 579–580, 582
      purchasing power parity, 580–582
    global business, 570–574
    introduction, 568–570
    political risk, 583–585
International finance, 7–8
International investments, 310
International Monetary Fund (IMF), 572
Internet stocks, 226
Inventory loans, 547
Inventory management, 72, 543, 547

Inventory turnover ratio, 72
Investment analysts, 17, 233, 239
Investment banks, 17, 256, 263t, 518,
    521–527
Investment grade, 199
Investment in operating capital (IOC), 43
Investments
    definition, 6–7
    fad, 125
    of idle cash, 549, 555–556
    interest rate effect on, 125–126
    over/underinvestment problems,
      474–475
Investors, 4, 226, 523; *see also* Corporate
    wealth-sharing; Shareholders
Invisible hand, 14
IOC (investment in operating capital), 43
IPOs (initial public offerings), 256,
    518–519, 523–527
IRAs (individual retirement accounts), 10
IRR; *see* Internal rate of return
IRS (Internal Revenue Service), 17, 393,
    394–395, 397–399

j

Japan, 342, 542, 555, 581
Jobs and Growth Tax Relief Reconciliation
    Act (JGTRRA), 493
Jobs, Steve, 19, 218
Johnson, Art, 264
J.P. Morgan Chase, 601, 602
J.P. Morgan & Co., 601, 602
Junk bonds, 199–202

k

Kaizen, 542
Kaufmann, Daniel, 584n
KeyBank Capital Markets, 256
Kraay, Aart, 584n

l

Lakonishok, Josef, 504n
Large investors, 523
Law of one price, 580
LBOs (leveraged buyouts), 470
Legal issues in cash management, 555
Lehman Brothers, 256
Leverage
    bankruptcy and, 471–477
    break-even EBIT and EBIT
      expectations, 469–471
    capital structure theory and, 459
    cost of equity effects, 460–461
    definition and overview, 32, 333, 459
    of hedge funds, 338
    market risk and, 333
    overinvestment/underinvestment
      problems, 474–475
    in a perfect world, 462–464
    re-leveraging choices, 466–469
    shareholders' expected return and,
      465–466
    WACC effects, 461–464
Leveraged buyouts (LBOs), 470
Liabilities, 30
Limited liability, 12
Limited liability companies (LLCs), 13
Limited liability partnerships (LLPs), 13
Limited partners, 13
Limited partnerships (LPs), 13
Limited partner venture capital firms, 517

Limit orders, 226
Lincoln National Corp., 605
Linear discriminant models, 617–618
Linear probability models, 618–619
Line of credit, 546, 548
Lintner, John, 332, 493
Liquidation, 611, 614
Liquidity, 30, 32, 263, 265–266
Liquidity premium theory, 276–278
Liquidity ratios, 70–71
Liquidity risk, 271
LLCs (limited liability companies), 13
LLPs (limited liability partnerships), 13
Loan commitment agreements, 515–516
Loan principal, 159
Loans, 157–163, 514–516, 546–548
Logit models, 618–619
Long position, 474
Long Term Capital Management
    (LTCM), 338
Long-term debt, 30, 521; see also Leverage
Lottery winnings, 153
LPs (limited partnerships), 13

m

MACRS (modified accelerated cost recovery
    system), 31, 398, 416–419
Managed-floating regime, 576
Marginal tax rate, 36
Market bubbles, 342
Market capitalization, 224
Market extension mergers, 601
Market makers, 222, 225
Market orders, 226
Market portfolio, 331–333
Market risk
    beta and, 333–334, 337–339
    definition, 304
    market portfolio and, 331–333
    security market line and, 334–336
Market risk premium, 331
Markets; see Financial markets
Market segmentation theory, 278–279
Market share, 15
Market-to-book ratio, 81
Market value, 32–33
Market value per share (MVPS), 35
Market value ratios, 81–82
Markkula, Mike, 19
Markowitz, Harry, 305
Master registration statement, 527
Mastruzzi, Massimo, 584n
Mattel Inc., 296–298, 300–309, 331, 333–334
Maturity date, 180
Maturity premium, 271–272
Maximum allowable payback, 427
MBS (mortgage-backed securities), 184–185
McCaw, Craig, 201
McDonald's, 221, 226, 229, 236–238
McGowan, Bill, 201
Merck, 45
Mercosur, 570
Mergers, 601–602
Mergers and acquisitions
    definition and introduction, 598–601
    motives
        cost of capital reduction, 607
        cost reduction, 603–606
        manager personal incentives, 607
        misallocation of capital, 608
        revenue enhancement, 602–603
        synergy, 602
        tax considerations, 606–607
    types, 601–602
    valuation of, 608–609
Merrill Lynch, 526

Merriman Curhan Ford & Co., 519
Merton, Robert, 338
Microsoft, 257, 494, 497
Midmarket business firms, 514
Milken, Michael, 201
Miller, Merton, 459–460, 461, 551n
Miller-Orr Model, 551–553
MIRR; see Modified internal rate of return
"MktProf" game; see Project cash flows
M&M theorem; see Modigliani-Miller
    theorem
Mobil Corporation, 603
Modern portfolio theory
    CAPM and, 332
    concept of, 305–308
    diversification and, 308–310
    portfolio return, 310–311
Modified accelerated cost recovery system
    (MACRS), 31, 398, 416–419
Modified internal rate of return (MIRR)
    calculating, 435–436
    with mutually exclusive projects,
        436–440
    strengths and weaknesses, 440–441
Modigliani, Franco, 459
Modigliani-Miller (M&M) theorem
    bird-in-the-hand fallacy, 493
    break-even EBIT and EBIT expectations,
        469–471
    with corporate taxes, 464–466
    with corporate taxes and bankruptcy,
        471–477
    definition and overview, 459–460
    dividend irrelevance theorem, 492–493
    equations
        Proposition I (perfect world), 459
        Proposition I (with corporate
            taxes), 464
        Proposition I (with taxes and
            bankruptcy), 477
        Proposition II (perfect world), 459
        Proposition II (with corporate
            taxes), 464
        Proposition IIa (perfect world), 461
        Proposition IIa (with corporate
            taxes), 464
    in a perfect world, 459–464
    reality versus, 477–478
    re-leveraging choices, 466–469
Money markets, 258–259
Moody's, 199, 270, 521
Morales, Evo, 583
Morgan, John Pierpont, 601n
Morgan Stanley, 256, 310, 524
Morningnotes.com, 519
Mortgage-backed securities (MBS), 184–185
Mortgage bonds, 200
Mullins, David, 338
Multinational corporations, 573, 583–584
Municipal bonds, 181–183, 196–197, 271
Mutual funds, 263t
Mutually-exclusive projects, 422, 436–440
MVPS (market value per share), 35

n

NAFTA (North American Free Trade
    Agreement), 570
Nasdaq 100, 342
Nasdaq Composite Index, 223–225
Nasdaq Stock Market, 221, 223
NASDAQ (National Association of
    Securities Dealers Automated
    Quotation) system, 257
Negotiated sales, 522
Net change in cash and marketable
    securities, 42

Net income, 34
Net present value (NPV)
    definition and overview, 402, 423–426
    in merger valuations, 608–609
    of mutually-exclusive projects, 436–440
    non-normal cash flows and, 433–434
    reinvestment rate assumptions, 434–435
Net proceeds, 524
Net working capital (NWC), 31–32,
    395–396, 540–544
New firm financing options, 514–519
Newmont Mining, 304, 307, 309
News and announcements, 340–341, 494,
    498, 502–504
New York Stock Exchange (NYSE)
    bond market operations, 202–203
    as publicly-traded company, 223
    as secondary market, 256–257, 264
    stock market operations, 220–221, 223
    trading volume, 258
NeXT Computer, 19
Nike, 573
Nominal interest rates, 266, 268–269
Nondiversifiable risk, 304
Non-normal cash flows, 422, 433–434
Normal cash flows, 422
North American Free Trade Agreement
    (NAFTA), 570
NPV; see Net present value
NPV profiles, 433–434, 436–440
Nucor Corp., 328–329
NWC (net working capital), 31–32, 395–396,
    540–544
NYSE (New York Stock Exchange); see New
    York Stock Exchange

o

Oneida Ltd., 614
Operating cash flow (OCF), 43, 394
Operating cycle, 541–542
Opportunity costs, 391, 543, 549–550
Optimal portfolios, 306
Options, 16, 343, 473–474, 578–579
Ordinary annuities, 143, 152–154
Organizational form of business, 11–14
Originating house(s), 526
Orr, D., 551n
Outflow, 112
Overinvestment problem, 474–475
Overseas Private Investment
    Corporation, 584
Over-the-counter (OTC) markets, 258

p

Page, Larry, 218
Partnerships, 12
Par value, 180
Passive capital structure management,
    458–459
Patriot bonds, 184
Payback (PB), 427–428, 430–431
Payment date, 498
Payout policies; see Corporate
    wealth-sharing
PD (probability of default), 618–619
Pegging, 577
Penny stocks, 339
Pension or retirement funds, 10, 146–147,
    263t
P/E (price-earnings) ratio, 81–82, 236–240
Percentage return, 296–297
Periodic payments; see Annuity cash flow
    analysis
Perks (perquisites), 16

Perpetuities, 152
Personal finance, 10
PI (profitability index), 441–442
Pixar, 19
Political risk, 583–585
Polkovichenko, Valery, 306n
Portfolio beta, 336
Portfolio design
    CAPM and, 332
    diversification, 304–305, 308–310
    modern portfolio theory concept,
        305–308
Portfolio return, 310–311
Portfolios, 304
Postal Savings Bank, 555
PPP (purchasing power parity), 580–582
Preferred stock
    on balance sheets, 30
    component costs, 362, 375
    constant-growth model and, 230–232
    firmwide versus project-specific WACC,
        365–366
    flotation-adjusted costs, 375, 405
    valuation, 230–232
Premium, 578
Premium bonds, 185
Prepackaged bankruptcy, 614
Present value (PV); see also Annuity cash
        flow analysis; Single cash flow
        analysis
    of an annuity due, 153–154
    of bond cash flows, 187–189
    definition, 113
    discounting and, 119–122
    future value and, 122–124
    of level cash flows, 148–151
    of multiple annuities, 151–152
    of multiple cash flows, 148–152
    of a perpetuity, 152
Price
    of bonds, 181, 185–187, 189–193
    of stock, 15, 225, 239, 498–501, 502, 504
Price-earnings (P/E) ratio, 81–82, 236–240
Price risk, 263–266
Primary markets, 256–257, 523–524
Principal, 15, 180
Privately-held companies, 514–519
Privately-held information, 340–341
Private placement, 522–523, 526
Probability, 328
Probability distribution, 329
Probability of default (PD), 618–619
Product extension mergers, 602
Profitability index (PI), 441–442
Profitability ratios, 79–81
Profit margin, 79–80
Pro forma analysis, 390
Project cash flows; see also Capital
        budgeting
    accelerated depreciation, 397–400
    calculating
        depreciation, 393
        free cash flow, 392–393
        gross fixed asset changes, 394–395
        net working capital changes, 395–396
        operating cash flow, 394
        total cash flows, 396–397
    cash flow estimation principles, 390–392
    cost-cutting problem, 401
    equivalent annual costs, 402–404
    flotation costs, 405
    half-year convention, 397–400
    introduction, 388–390
    replacement problem, 400–402
    sample project description, 390
Project WACC
    divisional WACC versus, 369–374
    firmwide WACC versus, 365–369
Prospectus, 526–527

Proxy betas, 367
Public corporations, 12, 519–523
Public information, 340–341
Purchasing power parity (PPP), 580–582
Pure-play proxies, 367
PV; see Present value

q

Quick ratio, 70

r

RadioShack Corp., 296–298, 301–309
Rajan, Raghuram, 16n
Rate-based decision statistics; see also
        Internal rate of return
    introduction, 422–423
    modified internal rate of return, 435–441
    profitability index, 441–442
Rate of return, 124n, 432; see also Internal
        rate of return
Ratio analysis
    asset management, 72–76
    cautions in using, 89–90
    debt management, 76–79
    definition, 68
    liquidity, 70–71
    market value, 81–82
    profitability, 79–81
Ratios; see Equations
RBC Capital Markets, 256
Real assets, 9, 420–422, 432
Real interest rates, 268–269
Real markets, 9
Record date, 498
Recourse, 547
Red herring prospectus, 526–527
Reinvestment rate risk, 191
Relative value, 236
Reorganization, 612–614
Replenishment level, 549
Repurchase of stock, 502–504
Required return, 330, 335, 343–344, 432
Residual claimants, 220
Residual dividend model, 495–496
Restricted stock, 19, 343
Restrictive financing policy, 545–546
Restructuring, 458, 610–611
Retained earnings, 5–6, 30, 44–45
Retention ratio (RR), 87–88
Retirement or pension income, 10,
        146–147, 263t
Return asymmetries, 126
Return on assets (ROA), 79–80, 83–86
Return on equity (ROE), 79–80, 83–86
Returns; see Expected return
Reverse stock splits, 502
Reyes, George, 13
Risk
    asset class, 302–303
    business, 366
    credit (default), 199–202, 269–270
    currency exchange rate, 261–262,
        576–577, 579
    definition, 8
    diversifiable, 304
    financial, 366n
    firm-specific, 304
    historical, 299–303
    interest rate, 190–192
    liquidity, 271
    market; see Market risk
    nondiversifiable, 304
    political, 583–585

    price, 263–266
    reinvestment rate, 191
    return and, 302–303, 328–331
    total, 299, 304
Risk-free rate, 331
Risk premium, 330–331
ROA (return on assets), 79–80, 83–86
Rodriguez, Alex, 151–152
ROE (return on equity), 79–80, 83–86
RR (retention ratio), 87–88
Rule of 72, 123–124, 126t

s

Safety stock, 549
Sales to working capital ratio, 74
Sallie Mae (SLMA), 184
Salomon Brothers, 604–605
Sarbanes-Oxley Act of 2002, 18n, 45–46, 617
Savings bonds, 184
SBA (Small Business Administration),
        516–517
SBICs (Small Business Investment
        Companies), 517
Schering-Plough, 297
Scholes, Myron, 338
S corporations, 13
Scott, Mike, 19
Sculley, John, 19
SEC; see Securities and Exchange
        Commission
Secondary markets, 256–258
Secondary securities, 266
Section 179 deductions, 399
Secured lenders, 471
Secured loans, 547
Securities and Exchange Act of 1934,
        522–523, 526
Securities and Exchange Commission (SEC)
    corporate governance by, 17
    hedge fund regulation by, 338
    Rule 144A, 523
    security registration, 522–523,
        526–527, 548
Securities firms, 263t
Security market line (SML), 334–336
Sell-side analysts, 233
Semistrong-form efficiency, 340–341
Senior bonds, 200
Separation principle, 374, 460
Sequoia Capital, 13
Shareholders, 12; see also Stockholders
Sharpe, William, 332
Shelf registration, 527
Shortage costs, 543–544
Short-term financial plans, 546–548
Short-term financial policies, 543–546
Simple interest, 114
Single cash flow analysis
    future value
        compounding and, 113–119
        definition, 112
        single period, 113
    interest rate computations, 124–126
    introduction, 110–112
    moving cash flows, 122–124
    organizing cash flows, 112
    present value
        discounting and, 119–122
        future value usage and, 122–124
    solving for time, 126–128
Single period future value, 113
Skipper, Suzanne, 519
SLMA (Student Loan Marketing
        Association), 184
Small Business Administration
        (SBA), 516–517

Small Business Investment Companies
        (SBICs), 517
Small firm financing options, 514–519
Smith, Adam, 14
Smith Barney, 605
SML (security market line), 334–336
Society for Worldwide Interbank Financial
        Telecommunication (SWIFT)
        system, 554
Sole proprietorships, 11
Sources and uses of cash, 39–42
S&P 500 (Standard & Poor's 500
        Index), 223–225
Specialists, 221
Special provisions or covenants, 271
Spot loans, 515
Spot transactions, 261, 574, 579–580
Spread, 546
Spreading the financial statements, 86–87
Stakeholders, 14
Standard deviation
        of asset classes, 302–303
        beta and, 334
        coefficient of variation and, 303
        definition and overview, 299–302
        expected return and, 328–330
        market risk and, 331, 333
        total risk and, 304–305
Standard & Poor's, 199–200, 202, 270, 521
Standard & Poor's 500 Index (S&P 500),
        223–225
Starbucks Coffee Company, 568–570,
        572–574, 579
Statement of cash flows, 39–43
Statement of retained earnings, 44–45
Stock dividends, 501
Stockholders; see also Corporate
        wealth-sharing
        definition, 12
        dividend or capital gains
                preferences, 493
        equity claims of, 30, 473–474, 615–616
        leverage and expected return of, 465–466
        maximizing wealth of, 14–15
        overinvestment problem, 474–475
        re-leveraging impact on, 466–469
        rights of, 220
Stockholders' equity, 30
Stock indices, 223–225
Stock market bubbles, 342
Stock markets
        bond market compared with, 178
        exchanges, 220–223
        Nasdaq, 221–223
        quotes, 222f
        tracking, 223–225
        trading stocks, 225–227
Stock options, 343
Stock price, 15, 225, 239, 498–501, 502, 504
Stock repurchase or buyback, 502–504
Stocks; see also Equity
        common, 220, 366
        introduction, 218
        preferred, 230–232, 362
        restricted, 19, 343, 523
Stock splits, 501–502
Stock valuation; see also Ratio analysis
        of bankrupt firms, 475–477
        cash flows, 227–229
        constant growth model, 230–232
        dividend discount models, 229–230
        dividend effect on price, 498–501
        estimating future prices, 238–239

expected return, 232–233
        of mergers and acquisitions, 608–609
        P/E model, 236–240
        preferred stock, 230–232
        variable-growth techniques, 233–236
Straight-line method of depreciation, 31
Strong-form efficiency, 340–341
Student Loan Marketing Association
        (SLMA), 184
Substitution and complement, 391–392
Sunk costs, 391
Sunstein, Cass, 306n
Surplus cash management, 555–556
Survivor (TV show), 461–462
Sustainable growth rate, 87–88
SWIFT (Society for Worldwide Interbank
        Financial Telecommunication)
        system, 554
Syndicate, 525–526
Synergy, 602

Take down, 515–516, 547
Target cash balances; see Cash management
Taxable equivalent yield, 197
Taxes
        business organization and, 11–12
        corporate income, 35–38
        dividends versus capital gains, 492–493
        as merger and acquisition motives,
                606–607
        M&M with, 464–466
        M&M with bankruptcy and, 475–477
        municipal bond interest, 181
        WACC and, 360, 363–364, 367
Technical insolvency, 609–610
Tender offers, 502–504
Term structure of interest rates, 192–193,
        271–274
Thaler, Richard, 306n
Theories; see also Modigliani-Miller (M&M)
                theorem
        agency, 15–19
        efficient market hypothesis, 340–341
        interest rate, 274–279
        liquidity premium, 276–278
        market segmentation, 278–279
        modern portfolio, 305–311, 332
        residual dividend model, 495–496
        unbiased expectations, 274–278
        yield curve, 274–279
Thrifts, 263t
Ticker symbols, 221
Tilton, Glenn, 613
Time lines, 112
Time series analysis, 88–89
Times interest earned, 77
Time to maturity, 180
Time value of money (TVM), 9, 420–422; see
                also Annuity cash flow analysis;
                Single cash flow analysis
Time Warner, 604
TIPS (Treasury inflation-protected
                securities), 183
Tombstones, 525
Total assets turnover ratio, 74–75
Total cost, 543–544, 551
Total risk, 299, 304
Toyota, 573
Trade-off between risk and return, 302–303

Trading cost, 550
Trading posts, 221
Trading volume, 258
Trailing P/E ratio, 237
Travelers Group, 602, 604–605
Treasury bills, 330–333
Treasury bonds, 182–184, 196
TreasuryDirect, 184
Treasury inflation-protected securities
        (TIPS), 183
Trustees, 611
Turner, Ted, 201
TVM; see Time value of money
Tyco International, 18n, 602

UBS Investment Bank, 527
Unbiased expectations theory, 274–278
Underinvestment problem, 474–475
Underwriter's spread, 524–525
Underwriting, 521–523
United Airlines, 598, 613
U. S. Department of Justice, 601, 603
U. S. government agency securities, 184–185
U. S. Treasury bills, 330–333
U. S. Treasury bonds, 182–184, 196
Unlimited liability, 11
Unsecured corporate bonds, 200
Unsecured loans, 546–547
Up-front fees, 515
Utkus, Stephen, 306n

V

Valuation; see Bond valuation; Dividends;
                Financial statements; Future
                value; Net present value; Present
                value; Stock valuation
Value Line Investment Survey, 337
Value stocks, 238
Variable-growth-rate technique, 233–236
Variable-rate loans, 516
Variance, 300
Venezuela, 583
Venture capital, 517–518
Venture capitalists, 11
Verizon, 583
Vermaelen, Theo, 504n
Vertical mergers, 602
Vidal, David, 26n
Volatility, 299–303, 462–467
Voyageur Fund Management, 605

W

WACC; see Weighted-average cost of capital
Wal-Mart Stores Inc., 264, 344
Weak-form efficiency, 340
Weighted-average cost of capital (WACC)
        component cost of debt, 362–363, 375
        component cost of equity, 360–361,
                375, 460–461
        component cost of preferred stock,
                362, 375
        definition and equation, 360
        divisional, 369–374
        financing costs and, 392

firmwide versus project-specific,
    365–369
flotation costs, 374–375, 404–405
leverage effect on, 461–464
leverage effect on cost of
    equity, 460–461
tax rates for, 363–364
weight calculations, 364
Weill, Sanford I., 604–605
Wisniewski, Mary, 613n
Working capital management
    cash cycle, 541–542
    cash management, 548–553
    credit management, 556–558
    float control, 553–555
    introduction, 74, 538–540
    net working capital, 31–32, 395–396,
      540–544
    operating cycle, 541–542
    short-term financial plans, 546–548
    short-term financial policies, 543–546
    surplus cash investment, 555–556

Workout, 611
World Bank, 584
WorldCom, 18n, 45, 598, 611
World Trade Organization, 572, 584
Wozniak, Stephen, 19
Wulf, Julie, 16n
Wynn, Steve, 201

X

X-efficiencies, 603, 606

Y

Yen carry trade, 581
Yield curve
    maturity and, 271–274
    term structure of interest rates, 192–193
    theories, 274–279

Yields
    credit risk and, 200–202
    current, 193–194
    dividend, 231
    interest rates and, 193
    summarizing, 198
    taxable equivalent, 197
Yield to call, 195–196
Yield to maturity, 194–195
YouTube, 13

Z

Zero-balance accounts, 554
Zero coupon bonds, 188
Zero-growth rate model, 230–232
Z-score models, 617–618

Connect core concepts by making use
indicators presented

Learning Goals appear at the beginning of each chapter and indicators are woven throughout the text in the headings, examples, summary, and end-of-chapter problems. This helps the student follow how larger concepts are built from smaller steps. It also helps instructors develop their classes and assign readings and homework based on these goals.

LG **Learning Goals**

LG1 Define the subareas of finance and their roles in corporate financial management.

LG2 Show why and how finance is at the heart of sound business decisions.

LG3 Apply finance in your personal life.

LG4 Compare and contrast the advantages and disadvantages of the three most common business organizational forms in the United States.

LG5 Differentiate between financial managers' appropriate and inappropriate goals.

LG6 Identify the firm's primary agency relationship and discuss why agency relationships can create conflicts.

LG7 Incorporate ethics into financial management.

LG8 Describe the complex and necessary relationships among firms, financial institutions, and financial markets.

---

summary of learning goals

Ratio analysis involves the process of calculating and analyzing financial ratios to assess a firm's performance and to identify actions needed to improve firm performance. The most commonly used ratios for ratio analysis fall into five groups: (1) liquidity ratios, (2) asset management ratios, (3) debt management ratios, (4) profitability ratios, and (5) market value ratios. This chapter reviewed these ratios, described what each ratio means, and identified the general trend (higher or lower) managers and investors look for in each ratio.

LG1 **Calculate and interpret the major liquidity ratios.** Liquidity ratios measure the relation between a firm's liquid (or current) assets and its current liabilities.

LG2 **Calculate and interpret the major asset management ratios.** Asset management ratios measure how efficiently a firm uses its assets (inventory, accounts receivable, and fixed assets), as well as its accounts payable.

LG3 **Calculate and interpret the major debt ratios.** Debt management ratios measure the extent to which the firm uses debt (or financial leverage) versus equity to finance its assets.

LG4 **Calculate and interpret the major profitability ratios.** Profitability ratios show the combined effect of liquidity, asset management, and debt management on the overall operating results of the firm.

LG5 **Calculate and interpret the major market value ratios.** Market value ratios relate a firm's stock price to its earnings and book value.

LG6 **Appreciate how various ratios relate to one another.** Many of the ratios we review are interrelated. That is, a change in one ratio may affect the value of several ratios. To see how these interrelations help evaluate firm performance, managers, analysts and investors often perform a detailed analysis of ROA and ROE using the DuPont system of analysis. The DuPont system of analysis uses the balance sheet and income statement to break the ROA and ROE ratios into component pieces.

LG7 **Discuss the differences between time series and cross-sectional ratio analysis and decide which is most appropriate given an analytical situation.** When managers, analysts, or investors review a firm's financial position through ratio analysis, they often start by evaluating trends in